W9-CLA-850

Emperor
Huizong

EMPEROR
HUIZONG

Patricia Buckley Ebrey

Harvard University Press

Cambridge, Massachusetts
London, England

2014

Library of Congress Cataloging-in-Publication Data

Ebrey, Patricia Buckley, 1947–
  Emperor Huizong / Patricia Buckley Ebrey.
      pages cm
  Includes bibliographical references and index.
  ISBN 978-0-674-72525-6 (hardcover : alk. paper)
  1. Song Huizong, Emperor of China, 1082–1135.
  2. China—History—Song dynasty, 960–1279.   I. Title.
  DS751.6.S97E37 2014
  951'.024092—dc23
    [B]   2013017623

Contents

Tables, Maps, and Illustrations

Figures   *page*

Color Plates *Following page 306*

Preface

$\mathcal{H}$UIZONG CAME to the Song throne in the first month of 1100, three months after his seventeenth birthday, and reigned almost twenty-six years, till the last month of 1125. Song China was at the time the richest and most advanced country in the world with about one hundred million subjects. Huizong is best known for his contributions to art: he was an accomplished poet, painter, and calligrapher; an avid builder of temples and gardens; a path-breaking collector of art and antiquities; a knowledgable patron of music, poetry, and Daoism. Few monarchs in world history can compare to him in the range of the arts he supported with his time and attention. With regard to his principal responsibility of governing the realm, however, he failed spectacularly, since it was during his watch that the Jurchen were able to consolidate power in the north, invade Song China, capture its capital Kaifeng, and take Huizong and several thousand of his kinsmen and palace attendants into captivity. Huizong's last eight years were spent as a captive far from his homeland.

The drama of Huizong's life owes much to the large role that chance played in it. Had his elder brother not died at twenty-three without an heir, Huizong would never have become emperor. Had his grand councilor Cai Jing died at sixty rather than living past eighty, the politics of his court would have been less divisive. Had the Kitans been able to suppress the insurrection of the Jurchens, the Jurchens would never have invaded Song and Huizong might well have reigned another decade or longer. Choices Huizong made had important consequences, but so did events and developments over which he had no control.

To Chinese historians of the Song period and later, the question that needed to be answered about Huizong and his reign was what went wrong. Huizong's failings had to be identified so that later emperors could be warned away from them. Looked at this way, Huizong's many cultural pursuits became his vices, not his virtues. His love of art was seen as self-indulgence and his faith in Daoism as self-delusion. Blame was variously placed on Huizong's reluctance to listen to dissenting opinion, his choice of Cai Jing as his grand councilor, his extravagant gardens, and his decision to ally with the Jurchens when they rose against the Kitans. The influence of this traditional moral interpretation of Huizong and his reign lingers on in both English and Chinese language works because it pervades the surviving primary sources. Most contemporary historians would admit that if only the Kitans had promptly suppressed the Jurchens, the Jurchens would never have become a threat to Song and there would have been no reason to view Huizong's reign as a failure. Yet historians still tend to write as though practically everything that Huizong did led directly and inexorably to the collapse of his government.

Why write a book on Huizong if there are no more Chinese emperors to admonish? I began studying Huizong and his reign in the mid-1990s, wanting to explore the more visual side of Chinese culture—it was Huizong as an artist, art patron, and art collector that first attracted me. The more I read, however, the more intrigued I became. I began to wonder whether one could take a different approach to Huizong. In European history, rulers were supposed to be magnificent. Kings who built great palaces, attracted talented artists, and formed huge collections were doing what great rulers were supposed to do and deserved approbation. Could one look at Huizong's pursuit of magnificence as an appropriate expression of sovereignty?

To try to reconsider Huizong and his reign, I turned to the earliest, least edited sources, especially ones dating to Huizong's reign. Gradually I piled up notes based on reading edicts Huizong issued, memorials submitted to Huizong, collections of anecdotes, and memoirs of various sorts. As my research on Huizong progressed, I began writing scholarly articles and conference papers on episodes or aspects of

Huizong's reign. I also organized a workshop on the culture and politics of his period and helped edit a volume from it, and more recently wrote a book on the collections of art and antiquities that Huizong assembled. All during this time, however, I was working on a more biographical book on Huizong that would look at his world through his eyes and tell his story in a fresh way, its aim to explain, not to exculpate or condemn. The result is a book much more sympathetic to Huizong than anything else that has been done, not only in Western languages, but also in Chinese. It shows Huizong to have been more complex but also more human.

How should we think about the Chinese institution of the emperor? In the twentieth century, with the development of the social sciences, many scholars set aside the old categories of Confucian historiography and adopted new Western ones such as autocracy, absolutism, and despotism. These concepts imply that the key element in emperorship is legal power and the limits or lack of limits on it. Scholarship connecting theories of autocracy or despotism to actual emperors is, however, very spotty. An alternative to thinking about emperors in terms of legal powers is to focus on their ritual roles. Royal rituals are well documented in Chinese sources, and studying these rituals and the cosmologies and ideologies underlying them can be seen as a more China-centered approach to the study of monarchy. Conceiving of the emperor as high priest helps correct the vision of the emperor as dictator, but it is, in its own way, just as one-sided. When the extremes of symbolic potency and unchecked power are emphasized, Chinese emperors seem a species apart from monarchs elsewhere.

In this book I try to shift the balance at least a little toward features of the Chinese monarchical institution that are not exceptional in comparative terms. Chinese emperors, like sovereigns many other places, lived in palatial settings; they had obligations as heads of complex noble families; they sponsored spectacles and entertainments; they gave employment to musicians, architects, painters, poets, scientists, and scholars; they met with officials, generals, envoys, and servants. Like courts elsewhere, the Song court provided a space where religion, art, literature, and politics all intersected, where style and taste were scrutinized, and where royal munificence was expected.

What was Huizong like as a person? In his early years he spoke often of his desire to continue his father's legacy, presenting himself as a filial son. His father had died when he was only two, so he did not have memories of him, but he cared enormously about his father's place in history. As the years passed, Huizong gradually referred to his father less often and took on projects that his father had never attempted, such as a revision of the ritual code and the collection of antiquities. Sometimes he would claim that his father had intended to get to a project but had not lived to see his hopes fulfilled.

Religion is, to me, one key to understanding Huizong. Not all Song emperors were drawn to religion in its many forms, but Huizong definitely was. Many strands in Huizong's life are easiest to understand when we acknowledge that he had strong religious inclinations. He had a deep interest in orthodox religious Daoism from early in his reign; he accepted the ancient conception of sacred kingship and the centrality it gave to rituals performed by the ruler; he saw ritual power in "recovering antiquity"; and he was open to new revelations about the heavens and his own connections to Daoist gods. These different strands of Huizong's involvement with the divine are central to my understanding of him.

Other keys to understanding Huizong are his taste for grandeur and delight in creating something new. He set others to work creating "ancient" rituals, elegant buildings, elaborate gardens, and up-to-date compilations of knowledge. Some of these projects survived the disaster that ended his reign, others did not.

Without question, Huizong deserves his reputation as a talented artist. He impressed his contemporaries with his poetry, calligraphy, and especially his painting, and enough of his works survive for us to make our own judgments. Many scholars have written about Huizong as an artist, as a teacher and patron of court artists, and as a collector who gathered together a broad range of cultural treasures. I engaged this literature in my earlier book on Huizong's collections, but this book takes me into other facets of it, especially art produced at court and Huizong's presentation of himself as an artist.

Like other Chinese emperors, Huizong never wrote a memoir. Nor did any historian of his own day or even later dynasties write a chronicle of his life. Thus to write this book I have had to piece together evidence of many types: both texts and visual materials, both edicts and anecdotes, both works from within the Daoist religious tradition and those from outside it. Naturally, these sources all pose challenges. An example here might help. A large painted portrait of Huizong survives in the collection of the Palace Museum in Taipei (Plate 1). It bears no date or artist's name, but the museum dates it to the Song period. Looking at it helps us imagine Huizong. He sits upright, not leaning against the back of his chair. His face is rounded, with full cheeks and a wispy beard and mustache. He is not a scrawny man, and might even be a bit plump, but his clothes conceal most of his body. His age is indeterminate, but he is not elderly. He seems to be gazing intently at something, or perhaps he is lost in thought. When I look at the portrait, I can imagine him as a sensitive, self-confident individual, but I recognize that other people could imagine him differently when looking at this painting, perhaps seeing someone affable and self-satisfied, for instance.

For the historian, it is at least as important to recognize what should *not* be inferred from this painting. It was painted after Huizong's death to be hung during ancestral rituals performed in the palace. We cannot infer anything personal from the choice of the color or cut of the robe he wears because this painting was one of a set of ancestral portraits in which the Song emperors were all depicted in round-collared red robes. Nor should we make anything of the decision to be portrayed seated instead of standing and the gesture of concealing his hands in his sleeves—it was not Huizong who chose to be portrayed those ways. We cannot even be sure how good a likeness it is. It would not have been made before news of Huizong's death reached his son Gaozong in Hangzhou. By then, no one in the south had seen Huizong in nearly a decade. This portrait would have been based on how painters and other people at the court, including Gaozong, remembered him and wanted him portrayed, and memories are never perfect.

Getting to know Huizong from written sources requires similar attention to what each source can tell us and what it cannot. The main collection of government documents, the *Song Collected Documents (Song huiyao)*, contains over seven thousand entries summarizing or recording in full documents that crossed Huizong's desk, either memorials to him or edicts he issued. There is a significant body of poetry, calligraphy, and painting that Huizong claimed to have done himself, and even a large set of letters he wrote to a Daoist priest. Collected works of people who worked in Huizong's administration also contain much valuable material, as do collections of anecdotes compiled in the decades after Huizong's reign. For the last twenty years of Huizong's life, the

Documents on the Treaties with the North during Three Reigns (Sanchao beimeng huibian) is an extraordinarily rich source, quoting from numerous first-person accounts that are no longer extant.

All of these sources need to be understood on their own terms first. The language used in edicts and poetry, for instance, was shaped by long-established conventions. Another challenge is to find ways to make use of sources that are biased against Huizong. Historians who work on social and economic history are accustomed to trying to wring useful information about women, peasants, merchants, and the like from recalcitrant sources: even biased observers may mention details likely to be based on accurate information. For the court as well, it is often possible to read sources in ways different than their authors or editors intended. For instance, memorials of indictment, which denounce men in favor at court, may not be very good sources for the person accused, but are excellent sources for thinking about the sorts of information the ruler received. Anecdotes are often our only source for personality traits and may contain elements of truth, even when they come from false rumors. Here, I have tried to scrutinize the basis for stories that circulated about Huizong, knowing that gossip and hearsay would have been the basis of many of them (see Appendix A on "Reasons for Rejecting Some Common Stories about Huizong and His Court").

In the chapters that follow, readers will get to observe Huizong involved in many activities: issuing proclamations, officiating at rituals, conversing with religious mentors, showing off his treasures, writing poetry with his councilors, and more. Like people of Huizong's time, today's readers may wonder how much of what Huizong did was a public performance, scripted by court officials, and how much reflected his personal feelings. These are questions that defy answers—we have similar questions about political figures today. There is no getting around the fact that we know much more about what Huizong said and did—his public side—than what he thought or felt. I have tried to include what I see as telling incidents and details, ones that have shaped my own understanding of Huizong, but usually let readers draw their own inferences.

I HAVE HAD a lot of help in writing this book. First, I have been able to draw on the work of many talented scholars. Song history is today a quite well-developed field. Besides more general works on the

Song government, religion, and art, there have been notable studies of Huizong's involvement in Daoism, his music reform, charitable ventures, the school system he established, his garden-building, his paintings and painting academy, the alliance with Jin, the Jin–Song war, Cai Jing as his grand councilor, and much else. My debt to the work of these scholars will be evident in my notes. It would have been much more difficult for me to cover such a wide range of topics if I had not had been able to benefit from the work of so many modern scholars.

Time I could devote to this project has been equally essential. Three times during the years I have worked on Huizong's life I was able to spend a year free from teaching to focus on research and writing. For this precious time, I am indebted to the John Simon Guggenheim Foundation, the Chiang Ching-Kuo Foundation, and the Alexander von Humboldt Foundation. The grant from the Humboldt Foundation enabled me to spend a year at the Sinological Institute of Münster University, where much of this book was written. At the University of Washington, the China Studies Program and the History Department helped fund research trips, illustration costs, and graduate student assistance. Near the end of the project Peyton Canary and Xiaolin Duan attended to many bibliographic details, and Marshall Agnew drew the maps. I am also grateful to the colleagues who read draft chapters and offered advice and encouragement. John Chaffee, Michael Chang, Ronald Egan, Peter Golas, Kent Guy, Charles Hartman, Susan Huang, Paul Smith, and Kyoko Tokuno all were generous with their time when I needed feedback. Two anonymous reviewers for the press also offered valuable suggestions. I turned to my husband, Tom, for a nonexpert's opinion, and he valiantly read the entire manuscript at three different stages.

Note on Ages, Dates, and Other Conventions

*C*HINESE TRADITIONALLY COUNTED ages differently than we do today. A person was said to be one *sui* during the first calendar year of life, two *sui* during the second, and so on. On average these ages make the person seem to be 1.5 years older than the use of Western years would. Accurate conversion is possible only when one knows the person's day of birth and for most purposes is not necessary. In the case of young people the difference is much greater, so ages have been converted when information allowed. By way of illustration, since Huizong was born in the tenth month of 1082, when his father died in the third month of 1085, he was two years and five months old, but four *sui*, and when he took the throne in the first month of 1100, he was seventeen years and three months old, but nineteen *sui*.

Dates mentioned in this book are Chinese dates, with the Chinese year converted to the Western year with which it overlapped most. Thus, the third day of the sixth month of the fourth year of the Da-guan reign period is given as 1110/6/3. It should be kept in mind that the sixth month would not be our June, since the Chinese year starts later than the current Western year and starts with spring. Thus the sixth month is the last month of summer. In addition events that took place in the twelfth month of the Chinese year would generally have fallen in the next year of the Western calendar. This leads to discrepancies in the dates given for the end of Huizong's reign, which occurred in the twelfth month of 1125, which if converted to the Western calendar would fall in early 1126. Another difference between the Chinese dating system and the current Western calendar is the use of intercalary months inserted every few years to keep the lunar calendar from diverging too far from the solar year. Thus 1105/i2/16 means the sixteenth day of the intercalary month that fell between the second and third months in the year 1105.

For the sake of ease of comprehension, Chinese units of weight, length, distance, and area have been converted to approximate metric units. These conversions aim to give the reader a sense of the scale of the number being discussed and should not be considered exact or even very close. Not only did units vary over time and place, but also authors regularly used large round numbers for dramatic effect. The exception is "foot," a unit used both in China and in English. Here when "foot" is used, the unit is the Chinese foot, which like the English unit is based on the human foot and thus roughly comparable (though generally smaller than our current foot measure).

To keep the text as uncluttered as possible, I have not added dates after each person's name but rather put them in the Chinese Character Glossary near the end of this book. Similarly, I have avoided inserting romanization after translated terms. Those who want to check the Chinese original should find them in the Chinese Character Glossary unless they are easily found in the References. As a convenience to readers who do not read Chinese or Japanese, in the notes I have indicated that a cited work is in English even though the author's name is Chinese or Japanese by using initials. Thus, an article by Jing-shen Tao in English is cited as "J. Tao date:page," but one in Chinese uses the Chinese order (with family name first) and is cited as "Tao Jinsheng date:page."

Chronology

Shang dynasty, ca. 1570–1045 BCE

Zhou dynasty, 1045–256 BCE

Han dynasty, 202 BCE–220 CE

Tang dynasty, 618–907

Five Dynasties, 907–960

Song dynasty, 960–1276

    Northern Song dynasty, 960–1126

        Taizu, r. 960–976

        Taizong, r. 976–997

        Zhenzong, r. 997–1022

        Renzong, r. 1022–1063

        Yingzong, r. 1063–1067 (wife, Empress
          Gao)

        Shenzong, r. 1067–1085 (wife, Empress
          Xiang)

            Xining period, 1068–1077

            Yuanfeng period, 1078–1085

        Zhezong, r. 1085–1100 (wives, Empress
          Meng, Empress Liu)

            Yuanyou period, 1086–1093

            Shaosheng period, 1094–1097

            Yuanfu period, 1098–1100

Liao dynasty
(Kitans),
907–1124

Huizong, r. 1100–1125 (wives,
  Empress Wang, Empress Zheng)
    Jianguo jingzhong period, 1101
    Chongning period, 1102–1106
    Daguan period, 1107–1110
    Zhenghe period, 1111–1117   Jin dynasty
    Zhonghe period, 1118   (Jurchens),
    Xuanhe period, 1119–1125   1115–1234
  Qinzong, r. 1125–1127 (wife, Empress
  Zhu)
    Jingkang period, 1126–1127
Southern Song dynasty, 1127–1276
  Gaozong, r. 1127–1162
    six more Song emperors
Yuan dynasty, 1215–1368

Ming dynasty, 1368–1644

Qing dynasty, 1644–1912

Cast of Characters

AGUDA (or WANYAN AGUDA) (1068–1123) Leader of the Jurchen, repudiated Liao overlordship and founded Jin dynasty.

BAI SHIZHONG (d. 1127) Councilor near the end of Huizong's reign.

CAI BIAN (1058–1117) Cai Jing's younger brother; reformer. On the Council of State during the later part of Zhezong's reign and also during the early years of Huizong's reign.

CAI JING (1047–1126) Huizong's long-term grand councilor.

CAI TAO (d. 1147+) Cai Jing's youngest son; author of several books about the period.

CAI TIAO (fl. 1100–1130) Cai Jing's son. Married Huizong's daughter. Accompanied Huizong in captivity and wrote about what happened.

CAI YOU (1077–1126) Cai Jing's oldest son. Had an active government career, rising to the Council of State. Involved with many of Huizong's projects.

CAO XUN. (1098–1174) Author of an account of the fall of Kaifeng and the ensuing transportation north.

CHEN, CONSORT. Huizong's birth mother.

CHEN, PRINCE (b. 1117) Qinzong's eldest son, Huizong's first grandson; made heir apparent.

CHEN CISHENG (1044–1119) Outspoken critic during Huizong's first two years; anti-reformer.

xxiii

CHEN DONG (1087–1127) Imperial Academy student who led protests and wrote inflammatory memorials concerning inadequacies of government, 1125–1126.

CHEN GUAN (1060–1124) Outspoken critic during Huizong's first two years; anti-reformer. On list of banned officials.

CHONG SHIDAO (1051–1126) Song general; fought in 1122 battle for Yanjing.

CHONG SHIZHONG (1059–1126) Song general, younger brother of Chong Shidao.

DA JINGZHI (1068–1113) Daoist priest, disciple of Liu Hunkang.

DENG CHUN (fl. 1127–1167) Author of *Painting Continued*, 1167.

DENG XUNWU (d. 1121) One of Huizong's councilors.

DONG YOU (fl. 1100–1130) Worked with Huizong's antiquities collection. Wrote books on paintings and calligraphies he had seen.

FANG LA (d. 1121) Led major uprising in the Southeast.

FUJIN, PRINCESS (b. 1103) Huizong's daughter, married to Cai Jing's son Cai Tiao.

GAO, EMPRESS DOWAGER (d. 1093) Mother of Shenzong; regent for grandson Zhezong after Shenzong's death.

GAOZONG (1107–1187, r. 1127–1162) Huizong's ninth son; the only one not captured by the Jurchen. First emperor of the Southern Song.

GE SHENGZHONG (1072–1144) One of Huizong's educational officials.

GONG GUAI (1057–1111) Active as critic, 1100–1101; anti-reformer.

GOU, PRINCE (1107–1187) Huizong's ninth son, Prince of Kang. Out of the palace when the Jurchen took control in early 1127. Succeeded to the throne in 1127/4/1, after which he is referred to as Gaozong.

GUO YAOSHI (fl. 1120s) Bohai commander under Liao who defected to the Song in 1122, and was treated as a hero when he arrived in Kaifeng in 1123. Later defected to Jin at Yanjing.

GUO XI (ca. 1001–ca. 1090) Court painter of landscapes during reigns of Shenzong and Zhezong.

HAN ZHONGYAN (1038–1109) Moderate conservative, grand councilor 1100–1102.

HE ZHIZHONG (d. 1117) One of Huizong's tutors; on Council of State 1105–1116.

HUAN, PRINCE Huizong's eldest son, born in 1100, made crown prince in 1115, succeeded to the throne on 1125/12/25, after which he is referred to as Qinzong.

HUANG BOSI (1079–1118)   Worked with Huizong's collections; author of major work on painting.

HUANG TINGJIAN (1045–1105)   Celebrated poet and calligrapher, friend of Su Shi. Huizong banned printing of his writings.

JIANG ZHIQI (1031–1104)   A councilor during Huizong's first year as emperor.

KAI, PRINCE (1101–ca. 1130)   Huizong's third son, talented in the arts, succeeded in the civil service examinations.

LI BANGYAN (d. 1130)   On Council of State 1121–1125.

LI GANG (1083–1140)   Involved with Huizong's abdication and became important official under Qinzong, in charge of defense of Kaifeng. Wrote account of his experiences.

LI GONGLIN (ca. 1041–1106)   Literati painter, much admired by Huizong and well represented in Huizong's painting catalogue; collector of bronzes, jades, paintings, and calligraphy.

LI JIE (d. 1110)   Official who specialized in building projects, favored by Huizong. Compiled *Building Standards.*

LI YAN   Eunuch included among the "Six Traitors."

LI YU (937–978)   Defeated ruler of Later Tang; poet, calligrapher, and painter, admired by Huizong.

LIANG SHICHENG (ca. 1063–1126)   Leading eunuch at Huizong's court. Known for expertise in the arts. Supervised building projects.

LIN LINGSU (1076–1120)   Daoist master whom Huizong favored. Exponent of Divine Empyrean Daoism.

LIU, EMPRESS (1079–1113)   Zhezong's second empress.

LIU BING (*jinshi* 1100)   Music expert.

LIU HUNKANG (1035–1108)   Patriarch of Highest Clarity Daoism; corresponded with Huizong when out of the capital.

LIU MINGDA (d. 1113)   Consort of Huizong's; Huizong was very upset when she died in 1113 and had her posthumously promoted to empress.

LIU MINGJIE (d. 1121)   A favorite consort of Huizong's, whose death caused him grief.

LIU ZHENGFU (1062–1119)   One of Huizong's councilors.

MA KUO (d. 1151)   Son of Ma Zheng. Song envoy to Jin who wrote of experiences. Military commander, active in resistance against Jin.

MA ZHENG   Song envoy to Jin.

MENG, EMPRESS / EMPRESS DOWAGER (d. 1135)   Zhezong's first empress; deposed in 1096, reinstated after Zhezong's death in 1100, only to be deposed again in 1102. Called on to confirm succession of Gaozong in 1127.

MI FU (1051–1107)   Eccentric calligrapher, painter, and collector; author of books on paintings and calligraphies he had seen. Briefly held office under Huizong.

NIANHAN (1079/80–1136/37)   Major Jin commander; nephew of Aguda.

QINZONG (r. 1125–1127)   Huizong's eldest son; succeeded when Huizong abdicated; taken captive.

REN BOYU (ca. 1047–ca. 1119)   Conservative critic during Huizong's first year.

RENZONG (r. 1022–1063)   Fourth Song emperor.

SHENZONG (r. 1067–1085)   Sixth Song emperor and father of Zhezong and Huizong.

SHEYEMA   Jurchen commander; son of Nianhan.

SI, PRINCE (1083–1106)   Huizong's second younger brother; son of Consort Zhu; full brother of Zhezong.

SIMA GUANG (1019–1086)   Major statesman and historian; leading opponent of the New Policies.

SSI, PRINCE (b. 1085)   Huizong's youngest brother. Prince of Yue.

SU CHE (1039–1112)   Official and literary figure; younger brother of Su Shi.

SU SHI (1036–1101)   Leading poet and essayist. Opponent of New Policies. Huizong resented him and banned his books.

TAIZONG (r. 976–997)   Second Song emperor, younger brother of Taizu.

TAIZU (r. 960–976)   Founding emperor of the Song dynasty.

TAN ZHEN   Song eunuch general.

TIANZUO (r. 1101–1125)   Emperor of Liao, overthrown and captured by Jurchen Jin.

TONG GUAN (1054–1126)   Eunuch general favored by Huizong.

WANG, EMPRESS (1084–1108)   Huizong's first empress, married to him before he took the throne.

WANG ANSHI (1021–1086)   Introduced the New Policies during Shenzong's reign.

WANG ANZHONG (1076–1134)   Served in central government during Huizong's reign; his collected works survive.

WANG FU (1079–1126)   Rose to grand councilor under Huizong.

WANG LAOZHI   Daoist master and seer favored by Huizong.

WANG MINGQING (1127–1214+)   Relatively reliable Southern Song author of several books of anecdotes that include many passages about Huizong, Cai Jing, and other members of his court.

WANG SHEN (ca. 1048–ca. 1103)   Husband of Huizong's aunt (father's sister). Painter and calligrapher; major collector of paintings and calligraphics.

WANG WENQING (1093–1153)   Daoist master, proponent of Divine Empyrean Daoism, favored by Huizong after Lin Lingsu was sent away.

WANG ZAO (1079–1154)   Served in palace library under Huizong; later served Qinzong.

WEI HANJIN (fl. 1030s–1100s)   Music theorist; proposed resetting the musical scale.

WOLIBU (d. 1127)   Jurchen general, son of Aguda.

WU, PRINCE (1083–1127)   Huizong's first younger brother. Prince of Yan.

WU JUHOU (1037–1113)   Served in fiscal posts under Shenzong and Zhezong; Huizong appointed to the Council of State.

WU MIN (1089–1132)   Involved with Huizong's abdication.

WU YUANYU   A court painter, specialist in bird-and-flower painting, who was Huizong's painting teacher while he was a prince.

WUQIMAI (r. 1123–1135)   Jurchen general who succeeded to the throne; later known as Jin Taizong.

XIANG, EMPRESS DOWAGER (d. 1101)   Shenzong's empress. Legal mother of Zhezong and Huizong. Selected Huizong to succeed in 1100 and co-ruled with him for six months.

XU ZHICHANG   Daoist court official; recommended Lin Lingsu to Huizong.

XUANZONG (r. 712–756)   Tang emperor; presided over a brilliant court, abdicated following start of An Lushan rebellion.

YANG JIAN (d. 1121)   High-ranking eunuch, involved in construction.

YE MENGDE (1077–1148)   Served Huizong in several offices; author of collections of anecdotes.

YELÜ CHUN (d. 1122)   Member of Liao imperial family put on the throne in Yanjing in 1123.

YINGZONG (r. 1063–1067)   Fifth Song emperor, father of Shenzong, husband of Empress Dowager Gao.

YUWEN XUZHONG (1079–1146)   Critic of alliance with Jin; discussed abdication with Huizong.

ZENG BU (1035–1107)   On Council of State when Huizong succeeded, raised to grand councilor under Huizong.

ZHANG BANGCHANG (1081–1127)   Councilor when Huizong abdicated. Made puppet ruler by Jin.

ZHANG DUN (1035–1105)   Councilor when Zhezong died, dismissed early in Huizong's reign.

ZHANG JUE (d. 1124)   Former Liao military officer who defected from Jin to Song, causing major crisis in Song–Jin relations in 1124.

ZHANG SHANGYING (1043–1121)   One of Huizong's grand councilors.

ZHANG XUBAI   Daoist master.

ZHAO LIANGSI (d. 1126)   Defector from Liao to Song. Played a major part in the negotiations that led to the Song–Jin alliance.

ZHAO LINGRANG (ca. 1070–ca. 1100)   Imperial clansman, painter, art collector.

ZHAO TINGZHI (1040–1107)   One of Huizong's grand councilors.

ZHENG JUZHONG (1059–1123)   High official under Huizong.

ZHENZONG (r. 997–1022)   Third Song emperor; son of Taizong.

ZHEZONG (r. 1085–1100)   Seventh Song emperor; son of Shenzong and elder brother of Huizong.

ZHU, CONSORT DOWAGER (d. 1102)   Zhezong's mother.

ZHU, EMPRESS (d. 1128)   Qinzong's empress. Committed suicide in captivity.

ZHU MIAN (1075–1126)   Given charge of collecting plants and rocks for Huizong's gardens; hated for his rapacity.

ZOU HAO (1060–1111)   Anti-reformer; exiled by Zhezong, briefly brought back by Huizong, then put on banned list.

Genealogy of the Song Emperors and Empresses

Emperors are preceded by a number; dates are dates of reign.

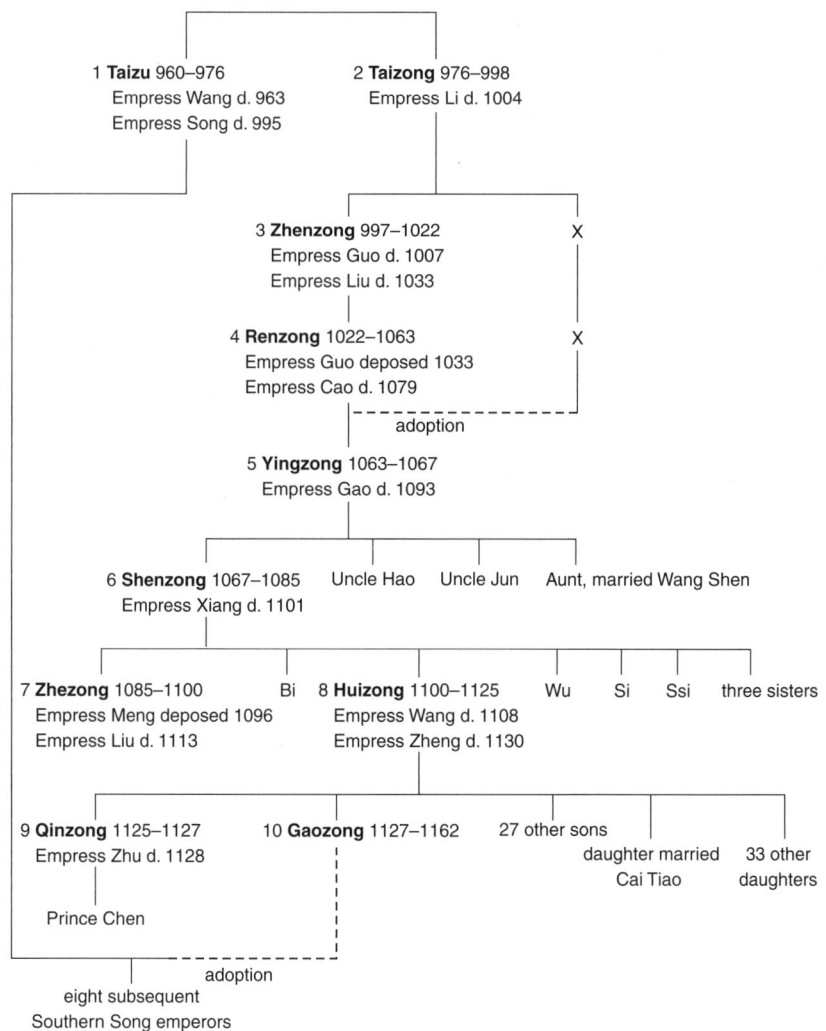

1 **Taizu** 960–976
Empress Wang d. 963
Empress Song d. 995

2 **Taizong** 976–998
Empress Li d. 1004

3 **Zhenzong** 997–1022
Empress Guo d. 1007
Empress Liu d. 1033

X

4 **Renzong** 1022–1063
Empress Guo deposed 1033
Empress Cao d. 1079

X

adoption

5 **Yingzong** 1063–1067
Empress Gao d. 1093

6 **Shenzong** 1067–1085
Empress Xiang d. 1101

Uncle Hao   Uncle Jun   Aunt, married Wang Shen

7 **Zhezong** 1085–1100
Empress Meng deposed 1096
Empress Liu d. 1113

Bi   8 **Huizong** 1100–1125
Empress Wang d. 1108
Empress Zheng d. 1130

Wu   Si   Ssi   three sisters

9 **Qinzong** 1125–1127
Empress Zhu d. 1128

10 **Gaozong** 1127–1162

27 other sons

daughter married
Cai Tiao

33 other
daughters

Prince Chen

adoption

eight subsequent
Southern Song emperors

I

LEARNING TO RULE, 1082–1108

1

Growing Up in the Palace, 1082–1099

> When I was a child Zhezong was very affectionate. He would often summon us to join him and we would eat and drink [informally] using only ceramic dishes.
>
> —*Huizong, looking back in 1102*

ON THE TWELFTH DAY of the first month of the third year of the Primal Talley reign period (which corresponds roughly to 1100 CE), Huizong's life took a momentous turn.[1] That day his elder brother, the twenty-three-year-old (twenty-five *sui*) Emperor Zhezong died after an illness that his physicians had failed to cure despite months of treatment.[2] No heir apparent had been appointed, and Zhezong's legal mother, Empress Dowager Xiang (the empress of his father Shenzong), selected the second oldest of Zhezong's five surviving younger brothers, Huizong, as the next emperor. Huizong had not been groomed to succeed to the throne, but he had spent fifteen of his seventeen years in the Palace City. He knew a lot about what an emperor did, even if he had never expected to be called on to perform the role himself.

Palace Life

What was it like to grow up in the palace? There was nothing else like it elsewhere in the country (Figure 1.1). To those who never got to enter the Palace City, its most striking feature was the five km-long brick-faced wall that surrounded it. These dimensions make the Song Palace City only slightly smaller than the Forbidden City in Beijing today. The uniformity of this stark, massive wall was interrupted by seven gates and four sixty meter-tall corner towers, designed for defensive

3

purposes. The most imposing of the gates was the central southern one, Virtue Revealed Gate. A huge structure, this gate had two watch towers on the wings of its upper story, their roofs of glazed tile. The gate's five sets of doors were painted red and decorated with gold-colored nails. Its walls were of stone blocks carved with dragons, phoenixes, and clouds, and its beams were all carved or painted.[3]

The Virtue Revealed Gate was the threshold marking the boundary between the emperor's quarters and the populace of the city of Kaifeng, indeed of the entire Song empire. The emperor regularly took advantage of the gate's symbolic significance to show his concern for his subjects by appearing there. Every year in the first month, at the Lantern Festival, the street in front of the palace became the site of a festival, and the emperor and a few members of his family would come to the gate to watch the display from the upper story. The emperor would also show himself at Virtue Revealed Gate to proclaim amnesties after he sacrificed to heaven and earth at the Suburban Altars.[4]

The Palace City was commonly called the "Great Interior," likening it to the inner quarters of ordinary homes, the part off-limits to strangers, where the family's women and servants could move around as they wished, without fear that outsiders would intrude on them. The emperor's servants included his civil servants, the officials; the clerks and other functionaries who worked under them; his expert servants, such as painters, astronomers, and physicians; his domestic servants, both palace ladies and eunuchs; and his military servants, who served as guards. Different sections of the Palace City were set aside for these different classes of imperial servants. Two roads, one east–west and one north–south, divided the Palace City into three large sections. The east–west road, running from the Western Splendor Gate to the Eastern Splendor Gate, divided the Palace City into a front, or southern section, dominated by officials and clerks, and a rear, or northern, more residential section. Civil officials who had access to the ritual spaces and office buildings in the front section did not enter the Palace City through the main southern gate—that was the privilege of the emperor and empresses. They would instead have used one of the other gates, such as the Right Side Gate, most dismounting their horses before entering.

In the center of the southern section was the compound with the largest and most formal hall, the Grand Celebration Hall, used on

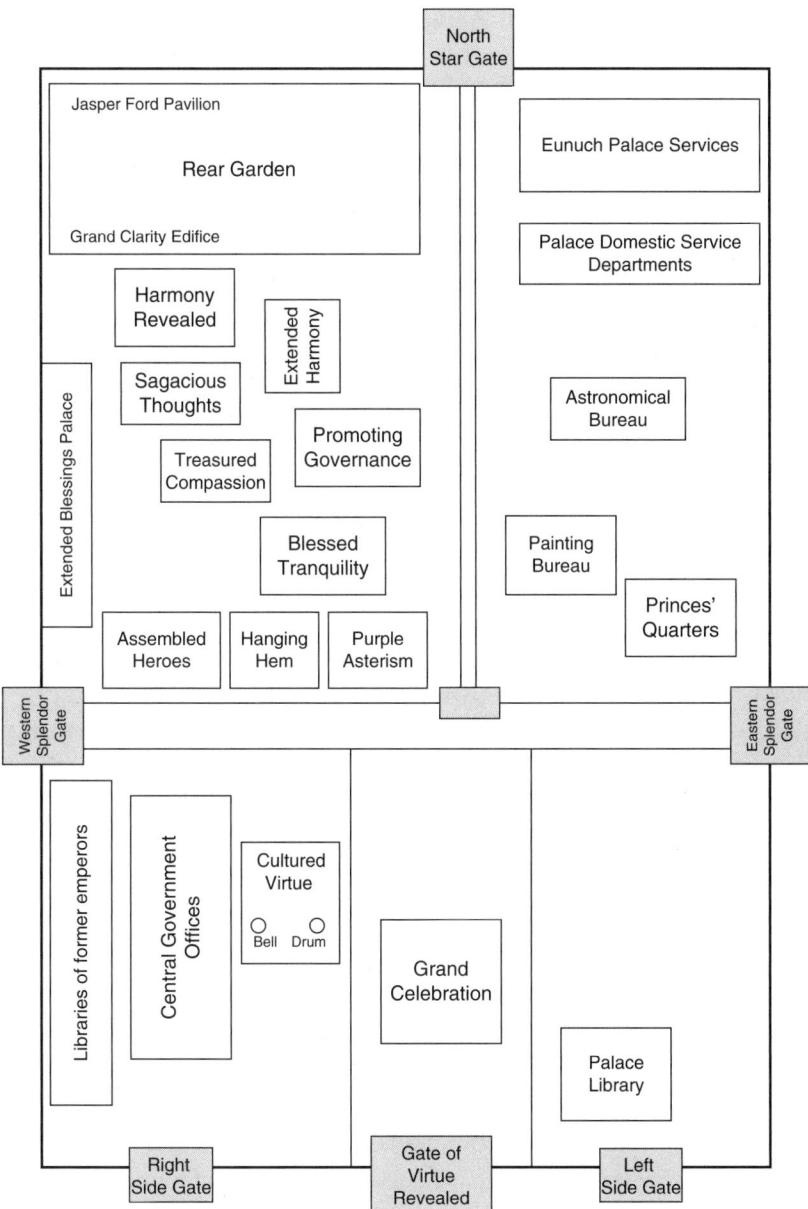

Fig. 1.1. Layout of the Palace City

major state occasions such as the New Year's audience. Six different gates led into this compound, which could hold twenty thousand or more people for major ceremonies. Grand Celebration Hall itself was nine bays across, making it on the order of fifty meters long. On either side of it were multistory side halls, five bays long, their arrangement reminding some observers of the layout of a temple complex with paired pagodas. Behind the main hall was another hall, used by the emperor during ceremonies, and on either side were galleries, each sixty bays long.[5]

To the east of Grand Celebration Hall stood the Palace Library, a complex of buildings holding on the order of forty thousand books. To the west was another large hall, Cultured Virtue Hall, in front of which stood the Bell Tower and the Drum Tower, used to mark time. The rear section, in turn, was bisected by a north–south road from the rear gate to the east–west road. Other halls sometimes used for ceremonies were Hanging Hem Hall and Purple Asterism Hall, behind Cultured Virtue Hall. Four celebrated painters were commissioned early in the reign of Huizong's father to paint the screen for Hanging Hem Hall, each of them doing one panel. Some of the same painters were called on to do screens for Purple Asterism Hall: Ai Xuan did four cranes, Cui Bo bamboo, Ge Shouchang crabapple blossoms, and Guo Xi a rock.[6] Higher officials entered these halls with some frequency. The emperor's closest advisors and ministers—called the Council of State—met him daily in Cultured Virtue Hall. Every five days a larger group of several dozen officials had an audience in Hanging Hem Hall. Then an even larger group of several hundred participated in the twice-a month audiences, on the first of the month in Cultured Virtue Hall, on the fifteenth in Purple Asterism Hall. They might also get to see other halls for banquets, to which the emperor invited officials with some regularity.[7]

To the west of the audience halls were the offices of the central policy organs, including, in particular, those for the Council of State, the Secretariat-Chancellery, the Bureau of Military Affairs, and the Hanlin Academy. Also nearby were the Censorate and the Bureau of Policy Criticism, whose officials were called "speaking officials" because they were charged with speaking up against misbehaving officials and misguided policies. These offices where officials worked, files were kept, and memorials and edicts were copied were naturally on a more modest scale than the halls where the emperor presided. Yet they were not necessarily shabby or cramped. The compound for the Hanlin academicians contained ten buildings: an office for clerks, four offices for academicians, an office each for express couriers and editorial assistants, two libraries, and a central hall, known as Jade Hall. The interior walls of Jade Hall had been decorated by several prominent artists. In the 980s, Dong Yu had depicted surging, whirling ocean waves on the eastern and western walls, each about eighteen meters long. A few years later, the monk painter Juran had painted a mist-enshrouded mountain on the north wall. In the 1030s, the high-ranking official Yan Su presented a six-panel screen of landscapes he had painted himself, which was placed behind the chair reserved for the emperor, should he choose to visit. The overall effect of these paintings, according to contemporaries, was to make the visitor feel that he was in some magical isle in the ocean where the immortals lived.[8]

As a child Huizong would have spent most of his time in the rear, more residential, section of the Palace City, with its exquisite gardens. During the reign of Huizong's father Shenzong, the eunuch Song Yongchen had supervised a renovation of Jasper Ford Pavilion in the Rear Garden. He had a special pavilion brought hundreds of kilometers from Hangzhou in south China and had a new pool dug out. When Shenzong expressed disappointment that there were not any lotus flowers in the pool, Song told him to come again the next day, then went out and bought up all the potted lotus plants in the city and sunk them into the pond. The next day when Shenzong visited, he was so pleased that he decided to get his favorite painter Guo Xi to paint a screen for the pavilion. Another garden favored by Shenzong was at Sagacious Thoughts Hall, kept cool in summer by the trees that surrounded it and a stream running through it. The screens made for this hall by Guo Xi depicted pines and rocks so successfully that they were used to elicit hundreds of poems by members of the court.[9]

Civil officials were the highest-ranking of the emperor's servants in the Palace City, but they were not the most numerous. Over two thousand military men were on duty there, charged with controlling entrance and exit through the gates of the palace and serving as the emperor's bodyguards. At one count there were 1,069 cooks and cooks' helpers working in the palace. Feeding everyone in the palace required

several thousand pounds of flour a day, and each year tens of thousands
of sheep and thirty-two tons of sugar.[10]

To manage paperwork, there were several thousand functionaries
and clerks who worked in the office compounds with the civil officials.
Following a quite different career path from the civil servants, these
men might work in the same office for decades, and could expect to see
their sons receive comparable jobs when they were of age. Of higher
status than the clerks, but still without the standing of the regular civil
officials, were the technical specialists, such as astronomers, physicians, and painters. Their buildings were concentrated on the east side
of the rear palace.[11]

Officials, clerks, and technical specialists merely worked in the Palace City, normally returning to their homes at night. Besides these
commuters into the Palace City, there were several thousand overnight residents, the most numerous of whom were the thousands of
women employed by the Palace Domestic Service.[12] No palace woman
would have reason to cross south past the east–west thoroughfare, but
those assigned to attend to members of the imperial family would have
frequently come and gone in and out of courtyards all over the northern two-thirds of the palace complex. Hundreds of them, however,
were not involved in such personal service, and stayed in the service
areas in the northeast, where clothing was made and laundered, and
where the utensils for meals and ceremonies were stored.

Palace women had titles and ranks, likening them to the men who
served in administrative or military posts, but this symmetry was
deceptive, as palace women were also a pool of potential mates for the
emperor. When Huizong was born in 1082, his father Shenzong had
been on the throne fifteen years, and in this time had acquired thirteen
consorts in addition to Empress Xiang, his wife.[13] Shenzong's consorts
all seem to have been promoted from among the palace ladies.

Shenzong's main residence was Blessed Tranquility Hall, located in
the middle of the western rear section, directly behind Hanging Hem
Hall where he saw officials. The halls occupied by mothers, grand-
mothers, and wives of emperors changed over time. Empress Dowager
Gao, Shenzong's mother and the highest-ranking woman in the palace
in Huizong's childhood, lived in Treasured Compassion Hall while
Shenzong was emperor, refusing his offer to build her a larger home.
Shenzong's wife, Empress Xiang, lived in Exalted Protection Hall.[14]

Besides the empress and empress dowager, there were probably fifty or so relatives of the emperor with their own quarters and their own servants. These would include Shenzong's step-mothers and step-grandmothers (widowed high-ranking consorts of his predecessors), his own higher consorts, his children, as well as his two brothers and their families.

Palace women could do most of the domestic service needed in the palace, but not all of it: eunuchs were needed to cross between the world of the women to that of the men. Eunuchs had played a role in palace affairs since antiquity, and had at times gained the upper hand through their capacity as the emperor's personal agents. In the ninth century, during the Tang dynasty, eunuchs had gained control of access to the emperors. Intent not to let that happen again, Song rulers severely limited eunuchs' numbers; the quota for eunuchs in the Palace Domestic Service and Palace Eunuch Service was set at 180 early in the dynasty.[15]

Like the palace women, eunuchs had their own career paths, involving promotion from one rank to another. The most important were much more than messengers; they could be sent outside the Palace City or even the capital city, and given tasks such as checking on military operations or tax collection in the provinces. A few eunuchs even became military commanders. Other eunuchs were given charge of agencies that were staffed by regular officials and clerks. Eunuchs kept track of and audited the many storehouses in the palace complex. One of these, the Inner Palace Treasury, contained the funds of the Privy Purse in the form of coins, gold, silver, and silk. Others held objects for the use of palace residents and for gifts, such as the Tea and Charcoal Storehouse, the Oil and Vinegar Storehouse, the Ritual Dress Storehouse, and the Import Storehouse, which held spices, medicines, and ivory received from tribute missions.[16]

When Huizong was born, the most powerful eunuch in the palace was Shi Deyi. He had been given charge of the construction of the new headquarters for the Department of State Affairs, four thousand room-units in size, a project begun in the middle of 1082 and completed at the end of the next year. The palace painter Guo Xi was charged with painting murals and screens for many of its buildings.[17]

Huizong's Immediate Family

Huizong was born to Consort Chen on the tenth day of the tenth month of 1082 in a side hall east of Blessed Tranquility Hall, Shenzong's main residence.[18] Even though Huizong is always listed as the eleventh son of Shenzong, he was hardly a superfluous child. Consort Xing had born four sons in 1071, 1073, 1077, and 1078, but not a single one was still alive in 1082. The same was true of the two sons born to Consort Song in 1069 and 1077. Of Shenzong's first ten sons, only four had lived to age three, and only one had reached five. When Huizong was born, he had only three siblings: his sister Xianmu, in her eighth year; his oldest brother Zhezong, in his seventh year; and his older brother Bi, then an infant of three months, and Bi hardly counted, given past experience with infant mortality. None of these children were born to the empress. Empress Xiang had given birth to a girl in 1067, but the girl had died at twelve *sui* in 1078 and Xiang had never had any other children. Succession invariably passed down along the male line, with sons of the empress favored over other sons, and age taken into account. It was common to select the eldest son of the empress as heir, but not required, and emperors could appoint any one of their sons as heir apparent.

Huizong was the first child born to Consort Chen, a woman who had entered the palace years earlier as a general palace lady and was first promoted to consort shortly after Huizong's birth (and undoubtedly because of it). Given the poor survival of royal children, we have to assume that Consort Chen made every possible effort to see that her son was given the best possible care. About all we know about how he was taken care of in this period, however, is that at least three women served as his wet nurses.[19]

Huizong's father, Shenzong, thirty-four years old when Huizong was born, had proved an activist emperor who oversaw a vast expansion of the activities of the government under the banner of the "New Policies" (Figure 1.2). Although Huizong would later identify with his father, he certainly could not have actually remembered Shenzong. By the time Huizong was a toddler, Shenzong was seriously ill; Huizong was only twenty-eight months old when Shenzong died in the third month of 1085.

The throne went to Huizong's older brother Zhezong. Zhezong was in his tenth year (ten *sui*), but only eight by Western ways of counting

Fig. 1.2. Portrait of Shenzong (anon.), hanging scroll, ink and colors on silk, 176.4 × 114.4 cm. (National Palace Museum, Taiwan, Republic of China)

age, since he was born in the twelfth month of 1076. He had been introduced to the leading officials at a banquet at Assembled Heroes
Hall the year before, but was not actually made heir apparent until
four days before his father died, his ill father reportedly nodding when
his councilors recommended this step. Shenzong had two adult brothers, the Empress Dowager's own sons, but the principle of succession
from father to son was so strong that they would not have been considered as heirs, given the presence of a son.[20] For ancestral rites, each
emperor needed to be succeeded by a son who would make offerings to
him at the Supreme Shrine.

Since Zhezong was still a child, it was expected that a regent would
make actual decisions. Earlier in the dynasty, when Shenzong's grandfather Renzong had succeeded to the throne at ten, his father's empress, his "legal" mother, acted as regent.[21] Zhezong's own mother was
Consort Zhu, outranked by his legal mother, Empress Xiang. She,
however, was in turn outranked by her mother-in-law, Empress Dowager Gao, then in her fifty-fourth year. It was Gao who took on the
role of regent for Zhezong.

Empress Dowager Gao was an old hand at palace affairs. From one
of the leading military families, she had been raised in the palace because her mother was the sister of Renzong's Empress Cao. In her teens
Gao was selected to marry an imperial clansman and left the palace
with him. Some fifteen years later, however, her husband was made
adopted heir to the sonless Renzong and ascended the throne. Known
as Yingzong, he died after only four years on the throne, and Shenzong as eldest son succeeded. As mother, Gao had not had much power
over her son Shenzong; at times she implored Shenzong to reverse his
political decisions, but without effect.[22] Once he died and she became
regent, however, she was free to turn to officials who had opposed Shenzong's New Policies.

Even if his grandmother could substitute for Zhezong in selecting
ministers and deciding policy issues, she could not take his place in the
funeral rituals sons were expected to perform for their fathers. Zhezong,
as the eldest son and heir, had specific roles to play, but Huizong and the
other younger brothers also had to be present at all the major funeral
rituals, spread out over nine months. For about seven months, while the
tomb was being built, the coffin remained in the palace and both family
members and officials would approach it and express their grief.[23]

For Huizong, at least as momentous a change as the death of his father would have been the departure of his mother, Consort Chen. When Shenzong's coffin was taken out of the palace to be buried at the imperial tombs in the tenth month of 1085, when Huizong had just reached three, she went with it, to continue her mourning at the hall built at the tomb. As it turns out, she never returned. The histories record that she went to stay at the hall at his tomb, and, preoccupied with her memories of him, wasted away to mere skin and bones. When those around her urged her to eat or take medicine, she told them, "My wish will be fulfilled if I get to serve the former emperor sooner."[24]

Once his father's coffin had been removed from the palace complex, Huizong's life probably settled down to a fairly quiet routine. During the next two or three years, 1085–1088, much went on at court, as Huizong's grandmother dismissed the ministers who had served under Shenzong and appointed ones to replace them who would dismantle Shenzong's New Policies. Huizong of course was much too young during this period to have had any inkling of what was going on.

Until he was five or six, Huizong's world would have been the women's quarters, the world of his step-mothers, step-grandmothers and even step-great-grandmothers, not to mention the numerous relatively young palace women and the dozens of wet nurses, both those currently nursing children and those kept on as children's nursemaids. Those in charge of these children looked for signs that they would grow up to be intelligent and well mannered. One of Huizong's brothers who lived only to four and a half was described as good looking and quick witted. "Before he could talk, his nursemaid would point to characters written on a screen, and after one or two times he could recognize them. As he got a little older and had his hair in a young boy's tufts, everyday he grew cuter, yet his demeanor was solemn, much like that of an adult. He did not carry playing too far, and he rarely had temper tantrums."[25] When this prince suddenly fell ill, we are told, Shenzong came to check on him every morning and evening, and was deeply grieved when he died.

Huizong had eight step-mothers, Shenzong's consorts who had borne children. First was Empress Xiang, his legal mother as wife of his father. Consort Xing had received her first title in 1068 and Consorts Zhang and Song in 1069. The next woman to bear a child and get the appropriate title was Consort Zhu, Zhezong's mother, followed by Consorts Lin, Wu, and Chen.

By the time Huizong was four, he had three younger brothers (Wu, Si, and Ssi) and four younger sisters, none born to his own mother.[26] Three of his brothers were very close to him in age; Bi three months his senior, Wu eleven months his junior, and Si fourteen months his junior.[27] In addition, his father's posthumous son, Ssi, was only about three years his junior. In terms of Chinese age reckoning, Bi and Huizong were the same age, Wu and Si one year younger, and Ssi three years younger. Like Huizong, Wu and Si lost their mother early in 1090. Although there may have been some rivalry among the surviving step-mothers, after Shenzong's death there was no longer much reason for the rivalry to be intense. These women were now all widows and did not have to compete with each other for the favor of their common husband. Although the consorts would all want to keep in the good graces of Grand Empress Dowager Gao and Empress Dowager Xiang, the throne was no longer at stake. It would be Zhezong's son, not one of their sons, who would be the next emperor.

Even as a very young child, it can be assumed that Huizong's nurse-maids took him on daily visits to Empress Dowager Xiang and Grand Empress Dowager Gao, his legal mother and grandmother, and probably also to his elder brother Zhezong. As the epigraph to this chapter shows, Huizong once remarked that Zhezong had been very friendly to his younger brothers and when they ate with him, they used ceramic dishes, not more expensive metal or lacquer ones.[28]

Along with his brothers, Huizong periodically received promotions in rank, title, and privileges. When just twelve months old, he was enfiefed as a duke with a nominal fief of three thousand households and actual income from one thousand households. His first appointment as prince *(wang)* came in 1085. Thereafter the list of his titles and the size of his fief were increased at regular intervals. For instance, in 1095, when Huizong and Bi were fourteen *sui*, Wu and Si thirteen *sui*, and Ssi eleven *sui*, they all received promotion after the Bright Hall ceremonies. The two older boys were ranked at 8000/2500 households, the next two at 7000/2300, and the youngest at 5800/1900.[29]

Diversions

The palace and imperial parks were full of things to fascinate a child. One of the more exciting entertainments was polo matches. Narrow ten-foot-high goals were set up on the east and west of the field, only a foot or so wide, held in place in lotus-shaped stone stands. Scorekeepers held small red flags that they raised when a ball was hit through the goal. Musicians were on hand, contributing to the festive atmosphere. The teams were drawn from princes, imperial sons-in-law, imperial clansmen, and higher-rank officials, who rode well-trained, decorated horses. To keep the teams distinguishable, players on the left wore yellow, those on the right purple. The emperor led the mounted players onto the field, the orchestra playing. Before play began, the emperor and the players toasted each other. Then the emperor set the ball in motion before leaving the field. The audience would cheer whenever a goal was made, and the player who scored would dismount to thank them.[30]

A child would also enjoy the Lantern Festival, on the fifteenth of the first month, when people throughout the capital would hang out decorated lanterns, then wander the streets to see other people's lanterns. Those in the palace viewed the Lantern Festival from the multistoried Virtue Revealed Gate in the center of the southern wall of the Palace City.[31] Virtue Revealed Gate would also have been a great place to watch the preparations for the Suburban Sacrifice to heaven, held every third year. Crowds would gather even for the rehearsals, needed to prepare the seven elephants, their handlers, and the musicians.[32] Clever businessmen took advantage of the crowds to sell pictures of elephants or wooden or ceramic models of elephants.

There would also have been much to watch on the day of the Suburban Sacrifice to heaven itself. About twenty thousand people lined up in the huge courtyard of the Grand Celebration Hall. An officer from the astronomical bureau stood on top of the drum tower, tending the water clock, and announcing each hour, to keep the preparations on schedule. The various participants in the procession were dressed in distinctive, colorful garb, so spectators would have been able to distinguish eunuchs from officials and soldiers. Civil officials wore scarlet court robes, their ranks made visible by their hats. As a prince, Huizong would have worn the nine-ribbed hat. The very highest officials would wear identical hats, but lower ranking officials would wear ones with fewer ribs, down to two ribs (see Plate 2).

Equally colorful were the banners, pennants, and streamers carried in the procession. There were also pennants for the wind, rain, thunder, lightning, wood, fire, earth, metal, and water star, white bird, and phoenix. The procession began to leave the palace at the third watch. When Huizong was ten, the prominent official Su Shi held the post of Commissioner of the Imperial Insignia, making him responsible for the procession to the Suburban Sacrifice. In the middle of the ceremony he submitted a memorial reporting that more than ten red covered carriages, carrying women from the palace, had followed the procession, competing for space on the road with the imperial procession. In his view women had no part to play in these sorts of ceremonies. It was bad enough that it had become the custom for the empresses to go out to welcome the imperial carriage back. But for them to show up before the sacrifices were complete and get caught up among the various pennants and flags was totally unacceptable. We are told that when Zhezong read the memorial, he sent a messenger to deliver it to Grand Empress Dowager Gao, after which greater solemnity was observed.[33]

Of the celebrations Huizong would have attended during his childhood, none would have been more festive than Zhezong's wedding. Yingzong and Shenzong had come to the throne already married, so the Palace City had not witnessed a full-scale imperial wedding since Renzong had married in 1024, nearly seventy years earlier. Empress Dowager Gao began planning for the wedding well in advance. She had more than one hundred girls from suitable families brought into the palace and eventually selected one named Meng as worthy of the title empress.[34] When Zhezong was thirteen in 1090, she appointed a group of high officials to study the precedents for imperial wedding rituals and prepare new step-by-step instructions.

The wedding itself took place over six days in the fourth month of 1092, when Zhezong was fifteen and a half. On the first day, Huizong and other princes, along with imperial clansmen, officials, and military officers, assembled in Cultured Virtue Hall in their scarlet court dress to observe the ceremonies of "presenting the gifts" and "asking the name," steps in the ancient marriage ritual. Four days later, after other preliminary rituals, the main emissary went to fetch the bride. Officials again wore their scarlet court robes to meet them on their return. Some lined up outside Virtue Revealed Gate where they could observe the formalities between the party bringing the bride and the party welcoming her. A place was marked off for Miss Meng's parents to take their leave of her using phrases from the classics. She then was carried through the palace grounds, part of the way in a sedan chair, part of the time in a carriage. Officials and clansmen lined up to welcome her at different gates, until finally she reached Blessed Tranquility Hall, where Zhezong had been brought, dressed in highly formal robes and the ancient-style "penetrating to heaven" hat. The rest of the ceremonies, including the requisite three sips of wine, were done with only a few palace attendants present.[35]

Education

What sort of life was Huizong being prepared for during these years? Brothers of emperors were in an awkward position. Because those who might wish to depose the emperor could latch onto them, it was dangerous to let princes have real power. But the cultural value placed on filial piety toward their common mother, not to mention fraternal love, required that an emperor treat his brothers amicably. In Song times, princes were not given substantive political or military assignments; they did not lead troops or govern provinces. They were given ample allowances and all the symbolic privileges of high rank, such as the right to large retinues and to wear the garments and other symbolic manifestations of high rank. But they had to guard against giving the impression that they had political aspirations. No emperor could allow ambitious or scheming officials to gather around a potential rival for the throne.

One way for princes to prove their lack of political ambitions was to give every indication that they enjoyed their indulged life—to immerse themselves in the pleasures of dogs, horses, wine, and women. The dissolute prince was a recognized and understandable social type.

An alternative way for princes to pass their days was to pursue learning and art. This was the route taken by Shenzong's two younger brothers (Huizong's uncles), Hao and Jun. As the only surviving sons of Empress Dowager Gao, during Zhezong's reign Hao and Jun were welcome in the women's quarters of the palace. Indeed, because Shenzong had repeatedly denied their requests to move out of the palace to their own quarters, these two uncles had stayed in the palace long after they were adult. They had minor ritual roles to play. The epitaph for Uncle Hao reports that he made the second offerings each of the times Shenzong performed the Suburban Sacrifice, two times when Shenzong had performed the Bright Hall sacrifices, and occasionally officiated at the Supreme Shrine ceremonies as a substitute for Shenzong.[36] As Huizong gradually became aware of his standing—that of younger brother of an emperor—he would undoubtedly have taken particular notice of these two uncles, who offered him an example of what he might be able to make of himself.

Both Uncle Hao and Uncle Jun were interested in religion. Jun, we are told, "enjoyed the words of the Buddha and Laozi. He gathered the essential [texts], and had blocks carved to print them." Hao was especially drawn to Buddhism and attended major Buddhist services on behalf of the emperor. He was also fond of medical books and would prepare prescriptions himself. Uncle Hao was skilled in both calligraphy and archery, and had a strong interest in music. For the Lantern Festival one year he composed some of the songs that were performed. He was also passionate about collecting rare books. Shenzong had encouraged this interest, and whenever he acquired an unusual book, he would have a messenger take it to Hao.[37] Uncle Jun had comparable interests in painting, calligraphy, and medicine. He did calligraphy in several script types and painted flowers, bamboo, fruit, shrimp, fish, old trees, and river reeds. He compiled a pharmacological book called *Collected Effective Prescriptions for Universal Benefit Compiled during Leisure* and would prepare prescriptions from his own supply of materia medica to treat those who fell ill. Uncle Jun's wife, Princess Wang, also painted. After she married the prince at sixteen *sui*, she interested herself in painting and literature, we are told, not jewelry or other luxuries. Uncle Jun died in 1088, when Huizong was six, but Uncle Hao lived another eight years to 1096, giving Huizong a much better chance to get to know him. Both Hao and Jun had quite a few sons themselves, cousins close in age to Huizong.[38]

Before Huizong could develop the sorts of refined hobbies his aunts and uncles had, he had to master the standard literary curriculum. The type of education he was given was probably influenced to some extent by the concerted efforts taken in the late 1080s to make sure that Zhezong received a thorough Confucian education. Three illustrated books that had been specially prepared some sixty years earlier when Renzong had ascended the throne as a child were reprinted for Zhezong. One of the books had selections on the famous rulers and ministers from history, another covered one hundred events in the first three reigns of the Song dynasty, and the last, in thirty chapters, illustrated the objects such as banners, flags, and decorated vehicles used in ritual processions. Since extra copies were made and distributed not only to the various palaces but also to high officials, it seems very likely that these books would have been among those used for Huizong's early education.[39]

One of Zhezong's teachers, Fan Zuyu, compiled a book in eight chapters titled *Learning for an Emperor*, which consisted of anecdotes about earlier emperors, showing that great emperors had respected scholars, teachers, and books, and were earnest in their studies. This book, still extant, includes no reference to anything that would seem forceful—emperors are not praised for being decisive, expanding the country, or improving the people's welfare, but rather for listening to their teachers. To give an example, the founder of the Later Han dynasty, Emperor Guangwu, is praised for inviting Confucian scholars to court, appointing one for each of the Five Classics, listening to lectures by them, and visiting the Imperial Academy where they taught. Once all rivals were defeated, he never again mentioned the armies. When his heir apparent asked about military strategy, he responded that Confucius had demurred when Duke Ling of Wei had asked about arraying troops.[40] Of the earlier Song emperors, special emphasis was given to Renzong because it was during his reign that the practice of Confucian scholars lecturing to the emperors was institutionalized.[41]

In 1091, when Huizong was nine, a Hanlin academician offered a plan for the education of imperial clansmen and princes. From age eight to fourteen, the students would memorize passages of twenty characters a day, according to a fixed plan. Each year they would be examined on their progress.[42] When Huizong was ten in 1093/2, Grand Empress Dowager Gao decided that it was time for the princes to begin studying with outside teachers. A school room was set up at a former prince's residence. Two officials were assigned to serve as teachers and four eunuchs to manage the establishment. Some six weeks later, when it was time for the princes to begin their studies, Zhezong gave them each a set of the Nine Classics as well as the writings of the Confucian philosophers Mencius, Xunzi, and Yang Xiong.[43]

In 1095 Zhezong asked his high officials to nominate older, virtuous men to serve as tutors for his younger brothers. Three men who served as Huizong's tutors are known: Fu Ji, Zhu Fu, and He Zhizhong. All three had civil service degrees, the first two getting them nearly thirty years earlier in 1067. All three were from the south, Fu Ji and Zhu Fu from the same prefecture in Fujian, He Zhizhong from a little further north in modern Zhejiang. Both Fu Ji and He Zhizhong had put in time in prefectural posts early in their careers but reached the capital by the 1090s. Zhu Fu served as a teacher at the princes' lower and upper schools from 1087 on. In 1094 when Zhang Dun became grand councilor, Zhu Fu was summoned for an audience. He lectured Zhezong on the doctrines of "rectifying the mind, making the intentions sincere, knowing men, and bringing peace to the people."[44] He continued as the princes' tutor for the next four years and was promoted twice.

Fu Ji was perhaps the most committed to Confucian learning of the three tutors. He had studied with well-known Confucian scholars in his youth and married the daughter of one of his teachers. While serving in a succession of local posts over the course of two decades, he assembled a large collection of books. Later he served as professor of the Imperial Academy for four years. During his five years as tutor to the princes, Fu Ji proposed that changes should be made to the established curriculum. In his view, the education of princes had stressed calligraphy and composition at the expense of the classics. He argued that the princes' education should focus on virtue and propriety, not minor accomplishments like calligraphy. Fu Ji requested approval of his plan to confine instruction to discussion of the *Analects, Classic of Filial Piety,* and *Mencius,* and to eschew any attention to Tang poetry and poetic composition.[45] Huizong's tutors would also have taught him and the other princes basic history, especially incidents where there was a clear moral lesson to be learned, such as famously profligate rulers like the First Emperor of Qin and the last emperor of Sui (Sui Yangdi), both of whom built extravagant palaces and gardens. Confucian teachings of restraint must have sometimes seemed at odds with the actual splendors of the palace in which they lived.

Not long after Zhezong's wedding, another major transition occurred—the death of the power at court, Empress Dowager Gao on

1093/9/3. Having no confidence in sixteen-year-old Zhezong's ability to rule, from her sickbed she summoned Fan Zuyu and other trusted ministers to urge them to resist Zhezong's likely efforts to reverse her policies after her death.[46] Her suspicions proved correct. It did not take Zhezong long to decide to get rid of his grandmother's leading officials and restore his father's program.

The Capital, Kaifeng

Once Huizong was studying with an outside teacher, he had more opportunities to get to know the city that surrounded the palace complex. As splendid and populous as the Palace City was, the young prince Huizong must still have been excited when he finally could travel more freely beyond its walls into the larger world of the capital city, Kaifeng.

Kaifeng was a city well worth exploring.[47] Like great cities before and after it, it brought together diverse sets of people—the most privileged and those without anything, long-term residents and the newly arrived, men of letters and merchants, soldiers, and students. It was a sacred city because it was the home of the emperor and the site of ceremonies that confirmed and recreated the emperor's role as intermediary between mankind and heaven. Kaifeng was also a military bastion. Not only did it have large walls and a surrounding moat, but about three hundred thousand soldiers were deployed in units spread out around the city. The military and their dependents made up a significant share of the city residents.[48]

The shape of Kaifeng reflected its origins as a prefectural seat and commercial hub. Chang'an, the capital of the Tang dynasty, had been planned from the start as a huge city, about nine kilometers on each side. It was symmetrically arranged with grand avenues, walls around wards, and government-organized and -supervised marketplaces. In contrast, Kaifeng had grown from a prefectural seat, did not have walls around wards, and had no fixed places for buying and selling.

The old city—demarked by a city wall—was less than three kilometers on a side, but so many people had settled outside the walls that in 955, a few years before the Song dynasty was founded, a new outer wall was constructed, approximately seven kilometers on each side, with twenty-one gates (see Map 1). This new wall quadrupled the size of the city. The whitewashed outer wall was twelve meters high and surrounded

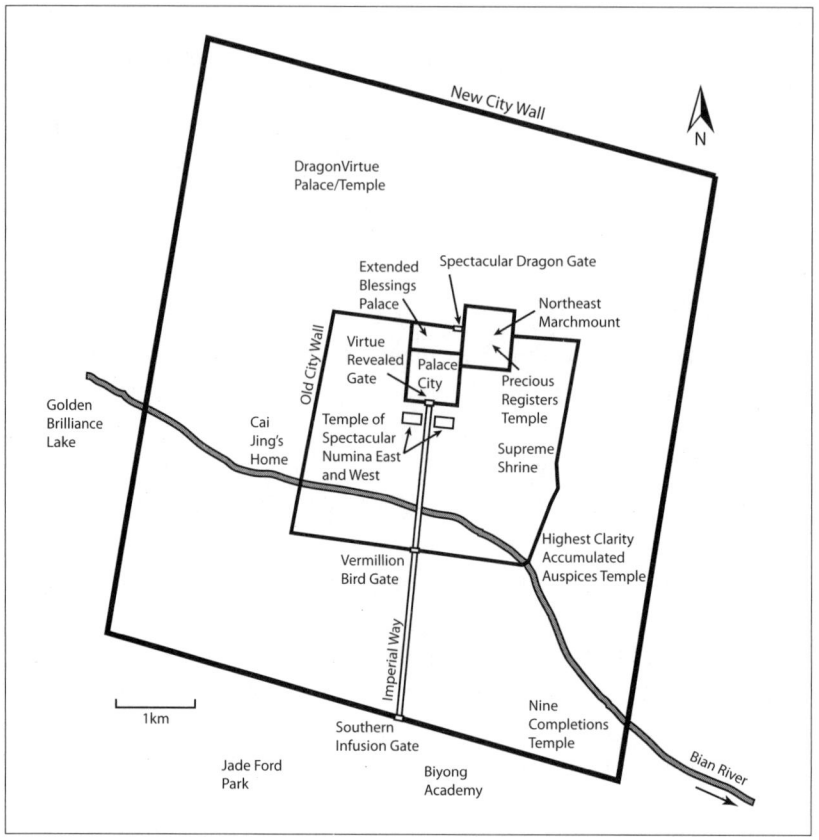

Map 1. Kaifeng

by a thirty-meter-wide moat. During Huizong's childhood the moat was enlarged to seventy-seven meters wide and almost five meters deep.[49] By that time Kaifeng had about 1.2 to 1.3 million residents.[50] Chang'an's population had been of similar size, but spread out over a larger expanse, making Kaifeng's population density about 50 percent greater (Kaifeng measured forty-nine square kilometers to Chang'an's eighty-four square kilometers).[51]

The Bian River crossed the city from west to east and was the main means of water transport in and out of the city as it linked up to the Grand Canal, which connected Kaifeng with the major cities of the south, such as Yangzhou and Hangzhou. Rice and other grain usually entered the city on boats. Jōjin, a Japanese monk who visited Kaifeng in 1072, was amazed by the "thousands and tens of thousands" of vessels he saw carrying goods on the river.[52] Goods also came in through the gates, such as the thousands of pigs driven in by pig herders every day. Traders in particular products tended to locate near each other; not only was there an alleyway where gold and silver were bought and sold, but also an inn where eagle and hawk merchants came to trade.

Symbolically, Kaifeng's most important street was the Imperial Way, which led south from Virtue Revealed Gate, on the south side of the Palace City, to Vermilion Bird Gate in the Old Wall, then the Southern Infusion Gate in the New Wall. The huge Vermilion Bird Gate was more than 150 meters wide and had a tower on its top. Shops of all kinds lined the Imperial Way and soldiers patrolled it day and night.

Entertainment was available around the clock outside the palace. Theaters, wine shops, restaurants, tea houses, and brothels were densely packed in the entertainment quarter. Meng Yuanlao reported that there were more than fifty theaters there. The Lotus Flower, Peony, Elephant, and Yaksa theaters could each accommodate an audience of several thousand.[53] Even small wine shops might well have a couple of singers to entertain customers.

Finding a place to eat in the city was never difficult. Night markets sold ready-to-eat foods such as baked sesame buns, candied fruit, rice balls, bean curd soup, crabs, and clams. Horse-Guild Avenue had especially raucous night markets, with so many lamps lit that mosquitoes and flies stayed away (or so it was thought). During the day food was even more abundant. One dumpling restaurant had more than fifty ovens and dozens of workers mixing dough, shaping dumplings, and taking them in and out of the ovens. In large markets, vendors called out the names of what they were selling in distinctive chants, making selling a performance. Large restaurants might specialize in regional cuisine, such as the Sichuan restaurant that served "noodles with meat, noodles with preserved meat; noodles with various forms of meat or vegetable topping, stewed meat, fried giblets of fowl, and rice served with toppings both raw and cooked."[54]

Huizong undoubtedly occasionally left the city, at least to go to the imperial pleasure gardens in the suburbs and the imperial tombs, further away. The Park of the Jade Ford, outside the southern gate of the New Wall, was used each year to entertain the envoys from Song's northern neighbor Liao with archery contests. Golden Brilliance Lake, outside the west wall, was originally dug to provide a place for the navy to practice maneuvers, but proved more popular as a place for boat races and other water games. Each year in the second month it was opened so that anyone in the city could visit it and enjoy the spring flowers. The reservoir was a pleasant place to stroll, with willow trees planted along its edge. Huizong would undoubtedly have accompanied Zhezong on his annual visit, along with an honor guard of mounted imperial soldiers, all wearing flowers in their hair and holding spears, swords, and colorful pennants. At the reservoir itself, there would be "flag twirling, lion and panther dances, the knife toss, the barbarian shield, and skits on ghosts and spirits."[55] Vendors would set up booths to sell wine, tea, soup, rice gruel, fruit, and souvenirs. There were games of chance and other ways to gamble. Boats on the lake served as stages for acrobats and puppets, all of these performances accompanied by music. The main events, however, were the appearance of the huge dragon boat and a capture-the-flag type of boat race. The three hundred foot-long dragon boat had a throne for Zhezong to sit on, behind which was a screen depicting dragons playing in water. Imperial consorts could watch the festivities from their cabins.[56]

Huizong would normally have traveled through the city on horseback (as did most officials), always with several men accompanying him. He would surely have visited some of the Buddhist and Daoist temples that were a prominent feature of Kaifeng. Some of the Buddhist temples had pagodas or other structures so tall that they were landmarks in the skyline. The Great Peace and Prosperous Realm Monastery southwest of the palace had an image hall seventy-four meters tall to accommodate a gigantic statue of the Buddha. Initiating Treasure Monastery, northeast of the palace, had a fifty-five-meter-tall pagoda covered in glazed brick.[57]

Not far from the southern gate of the palace was Assisting the State Monastery (Xiangguo si). Emperors made frequent visits to this state-sponsored Buddhist monastery, sometimes to view lanterns, sometimes to pray for rain. Officials went there to offer incense on imperial birthdays. It was also notable for its artworks, which included a set of gilded bronze statues of the five hundred lohans. Jōjin, the Japanese monk who visited in 1072, mentioned a sixty-foot-tall statue of Maitreya in the main hall. In Huizong's youth it would still have been possible to see the wall paintings by Gao Wenjin of the appearances of Wenshu

(Mañjuśrī) and Puxian (Samantabhadra) on Mounts Wutai and Emei respectively. He could also have seen the more recent paintings by Cui Po of Tejaprabha Buddha with the Eleven Luminaries depicted as seated deities.[58] Assisting the State Monastery was nearly as famous for its periodic market which assembled in the huge courtyard five times a month. Dealers in different commodities each had their section of the grounds. Dealers in rare birds were at the gate; in another section were booths selling saddles and bits, bows and swords. There were also dealers in honey, brushes, inks, hats, books, curios, and paintings, not to mention fortune-tellers.[59]

To truly enjoy the city, Huizong needed to set up his own residence outside the Palace City. In the tenth month of 1095 when Bi and Huizong were just turning thirteen, Zhezong announced that the five imperial younger brothers would soon be moving out. Four months later, the director for public buildings submitted plans for housing the five princes. Following precedent, their mansions would be lined up in order, with the easternmost for the most senior.[60] Construction took approximately two years. The man given charge of this construction project was Li Jie, the most famous architect in Chinese history because during these same years he compiled the oldest extant architectural manual.

On 1098/3/20, Huizong and Bi, both fifteen, moved into their mansions. Zhezong visited Bi's home the next day, Huizong's the day after. At the same time, the annual stipends for Bi and Huizong were set at an ample eight thousand strings of cash.[61] Huizong still came back to the palace regularly for the frequent rituals of audiences, both the very grand ones on New Year and other major occasions and the more routine ones held twice a month or every five days. On all these occasions the hierarchy of the government and monarchy were fully displayed with much pageantry. Everyone lined up in order, from the first-degree princes such as Huizong on down. The supreme authority of the emperor was visually confirmed when he took the throne and everyone else, including princes, kowtowed to him in groups. Huizong also occasionally represented the throne in ceremonies outside the palace. In 1098, he was selected to make the second offering at the grandest of the ceremonies, the Suburban Sacrifice, a role his uncles had performed in his childhood. The next year Huizong was called on to make a report at the Supreme Shrine to inform the ancestors that Qingtang had been recovered, a major military victory.[62]

Talented Friends and Acquaintances

Once Huizong had a house outside the palace, he could enter more fully into elite society, the world where men of wealth, learning, talent, accomplishment, and connections all mingled. Historical sources preserve several anecdotes about Huizong during this period of relative freedom when he was known as the Prince of Duan. One mentions that he was fond of pet birds. Another records that when he left court he would exit the palace city by the north gate where a young man hoping to make his acquaintance would wait till he saw him, then dismount his horse and salute him, eventually attracting his interest.[63]

The most interesting of the anecdotes about Huizong as a prince portrays him playing kickball. The point of the anecdote is to explain how Huizong became acquainted with Gao Qiu, the man who would eventually rise to commander of the imperial guard.

> Once Wang Shen and Huizong met unexpectedly at the palace while waiting to line up for an audience. Huizong said: "Today I inadvertently forgot to bring my razor. I'd like to borrow one to trim the hair at my temples. Could I?" Wang Shen took one out from his belt. Huizong said, "This type is very new and attractive," to which Wang Shen replied, "I recently had two made, one of which has not yet been used. In a little while [text missing]." That evening, Wang sent Gao Qiu to deliver it.
>
> When Gao arrived, Huizong was in his garden playing kickball. As Gao Qiu waited for an opportunity to report, his eyes darted back and forth. Huizong called him over and asked, "Are you familiar with this game?" When Gao Qiu responded that he was competent at it, Huizong good-naturedly asked him to return the kick, and Qiu did as requested.
>
> Huizong was very pleased and told the underlings who had accompanied Gao, "You can return and tell the commandant that I thank him for the razor and will keep both it and the man he sent with it."[64]

The man who sent Gao Qiu with the razor, Wang Shen, was a relative of Huizong's (his father's sister's husband), a collector of paintings and calligraphies, a skilled painter, and a friend of many of the leading

cultural figures of his day, most notably Su Shi and Mi Fu.[65] Su Shi
was a leading poet and vocal opponent of the New Policies. Mi Fu was
an artist, collector, and connoisseur who wrote extensively about the
paintings and calligraphies he saw, including many that Wang Shen
owned.[66] Wang Shen's friendship with Su Shi embroiled him in the
struggles between the reformers and anti-reformers at court. In the
1070s Wang Shen had financed the printing of an anthology of Su
Shi's poems, some of which later were used as grounds for charging
the poet with slandering the emperor. Wang Shen was charged as an
accomplice, and the deposition chronicles his relations with Su Shi over
the previous ten years, recording that Wang Shen repeatedly sent the
poet valuable gifts, supplied him with materials to mount his own paintings, and even lent him money for his niece's dowry. That Su Shi's
poems were popular added to the censors' irritation: "The common
people," the censors complained, "expect that as soon as there is a flood
or a famine or an outbreak of banditry Su Shi will surely be the first to
criticize the situation, attributing all blame to the New Policies." When
Su Shi was exiled, Wang Shen would have been as well, had not the
princess begged her brother Shenzong to let her husband keep his political post. But the next year the princess died, and Shenzong then
had Wang Shen banished.[67]

Wang Shen returned to Kaifeng in 1085. To the youthful Huizong,
he was a fascinating uncle who knew famous people, had traveled
across the country, was an accomplished painter and calligrapher, and
had one of the most notable collections of paintings and calligraphy in
the country. Huizong also started collecting in this period and once
helped Wang Shen acquire a painting he wanted.[68]

Under the influence of Wang Shen, Huizong took up painting himself. According to Cai Tao, those with the most influence on Huizong's
amateur practice of painting and calligraphy during his years as a
prince were Wang Shen, Zhao Lingrang, and Wu Yuanyu.[69] Zhao
Lingrang was a descendant of the first Song emperor and thus a distant relative of Huizong (one of 3,488 members of the fifth generation
of clansmen, the generation of Huizong's father). Zhao Lingrang grew
up in the crowded clansmen's quarters in the capital, and was said to
have lived his whole life within the geographical restrictions imposed
on members of the imperial clan, who were allowed to leave the capital
for visits to the imperial tombs halfway to Luoyang, but not to travel at

Fig. 1.3. Wang Shen, *Rivers and Mountains in Mist*, handscroll, ink and colors on silk, 45.2 × 166 cm. (Shanghai Museum)

will. Zhao Lingrang did, however, have a large collection of paintings to draw on. As a painter, he was best known for his landscapes, done in a style associated with men of letters, such as river landscapes and "small scenes." Wu Yuanyu, by contrast, was not an amateur painter like Wang Shen and Zhao Lingrang but a professional who had studied with the court painter Cui Bo, generally recognized as one of the best bird-and-flower painters of the Northern Song period. Huizong would have seen screens Cui Bo had painted in the palace.[70]

Two of Wang Shen's paintings that once were owned by Huizong have survived and are today much admired. Wang Shen's *Rivers and Mountains in Mist* (Figure 1.3) opens with an empty mist and two faint, barely visible boats. Across the river blue-green mountains rise up. In 1088 Su Shi wrote a twenty-eight-line poem for this painting. When Wang Shen saw the poem, he responded with one of his own, using all the same rhymes. Delighted, the poet matched it with another poem, and Wang Shen again responded. In his first poem, Wang Shen contributed to the then emerging theory of painting as an art suited to educated men of ideas, and listed a series of scholar-official painters whom he took as his models. In the poem he sent back, Su Shi also commented on painting as an art, noting that one did not have to live in the mountains to paint mountains, any more than one had to work the fields to write poems about farming. He flattered Wang Shen by comparing him to Zheng Qian, a Tang official who presented a scroll of poems and paintings to Emperor Xuanzong, who inscribed at the end, "Zheng Qian's three perfections," referring to his poetry, calligraphy, and painting.[71]

What did Huizong get from Wang Shen and his circle? He would have learned that one did not have to be a professional painter who devoted years to perfecting his craft to produce elegant and meaningful paintings. He would have seen the ways the practice of poetry, calligraphy, and painting complemented each other and formed an agreeable element in the social life of men of letters. He would have seen what a great resource a collection of paintings and calligraphies was, not only as a source of inspiration for one's own practice of the arts but also because it would draw interesting men like Mi Fu to one's home in order to view one's masterpieces.

Family Drama

In 1096, before Huizong got to move into his princely mansion, the palace was thrown into an uproar because of accusations of witchcraft brought against Zhezong's young wife, Empress Meng, married to him four years earlier. Zhezong never liked Meng, possibly because Empress Dowager Gao had picked her. He tolerated, perhaps even encouraged, his favorite, Consort Liu, to act rudely to his young empress. He also did nothing to tamp down accusations of occult dealings made against her. The incident began when Meng's infant daughter became ill and Meng turned to her older sister who had some expertise in medicine for help. When the medicine given the baby had no effect, the sister brought some "talisman-water," which Daoist priests used to cure illness. When she showed it to the empress, the empress was aghast and told the sister that this sort of thing was strictly prohibited in the palace. Before long Zhezong came to check on the baby, and did not seem upset about the talisman-water, saying that offering it was a normal human response. Still, rumors began spreading through the palace, giving rise to fear of demonic forces. When the baby's illness took a turn for the worse, the empress noticed token paper money (used as offerings to gods) by the baby's side and began to suspect that her rival Consort Liu had sent someone to do something. Then three people—the empress's adoptive mother, a nun, and a eunuch—were accused of using sorcery to help the empress.

Zhezong ordered one of the chief eunuchs to conduct a judicial investigation into the alleged conspiracies in the women's quarters. After thirty of the palace women and eunuchs were tortured, some ending up with broken bones or their tongues cut out, all sorts of accusations surfaced. The nun was charged with conducting voodoo-like occult ceremonies using the words "the one you despise will submit; what you seek you will gain." The eunuch was accused of drawing a picture of Consort Liu and then driving a nail through her heart in the picture, hoping in this way to kill her. The adoptive mother was accused of writing "happiness" on a piece of paper, burning it, and putting the ashes into tea to be served to Zhezong as a way to get him to shift his affections. Zhezong's officials discussed the findings with him at length, clearly recognizing that interrogations under torture did not necessarily uncover the truth. Recognizing that Zhezong believed himself to be in danger, in the end they acquiesced to his decision to depose Meng and send her to a Daoist nunnery. The three accused of sorcery were executed.[72] Huizong, Empress Dowager Xiang later reported, was brought to tears when he heard that a palace woman had died during these investigations.[73]

The year 1099 was another eventful one for Huizong and his family. In the second month the youngest of Huizong's brothers, Prince Ssi, began preparations for moving out of the palace to his own mansion. In the fourth month, Zhezong brought a considerable retinue with him for a visit to the princes' mansions. On this occasion a feast was held at the home of Wu, the eldest of Huizong's younger brothers. Two weeks later Zhezong called again. This time it was Prince Si, Huizong's second younger brother, who was the host. Given that this time Zhezong's two mothers, his legal mother Empress Dowager Xiang and his birth mother, Consort Dowager Zhu, accompanied him, in all likelihood one item of business was the marriage arrangements for the two older princes, Bi and Huizong.[74]

The girl selected to marry Huizong was then in her sixteenth year, making her two years younger than Huizong. Surnamed Wang, all that is known of her family is that they came from the capital and her father served as a prefect. Wives of princes would be selected from respectable families, but Huizong, of course, would not have been involved in the selection of this particular young woman. In the sixth month of 1099 Huizong's wedding took place, and Miss Wang was brought to Huizong's mansion to become his wife. Once he was married, Huizong's legal mother Empress Dowager Xiang made him a gift of two concubines, Miss Zheng and another Miss Wang. He already knew them, as Empress Dowager Xiang had some time ago assigned them to look after Huizong during his visits to the palace and he had become very fond of them.[75]

In the palace people were beginning to worry about Zhezong's health. From the diary kept by a member of Zhezong's Council of State, Zeng Bu, we know that Zhezong readily talked about his ailments to his councilors, so it is likely that his mothers and brothers heard about them as well.[76] At the start, the symptoms were more annoying than alarming. On 1099/5/18, Zhezong reported that he was bothered by a persistent cough and constipation. Although he had taken many medications, none had had much effect. He asked his councilors to recommend physicians well-versed in the fundamentals of medical science. The court physician Geng Yu was recommended as knowledgeable in pulse theory and good at using ancient prescriptions. Even though Zhezong followed his doctors' advice scrupulously, his health did not improve. In the seventh month doctors who came to examine him stayed three days. By then Zhezong was troubled by severe diarrhea and a full chest, and couldn't get down any porridge or medicine. Geng Yu supplied spleen-warming pills, a medicine Zhezong's mother also recommended.[77]

As the weather cooled, Zhezong's health improved, and he could join in the excitement about the impending birth of a child. Zhezong's consorts had so far borne him four children, but all of them were girls, and one had died in infancy. When his first son was born on 1099/8/8, Zhezong was healthy enough to participate in the celebrations. The moment the baby boy was born, Zhezong immediately had a eunuch carry the news to his councilors. When they saw Zhezong next, he told them that his two mothers were overjoyed, to which they added that it was not just the two royal women who were happy; the entire realm was celebrating. A eunuch was sent to make a report at the imperial tombs, and arrangements were made for senior officials and imperial clansmen to make reports at the northern and southern Suburban Altars and the Supreme Shrine. In addition, the Hanlin Academy drafted an edict proclaiming an amnesty for everyone whose crime warranted a punishment no heavier than exile. Then Zhezong fell ill again. For two days he canceled his audiences. When he saw his councilors on 8/14, he told them that Geng Fu had given him medicine to induce vomiting. He was somewhat better but still had no appetite and his belly hurt from time to time.[78]

Huizong naturally attended the banquet held in honor of his new nephew, which took place on 1099/8/21 in Assembled Heroes Hall. Zhezong was in a very good mood and he showered his councilors and his brothers with gifts, including clothes, finely worked gold belts, and fully harnessed horses. The clothes, made in the imperial workshops, included red gauze embroidered sashes, white damask trousers, yellow damask inner robes, and purple gauze official robes. Later, when the councilors came to thank Zhezong for these gifts, they wore the clothes and rode the horses. Huizong and the other princes, for their part, wore theirs when they returned to their mansions. The banquet does not seem to have been a success as a literary event, however. Zhezong later agreed with his councilors that none of the lyrics composed to celebrate the happy event was very good, and they discussed possible appointees who could raise the literary standards of the court.[79]

Zhezong's new son was warmly welcomed by everyone. Not so his decision to promote to empress the baby's mother, Consort Liu, whom many blamed for the downfall of Empress Meng. On 1099/9/27 Liu was officially appointed empress. Huizong would have stood with the other princes at Cultured Virtue Hall to greet her. The ceremony would not have been as elaborate as that for Meng seven years earlier, since the new empress already lived in the palace and would not enter through the main south gate.[80]

Huizong indirectly lost two of his tutors as a result of the promotion of Consort Liu to empress. The remonstrance official Zou Hao submitted a memorial objecting to the promotion, which incensed Zhezong.[81] Zhezong argued with Zou Hao in court, telling him that earlier Song emperors had done the same thing, to which Zou Hao rejoined, "Your ancestors have many virtues worth adopting, but instead of Your Majesty selecting one of their virtues to copy, you copy their minor faults."[82] Zhezong not only had Zou Hao demoted, but also had him removed from the ranks of officials and sent into detention in the far south, one of the "deadly" regions, where men from the north could catch tropical fevers to which they had no resistance. To make the penalty more severe, the governor of Kaifeng was ordered to see that Zou left the city that very day. Zou Hao's many friends, however, came to his aid, among whom were Huizong's two tutors, Fu Ji and Zhu Fu, and this slowed things down. Zhezong, in his anger, had the tutors dismissed from their posts for giving Zou Hao money to help cover his travel expenses. Zhezong even dismissed one of his councilors, Huang Lü, for defending Zou.[83]

Possibly contributing to Zhezong's bad mood was the poor health of his new son. On the fifteenth of the intercalary ninth month, Zhezong told his councilors that the baby had had a fright, and the doctors were treating him with medicines for intestinal disorders. From then on the councilors asked about the royal heir every day, and regularly offered advice on his medical care. On i9/26, the baby (still not yet named) seemed to be improving, but later that day a messenger informed the councilors that the child had died and Zhezong would cancel his audiences for the next three days. Three days later, one of Zhezong's young daughters died as well, only two years old.[84]

Despite the grief that Zhezong had trouble containing, the more ordinary routine of palace life continued. In the ninth month, Prince Ssi finally moved into his mansion. Members of the imperial clan formed an honor guard to accompany him from the palace to his new home. With this move all five imperial younger brothers were settled outside the palace walls.[85]

Zhezong's birthday fell on the eighth day of the twelfth month, and its annual celebration was a major occasion for banqueting in the palace. Two days in advance the ceremonies were rehearsed.[86] Among the many guests for the elaborate banquet held in Purple Asterism Hall were the foreign envoys from Liao, Koryŏ, and Xi Xia, all of whom had made the trip to Kaifeng especially to participate. Most other officials in Kaifeng attended, seated in ranks by seniority. The princes sat in order of rank in the most honored position just to Zhezong's right. The festivities were organized in terms of nine rounds, each round including entertainment and food or drink. Officials in the Hanlin Academy each year wrote new phrases to be used for toasts and songs. The musicians wore colorful costumes—crimson, purple, or green—depending on which instrument they played: clappers, lutes, harps, drums, chimes, mouth organs, ocarinas, or flutes. Both boy and girl dance troupes performed. Other entertainment included acrobatics, comedy sketches, and a kickball game. Before the day was over numerous gifts were bestowed on the guests.[87]

Not long after his birthday party, Zhezong fell ill again. He was vomiting all day long and could keep nothing down. In addition, he was coughing. His councilor Zeng Bu told him that these were symptoms of depletion and required fortifying food. When Zhezong told him he had taken some hundred fortifying pills, Zeng Bu said that given his youth he should not take warming medicines which might deplete his yang forces even more. The next day Zhezong had laryngitis and could talk only with great effort. For the next three days, Zhezong continued to come to court even though his condition failed to improve. To avoid breathing cold air, he was staying indoors except for a single trip to visit his mothers each day. By 12/21 the doctors were keeping the councilors informed of the seriousness of the emperor's condition, which now included a weak pulse. Still, the councilors did not talk to each other about the inauspicious topic of what would happen if Zhezong died.[88]

On New Year's day, 1100, Zhezong was too ill to hold the usual grand New Year's audience. On the fourth, it was announced that the usual banquet in Purple Asterism Hall would be canceled. Not only was Zhezong still coughing and vomiting, but the pain in his belly was getting worse. The councilors proposed that Buddhist and Daoist temples in the city begin a seven-day prayer service and that a general amnesty be announced, pointing out that Renzong had recovered after such an amnesty in 1056. The councilors were allowed to go into the living quarters of the palace to see Zhezong, where he lay in the eastern side chamber of Blessed Tranquility Hall. He was wearing a cap and jacket and sitting in a chair, but said that his intestines still were in distress and none of the medications had helped the situation. On their suggestion, Zhezong agreed to the religious services, the amnesty, and to undergoing more moxibustion treatment. That day moxa was burned all over him until the pain became intolerable. The next day his officials brought more medicines for him to try, but they too proved of no benefit, and by the morning of 1100/1/12, Zhezong had died, just a month past his twenty-third birthday.[89]

꙳ How DID THE PALACE in which Huizong grew up—the Song palace—compare to royal residences in the Western world?[90] Both similarities and differences are worth noting. As an architectural space, the Song palace, like palaces elsewhere, resembled the homes of the elite, but on a much grander scale. As a social space, it was filled with people, from the very high-ranking to servants of many sorts, their interactions regulated by elaborate court etiquette and ritual, much like palaces elsewhere. Some of the rituals that took place at court had structural similarities to rituals performed in much more explicitly religious settings. These rituals bear on both the sacral quality of the ruler and the finely graded social hierarchies of court society. There are often even similarities in the form of rituals. For instance, across much of Eurasia, canopies of various sorts were carried or erected for the ruler when he was in more public places, and people who came into the presence of the ruler knelt.

As in other countries, news of what happened in the Song palace could spread quickly, some of it gossip about individuals, some of it reporting on new fashions—innovations in etiquette, entertainment, and clothing that appeared first at court. In this case, also, it is useful to note a few differences. Although people outside the Song palace seem to have quickly copied styles of women's clothes worn there, that was not the case with men's clothing. The garments men wore at court seem almost never to have been a topic of interest, probably because all of the men, from emperor on down, were, in a sense, in uniform, wearing the robes that those of their rank were expected to wear.

In the Song palace, segregation by gender was the rule. At the major palace banquets, neither consorts nor princesses were present. Sometimes titled women (such as the wives of high-ranking officials) were invited to women's parties in the palace. Events that would bring together unrelated men and women, however, were avoided as much as possible. Princesses would be supplied with generous dowries, often including a house, and would be married out at what was considered an appropriate age, generally fifteen or sixteen. But they played at best a minor role in court culture. There was not even very much gossip about whom they might marry.

Princes and princesses growing up in the Song palace did not have many chances to get to know unrelated children their own age. In Europe, from the Middle Ages on, the nobility were a regular presence at court, and nobles' sons were sent to court to serve as pages or simply to complete their educations. There was nothing comparable in the Song palace. There was almost no hereditary nobility other than the imperial clan. Huizong's only known playmates as a child were his brothers and sisters; officials' sons or clansmen's sons did not grow up with him in the palace. The adults in the palace were similarly isolated from peers. Zhezong and his empress did not have noble men and women to attend them, the way European monarchs did. Zhezong spent time with his councilors, but they did not help him change his clothes—the people who performed such personal services were eunuchs or palace ladies. Thus, the Song court was not nearly as public a space as European courts. Zhezong did not go out riding or hunting with his cousins or other noble relatives with whom he might interact relatively informally. Like his predecessors, Zhezong held banquets, but only those explicitly invited could attend. Not even imperial clansmen could just show up at the palace and expect to be allowed to join a gathering, as noblemen could at Louis XIV's Versailles.

One of the most striking features of Song court culture is the relative immobility of Song rulers. Through the eighteenth century most European rulers had several palaces and spent much of their time moving from one site to another. Rulers even sometimes visited other rulers. Royal entries to cities were major spectacles, celebrated in words and pictures. Part of the creation of royal majesty there was putting it on display to broader publics during such journeys. By contrast, although the Song had designated four capital cities, the emperor did not spend any time at the western, northern, or southern capitals, remaining almost exclusively in Kaifeng, which technically was the eastern capital. The previous Tang dynasty, by contrast, made much more use of its secondary capital Luoyang, at times moving the court there. It is true that in Song China there was considerable spectacle when the ruler left the palace to perform a ritual, but such trips did not usually go far from the capital. People in other parts of the country were unlikely ever to catch a glimpse of the emperor's carriage.

After Huizong was allowed to move out to his princely mansion, he escaped many of the social restrictions of palace life. Still, as Chapter 2 relates, he offered only token resistance when he was called back.

2

Taking the Throne,

1100

All [of Zhezong's brothers] from the Prince of Shen on down are equally Shenzong's sons. It would be difficult to distinguish among them [on the basis of parentage]. The Prince of Shen has sick eyes. The next is [Huizong] the Prince of Duan, so he should succeed.

—*Empress Dowager Xiang after announcing*
Zhezong's death to the councilors

IN ANY MONARCHY, the death of the ruler creates a crisis. Even when the death is expected and an heir apparent in place, no one knows how effectively the new ruler will handle his position, whether he will be able to assert control over the machinery of government and manage the intricate interpersonal relations between ruler and ministers to his advantage. When the death is unexpected or there is no heir apparent, the possibility of a succession struggle looms. High officials, senior consorts, and principal palace servants know that they will fare better if their candidate takes the throne and so have incentives to try to make that happen.

During the first 140 years of the Song dynasty, there had been six successions, and no two were alike.[1] For reasons we will probably never be able to fathom, the Song imperial line was plagued with mental and physical health problems, and the survival rate of sons born in the palace was remarkably low. The founding emperor, Taizu, did have two sons alive at his death, but the succession did not go to either of them. Taizu's younger brother Taizong seized the throne and had his mother claim that Taizu had wanted him to succeed. This lateral succession violated a long-established principle that rulers were succeeded by their sons, as the sons were the ones qualified to serve as heirs in the ancestral cult. Taizu's eldest son, who would normally have become heir, soon committed suicide, and his younger son died suddenly less than two years later at age twenty-three *sui*.

The second emperor waited a long time before making it explicit that he would be succeeded not by a descendant of his elder brother, the dynasty founder, but by one of his own sons. He was fifty-seven and suffering from an old wound in his leg when he chose Zhenzong, his third son, as his heir. His appointment of an heir did not prevent a struggle between his widow and his grand councilor when he died. The empress dowager and her allies tried to put their own candidate, the oldest son, on the throne, but the grand councilor Lü Duan forced adherence to Taizong's wishes, which naturally put him in a good position with the new emperor.

Zhenzong in turn did not establish an heir until 1018, when he was fifty-two *sui* and had been on the throne twenty years. At that date only one of his six sons was alive. But it probably was not just the sickliness of his sons that led Zhenzong to delay so long naming an heir. He apparently feared being pressured to abdicate. In fact, when he became ill in 1020, his grand councilor and chief eunuch asked him to retire and pass the throne to his heir. Not only did he refuse, but also he had the audacious eunuch executed and the grand councilor dismissed.

Zhenzong's successor Renzong lived long enough to be survived by adult children, but not one of his three sons survived (and only four of his thirteen daughters). In 1056, when he was forty-seven and had sat on the throne for thirty-five years, he became gravely ill. For ten days he had bouts of insanity and could not recognize people; even his empress was frightened by him.[2] After Renzong recovered, a censor submitted a series of seventeen memorials urging Renzong to choose an heir, and other officials joined in. Finally Renzong settled on a son of a first cousin as the heir (Yingzong). Yingzong was already an adult, and was well known to both Renzong and his empress because as a child he had spent several years in the palace as a potential adoptee.

Yingzong came to the throne as an adult with three sons, ages eight to fifteen. Unfortunately, he immediately developed both mental and physical maladies and died after only four years on the throne.[3] On his death, his eldest son, Shenzong, then nineteen, was made emperor. Although this succession was the logical one, the grand councilor Han

Qi felt it made things smoother to have Yingzong write out Shenzong's name in a moment of lucidity. Shenzong thus was indebted to Han Qi and the other grand councilors, which added to the deference Shenzong paid to the councilors, all much older than he was.[4] Shenzong also died in early middle age and had not named Zhezong as heir until near death (if, in fact, he still knew what was going on by that time).

Huizong's succession was in some ways like Taizong's: he was his predecessor's younger brother, not his son. But Huizong came to the throne much younger than Taizong (just over seventeen) and was never suspected of doing anything to bring about the lateral succession.

The Day of Succession

The fullest account of the events surrounding Zhezong's death and Huizong's accession is found in the administrative diary kept by Zeng Bu, then the head of the Bureau of Military Affairs, which gave him a

Table 2.1. Main players at Huizong's accession

Deceased Emperor Zhezong	Dies before dawn on 1100/1/12
Senior women	
Empress Dowager Xiang	Zhezong's legal mother, Shenzong's widow
Consort Dowager Zhu	Zhezong's birth mother
Potential heirs	
(Zhezong's younger brothers)	
Bi, b. 1082/7	Prince of Shen, bad eyes
Ji, b. 1082/10	Huizong, at the time Prince of Duan
Wu, b. 1083/9	
Si, b. 1083/12	Son of Consort Dowager Zhu
Ssi, b. 1085/8	
Council of State	
Zhang Dun	Grand councilor
Cai Bian	Cai Jing's younger brother
Zeng Bu	Author of key account
Xu Jiang	
Other officials	
Cai Jing	Hanlin academician, recipient of edicts
Leading eunuch	
Liang Congzheng	

place on the Council of State.[5] The most detailed narrative history of the period, the *Long Draft of the Continuation of the Mirror for Government*, drew heavily on this diary but also incorporated other sources.

The four members of the Council of State when Zhezong died were Zhang Dun, Cai Bian, Zeng Bu, and Xu Jiang (see Table 2.1). All had been on the Council of State together for five years. On the morning of 1100/1/12, the councilors went to the Inner Eastern Gate to wait to be summoned. They were aware that Zhezong was gravely ill, and plans had been made to spend part of that day holding prayer ceremonies in the palace and at Buddhist and Daoist temples in the capital.[6] When they reached the gate, however, the eunuch manager Liang Congzheng told them they could not enter there. They then went to Blessed Tranquility Hall, Zhezong's primary residence, where they found that a screen of state had been set up so that Empress Dowager Xiang could receive them. She told them that Zhezong had died, and since he had no sons, a decision had to be made concerning the succession. According to Zeng Bu:

> Before the others could answer Zhang Dun said in a harsh voice, "According to the rites and the statutes, [Si] the Prince of Jian should be installed, since as a brother with the same mother, he is the closest." I was surprised and had not yet responded when the empress dowager said, "All of them from [Bi] the Prince of Shen on down are equally Shenzong's sons. It would be difficult to distinguish among them [on the basis of parentage]. The Prince of Shen has sick eyes. The next is [Huizong] the Prince of Duan, so he should succeed. Moreover, the late emperor once said that the Prince of Duan would have a long and prosperous life. [Huizong] once answered 'For some reason the emperor is unhappy. What has happened?'"[7]
>
> I [Zeng Bu] quickly responded [to the Empress Dowager], "Zhang Dun has not talked this over with the rest of us. Your Majesty's instructions are entirely appropriate." Cai Bian also said, "It is up to Your Majesty," and Xu Jiang concurred, which silenced Zhang Dun.[8]
>
> At this time more than a hundred palace eunuchs from the director, manager, and imperial pharmacist on down were standing in ranks outside the screen and they all could hear the conversation.

At the conclusion of our deliberations, we left. [The eunuch] Liang Congzheng led us to sit in the tents set up in the courtyard in front of the adornment office by Compassionate Virtue Hall's south wing. From time to time we could hear someone wailing. Congzheng and the others hushed them, telling them it was not yet time to wail aloud. I called to Congzheng and ordered him to summon the commander of the guards as well as the five princes. Congzheng said, "Before the five princes are brought in, we should summon the Prince of Duan to take the throne. After he has taken the throne, we can bring the other princes in." He selected a few drink attendants to go attend the empress dowager. A note was received which said "Three of the princes are here. But the Prince of Duan had asked for the day off." Congzheng was then told to quickly ask the empress dowager to send someone to summon him.[9]

While they were waiting for Huizong to arrive, Zeng Bu told the eunuchs that the councilors needed to see Zhezong's body to verify his death. The empress dowager gave permission and Liang Congzheng led them in.

The curtains were parted and we saw that the late emperor had already been prepared for the first laying out, his cap and comb in place and a shroud covering him. Congzheng ordered them to lift the white cloth covering his face, and we saw the late emperor's face, which looked as though it had been powdered.[10]

Before leaving, Zeng Bu told Liang Congzheng to have the hat and imperial robe ready so that Huizong could be immediately enthroned, and Liang Congzheng told him that he already had that matter in hand.

In contrast to many societies where senior men in the royal family would be expected to choose the heir when one had not been designated in advance, in China the senior empress was the "kingmaker."[11] Still, as in this case, it was best to get the councilors to agree with her choice.

While waiting for Huizong's arrival, the councilors worked on the text of Zhezong's final testament. When they heard that Huizong had arrived, they followed him into the hall.

When we got to the chamber with the curtain of state, the empress dowager seated behind the curtain said to the prince, "The emperor has abandoned the world and has no son. You, the Prince of Duan, should succeed." The prince, shaking, strongly declined, saying, "[Bi], the Prince of Shen, is the oldest. I dare not accept." The empress dowager said, "The Prince of Shen has defective eyes. The next should be established. You should not decline." I also said that for the sake of the dynasty he should not refuse. The manager and others pulled up the screen curtain and took the Prince of Duan behind it. He was still strongly protesting. The empress dowager told him to stop. I also parted the curtains and said, "For the sake of the country, you should not decline." From behind the screen, we heard the eunuch managers and the others transmitting the message to take the hat. Then we left and stood below in the courtyard for a while. When the curtain was rolled up, the emperor was wearing a hat and a yellow jacket, sitting on the throne. The councilors and the eunuchs from the manager on down all lined up. After congratulating [Huizong], the wailing [for Zhezong] began.[12]

The councilors retreated to work on the final testament to be issued in Zhezong's name, calling on Cai Jing, as the Hanlin academician recipient of edicts, to wield the brush.[13] Cai Jing, later to be a major figure at Huizong's court, thus was already playing a part in Huizong's story, though at this point he was outranked by his younger brother, Cai Bian, then on the Council of State.

Once the final testament was ready, they had the eunuchs summon the court officials, but before the testament could be read to them, Huizong summoned them.

Huizong was sitting on the throne and our names were announced. We said "ten thousand blessings," then ascended the hall. The emperor said something confidentially to Zhang Dun in so low a voice that those of us in line could not hear it. I said, "We could not hear the emperor's words." Dun said, "He asks that the empress dowager temporarily govern with him." The emperor also turned to look at us and said, "Just now I repeatedly asked my mother to govern with me." I said, "Your Majesty is virtuous and humble and thus wishes to proceed in this way. However, there is no precedent for doing this when the ruler is full grown. I don't know what the empress dowager thinks about this." The emperor said, "The empress dowager has already agreed. I just thanked her. That is why I presumed to order you here. Since the final testament has not yet been issued, this provision can be added to it."[14]

The councilors called back Cai Jing and had the final testament revised. This testament has been preserved, and besides naming Huizong as his successor, it discusses Zhezong's illness and his desire for a frugal funeral and burial, with officials to observe only a brief mourning period, all conventional in final testaments.[15] Convention also governed how it was proclaimed:

> When the officials had lined up, the grand councilor was led up into the hall to receive the final testament. He faced west and read it aloud. He then went down the stairs and bowed twice. Next the councilors burned incense and made an offering of tea and wine, then bowed another two times. The one reading the final testament at times would stop to weep. Everyone, high and low, inner and outer, wailed; it was impossible to restrain them. The ranks of officials then went to the eastern side chamber to congratulate the emperor on taking the throne. They also offered their condolences. Then the councilors and the first and second generation princes all ascended the hall and wailed. Huizong also covered his face and wept.[16]

After the councilors urged Huizong to curb his grief for the sake of the dynasty, they went to see Empress Dowager Xiang to tell her about the added passage in the final testament. She responded, "The emperor is full grown and intelligent. How could I manage his affairs?" When they told her that Huizong said she had agreed, she said, "Only because he asked two or three times."[17]

From Zeng Bu's testimony, Xiang was quite definite that she wanted Huizong to succeed Zhezong. In other quoted conversations she mentions how intelligent he is, and in one she explicitly says that none of the other princes could compare with him.[18] Once when Zeng Bu mentioned how diligent Shenzong had been, she said that Huizong was similar.[19] There is no reason to doubt that she both liked Huizong and considered him the most capable of Shenzong's surviving sons. He had been left motherless at a young age (his mother Consort Chen dying at Shenzong's tomb), so she may have taken particular interest in his education. Moreover, the fact that he did not have a living mother may have contributed to his appeal: there would not be another imperial mother (like Zhezong's mother Consort Dowager Zhu) to compete in any way for parental authority. Since Huizong was only three months younger than Bi, the age difference between them had little more than symbolic significance. If Bi had an eye disease or even just poor eyesight, he would have made a poor candidate for emperor, since emperors had to read through piles of memorials and other documents on a daily basis. On the day of Huizong's accession, Zeng Bu discussed his selection with Xu Jiang and Cai Bian, and all three concurred that Huizong was the obvious choice and that Zhang Dun was pursuing a private agenda in proposing the fourth brother Si. It is also possible that other people in the palace, such as leading eunuchs, had talked up Huizong to Xiang. She suspected Zhu of colluding with a couple of the top eunuchs to try to get her younger son Si to succeed rather than Huizong. Zeng Bu reports a later conversation with Xiang in which she said that when she asked the eunuch Liang Congzheng what to do about the succession, he told her to listen to Zhang Dun, probably knowing that Zhang Dun favored Zhu's son Si. It is not inconceivable that another eunuch made similar arguments in favor of Huizong.[20]

It is significant that no one at court proposed setting aside Zhezong's brothers and looking for a clansman of the same generation as Zhezong's children. There were no living grandsons of Shenzong, and perhaps no living great-grandsons of Yingzong. However, there were definitely descendants of Taizong of the right generation and there were also many descendants of Taizu of the right generation.[21] The choice Xiang made was probably the most human, however. Placing one of Shenzong's sons on the throne meant that the succession would go to a descendant of her husband, someone she had herself helped rear.

The decisions made on 1100/1/12 changed almost everything in Huizong's life. Had succession gone to one of his brothers, he would have continued in his old status as the brother of an emperor, a position that entailed some duties but allowed much time for cultural pursuits. From the moment Huizong assumed the imperial robes and mounted the throne, however, he was surrounded by officials and eunuchs attempting to shape how he performed his new role.

Empress Dowager Xiang's Participation in the Government

When Huizong was asked to take the throne, his first response was to beg his legal mother Empress Xiang to help him.[22] Although to us today, it is not surprising that someone just past seventeen might be intimidated by the prospect of presiding over an enterprise as large and complex as the Song empire, to his contemporaries he was a full adult of nineteen *sui* and his reaction was unexpected.

Immediately after Huizong told the councilors that he wanted Xiang to govern with him, they retreated to discuss among themselves how this would be arranged. They found two different precedents. In the case of two previous child emperors, Renzong and Zhezong, the empress came to the audience hall where a screen was erected and she and the boy emperor both sat behind it. The councilors spoke to both of them at the same time, but in reality were discussing the matters with the empress dowager. Moreover, the empress dowager was treated ritually as the ruler in that her birthday was given a name and celebrated and her rule was announced to the Song's principal diplomatic partner, the state of Liao. The alternative precedent that the councilors found was the period of Yingzong's illness when the councilors would first call on Yingzong in the audience hall, then go to call on the empress dowager in a rear hall, telling her what had been discussed with Yingzong and letting her have the final say. This measure was treated as a temporary expedient and the empress dowager was not treated ritually as the ruler. Zeng Bu contended that the Yingzong precedent was the most applicable, since both Huizong and Yingzong were adults. His fellow councilors raised some objections, but eventually concurred.[23]

Once Zeng Bu had convinced the other members of the Council of State, he brought the matter to Huizong, describing for him the arrangements during Yingzong's reign and how the circumstances matched his because in both cases it was the emperor himself who involved the empress dowager. "When [Zhenzong's widow] Empress Zhangxian ruled, Renzong was only thirteen [*sui*], and when [Yingzong's widow] Empress Xuanren [Gao] ruled, the late emperor was just ten *sui.* How could Your Majesty sit behind a screen [like they did]?" Huizong and the councilors then went together to see Xiang, who after insisting that none of this was her doing, agreed. After the councilors praised her wisdom, the details were settled, including the fact that she would not go to the forward or rear audience halls, nor would she receive the full range of memorials. The members of the Council of State would go to the Inner Eastern Gate to report to her after they had met with Huizong. Moreover, nothing would be done about her birthday, nor would her participation be announced to Liao, all things done when Gao was regent.[24]

Over the next couple of days, Xiang was active in bringing up issues concerning women in the palace, such as honors for Huizong's deceased mother and living arrangements and titles for Zhezong's widowed consorts. On 1/14 she wrote out in her own hand a pledge that before long she would give up participating in the government and that she would not hold audiences. Within a few days, she ceased taking much initiative, rarely doing more than express approval of what the councilors and Huizong had decided. On 2/5 she wrote out another document that she sent to the Department of State Affairs and the Secretariat-Chancellery stating that she had decided to give up participating in the government once Zhezong was buried and his tablet was placed in the ancestral temple.[25]

In his administrative diary, Zeng Bu records a few substantial conversations with Xiang. All are concerned more with palace affairs than government policy. On 2/2 she talked about Zhezong's final days and his medical treatment. That day she also complained that her reading ability was not up to handling government paperwork. She did not know the character *xia* (blind) until she saw it as part of a name on a border affairs memorial. Zhang Dun assured her that she was intelligent enough to handle matters and reminded her that the Sixth Patriarch of Chan Buddhism had been illiterate. On 2/12 she talked to Zeng Bu about her suspicions that Zhezong's birth mother, Zhu, had tried to arrange with Zhang Dun and a eunuch to have her son Si succeed to the throne. About a month later, Zeng Bu and Xiang exchanged similar stories implicating Zhu and another eunuch, this time saying the eunuch had brought her things to the hall where Zhezong lay ill, apparently because she wanted to be present when he died to see that the succession went her way.[26]

One of the few issues on which Xiang did take a strong stance concerned the women's quarters: she wanted to find a way to reverse Zhezong's ouster of Empress Meng and appointment of her rival Liu as
empress, discussed in Chapter 1. At the end of Zhezong's reign, three
women had particularly strong claims to honor: Xiang, who was Shenzong's widow and the legal mother of Zhezong and Huizong; Zhu,
who was a senior consort of Shenzong and Zhezong's actual mother;
and Liu, Zhezong's widow, promoted to empress less than three months
earlier. Huizong's accession changed their status along with so much
else. Each had her own establishment, with eunuchs and palace ladies
assigned to her. In 1100 there were seven hundred people living with
Zhu in Sagely Good Omen Hall.[27] Xiang's position had if anything
been enhanced with Huizong's accession, as she was the only one with
status as Huizong's mother, his own mother having died more than a
decade earlier. Xiang showed little warmth or empathy for Zhu, with
whom she had been living in close proximity for many years. Xiang
even more clearly disapproved of Liu. Zhu and Liu were no longer
closely tied to the main line of succession, and they could probably
anticipate that some of those who had sought their favor in the past
would now turn their attention to more promising patrons, such as
Huizong's young wife, soon to be the new empress.

Xiang did not care much for her daughter-in-law Liu. Xiang compared Liu unfavorably to Meng, who came from a literati family and
had from her first introduction to the court been taught wifely etiquette.
Xiang did admit that the rivalry between Meng and Liu was both their
doing, as both had tempers. Yet she argued that Meng's ouster was never
legal because the edict demoting Meng, presented as a hand-drafted
edict by Xiang, had been forged. She had not even seen, much less
written it.[28]

Because Xiang felt so strongly about this issue, she discussed it with
both Han Zhongyan and Zeng Bu, neither of whom was comfortable
with Xiang's line of thought. When they discussed the matter with
Huizong, he asked them to explain to Xiang the principle that a
younger brother could not change the status of his elder brother's
widow.[29] The biography of Han Zhongyan records the resulting discussion with the councilors, the empress, and Huizong this way:

> When Empress Dowager Xiang first rolled down the curtain and
> shared in governance, the former councilor Zhang Dun was still

in office. Han Zhongyan and Zhang Dun went to talk to her, and she said, "Favors have been distributed broadly since Huizong's accession, reaching everyone. The deposed Empress Meng should be restored." Afterwards Han asked Zhang Dun, "Is there any precedent for this? Would this have no bad consequences?" He said, "It would cause no harm." Then the two talked about it with Huizong, who said, "It would be fine to restore Miss Meng, but what about the empress dowager's desire to restore Miss Meng and depose Miss Liu? To restore one and depose one, wouldn't this be disrespectful to Zhezong? You are managing the government, so you ought to be able to take care of this." Han Zhongyan said, "Your Majesty's words are wise, so we must act on them." They then called on the empress dowager, who kept talking about deposing and restoring and would not budge. Han cited cases from the past and present, fully bringing out the rationales for each one, doing everything he could to persuade her, until she finally relented.[30]

In Zeng Bu's version, Xiang insisted that the long-established principle was one emperor, one empress, which Zhang Dun supported while the other councilors remained silent. Another councilor, Jiang Zhiqi, added the arguments that deposing Liu would publicize Zhezong's errors and that it was not appropriate for Huizong as a younger brother-in-law to change the status of his older brother's widow. Xiang reluctantly agreed to dual empresses as a compromise. On 1100/6/23 an announcement was made at the Suburban Altar that Meng had been reinstated.[31]

Within a few months Zeng Bu began to worry whether Xiang would in fact give up participating in government decisions as early as she had said she would. On 5/9, after Huizong's first son was born, Zeng Bu warned Huizong, "Your Majesty now has a son, and the empress dowager dotes on her grandson. There is no longer any reason for a regency." Huizong repeated that the regency had never been her idea and that she had put in writing that she would give it up when Zhezong's tablet was installed in the ancestral temple, which was only another month or two away. Zeng Bu took this as an opportunity to teach Huizong about the complexities of power. Those around the empress, he warned Huizong, might not want her to lose influence. Huizong should be prepared for them to create some sort of incident.

Huizong discounted the idea that his legal mother could be so easily deceived, but agreed to be on his guard.[32] Zeng Bu then urged Huizong to decide in advance exactly which issues would be brought to the empress's attention after her retirement. To Zeng Bu's relief, Huizong replied that other than issues concerning the princes and princesses, no external matters would have to be reported to her.

After the end of this conversation, Zeng Bu begged Huizong to make sure that no one learned what they had said. He cited a well-known saying: "If [this conversation] is not kept secret, the ruler loses his minister, but the minister loses his life."[33] He went on, "I would like Your Majesty to pay special attention to this. If it is in the slightest exposed, I will have no place to put my body." Huizong answered, "I get it. I get it. How could I leak it?"[34] Zeng Bu clearly did not trust some of those around the empress dowager and perhaps the empress dowager herself.

In their accounts of Song political history, many historians make the assumption that Xiang was the person making the decisions during Huizong's first year on the throne and that it was she who brought back the conservatives. They assume that her views must have been much like those of her mother-in-law, Gao, when she became regent fifteen years earlier. Close examination of the evidence, however, shows that this was not the case. Xiang's role was relatively minor and as is shown below, she was more interested in keeping the reformer Cai Jing in the capital than bringing back any particular conservative.[35]

Factional Politics

Once on the throne, Huizong set himself the task of ameliorating the bitter factional strife that had marred political life for a generation. At the start, he was somewhat naïve about what he could accomplish. In theory the emperor possessed all power: he could announce laws and appoint and dismiss his officials at will. In reality, however, he had to work through officials who had many ways to resist things they did not want implemented. Dealing every day with officials who tended to be highly critical of each other, Huizong had to learn how to sort out and evaluate the often conflicting advice they gave him.

During the preceding three decades, shifts in the occupant of the throne had three times led to the ouster of the top few dozen governmental officials, first with Shenzong's accession, second with the succession of the child Zhezong with Empress Dowager Gao as regent, and third with Zhezong's personal rule after the death of his grandmother. Those who had been out of power during Zhezong's last six years saw Huizong's succession as an opportunity to regain court posts, while those in power during Zhezong's final years, who had just facilitated Huizong's succession, were just as determined to stay there.

As in many other times and places, Song court politics was very capital-focused. The vast majority of those in the civil service were serving outside of the capital and were largely outside the competition for influence at court. The few hundred working in the key posts in the central administration tended to view assignments outside the capital as a kind of banishment, a forced removal away from the action. Although most of those who had risen to key posts in the central government had earlier spent time in the provinces, once they had risen to the upper reaches of the bureaucracy they rarely wanted to return to hands-on administration of the three hundred or so prefectures and twenty-six circuits.

One way to think about politics in this period is in terms of two principal political arenas, which can loosely be termed the audience hall and literati opinion circles. The small group of a couple dozen officials who met regularly with the emperor—members of the Council of State, censors and remonstrance officials, and the top officials of major bureaus and agencies—had the most direct say on the issues regularly referred to the emperor. Chief among these were personnel issues, such as whom to appoint or promote, whom to dismiss or demote. The emperor also had to give explicit authorization for major initiatives, ranging from military campaigns to tax reforms. Decisions made in the audience hall were high-stakes decisions, ones on which men's careers depended; they could result in major expenditures and affect the economic fate of different sectors of the economy. It is not surprising that many people were intensely interested in what went on in the audience hall and who had influence there. News of decisions made there spread quickly, both through an official gazette and through word of mouth and letters.[36]

The primary rival power center was a much less concrete entity variously called "outside discussion," "the common opinion," the "literati," or "scholar-officials." To some extent, these terms referred to what was discussed among educated men not in office. But it was not restricted to those out of office. Indeed, "speaking" officials were strongly associated with the expression of outside opinion. These men, serving in censorial and remonstrance posts, were charged with criticizing both policy proposals and the actions of incumbent officials. Many memorials by censors and remonstrance officials circulated widely among those interested in politics, and their authors often wanted to sway this audience as much as the emperor and his main advisors. The language of these memorials tended to be strident. Authors claimed moral legitimacy for themselves and labeled their opponents selfish, wicked, evil, obsequious, and the like. The notion that good people might analyze a situation differently was never given much consideration. If a proposal was unwise, its author must be of inferior character; if a political actor was of poor character, whatever he proposed must be detrimental.[37] This was not the language of the oral discussions of politics in the audience hall, nor was it necessarily the language literati used when talking about politics with their friends and relatives. Its place was the literary genre of memorials of indictment, which could not have been pleasant for emperors to read.

For three decades the principal political cleavage had been between supporters and opponents of the New Policies, which had been set in motion by Shenzong and his grand councilor Wang Anshi in 1069, more than a decade before Huizong was born. These policies touched almost every facet of government, from the examination system to compulsory labor demanded of commoners. Among the most controversial of the New Policies were the Green Sprouts Loans to farmers, the Hired Service Policy commuting labor service to a tax, and the State Trade Policy that levied commercial taxes and got the government involved in trade.[38]

Instituting the New Policies had proved difficult. The officials who had served Shenzong's father and grandfather barraged each proposed policy with criticism as soon as it was announced. Opponents saw in the New Policies not innovative ways to make the government better serve the needs of a growing economy, but a bureaucracy gone wild, issuing a mass of new government regulations. To the critics, Wang Anshi and his supporters did not understand the Confucian principle that good government depends on good men, not good laws. Opponents were incensed as well that they could not make their criticisms heard without jeopardizing their careers. Wang Anshi, with Shenzong's consent, had one dissenting official after another reassigned out of the capital. Maintaining avenues for policy criticism had been a fundamental element in Chinese government organization since Han times, so silencing opponents was viewed as outside the bounds of legitimate political behavior. The senior statesman among the dissenters, Sima Guang, resigned from office in 1071 and resettled in Luoyang (170 kilometers west of Kaifeng), where he was soon joined by many others unhappy with the direction of the government. Another prominent figure, Su Shi, mentioned in Chapter 1 as a friend of Huizong's uncle Wang Shen, was assigned to a series of provincial posts, then in 1080 exiled without a post because poems he had written were judged libelous.[39]

A principle reason for Shenzong's support of the New Policies was his desire to raise revenues so that he could launch an offensive against his northern neighbors, the Kitans and Tanguts, in the hope of taking back territory that had been controlled by the Tang dynasty (618–907) but not since then. Although the government was devoting more than half its revenue to military expenses, it still had difficulty fielding armies that would win decisive victories against these foes. In 1080 the new Yuanfeng Treasury was built to hold the surpluses generated by the New Policies, and by 1082 eight million strings of cash had been deposited in it.[40] Progress on the military front was, however, less satisfactory. The campaign of 1081–1082 against the Tangut state of Xi Xia in the northwest (modern Gansu) resulted in the capture of six towns but at the cost of six hundred thousand men.[41]

After Shenzong's death in 1085, Gao brought back the senior statesman among the opposition, Sima Guang, who by then was in his midsixties and ailing. Many other officials were also called back, including Su Shi and his brother Su Che. The name for the new reign period was Yuanyou (Prime Safekeeping), and those who came back to office in this period came to be known as the Yuanyou faction or Yuanyou partisans.[42] In this period, Wang Anshi's policies were not considered separately, each on its own merits, but were abolished wholesale. As quickly as possible, virtually the entire financial apparatus established under Shenzong was dismantled, and by the time Wang Anshi died in the fourth month of 1086, most of his initiatives had been reversed. Relentless personal attacks were directed at Wang Anshi's followers, especially Lü Huiqing and Zhang Dun, who were sent into exile.

Literary inquisitions were now used against the reformers. Cai Que was accused of libeling the empress dowager and banished to the far south, where he died a few years later.[43]

The conservatives could not maintain their unity once their opponents were ousted and soon were nearly as vicious in their attacks on each other as they had earlier been toward the reformers. In 1091, after returning from service outside the capital, Su Shi was accused of misconduct by a student of Cheng Yi, the evidence a poem he had written.[44]

When Zhezong began to rule on his own in 1093, he brought back the reformers, who promptly worked to remove from power those who had eight years earlier ousted them. They even wanted punishment for those no longer alive. On their urging Zhezong approved the destruction of the stone stele that marked Sima Guang's grave.[45]

Zhang Dun, Zeng Bu, and Cai Bian, three of those present when Huizong was put on the throne, all had strong claims to leadership of the reform faction. Cai Bian had the additional distinction of being selected by Wang Anshi as his son-in-law. By the late 1090s, however, these three leaders of the reform movement had relatively little sympathy for each other and in Zhezong's presence acted more like rivals than allies. Although to those excluded from Zhezong's court, it probably seemed that those serving there were a coherent faction, those on the inside were aware of all sorts of animosity, jealousy, and personality conflicts. No two men seem to have consistently sided together, not even the brothers Cai Bian and Cai Jing.[46]

The Song period was, of course, not the only time in Chinese history when factional strife grew unpleasant. There were at least as divisive struggles in the Han, Tang, and Ming periods, and bitter rivalry among the key players at court was far from rare in other monarchies as well.[47] Generally speaking, the longer a chancellor was in power, the more criticism he would attract and the more enemies he would make. These were among the political facts of life that Huizong had to confront. Reducing or overcoming antagonism would be a challenge.

On-the-Job Training

Most of the actions Huizong had to take in the first couple of weeks on the throne were required by ritual. The day after Zhezong died, an amnesty was issued, which reduced the penalties placed on officials who had been demoted, suspended, or banished by Zhezong. On the same day an emissary was dispatched to announce Zhezong's death and Huizong's accession to the Liao court. Word of Zhezong's death also needed to be sent to officials, soldiers, and ordinary subjects in the provinces. A series of officials were appointed to take charge of Zhezong's funeral, with Zhang Dun assigned the prime responsibility. Two days later, the physicians who had treated Zhezong were dismissed and fined. The next day Huizong's birth mother was given a posthumous promotion and a call sent out to locate her relatives. A day after that (1/17), Huizong summoned two of his former tutors, Fu Ji and Zhu Fu, both of whom had been banished two months earlier as a result of the Zou Hao affair (discussed in Chapter 1). The next day, personal objects of Zhezong's were distributed among his top officials. The day after that (1/19), Huizong's older brother Bi was given a promotion in title, to Prince of Chen. His younger brothers got their new titles three days later, on 1/22.[48]

Much more important than these routine orders was the selection of officials for important posts. During Huizong's first few months as emperor, he was repeatedly told that the secret to governing was appointing men of character and talent to key posts, especially remonstrance and censorial posts and the Council of State. Once he had the right people in place, his advisors assured him, he would be able to rule without taking action *(wuwei)*. Councilors had similarly urged earlier Song emperors to rule through nonaction, which can be taken as a polite way to say let us run things for you.[49]

Huizong's first appointments went largely to men who had been banished by Zhezong. He clearly was familiar with their cases in rough outline and had heard the arguments against their banishment. Moreover, the amnesty issued on his accession authorized lifting the penalties on them.

Not surprisingly, the reformist members of the Council of State that Huizong inherited felt threatened by his interest in anti-reformers. Zhang Dun and Cai Bian stressed the need to preserve Zhezong's policies and keep out of office those who had slandered Shenzong or Zhezong.[50] Huizong, however, repeatedly expressed interest in them. On 1/19, only seven days after Zhezong's death, Huizong asked his councilors to prepare a list of men qualified to fill high posts, including

those who had previously served in them. When the list was presented
the next day, Huizong discussed the names one by one with his councilors. In Zeng Bu's account, Huizong demonstrated knowledge of all
of these men and had his own ideas about which ones to employ:

> We went for the morning viewing [of Zhezong's coffin], then
> went to ask for a meeting. We reported to the emperor in person
> the names of former councilors and attending officials. Lü Hui-
> qing was listed first. Huizong abruptly pointed to his name and
> said, "Let him stay on the border for the time being." The next
> was Han Zhongyan. Huizong said, "This one should be sum-
> moned." . . . When he reached Huang Lü, Huizong said, "These
> three men [Han Zhongyan, Li Qingchen, and Huang Lü] can all
> be summoned."[51]

Huang Lü had been dismissed when he defended Zou Hao, who had
angered Zhezong by protesting the promotion of Empress Liu. An
Tao was discussed next, then Jiang Zhiqi.

> The emperor said, "He should be summoned and his appoint-
> ment as concurrent [Hanlin] academician restored. He should be
> given an audience."[52] When we got to Ye Zuqia, I said, "He is not
> in any faction and could be used," which Huizong approved. On
> reaching Lü Jiawen and Jian Xuchen, I repeated, "Your Majesty
> must know these people," which Huizong confirmed.
>   Next came Ye Tao. I said, "He was a secretariat drafter of moral
> fortitude and ambition, who was courageous enough to express
> his beliefs and opinions. He could be used." After him were Xing
> Shu and Zhu Fu.[53] Huizong was aware how these three flip-flopped.
> Zhang Dun pointed to Ye Tao and said, "Only this man can be
> employed."

The group proceeded to discuss eight more men, selecting five for
appointment, among them Zeng Bu's younger brother Zhao. Zeng Bu
explained that his brother was not really in any faction and had been
dismissed solely for his work on the compilation of historical records.
After these discussions, the councilors went to see the empress dowager who "concurred with all of the emperor's choices." Zeng Bu tried a

little flattery on her: "With the emperor and the empress dowager so perceptive in judging people's talents, what is there for us officials to add?"[54]

The political implications of these initial appointments did not escape Cai Bian and Zhang Dun. Zeng Bu tried to reassure Cai Bian that he could at least count on the emperor not bringing back Su Shi or Su Che.[55] Apparently Zeng Bu had already perceived Huizong's antipathy toward them, which cannot have been based solely on their politics since he was bringing back other men just as spirited in their opposition to the reform program.

It naturally took a while for Huizong to get a good grasp of the interpersonal dynamics of the Council of State he had inherited. Zeng Bu records many conversations in which he tried to coach Huizong on these matters. When Huizong asked about Huang Lü, Zeng Bu reminded him that Huang had been dismissed because he had defended Zou Hao. Huizong then asked what Zou Hao had said that gave offense, and Zeng Bu said it had something to do with Zhezong's empress Liu, but that the councilors were never given all the particulars. He explained that Huang Lü had made a strategic error by presenting his opinion to Zhezong without first discussing the matter with the other councilors. "If the senior officials had presented a unanimous opinion, the emperor might have gotten angry, but he would not have dismissed all of the councilors at once." When Huizong nodded at this, Zeng Bu brought up the issue of the many vacancies in the remonstrance and censorial posts. On another occasion Zeng Bu suggested three people he thought would be good in these "speaking" posts. Huizong on his own brought up Zou Hao and remarked on the injustice of his having been banished to a deadly place. Zeng Bu added that he was not the only one. Nan'an, where Chen Cisheng had been sent, was plagued by tropical diseases that killed over half the soldiers and officials sent there. Eight days later Zeng Bu stressed to Huizong the importance of haste in bringing back those sent to deadly places. "It would not be good if by chance Zou Hao never gets to return," was the way Zeng Bu put it.[56]

From Zeng Bu's account, Huizong was a curious student and ready to ask questions. For example, one day in the fifth month, after Zeng Bu had presented some recommendations on appointments, Huizong questioned him about the paperwork:

That day Huizong mentioned that documents of the Three Departments were often delayed. I replied that it was because of the number of places documents had to pass through. Each of the Three Departments and the Six Sections was supposed to handle each piece within a day or two, but then there are days off, so each document requires ten days to be issued.

Huizong said, "How would you compare the quantity of documents handled by the Three Departments and the Bureau of Military Affairs?" I answered, "The Bureau of Military Affairs only gets one- or two-tenths as many. The Department of State Affairs is the place that handles endless critical matters. Unless a war is going on, the Bureau of Military Affairs handles much less. They are really not comparable. Many days the only documents submitted to us are the papers for the appointment of one or two eunuchs or military officials. The deliberations of the Three Departments result in statutes that concern the joys and sorrows of the people of the empire. Those agencies also handle the promotion and demotion of talented men and the memorials and requests from officials inside and outside the court making claims about right and wrong on important matters. How could the Bureau of Military Affairs compare to it?" Huizong seemed impressed.[57]

Tensions and rivalry among Huizong's councilors were never well hidden, and Huizong had to learn to deal with them. Because Zhang Dun was put in charge of Zhezong's burial, he had to be away from court for extended periods, giving the others the opportunity to undermine Huizong's trust in him. In his diary Zeng Bu did not conceal his efforts to disparage Zhang Dun. On 2/21, for instance, Zeng Bu remarked that Zhezong was intelligent but had been overly influenced by Zhang Dun's opinions and had even adopted his way of talking. Early on, when Zhang Dun had said that Fan Chuncui should be executed for advocating giving up territory, Zhezong had responded by asking how a person could be discarded for a single comment. Yet later, having gotten used to Zhang Dun's ways, Zhezong would say "Slash him! Chop him down!" just like Zhang Dun did. Zeng Bu went on to say that in banishing the conservatives, Zhang Dun had often gone too far. What really motivated Zhang Dun was the desire for revenge, Zeng Bu claimed.[58]

As emperor, Huizong's behavior was open to scrutiny and comment by officials submitting memorials.[59] Huizong was not yet inured to this and got upset when people learned that he had been flying kites in the palace grounds. Huizong wanted to find out who was responsible for a paper kite of his ending up outside the palace. Zeng Bu tried to dissuade him from starting an investigation: "Your Majesty has just taken the throne and is in the prime of life with many years to come. If in your leisure after audiences you divert yourself with amusements, no great harm will come of it. But I worry that once you initiate an investigation, the authorities will be on their guard and your officials will make false accusations, which I fear will lead to widespread lying, to the detriment of your reputation for sagely virtue." Huizong, we are told, took this to heart.[60]

The Return of Anti-Reformers

The first anti-reformer to be placed in a court post was Han Zhong-yan, given an assignment in the second month. Zeng Bu told Huizong that someone had printed the edict appointing Han Zhongyan and seven others, citing this as evidence of literati approval of the course he was taking.[61] At his first audience with Huizong, Han Zhongyan outlined a moderate position that placed priority on four matters: broadening favor, expanding opportunities to speak out, eliminating suspicions, and ending military operations. In his view, in recent years the administration had been too quick to impose penalties because of political offenses, which could lead to the government losing support. To secure the hearts of the people (by which he meant the educated elite), the government should be more tolerant. His argument for expanding avenues for speaking up was the familiar one that the ruler had to depend on others as his eyes and ears. Han Zhongyan said that in recent years if an official brought up something that conflicted with the grand councilors, other people would expect him to be dismissed. To remedy the situation, Huizong should reward those who bring up issues in constructive ways. On the third matter he said, "In terms of policies, make no distinction between the old policies and the New Policies. If something benefits the people, it is good. In terms of people, make no distinction between us and them. Employ those who are talented." His argument about military campaigns was that nothing of any real value had been obtained during the recent northwestern campaign, though it had been extremely costly.[62]

The military campaign that Han Zhongyan wanted to end had been initiated the year before. It concerned Qingtang, a region settled by Tibetans located to the northwest of the Song borders, just south of land controlled by the major adversary Xi Xia (see Map 2). Within a few days of taking the throne, Huizong was getting reports on the situation there.[63] Because the issues were complex, a few days later Zeng Bu gave Huizong a series of memorials that had been presented to court during Zhezong's last couple of months concerning whether or not to abandon Qingtang. Zeng Bu explained to Huizong the origin of the campaign in a succession dispute among the Tibetan tribes and his own misgivings about it. He saw no easy solution. Keeping the area, he pointed out, would be a way to fulfill Shenzong's ambitions.

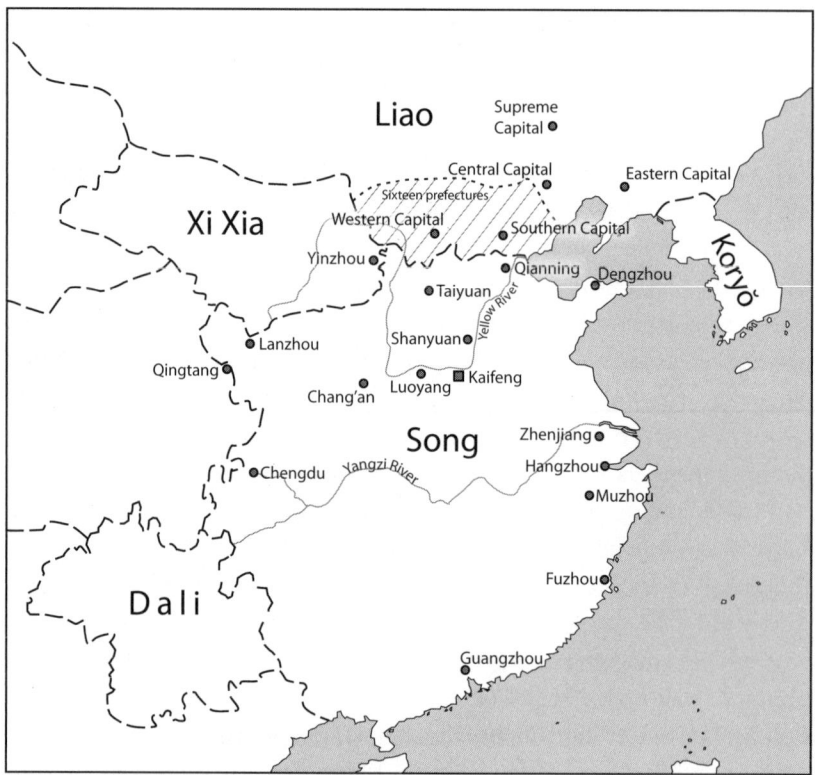

Map 2. Song China and its neighbors

Moreover, abandoning land that had been so publicly proclaimed as a symbol of Song success would open them to ridicule both within the country and without.[64]

The memorials that Huizong was given to bring him up to speed on Qingtang would not have made easy reading, as they were filled with obscure place names, confusing kinship connections among the rival Tibetan warlords, and odd-sounding Tibetan names. But the divergence in opinions among the memorials' authors would not have been difficult for Huizong to discern. After Tibetan resistance emerged, Zhang Dun urged the court to extend the campaign to include a punitive raid on Xi Xia because it had aided the Tibetans. In response, Zeng Bu argued that the armies and local population were already exhausted, and opening a new front would make things much worse. He had reminded Zhezong that the effort to extend Song suzerainty into Vietnam in 1075 had failed, and that Xi Xia was a much stronger country than Vietnam.[65] As casualties mounted, the military commissioner of a nearby circuit had submitted a long memorial criticizing the entire Qingtang campaign. He described the region as so remote and mountainous that provisioning troops was almost impossible. Moreover, local Tibetans had a huge advantage because they knew the territory and could scatter when the Song troops appeared. Zeng Bu again joined in, this time presenting the Qingtang campaign as an enormous mistake. He claimed that the Song empire had no shortage of land and that desolate land of this type was of little use. Moreover, since the subordinate tribes were as much as sixty-three days by horse away from the seat of Qingtang and the Chinese language was not understood there, they were very difficult to administer. "How can we guarantee that they all are willing to turn their hearts to the Han?"[66] Other officials echoed these concerns, even suggesting that it would be wise to give the newly acquired territories back to the Tibetans.[67] For the time being, Huizong deferred making any decisions.

In the second and third months of 1100, several men who had gained fame as critics of the reformers in Zhezong's court were appointed to "speaking" posts, including Chen Guan and Gong Guai. Other prominent men brought back for other posts included Su Che, Cheng Yi, Huang Tingjian, and Zhang Lei.[68] As soon as Chen Guan was back in office, he wrote a memorial to Huizong stressing the importance of selecting the right people and urged him to bring Zou Hao back and dismiss An Dun, who had been arguing against reversing the decision on Zou Hao.[69]

One of Gong Guai's early memorials stressed the need for the emperor to distinguish clearly between right and wrong, good and bad. His memorial is a good example of factional discourse—strong in its moral indignation, but weak on specifics:

> Your subject has heard that when good and bad are not made clear, people do not know which way to turn, and that when the loyal and the treacherous are not distinguished, people inevitably suspect what they hear. Recently I have been serving outside, where I heard indirectly how the court under your sage government is renewing itself daily, to the joy of those far and near. When I received the order to come to court, I also heard that the promotions and demotions on the basis of talent have all been your sagacious decisions. This definitely is a very positive step.
>
> And yet, the treacherous faction, having been smashed, will be plotting from morning to night to come up with strategies to secure their comfort. You must be on guard against this. Some will quickly change their countenance in order to get back in; some will hold fast to their deviant theories to resist the correct views; some will wildly predict disasters in order to agitate the court; some will cite your ancestors in order to put pressure on you; some will cleverly fawn on the high-ranking and [imperial] relatives; some will secretly make connections with those in attendance [on the emperor]. It is in the nature of the wicked to come up with hundreds of ploys, so I cannot list them all. In essence, they wish to confound right and wrong, crooked and straight, to confuse the court, and arrange it so that those who have been ousted will be employed again and those who have been brought back will be sent away again.[70]

In response to this memorial and similar ones from other recently appointed conservatives, on 3/24 Huizong issued an edict drafted by Zeng Zhao calling for frank advice. Asserting that he was "opening the avenue of remonstrance," he declared that nothing was out of bounds, including his own shortcomings, his policies, his associates, and conditions in the country. He promised to reward those whose advice was used and not penalize those whose charges turned out to be inaccurate. "Given the huge size of the realm and the complexities of the myriad affairs, how can I as a single individual inspect it all? I must depend on the officials and common people to keep me informed."[71]

In the fourth month Han Zhongyan was put on the Council of State as the junior councilor. In a casual conversation with him after this promotion, Huizong asked him what he saw as the most urgent matter. Han Zhongyan made a strong plea for abolishing the office for the classification of memorials, which could class as slander something an official had written with sincere intentions. According to Han, the office had more than five hundred memorials under consideration. Appeals for frank advice, like the one Huizong had recently issued, would not be effective as long as this office remained in operation, he argued. Huizong was apparently persuaded and later told Han Zhongyan that he had had the files brought into the palace and burned. It also seems to have been Han Zhongyan who convinced Huizong to abandon claim to the two northwestern prefectures acquired at such a cost the year before. In 1100/4 Shanzhou was returned and a year later in 1101/3 Huangzhou was also.[72]

Ousting the Top Reformers

Despite having brought many conservatives to court, Huizong found it far from easy to remove the reformers at the top of the administration. On 3/14, after Huizong brought up the topic of Zhang Dun, Zeng Bu said that if he wished to dismiss him, he should first dismiss Cai Bian. Huizong responded. "That would not be difficult. All that is needed is to write a rescript sending him away and he is gone." Zeng Bu countered that the matter was not so simple: "There are established ways to advance and demote high officials. New censors must be appointed and they must speak up. If they bring up a matter, documents can be issued. The person accused then becomes uneasy in his position, and there is no problem getting him to leave. Once Cai Bian is gone, Zhang Dun will not be able to harm the government any more."[73] Huizong, we are told, complimented Zeng Bu on the shrewdness of his strategy. Huizong also told him of a conversation he had had with An Dun, who proposed having everyone in the Censorate attack Zhang Dun. Huizong had told him that attacking him was one thing, but he should not first seek permission.

Not long after this conversation, Zeng Bu and Han Zhongyan found a way to get Zhang Dun and Cai Bian to approve reassigning Cai Jing out of the capital. They spoke to Huizong of the importance of filling the post of prefect of Taiyuan with a high-ranking official with experience in border affairs. They gradually eliminated one possibility after the other until they got to Cai Jing. When Zhang Dun insisted that he be sent with a high rank, Zeng Bu proposed an even higher one. Eventually Zeng Bu explicitly asked Huizong which official he wished to appoint and Huizong responded, "Cai Jing." Zeng Bu gave Huizong the appointment papers to sign, after which Cai Bian said, "My older brother will not decline to go, but since he has often differed from the current councilors, people will say the councilors are sending him away," which provoked no response from Huizong. At a later audience Huizong spoke openly to Zeng Bu of the progress they had made in removing the reformers Cai Jing, Zhang Shangying, and Fan Tang, and listed several others they still had to deal with.[74]

The effort of Zeng Bu and his allies to send Cai Jing away soon ran into a greater obstacle than his brother Cai Bian: Empress Dowager Xiang. On 4/2 when Huizong met with Zeng Bu, he warned Zeng Bu that Xiang wanted to keep Cai Jing, and when Zeng Bu later went to see her, she in fact insisted he be kept. Zeng Bu warned her that he himself might resign if she did not give in, but she responded, "What does this have to do with [your job at] the Bureau of Military Affairs?" When Zeng Bu said, "Gentlemen and inferior men cannot abide in the same place," she countered, "During the late emperor's reign you were together." Zeng Bu was so stubborn that finally the empress had to tell him it was time for him to go.[75]

When people outside the court learned that Cai Jing would stay in the capital after all, they assumed Zhang Dun had used his influence to keep him there. As Zeng Bu explained to Huizong, this was evidence that outsiders do not understand what happens at court, since in reality Zhang Dun detested Cai Jing. Moreover, he added, the other members of the Council of State do not obediently do whatever Zhang Dun tells them to do.[76]

Those Zeng Bu was accusing of factional politics also, of course, lodged similar charges against him. Once Cai Bian had urged Huizong not to appoint Chen Guan on the grounds that he was too close to Zeng Bu. On another occasion, Huizong told Zeng Bu that An Dun and Wu Juhou had charged that he, Han Zhongyan, and Jiang Zhiqi had formed a faction that included all the recently appointed censors and remonstrance officials. Zeng Bu responded by bringing up his desire to retire, which he would do many more times and which Huizong would keep insisting he did not seek.[77]

Huizong was getting advice not only from a handful of councilors and a similar number of censorate and remonstrance officials but also from many others in the administration. On 4/13 Huizong let Zeng Bu know that he had already received more than a hundred memorials vilifying Zhang Dun, and the next day he said he had two to three hundred attacking Zhang Dun and Cai Bian.[78] Just reading so many memorials must have been discouraging.

As the fourth month progressed, more and more new appointments were made, in most cases bringing in conservatives and sending away reformers. One day Huizong even asked Zeng Bu about Su Shi's friend Huang Tingjian, and Zeng Bu said he had literary talent and would be a suitable appointment. By the end of the fourth month officials of the Censorate and Remonstrance Bureau were playing their assigned part and attacking Zhang Dun. Chen Guan, with his typical fervor, charged Zhang with deceiving the country and the dynasty, and claimed that all the wrath and resentment of the realm was directed at him. He accused Cai Bian of being the strategist behind Zhang Dun's measures and charged that he would label anyone who opposed his ideas as disloyal to Shenzong.[79] First among Cai Bian's crimes, the censor Gong Guai charged, was marrying Wang Anshi's daughter and mastering his learning "in order to deceive the state." Gong Guai urged that he be banished. Ren Boyu labeled Cai Bian even more wicked than Zhang Dun, charging him with slandering Empress Dowager Gao and spreading rumors about Zhezong's first empress. He also alleged that Cai Bian had been involved in finding several thousand men guilty through an analysis of their memorials.[80]

Cai Bian was finally dismissed from the Council of State and sent out of the capital to a prefectural post on 5/19. Since Huizong had not yet dismissed Zhang Dun, censors continued to attack him. In 1100/5/28 Chen Guan pointed to Zhang Dun's cooperation with the now discredited Cai Bian, and said that the source of his treachery lay in his misuse of the two words, "continuing" and "legacy."[81] By the sixth month Huizong had assigned the followers of Zhang Dun and

Cai Bian out of the capital and brought back many of those they had ousted just a few years earlier.

The new conservative appointees disappointed Huizong. On 6/8 he told his councilors that he deplored the extreme language the new appointees used: "You councilors ought to tell them not to exaggerate." Zeng Bu told him that speaking officials did not like being warned and suggested that Huizong cope by taking their hyperbole into account when assessing their charges. The next day Huizong remarked to Zeng Bu that Li Qingchen was extremely biased. To him, "everything done under Empress Gao was right." A day later Huizong came up with a way to make his disapproval of vituperative language known: he would explicitly dismiss the censor Xing Shu for it. This step did not yield much in the way of moderation, however. On 6/16 Gong Guai's impeachment of Cai Jing rankled Huizong.[82]

On the first day of the seventh month, Empress Dowager Xiang withdrew from participating in the government. The pressure on Huizong to dismiss Zhezong's top officials if anything grew more intense. In 1100/7 a long series of officials charged Zhang Dun with holding on to power too long and "harboring sinister schemes." On 1100/9/8 Huizong finally accepted Zhang Dun's request to retire. A few months later, in 1101/2, at age sixty-seven, Zhang Dun was banished to Lingnan.[83]

With Zhang Dun gone, Chen Guan now took as his target Xiang and her relatives. When Chen Guan submitted a memorial on 1100/9/15 criticizing Xiang's relatives and also charging that she had not in fact given up participating in the government, she became extremely upset and would not eat. Huizong tried to console her by saying he would banish Chen Guan. When her anger still did not abate, her companions suggested that the way to calm her down would be to appoint Cai Jing to a councilor position. Huizong did not go that far, but the next day Chen Guan was assigned a post out of the capital.[84] Huizong said he would not keep him out for long and sent someone to give him one hundred ounces of gold for his expenses. This demotion did not stop him from continuing to submit memorials, however. One of them, on Cai Jing's friendship with relatives of Xiang, persisted in portraying her as holding on to power.[85]

The last of the major reformers to be sent away was Cai Jing. On 1100/10/3 Huizong had Cai Jing sent out to serve as a prefect. Zeng Bu told Huizong that the whole realm had been hoping for Cai Jing's dismissal, but he had been afraid to open his mouth about it ever since Xiang had gotten angry at him for his earlier attempt.[86] This opened the way, on 1100/10/9, for Zeng Bu finally to be promoted to junior grand councilor, ranking just below Han Zhongyan, then the senior grand councilor. According to Zeng Bu's *Song History* biography, when he was second to Han Zhongyan, he was in fact the stronger of the two, and most initiatives were his. He argued that both the reformers and the conservatives had shortcomings, and urged Huizong to try to defuse factional antagonisms. In that spirit, Huizong chose his first reign name: "Establishing the Mean and Stabilizing the State." Members of both factions would be employed together. An edict of 1100/10/26 began by asserting Huizong's impartiality: "My approach to governing is to select men without regard to differences between this period and that period [that is, Yuanyou and Shaosheng], and paying attention only to ability, loyalty, and the like."[87] Not everyone approved this message. Ren Boyu, then a "speaking" official, objected that "Since ancient times there have been no cases when mixing together men of virtue and petty men resulted in good order. The reason is that the man of virtue readily withdraws but the petty man only reluctantly withdraws, so when both are employed together it will end up that all of the men of virtue depart, leaving only the petty men."[88]

One reason it took so long for Huizong to oust Zhang Dun and Cai Bian was propriety: it was considered disrespectful of his predecessor for a new emperor to act too hastily in removing the ministers who had served him. In the common case of a son succeeding to his father, filial piety was at stake. In the *Analects*, Confucius says, "When your father is alive observe his intentions. When he is deceased, model yourself on the memory of his behavior. If in three years after his death you have not deviated from your father's ways, then you may be considered a filial child" (1.11). Another passage in the *Analects* makes specific mention of the father's ministers: "Zengzi said, 'I have heard from the Master this about the filial piety of Meng Zhuangzi: Other dimensions of it can be attained by others, but his not changing his father's ministers or his father's government is difficult to match'" (19.18). So long as Zhezong's body had not yet been buried, Huizong was expected to move slowly in his efforts to distinguish himself from his predecessor and alter the direction of the government.

Zhezong's Funeral

The funeral of an emperor was a major event, costly in men and materials. Because the "inauspiciousness" associated with death and mourning conflicted with the emperor's ritual obligations, many compromises had to be made. Soon after taking the throne Huizong called on his officials to research appropriate precedents for how he should mourn Zhezong: Should it be at the one-year level of a younger brother for his elder brother or the three-year level of a son for his father and a subject for his ruler? The decision, argued by Cai Jing, was that it should be the three-year level because Huizong had been a subject of Zhezong. Since in the case of a reigning monarch, each month was converted to a day, the twenty-five months of the three-year mourning became twenty-five days.[89]

Huizong got regular reports on the progress made with Zhezong's coffin, tomb, and portraits. The coffin was somewhat over nine feet long, five feet high, and four feet wide. Lacquering it took several days, but it was finished on 1/17, which made possible the laying out ceremony the next day. While Huizong performed the laying out, officials gathered at the entrance of Blessed Tranquility Hall where they offered their condolences to Huizong. Afterwards they went to the Inner Eastern Gate to submit their condolences to Empress Dowager Xiang, Empress Dowager Liu (Zhezong's widow), and Consort Dowager Zhu (Zhezong's mother). Next, messengers were sent to report the laying out ceremony to heaven, earth, the Supreme Shrine, and the Altar of the Soil. By the end of the month the schedule for the burial had been set, with auspicious days chosen to break ground, to finish the tomb, to take the coffin out of the palace, and for the burial.[90]

Because of the complexities of imperial funerals, ritual specialists made most of the decisions. While preparing for the Second Sacrifice of Repose, Zhang Dun and Cai Bian got into a protracted argument about the correct color for their head coverings, and finally had to call in a ritual specialist to arbitrate (he ruled that black was correct).[91] An issue on which the councilors' opinions were sought was the portraits made to represent Zhezong in ancestral rites. On 4/23, the day after the hundred-day service, Zhang Dun brought in a portrait that an official named Lin Xi had commissioned. The councilors commented that the one submitted by one of the eunuch agencies did not at all resemble Zhezong. Huizong said that Cai Jing had also presented a portrait that did not resemble the former emperor. When he mentioned that he would be satisfied with one that caught 50 or 60 percent, the councilors recommended the one that Lin Xi had presented. Huizong inspected it and agreed that it was the best of them. In a discussion with Xiang, Zeng Bu urged using Lin Xi's portrait as the model for the clay statue to be made of Zhezong (presumably for the Temple of Spectacular Numina).[92]

The transportation of the coffin from the palace to the tomb in the seventh month ran into serious weather problems—it rained steadily for several days in a row. On 7/22 Buddhist and Daoist temples were ordered to pray for clear weather and residents of the capital were asked to desist from slaughtering animals for three days in hopes of securing divine help. Despite the rain, the cortege reached Gong county, where the imperial tombs were located. However, once there, the rain and mud made it impossible to proceed, forcing the party to stay overnight outside as the stop was unanticipated and no arrangements had been made for shelter. Still, the next day (8/1) Zhezong's coffin was placed in the tomb. The spirit tablet was welcomed back to the capital in stages: the officials met it at Plank Bridge, Zhezong's widow now Empress Dowager Meng met it at Rose-Quartz Grove Park, and Huizong met it at Assembled Heroes Hall within the palace.[93]

WHAT DID HUIZONG ACCOMPLISH in his first year on the throne? By asking his mother to co-rule with him he avoided any significant resistance to his succession. Consort Dowager Zhu's son Prince Si was not happy that Huizong had been chosen, but his displeasure never became a crisis. Another accomplishment was quickly gaining the goodwill of leading conservatives. Huizong was not simply making a gesture when he brought so many of them back to court: he genuinely thought their presence at court would be a good thing. Huizong listened to their concerns and issued statements that they wrote. He made a public commitment to allowing differing opinions at his court. What must have pleased the conservatives the most was his slow but steady efforts to reduce the power of the top reformers Zhang Dun and Cai Bian, to the point when they could be dispatched out of the capital.

At least as important as what Huizong did in his first year is what he learned. From seventeen to eighteen, he spent much of his time and energy on the two activities viewed as compulsory for emperors: performance of major rituals and selection of senior officials. Tacitly acknowledging that his ministers had much to teach him, Huizong listened to what they had to say as he tried to master the interpersonal complexities of occupying the apex of the government structure. In Zeng Bu he found a teacher to his liking, a man willing to speak candidly and explain the politics behind many court customs. Huizong began his second year on the throne quite a bit wiser in the ways government actually worked.

Huizong's first year on the throne was not entirely taken up with politics. He held long conversations on Daoist principles with the distinguished Daoist master Liu Hunkang. He found time and occasions to continue his love of the arts of painting and calligraphy. His old princely mansion was no longer needed for its original purpose, and Huizong had it redecorated as Dragon Virtue Palace/Temple, occasionally visiting to inspect the work of the artists decorating it and give them pointers. He also found time to spend with his consorts. By the end of his first year Empress Wang had given birth to a boy and Consort Zheng to a girl.

These sources of satisfaction will all be examined more thoroughly in later chapters. First, however, it is necessary to examine Huizong's experience trying to rule with a coalition government during his second and third years on the throne.

3

Trying for Balance,
1101–1102

> The other day I, your subject, heard a rumor on the street
> that some high-ranking men including one named Jia entered
> the Rear Garden with falcons on their shoulders to hunt
> birds. This I could not believe. . . . How could a ruler who is
> benevolent busy himself with going hunting? How could
> anyone devoted to the dynastic ancestors have the leisure to
> pursue the pleasure of hunting!
>
> —*from an 1101 memorial submitted by Jiang Gongwang*

*H*UIZONG'S SECOND YEAR on the throne was a demanding one that entailed even more ritual obligations than his first year. Not only was there Empress Dowager Xiang's funeral, but also provision for Zhezong's portrait hall and Huizong's first performance of the Suburban Sacrifice to heaven. As he fulfilled these obligations, Huizong attempted what would be termed today a coalition government, one in which members of opposing factions work together. He kept in place the moderate conservative Han Zhongyan and the moderate reformer Zeng Bu to head the Council of State. Many less moderate men were also brought to court. In 1101/3 the eloquent critic Chen Guan was brought back and appointed to a court history post.[1] Huizong had said he would not keep him out long, and he was true to his word.

A large number of memorials submitted to Huizong during this period have been preserved, especially ones written by anti-reformers. This allows us to put ourselves imaginatively in Huizong's place and ask what information and ideas were reaching him. What problems did writers identify? How did they convey a sense of urgency? What did they propose should be done to solve the problems they identified? What did they advise against doing?

Coalition Government

Zeng Bu, during the more than a year and a half that he was junior grand councilor, consistently spoke to Huizong of the need to circumvent factional hostilities, to make use of the best ideas from both sides and employ men with connections to each side, so long as they were not incapable of compromise. Although a few other officials made similar arguments, Zeng Bu does not seem to have been able to attract many officials to his position. Instead, both sides viewed him as an opportunist who changed his position depending on circumstances.

Within weeks of Zeng Bu becoming junior grand councilor, Huizong had to listen to objections to his appointment. The attending censor Chen Cisheng charged Zeng Bu with evil intentions, monopolizing power, looking down on his colleagues, favoring friends, and the like. Zeng Bu was also accused of having been friendly with Cai Bian.[2] Zeng Bu was not at all indifferent to this criticism, and did what he could to prepare Huizong's response to it.[3] When Huizong appointed Zeng Bu to undertake responsibility for Xiang's tomb soon after her death in 1101/1, the councilor knew he would be vulnerable to attack while away and warned Huizong, who told him not to worry. In the sixth month of 1101, just as Zeng Bu predicted, criticisms of him intensified. The remonstrance official Chen You submitted several memorials laying out Zeng Bu's failings. When Zeng Bu returned, he collected documents to try to refute the charges item by item, and he reminded Huizong that he had warned him that this would happen. He told Huizong that the conservatives wanted to get rid of him so that they could "revive the policies of the Yuanyou period, which is not at all what Your Majesty wants." Huizong responded, "How could we let that happen? If Su Shi or Su Che were made councilor, that would be the end of Shenzong's policies."[4]

All through 1101 Huizong consistently supported Zeng Bu, often seeing to it that his critics were dismissed. Supporters of the cast-off officials often would approach Huizong and try to get him to change his mind. After Chen You was reassigned to a prefectural post on 1101/6/15, the remonstrance official Jiang Gongwang, at an audience, asked what Chen You had said that had offended him, and Huizong said he wanted to oust Zeng Bu and appoint Li Qingchen in his place. Huizong added, "How can that be allowed?" Jiang Gongwang cautioned Huizong that he had already replaced three censors and seven remonstrance officials, "which is not what the world had hoped for."[5]

In the middle of 1101, Huizong dismissed two of the anti-reformers on his Council of State (Fan Chunli and An Tao), and was eager to learn more about potential reformer replacements. During an audience on 1101/7/3, Huizong asked for two lists, one of men who had slandered Shenzong's government during the Yuanyou period, the other of officials holding regional posts who could be brought to court. Zeng Bu responded by encouraging Huizong to maintain a bipartisan attitude and favor neither the Yuanyou nor the Shaosheng faction. He cited another official's advice: "On the left do not employ [Su] Shi or Che; on the right do not employ [Cai] Jing or Bian."[6]

Chen Guan waited several months before attacking Zeng Bu, but on 1101/8/23 he submitted a letter to Zeng Bu criticizing him, which he subsequently submitted through channels. When Huizong got it, he said to Zeng Bu, "Is this how he repays you?" Zeng Bu went on to explain his view on several of the issues raised. One was the use of Wang Anshi's administrative diary in the writing of the *Veritable Records* for Shenzong's reign. To Zeng it was a good source since it recorded the face-to-face conversations of the ruler and his ministers. Huizong responded, "You formerly recommended Guan and wanted him to be appointed as a close attendant. I said he would not be impartial in his discussions. What do you think now?" Zeng Bu had to agree that he had been mistaken. Han Zhongyan and the others present urged that Chen Guan be reassigned to a prefectural post. When Huizong proposed a heavier punishment, Han Zhongyan and Lu Dian tried to dissuade him, arguing that "What Guan said was definitely not appropriate, but if he is punished for it, he will become famous as a result. It would be better for Zeng Bu to bear it."[7] Zeng Bu had hoped that by giving appointments to prominent conservatives, he would get them to support his coalition strategy. In Chen Guan's case, Zeng Bu clearly had not succeeded.

A few days later Huizong told two of his councilors, "More than half the Yuanyou men have been dismissed and yet [Chen Guan] still dared to act this way. For Zeng Bu to stand up against such a group by himself is not very easy. You ministers should give him some encouragement on my behalf." Later that day Zeng Bu saw Huizong alone. Huizong revealed to him that he was no longer interested in preserving a neutral stance, saying both that projects of the previous reign were not yet complete and also that "the inferior men of the Yuanyou faction must be dismissed." Zeng Bu still was not ready to give up and tried to deflect some of Huizong's anger by taking blame himself. Huizong then asked, "What are you afraid of? Some say you usually comply with the Yuanyou people." Clearly some of the reformers Huizong talked to were portraying Zeng Bu as too close to the anti-reform side. Zeng Bu denied being afraid of anyone but admitted that few people were as independent as he was. He was troubled enough by Huizong's remarks, however, to ask him his own opinion. Huizong then laughed and said that he had only raised the question because other people were asking it.[8]

Warnings of Heaven's Displeasure

Huizong never lacked for advice. Officials could indirectly criticize Huizong by saying they had heard a rumor that Huizong had done something that they could not believe he had really done. As the epigraph to this chapter shows, Jiang Gongwang took that tack on the issue of hunting. Surely a ruler as devoted to duty as Huizong would not waste time and energy killing birds and animals. To Jiang Gongwang, the only justification for hunting was to obtain meats for ancestral offerings. He provided two other arguments against hunting: it is dangerous and it is expensive because once someone gets a bird, the emperor has to reward him. Spending money on things like that does not show respect for the hard work of ordinary people that lies behind government funds. Jiang Gongwang ended by encouraging Huizong to do his hunting in "the fields of benevolence and righteousness" and his roaming in "the gardens of the Six Classics." There was a long tradition of Confucian advisors protesting royal hunting, so perhaps Huizong did not take Jiang Gongwang's memorial too personally.[9]

Among the most strongly worded memorials that Huizong received during his first two-and-a-half years on the throne were alarmist calls to reconsider his appointments and other decisions in light of heaven's clear displeasure. In this, the memorial writers were continuing a long tradition, dating back to the Zhou and Han periods, in which the ruler serves as a scapegoat.[10] The language used by both critics and the emperor in his responses was highly ritualized, but that did not keep the parties from using omens for their own purposes or imputing their own meanings to them.[11] Huizong was required to respond to such memorials with due humility and willingness to take on the blame. By way of illustration, three months after Huizong took the throne, the Astrological Service predicted a solar eclipse. Even though solar eclipses were by then highly predictable, Huizong was still expected to say that he took the eclipse as a warning from heaven. Zeng Zhao drafted an edict for Huizong to issue to show that he was properly chastened by the impending event. He said the anomaly could not be meaningless and to "remedy deficiencies in my initial rule and dissipate this heavenly calamity," he wanted "frank words on everything: my personal faults, the disloyalty of those around me, flawed government laws, undesirable customs, shortfalls in government assistance, and suffering of the unfortunate. Do not hold back."[12]

Over the course of the next two years there were other astral anomalies, such as a deviation in the path of Mars in the seventh month and a red vapor (probably aurora borealis) seen in the sky in the first month of the following year (1101).[13] Memorials commenting on them have been preserved by Han Zongwu, Chen Guan, Zou Hao, Zhu Hong, Jiang Gongwang, Zeng Zhao, Wang Di, and Ren Boyu.[14] Chen Guan, for instance, in the seventh month of 1100 wrote a long memorial after consulting the astrology monographs in the dynastic histories. He saw the deviation in the path of Mars as especially ominous coming so soon after the solar eclipse. He cited the Han dynasty Confucian scholar Dong Zhongshu: "When the state is about to suffer a loss of the Dao, heaven will send warnings in advance in the form of disasters. For those who do not use this to reflect on their situations, heaven will send abnormalities to startle them. Destruction will come to those who still do not change." Chen ended by reporting that Renzong had compiled a book in twelve chapters on disasters and anomalies in earlier ages, titled *Mirror for Governing along the Lines of the "Great Plan" Chapter of the Book of Documents*. Whenever there was a change in the heavens, Renzong would consult the book, Chen asserted. He thought the book probably was still in the palace and advised trying to locate it.[15]

Ren Boyu wrote in response to the red vapor. Colored vapors had been reported many times in earlier reigns (and in earlier dynasties as well), and there does not seem to have been a consistent interpretation of them. The most recent observations recorded in the *Song History* occurred in 1088 and 1099. During Shenzong's reign (1069/11), Wang Gui interpreted red vapor as a positive sign that a son would soon be born to the emperor, and composed a poem about it at a court banquet.[16] At the end of Huizong's first year, however, Ren Boyu was convinced that this time the red vapor was a dire warning, "Because heaven, in its heart, loves Your Majesty, it wants you to learn fear and trepidation."

> Now, the beginning of the year, the first month, corresponds to the hexagram "peace" *(tai)*. The year having changed its start and being in the first month of spring, the moon is in its starting position. Moreover, the day is *renxu*, Your Majesty's Personal Destiny day.[17] And yet the red vapor arose in the darkness of the night. In terms of sunshine, the sun is yang, the night is yin. Among directions, the southeast direction is yang, the northwest is yin. Among the Five Colors, red is yang and black and white are yin. In terms of affairs, the part of the palace where government is conducted is yang and the part that is restricted [where women live] is yin. China is yang, barbarians are yin. The gentleman is yang, the inferior person is yin. Virtue is yang, weapons are yin. Now, the red vapor arose in the most yin direction, and the black vapor also appeared below it. This is evidence that there are yin plots in the women's quarters, that inferiors are opposing superiors. The vapor gradually moved west, scattering and becoming white. Since white is the quality of weapons, this is evidence that barbarians will raid.[18]

Ren Boyu, in this memorial, draws on many sources in his efforts to alarm the emperor. He considers the date, the direction, and the color of the vapor. To show that each of them bodes badly, he draws on yin and yang, Five Phases, and Personal Destiny ideas. He cites the *History of the Han* monograph as an authority and verifies the negative prediction by pointing to a period during the Tang dynasty when red vapors were frequently seen and the government was in decline.

Red itself was not a baleful color; to the contrary, it was associated with celebration. Consequently, other officials took the red vapor as a positive augury. Half a month later, after Empress Dowager Xiang died, Ren Boyu submitted a supplemental memorial to refute them:

Let me note that less than half a month after the red vapor on the night of the first day of the month, there was in fact the calamity of the empress dowager [dying and] becoming an immortal. That this was what the anomaly augured is now clear. Recently, officials from Hao, Yan, and Hezhong prefectures have memorialized that you should perform ceremonies to acknowledge this [red vapor] as a positive augury. However, the direction from which the red vapor arose was seen by everyone in the realm. How do they dare move its direction and add to its form, blatantly deceiving and flattering, in order to sway the stupid! In my humble view, at the intersection of heaven and man, the Dao is very faint, and when auguries emerge, they are not likely to be empty of meaning. How can we let flatterers and schemers destroy the state by using deceptive phrases and erroneous theories to mislabel calamities as auspicious signs, thus treating heaven's mandate lightly and duping the ruler?[19]

According to the *Song History*, Ren Boyu, in his half year as a "speaking" official, submitted 108 memorials. The high officials suggested that he use a bit less ink, but he was not deterred.[20]

In the sixth month of 1101 a Daoist temple in the capital with strong ties to the throne was hit by lightning and burnt down. The memorial submitted by Wang Di mentions that Huizong's immediate response to the conflagration was to conduct a Daoist religious ceremony: "Your Majesty did not wait for dawn to break but summoned those in charge to perform a repentance offering in Extended Blessings Palace." The author approved of the seriousness with which Huizong responded to the message from heaven, but implied he was not taking the right action. Wang Di cited Han dynasty sources to argue that fires occur when rulers do not clearly distinguish the worthy from the duplicitous and the deviant from the proper and when rulers are not frugal. As he saw it, auspicious signs will not appear and inauspicious ones will not become rare until Huizong has looked for these faults in himself.[21]

Surviving omen-reporting memorials from Huizong's first two years on the throne are mostly by anti-reformists raising alarm.[22] But the rhetoric and strategy was available to both sides, and the disproportion may simply reflect differences in the survival rates of writings by reformers and anti-reformers. In mid-1102, the reformer Qian Yu declared in an impeachment of Zeng Bu, "How can solar eclipses, earthquakes, comets, and drought be the ordinary failings of a prosperous age? They are caused by high officials not being public-minded. Men and spirits rage in unison, and heaven and earth will not tolerate it."[23] Huizong was still, of course, ultimately responsible, because he had appointed Zeng Bu, but he could easily rectify the situation by ousting him.

Records of positive signs reported in Huizong's first two years as emperor are much rarer. In 1100/9 both Chen Guan and Chen Shixi submitted memorials because Huizong had taken out the imperial carriage to call on his brother Si after a report that numinous mushrooms were growing at Huizong's old mansion, now converted to Dragon Virtue Palace/Temple. Someone must have reported this auspicious event, but Chen Shixi used it to warn Huizong not to be taken in. Although he granted that the spirits send auspicious omens in response to sages, he wanted to stress to Huizong that the previous emperors had told officials not to submit memorials about auspicious occurrences, since it is better to think about what is not yet perfect than become overconfident: "The appearance of sweet dew, the gushing of sweet water springs, the arrival of unicorns and phoenixes, the growth of vermilion herbs—these are natural phenomena that occur according to the intrinsic nature of things. Flatterers label them auspicious omens and sing their praises in order to appeal to the ruler's vanity. This is what your ancestors guarded against."[24]

Chen Guan took a different tack: "I have heard that when the imperial carriage went to the home of the Prince of Cai, word passed quickly among the residents of the capital, both young and old, and there were shouts of joy, drumming and dancing, as everyone tried to catch a glimpse of your heavenly visage. From this you can see where the people's hearts are." There was nothing the matter with letting his subjects see him, but it should have been for something worthy, such as praying for the people. If Huizong was not careful, word that he was interested in auspicious signs would spread and "throughout the realm people will come presenting numinous mushrooms, not considering a myriad *li* too long a journey."[25]

What was the impact of these memorials on Huizong? They do not seem to have led him to conclude that omen reporting was a waste of time or energy. Rather, he seems to have developed an appetite for reports of auspicious omens to counter all of the negative ones he was hearing.

The Temple of Spectacular Numina

Less than five months after Zhezong was buried, Empress Dowager Xiang died (1101/1/13) and the palace again had to manage a major funeral. The ritual sequence for the empress dowager was more compressed than for Zhezong, probably in part because she was buried in a side chamber of Shenzong's tomb. Work was begun on the tomb on 1101/2/19, the coffin was sent off on 1101/4/17, and it was interred on 1101/5/6.[26]

Some issues connected to Zhezong's demise had not been fully resolved a year after his death, above all provision for him at the Temple of Spectacular Numina, the site for the portrait statues of imperial ancestors. By Huizong's day, there were two principal places in Kaifeng outside the palace itself with representations of imperial ancestors— the Supreme Shrine where ancestors were represented by their names and titles inscribed on wooden tablets, which adhered to rituals described in the Confucian classics, and the Temple of Spectacular Numina, where ancestors and ancestresses were represented by painted clay statues and Daoist ceremonies were performed.[27] The portrait temple complex had no connection to the ancient ritual classics, but was a Song innovation. The early Song emperors had put painted portraits of their parents in a dozen or so Buddhist and Daoist temples around the capital so that the priests and monks there could pray for them. When Zhenzong discovered that the founder of the Song imperial line was an incarnation of the Jade Emperor/Yellow Emperor, whom he then referred to as the Holy Ancestor, he built a large temple dedicated to him, the Temple of Spectacular Numina, just south of the Palace City. This temple later came to hold other imperial portrait sculpture, but not in a systematic way until Shenzong, in 1082, decided that images of all the Song emperors and empresses should be consolidated at the Temple of Spectacular Numina. To do this, the site had to be expanded, and 120,000 strings of cash were spent to compensate the people whose houses were confiscated.[28]

Once construction was finished in 1082, all the ancestors and ancestresses were represented by painted clay statues that depicted them

seated on dragon-decorated chairs. The halls were lined up in genea-
logical order in three tiers. The front tier had the hall for the Holy
Ancestor, the middle tier had six halls, one for each of the five prior
emperors plus the father of Taizu and Taizong, and the third tier had
five halls, one for each of the five sets of prior empresses (as Yingzong's
empress, Shenzong's mother, was still alive). Inside the hall for each
emperor were three statues: the emperor and his two most eminent
councilors who thus would receive offerings alongside him. On the
walls of the hall were paintings of other officials who had served him.
Four times a year the emperor would go in person to conduct the seasonal sacrifices at the Temple of Spectacular Numina, accompanied by
huge processions of officials and palace personnel. On anniversaries
of the deaths of both emperors and empresses, Buddhist and Daoist
clergy conducted services at the appropriate hall, and the grand councilors led processions of officials there to offer incense. In Huizong's
era, there would have been about twenty of these days in the year,
more than one a month on average. The day after these death-day ceremonies, the empress would lead the palace ladies in supplementary
ceremonies.

When Shenzong expanded the Temple of Spectacular Numina, he
did not make any provision for a hall for himself or any future Song
emperors. After he was buried and his tablet was installed in the Supreme Shrine, an official submitted a memorial proposing a frugal way
to handle the installation of a statue of Shenzong. He argued that expanding the temple complex would disrupt the livelihood of the people
who lived nearby. Instead, the portrait sculptures of the empresses
could be moved to the halls of their husbands, freeing several halls.
Empress Dowager Gao, then the regent, did not consent to moving
the empresses' statues, but she did not want to expand the site either,
so she proposed building a hall for Shenzong behind the hall for his
father Yingzong.[29]

Every time Huizong as a prince participated in seasonal offerings at
the Temple of Spectacular Numina he would have been made aware
of differences in the space given to earlier emperors and that given to
his father. Once he was emperor, he decided to rectify this slight.
The solution Huizong decided on was to build a second temple complex across the Imperial Way from the first, to be called the Western
Temple of Spectacular Numina (see Map 1). Shenzong was made the

primary ancestor of this complex and Zhezong was positioned as the first of his descendants.[30]

How this decision was reached is described in an inscription for the new temple signed by the grand councilors Zeng Bu and Han Zhongyan but actually drafted by Zeng Bu's son Zeng Yu. The way they tell the story is undoubtedly the way they thought Huizong wanted it to be told. It begins with a history of the Temple of Spectacular Numina, including its founding by Zhenzong. Special praise is given to the beauty of the buildings that Shenzong had added. The names of each hall are explained in terms of the accomplishments of the emperor enshrined in it. Then the authors turn to Huizong:

> In the seventh month after the current emperor succeeded to the throne, Zhezong was interred in Tai Mausoleum, and it was proposed that his portrait shrine go to the left of [Shenzong's] Xiancheng Hall. One day [Huizong] turned to his advisors and said, "My deceased father Shenzong's virtue and achievements were above and beyond anyone else's in history, and yet, in the system of portrait halls which he created during his Yuanfeng reign, [his own hall] Xiancheng Hall is cramped in a corner, pressed in by the city and its clamor. This is totally at odds with the importance I give to honoring and repaying him. We should build a new temple to the west of the Imperial Way where honoring my deceased father Shenzong would occupy the central position. This would express my intention to give exceptional honor to him in perpetuity." The officials present were uniformly enthusiastic. They went back and drafted a request, which Huizong promptly approved.[31]
>
> Some unscrupulous scholars argued that [Shenzong's temple] should not be relocated. His Majesty was resolute in his decision and in the end demolished their unfounded counterarguments.

The authors then turned to praise of Shenzong and his New Policies, such as the reforms of the school, examination, mutual responsibility, and militia systems. They also touched on the two political reversals since then. Next they praised Huizong for his virtue, intelligence, determination, and sense of priorities. In building the new temple complex, they reported, in all matters the model of the older temple complex was followed, with nothing superfluous added. The names of the new halls and gates for Shenzong, Zhezong, and Shenzong's empresses were explained. Altogether there were 640 room-units of new buildings.[32] The construction, we are told, was completed in less than a year without complaints from either the workers or the neighbors. The new buildings could be seen from a hundred paces outside the main front gate of the Palace City, and people bumped into each other looking up at them. The authors added some typical flattery: "How could this have been accomplished if it hadn't been for His Majesty's in-born wisdom and sincerity and his refusal to give in to the views of the small-minded!"[33]

The small-minded critics referred to in this inscription undoubtedly included Chen Guan, who wrote several memorials against the project. Chen Guan laid out five objections to the new temple complex. First, left is the honored direction in ancestral shrines, but this gets reversed by building the new building to the west. Second, the new complex is being built on the site of the former Justice Ministry, which, connected as it was to judicial executions, has been said to give off a "killing" *qi*. Third, even though the site is now occupied by offices, not homes, those offices would have to be moved, which would require uprooting people. Fourth, Shenzong had worked to bring the shrines together, but the new plan would divide them. And fifth, one should not disturb the dead. Chen Guan blamed the idea of expanding the Temple of Spectacular Numina on Cai Jing, who claimed that Shenzong had spoken of the need for later expansion and pointed to a passage in the authoritative *Veritable Records* as proof. Chen Guan was convinced that Cai Jing must have fabricated this evidence.[34]

In the twelfth month of 1101, Shenzong's portrait statue was installed in the Western Temple of Spectacular Numina, followed by Zhezong's in the third month of 1102. As before, leading officials who had served under Shenzong and Zhezong had their portraits painted on walls of the shrine. As Huizong was at the time employing both reformers and conservatives, members of both factions were represented on the walls. In the fourth month of 1102, Huizong wrote an appreciation *(can)* for the Western Temple of Spectacular Numina. His grand councilors made their contribution nine days later in the form of hymns of praise *(song)*.[35] None of these compositions is extant.

The Suburban Sacrifices

Before Shenzong's portrait was installed, Huizong had to perform his first sacrifice to heaven at the southern Suburban Altar. Huizong had made the second offering at the Suburban Sacrifice three years earlier in 1098, something common for a younger brother or son of the emperor to do, so he was already familiar with the overall choreography of the ritual, the procession that accompanied the emperor to the site, the height of the altar he would have to ascend several times, the music played, the dances performed, and so on. Still, he had much to learn.

Although the Suburban Sacrifices to heaven had been performed by emperors for centuries, much remained debatable about exactly where, when, and how they should be performed. The classical *Rites of Zhou* mentions sacrifices to heaven at the round altar on the winter solstice and sacrifices to earth at the square altar on the summer solstice. The *Record of Ritual* refers to Suburban Sacrifices, but does not refer to the shape of the altars. Many earlier dynasties had separate open-air altars for heaven and earth, used on the two solstices. During the first century of the Song, however, the two sacrifices were combined, with both heaven and earth receiving sacrifices at the southern Suburban Altar on the winter solstice every third year.[36] Shenzong had doubts about the classical basis for the combined rites and asked his officials to deliberate on whether joint rituals were appropriate or not. Substantial numbers lined up on each side. Shenzong decided to separate the rites, and in 1080 at the winter solstice sacrifice no altar was set up for earth, and in 1083 the two rites were performed separately. After Zhezong succeeded, the issue was debated again, with substantial numbers of officials again on each side. Empress Dowager Gao decided on joint sacrifices as a temporary expedient. When Zhezong was ruling on his own, Zhang Shangying and many others, including Cai Jing, persuaded Zhezong to restore the separate sacrifices. As this case shows, even though rituals were supposed to create order, at court they easily could become a source of contention or a vehicle for expressing opposition.[37]

In 1101, Huizong had to consider these issues. He reportedly had wanted to personally perform the sacrifice to earth at the northern Suburban Altar on the summer solstice, but his high officials rejected the idea. In the eighth month the idea of returning to joint sacrifices was raised, and Huizong first issued an order for joint sacrifices, but reversed himself five days later.[38] An official with considerable experience in ritual matters, Zhou Chang, explained to Huizong the concerns behind the arguments made during Shenzong's and Zhezong's reigns and who had made them. Some officials were concerned especially with expense, others objected to holding major rituals in the heat of summer and offered alternative dates, some said an official should preside at the summer rites rather than the emperor, and so on. Zhou Chang argued that since Huizong wanted to continue his father's practices, he should ask for debate on the issue. After the censor Peng Rulin opposed joint sacrifices, Han Zhongyan expressed doubts about debating a religious matter, saying, "Gods are not appointed or removed depending on the attacks of censors." Zeng Bu supported separate rites, noting that fear of the heat of summer should not keep one from serving heaven and earth with full sincerity. Huizong sided with Zeng Bu and provisionally abolished joint rites.[39]

Preparing for the rites was a major undertaking, as numerous small issues had to be settled. For instance, Lu Dian, then on the Council of State, asked Huizong for permission to decorate the case for the great fur coat with silver rather than gold, to which Huizong responded, "Must the case be decorated?" Lu Dian admitted that it was not required by ritual but had been the earlier practice. Huizong decided to leave the case plain.[40] On 1101/11/14 Huizong approved the request of the Secretariat-Chancellery to set the honor guard at 21,575 people. That same day, the Imperial Music Service reported that since the Jingyou period (1034–1037), a single set of hymns had been used, but now that the sacrifice to heaven and earth were no longer joint, some were inappropriate and new ones needed to be written. Huizong personally helped by writing one hymn for "calling down the spirits" and another for "sending off the spirits."[41]

The ceremonies themselves fully occupied Huizong and his top officials for several days, as three days in a row the emperor performed dawn rituals at different places. Zeng Bu recorded in some detail several complications that occurred. Snow was a problem on the day of the announcement at the Temple of Spectacular Numina:

> On 1101/11/21, before dawn, I led the vehicles and officials that had lined up in front of Grand Celebration Hall as we walked

with the sedan chair [for the emperor] through Virtue Revealed Gate [in the south wall of the palace], where the emperor got into the Jade Carriage. I mounted my horse and rode it to the Temple of Spectacular Numina. After completing the rituals, we proceeded toward the Supreme Shrine. By then the sun was up and it was snowing heavily. As we entered the shrine compound, the storm became a blizzard. When the honor guard reached Vermilion Bird Gate [in the old city wall], it was still snowing and the guards were soaked. The emperor turned to me and said: "The snow is great but the timing is not the best." After arriving at the Supreme Shrine, the snow became even worse, and it hadn't stopped by the second drumbeat. The emperor sent the [eunuch] imperial pharmacist Huang Jingchen to our station to ask us, "If the snow does not stop, or if there is a blizzard tomorrow, how will we get out to the suburbs?" I said, "Today is the twenty-first; the Suburban ritual is the day after tomorrow. There is no reason for it not to clear by then." Huang Jingchen said, "The emperor is just concerned that the wind and snow will make walking difficult." I said, "Even if the snow is deep, those in charge will clear the roads, so there will be no obstacles. There may be some slipping and bumping into each other, which we can do nothing about. Any really bad snow will not last long. It is best to mount the carriage and proceed, as there is no reason it will not be clear. Even if there is more snow, we still must go out to the suburbs. If it turns out we definitely cannot ascend the altar, then we would need to perform the ceremony looking at the altar from Proper Sincerity Hall [at the suburban site]. This is an unchangeable principle. Since the emperor has already issued the announcement [of the ritual] and it has been distributed throughout the realm, how could the ritual be delayed now?" Huang Jingchen said that was fine but added, "The left councilor Han Zhongyan wishes to perform the ritual looking toward the altar from Grand Celebration Hall [within the palace]." I said, "That is definitely not acceptable. Simply convey that [to the emperor]."

After Huang Jingchen left, the councilors, who were gathered at the left councilor's room for ritual purification, drafted a note. The senior grand councilor [Han] still advocated using Grand Celebration Hall, but the assistant director of the Department of

State Affairs Lu Dian said, "The junior grand councilor [Zeng] says alteration is not possible and that there is no reason the weather won't clear. If we go back to Grand Celebration Hall and the sun does indeed come out, what then?" I then drafted the note, and signed it along with the other council members, then went to see the emperor, where the decision was finalized. Huizong was pleased to hear our opinion. Someone familiar with the situation said, "This is how major events should be handled."

On the second day Huizong had to make the announcements at the Supreme Shrine.

In the middle of the night the snow in fact stopped. At the fifth watch, the emperor made the offerings in the nine chambers [of his nine ancestors]. As I was serving as the ritual commissioner, I assisted by holding the pitcher and washbasin. The moon could be seen and the emperor cheerfully commented, "The moon is pure white." I did not dare reply and went back to the pitcher and basin. The emperor said, "We can already see the moon's color," to which I responded, "There is no reason it won't be a clear day." When the emperor made the offering at Shenzong's chamber [at the Supreme Shrine], tears streamed down his face. When he went a second time to pour the libation of wine, he again wept ceaselessly, which brought tears to the eyes of those around him.

On this day, we heard that the emperor did not take his normal food but ate only vegetables as a pious act. Before 7 a.m., as the sky began to brighten, he walked from the purification hall at the Supreme Shrine to outside its gate, where he got into the Jade Carriage. By then the sky had brightened and the color of the sun could be seen. Before 1:00 p.m. we arrived at the Green Enclosure. As the day progressed, it remained bright and we could see the sun. When the honor guard of the five commissioners reached Jade Ford Park, the sunset glow filled the fields, pleasing everyone.

After resting overnight at Green Enclosure, the Suburban Sacrifice itself took place early in the morning.

The next day, 11/23, at the fourth drumbeat, we reached the canopy by the Suburban Altar, and after a while we went to the starting stations. I knelt in front of the screen to ask the emperor to perform the ritual. I led him to the second station from which he would climb the altar and make the offerings of silk. Again I assisted with the pitcher and basin. The emperor then ascended the altar to make the libation of wine. By then the sky was bright and clear, and the polar star glistened, no clouds obscuring it. Huizong turned to say, "The polar star is sparkling." When we got to the second station, he said to me, "This must be the response of heaven to my feelings of reverence."

The banquet that followed was disrupted by one of the councilors falling down, possibly from a stroke. Huizong had people assist him and sent the physician to tend to him.

When it was time for the ascension for the second offering, those in charge invited the emperor to go to the second station, but he was unwilling and stood erect facing east [while his brother made the second offering]. After the offerings were burnt, I knelt to report that the ritual was complete and led him back to the first station. The precedent was that the ritual commissioner would stand outside the curtain and wait for the Ministry of Rites to announce that we could relax before returning. Huizong told the office managers Yan Shouqin and Yan Anzhong to take care of us till we got outside the entrance to the mound, concerned that the horses might have a difficult time exiting. This was an exceptional favor, causing us all to sigh at its generosity.

At the fifth drumbeat, the Two Departments offered their congratulations in Proper Sincerity Hall. When it was fully bright, the emperor got into the carriage and returned to the palace. Before that, at the completion of the ceremony, he had sent a eunuch messenger to tell me that when the carriages get back to the palace, the honor guard should form a single column so as not to get in each other's way. I passed this order on to those in charge of the procession, then reported it to the three commanders, so that they would arrange things the way the emperor wanted. When he got into his carriage there was a single column of guardsmen and no traffic jams. After several hours we arrived at the central gate [of the palace]. The senior grand councilor [Han Zhongyan] as commissioner for the great ritual reported to me, which seemed strange to everyone. After a while [the emperor] ascended the [gate] tower and proclaimed an amnesty.[42]

From his first performance of the Suburban Sacrifice to his final one, Huizong makes no complaints about the ritual obligations that the role of emperor entailed. He is never criticized for treating rituals lightly or performing them in a perfunctory manner, much less refusing to perform them. From the many edicts Huizong issued connected to the rites he performed, one can infer that Huizong was well versed in the language of the state cult and comfortable using it. Religious feelings probably played a part in Huizong's performance of these rituals, but that does not mean that political considerations were not also involved. Performing major rituals was something Huizong did collaboratively with his officials, something that had the potential to strengthen their emotional ties.

Financial Matters

In Huizong's day, people knew that their society was wealthier than any that had existed earlier—that more money circulated, that more was available by way of material goods, that more people could afford educations, and so on. Still, the government often was short of funds.[43] Much more ink seems to have been spilled over inadequate government revenues and the constraints they posed than on topics we might consider elements of the overall economy—such as the growth of trade, agriculture, and transportation.

During Huizong's first three years on the throne, he had to authorize some of the largest expenditures that Song emperors were called on to make: the construction of a tomb for his predecessor, the funding of armies on the frontier, and a performance of the triennial Suburban Sacrifices. This major ceremony traditionally involved substantial gifts to both soldiers and officials, running its costs up to more than ten million strings of cash (out of total annual revenues of at least one hundred million strings of cash).[44] Huizong also had new buildings constructed, most notably the Western Temple of Spectacular Numina, which was another substantial expense. Even routine promotion of widowed consorts of former emperors involved substantial outlay as their stipends were several thousand strings of cash a month.[45]

How did Huizong understand these financial matters? In his first few months, many decisions that involved substantial outlays were presented to him as questions of ritual or precedent, without reference to their budgetary implications. Thus, the widowed consorts of previous emperors were all given promotions in rank that would result in larger stipends, and those who had served on Zhezong's Council of State were given rewards that included two hundred to four hundred ounces of gold, without any mention of less costly alternatives. Even the cost of the construction of Zhezong's tomb does not seem to have been directly addressed.

Probably part of the reason that his councilors put off discussing in any detail government revenues and disbursements was that accounting was so complicated. First of all, accounts were not kept in a single unit, but in many different ones: strings of cash (nominally one thousand coins strung through the hole in their middle), ounces of silver, piculs of grain, bolts of silk, and a long list of other commodities collected as tribute from the prefectures and foreign countries. Although there was a rough equivalency between the key units of cash, silver, grain, and silk, fluctuations in price of the different items regularly occurred. Moreover, revenues were collected and disbursed in all of these commodities, and had to be transported and stored in appropriate manners. Even the councilors would have found it difficult to summarize how much money the government had coming in or where it came from. There was nothing like a one-page national budget that the councilors could show Huizong, with sources of income on one side and expenditures on the other, nor a one-page statement summarizing total assets.

Huizong would certainly have come to understand the distinction between the revenues assigned to the government and those assigned to the Privy Purse (or, in the vocabulary of the time, to the Inner Treasury). Tax receipts and disbursements classed as belonging to the government were handled by the regular civil service. Officials of the Ministry of Revenue took charge of them and relevant officials discussed them in memorials and made recommendations about how they should be used. By contrast, civil service officials were not kept informed of the accounts of the Privy Purse, which was treated as though it was the private property of the emperor. A small group of eunuchs handled the Privy Purse accounts and monitored deposits and disbursements, which were treated as confidential. Because there regularly were better balances in the Privy Purse than the government coffers, it had become established practice for the emperor to make annual transfers to government accounts and from time to time authorize loans.

About two-thirds of the revenue collected through the land tax was kept at the local level for the expenses of the counties, prefectures, and circuits. If the calculations and projections made by Robert Hartwell are reasonably accurate, then in 1093 the third that did make its way to the capital made up about 30 percent of the total income of the central government and Privy Purse put together. The other 70 percent came from the various state trade agencies and monopolies, the hired service exemption fee, the sales tax on urban merchants, the profits from minting coins, and other miscellaneous sources. On the disbursement side, the salaries of the half million or more soldiers was by far the biggest expense, accounting for over 30 percent of expenditures. Palace expenses, by contrast, came to less than 5 percent.[46]

The income of both the emperor and the central government was stored in more than a hundred storehouses and treasuries, some within the palace complex itself but most scattered through Kaifeng and its suburbs. Since the beginning of the dynasty, the Left Treasury had been the main repository for government revenues in coins and precious metals. It was located just south of the palace complex, between the Assisting the State Monastery and the Imperial Way. In 965 the dynastic founder had set up the Reserve Treasury as a Privy Purse treasury to build up resources that would be needed in case of war. For more general Privy Purse expenses, there was the Inner Treasury and the Jingfu Palace Treasury, set up by the second emperor, Taizong. Both were located within the Palace City. Renzong, in 1040, consolidated several storehouses holding domestic and foreign tribute to make the Imperial Apartments Storehouse, another Privy Purse storehouse.[47] And Shenzong had started a new storehouse, called the Yuanfeng Treasury, situated to the east of the New City Wall, by the Rainbow Bridge. Established in 1080, it was started with the profits from state wine and ferry operations and was to be set aside for a future campaign to regain the Yan-Yun region (the Sixteen Prefectures) in what had been Tang China that had been occupied by Liao since the midtenth century. In time the Yuanfeng Treasury also received funds from other state enterprises, and disbursements could be made only with the approval of both the grand councilors and the emperor. Thus, it was thought of as the grand councilors' treasury. Outside the palace along the Bian canal were storehouses for the tax grain coming from specific prefectures. For instance, by the Eastern Water Gate was Broad Supply Granary, for grain coming from Henan, and between that gate and the road coming in from Chen Prefecture Gate on the south wall were five granaries for grain from the Jiang and Huai regions.[48] Most of the tax grain went to the government, but the taxes from certain prefectures were assigned to the Privy Purse.

The revenues set aside for the Privy Purse included the commodities that prefectures sent to the emperor, both as standardized gifts and because they were needed for palace use; items received as tribute from foreign countries; profits from government monopolies in salt, wine, and tea; duties on maritime commerce; coins from imperial mints; proceeds from government gold and silver mines; specified shares of other tax income; and any surpluses in the government accounts.[49]

Before the New Policies were instituted in 1069, on the order of 10 to 15 percent of state revenues were under the control of the emperor.[50] Decisions about whether the government or the Privy Purse should pay for an expense seem often to have been made on an ad hoc basis. Thus, although the Privy Purse paid for construction and repair of palace buildings and gifts necessitated by the birth, marriage, or death of members of the imperial family, the government paid the salaries of many of those who worked in the palace, including the guards, cooks, and the employees of many of the palace stockrooms and workshops; it even covered the stipends of princes and princesses and payments made to palace ladies when they were released from service. The government treasuries also paid for the housing and stipends for members of the imperial clan. On the other hand, although the government covered the salaries of soldiers, the Privy Purse was expected to make large contributions in time of war, particularly to pay for rewards to soldiers after victories. The Privy Purse was also the principle source for relief funds in case of famine, flood, or natural disaster. The huge expenses associated with the death of an emperor, both for the construction of the tomb and for the gifts given to those who took part in the funeral were divided; the state covered most of the burial cost, the Privy Purse most of the ritual expenses. Surpluses in the Privy Purse gave emperors leeway in undertaking projects despite bureaucratic opposition. According to Hartwell's analysis, enough surpluses had accumulated in the Privy Purse by 1069 that Shenzong could fund the new fiscal measures from it.[51]

After Huizong had been on the throne a few months, officials began bringing up budgetary issues to him, especially the costs of holding Qingtang in the northwest. In the fourth month of 1100, during an audience, Huizong approved a request from the Shaanxi army for the equivalent of one million strings of cash. In the fifth month during an audience reference was made to Lü Huiqing's report that there was not enough grain on the border to feed the soldiers. The next month, when the court learned that a prefecture in Shanxi had less than ten days of rations left for its army, the fiscal commissioner was asked to report on the availability of supplies elsewhere. Later that month Huizong learned that tax revenue was not sufficient to cover expenses in seventeen prefectures along the border in Hebei, so each year the government had to provide the equivalent of two million strings of cash. In the sixth month, Zeng Bu discussed the New Policies fiscal measures with Huizong during an audience. He told Huizong that the Tea-Horse Agency annually brought in two million (strings of cash, presumably), which was used to purchase twenty thousand horses a year. Huizong responded that the labor service exemption fees were also an essential component of the budget. In the eighth month, Huizong approved transferring from the Privy Purse the equivalent of two million strings of cash to supply the army in Shaanxi.[52]

By the tenth month of 1100, Huizong was receiving memorials devoted to fiscal matters. Yu Ce, then in the Ministry of Revenue, claimed that the government was receiving much less in revenue than in decades past, and therefore severe economies were warranted. In the first month of the following year Fan Chuncui wrote in a memorial that better men needed to be selected for fiscal positions, pointing out the problems with the policy of selling official ranks to raise revenues that had been adopted in three circuits in the northwest. According to Fan, "a rich merchant who pays ten million cash can get positions for three sons." A few months later he wrote on the strain caused by building fortifications in Hebei; because grain prices had risen, the wages paid the soldiers were not enough to keep them adequately fed.[53] In the third month of 1101, Chen Cisheng submitted a multipart memorial of moral advice on topics such as cultivating oneself and extending benevolence to the people. Under the rubric, "honoring frugality," he brought up examples from history of rulers who had spurned luxuries and thus prospered and those who had indulged themselves only to lose everything. The taste for luxury and novelty was especially bad in their own day, he claimed. Huizong should consider morality *(daode)* to be beautiful and kindness *(renyi)* to be decorative, rarities to be the axes for chopping down countries, and pearls, jade, and brocades to be the poisonous addictions that lead one astray.[54]

In the middle of Huizong's second year on the throne, An Tao submitted a memorial claiming that, under Shenzong, the treasuries of both the Privy Purse and the government had been full, but now they were all empty because of the demands of supplying the border region. He advised Huizong to dismiss unnecessary people, encourage savings at all levels, and curb spending by sticking to budgets.[55] The next month Chen Guan also claimed that government coffers were empty in a lengthy memorial on "what needs to be known about national finance." The memorial cites five edicts issued between the ninth month of 1100 and the third month of 1101 which had ordered circuits to send half of the surpluses from the wine monopoly and the price stabilization authority to the capital. To Chen Guan, this was a case of taking from the people but not giving them anything in return.[56] Surpluses built up in the counties and prefectures should be left there for future emergencies, he contended. When Shenzong, in 1084, took two million strings from the price stabilization and other agencies to fund border expenses, he said it was a temporary measure, to last only three years. How could it be fair to take the surpluses built up over thirty years to help only one part of the country? Chen Guan felt that the wealth of the entire realm was all being moved to the border. He also tried to insist that Shenzong would never have acted this way. "Today supplying the borders cost a hundred times what it did in the past; the fiscal intendants are more stressed than in normal times." In less than a year, through these five edicts, the entire savings of counties and prefectures has been confiscated, but the problem of shortages still had not been solved.[57] Chen Guan admitted that there were lots of details about government finance that he did not know, so could offer no solution. But he does imply that a resolute ruler would solve these problems without taxing the richer parts of the country so heavily.

When Chen Guan submitted this memorial, he also sent in another objecting to the way the *Veritable Records* was being compiled and a third indicting Zeng Bu. When Huizong next saw Zeng Bu, he commented that Chen Guan had not proven grateful to Zeng Bu for recommending him. In his response Zeng Bu countered the charge that he had spent the savings of thirty years. "When Shenzong was managing finance, even though there were many years with military expenses, the storehouses and treasuries were all full. In the Yuanyou period [the anti-reformers] spent it all for no good reason, making withdrawals but not deposits until the storehouses and treasuries were empty. So it is not exactly fair to say I destroyed the results of thirty years of planning."[58] In other words, Zeng Bu did not dispute the characterization of the treasuries as empty, only whose fault it was.

How successfully did Huizong and his councilors learn to work together? During Huizong's second and third years on the throne, a group of experienced officials, each old enough to be Huizong's father or grandfather, continued to educate him in the complexities of governing. Learning was a two-way process: just as Huizong was acquiring a better sense of how things got done, his councilors were figuring out what would catch his attention or stir his interest. They would hope to be a good influence on him, but also had to take into account his personality and preferences. They could not control all of the information that reached him since hundreds of officials could submit memorials to him. Moreover, Huizong could have strong feelings on an issue that was not uppermost on their agenda. An example would be the arrangement of the ancestral portrait halls, which Huizong took personally. By the time the new extension of the Temple of Spectacular Numina was completed, it is likely that his councilors had come to realize how much Huizong enjoyed the process of planning construction and seeing new buildings take shape.

During these two years Huizong had to read a huge number of memorials from his officials. He had to get used to being held responsible for any defect in the government, even for strange weather or eclipses of the sun. He was told to take exaggeration into account when reading officials' memorials, but it still must have been difficult to figure out when the authors were exaggerating only a little and when they were blowing things totally out of proportion—Were all of the treasuries really empty? Or did they just have less than at some earlier time? Or less than one would like? As he found out, the role of emperor entailed much that was irksome.

During 1102, Huizong gradually dismissed most of the conservatives he had summoned in 1100. In 1102/5 he dismissed Han Zhongyan. A few weeks later, Zeng Bu, no longer accepted by either side, was dismissed (1102/i6). At the same time, several reformers were put on the Council of State, including Zhao Tingzhi in 1102/i6, Cai Jing in 1102/7, Zhang Shangying in 1102/8, and Cai Bian in 1102/10.[59]

In contrast to those who see the death of the empress dowager as the primary reason Huizong gradually eased the conservatives out of his court, I see Huizong himself as slowly changing his mind as he gained experience. Trying to bring diversity to his court and manage the inevitable conflicts himself had not proved rewarding to Huizong, who lost some of his initial enthusiasm for the political process. Rather than a change in personnel, I think a more likely explanation is a change of heart.[60]

Zeng Bu saw it that way. In late 1101, Zeng Bu tried to explain to his brother Zeng Zhao why Huizong changed his mind about the sorts of officials he wanted at his court. In an earlier letter, Zhao had voiced his concerns that "good and upright scholars" had been leaving the court, while those taking their places mostly had served under the reformers. Zhao warned his brother that, since he had previously worked so hard against the reformers Zhang Dun and Cai Bian, he should not expect their followers to be willing to work with him now. Thus, it would be a disaster for the entire Zeng family if the reformers returned to power. Bu, in his reply, stressed that Huizong had genuinely wanted to "destroy factional thinking" and "unite the scholar class." What made him lose hope was the anti-reformers' unwillingness to compromise and their persistence in denigrating everything connected to Shenzong's reign.[61]

Even granting that Huizong concluded that it was not worth the effort to try to get the long-time opponents to work together in harmony, one can still ask why he ended up choosing the reformers rather than the anti-reformers. Here I think it is useful to consider the contrast between Cai Jing and Chen Guan. In the traditional histories, strongly influenced by the Learning of the Way (Zhu Xi's strain of Neo-Confucianism), the most admired man of this period was Chen Guan.[62] He is seen as a man of unquestionable probity, consistently standing up for what was right. More than forty of his memorials to Huizong during his first two years have been preserved as model memorials. Quite a few have been cited here—the ones against Zhang Dun, Cai Bian, Cai Jing, Zeng Bu, An Dun, and Empress Dowager Xiang's relatives; the ones in favor of Zou Hao and Gong Guai; the warning that should be read into the deviation in the path of Mars; the mistake Huizong had made in visiting his brother to see auspicious mushrooms; the error of the plan to expand the Temple of Spectacular Numina; and the need to economize. Some of his other memorials offered more general advice. In one he urged Huizong to read Sima Guang's monumental history, the *Comprehensive Mirror for Aid in Governing*; in another he told him that, of the forty Han and Tang emperors, only three were worth emulating: Wen and Xuan in the Han and Taizong in the Tang. These three came to the throne as young men and had admirable traits: Wendi was frugal, Xuandi had sympathy for ordinary men, and Taizong was good at accepting criticism.[63] Chen Guan also offered his analysis of the political reversals of the last few decades, claiming that the retirement of Wang Anshi in 1076 was a key turning point, as after that point Shenzong turned away from the extreme factionalism of his earlier years and began to bring conservatives back. Thus, if Huizong truly wanted to "continue the legacy," he should follow Shenzong's final direction, not his initial reform program.[64]

Chen Guan wrote cogently and elegantly, and Huizong seems to have liked him as a person. The first time he dismissed him in 1100/10, he did so solely because he had infuriated Empress Dowager Xiang with his criticism of her relatives and his charge that she was still participating in the government. To make sure that Chen Guan knew he still appreciated him, Huizong sent him off with the very sizable gift of one hundred ounces of gold. When Huizong brought him back five months later, he was not assigned to a "speaking" post and so did not write as many memorials. But the ones he did write were direct and forceful.

Why did Huizong in the end decide he would rather work with Cai Jing than Chen Guan? From Huizong's perspective, a key difference between the two was that Cai Jing was positive, telling Huizong what he could accomplish, and Chen Guan was negative, preferring to point out the things he should not do. Chen had a low opinion of most emperors and didn't want Huizong to make expenditures, even for good causes. Cai Jing was traditionally criticized for knowing how to approach Huizong, for knowing what would appeal to him, but that surely is not an entirely bad trait. Chen Guan and other conservatives often seem lacking in such basic people skills. Chen Guan had numerous audiences with Huizong and yet apparently did not come to realize that Huizong did not respond well to extreme exaggeration and was annoyed rather than persuaded by memorials that condemned people in sweeping terms. Could it be that Chen Guan did not adapt his message to his audience as a matter of principle? That is, did he think that the truth should not be phrased differently because a ruler was new to the throne, young, or had high ambitions? A less flattering possibility is that Chen Guan cared more about impressing his fellow conservatives than persuading Huizong. Unfortunately, none of Cai Jing's memorials from the same period have survived, so direct comparison is not possible. But we do know that, soon after Cai Jing was appointed, Huizong initiated major charitable and educational projects. It seems likely that the two had talked about what they could accomplish before Huizong announced his appointment. Moreover, by putting a strong individual in the position of senior grand councilor and letting him manage affairs as he saw fit, Huizong could put more of his energies into the ritual and cultural side of the role of emperor.

The consequences of Huizong's gradual conclusion that a coalition government would not work are taken up in Chapter 4, which covers the appointment of Cai Jing as grand councilor in mid-1102 and what followed, with particular attention to the more autocratic policies put in place.

4

Choosing the Reformers, 1102–1108

> Now, a king has power over life and death and can confer
> benefits and impose penalties. How can anyone resist his
> orders? I must warn against subordinates who deliberately
> procrastinate: From now on, when I issue special instructions
> and decisions, it is acceptable to exhaustively discuss their
> pros and cons in memorials, which I will consider with an
> open mind. But it will be classed as a case of great disrespect
> if orders are simply not carried out on the grounds that they
> conflict with the usual practice.
>
> —*Huizong's edict of 1106*

WITHIN THE LONG SPAN of Chinese history, the Song period has commonly been perceived as a time when both emperors and
the educated elite gained greater powers. Emperors are said to have
become more autocratic, concentrating more authority in their own
hands and delegating less to their officials. At the same time, the
scholar-official elite, recruited through the competitive civil service
examination system, is said to have come into its own, its morale and
sense of worth strengthened through the reenergizing of Confucianism. To James Liu, the autocracy of the ruler and the factionalism of
the officials exacerbated each other: "The more bitter the power struggle among the bureaucrats became, the greater was the probability of
their depending upon the support of the emperor, or their playing into
the hands of those around the emperor and in the palace, and of their
helping, by design or by force of circumstances, the growth of absolutism."[1] A key element in absolutism to Liu was the suppression of dissent: "When an autocrat or an extraordinary official elevated to be an
autocratic surrogate disallowed or even suppressed competing views

from other officials as well as from intellectuals no longer in the bureaucracy and private scholars who expressed strong beliefs, autocracy
escalated into absolutism."[2]

In recent years scholars have begun to question the idea that Song
emperors were autocrats. Wang Ruilai emphasizes the ways the civil
service could limit the emperor's power; the emperor was constrained
by the system which gave him symbolic power but not much administrative power.[3] Intellectual historians argue that Song Confucianism,
rather than providing grounding for the absolute power of emperors,
justified the supremacy of scholars; the authority for truth was to be
found in the classics and scholar-officials were the authoritative interpreters of the classical tradition, not the emperors. As a result, the
impulse to limit imperial authority is evident in much of the Confucian rhetoric of the period.[4]

Where does Huizong fit in these larger schema? Huizong is not
considered one of the strongest of Song emperors—that distinction
would go to emperors like Taizong, Shenzong, and Xiaozong who
worked to strengthen the throne. As an imperial surrogate, however,
Cai Jing falls clearly on the autocratic side. Cai Jing was able to dominate
the government for a decade and a half and was unusually effective at
suppressing dissent. Between 1102 and 1104, a series of blacklists were
issued, the last naming 309 men as so recalcitrant that they should be
deprived of posthumous honors if already deceased and if still alive sent
away from the capital and excluded from the pool of candidates eligible
for office. To the conservatives, this was an egregious act, out of the
bounds of acceptable political behavior.

This chapter tackles the issue of autocracy head on. It looks closely
at the measures taken in the first few years of Cai Jing's tenure, especially those that can be interpreted as strengthening the power of the
ruler and his agents. In addition to the blacklists, these would include
the expansion of the government school system in the hope of increasing ideological conformity and the practice of the emperor issuing edicts directly in his own hand, rather than letting officials process
them.

Looked at closely, Huizong's case tends to support the view that
emperors were limited in their ability to act autocratically. However
much Huizong may have wanted to be obeyed, he discovered that
there were real limits to what he could accomplish by issuing orders,

even quite explicit ones. His efforts to identify unambiguously the men he did not want in his government largely backfired. Less than a year after his final blacklist, he began lifting the formal sanctions. The scholarly elite never lost their ability to challenge his decisions and in effect forced Huizong to back down.

Cai Jing as Grand Councilor

In the Song period, shared governance was the ideal, at least among the scholar-official class. Emperors should share power with their councilors, no one councilor should dominate the Council of State, and an independent Censorate and Bureau of Policy Criticism should keep them all in check. In reality, however, letting numerous voices be heard often led to rancor and stalemate. Thus, most emperors at some point put one councilor clearly in charge and left him there year after year. Earlier Song dominant councilors included Wang Dan under Zhenzong, Lü Yijian under Renzong, Han Qi under Renzong and Yingzong, Wang Anshi under Shenzong, and Zhang Dun under Zhezong. These powerful ministers all had critics, and the histories often reflect their critics' views.

The historical record on Cai Jing was definitely shaped by his critics, as Charles Hartman has shown.[5] Cai Jing's collected works have not been preserved and his biography in the *Song History* was based on the memorials of indictment written against him. Thus understanding the role of Cai Jing in Huizong's life requires carefully weighing evidence from often biased sources.

Cai Jing was a part of Huizong's story from the day of his accession when Cai Jing wrote out the posthumous edict making Huizong Zhezong's heir. During Huizong's first year on the throne, Zeng Bu and Han Zhongyan had wanted to send Cai Jing out of the capital, but Empress Dowager Xiang wanted him to remain to work on the history of Shenzong's reign. It wasn't until 1100/10 that they were able to reassign him to a prefectural post. Seventeen months later, in 1102/3, Cai Jing was brought back to the capital to serve once again as Hanlin academician recipient of edicts and to work on the compilation of the *National History*. The next month, 1102/4/10, he was granted an audience, but no record survives of what he and Huizong discussed. Within a month, Han Zhongyan was dismissed as grand councilor. A few weeks later, on 1102/5/25, Cai Jing was promoted to assistant director of the Department of State Affairs, making him a member of the Council of State. A few weeks after that, on 1102/i6/8, the palace censor Qian Yu impeached Zeng Bu, charging that he was not loyal to the cause of reform. He had favored his friends and relatives and conspired with the now discredited Han Zhongyan and Li Qingchen. "No minister has ever been more disloyal." That there had been eclipses, earthquakes, and comets was evidence enough that heaven and the spirits were angry with his appointment. As expected, Zeng Bu submitted a request to retire, which was promptly accepted. Like Zhang Dun before him, Zeng Bu was sent out with a respectable prefectural appointment, but over the next several years was repeatedly demoted and transferred.[6]

With both Han Zhongyan and Zeng Bu off the Council of State, on 1102/7/5 Cai Jing was made junior grand councilor, then seven months later promoted to senior grand councilor.[7] Off and on over the next eighteen years he was the dominant figure at court. Because Cai Jing would play such an influential role in Huizong's court, a variety of stories eventually circulated about who recommended him to Huizong. One story was that Han Zhongyan recommended him as a counter to Zeng Bu; he felt Zeng Bu had too much influence and wanted to get someone who was an even stronger reformer than Zeng Bu to counter him. Another story is that Fan Zhixu and the Daoist Xu Zhichang spread word among palace ladies that Cai Jing would be good and they recommended him to Huizong.[8] A text completed in 1172 made Zeng Bu the unwitting agent because he passed to Huizong the chart prepared by Deng Xunwu, which listed on one side officials associated with the New Policies and on the other those against them. The chart had seven rows, one each for key offices, showing alternative candidates in the two camps. Only a handful of men were listed from the reformer side, among them Wen Yi, Zhao Tingzhi, Fan Zhixu, Wang Nengfu, and Qian Yu. There were over a hundred in the anti-reformist column, showing that the two factions were not balanced. Deng had written one person's name in the grand councilor line for the reformers, but had covered it over with a paper tag. When Zeng Bu presented this list to Huizong, Huizong looked under the tag and saw that the name was Cai Jing. Huizong, we are told, then made up his mind to put Cai Jing on the Council of State.[9]

The *Song History* records a shorter version of this last story, then adds that on the day the edict was issued appointing Cai Jing to replace Zeng Bu, Huizong granted Cai Jing a seated audience in Extended Harmony Hall and said to him, "Shenzong created the [New] Policies and the former emperor [Zhezong] continued them. Twice there were reversals, so that our national destiny is not yet fulfilled. I wish to return to the goals of my father and elder brother. What advice do you have to give me?" Cai Jing, we are told, bowed his head and promised to devote his life to meeting these goals.[10]

More important than how Cai Jing entered the Council of State is what happened once he got there. In his first year as grand councilor Cai Jing put through ambitious programs to reform education, public welfare, and the imperial clan. Probably Cai Jing and Huizong had discussed these projects before his appointment, as he moved quickly with detailed proposals once in charge. Moreover, these reforms were closely connected to Cai Jing; they were initiated as soon as he entered office, curtailed when he was out of office, reintroduced when he returned, and abolished for good when he retired in 1120.[11] These are projects we have to identify with Cai Jing even if Huizong was fully persuaded of their value. In other cases there is little basis for labeling a decision Huizong's or Cai Jing's. A few months after Cai Jing became junior grand councilor, the decision to restore Empress Meng was reversed and she was sent back to the nunnery.[12] Empress Dowager Xiang was the one who had wanted so badly to bring Meng back, but she had since died. But was it Huizong or Cai Jing who was most eager to reaffirm Zhezong's original decision? Sources do not offer much help in this regard.

In Cai Jing, Huizong found an efficient administrator who could quickly sort through the huge number of issues referred to the throne, identify the significant elements, and make recommendations on them. Cai Jing repeatedly tried to rationalize the government by extending measures to the entire country. Most of the measures he introduced had been tried before, but only in certain places: he wanted them to be extended everywhere. Cai Jing was well aware of the ways policies could fail, especially because officials would be tempted to divert resources for private purposes, and he generally proposed elaborate rules and penalties to try to keep officials honest. In the case of the Salt Administration, his reforms involved tighter regulations, with each stage requiring more inspections, receipts, and guarantees than before. For the school system, he had elaborate rules for promotion and demotion not only sent to each school, but also carved on stone there so that all students would see them.[13]

Cai Jing was also something of a financial whiz. He considered the fiscal demands of programs and designed them so that they would not become drains on central government funds. The school system and the expansion of housing for imperial clansmen, for instance, were funded by getting local governments to endow them with unused land.[14] Some charitable programs were funded in part by turning operation over to Buddhist monks, who would be compensated with ordination certificates. Monasteries and convents were also encouraged to take in orphans and raise them as novices.[15] Just as important were expanded sources of revenue. Soon after taking office Cai Jing quickly set about restoring and retuning elements of the fiscal structure associated with the New Policies. In 1102/7 trade superintendencies were created for Hangzhou and Mingzhou and the salt monopoly was extended to the southeast. The next month, 1102/8, the Hired Service system was revived, using the regulations that had been in effect during Zhezong's later years. A few months later, Cai Jing revived the long-defunct monopoly on southeastern tea, which soon was bringing in about 2.5 million strings of cash a year and made possible the acquisition of fifteen to twenty thousand horses annually.[16] In 1104/7 the land tax system associated with the New Policies, based on resurveying land, was revived.[17] By the time Cai Jing had been grand councilor two or three years, he seems to have eliminated government deficits and perhaps even started generating surpluses. Of course, what would have looked like remarkable improvements in government revenue streams to Huizong could have seemed like oppressive extraction at the local level.[18]

Although everyone on Huizong's Council of State after 1102 was a reformer, Cai Jing was not always able to get them to work together as a team. He and his brother Cai Bian still treated each other as rivals, and Huizong finally decided to transfer Cai Bian off the council in 1105/1. Although Huizong and Cai Jing took exceptionally thorough measures to stop the intemperate name-calling, Cai Jing by no means escaped criticism himself. Most of the time Huizong ignored the accusations that Cai Jing monopolized access to the emperor and pursued his own agenda, which were voiced from early in his tenure.[19] His fellow grand councilor, Zhao Tingzhi, submitted eight or nine memorials saying he did not want to serve in the same government with Cai Jing. Finally, in 1105/6, by staying home on the excuse of illness, Zhao Tingzhi obtained permission to retire. He was still packing up to return to his hometown when a huge comet appeared in the western sky in 1106/1. This unusual astronomical event shook Huizong. He took it as a sign that heaven disapproved of his government and its recent actions. He wrote out in his own hand a note summoning Zhao Tingzhi back, and on seeing him said, "Everything you said about Cai Jing's actions is right." Zhao Tingzhi then submitted memorials criticizing all of Cai Jing's initiatives, each of which Huizong promptly canceled.[20]

Most of the criticisms leveled against Cai Jing by his critics were general attacks on his motivations and character, much like the ones earlier leveled against Zhang Dun, Cai Bian, and Zeng Bu. Occasionally, however, specific charges were made. Zhao Tingzhi, for instance, argued that Cai Jing's plan to replace the civil service examinations with a school promotion system did not have roots in Shenzong's program and threatened the principle of fairness rooted in the practice of covering over candidates' names on the examination papers. An official named Fang Zhen also made some specific charges in 1106, though in his case rather inflammatory ones. He accused Cai Jing of planning to usurp the throne himself, the way Wang Mang and Cao Cao had in Han times. Another charge was that he treated Huizong like a child, easy to fool; he could convince Huizong of any crazy project by saying either that it was ancient or that it was an unfulfilled part of Shenzong's plans. He sent his son Cai You to amuse Huizong, we are told, with the result that a steady stream of flowers, strange rocks, and caged birds and animals were brought into the palace. Moreover, Fang Zhen charged, whenever Cai Jing made a report or request, he would ask Huizong to write out an edict in his own hand so that he could show the scholar-officials that the matter was the emperor's idea. None of the recent projects, Fang Zhen maintained, were useful. This included casting the Nine Cauldrons, the new large cash, the Three Hall schools system, the music bureau, and the sacrifices at both the northern and southern suburbs. Fang Zhen claimed that the classification of officials as deviant had deterred policy criticism: "ten thousand men have been condemned for speaking out, so no longer is anyone willing to speak frankly to the emperor."[21]

Despite this barrage of criticism, or perhaps because of its hyperbole, within a few months of dismissing Cai Jing in 1106 Huizong concluded that he had overreacted to the comet. The other members of the Council of State (Wu Juhou, Zhang Kangguo, Deng Xunwu, Liu Kui, and He Zhizhong) had not been dismissed with Cai Jing. Liu Kui sided with Zhao and helped him get Cai Jing's reforms abolished en masse, but the others tended to side with Cai Jing. Officials not on the Council of State began expressing reservations about the decision to abolish all of the reforms Cai Jing had instituted. The Hanlin academician Zheng Juzhong learned from his contacts in the women's quarters that Huizong was ready to make a change. He requested an audience at which he argued that heaven could not have been angry at projects that promoted culture, such as schools, rituals, and music, or at ones which aided people in distress, such as the poorhouses and clinics. Soon Huizong was preparing the way for Cai Jing's return. By 1106/7 Huizong was reinstituting measures which had been canceled only a few months earlier, especially those related to schools.[22] Cai Jing rejoined the Council of State in 1107/1.

Charitable Ventures

Although Huizong and Cai Jing regularly referred to their project as "continuing the legacy," they did not merely retain or restore measures instituted by Shenzong and Zhezong, but went beyond them in many ways. Cai Jing inspired Huizong by talking about the noble projects they could undertake: charity for the indigent, disabled, or ill, schools in parts of the country where none existed, and new housing for the rapidly expanding imperial clan.

Just six days after his appointment as grand councilor, Cai Jing was put in charge of a new office, the Advisory Office. Modeled on the Finance Commission of Shenzong's reign, this new office was designed to overcome bureaucratic resistance to innovation.[23] When the organization of the Advisory Office was announced in 1102/8, it had seven units, one each on the imperial clan, supernumerary officials, government budget, taxation, merchants, salt, and livestock management (concerned with horses for the army). Each unit was assigned a consultant of middle rank and one or two editors of low rank (rank 8 or 9). Among the consultants were Wu Juhou, Zhang Shangying, and Fan Zhixu, men who would form the core of the committed reformers in the central government. For the next several weeks, a whole series of new projects were announced reforming welfare for the poor, education, recruitment to office, the imperial clan, and several fiscal matters, including currency, the tea monopoly, taxation, and labor service impositions.[24]

It was an ancient idea that the benevolent ruler would make arrangements for the care of those with no relatives to support them—widows, widowers, orphans, and the childless—and earlier Song rulers had made sporadic provisions, especially for the needy in the capital. Once Cai Jing began his term as grand councilor, however, these measures were extended to the entire country and ways were found to fund them on a permanent basis. On 1102/8/20, all prefectures and counties were ordered to set up charity clinics to treat the poor. Twenty days later the poorhouse system, which had been introduced under Zhezong in 1098, was extended to the capital. In 1103/5 public apothecaries were ordered established throughout the country. In 1104/2/3 orders were issued to establish paupers' graveyards, expanding a project that Shenzong had initiated.[25] In 1107/110 the charitable ventures were expanded to include housing the homeless during the winter when exposure to the cold was most dangerous. As John Chaffee notes, there were precedents for government welfare programs, but under Huizong they were extended much more systematically, which "represented a radical assumption of responsibility for at least minimum levels of welfare for the poor."[26]

The poorhouses were meant to provide food, clothing, and shelter for those who had no means to support themselves, above all widows and widowers without grown children, as well as orphaned or abandoned children. Rules were issued specifying the food and money they should be given (0.7 liters of rice a day for an adult, a half ration for a child, along with small cash allowances of ten cash a day with a winter fuel supplement of five cash). Special efforts were made when the weather was coldest and the need for shelter greatest.[27]

Concern with the spread of epidemics seems to have been part of the motivation behind the charity clinics. The memorial that proposed these hospitals for the poor, written by Wu Juhou, specifically mentions quarantining the ill: "The Rest and Recuperation Houses ought to take the sick and separate them according to the severity of their illnesses and then place them in different wards. This is done to prevent contagion. There should also be a kitchen to decoct drugs and prepare food and drink for the patients. The living quarters of the attendants and the wards of the patients should be separated. The wards, which are differentiated based on the severity of the patients' disease, can contain up to ten rooms."[28] Rules issued for these clinics required physicians to keep records of the number of patients they treated and how many of them died, information used to reward and promote the more successful. For instance, an official who treated between five hundred and a thousand patients in a year and did not lose more than 20 percent of them would be given fifty strings of cash.[29]

The paupers' cemeteries, instituted in 1104, were needed above all for the urban poor. The rules issued specified that officials keep track of who was buried in each plot and that the graves be dug at least three feet deep. Markers buried with the body were to list the person's name, age, and date of burial. The operation of the poorhouses and the paupers' cemeteries has recently been confirmed by archaeologists. At a site in modern Henan province, a graveyard was found with 849 vertical shaft tombs neatly arranged in rows and all facing south. Most were buried in ceramic vat coffins. Also found were 372 brick epitaphs which identified the subjects' names, ages, dates of death and burial, and a code indicating where they were buried. Those buried there ranged in age from nine to eighty-two, and many had been living in the charity clinic or poorhouse. Others had been working as soldiers or fulfilling labor service obligations.[30] How could the government pay for such wide-ranging welfare measures? Cai Jing's financial wizardry seems to have made it all work.

The Ban on Opponents

Because critics of Huizong's reign assign particular opprobrium to the blacklists issued from 1102 to 1104, they need to be carefully examined. It was not the case that a blacklist was announced and left in place for the rest of Huizong's reign. Rather, the rules and lists were repeatedly revised and these revisions are an important part of the story. Lists of men barred from certain posts had been issued in the two prior administrations (that is, both those headed by Empress Dowager Gao and by Zhezong).[31] Huizong's final blacklist, however, was the longest. It was designed to ensure that those serving in posts of much importance, particularly the top four or five hundred posts, in fact supported his programs and would not attempt to sabotage them from within.

The timing of the blacklist announcements does not correspond as closely to Cai Jing's tenure as grand councilor as the school, charity, and imperial clan reforms. The first measures were taken when Zeng Bu was still dominant, and many of the steps of the reversal took place while Cai Jing was grand councilor. In addition, the frequent reversals and emendations seem less characteristic of the very experienced Cai Jing than the nineteen-year-old Huizong, still perhaps under the illusion that he could get whatever he wanted by issuing an edict.[32]

Huizong's rupture with the conservatives was rather abrupt. The same month that Han Zhongyan was dismissed (1102/5/6), the first blacklist was issued. Just days later, on 1102/5/10, after Cai Jing was back in the capital but before he had joined the Council of State, a memorial was submitted asking Huizong to expel from court all the petty men opposed to reform. Its author is not listed, but Cai Jing is a likely candidate. The memorial argued that the leaders of the Yuanyou period had "committed crimes against Shenzong." When they had been brought back after Huizong first took the throne, they devoted themselves to indicting the true reformers. Once the guilty parties were clearly identified, everyone else would be able to devote themselves to loyal service to the ruler and achieving Shenzong's great enterprise.[33] Ten days later, on 1102/5/21, Huizong demoted more than fifty leading members of the Yuanyou faction (many of them long deceased, such as Sima Guang and Lü Gongzhu), and ruled that those living could no longer be given assignments in the capital. The next day charges were brought against men who had recently asked that these men's honors be restored.[34] Two days after that, 1102/5/23, Huizong issued an edict drafted by Zeng Bu designed to explain his position and reassure his officials:

> Formerly, during the Yuanyou period, powerful officials monopolized power and led evil factions to slander the former worthies' good government and excellent institutions and made reckless changes to them. During the Shaosheng period when [Zhezong]

personally took charge of the government, he clearly saw through this group's deceptions and banished them in full accord with the law. When I took over, the slate was wiped clean and they were all taken back and brought to court. And yet they conspired to restore [the Yuanyou system]. Stubbornly they took ruining [the New Policies] to be payback and hostility to be their responsibility as they slandered and slandered.[35]

The edict went on to point out how well Huizong had treated the conservatives, giving them positions as good or even better than they had had earlier. Yet those in censorial and remonstrance posts continually vilified the reformers. Unable to restrain them, there was no choice but to remove the most extreme of them. To calm those worried by this turn of events, Huizong clarified that no new charges would be brought against the Yuanyou or Yuanfu partisans (the "Yuanfu partisans" were those who in the last year of the Yuanfu period, that is, Huizong's first year on the throne, heaped calumny on the reformers). A few days after this edict was issued (on 1102/5/25), Cai Jing entered the Council of State.

In his first year on the throne, Huizong had expressed concern about the fate of Zou Hao, abruptly banished and deprived of government rank during Zhezong's last year, and he had brought him back in 1100 to serve in a "speaking" post. After Cai Jing was on the Council of State, on 1102/i6/15, Huizong issued an edict demoting Zou Hao to a prefectural post.[36] Just five days later, Huizong wrote out an edict in his own hand, going into more detail about why Zou Hao deserved to be penalized:

> I know Emperor Zhezong to have been stern and reverent, diligent in the pursuit of virtue. Late in the Yuanfu period [1098–1100], he begat the Prince of Yue. Treasonous men created rumors that the baby was not the empress's. Recently I have been looking at officials' old memorials and happened to see accusations concerning the empress's private apartments. Examined more closely, they all are clear proof [of wrongdoing]. At that time, the two palaces were close and in constant contact.[37] Palace lady attendants were at the empress's side. How could an outsider gain access to the forbidden parts of the palace, kill a mother, and take

her child? This charge is without any basis. In my capacity as younger brother, I am his successor, continuing the sacrifices to him. How could I allow a treacherous official in search of a reputation to bring severe harm to the great principles of friendship and respect? There is no crime greater than false accusations. Zou Hao should be demoted again to show my feelings toward my illustrious predecessor. Anyone who dares bring up this issue again will be dealt with in the same way.[38]

In 1100 when Huizong had asked why Zhezong had originally dismissed Zou Hao, Zeng Bu had said it had something to do with Zhezong's second empress. By this point, after Huizong had more experience himself in reading inflammatory memorials, he reread the memorial in question and decided Zhezong had been right.

Once Cai Jing was made grand councilor, the attempt to identify opponents seems to have proceeded more systematically. On 1102/9/12 the results of an analysis of the memorials submitted during Huizong's first year as emperor was announced, and their authors were classified as either proper or improper to varying degrees (see Table 4.1). There had been similar earlier scrutiny of memorials for deviance and slander first during the early Yuanyou reign, then again after Zhezong began his personal rule.[39] This time, 583 people were divided into seven categories. It included several men who had recently served as speaking officials, such as Ren Boyu.[40]

Table 4.1. Numbers of men on the 1102/9/12 blacklist

Category		Number
Proper or correct		41
Proper to a high degree	6	
Proper to an average degree	13	
Proper to a slight degree	22	
Improper or deviant		542
Improper to a slight degree	312	
Improper to an average degree	150	
Improper to a high degree	41	
Improper to an extreme degree	39	
Total		583

In the next month, long lists of specific demotions were issued. In 1102/11/22 the classification of 583 officials was used in a systematic way to assign new posts. For instance, the thirty-nine in the worst category were sent to small remote places and the forty-one in the next-to-worst category were sent to remote places. The edict justified this action in terms of their lèse-majesté: they had odiously slandered the government of the former emperor. The next month local officials were ordered to keep under supervision those banished to their jurisdictions.[41]

Much more famous than this list of more than 500 deviant officials was the much shorter list of 119 men issued a few days later (1102/9/16). Most of the men on this list had served in prominent posts during the Yuanyou period, and many were no longer living. It included such prominent people as Wen Yanbo, Sima Guang, Su Shi, Su Che, Fan Zuyu, and Cheng Yi, as well as some of those who had recently served Huizong, such as Ren Boyu, Chen Guan, Chen Cisheng, Zou Hao, and Gong Guai. The *Song History* says that this list was written out by Huizong himself and carved on a stone erected near the gate on the south side of Cultured Virtue Hall compound.[42]

In 1103 efforts were made to enforce and extend these bans. The sons and younger brothers of the banned Yuanyou and Yuanfu partisans were forbidden to enter the capital in the third month.[43] Next came an order that the portraits of Sima Guang, Lü Dafang, Fan Chunren, Liu Zhi, Fan Bolu, Liang Tao, and Wang Yansou be removed from the walls of the hall dedicated to Zhezong at the Western Temple of Spectacular Numina, completed less than two years earlier. In the fifth month twelve officials who had recently served Huizong, including Chen Guan and Zou Hao, were stripped of official rank and placed under administrative supervision in distant prefectures.[44]

There is very little record of officials speaking up against these measures, but some must have. The funerary biography of Zhang Fu (1045–1106) reports that although even highly principled scholars remained silent, Zhang Fu, during an audience with Huizong, did protest, telling the emperor that in the first years of his reign people had congratulated each other on the road when so many of those banished had been allowed to move closer, but now that he had reinstituted a purge and extended it to sons and grandsons, he was reversing his original policy. Huizong did not rebuke Zhang Fu, but neither did he act on his advice.[45]

Men who publicly supported the penalties are easier to find. On 1103/9/25 an official complained that the list of those barred from office was not widely available and proposed that every circuit and prefecture erect stones inscribed with the list. His request was approved, and a revised list was compiled, bringing the total down to ninety-eight men, nearly half of them deceased.[46] There is no evidence that any stones were actually erected in response to this order, perhaps because before local officials got around to acting on it a new list was issued. On 1104/1/6 Huizong's former tutor He Zhizhong proposed that those who had been classed as deviant be sent out of the capital, implying that the previous orders to that effect had not been effective. The next month (1104/2/6) it was decided to treat Zhang Dun and Wang Gui the same way the anti-reformers were being treated on the ground that officials judged them as similarly treacherous.[47]

In 1104/6/3 Huizong issued what came to be the final and most famous blacklist. This edict named 309 former officials as "the treacherous faction of the Yuanyou period." The list was divided into six tiers (see Table 4.2). Civil officials who had once served on the Council of State began with Sima Guang and Wen Yanbo, both long dead, and ended with several who had served in Huizong's own Council of State, most notably Han Zhongyan and Zeng Bu, but also Li Qingchen, Fan Chunli, An Tao, Lu Dian, Huang Lü, Zhang Shangying, and Jiang Zhiqi. The next category was men who had formerly served in high court posts, and began with a long list of deceased officials beginning

Table 4.2. Living and deceased officials on the 1104 blacklist

	Living	Deceased	Total	On earlier 1102 list
Former councilors	7	20	27	21
Other former court officials	22	27	49	35
Other civil officials	151	26	177	37
Military officials	21	4	25	4
Eunuchs	24	5	29	7
Disloyal subjects	1	1	2	1
Total	226	83	309	105

Sources: CBSB 20.714–717; YYDRZ 10.9b–25b; JSCB 144.13a–32a. The column "On earlier 1102 list" refers to those on the 1104 list who were also on the 1102 list; it does not add up to 117 (the number on the 1102 list) because some of those on the first list were not on the second.

with Su Shi. It too ended with officials who had recently served under Huizong. The next category of "other officials" began with men known to be friendly with Su Shi, including Qin Guan, Huang Tingjian, Chao Buzhi, and Zhang Lei, and included many who can no longer be identified. Next came a group of men with military ranks, including two imperial clansmen. After that was a list of twenty-nine eunuchs, who had probably served Empress Dowager Gao. The final tier consisted of two men who were identified as "disloyal ministers who once served as grand councilors," Wang Gui (Shenzong's long-deceased councilor) and Zhang Dun.[48]

A copy of this list was written out by Huizong, then carved into a stone placed on the east wall of Cultured Virtue Hall. Soon replicas of it were ordered erected in all prefectures. Most of the people on this 1104 list who had not been on the earlier lists with 119 or 98 names were lower rank officials, but there were also some like Zeng Bu and Zhang Dun who, while opponents of Cai Jing, were not anti-reformers.[49]

Naming those he did not want in his government was only one part of Huizong's effort to bring peace to his court. He also tried simply ordering his officials to put an end to accusing each other of partisanship. The edict of 1104/6/3 that listed the 309 to be blacklisted also declared that "officials should cease impeaching anyone not already on the list or who has been removed from the list."[50] This order apparently did not meet with instant compliance, because fourteen days later he had to reiterate it. On that occasion Huizong justified the proscription of specific officials and reiterated his determination that officials stop trying to get more people added to the list:

> When I first took the throne, the respectful and quiet were not yet speaking up. The treacherous factions of prior years got themselves activated again and took to spreading deviant ideas and gathering followers. Some in important positions attempted to make major changes. Others submitted sealed memorials to make crazy libelous accusations. Sharing the same malicious intentions, they aided each other. . . . Recently I ordered the compilation and classification [of the memorials they wrote] and have a full list of their names, which has been issued through channels. After exhaustive discussion the names were divided into three levels. Each of those participating in the discussion heard everything and

agreement was nearly complete. No one has been left off the list
[who deserves to be on it]. . . . All of this I have written out in my
own hand, putting it together to make a single list. It has been
carved into a stone placed at the court. We created the category of
disloyal minister and added it at the end. Although those men's
statuses differ, their crimes are equally grievous. Out of consideration I have distributed this list throughout the realm. . . . The
list is now fixed and immutable. Everyone should listen respectfully and not discuss these matters further. . . . From now on officials may not impeach anyone else. This edict is to show that I
want everyone to be informed.[51]

In this edict Huizong keeps returning to his goal of ending the use of
abusive language and the cycles of retaliation. He tries to assure his
audience that making the list was done carefully and for goals that
reasonable people would share.

Cai Jing wrote a preamble for the version of this stele distributed to
the prefectures. In it he began by stating that the emperor has a responsibility to distinguish the good from the evil. This had been done
by scrutinizing the memorials of a very large number of officials, only
309 of whom were judged unworthy of further appointment or posthumous honor. Cai Jing reported that Huizong had written out the list
carved on a stone in the palace and that he had received an order to
write out this one for distribution to the prefectures, which he was
happy to do because it helped publicize the emperor's filial and fraternal desire to continue the legacy.[52]

Huizong and Cai Jing had not given up on using less coercive ways
to win the support of officials and potential officials. They heaped
honors on Shenzong and his leading officials, especially Wang Anshi.
In 1104/6, Huizong announced that more than 9,800 of Shenzong's
state papers had been collected and that pictures of the leading officials
of his reign would be painted on the walls of the building holding them.
That same month an edict was issued enshrining Wang Anshi as a cor-
relate in the Confucian temple, placing him after Mencius. The Directorate of Education was ordered to make pictures of his statue, print
them, and have them distributed throughout the country.[53]

The full form of the blacklist was short-lived. Less than a year after
the final, 309-person list was issued, the process of reducing the penal-

ties imposed on the listed men and their families was initiated, following established precedents.[54] On 1105/5/11, the restrictions on the travel of fathers, sons, and brothers of those banned were removed. Two months later, on 1105/7/22, Huizong wrote out an edict permitting those who had been banished for nothing more than writing memorials to return home. Local officials were to have their relatives serve as guarantors for them. The next month a clarification was issued: the guarantors were to be held equally liable if those who returned home again engaged in slander.[55] Six weeks later, on 1105/9/5, a different sort of reduced penalty was announced for fifty-eight men whose offenses were deemed more serious. Because of recent auspicious events including the casting of the Nine Cauldrons, an amnesty was being extended even to the slanderers. Those in Lingnan should be moved to Qinghu, those in Qinghu to the Jianghuai area, those in Jianghuai to regions near the capital, and so on. However, those already in close regions were not to be moved to the suburbs of the capital. Each of the fifty-eight men is listed with his previous place of banishment and his new assignment.[56]

Before the end of the year, on 1105/12/24, Huizong issued an edict restoring the eligibility for appointments to the Yuanyou and Yuanfu partisans on the grounds that they had been punished enough. He had had the inscribed stone at court destroyed and had instructed any prefectures that had set up a copy to demolish it. Once again Huizong restated his demand that officials stop accusing each other of factionalism. This time he went so far as to ask the Censorate to report anyone who submitted such a memorial.[57]

A few days later, on the last day of 1105, in an imperial brush edict Huizong reported frustration with getting officials to carry out his reduction of penalties on those formerly blacklisted:

> Recently I issued a directive in my own hand which ordered those under supervision and registration for submitting memorials to return to their native places and charged their relatives with guaranteeing them, and yet the authorities merely moved them to closer assignments.[58] . . . At the end of the Yuanfu period [1100], the literati overstepped their position and took the opportunity to "strike at the mountain," in hope of gaining a high post. It has already been three years since they were sent to distant regions.

Their crimes are not minor, excusable ones, but good and evil have already been made clear and their punishment has already been lengthy. We should be lenient and show that they will not be permanently abandoned. . . . Each should make a new start and not fear later trouble.[59]

Huizong's decision to lessen the penalties on the partisans was strengthened by the appearance of a comet a few days later on 1106/1/5.[60] The first edicts after the comet called for frank advice and criticism, allowed those who had been banned to serve in office again, and reiterated the order that local governments that had set up steles with the lists of partisans should have them destroyed.[61] Two days later Huizong issued a general amnesty and said that even officials whose offense according to the statutes should not be reduced by an amnesty could have their penalty reduced.

> I know that the stars convey messages from heaven, which makes me stand in awe, uneasy. Because of [such a message], I am specially offering clemency and pardoning those under restrictions. All may start anew; we welcome them with a harmonious spirit. I have already issued directives that besides destroying the inscribed stone on the Yuanyou partisans also restores priority for appointments to those who were under registration.
>
> Yet I shudder to think that shallow, foolish people will wildly speculate, spying through cracks, rushing to "strike the mountain." My deepest wish is that we could once again attain the good government of the Xining and Yuanfeng reigns [of Shenzong]. Those who stubbornly obstruct the policy of continuing the legacy will be dealt with according to the law. This needs to be explained to all, far and near, so that they will understand my intention.[62]

What message was Huizong conveying here? Former critics now willing to live with the reform program could get new assignments, but they should not infer that Huizong had changed his mind on the New Policies or welcomed criticism of it. Obstructing the reform program would still be a punishable offense.

On 1106/1/17 the Three Departments made the restoration of the privileges of those who had been banned concrete by listing new ranks and appointments for them. They were divided into categories, and ranged from those given only a promotion in personal rank, to those assigned a sinecure such as a temple guardianship, to those assigned a substantial office such as prefect. On 1106/1/20 the Ministry of Justice was ordered to destroy the pamphlets of the blacklist as well as the woodblocks used to print them.[63]

Not everyone understood Huizong's intentions and he had to issue repeated clarifications. On 1/24 he insisted that he had not changed his mind about the seriousness of the offenses of the Yuanyou and Yuanfu partisans, and although he was giving the listed men another chance for employment, they would not be regaining control of the government. The next day he brought up the fact that most of the memorials he had received in response to his call for frank criticism had attacked the idea of continuing the legacy. Although it was "regrettable that speaking up had become a crime," everyone needed to realize that slander of the imperial ancestors was out of bounds, a punishable transgression.[64]

On 1106/3/6, after Cai Jing had been dismissed, the penalties on the banned partisans were further reduced by dividing them into three levels, with the third level again allowed into the capital. Even before those men had the chance to arrive, the effects of the previous year's lifting of the travel restrictions on partisans' sons and brothers were being felt and twice that year (1106/7/3 and 11/26) the court had to issue clarifications of how to treat those arriving in the capital in search of new appointments.[65]

From this point on, names were gradually removed altogether from the blacklist. For instance, on 1108/3/28 it was reported that of forty-five people examined, all but three could be removed from the blacklist, and on 1108/6 some ninety-five people were taken off the list. In 1110/3 it was ordered that those who had been classed as less seriously deviant should be treated just like anyone else in appointments and promotions.[66] A few men once on the list even reached high office, most notably Zhang Shangying, who rose to grand councilor in 1110.

Over the course of the years 1102–1104, Huizong articulated several arguments to justify the blacklists. A key one was that with a definitive list, officials could cease indicting each other and turn their energies to other tasks. From 1105 to 1110, Huizong kept scaling back the penalties, explaining that right and wrong had been made sufficiently clear, thus allowing him to be lenient. He did not admit that imposing the bans had been wrong or that the men labeled as offenders were blameless. Rather, their punishment had served its purpose and the men involved could be given another chance.

Why did Huizong begin modifying the blacklists so quickly and make revisions so many times? The only reasonable inference is that there was a storm of protest against the lists. At first Huizong thought fuller explanations would defuse the situation, but later he tried backpedaling step by step, trying to determine how much he would have to undo to placate the disaffected.

Suppression of the Writings of Su Shi and His Circle

During the Yuanyou period, when the New Policies were quickly dismantled, orders were issued to destroy all copies of Wang Anshi's *New Interpretations of Three of the Classics* (the *Book of Songs*, the *Book of Documents*, and the *Offices of Zhou*), a book which had been widely studied by those preparing for the civil service examinations.[67] Huizong thought the writings of the anti-reformers merited similar suppression.

Huizong, in many of his edicts, condemned what he called "Yuanyou learning" without defining it. He did not want it taught in the schools and did not want its advocates to serve as teachers. He also singled out some particular books for suppression. The first edict to this effect was issued on 1103/4/9. It said, "Burn the wooden printing blocks for Su Shi's *Dongpo Collection* and *Later Collection*."[68] A Southern Song source says that an official proposed also destroying steles with Su Shi's books, which was approved.[69] The next order, on 1103/4/27, was not limited to Su Shi. It ordered the burning of the printing blocks for the collected works of the "Three Su" (meaning the brothers Su Shi and Su Che and their father Su Xun) as well as those of Su Shi's disciples Huang Tingjian, Zhang Lei, Chao Buzhi, Qin Guan, and Ma Juan, as well as specific books by Fan Zuyu, Fan Zhen, Liu Ban, and the monk Wenying.[70]

Little is heard about the implementation of these orders until much later in Huizong's reign. In the seventh month of 1123, one source reports, an edict ordered the destruction of the printing blocks for the collected works of Su Shi and Sima Guang, which someone in Fujian had had the audacity to have carved. Another source says that the following year, 1124, Huizong issued an edict that said, "From the start I outlawed Yuanyou learning. In recent years, however, people are again honoring Su Shi and Huang Tingjian. The two have offended the imperial ancestors and their ideas do not conform to heaven. Even scraps of their writings ought to be burned and not preserved. Those who defy this will be charged with disrespect."[71]

Perhaps issuing this reminder was spurred by the discovery that Cai Tao, the youngest of Cai Jing's sons, had written a book of anecdotes about poems and the incidents that led up to them that treated Su Shi and Huang Tingjian as major poets. As a result, in the ninth month of 1123 Cai Tao was stripped of all his titles and privileges.[72]

One implication of these two incidents is that people had come to think of the rules against Yuanyou learning as dead letters. In the case of Cai Tao, at least, the penalties did not last very long. The next year he was again assigned to office and acted on his father's behalf when he was returned to the Council of State for a few months.

Did Su Shi's writings or the writings of his followers ever become hard to find? The anecdotal literature says little on this topic. Perhaps Huizong was issuing orders his government had little capacity to enforce. Certainly writings of the prescribed men all survived. By contrast, the collected works of most of Huizong's leading officials did not make it.

Expansion of Government Schools

At much the same time that Huizong began issuing lists of a couple hundred men whom he did not want in his administration, he offered thousands of men places in government schools and the chance to enter government service based on promotion through the school system. Places in schools can be seen as the carrot to the stick of the blacklist. If both worked as intended, it should have been easy to staff the government with men who supported the New Policies.

Government education had begun early in the Song and was an important part of the reform agenda of both the "minor reform" of Fan Zhongyan in 1043 and of Wang Anshi after 1069.[73] Under Shenzong, the New Policies had involved a reorganization of government education in the capital through the Three Halls system of graded levels at the Imperial Academy. Huizong's policies went much further because they extended the system to the entire country.

Cai Jing proposed the educational initiatives soon after becoming grand councilor. His ten-point proposal, submitted on 1102/8/22, asserted that schools needed to be opened throughout the country because education was a high priority. He proposed increasing the numbers of teachers, students, and schools, as well as the size of land endowments. Not only prefectures, but also counties should get schools, including primary schools for elementary education. Students would be divided into three grades (the lower, inner, and upper halls), and tests would be used to promote them from one grade to the next within schools and from lower to higher schools. The system thus was called the Three Hall system. Students who reached the upper hall of the Imperial Academy could test directly into office.[74]

To handle the increase in students, a new campus was built for a new lower school for the Imperial Academy. Given the name Biyong, after the schools of the Zhou kings mentioned in the classics, it was located outside the southern walls of the city. The architect Li Jie, the same official who had designed the mansions for Huizong and his brothers a few years earlier, was given charge of constructing the Biyong's four lecture halls and one hundred residence halls, each to house thirty students.[75]

From 1103 through 1105, Huizong issued many details of how the schools would be run, ranging from land allocations, to testing, selection ratios, numbers of teachers, and avoidance of heterodox thought. In 1103 and 1104 specialty schools were established in the capital for medicine, mathematics, painting, and calligraphy. Although there is no evidence that Huizong took a particular interest in mathematics, he did have personal interests in the other three subjects. In 1104/1 the stipends for students at the government schools were increased. There were also calls to increase the number of county schools and the enrollment at them. Large counties could have fifty students, medium-sized ones forty, and small ones thirty. That year the Three Hall system accommodated 210,000 students across the country, and cost 3.4 million strings of cash and 500,000 piculs of rice (ca. 1.35 million bushels).[76] By the eleventh month Huizong and Cai Jing apparently felt that the development of the school system had been so successful that its examinations could be used for civil service recruitment. Early in 1105 Huizong issued an edict that permitted schools with adequate funds to increase the number of students they supported. Eleven days later another edict clarified an important privilege granted students in the schools: students in prefectural and county schools did not have to perform labor service in person; those at the intermediate level (the inner hall) did not have to hire replacements, and those in the highest level (upper hall) would be treated on a par with official households.[77]

Huizong chose to identify himself closely with this expansion of the school system. Once construction of the Biyong Academy was complete in the eleventh month of 1104, Huizong paid a visit. By this time, the two divisions of the Imperial Academy together had 3,800 students. Huizong paid his respects to the image of Confucius in Great Completion Hall, then summoned the two directors of study to tell them that he was making a donation to the school of some of his own calligraphy and inviting everyone at the school to view it. Evidently, in his fifth year as emperor, Huizong expected his subjects to be excited to get the chance to look at texts he had written out. After Huizong's visit, thousands of congratulatory verse and essays were submitted to the court by scholars from all over the country. Huizong told the Secretariat-Chancellery to rank them, and they rated a long essay by Ge Shengzhong as the best.[78]

After this visit, Huizong issued a hand-drafted edict extolling the virtues of the new school system. This edict was then carved on a stele erected at the Biyong Academy. Cai Jing did the calligraphy for its title, "An Edict Bestowed by the Emperor on the Biyong." He also proposed that copies of the stele be made and distributed to all the prefectural schools so that they could replicate it.[79] The timing of Cai Jing's suggestion, late 1104, just a few months after the stele listing the banned partisans was ordered duplicated, suggests that the new stele was intended to counter any sense that Huizong was an enemy of literati, education, or Confucian principles.

Huizong's edict, on display at schools all over the country, begins by asserting that ancient schools were wonderful institutions that improved customs, encouraged hard work, and led people to honor their rulers. Teachers would recognize talented and virtuous students and recommend them for office. Shenzong had appreciated the need for such a school system and had made a good beginning in the capital, but he had never been able to implement his ideas fully. The new Biyong Academy, Huizong announces, will follow Shenzong's Three Hall system. With the eventual abolition of the civil service examination system, students will rise through recommendations from people who know them at the local level. All this should eliminate dissension: "Books not by the sages and worthies, plus the learning of the Yuan-you period, are forbidden and not to be studied."

After 1106, as Huizong backpedaled on the use of a blacklist, he devoted more effort to his school initiatives. In 1107 a way of recruiting students outstanding for their virtue was introduced. Based on the system described in the *Rites of Zhou*, this "Eight Virtues, Eight Offenses" school promotion system was intended to allow the rapid promotion of students nominated for their excellence in eight specified virtues. An edict that Huizong issued on this system in 1107/9 was soon inscribed on stones erected at government schools around the country, most of them again in his calligraphy. This edict argued that the school system described in the *Rites of Zhou* was the ideal one as men were advanced on the basis of such virtues as filial piety, fraternal love, solidarity with relatives, and loyalty to the ruler.[80] Students recommended by their villages or county or prefectural schools for two or more of the virtues would attend those schools for a year, after which they could be directly admitted to the upper hall of the Imperial Academy without taking an exam. Once they had been vetted there, they could be given degrees and official rank. The other side of bringing morality into the school system was the Eight Offenses, the crimes or improprieties that would warrant expulsion from the schools, ranging from murder, arson, and rape, on down to theft.[81]

Even when Cai Jing was out of office for three years, 1109/6 to 1112/5, the new schools continued, though efforts were made to tighten the rules on attendance and teachers' qualifications. In 1111 or 1112 Ge Shengzhong submitted a twenty-five volume report giving detailed statistics on all of the government schools. He pointed out that nothing had been attempted on this scale since high antiquity; certainly neither the Han nor the Tang dynasty had done anything so magnanimous. Altogether 105,990 *qing* (each *qing* is 100 *mu*, or about 7 hectares) of land had been set aside to support the schools, attended by 167,622 students from elementary school on up.[82]

Did the schools succeed in indoctrinating students, winning them over to the New Policies? The evidence is mixed. On 1108/1/30 Huizong issued an edict in his own hand that revealed his foreboding that the government schools could provide a place for the Yuanyou partisans to spread their ideas. He had learned that partisans had attracted large numbers of students and "instructed them in their heterodox ideas." Since what they study is not correct, "it will not further the unification of moral virtue and the standardization of customs." He ordered that all teachers, even ones in towns and villages, should report to the county or prefectural authorities and explain what they taught.[83] On the other hand, some school officials did make efforts to promote adherence to the New Policies agenda. In 1114 an official submitted a memorial which complained that the major criterion used by counties and prefectures in selecting students was the orthodoxy of their views. "If the language of a candidate's essays touches on tabooed subjects, then no matter how well he writes, they do not dare pass him." Such phrases as "Rest the military in order to rest the people" or "regulate expenses to increase wealth" were taboo.[84]

Even if the schools did not turn out to be everything Huizong had hoped that they would be, neither were they failures. Two generations later, Zhu Xi said the school system had largely succeeded in its goal of gaining the good will of scholars. In a discussion with a disciple, he mentioned that after Cai Jing expanded the school system, "current discussion" came more and more to favor Cai Jing. He would visit the schools and eat with the students, earning praise for the attention he devoted to the school system. A contemporary of Zhu Xi's, Zhao Ruyu, also noted positive features of the Three Halls system and its extension throughout the country, remarking that the system came close to the ancient ideal of selecting men on the basis of their local reputations. On the other hand, he disapproved of requiring students to study Wang Anshi's commentaries and skip the *Spring and Autumn Annals*.[85]

Imperial Brush Edicts

From early in his reign, Huizong wrote out some edicts himself. He did this more frequently after Cai Jing joined the Council of State, and it is quite plausible that Cai Jing encouraged him in the practice. Cai Jing was well aware that Shenzong frequently wrote out his own edicts, since he was the one to edit a volume of them in 1082. During 1105–1108 Huizong wrote out many edicts that underlined his commitment to Confucian virtues. They covered all sorts of issues connected to schools: village teachers, the income and expenses of schools, the

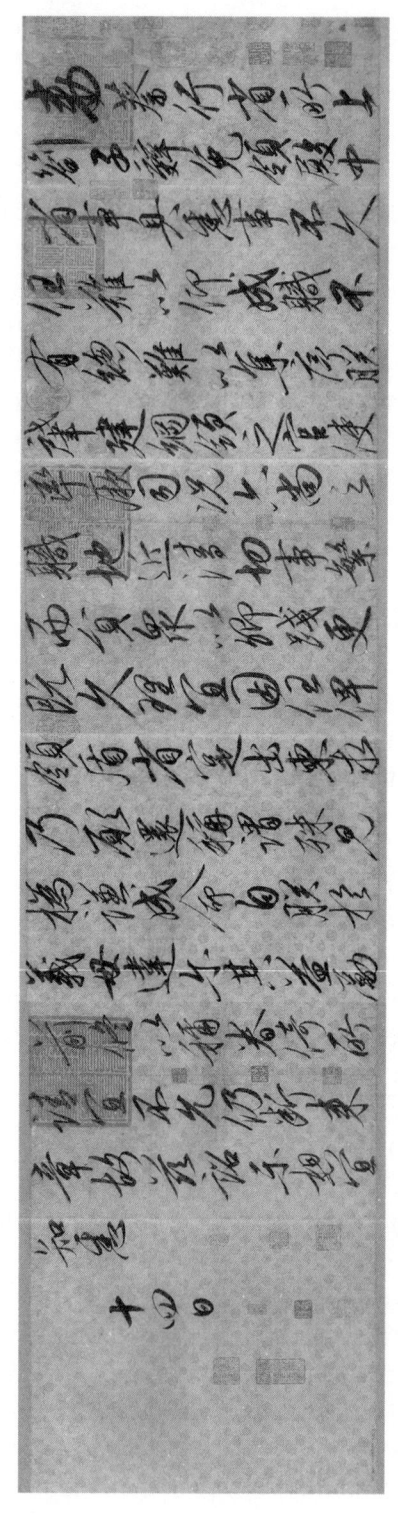

Fig. 4.1. Huizong, *Hand-Drafted Edict for Cai Xing*, handscroll, ink on decorated paper, 35 × 214.6 cm. (Liaoning Provincial Museum)

music to be used at banquets at the Biyong Academy, and the books to be distributed to schools, including sets of imperial edicts and of the classics.[86]

Writing out edicts was a way for Huizong to underline his personal interest in an issue. In other words, he did not write out these edicts simply as calligraphy practice, or because he took pride in his writing, but because he thought clear evidence of his personal concern would help accomplish his objectives. An edict of exhortation, for instance, derived its force from the moral authority of the emperor, and thus would be that much more effective when it in fact came directly from the emperor, in his own handwriting. This would be true as well when the goal was nothing more than to gratify an official—an edict of congratulations carries more honor when written out by the emperor himself. Observers of the time noted that Huizong used imperial brush edicts for minor matters rather frequently. Huizong is said, for instance, to have written many imperial brush edicts granting individuals an extension of the protection privilege (by which higher officials could nominate sons and other relatives for office).[87] Wu Zeng (d. 1170+), in his *Free Recollections*, records a variety of imperial brush edicts issued by Huizong on less than urgent matters, including one in 1113 that granted a name to the wine made by the empress's brother.[88] Two of Huizong's hand-drafted edicts are still extant, and both deal with minor matters of this sort and are directed to particular individuals (see Figure 4.1). The surviving edicts are in running script, but many were also written in Huizong's Slender Gold calligraphy, including a few that have been preserved because they were carved into stone.[89]

There is another side to the politics of hand-drafted edicts, however. Huizong, like Shenzong before him, used this system to get around the usual bureaucratic procedures for issuing orders.[90] That is, rather than let the appropriate government organs draft edicts and review each others' drafts, the emperor could write a version that would be sent immediately to the department that would enforce it. Moreover, the emperor did not have to wait for a memorial—on an issue he felt strongly about, he could take the initiative. To make these edicts more effective as law, they were collected and published twice a year, beginning in 1106. These compilations of hand-drafted edicts were widely distributed so that magistrates and prefects would be able to conform to their stipulations.[91]

From time to time Huizong used hand-drafted edicts to circumvent appointment procedures. The *Song History* records that in 1108 Cai Jing had recommended giving a post to Wu Min, who had come in first in the examination at the Biyong Academy. When other officials resisted because they thought he did not yet have the appropriate experience, Cai Jing proposed that Huizong issue an imperial brush edict inviting Wu Min for an audience. At the audience, Huizong gave Wu Min the post. We are told that from then on, those who met personally with Huizong clamored for imperial brush edicts.[92]

Modern scholars have argued that the system of imperial brush edicts was a key element in allowing Cai Jing to gain control over the government.[93] Zeng Minxing's *Miscellany* of ca. 1175 reports that as early as 1105 Cai Jing was tired of having his recommendations debated, so would secretly present drafts of edicts to Huizong and beg him to write them out in his own hand. Once Cai Jing is said to have requested an imperial brush edict because he did not like a proposal to reduce the number of officials in the Three Departments. He supplied a line to Huizong: "In this great and prosperous age, he proposes retrenchment suited to a period of decline."[94] Since "brush" can refer to both composition and calligraphy, the term "imperial brush" would have covered an edict that Huizong merely transcribed. Still, people thought it should mean that the emperor authored it as well, and for Cai Jing to supply even one line was perceived as a bit illegitimate. In the Southern Song some people speculated that imperial brush edicts were not always written by the emperors themselves, some suspecting that eunuchs were responsible, others female palace officials. The *Song History* biography of Liang Shicheng says that he handled imperial brush edicts and trained some clerks to write in Huizong's style so well that no one could distinguish the writing.[95] On the other hand, there is nothing inherently unlikely in Huizong drafting an edict or two a week himself. Some, after all, were very short, done for a waiting official, requiring little effort. In Cai Jing's account of Huizong's visit to his home in 1115, Huizong asks for paper and brush and proceeds to write out an edict on a matter that was troubling Cai Jing.[96] At the same time, there was nothing to stop Huizong from assigning eunuchs or palace ladies the task of writing out an imperial brush edict for him if he so chose.

Huizong found getting officials to enforce edicts a perennial problem, and in desperation increased the penalty for ignoring imperial brush edicts. Even though officials know that laws are defined at court, he wrote, they do not automatically obey them. "Recently we have issued special orders and decisions and yet the Three Departments cite the statutes to create obstacles, to keep from carrying the orders out. This has become the routine behavior of the officials, who resist the ruler's function to reward and punish." Once the issue has been decided by an edict, not enforcing it on the grounds that it conflicted with earlier laws would be treated as obstruction. The next year Huizong ruled that an imperial brush edict on a legal case was final; no appeals were to be sent to the Secretariat. This edict was followed up by a statute specifying punishment for delaying imperial brush edicts on the part of the officials responsible for seeing to their distribution. Delaying even one day could result in two years of penal servitude, and delaying two days to banishment to 3,000 *li*.[97]

Naturally, no emperor looked on bureaucratic procedures from the same perspective as the bureaucrats. It is easy to understand how Huizong would be willing to pick up the brush for a variety of purposes—to please someone he liked, to circumvent a bureaucracy he could not tame, or even to appeal directly to his officials and subjects. As time went on, he wrote on a wider range of subjects and in a less restricted style. For him, the imperial brush was too potent a political tool to leave idle for long.

꩜ WERE HUIZONG'S ATTEMPTS to exclude well-known conservatives from his government especially egregious cases of the exercise of autocratic power, as traditional historians have usually viewed them? From the perspective of those listed on the ban, plus their friends, neighbors, and relatives, for the emperor to list those he would not appoint to office was beyond the bounds of accepted practice. The fact that the lists included many of the most prominent literati of the day was evidence of how mistaken the policy was. Those banned would have agreed that they resisted many of the emperor's policies, but that was because in their opinion the emperor was listening to the wrong advisors. That they spoke up bluntly against the emperor's actions was proof of their loyalty. If the emperor did not employ critics of his policies, he would never learn of their shortcomings.

If we view the bans on the Yuanyou and Yuanfu partisans from Huizong's perspective, however, they look different. The bans were assertions that the emperor has the right to choose his subordinates, that he does not have to employ men opposed to his program. More-over, they were relatively limited: they affected only 226 living men, a miniscule fraction of the circa 20,000 on the civil service rolls; the full penalties lasted only a year and the list got progressively shorter. How could the emperor accomplish anything if he had to appoint men not only adamantly opposed to his plans but also outspoken in their con-demnation of them?

Huizong spent more energy trying to win over members of the edu-cated elite than he did identifying ones he had given up on. He em-ployed thousands of teachers in his school system, and through the system of stipends provided opportunities to hundreds of thousands of students from less wealthy families to study full time. He appealed to the Confucian values of these teachers and students in many of the edicts he wrote out in his own hand and had carved on stones placed at their schools. But he remained frustrated at how difficult it was to get the educated class, even his own officials, to do what he wanted. He apparently thought that if men of learning saw with their own eyes what he was trying to convey to them, they would be persuaded.

Serving as emperor entailed more than appointing high officials and accepting or rejecting their proposals, even if that is the side recorded most fully in the histories. By Song times the sacred and moral side of kingship broadly conceived authorized a wide range of imperial activity, from gifts to Buddhist and Daoist temples to revitalizing court music and ritual. The next several chapters shift attention to Huizong's activities in the cultural sphere—religion, ritual, art, music, and architecture—where he had greater leeway to pursue his own passions and agenda. In this sphere Huizong did not so regularly evoke his father's legacy and in fact plunged into things Shenzong had largely ignored. Trusted se-nior officials may have given Huizong advice, but the ambitions under-lying these projects originated with the emperor.

II

STRIVING FOR MAGNIFICENCE, 1102–1112

5

Placing Faith in Daoism,
1100–1110

> To Liu Hunkang:
> I have received several of your memorial-letters, full of
> earnest and reverent thoughts. It was just as though I was
> listening to your gentle voice. In accord with the seasons one
> eats and rests. Wouldn't it be good if this coming spring you
> were to fly west by boat? We could plan for marvelous
> discussions. The talismans required by the Precious Consort
> need to be managed and we haven't been able to handle it
> expeditiously. The picture of the Three Mao Lords is
> finished. We just wait for you to come to the capital to hand it
> to you in person. Let me request several dozen of the "curing
> illness, carry at the belt" talismans.
>
> —*letter from Huizong to Liu Hunkang, dated 1107/11/6*

ITHIN THE WORLD OF Song culture, a great many ideas
circulated concerning what we might consider cosmology, natural science, and religion. Some people were highly eclectic in their thinking,
accepting most of what they heard. They had confidence in the powers
of many gods they knew by name, whether of Buddhist, Daoist, or local origin. They knew that natural disasters could be warnings from
heaven. They took for granted ideas about yin and yang, *qi* (vital energy, vapor, pneuma), and the Five Phases (wood, fire, earth, metal,
and water) that were used to discuss biology, music, geomancy, and
weather. They did not doubt that rare individuals had exceptional
powers to foretell the future, communicate with the dead, or summon
gods or demons. Besides such eclectic believers, there were skeptics who
reserved judgment, thinking it likely that some ideas were mistaken and
some claims of extraordinary powers were fraudulent. Those learned

in the texts of a single tradition, whether Buddhism, Daoism, or Confucianism, often thought that the ideas associated with their tradition were true but that the others were deficient in one way or another. But such experts were only a small proportion of the population, probably even a small portion of the broad educated class.[1]

In the history of Daoism, the Song period was an especially active and creative period, with many new deity cults and revelatory traditions emerging.[2] Daoism was in transition from the more hierarchal and aristocratic traditions of the early Tang court to a more diverse and encompassing form that was widely diffused through society. At the local level, people turned regularly to Daoist masters to help them deal with a wide range of problems that could be attributed to ghosts, gods, and demons. Therapeutic and exorcistic teachings proliferated. Revelations continuously provided new elements—new heavens, deities, talismans, and scriptures. Daoist masters armed with talismans and Thunder Rites helped provide a sense of divine justice by keeping demons and other unruly spirits in line.[3] Officials and others with comparable Confucian educations were among those who found use for Daoist rituals.[4]

Beginning well before Song times, the throne had been a major patron of both Buddhism and Daoism, with the balance shifting from time to time when an emperor strongly preferred one religion to the other. Daoism had much that would appeal to an emperor, ranging from the early Daoist notions of the ruler who achieves everything by doing nothing, to grand Daoist rituals of cosmic renewal. The state cult over which the emperor presided drew from the same body of cosmological ideas as Daoism, not only yin and yang and the Five Phases, but also star lore and concerns with auspiciousness.[5] Many of the high gods of Daoism were conceived of as emperors; they had titles redolent of imperial majesty, sat on thrones wearing imperial garments, in temples called palaces. Those who wished to communicate with them used the ritual forms (prostrations, written petitions) employed by those addressing emperors. The Tang royal house claimed a special relationship to Daoism on the grounds that the imperial Li family was descended from the early Daoist philosopher Laozi (also surnamed Li). The Tang emperors supported the Daoist religion by building temples, adding Daoist texts to the civil service examination curriculum, setting up Daoist schools, inviting leading Daoist masters and holy men to court, and making copies of the Daoist canon. The Tang emperor Xuanzong (r. 712–755) even wrote commentaries on Daoist texts. Some of his successors pursued immortality through Daoist alchemy and were ordained as Daoist priests.[6]

During the Northern Song period, Daoism continued to receive imperial favor. Yet, of Huizong's seven predecessors, only one, Zhenzong (r. 997–1022), was as active in his patronage of Daoism as several Tang emperors had been. In 1008 Zhenzong ordered every prefecture to establish a Heavenly Felicity Daoist Temple to celebrate his receipt of a document from heaven, an important step in extending the local reach of Daoism. In 1012 Zhenzong had two dreams from which he learned that an ancestor of the Song imperial family was an incarnation of a descendant of the high gods of Daoism, the Jade Emperor and the Yellow Emperor. Zhenzong got to see them in person after purifying himself and performing a ritual. To honor this "Holy Ancestor," Zhenzong built a truly enormous temple in Kaifeng, called the Temple of Reflecting and Responding to the Realm of Jade Clarity. All of its buildings together came to 2,610 room-units. Zhenzong also undertook to collect and catalogue Daoist texts for a new Daoist canon. He wrote the preface to the resulting canon, 4,565 *juan* (rolls or chapters) in length. Multiple handwritten copies were made and distributed to temples across the country.[7]

Huizong proved just as dedicated a patron of Daoism as Zhenzong had been, if not more so.[8] This was especially true after he met Lin Lingsu in 1115 or 1116. Because Lin Lingsu told Huizong that he was an incarnation of the Great Lord of Long Life, this episode is also notorious as an example of the bad things that can happen when a ruler believes the flattery that he hears. In this chapter I make every effort not to let these events of Huizong's later years shape our understanding of his relationship with Daoism in his first decade on the throne. Huizong was already a strongly committed Daoist long before the arrival of Lin Lingsu.

Liu Hunkang

Huizong's early interest in Daoism was closely tied to his relationship with Liu Hunkang (1035–1108), the twenty-fifth patriarch of the Highest Clarity (Shangqing) lineage at Mount Mao (in modern Jiangsu province).[9] In the 1080s and 1090s, Liu Hunkang was well known in elite circles in the capital and had met both Wang Anshi and Cai Bian. According to his biography in the *History of Mount Mao*, he was summoned to the palace when none of the palace doctors could remove a needle that had gotten stuck in Empress Meng's throat. Liu presented a talisman (slip of paper with strange, often illegible words) which caused her to vomit it up. In gratitude, Zhezong conferred on him a title and declared his intent to construct a temple for him at Mount Mao.[10]

When Huizong came to the throne, he summoned Liu Hunkang, already an old man in his sixty-sixth year. According to an inscription that Huizong had Cai Bian write a few years later, Liu Hunkang was impressed by Huizong's insight and virtue: "Over a period of several years, he was frequently summoned to come to court and have audiences in the palace. The two of them would spend the entire day together. What they talked about together so intimately was the wondrous principles of the cosmos."[11] Over the course of the next eight years, Huizong repeatedly demonstrated his high regard and affection for Liu Hunkang and his wish to learn from him.

On one occasion, Huizong asked Liu Hunkang for information about the Three Mao Lords.[12] According to Highest Clarity traditions, the Mao Lords were brothers who lived during the Han period. The eldest, Mao Ying, retired to Mount Heng to study the *Laozi* and the *Changes*. There he communicated with immortals and gods, including the Queen Mother of the West, who gave him seals, talismans, and two texts that named the deities of the Nine Heavens. Mao Ying and his brothers then moved to Mount Juqu, south of Nanjing, which came to be known as Mount Mao after them. By Huizong's time the Three Mao Lords were seen as gods who administered the underworld beneath Mount Mao where the spirits of the dead resided. After Liu Hunkang elaborated for Huizong the significance of the Mao brothers, the emperor had the titles of each of them raised and instituted sacrifices to them.[13] The rescript Huizong issued announcing the new titles described the spiritual power of the Mao Lords as unfathomable, lasting for more than a thousand years, and producing auspicious signs and benefits for the populace. Huizong concluded by claiming that this measure would help attain "the limitless blessing of great peace for our country."[14]

Liu Hunkang proposed to Huizong that a temple be established for the star deity that corresponded with Huizong's year of birth (known as his Personal Destiny star god, or *benming*). The concept of Personal Destiny is based on the sixty combinations of the ten celestial stems and the twelve earthly branches.[15] The sign of the year of one's birth corresponds to the lord of one of the seven stars of the Dipper, which determines one's destiny. Thus, the cult of Personal Destiny was connected to the cult of the Northern Dipper, an important element in early Daoism. By the early Tang period, Daoists were performing ceremonies six times a year (every sixty days, each time the sign of the day corresponded with their Personal Destiny). The ceremonies involved making offerings of fruit and tea and reciting prayers before images of the Northern Dipper and their Personal Destiny star.[16] Another sign of Huizong's interest in the practices associated with Personal Destiny was his copying of the *Scripture of the Northern Dipper* to give to Liu Hunkang.[17] This popular scripture, whose full title is *Scripture of the Northern Dipper of Mysterious Power Prolonging the Original Life Span*, includes talismans and spells, stresses the correspondence between the sign of one's birth and one's natal star, and specifies the rites that must·be performed on one's Personal Destiny day.[18]

Liu Hunkang's first stay in the capital during Huizong's reign was short. In 1102 Huizong reluctantly consented to Liu Hunkang's repeated requests to return to Mount Mao. Among the gifts Huizong gave him on his departure were a rosary, incense, a red silk dragon fan, a jade seal reading "Lord of the Nine Old Immortals," and Huizong's own transcriptions of several Daoist scriptures: the *Book of Salvation*, the *Scripture of Purity and Tranquility* and the *Divine Talismans of the Sexigesimal Jia*. Huizong also conferred a more elevated title on Liu Hunkang and gave ordination certificates for ten of his disciples along with gifts of purple robes.[19]

The list of the scriptures Huizong transcribed and presented as gifts to Liu Hunkang in 1102 shows that Huizong was studying central works in the Daoist canon. The brief, one-chapter *Scripture of Salvation* was one of the most central of the original revealed Numinous Treasure scriptures. Written largely in verse, it was meant to be recited in private. The scripture traces the workings of the Dao and the multitude of heavens, gods, and demons, and promises a place in paradise to those who recite it. It includes long lists of celestial deities in a secret, unintelligible language, inspired by Buddhist mantras. By Huizong's day, many commentaries had been written for it, and stories circulated of the miraculous benefits of reciting it.[20] The *Scripture of Salvation's* portrayal of the heavens is exuberant:

> The completely perfected heaven-soaring spirit kings and all of the countless greater deities who provide long life and salvation in the ten directions are all alike borne by carriages with cinnabarred compartments, green shafts, feather canopies, and red-gem wheels, all formed of soaring clouds. To these are harnessed vermilion phoenixes and pentachromatic mystic dragons. Held aloft are blazons of nine colors and spirit banners of ten striations. Before, nine whistling phoenixes sing out in unison. Behind, eight trumpeting simurghs [mythical flying creatures] sound at once. Lions and white cranes whistle and sing in austere harmony. The Five Ancient Ones clear the road ahead, while the masses of Transcendents flank the carriage shafts. In myriad conveyances, on thousands of mounts, the procession arrives, floating through the void. Then, on slanting beams of light, they ride back to oversee the perfection and salvation of mortals.[21]

The second scripture that Huizong transcribed, the *Scripture of Purity and Tranquility*, is a short, popular scripture written in verse that dates from the Tang period and had a commentary by the tenth-century master Du Guangting. Quite different in style from the *Scripture of Salvation*, it uses language reminiscent of the *Laozi* to urge observation of the self, others, and the mind to free oneself of desires and achieve oneness with the Dao.[22] Here is an example:

> The human spirit is fond of purity,
> But the mind disturbs it.
> The human mind is fond of tranquility,
> But desires meddle with it.
> Get rid of desires for good,
> And the mind will be calm.
> Cleanse your mind,
> And the spirit will be pure.[23]

There is no book in the present Daoist canon with the exact title *Divine Talismans of the Sexigesimal Jia* though this may be a short title for a work better known under a longer title.[24] Sexigesimal *jia* was a system of divination that used the sixty combinations of stems and branches, and had been a part of Daoism since the fifth century.

After Liu Hunkang left the capital in 1102, Huizong began writing letters to him regularly, fifty-nine of which have been preserved in the *History of Mount Mao*.[25] Fourteen letters survive dated between the first month of 1103 and the ninth month of 1105, during Liu Hunkang's first absence. This letter of 1103/3/21 can serve as an example:

To Liu Hunkang:

Since you left the capital, the seasons are quickly passing. [I note that] the renovations of the shrine hall have been completed, thanks to the full and earnest effort of those involved. Recently as I read over your memorial-letter, I see that you are at peace and prospering. As for your question about the name for the hall, a good choice would be "Heavenly Calm, Myriad Blessings."[26] With regard to the *Scripture of Purity and Tranquility*, what you propose is fine.

Your serene and reverent offerings reach to the highest realm. Why don't you provide a full account of the omens and auspicious signs you have seen? Here, when it is time for the barley to sprout, rain is critical, but since the first month of spring, the seasonal rain has been inadequate. The farmers in the suburbs no longer have any hope of a good harvest. This troubles me; day and night I fret. You should wholeheartedly tackle this problem. My wish is that you offer prayers that carry to the utmost my heartfelt entreaties.

If you did not have the reputation of a lofty Daoist, how could you attain such purity? Lastly, you should take good care of yourself as you go ever deeper into the workings of the marvelous. As you seclude yourself in the mountain forests, you should give extra effort to preserving the constant true principles.[27]

Since the scripture mentioned in this letter, the *Scripture of Purity and Tranquility*, was one of those that Huizong had copied for Liu Hunkang, most likely the priest had asked Huizong's permission to show it to others or have it reproduced in Huizong's calligraphy.

Huizong refers in this letter to a temple being built by the government at Mount Mao, called Primal Tally Myriad Calm Temple. Huizong freely provided funds for the construction of buildings, helped with logistical details, and made gifts that would add to the prestige and drawing power of the temple. At one point Liu Hunkang asked permission to have some of the calligraphy Huizong had done for him carved on stone at the temple. Huizong responded that the ode he had written for the temple and the seeing-off poem he had recently sent could be engraved, but not the letters that were in his hand.[28]

In building on Mount Mao, Huizong was carrying out a project Zhezong had initiated. Construction was started on 1103/1/9 and finished two and a half years later on 1106/8/15. Huizong himself wrote out the title plaque for each of the buildings. As shown in Table 5.1, three of the four main halls had close ties to Huizong himself. The total complex measured more than four hundred room-units. On its completion in 1106, we are told by the local magistrate, cranes gathered overhead, clearly an auspicious sign and one that was visible to all. For the temple's long-term support, Huizong had lands set aside and established a generous quota of ordination certificates.[29]

After much urging on Huizong's part, Liu Hunkang returned to the capital a second time in the autumn of 1105 and stayed until spring 1106. On his departure in 1106, Huizong gave him a painting of Laozi

Table 5.1. Main halls at Primal Tally Myriad Calm Temple at Mount Mao

Name of building	Deities enshrined/contents	Location
Heavenly Calm Myriad Blessings Hall	Three Mao Lords	Center
Spectacular Blessings Myriad Years Hall	Huizong's Personal Destiny Star God	East
Flying through the Heavens, Collection of the Law Hall	Huizong's transcriptions of scriptures and other original calligraphy	West
Honoring Calm Pavilion	Engraved stones or boards of Huizong's calligraphy	Adjacent

Source: QSW 129:188; 137:8–9 (MSZ 26.2a–3b; DZ 5.665A–B).

he had done himself as well as more copies of scriptures. This was not the only painting Huizong made for Liu Hunkang. In 1107, when Huizong was sending a group of presents, he included two paintings he had done himself of two of the most important Daoist deities, the Venerable Celestial of the Primal Beginning and the Most High Lord of the Dao. Huizong said that, if these were put together with the painting he had done the year before of Laozi, they would make a complete set of the Three Clarities. In another letter, Huizong mentioned completing an image of the Three Mao Lords, which he was holding for Liu Hunkang's arrival in the capital.[30]

Another gift Huizong gave Liu Hunkang on his departure in 1106 was a poem Huizong had written for him "to send him off":

> During these years you have inquired about the Dao in
>   the company of lofty men.
> Disturbing your rosy garments, you came to Purple
>   Asterism [palace hall].
> You are in person a companion from beyond the clouds of
>   the Three Mountains.[31]
> Your heart has not a fleck of worldly dross.
> Like a migrating swan you gaze toward the extremities,
>   finding your perch in the isolated distance.
> Congratulatory swallows fly back to your new grotto office.
> My great appreciation for your heart-and-mind methods
>   is passed along.
> Truly there is no truth beyond the truth.[32]

Huizong also wrote a formal 32-line ode in praise of the temple built at Mount Mao which he sent it to Liu Hunkang.[33] It concluded with these lines:

> The Dao is large and lacks directions
> But there are constant principles to its substance and
>   function.
> Through virtue [the ancient greats] become thearchs,
> Through accomplishments they become kings.
> Without stirring from their seats they advance this Dao.[34]
> Like the Dao, they have no ultimate limit.

With the spirits they hear it,[35]
And they comprehend the myriad countries.[36]

Once Liu Hunkang was back at Mount Mao, Huizong renewed their correspondence, the frequency of his letters if anything increasing. In the year and a half from 1106/5 to 1108/2, Huizong sent forty-two letters.[37] On 1106/6/20, Huizong sent two letters. The first mentioned that Liu Hunkang had resisted Huizong's request for him to return. The second touched on the work being done on the new temple at Mount Mao: "If there is anything your temple lacks, just make an itemized list and submit it. The work of the hidden gods is not yet at an end. Does the work completed so far match your expectations?"[38]

Several of Huizong's letters refer to his concern with portents and auspiciousness. Liu Hunkang's biography in the *History of Mount Mao* states that he submitted numerous memorials on the issue of disasters.[39] We do not have these, but we do have some of the requests that lay behind them, such as the one already cited in which Huizong asks Liu Hunkang for an update on new anomalies and portents. In a letter dated 1107/2 Huizong mentions his own efforts to induce auspicious signs: "I am constantly thinking about the weightiness of my responsibilities to the numinous and how to bring about auspicious signs." Once Huizong mentions that Liu Hunkang had sent an auspicious emblem and asked him to send anything else like it that he found. In a letter dated 1106/12/18, Huizong cited Liu Hunkang's report that divine lights were seen at the new temple at Mount Mao during the performance of a ceremony, which Huizong took as an auspicious omen that the gods were pleased.[40]

Rulers had paid attention to portents since ancient times: there was nothing innovative or remarkable in that. What is worth noting, however, is that Huizong turned to a Daoist cleric to help him in this regard. He did not think that the traditional interpretations of portents provided all answers, especially, perhaps, in the case of negative portents (anomalies and disasters). That they were bad was self-evident, but what precisely they were a response to and how one could counter them remained real questions for Huizong, questions he thought Liu Hunkang could help him answer.

Gift-giving was an important element in Huizong's relationship with Liu Hunkang from the beginning. The letter below refers to gifts in both directions:

I have already given instructions on the matters you raised in your memorial-letter. If there is anything else found wanting, show a list to the supervising official. I have sent Yang Jian with the title, which is already written. Cai Bian has written the essay.

Send me a close and detailed analysis of any cases of fortune or misfortune that you have learned about since returning to the Gan region.

I have already received the flowering tree; its auspicious fragrance is especially fine. Fu Xilie has returned; the edict concerning him has been sent to the Bureau of Sacrifices. The rest of them will be given purple robes and titles. The fans with my personal calligraphy and painting can be used to summon a breeze and protect your heart in this hot weather.

I would like to request several talismans. Fu Xilie and the others are returning with the following items: twenty catties each of heavy sandalwood letter paper and incense, five catties of fresh mature camphor, ten catties of Descending Truth incense, twenty pieces of Four Flavor sweets, ten fans with imperial calligraphy and painting, and two packs of fragrant medicinal herbs.[41]

Some gifts Huizong gave were valued because Huizong had taken the time to make them—his calligraphy and painting, his transcription of scriptures, for instance. These were the type of gifts anyone could give. Huizong sometimes conferred gifts that he as emperor was especially positioned to make. A good example would be the gift of a convenient place to lodge while in the capital—a cloister within the major Daoist temple, Highest Clarity Accumulated Auspices. Huizong explained the gift in a letter dated 1107/2:

Mounted on a crane many times you went out of your way to visit me here in the palace. You courteously offered perfect words on names and principles and advised me on the essential marvels of the heart-and-mind methods. You protect your spirit through tranquility and dislike the clamor of the marketplace. When you lodged at Accumulated Auspices, [the quarters] proved barely acceptable. We some time ago ordered Dong Zhi[text missing] to assemble workers and begin construction [of new buildings]. Thus in the eastern corner of Highest Clarity we have built a detached cloister of Myriad Calm as a lodging that will be kept tranquil and ready for your arrival. You should select a disciple to come to manage it, which is why I am informing you now, thinking that you should know all about it.[42]

Talismans are another issue that comes up in many of Huizong's letters. Talismans were conceived of as orders from high gods that controlled lower gods and had been a part of the armament of Daoist adepts since the Han period.[43] They could be read by spirits but were not intended to be comprehensible to ordinary mortals (see Figure 5.1). Liu Hunkang was considered an expert in the therapeutic use of talismans. Cai Bian, in his epitaph for Liu, praised his devotion to helping others: "Innumerable times he cured people of their illnesses by using Highest Clarity talisman-water." Huizong sometimes requested particular types of talismans, such as "carry at the belt" talismans kept in a small pouch

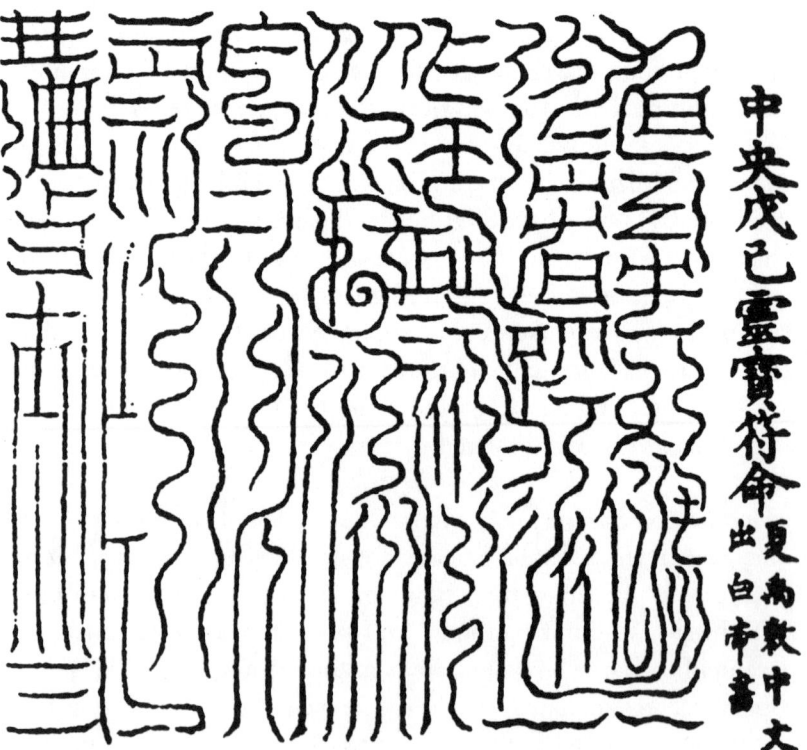

Fig. 5.1. Talisman of the Center in *Five Talismans, Powerful Treasure of the Most High* (TSLBWFX 4; DZ 6: 338c)

attached to one's belt. Huizong also asked for ones to cure colds, to quiet the mind, to allay fears, and to heal "the hundred ailments." Once Huizong mentioned that he was not keeping the talismans previously sent for himself, but giving them to those who took ill.[44] It is noteworthy that Huizong asks for prepared talismans rather than instruction on how to make his own talismans. In his letters to Liu Hunkang, Huizong seeks the help of an expert, not advice on becoming an expert himself.[45]

Huizong's strong opinions on the need to keep Buddhism and Daoism separate come through in a couple of letters. He explained his concerns to Liu in a letter of 1107/2/9:

> Recently Daoism and Buddhism have been confusedly mixed. You should keep them separate, correcting the errors in line with my thinking. For instance, paintings or sculpture of the Three Clarities will be set out at a [Buddhist] Water-and-Land cere-mony,[46] or the Original Destiny will be enshrined at a Buddhist temple—I cannot list all the problems of this sort.
>
> I am at present planning to lay out the relationships [between Buddhism and Daoism] and clarify their teachings. I will investi-gate which came first and explain the origins of the practices that have accrued, so that I can instruct government officials to make clear distinctions when performing rites. This should result in blessings for everyone.
>
> Keep in mind that on profound matters there needs to be delib-eration, and when revising the annual codes it is best to be con-servative. Thus I am thinking that this instruction should be widely publicized.[47]

Six days later Huizong referred to the letter above and noted that he had already taken steps to deal with the indiscriminate mixing of Bud-dhism and Daoism. He enclosed a draft of the policy statement for Liu Hunkang to read.[48]

In response to Huizong's repeated pleas, Liu Hunkang returned to the capital a third time at the beginning of 1108. Cai Bian reported what then transpired:

> In the spring of 1108, the emperor summoned Master Huayang [Liu Hunkang] to come to the capital. In the summer, on the day

dinghai of the fourth month, he arrived from Mount Mao. The emperor ordered two hundred Daoist priests to form a welcoming honor guard to accompany him to his lodgings at Primal Tally, the newly built detached temple within Highest Clarity Accumulated Auspices Temple. Because the Master was ill, he could not attend court. Messengers from the court were continuously on the road to inquire about his condition [on Huizong's behalf].

On the tenth of this month, Huizong paid a visit to Accumulated Auspices Temple to visit the Master. They talked for a long time. Two evenings before the Master had dreamed of attending the Emperor of Heaven and discussing with him the *Perfect Scripture of the Great Profundity*. When he awoke, he marveled at [the dream]. When he in fact got to see the emperor, he made a gift to him of his own long-used copy of the *Great Profundity Scripture*. As the emperor looked through it, he changed color and said, "I have been purifying myself to copy this scripture and have just finished. I now wish to give [my copy] to you along with the painting[s] I have done myself of the Three Mao Perfected Lords." That day those gifts were exchanged. After the Master had handed over the scripture to the delighted emperor, he was relaxed and happy. When the emperor was about to return to the palace, he asked to see the Master again, and treated him with special kindness.[49]

Needless to say, it was a special honor for Huizong to call on Liu Hunkang at his temple. Just seven days later, Liu Hunkang died.

The scripture mentioned in the passage just cited, the *Great Profundity Scripture*, is another of the basic Highest Clarity texts. The great profundity is the "supreme, unlimited darkness where one attains the void and guards tranquility." During recitations of it, heavenly gods are brought down to the adept's body through visualizations. Much of the scripture consists of stanzas on the "wanderings of the deities in the heavens, their manifestations in the human body, and their intercession for the salvation of the adepts and their ancestors."[50] The current version of the scripture is copiously illustrated, showing seated adepts and what they are visualizing rising from their heads (see Figure 5.2).[51]

Even before Liu Hunkang died, Huizong occasionally turned to other Daoist masters. In 1107, when Liu Hunkang strongly resisted

Fig. 5.2. Visualizing the Six Guardians in the *Great Profundity Scripture* (SQDDZJ; DZ 1:539C)

returning to the capital, he sent in his place his disciple, Da Jingzhi, who had been with Liu Hunkang since he was six or seven and had accompanied him on his visits to Zhezong and later Huizong. Liu Hunkang instructed Da Jingzhi in Daoist scriptures, talismans, spells, exorcism, and other healing techniques. Nine of the letters Huizong sent Liu Hunkang mention Da Jingzhi, usually as someone who could carry messages or gifts between them. In one, Huizong lists many things he was entrusting to Da Jingzhi, including a "petition" on behalf of one of his consorts that he wanted Liu Hunkang to present to the gods in a ceremony. Other items included food, tea, candles, and his copy of the *Scripture* of the *Northern Dipper* in five booklets.[52]

In 1110, after Liu Hunkang had died, Da Jingzhi traveled from Mount Mao to the capital. Huizong arranged for him to give sermons at a capital temple, which reportedly attracted large numbers of scholar-officials. When Da Jingzhi took leave before returning to Mount Mao, Huizong gave him pieces of his own calligraphy and a portrait of Liu Hunkang. He also seems to have given him a copy of an essay he wrote on the Dao, which Da Jingzhi later had engraved on a stele at Mount Mao. Huizong's essay, titled "The Dao of Transformation," described the need to understand the fundamental nature of the Dao and lamented the prevalence of ignorance among the common people. If everyone were to honor the Dao, he asserted, the benefit would be universal.[53]

On his deathbed in 1113, Da Jingzhi wrote a two-part farewell letter to Huizong. It is worth quoting as an example of the counsel Huizong received from Daoist masters.[54]

> Bequeathed memorial of your subject Jingzhi to His Majesty.
>
> Months have passed since I left the capital. As I think back on my many days in your sagely presence, I am filled with warm feelings. My plan had been to leave the mountain forests to see you again, but my wishes conflicted with my destined lifespan. I am pained by my debt to the court, but although my time here is short and the path of the immortal diverges [from that of the living], how could I forget the generous way you have treated me throughout my life? I hope that Your Majesty will secure the fundamentals of the state and take good care of your health, on the one hand to assist the kindness of the august vault and precious

sequence, on the other to soothe the hopes of society and the spirits. Unable to call on you, I respectfully submit this memorial. [This is followed by date and Da Jingzhi's full title]

In the time since I, your subject, in my extreme ignorance, met you in the company of my late teacher, the temple has been built and the teachings have been spread. Moreover my every request has been more than filled. I am burdened with guilt for annoying you with requests. Now that I can no longer offer you my humble services, [it is clear that I have] repaid only one part in ten thousand [of what I owe you]. I did not anticipate contracting this spleen disease. I have reduced what I eat and drink and forced myself to take medicine, but there has been no respite. We have recently performed an offering *(jiao)* ceremony to pray to heaven above, and although we obtained a response I must bid farewell to the world. On the matter of departing, I really have no regrets, but I do feel frustrated that I will never have another opportunity to see you and all your children again. The disappointment is overwhelming.

Your Majesty has the intelligence of heaven and the wisdom of the sages. In honoring and promoting Daoism, no ruler since antiquity has gone further than you. But keep in mind that there are differences between a ruler and a subject in serving the Dao. [With a ruler], when each word and act conform to heaven's heart-and-mind, then all receive blessings.

It is best not to disturb the perfect through adornment, thereby diminishing the sacred canon. The five thousand words of Taishang [Laozi] place priority on getting rid of extravagance and loving frugality. This is a teaching you should treasure as it lays out a way to extend the Dao. I would like Your Majesty to purify your heart and reduce your desires to protect your health and cut back on expenses to firm up the fundamentals of the state. If you listen to honest advice, thereby encouraging criticism, the whole realm will benefit greatly.

Given my limited intelligence, I certainly should not be risking death to set forth my views. It is just that I remember the heavy responsibility that my teacher laid on me to always put first repaying the country with full loyalty. If in the current situation I said not a word to foster your sagely virtue, I would be opposing heaven and turning my back on my teacher and bear regret in the underworld.

I have entrusted the rites and registers, the perfect scriptures, the jade seal, and all the calligraphy and paintings that you have conferred on us to my disciple, Yu Xiyin. I would like to remind Your Majesty of my late teacher's never-ending desire to spread the Dao and its blessings and his never-deviating commitment to orthodoxy. If you keep them in mind, although I will never see your countenance again, I will die without regrets.

I have taken up my brush and put my feelings into words out of deep gratitude.[55]

Huizong's correspondence with Liu Hunkang and his disciple Da Jingzhi offers some glimpses of Huizong and his everyday life. We learn something of what went on in the palace, such as ill consorts who want petitions made to Daoist gods on their behalf and that Da Jingzhi met Huizong's children. We see Huizong writing letters that are much like the letters educated men of his era wrote to each other—Huizong is not denying his rank as emperor, but he tries not to let it interfere with his relationship with a man he holds in high esteem. He is attentive to details about the gifts he was sending and the buildings he was having made.

Above all what we learn from these letters is the depth of Huizong's commitment to and understandings of Daoism. Huizong was not exceptional in taking an interest in Daoism. Virtually all educated men in Huizong's day had read the *Laozi* and *Zhuangzi* as well as stories of gods and immortals in other books in general circulation. Much of the great poetry of the Tang period, highly esteemed by Song men of letters, alluded to ideas about the stars closely tied to Daoism. Some Song literati were intrigued by Daoist methods for promoting health through dietary restrictions.[56] Huizong went further, however: as a more devoted lay believer, he made offerings to deities, he read and recited scriptures, he made frequent use of talismans, and he painted religious icons, both of the "Three Clarities," the very high gods, and also of the Three Mao Lords, Transcendents who had once been human. We can also see that Huizong saw Daoism as a means to fulfilling his obligations to his subjects: Daoism offered help in averting bad fortune, not just for himself but also for his subjects. It is also worth noting the aspects of Daoism that Huizong did not pursue in any depths with Liu Hunkang and other Daoist masters: he does not seem to have been preoccupied with ways of achieving immortality and shows no interest in alchemy.[57]

Temples and Rituals

Even during Liu Hunkang's lifetime, Huizong consulted other Daoist masters. In 1105 he summoned the head of one of the other main traditions of Daoism, Zhang Jixian, the thirtieth Celestial Master from Mount Longhu. According to one Daoist source, he also called on Zhang in later years to deal with various crises.[58] Daoist hagiographies of holy men who lived during Huizong's period often record at least a brief encounter with Huizong. For instance, Huizong frequently summoned Zhang Xubai and tolerated his getting drunk. Liu Yi responded to Huizong's summons but soon requested to return to the mountains. After Rong Yang responded to Huizong's questions about his learning, Huizong gave him one hundred thousand cash. Others like Liu Biangong were summoned by Huizong but declined to go.[59]

Huizong's commitment to Daoism led to his reshaping several established dynastic practices in more Daoist directions. The clearest case concerns temples designated for the celebration of his birthday. Imperial birthday celebrations had evolved gradually over the course of the Tang and Song dynasties. Emperor Xuanzong in the mid-Tang period was the first to give his birthday a name and to issue instructions on how it should be celebrated at court, in temples, and in localities.[60] Tang emperors hosted banquets on their birthdays, and several of them organized debates between Buddhists, Daoists, and Confucians as entertainment for their guests. During the Five Dynasties, when Kaifeng was the capital, on rulers' birthdays, it became common for ceremonies to be performed at the Assisting the State Monastery just south of the palace and for officials to attend those ceremonies before joining banquets in the palace, practices that the Song rulers maintained.[61]

What makes Huizong different is that he systematically extended the cult throughout the empire and fully incorporated Daoist temples in it. In 1103 he ordered one Buddhist and one Daoist temple in each prefecture to be given the name Honoring Calm (Chongning, the name of the reign period at the time) as well as responsibility for conducting imperial birthday services. This was a major expansion of the system of conferring names (and name plaques) on Buddhist and Daoist temples, which gave them both recognition and some privileges.[62] Regulations for the Honoring Calm Temples issued in subsequent years provided ordination certificates, tax exemptions, endowments of ten *qing* of land, and protection from encroachment by officials. In 1111 the name of these temples was changed to Heavenly Calm to match the name of Huizong's birthday.[63]

The Daoist versions of these temples held services not just on Huizong's birthday, but also on each *renxu* day, his Personal Destiny days. Earlier Song emperors had celebrated their Personal Destiny days at Daoist temples in the capital, but Huizong had his celebrated in Daoist temples throughout the land. In 1104 he decreed that Honoring Calm Daoist temples designate a special hall for the Personal Destiny day ceremonies and name it Heaven's Protection Hall. In response to an official's request, Huizong himself wrote out the name plaque for the hall and had copies of it distributed throughout the country.[64]

From Song local histories, it is clear that local governments followed these instructions and designated Honoring Calm/Heavenly Calm Temples.[65] Sometimes the chosen temple was quite grand. In 1107, on imperial command, He Zhizhong, then on the Council of State, wrote a commemorative account of a Daoist Heavenly Calm Temple in the southeast that was 369 room-units in size. Huizong had conferred on it a copy of the Daoist canon, ten *qing* of land, two ordination certificates per year, Huizong's own calligraphy for two plaques, and other gifts.[66]

In 1116 officials recommended opening Heavenly Calm Temples on Huizong's birthday. They proposed that both in the capital and in the provinces, on both Huizong's birthday and on his Personal Destiny days, Buddhist and Daoist temples stay open for three days to allow both literati and commoners to burn incense and pray for the long life of their sovereign. In 1118 a ritual official proposed distributing a protocol for the prefectural ceremonies on Huizong's Personal Destiny day. These protocols specified that seven days in advance the prefect and his subordinates would visit the Heavenly Calm Daoist temple to bow and burn incense, then take turns making visits on subsequent days. On the day itself, the prefect, attended by his subordinates, would read a prayer and make three offerings, after which they all would bow twice.[67]

These were not the first ritual protocols prepared at Huizong's court. In 1108 he ordered the collection of liturgies for the Rite of the Golden Register, his goal to prepare an edited version to send to each county and prefecture with a Daoist temple. According to Michel Strickmann, the purpose of the Rite of the Golden Register was "to guarantee the welfare of the imperial house," and by distributing a newly codified redaction of the rites the government was ensuring that "a vast chorus of supplication in the interests of the Song would rise from every corner of the empire."[68]

Before distributing a new version of the Golden Register liturgies, textual issues had to be addressed. In 1110, after two years of work, Huizong handed over to his grand councilor Zhang Shangying the unfinished manuscript. He told Zhang Shangying:

> Some time ago I commissioned a few Daoist masters to emend the rules of the liturgy on the basis of the standard works in the Canon. They recently completed the book and submitted it. Thereupon I handed it to the Daoist officials for their judgment. It is now clear from their written comments that there are many points of disagreement. Hence I forward the whole matter to you, so that you may in the spare time which the affairs of state leave you examine it and decide what is right or wrong. If anything has not been thoroughly revised, if the sense of a passage is erroneous, or if anything is incomplete, you should supplement, alter, shorten, or polish the text and then present it to me.[69]

The final section of Zhang Shangying's edited text has been preserved in the Daoist canon. Called *Ritual of Casting Tablets of the Golden Register Retreat*, it concerns throwing tablets with images of dragons on them into specified mountains or bodies of water to announce to the gods that the rituals have been performed.[70]

Hymns

Huizong wrote on Daoist themes in letters, poems, and essays. Particularly interesting is a book of hymns by three Song emperors—Taizong, Zhenzong, and Huizong. According to the preface, in 1111 Huizong summoned two officials in charge of Daoist clergy to Harmony Revealed Hall where he took out the sixty hymns he had written to show them. While they were considering the musical tunes, "suddenly words came down from heaven, authorizing the permanent use [of the hymns] as part of the *jiao* service." From this it would seem that Huizong not only wrote the words to the hymns but also selected the music. Huizong instructed Xu Zhichang to prepare the collection of hymns, which was later distributed to Daoist temples large and small.[71]

Huizong's hymns are in six series, each consisting of ten hymns of four lines each. Five of the topics use seven-word lines: Jade Clarity, Highest Clarity, Great Clarity, Pacing the Void, and White Cranes. Scattering the Flowers instead uses five-word lines. These hymns are richly descriptive, not unlike some of the scriptures cited earlier. This one belongs to the White Cranes series:

> Amid Five Clouds in the palace halls we pace the void
>   at length.
> The Dipper revolves and reveals the empyrean before the
>   night is done.
> The white crane flies here carrying an auspicious missive.
> The pure sounds one after the other—the fragrance of
>   returning spirits.[72]

The following three hymns belong to the Great Clarity series:

> Incense burnt down to the fifth notch signals the night
>   half over,
> Celestial beings and jade maidens can be heard in the
>   far-off distance.
> When scents and auras match, they respond to each other
>   from afar.
> Crimson tablets and rainbow banners descend from the
>   five clouds.

As the Primal Lord of the Great Ultimate rides in a
    kingfisher plume chariot,
The myriad demons scatter in all directions hearing the
    dreaded spells.
Nine dragons walk slowly together with heads high,
From time to time you can see them spitting out fiery pearls
    into the sky.

Cliffs and hills of primal phosphor rise into the great
    emptiness.
So many are the rooms of the Transcendents in the midst
    of rosy clouds.
The nine spirits transform, suddenly separate or join.
Feathered chariots sail all about, no end to their number.[73]

The use of these hymns in Daoist services continued into modern times.[74]

Local Shrines

Huizong's involvement with religion was not restricted to Daoist
clergy, temples, and rituals. It extended also to local gods and the
shrines where they were worshipped. The Song government had long
kept a register of approved shrines and granted titles to their principle
deities, which included mountains, streams, dragons, and local gods that
had once been human men or women. Huizong's reign was a highpoint
in the Song government's efforts to standardize and routinize supervision of popular religion. More temples received plaques and more gods
received noble titles during Huizong's reign than any other. At the
same time, cults not on the register were abolished in large numbers.

Huizong must have been approving a new temple plaque or noble
title every few days. The *Song Collected Documents* records 764 awards
of name plaques for temples and noble titles for gods during Huizong's
reign.[75] Most of the records in it are very brief. For instance, in the
section on mountain gods we find: "The god of White Dragon Mountain is General He Lu of the Northern Wei period. The shrine is in
Fen prefecture, Xihe county. In the fifth year of Huizong's Chongning reign period [1106], the shrine was granted the name plaque
'Permanent Benefit.'"[76] What Huizong would have read, however,

would not have been such brief, dry records, but rather enthusiastic petitions that detailed the god's response to people's prayers for rain, clear weather, protection during epidemics, and so on. Occasionally traces of these original petitions have survived in the inscribed stones local people erected to commemorate the reception of a name plaque from the throne. For instance, two months after the shrine for General He Lu received its title, the community erected an inscribed stone which told the story of the god and his shrine. It relates that the general had always answered people's prayers, and in the past the local officials had wanted to request a noble title for him, but none of them ever got it done. In 1105, however, a new prefect arrived. The following year, when there was no rain, he prayed at the shrine, as a consequence of which clouds appeared and rain fell, leading to an excellent harvest. The prefect then remarked, "How wondrous! The gods of mountains and rivers instantly producing clouds and rain to save a place from drought! What a blessing for mankind! The benefit extends a thousand *li!* He should be rewarded with a noble title to dazzle this place, so that for ten thousand generations the offerings will be made without remiss." The prefect then wrote a report and submitted it through channels. Huizong then did his part: "The Son of Heaven, impressed with [the god's] numinous powers, on the day *yisi* in the seventh month, conferred the name 'Permanent Benefit' on the shrine. Thereupon, the name was written out and displayed. Young and old excitedly gazed at it, far and near hurried there, all wanting to rebuild the shrine." The inscription went on to discuss the rebuilding of the shrine and also to mention that the local people had long wanted a noble title for their god, but had been informed that it was first necessary to get a name plaque for the shrine.[77]

One reason so many names and titles were approved during Huizong's reign was that he repeatedly called on people to identify every powerful and benevolent god in the country. The first call came during Huizong's second year on the throne. On 1101/3/24 prefects were instructed to submit reports to the fiscal intendants on all the gods in their jurisdictions that had been given noble titles or name plaques. The intendants then were to investigate whether the gods deserved their honors, that is, had they responded to prayers or performed meritorious deeds.[78]

A second such call was issued in 1107. An inscription for a temple in Fujian records that "In the first year of the Daguan period [1107], Emperor Huizong conducted the sacrifices at the southern Suburban Altar, and made offerings to the 'hundred gods.' On its completion, he announced that people could submit reports on mountains, rivers, and other gods that have benefited the people but were not listed in the register of sacrifices."[79] About a year later, Huizong approved a request to compile a thorough list of temples, with full details on their location, when they were built or repaired, the titles they had been awarded, and what had distinguished them. Huizong's note on the request commented that, "The number of shrines to gods in the realm is not small, but until now there has not been a full record of them. I wish that this be carried out as requested."[80]

The desire to rationalize government supervision also comes though in a ruling of 1111/7/27. Those compiling an ambitious country-wide gazetteer were instructed to include information about shrines and to compare it to the information in the register of sacrifices. Inconsistencies in the system were to be identified, such as the same god having different titles in different places. Those working on the project were instructed to classify shrines into three categories: those that had already been granted plaques and titles; those that deserved plaques and titles but had not yet received them; and those that had been set up by commoners and did not deserve recognition, "the so-called illicit cults."[81]

Huizong's primary engagement with local shrines may well have been reading accounts of the good work that their gods did and approving honors for them, but surviving records are considerably fuller on the subject of illicit religious activity. The Song government, like the Tang before it, outlawed a variety of vaguely described religious practices, ranging from "heretical beliefs" to black magic and false claims of supernatural power.[82] Harsh punishments could be justified on the basis of a passage in the *Book of Rites*, "Royal Regulations," which describes several categories of people who must be promptly executed, among them those who practice heterodox ways and thus bring disorder to the government, and those who bewilder the multitudes through false reports of gods and ghosts, divination, or prognostication.[83]

Secrecy and immorality were commonly cited as reasons to outlaw a cult. On 1108/8/14, Xinyang Military District (modern Henan) reported that they had found cases of groups that met at night, men and women together, and transmitted and practiced demonical teachings. Huizong approved their request for a clear statement that this behavior was illegal and instructions that prefectural and county authorities regularly check for such groups, so that they could be effectively suppressed.[84]

Cult activities in the capital were especially worrisome. An 1109/8/26 edict referred to abolished shrines in the capital not on the register of sacrifices. If any of their priests "deceive the multitudes with wild talk of gods and ghosts," the Kaifeng government should arrest them, assess their crimes, and then sentence them to penal registration in nearby prefectures. The most serious offenders were to have their cases submitted to the central government for sentencing. Apparently many shrines in the capital were closed down. An 1111/1/9 edict referred to 1,038 shrines that had been abolished and ordered that the images in them be moved to Buddhist or Daoist temples or the god's primary shrine. The edict gives the example that images of the god of the soil should be moved to the City God Temple. The ruling explicitly stated that people could not establish shrines on their own, without permission.[85]

Heretical books were also seen as cause for alarm. In 1104/4/19 Huizong approved a request to proscribe the *Sutra on the Final Kalpa as Preached by the Buddha* because "its language is full of falsehoods designed to delude the multitudes." The judicial intendants of the two circuits where it circulated were instructed to find out who wrote and who printed this book. "They should fully interrogate them, then report back. All copies currently in people's hands should be turned over within ten days to the county, prefecture, or military camp authorities for burning, and the authorities must inform the Department of State Affairs [of the texts destroyed]. This order is based on our fear that the book mentioned above could begin to circulate in other circuits and prefectures, leading originally good people to act improperly and transmit it by chanting, which would be highly regrettable."[86]

Several measures taken in 1114 show the seriousness with which suspect religious activity was taken. In one, rewards of one hundred strings of cash were offered to anyone informing on priests or shamans of illicit cults who "falsely say they were speaking the words of gods, thus stirring up the ignorant folk and leading them astray." The punishment for the miscreants was two years of penal labor. In another measure, Huizong granted a request to clearly prohibit certain religious groups and practices "in order to stop heresy before it has taken form and to enable ignorant people to avoid committing a capital offense." The objectionable activities are described as "groups that call themselves societies for discussing doctrines, burning incense, and fasting, and then privately set up Buddha Halls and Dao Quarters to gather lots of people." The government officials did not have any easy solutions to the problem; they urged notifying the local people that the activity was illegal, offering rewards to informants, and having local officials make regular inspections. A third case involved suspicious texts. On 1114/8/30, Huizong issued an edict that lamented the prevalence of heretical teachings in Hebei. "Even though the punishment is severe, practitioners never repent." Not only should copies of the books be destroyed, but it was also important to seize any printing blocks or inscribed stones that had been used to duplicate their holy books. Local officials were instructed to send any books they discovered to the central government authorities.[87]

Do these measures both to honor local gods and police suspicious cults have a connection to Huizong's adherence to Daoism? None of the extant memorials or edicts on these subjects uses Daoist language, but surely there was a connection. Huizong's religious inclinations made him open to the idea of benevolent local gods. He was happy to celebrate them and bring them under greater state supervision. At the same time, Huizong supported the established Buddhist and Daoist churches when he used the power of the state to curb religious practitioners not affiliated with them. There is another motivation at work here as well. The desire for routinization and standardization, for reaching down to the local level, was characteristic of the New Policies and the initiatives undertaken by Cai Jing. Huizong's religious beliefs and the New Policies concern for extending the reach of the government to the local level both contributed to Huizong's policies on local shrines.

☙ WHAT ATTRACTED HUIZONG so strongly to Daoism? As likely as not, there were multiple attractions. Huizong, like other rulers in Chinese history, saw Daoism not only as a means to personal goals, but also as a set of techniques that could help him rule. In his conversations with Liu Hunkang he showed a strong interest in Daoist insight into messages from heaven in the form of positive and negative omens. He brought Daoism into some of the most sacred of the Chinese rituals of kingship. In addition, Daoism has a much more expansive cosmology than the Confucianism of Huizong's day, with multiple heavens and hundreds of deities. Perhaps Huizong found in Daoism a basis for royal grandeur and magnificence that was not so easily justified from a Confucian perspective.

Daoism's visual power must have been one of its attractions. Many of the scriptures Huizong studied or transcribed were rich in imagery, with description of the colors of clouds, decoration of carriages, and so on. The beauty of the Daoist temples that Huizong had built and the art of the sculptures of deities in them, plus the ephemeral splendor of the ceremonies held in them, would all have appealed to Huizong. Certainly there was visual appeal to the paintings of divinities that Huizong made for Liu Hunkang. There would also have been a visual dimension to the hand-copied scriptures that Huizong and Liu Hunkang gave each other—though we don't have any specific information about them as works of calligraphy, such as the script they were written in.

There are alternatives to viewing Huizong as a serious lay Daoist. From a Daoist perspective, one could question the depth of his knowledge and view him as a shallow dilettante. From a Confucian perspective, one could, to the contrary, view him as overly credulous, easily misled by the florid rhetoric of Daoist masters, or perhaps drawn in by the visual splendor of Daoist temples. Yet another approach would be to question his sincerity, to posit that he was cynical in his use of Daoism, trying to gain political advantage from his patronage. In my view, there is no reason to see only one of the probably many strands in Huizong's Daoism, or to see one as explaining all the others. Surely his knowledge of Daoist scriptures would not have matched that of learned priests, and he undoubtedly at times made political use of his support of Daoism. Still, we should not reduce his involvement with Daoism to political expediency, artistic attraction, naiveté, or delusion (even if there was a little of each from time to time).

It was not only in Daoism that Huizong found ways to enhance the magnificence of his court. Chapter 6 looks at his involvement in reform of court music and celebration of auspicious signs, both activities with connections to antiquity and each contributing to the splendor of life at court.

ᴄ 6

Embracing and Revitalizing Tradition

After the emperor encouraged him to continue, Zhang Shangying said, "Disregarding my lack of talent, I presume to present *Picture of Auspicious Grain*, along with thirteen verses of *Song Dynasty Greater Elegantia Poems* to depict the eminent signs of great peace achieved under Your Majesty."

—*Song Collected Documents record of 1110/9/27*

ꞮꞞꜰ ᴀᴛ ᴄᴏᴜʀᴛ required performances of many kinds, both by the ruler and by those who came into his presence. On the simple side were daily courtesies that people largely took for granted. Musical entertainment and religious rituals were much more complex and shaped not only by conventions of many sorts but also principles laid down in such sacred books as the *Record of Ritual* and the *Rites of Zhou*. Despite these layers of tradition, there was generally room to creatively reimagine how performances could be improved or enhanced. Reattaining the perfection of antiquity carried great prestige, but there was no single unified understanding of how rites and music had been performed in ancient times, or even which period of the past to emulate. Should it be the early Zhou court, praised by Confucius and described in some detail in the *Rites of Zhou?* Or should one aim to achieve levels of excellence associated with the ancient sage kings of high antiquity, such as the Yellow Emperor, Yao, Shun, and Yu? Could traditions dating back only to Tang times be worth maintaining?

This chapter does not aim to look comprehensively into all of the ways tradition was honored or modified at Huizong's court. Instead it takes three cases, each of which shows something different about Huizong's embrace of tradition. Achieving the excellence of high antiquity inspired Huizong to cast a set of the Nine Cauldrons and also to reform court music. As counterintuitive as it might seem, one of the best ways to make court protocol and music seem new and fresh was to attempt to return them to their pristine ancient form. Relatively recent history—the Han and Tang dynasties—provided most of the traditions relevant to the reporting and celebrating of auspicious omens. These traditions provided considerable room for the expression of individual talent and initiative, and made possible a political theater where performances attested to political allegiance.

The Music of Great Brilliance

Music had long been a part of most court rituals. For the Suburban Sacrifices not only was an orchestra needed but also a troupe of male dancers. The music performed for sacred rituals was more formal and conservative than the music performed for banquets and other entertainment, which was open to new tunes and musical styles. Both types of music, however, added to the brilliance of the court.

In the Confucian classics, music could be either very good or very bad. Good, elevating music improves social harmony, while vulgar, seductive music encourages dissipation. The "Book of Music" in the *Record of Ritual* claims that music is a means by which "the hearts of the people are unified and the orderly way attained." The *Rites of Zhou* extends the power of music to the entire cosmos, asserting that "Rites and music are the means to adjust the transformations of heaven and earth and the production of all creation, to serve the ghosts and gods, bring harmony to the myriad people, and perfect all creation."[1] In this way of thinking, one of the most important steps a ruler can take is to establish proper music.

When Huizong called for a music reform in 1102, he was thus doing something many rulers before him had done. Huizong noted several deficiencies in music as played at his court: musical instruments were broken or tuned too high; many of the musicians were temporary recruits unfamiliar with the music and not able to follow the notation; and government music officials argued endlessly about music theory to no avail. Huizong called for a nationwide search for music masters whose knowledge of music came from personal transmission rather than books.[2]

Cai Jing recommended the nonagenarian Wei Hanjin as a music expert. In Song sources, Wei Hanjin is identified as a *fangshi*, a man capable of tapping into mysterious powers to work wonders. He created something of a stir at court, and some of the incumbent music officials tried to argue against his ideas. Wei Hanjin was not deterred, however, and in 1104 submitted a memorial proposing to reset the musical scale. He traced the changes in calibrating the pitch pipes from the legendary Fuxi down to the great sage king Yu, founder of the Xia dynasty, who according to Wei Hanjin had used the length of the different fingers of his left hand to set the length of the pitch pipes. With the Qin burning of the books, knowledge of Yu's method was lost. Wei Hanjin proposed reviving it and measuring Huizong's fingers to set the ruler for the pitches. He also advised the court to cast three sets of bells: the imperial big bells, the four clear-tones bells, and the twenty-four solar-term bells. On that basis, the string and wind instruments would be retuned "to make new music for this generation."[3]

Around the time Wei Hanjin was propounding his ideas about how to set the pitch pipe, a set of six ancient bells was discovered in a tomb. From the drawings of them later included in the catalogue of Huizong's antiquities collection, *Antiquities Illustrated* (Figure 6.1), they had flat bottoms, bosses with spiral designs, and opposed dragons at the top that formed a hook. The discovery of these bells was especially auspicious because of the words inscribed on them, read as "bell of Duke Cheng of Song." Moreover, they were found in Yingtian prefecture, which meant "responding to heaven" prefecture. In Tang times this prefecture was called Song prefecture (after the ancient state in the same place), and was given the new name because it was where the founder of the Song dynasty began his rise (that is, responded to heaven's intentions for him). In 1105 Huizong described the creation of the new music as resulting from the combination of Wei Hanjin's ideas about how to set pitches and the bells acquired "from the land where the Mandate was received." Another time he expressed the same idea but added more explicitly that the excavated bells made possible discovering the proportions used in their design.[4]

Huizong had experts on ancient artifacts in the Palace Library who probably alerted him to the potential value of the excavated bells. The study of actual ancient artifacts was in Huizong's day an exciting field,

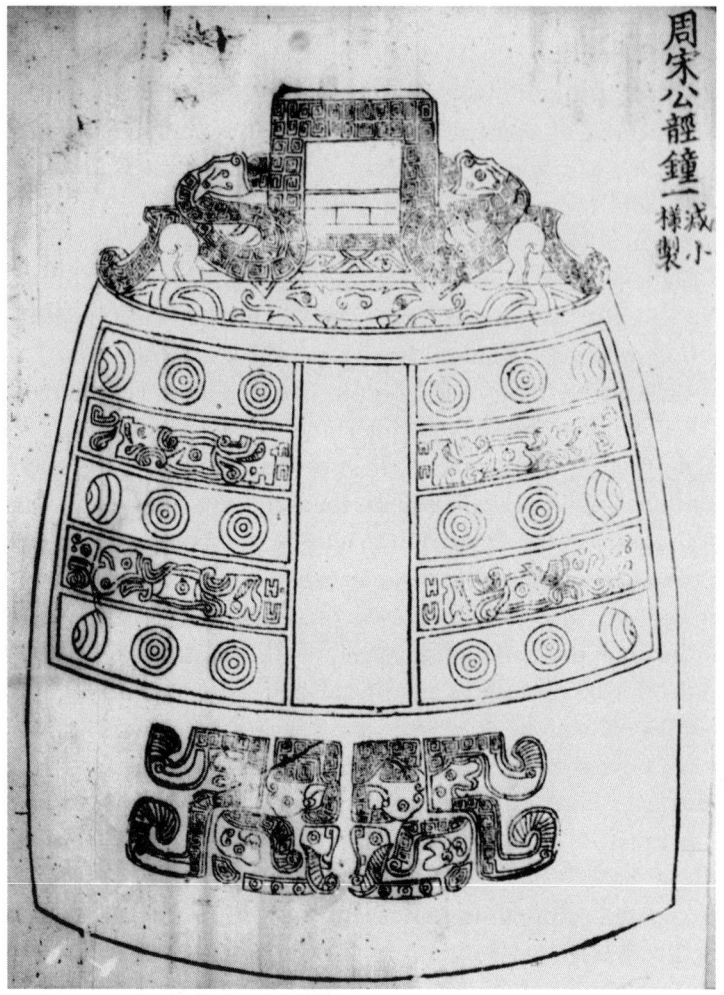

Fig. 6.1. Illustration from *Antiquities Illustrated* of the First of the Duke Cheng of Song Bells. (BGT 1528 ed. 22.27a)

and Huizong employed several men expert in it. One of those who examined the bells, Dong You, wrote about their music-making function. He gave six dimensions for each bell (height, length and width of top, length of sides, length and width of bottom opening). He also gave both the name of each bell's absolute pitch and the name of its note (assuming that the tuning bell, the largest and lowest, was the note *gong*), showing that officials at the Palace Library had tried play-

Fig. 6.2. Bell cast at Huizong's court, height 28.2 cm., weight 6.5 kg. (National Palace Museum, Taiwan, Republic of China)

ing them. Dong You remarked that even though there were quite a few bells that had survived from the Zhou period, officials at court had not been able to cast bells that worked properly as musical instruments. Some did not hang properly on their frames, some did not give their full sound, and so on. It was only after Huizong ordered that the Duke Cheng bells be used as the model that the responsible officials were able to cast bells that could be played in tune.[5]

More than two dozen of the bells cast as part of the new music are still extant and several scholars have studied them closely (Figure 6.2).[6] Typically these bells have the phrase "Great Brilliance" inscribed on one side and the name of the pitch on the other.[7] They belong to three types of chimes, one with just the name of one of the twelve pitches, one with the name of one of the twelve pitches with "middle sound" added to it, and one with the name of one of the four "clear tones." These three series correspond to the bell series that Wei Hanjin had asked to have cast.

To administer this new court music, Huizong created the Bureau of the Music of Great Brilliance. Besides making new instruments and retuning old ones, this bureau issued notated scores and illustrative diagrams to help musicians cope with the changes. Musicians in the employ of the government were ordered to follow these instructions closely and threatened with punishment if they dared to alter the tuning or designs of the new instruments. On Cai Jing's recommendation, Liu Bing was put in charge of the bureau. In that capacity, Liu Bing compiled *The Book of the Music of Great Brilliance*. Some suspect that Liu Bing made modifications to Wei Hanjin's pitches, but he did not just reimpose the old system, as people recognized something new about the Music of Great Brilliance when they heard it.[8]

In 1105/8, after the sets of bells had been cast and the new music written, Huizong called on the court orchestra to demonstrate the difference between the old and new music. First three pieces of the old music were played. Huizong interrupted the performance, declaring that it sounded like someone weeping. When the new music was then played, Huizong approved. The next month the new music formally premiered at a court banquet. As the officials offered toasts to the emperor, the *Song History* reports, cranes flew in from the northeast, circled over the imperial terrace where the music was being performed, signaling their approval.[9] Delighted by this auspicious omen, Huizong issued an edict explaining the reasons and goals for launching this new music. It was an opportune time to institute new music, he proclaimed, because the world had been at peace for a hundred years, he had encountered the hermit Wei Hanjin, and there had been the fortuitous discovery of ancient bells. The next day at an audience with four officials Huizong asked them what they thought of the music performed the day before. Not surprisingly, they were ready with praise, commenting on the use of ancient-style instruments and the response of the cranes, which they compared to the appearance of phoenixes in the classics. When Huizong asked if the sounds were harmonious, they told him they were indeed, all due to his good government.[10]

Several years after the Music of Great Brilliance was inaugurated on 1110/8/1, Huizong wrote an essay on it. He began with the loss of the ancient forms of music and the difficulties earlier Song emperors had had trying to reform court music. Because he encountered a disciple of the famous master, Li Liang, and acquired the bells of Duke Cheng, he was able to use his fingers to set the pitches. It took three years to be ready to play the new music, but in 1105/8 it was successfully played in Promoting Governance Hall. Nine months later, when the officials heard it in Grand Celebration Hall, cranes again responded to the performance. This also happened the following year when it was played as part of the winter sacrifice, and from then on cranes regularly appeared when the music was played. The music had been widely distributed, Huizong claimed, even to foreign countries, and was being taught at the government schools. Huizong said he wrote out edicts in his own hand to spread knowledge of the music and to fulfill the intentions of his predecessors.[11]

Huizong took further steps to spread knowledge of the new music in 1113 when he instructed the Bureau of the Music of Great Brilliance to print collections of musical compositions.[12] The new instruments and the new music all helped Huizong present his court as one that magnificently captured the essential elements of antiquity. There does not seem to be any way to determine what was more important to Huizong: that the music was "ancient"; that cranes testified to its auspiciousness; or that it gave a new feel to performances of court entertainment and ceremonies. Huizong could only admit to the first two, but the third probably contributed as well.

The Nine Cauldrons

Besides resetting the musical scale and casting new bells, Wei Hanjin proposed that the court should cast a set of the famed Nine Cauldrons, vessels that had been associated with the true ruler ever since they were fashioned by Yu. The *Zuo Commentary* records that, after the cauldrons were cast by Yu, they were passed down from the Xia to the Shang dynasty and later from the Shang to the Zhou, their weight changing in accord with the virtue of the rulers—heavy under virtuous kings, light in times of disorder.[13]

In Wei Hanjin's plan, the newly made cauldrons would be treated as objects of worship; he gave them names and described the seasonal, color, and directional symbolism of rites to them. Huizong agreed to take on this project and had metal collected from the nine ancient provinces of China for the casting.[14] In all likelihood some officials added their support to Wei Hanjin's plan, but the histories do not record any memorials either for or against casting a new set of the Nine Cauldrons.

While the cauldrons were being prepared, Huizong built a new Daoist temple to house them in the southeast part of the New City, using some land to the south of the existing Daoist temple of the Grand Unity. He employed the architect Li Jie to design and supervise the project, and gave the temple the name "Nine Completions."[15]

Casting the cauldrons took almost a year, from 1104/10 to 1105/8. When the first cauldron was cast, Cai Tao reports, the sky was lit up with colored light visible as far away as the palace, confirming that something very special was taking place.[16] Once the temple and the cauldrons were ready, Huizong appointed Cai Jing as the "commissioner for settling the cauldrons" and had him supervise the ritual of their transfer. When they were installed on 1105/8/20, cranes again appeared overhead. The next day Huizong went to the temple to make offerings and more cranes came, flying in front of the multicolored clouds, in apparent response to the music. Officials at court, not surprisingly, readily submitted congratulations.[17]

A Daoist master named Wang Yuzhi submitted a text titled *Secrets of the Ritual Forms for the Yellow Emperor Honoring Heaven and Sacrificing to the Cauldrons.* Huizong asked the official Zheng Juzhong to examine this text to see if it could be used to prepare a step-by-step guide to sacrificing to the cauldrons. He stated that the proper methods had not been transmitted but Wang Yuzhi's book may convey some of it as it "is not something people today would be able to write." Zheng Ju-zhong reported back that Wang Yuzhi's rituals seemed to draw on established Daoist ritual traditions combined with Wei Hanjin's ideas, as well as Five Phases, Six *Qi*, and other cosmological ideas. Huizong then approved using Wang Yuzhi's book for preparing the ritual instructions. The next month officials proposed musical pieces that would work well with the Nine Cauldrons because they corresponded to the different geographical directions.[18]

Huizong took credit for writing a commemorative account of the cauldrons, as well as two inscriptions, one for the first of the cauldrons and another for the other eight.[19] The commemorative account survives in abbreviated form. It begins by asserting Huizong's sincerity and complaining about the one-sided literati who spread dissension, undoubtedly referring to the factional strife of the period. The first and largest cauldron, for the central tone, was a huge nine feet tall and reportedly made from 220,000 *jin* of metal [on the order of 100,000 kilograms]. "At the middle of the night when it was cast, I rose and saw the fire which illuminated the sky. [The cauldron] was made in a single casting. At the top it has the sun, moon, stars, constellations, and clouds. In the middle it has the ancestral shrines, the court, and the subjects. At the bottom it has mountains, rivers, springs, marshes, and mounds." After it was installed in the double-roofed Nine Completions Temple, two auspicious signs manifested themselves: a flock of cranes came and danced in the air above the temple and sweet dew was found near the largest cauldron.

Huizong's account goes on to explain the connections between each cauldron and the seasons and colors. For instance, it states: "Because the ten thousand things start in the east and there is the season of spring, we made the Blue Cauldron in order to make offerings to [the eastern states of] Qi and Lu. Because the ten thousand things move to the south and there is the season of summer, we made the Vermilion cauldron in order to make offerings to [the southern states of] Qing and Chu." The account ends by evoking the positive outcomes of these awe-inspiring cauldrons: they would assist in the transformations of heaven; bring regularity to the four seasons; bring an end to floods, droughts, and wars; unify the hearts of the Chinese and the barbarians;

and secure the imperial succession for all time.[20] When the *New Forms of the Five Categories of Rites of the Zhenghe Period* was compiled in 1111–1113, rituals were included for annual offerings to be made at this temple both to the largest of the cauldrons and on a different day to the other eight cauldrons.[21]

Huizong was not satisfied with only one Daoist temple linked to his Nine Cauldrons. In 1109 he had another Daoist temple built at the site where the cauldrons were cast, and gave it the name Treasured Completion Temple. It had several halls, coming to seventy-one room-units, with the central hall dedicated to the Yellow Emperor, the eastern one to the founder of the ancient Xia dynasty, the western one to three early Zhou dynasty figures (King Cheng and the Dukes of Zhou and Shao), and the rear one to the recently deceased Wei Hanjin and his teacher Li Liang.[22] Huizong must have felt very positively about the contribution of Wei Hanjin to want to institute regular offerings to him.

What is the connection between the Nine Cauldrons and the newly cast bells? Wei Hanjin was the one to propose both, but what the bells and the cauldrons had to do with each other is somewhat obscure. Several sources include the sentence "the Jing bell, when suspended was a bell, when turned face up was a cauldron." The earliest use of the sentence may date to 1146, when the Southern Song government wanted to cast new bells, and officials tried to figure out how the bells had been cast during Huizong's reign. Someone cited a *Book of Music* as including the sentence in question. A contemporary, Cheng Dachang, attributed the line to the *Dasheng Book of Music*, and later sources quoted him to that effect. The sentence eventually made its way into the *Song History*.[23]

The problem is that the surviving Great Brilliance bells that Huizong had cast look nothing like cauldrons, and most references to the cauldrons make no mention of music. Rather than being kept in the palace to use during musical performances, the cauldrons were taken a considerable distance away to be enshrined in their own temple. Huizong in his own edict mentions using the largest cauldron to set the pitch. What seems most likely is that the largest of the cauldrons originally was used for its pitch, but after the casting of the other cauldrons and bells, each set had quite separate histories.

The Celebration of Auspicious Signs

The repeated appearance of cranes during the performances of the new music was taken as an auspicious sign. Huizong's officials reported many other positive signs during the same years, providing occasions for the political theater of congratulations. In doing so, they were continuing a long tradition, dating back to the Zhou period but formalized largely in the Han dynasty. The language used by both the emperor and his officials was highly ritualized, but that did not keep those involved from using it for their own purposes or imputing their own meanings to it. As discussed in Chapter 3, Huizong received many warnings that heaven disapproved of his political acts in his first three years on the throne. Thereafter, positive signs get much more attention. These excuses to celebrate and glorify the throne broke the tedium of life at court.[24]

The ancient theory of the Mandate of Heaven lay behind the reporting of both auspicious and inauspicious phenomena. Heaven sends warnings in the form of unusual events, such as comets, eclipses, or earthquakes, when the ruler's management of the realm is deficient. When peace prevails or a new dynasty is about to rise, heaven signals its approval through such auspicious signs as colored vapors in the sky or sweet dew. These ideas were elaborated at considerable length in the Han period, using the cosmology of yin and yang and the Five Phases and traditions of prognostication associated with the *Changes*, the "Great Plan" chapter of the *Documents*, and the *Spring and Autumn Annals*.[25] Han scholars assumed that with enough study, they could discover the meanings of signs, and toward that end, records were kept of each anomaly and the event it was believed to explain. The *Luxuriant Dew of the Spring and Autumn Annals*, traditionally attributed to Dong Zhongshu (ca. 195–ca. 105 BCE), mentions such favorable signs as the auspicious star, yellow dragon, sweet dew, vermilion herb, wine springs, fine grain, empty prisons, phoenixes, and unicorns.[26] The three histories of the Han period, the *Shi ji*, *Han shu*, and *Hou Han shu*, all include extensive records of the reporting and interpretation of portents in their treatises on astronomy and the Five Phases.[27] During certain periods, reports of portents arrived in exceptionally large numbers, especially during the reign of Emperor Wu, the years leading up to the usurpation of Wang Mang, and the years leading to the restoration of the Han dynasty a couple of decades later. As several scholars have demonstrated, Han Confucian scholars used the occasion of anomalies to criticize the ruler, the people around him, their policies, and so on. At the same time, auspicious images were celebrated in verse and made into occasions to extol the grandeur and magnificence of the court, indeed to create it.[28] In 53 BCE the reign name was changed to "sweet dew," the first of many reign period names that attested to auspicious events.

Auspicious events and objects were in Han times also commemorated visually; pictures of them appeared on chariots, mirrors, incense burners, goblets, houses, and tombs.[29] Already by Emperor Wu's time there were books with annotated pictures of specific auspicious omens. In 109 BCE, when numinous mushrooms were found growing on a palace building, Emperor Wu was so pleased that he wrote a poem that mentioned the mushroom's nine stems and joined leaves and said he had identified it by reference to pictures.[30] Over time, many competing texts were written that provided specific prognostications for each portent, drawing on several traditions. The fullest version to survive was included in the history of the Southern Dynasties' Song dynasty. From it we learn, for instance, that intertwined trees, "grow when a ruler's virtue is pure and harmonious, and when the eight directions are unified into a single family." The dark tablet "arrives when rivers and springs flow into each other, and when the four seas join together." Sweet dew descends on vegetation when the ruler shows virtue and benevolence or when elderly people are respected and worthies honored.[31]

The multiplicity of omen interpretation meant that commentators not infrequently disagreed on the interpretation of particular signs: Was a negative sign an indication that officials were negligent, the emperor extravagant, the women's quarters unruly, or a warning that something bad was about to happen? A bad omen could predict disaster for the Han's enemies rather than for the Han.[32] Already in Han times, many people suspected that signs were manufactured for political purposes, even those who believed that heaven in fact sent messages. There were also skeptics who did not think there was anything to gain by looking for signs of heaven's approval or disapproval. During the Northern Song, Wang Anshi was a notable skeptic. Adding to the complexity of omen analysis, some people did not see omens as revealing ineluctable fate, instead believing that virtue could overcome the inauspicious and righteousness reverse unfavorable portents.[33]

During Tang times, the government identified sixty-four types of "grand" auspicious portents. Local officials were to report them to the throne as soon as they were discovered and court officials were to promptly offer their congratulations. Reports of the three lesser ranks of portents could be gathered and reported together at the end of the year. Among the major portents were unicorns, phoenixes, divine tortoises, dragon-horses, white elephants, the dark tablet, vermilion herbs, divine tripods, and the clearing of the waters of the Yellow River. The next grade of omens included red hares, three-legged crows, sweet dew, purple jade, and white jade with red text on it. Below that were several types of white (or albino) birds, five-colored geese, and pearls from the earth. Examples of the lowest grade included some of the oldest, such as fine grain, numinous mushrooms, and trees that grow intertwined. Local officials were required to scrutinize the evidence to make sure the omens were genuine, then submit a picture to the central government.[34]

The Song government followed a similar system. As in most earlier dynasties, portents were frequently reported in the early years of the dynasty as a way to show that the Mandate of Heaven had been properly transferred. Taizu had procession flags made to commemorate the auspicious sighting of a golden parrot and a jade rabbit as well as the diplomatic gift of a trained elephant. Taizong in 987 wrote two poems to celebrate the receipt of the auspicious sign of fine grain. The next year, however, he issued an edict telling local officials not to send unusual animals or birds, both because confining them was a violation of their nature and because the ultimate auspicious sign was a good harvest.[35]

His successor Zhenzong was enthusiastic in welcoming news of a wide array of auspicious omens. Zhenzong celebrated auspicious signs by having them painted on the wall of the magnificent Daoist temple he had built in the capital, the Temple of Reflecting and Responding to the Realm of Jade Clarity.[36] One source reports that he was advised not to concern himself with whether a sign had been manufactured or not.[37]

Why was Huizong so fond of auspicious signs? While still a prince, he would have become familiar with the language used at court to discuss portents, as portent reports were an established part of court ritual. To give an example, in 1098 when Huizong was seventeen *sui*, an ancient jade seal was presented to Zhezong and treated as a very positive augury, especially because its inscription read "Having received the mandate from heaven, longevity and everlasting glory." Receipt of the seal was announced at the Suburban Altar, the Supreme Shrine, and other temples, then formally accepted at a major audience, after which Zhezong's officials congratulated him. To further mark the receipt of this ancient seal, Zhezong decided to change the name of the reign period to "Primal Tally" (*yuanfu*). Zhezong further celebrated this discovery through the creation of new procession flags picturing the ancient seal. An official who wrote to congratulate Zhezong was effusive, "Because the sun, moon, and stars look after you, auspicious responses of all sorts keep arriving. Because your brilliance shines down to the ground, divine light illuminates the sky. Because you bring benefits to the people, sweet dew is as abundant as rain."[38] Officials at Zhezong's court knew when they should tell the emperor that he was a sage and that heaven was making clear its approval of him.

Huizong evidently enjoyed this sort of political theater. In other words, I see his celebration of auspicious signs not so much as evidence of his belief in a body of religious or cosmological ideas, but as evidence of his ability to play with court ritual, to temper the grave and solemn side of government with something lighter and brighter. While Huizong undoubtedly did believe that there were forces beyond the human sphere and that heaven could in fact send messages, I doubt that he assumed that every phenomenon reported to him as auspicious was indeed such a message. In the routine of court life, these reports were entertaining, a kind of play-acting that authorized pleasantries at little cost. Huizong's poems and other writings on auspicious signs show little sign of a serious struggle to find meaning. Rather, what I see is an embracing of the cheerful side of auspicious signs. There may also have been some wishful thinking: Could one invite good luck by identifying and applauding its signs?

Omen reporting certainly also had a political side. After Huizong chose the reformers, officials were much more likely to point to positive signs and congratulate him on them than dwell on negative signs. Presumably they had discovered that Huizong enjoyed hearing of positive signs and were happy to oblige him in that way. Doing so also was a statement that they sided with the reformers, that they supported Huizong's policies. Men who served in Huizong's court after 1102 would all have joined in congratulating Huizong on auspicious signs. Only a few of the authors of these memorials have had their collected works preserved. The fullest surviving set is in the collected works of Wang Anzhong. According to his biography in the *Song History*, Wang Anzhong first attracted Huizong's attention because of the congratulatory memorials he wrote about auspicious responses.[39] Most of Wang Anzhong's congratulatory memorials are undated, but from the events commemorated several can be assigned dates ranging from 1104 to 1118. The occasions of the memorials are summarized in Table 6.1.

Congratulating the ruler on auspicious signs customarily involved praise of the ruler's accomplishments or fine qualities. Zhang Shangying drew attention to this practice in 1110 by citing the sentiment in the poem, "Heaven's Reciprocity" (in the *Book of Songs*) that just as the lord helps his ministers complete the government, the ministers praise the lord as a way to repay him. In this case, Zhang Shangying as grand councilor submitted a report on the discovery of fine grain. Huizong

Table 6.1. Subjects of Wang Anzhong's fifty memorials congratulating Huizong on good omens

Subject	Number of memorials
Multiple auspicious signs in a single prefecture	10
Numinous mushrooms	9
Auspicious metal	3
Fine grain	2
The clearing of the Yellow River	2
Five-colored clouds	2
Auspicious movements of stars	2
Intertwined and other unusual trees	2
White hares	2
A belt of vapor around the sun	1
The placidity of the Yellow River	1
Solar eclipse that did not reach the predicted degree	1
The lack of prisoners in the Kaifeng jails	1
The empty docket of the Court of Judicial Review	1
Red grass	1
Red salt	1
The word "bright" found inside a stone	1

responded in a gracious way, using "the imperial brush" and thus probably either writing a poem or painting a picture. Zhang Shang-ying decided to respond to the emperor's response with thirteen poems modeled on poems from the "Greater Elegentia" section of the *Book of Songs*.[40]

Huizong occasionally brought up auspicious omens in his own poems. For example, he mentions summoning painters to make visual records of auspicious phenomena:

> No day passes without auspicious items brought for
>   submission.
> With bows they present numinous mushrooms, each
>   different in some way.
> Sometimes I call for an expert in red and green pigments.
> In each case I give him the plan and have him make the
>   painting.[41]

Signs from heaven could be read in the skies, which was one of the responsibilities of the Astrological Service. In general, events that were understood to be periodic and predictable were not treated as messages. For instance, eclipses of the moon were understood to recur in predictable ways. At the other extreme, the appearance of comets and meteors were among the most worrisome auguries, since there seemed to be no logic to their appearance. The principal exception was solar eclipses. By Tang times, with the improvement in computational astronomy (due in no small part to Buddhist texts that introduced Indian and Central Asian astronomical knowledge), solar eclipses could be predicted with a high degree of accuracy and yet they continued to be viewed as negative portents for the ruler, probably because the sun was seen as a counterpart to the emperor (and because much of court ritual was established in Han times before solar eclipses could be predicted accurately).[42] The sun was not the only counterpart of the ruler. The Northern Dipper and the Pole Star were also regularly likened to the emperor. These stars also played a central role in the Daoist pantheon, adding to their significance.[43]

A few examples of astronomical signs should suffice. On 1103/4/19, "the Grand Astrologer memorialized, 'The Five Planets are all traveling along the Yellow Path [that is, the path of the sun]. When we investigate ancient precedents, we find that this is surely an auspicious response to Great Peace. According to the monograph in the *Han History*, when there is great peace in the subcelestial sphere, the five stars are obediently ordered.'" Cai Jing and the other councilors submitted a memorial offering congratulations.[44] On several occasions officials congratulated the emperor because a predicted solar eclipse was less total than predicted or was not visible because of clouds. In 1110 a green, red, and yellow vapor appeared first above and then below the sun. This was treated so positively that procession flags were made to commemorate the event.[45]

Sweet dew was another time-honored auspicious sign. The *Laozi* mentions sweet dew as descending when heaven and earth are in harmony. Early medical texts say sucking sweet dew prolongs life. The Southern Dynasties compendium states that "sweet dew descends when the king's virtue is extremely large and the *qi* of harmony prevails."[46] The idea of sweet dew was so strongly established that it was widely used in both Buddhist and Daoist literature as a positive sign.[47] Huizong wrote a poem for his officials in 1109 in response to the appearance of sweet dew by a government building. The story is recounted this way by Wu Zeng in 1157:

On the day *renzi* in the fourth month of 1109, sweet dew came down at the Department of State Affairs. An imperial brush edict issued at the place for announcing policy in the central pavilion declared that heaven's intention blazes forth, providing this fine auspicious sign. Accordingly, [the emperor] wrote a poem with four rhymes to record these facts, which he conferred on his high officials:

> The government completes heaven and earth; nothing
>   is in opposition.
> The auspicious responses in the Central Pavilion assist
>   the workings of the cosmos.
> At night, moisture falls in pearls and moistens the green
>   leaves.
> At dawn, it congeals as glossy jade, making it gleam.
> With this immortal pan [of moisture] beyond the
>   clouds, autumn cannot compare.

The dew that fell at night on the luxuriant plants has not
    yet been dried out by the sun.
Its origin is in the harmonious union of the ruler and his
    ministers.
They once more happily report that excellence has
    returned.[48]

Since Huizong was so open in his embrace of sweet dew, we should
not be surprised that his officials were quick to celebrate it. Wang Anzhong wrote a congratulatory memorial on the occasion of a sacrificial
ceremony marked by both sweet dew and a pair of cranes. In it Wang
Anzhong assures Huizong that the sweet dew and cranes had come in
response to his ritual and music projects.[49]

The clearing of the Yellow River provided other occasions for re-
joicing. The Yellow River was normally muddy, a result of the loess silt
that it carried. Since early times, the river turning clear (*qing*) was
considered a positive augury—perhaps in part because clarity/purity
was such a positive quality—something to which the government should
also aspire. The clearing of the river had been reported not only in earlier dynasties, but also during Taizong's and Zhenzong's reigns. But
more instances were recorded in Huizong's reign than in that of any
earlier Song emperor. These occurred in 1107, 1108, 1109, 1116, 1117,
and 1119.[50]

One of the many officials who offered congratulations on the clearing of the Yellow River at Qianning in 1107 was Murong Yanfeng, who
wrote on behalf of the councilors. His memorial begins: "Heaven's
mind assists virtue. The Goddess of the River [in the *Book of Songs*]
offers auspicious signs. Just now, when the banks are full to overflowing, we get this auspice of once-in-a-thousand-years clarity. Responding to the moral standards [of the ruler], blessings of many sorts mate-
rialize." He then likened this auspicious sign to the way Huizong had
recently performed the Suburban Sacrifice, in particular the way the
connection to antiquity had been strengthened. He also pointed out
that no one would have been able to turn the river clear—it had to be
heaven's doing.[51] Huizong himself celebrated the clearing of the Yellow River at Qianning in a poem:

On a clear morning, the post messenger announces a
    phoenix report.

> Congratulations are exclaimed at Purple Asterism Hall,
>   where the [officials with their] hatpins and tassels gather.
> From Qianning comes news of the latest auspicious sign,
> For several nights the Yellow River flowed clear, right down
>   to the bottom.[52]

Individuals outside the court also sometimes celebrated auspicious signs in verse. Chao Duanli, a man who had passed the civil service examinations forty years earlier, wrote a long song which Cai Tao reports became very popular with people of all ranks. It includes these lines:

> When the high officials report,
> The heavenly visage shows pleasure.[53]
> During the night successive memorials had arrived
> Reporting that the Great River had turned entirely clear.
> May the ruler live as long as heaven.
> The fragrance [of his virtue] stirs the sky above,
> Which unceasingly sends down auspicious signs.[54]

The popularity of this song suggests that pleasure in auspicious signs extended beyond the palace.

Undoubtedly localities could benefit from reporting an auspicious event such as the clearing of the Yellow River. According to the stone inscription erected where the river turned clear in 1109, Huizong agreed to pay for the construction of a thirty-four-room-unit shrine at the site. The inscription, not surprisingly, linked the clearing of the river to all of the other achievements of Huizong's reign, including revising imperial sacrifices, planning the Bright Hall, and reforming music.[55]

Plants could also be auspicious, none perhaps more than numinous or magical mushrooms (*zhi*, or *zhicao*). Since at least the time of the First Emperor of Qin, a certain type of mushroom had been considered to have special powers, above all to extend life spans. The *Comprehensive Discussions in the White Tiger Hall* of 79 CE claimed that "When the ruler's virtue affects the mountains and the hills, the luminous cloud appears and the divine mushrooms grow luxuriant." The Southern Dynasties compendium reported that the mushroom grows when the king is compassionate and that eating it allows people to transcend the world.[56] Numinous mushrooms were absorbed into Daoist lore as well. The Daoist canon preserves a Song text, *Catalogue*

Fig. 6.3. "Cloud Mushroom" in *Catalogue of Numinous Mushrooms.* The caption reads: "Cloud mushrooms have a green cover and a yellow stem and taste like honey. Consuming them for a thousand years, one becomes a Transcendent. Above, five-colored clouds cover them." (TSLBZCP; DZ 34.328B)

of Numinous Mushrooms of Most High Numinous Treasure, which has illustrations of more than a hundred types of numinous mushrooms, with names like yellow jade mushroom, metal essence mushroom, or cloud mushroom, each depicted and described (see Figure 6.3).[57]

In a poem Huizong wrote about numinous mushrooms, he alludes to an occasion when a nine-stalked mushroom was found at a Han palace building and Emperor Wu was inspired to compose a song to celebrate it. Huizong wrote:

> From Cloud Terrace an auspicious force brings forth a
>   treasure from the earth.
> At Dragon's Horn are layers of auspicious mushrooms,
>   jade-colored and fresh.
> From this occurrence, how are the Nine Stalks [of the Han
>   emperor Wu] worth admiring?

The paintings and calligraphy of the Unicorn Pavilion
forever pale in comparison.[58]

Wang Anzhong wrote a memorial to congratulate Huizong when numinous mushrooms were found growing by the buildings of the newly
founded Medical School. His conclusion is Daoist-tinged: "I humbly
note that Your Majesty clasps kindness as a treasure, embodies benevolence like heaven. You consistently do good to save other people,
extending the wonders of revolving the pivot of the Dao to aid everyone, who can together attain the peace of ascending to the regions of
longevity. Luminous the flowering of the numinous mushrooms, glorious the total response! We are fortunate to be among your staff and to
see with our own eyes this excellent auspicious sign."[59]

Among animals, birds were probably the most often viewed as auspicious signs. White birds were especially revered. As the dynastic histories from Han times on document, provincial officials regularly sent to
the capital albino birds that could be interpreted as signs of the success
of the current monarch.[60] One painting done at Huizong's court provides evidence that he appreciated this tradition. The inscription by
Cai Jing, dated 1114, attributes the painting to Huizong and discusses
the Five Phases principles underlining auspicious phenomena, then
turns to its connection to Huizong: "I had never heard of a white hawk.
But the moral authority of Your Majesty, our August Sovereign, moves
heaven and earth, and your benevolence extends [even to the creatures
that] run and fly. You equalize the transformations of *yin* and *yang* and
unify the life-forces of north and south so there are no differences between boundaries here and borders there. Birds, animals, and plants
change their features and their colors in response to the prodigious
power of your virtue and become auspices of good omen for the State."
Cai Jing mentions that he had seen the white hawk in the Rear Garden
and also praises Huizong's painterly skill, the "marvel of divine brushwork to which nothing can be added."[61]

The bird most celebrated at Huizong's court was the crane. Cranes
had no place in the ancient system of auspicious portents; no cranes are
among the auspicious items in the Southern Dynasties list; nor are any
among the auspicious birds recorded in Tang times. In all likelihood,
what made cranes worth celebrating were their associations with
Daoism. Over and over during Huizong's reign reports arrived of the

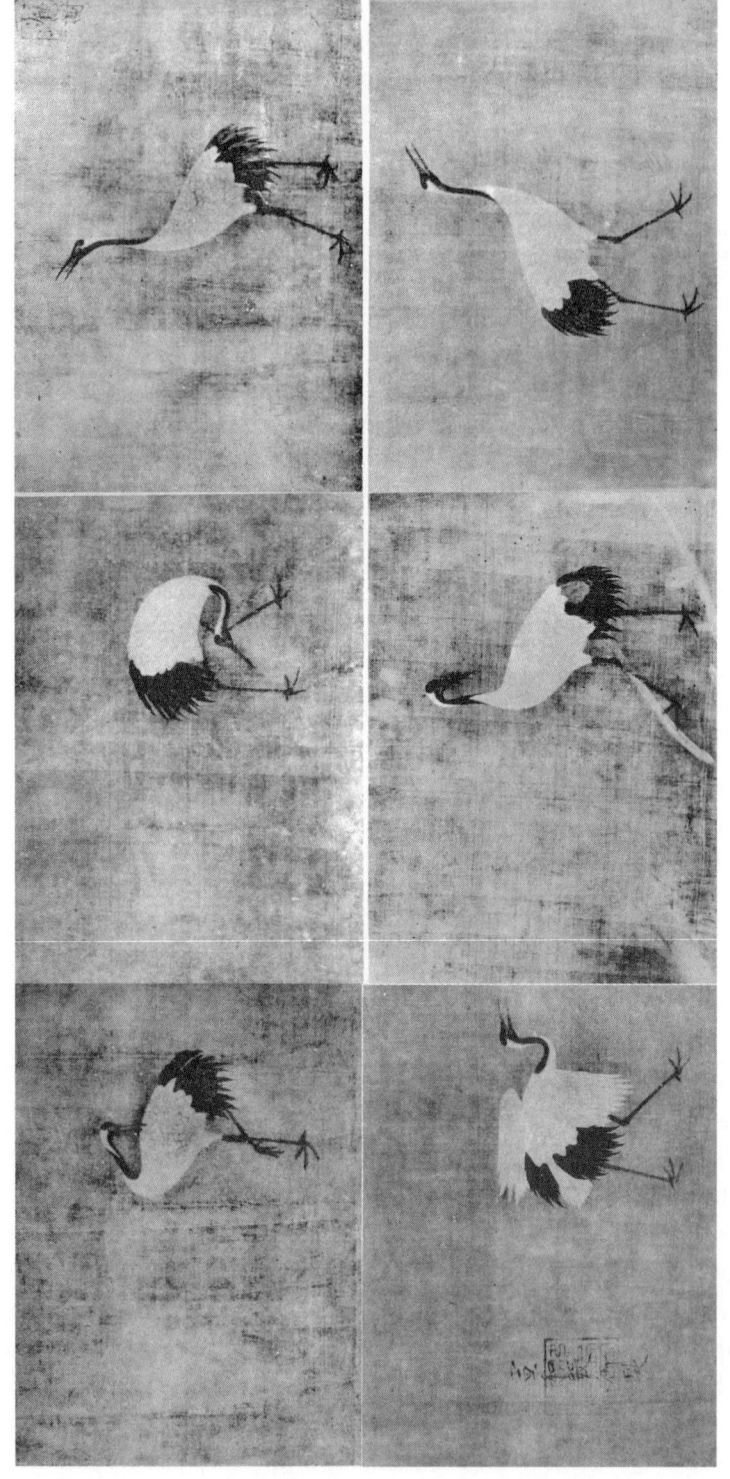

Fig. 6.4. Huizong, *Six Cranes*, album leaves, ink and color on silk. Location unknown. (After Kawai 1937 6:15–17)

appearance of cranes at the palace or other buildings associated with the throne. To give a later example, on 1118/9/12 several thousand cranes flew from Longevity Mountain (in the Northeast Marchmount) to Highest Clarity Precious Records Temple nearby.[62] Cai Jing wrote a poem to celebrate this event, which Huizong responded to with a poem of his own using the same rhymes. Huizong's poem begins with a preface:

> On the first day of winter, following the sermon at Highest Clarity Precious Records Temple, several thousand cranes soared through the sky, causing everyone—high and low—to look up at them. When you saw this splendid sight, you wrote a poem to record it and submitted it. I have used the same rhymes to write one for you.
>
> > At Highest Clarity's lecture space at Melancholy Terrace
> > Suddenly there came a myriad companions of the green
> >   fields.
> > Their feathers obscured the clear sky and made them
> >   seem like dancing snow.
> > Lingering and loitering, their revolving shadows resemble
> >   parting clouds.
> > As they flew up their pure cries came one after the other
> >   from far away.
> > Since such an auspicious responses may never come again
> > We laud it in a song suited to the happy event.
> > How joyous that we now once more experience the tune
> >   of the banished immortal talents.[63]

Huizong also painted cranes. An album of six depictions of cranes in various poses signed by Huizong was published in the 1930s, though its current whereabouts is unknown (Figure 6.4).[64]

❧ WHAT SORTS OF KNOWLEDGE of the past did members of Huizong's court draw on in their efforts to enliven court culture? In the case of music, Wei Hanjin claimed to know the way the ancient sages had set the pitch pipes, thus allowing him to adjust the musical scale so that music made in his day would sound like music in high antiquity. He did not claim a deeper understanding of the classical texts but rather direct transmission of ancient knowledge from his teacher. That musical tunes and techniques are best conveyed from master to student is certainly plausible—the texts on music that survive from Huizong's day offer us little help in imagining the sounds produced by his orchestra.

Before long, however, an alternative way to recapture the true sounds of antiquity became possible because of the discovery of a set of six bells. Using the proportions of these unearthed bells to cast a new set of bells made it possible to set the scale on the basis of actual ancient objects. Huizong had at his court several men who had kept abreast of the many advances in the study of ancient artifacts and they saw the potential of the bells. Thus, in the case of music, books were not treated as the primary source of knowledge about what had been practiced in ancient times—both artifacts and personal transmission were viewed as superior.

In the case of the reporting and analysis of omens, textual traditions were much more dominant than oral transmission. Although those writing on omens often found passages to quote from the classics, more important sources were earlier histories, especially the three histories of the Han period (*Shi ji*, *Han shu*, and *Hou Han shu*). These histories offered a wealth of material to draw on, enriching literary possibilities. Analysis and celebration of omens were above all verbal activities.

Both music and omens at Huizong's court had complicated connections to Daoism. Wei Hanjin acted much like a Daoist priest, and Huizong had a Daoist temple built to enshrine the Nine Cauldrons. He later had another Daoist temple built after Wei Hanjin's death at the site of the casting of the cauldrons and at that site Daoist offerings were made to Wei Hanjin and his teacher.

The connections between Daoism and omen analysis require more unpacking. Here, I have presented them as to some degree separate, each with its own traditions and expectations. Moreover, whereas I presented Huizong as a sincere lay Daoist in Chapter 5, someone who fully embraced its core teachings and practices, in this chapter I have presented Huizong as less than a full believer in the ideas underlying messages from heaven, though still someone who took pleasure in the pomp and ceremony of announcements of auspicious omens. Let me review the evidence for making this distinction.

First, the Daoist religion that Huizong embraced was a living religion, with a large clergy and millions of followers. New scriptures were being written, new traditions were being developed: in no sense was the religion out of touch with life in the early twelfth century. That its teachings spoke to Huizong is no cause for wonder.

By contrast, much of the lore of omens dated to the Han dynasty, a thousand years earlier, and was rooted in sets of ideas that no longer seemed so compelling to people of Huizong's age, such as Five Phases correlative cosmology and the idea that all knowledge could be integrated into a single comprehensive system. The correct thing to say about the appearance of omens had been established through centuries of edicts and memorials, this language gradually becoming more and more ritualized, if not ossified. From their memorials, we can infer that Cai Jing, Wang Anzhong, Zhang Shangying, and Murong Yanfeng were willing to tell Huizong that he was a sage and heaven approved his actions, but earlier officials had said much the same thing to earlier emperors, including Zhezong during Huizong's youth. There is no need to infer that either Huizong or his officials worried about whether what they said was in fact the case. Because the classics and early histories were full of references to messages from heaven, Song officials could not treat them as superstitious and refrain from participating in the offering of felicitations. Much the way we politely praise our host's cooking, no matter what we actually think of the food, Huizong's officials recognized that the occasion required that they declare the meaning of signs to be indisputably positive and to do so in artful language.

Rather than just claim Huizong did not take omens too seriously, I have gone further and suggested that he enjoyed the political theater that surrounded the reporting and celebrating of auspicious omens. In quite a few poems, Huizong presents himself as savoring the moment. Although, following established ritual norms, in edicts he had to say he was in awe of heaven, worried by the heavy burden he had to bear, outside those documents he does not come across as anxious about heaven's judgment of his policy decisions. The one omen that historical sources depict him as indeed frightened by—the comet of 1106—in the end led him to question the expertise of the omen interpreters. At first Huizong accepted the conclusions of those who told him heaven was showing its displeasure with Cai Jing and his program, and he not only dismissed Cai Jing but canceled most of the policies he had put in place during the preceding three years. Within months, however, Huizong began to have misgivings. The Hanlin academician Zheng Juzhong requested an audience at which he argued to Huizong that heaven could not have been angry at such noble projects as expanding schools and aiding orphans. Others made similar arguments, and soon Huizong began to reverse his earlier decisions. If politically motivated interpretations of inauspicious omens could be so far off the mark, omen interpretation was no science and its exponents were hardly experts.

What did officials gain by participating in these court performances? By submitting reports of auspicious omens, local officials drew attention to themselves and also to their region, which might stand to gain concrete benefits (as in the case of the shrine built where the Yellow River had cleared). Officials at court could enhance their reputations as writers by submitting poems or memorials about auspicious events that seemed fresh and original. Wang Anzhong was said to have gained notice that way. To put this a different way, the multiple participants in these dramas were performing different scripts and could well be giving them different meanings. There was no single unified meaning to which all had to subscribe.

Even if we should approach the issue of convictions differently in the cases of Daoism and omen interpretation, it is worth noticing the ways Daoism had enriched the analysis of omens, revitalizing it and keeping it from becoming totally frozen in patterns set during the Han dynasty. Ancient omens such as sweet dew and numinous mushrooms maintained their power in part because they played a significant role in Daoist traditions. And cranes, so widely associated with Daoist immortals, were absorbed into the omen traditions. Moreover, Huizong's personal interpretations of anomalies and other signs from heaven probably was formed more through his discussions with Liu Hunkang than through the memorials submitted by his officials—that is, his interpretations may have had more of a Daoist cast than those of his officials, who drew more on Han dynasty traditions.

This chapter has concentrated on the period 1102–1110, but Huizong did not lose interest in either court music or the pleasantries of auspicious signs in the years that followed. It was probably after 1110 that Huizong began a huge project to have paintings made of auspicious signs. Most of the reports of massive finds of auspicious mushrooms were made in later years. In 1115, Qi prefecture reported 12,060 sprigs of magic mushrooms, then Wusheng prefecture reported 50,000.[65] The next year Huizong instructed Confucian officials to write poems on the major auspicious events since 1102. He planned to have them set to the new music and sung as hymns during the Suburban Sacrifices.[66]

We know very little about the musicians who performed these hymns and other music at court. We know somewhat more however about other artists and experts that Huizong put to work at his court. They are the subject of the next chapter.

7

Welcoming Masters and Experts

> Eighteen-year-old [Wang] Ximeng is a student at the
> Painting School with an appointment in the Documents
> Storehouse. He submitted his paintings to Huizong, who
> considered them not yet very accomplished. Still His Majesty
> recognized Wang's aptitude and thought he might be
> teachable. He began to instruct him personally in technique.
> In less than half a year, Wang submitted this painting, which
> the emperor thought very fine. He then conferred it on me.
>
> —*Colophon written by Cai Jing in 1113 on a long landscape*
> *handscroll by Wang Ximeng*

*H*UIZONG'S COURT—like courts elsewhere in his age—
was not only a consumer of culture; it was also a producer. Huizong
could not achieve a magnificent court on his own: he needed to recruit
talented craftsmen and specialists in many fields and give them opportunities to shine.

The ways Huizong went about selecting, training, and rewarding experts for his court can be viewed in terms of the options open to him.
What could he do to make his court magnificent? Where did the court
have competitive advantage, so that investment in training and materials would pay off? To the extent that Huizong accurately understood
the requirements for excellence in each field of culture, he would have
adapted his strategies to match the circumstances. For instance, in many
fields of culture, people are the key resource. No one can own a poem
committed to memory. And if one needs to turn to a book for it, any
book reproducing it will do. For the court to be a creative center of poetry, human capital is the key: it has to gather poets, not poetry books.

For some scholarly fields, books are as necessary as experts. Until
the spread of printing, government historians with access to the archives and palace book collections had a tremendous advantage. Thus

until late Tang much of the best work in classical scholarship and history was done by scholars in the employ of the government.[1] By Song times with the spread of printing there were enough books in circulation that excellent histories and other works of scholarship were increasingly written by scholars acting independently of the government. Still, during the Northern Song the court sponsored important books in several fields such as medicine, military technology, mathematics, and geomancy.

Then there are fields in which objects other than books greatly aid creative work. The court painters who got to see and closely copy the paintings in Huizong's collection had access to a resource outside painters were denied. The court had less of an advantage with the art of calligraphy because the most prized works had been reproduced via rubbings and widely circulated. With painting, however, not only was printing not much used for reproduction, but copying was done on a much smaller scale. Thus as the technologies of transmitting culture changed in Song times, the court retained advantages in the field of painting longer than in the fields of scholarship or calligraphy, and an emperor who wanted his court to produce masterpieces would find painting a particularly suitable field for investment. The court could support lengthy, exacting artistic training. It could provide artists with a rich array of expensive pigments, plus silk, screens, and mounting facilities. And the large collection of earlier masterpieces could be made available for study.

For painting, music, and many crafts, the court in Huizong's time could successfully train its own experts. The court Music Bureau could devote more resources to the training of a flute player than a commercial establishment would find profitable. Quality materials also would help. Court weavers and embroiders could do superb work not only because of their lengthy training, but also because of their access to the high-quality raw materials and the generous allotments of time given them to complete their work.

Specialists in certain fields—such as astronomy, medicine, calligraphy, and religion—had to be experts in texts. Nevertheless, appointments to technical offices did not require success in the civil service examinations. In the Song, as the prestige of the civil service examinations rose, the gap between literati officials and technical officials consequently widened.[2]

The career paths of technical officials differed significantly from those in the civil service. One could prepare for the civil service examinations anywhere in the country and could take a decade or longer trying to pass them. Technical officials more often underwent training programs or apprenticeships run by the relevant government agencies. In the regular civil service, officials could progress through a dozen or more posts, in the capital and outside it, occupying none more than three years. The possible appointments for technical officials were much more limited, and they could remain at court for decades, in this regard more like clerical staff than administrators. Technical officials were given low-rank titles in the military rank system. This set them apart from those who entered through the exams and received civil-rank titles and also from officials who entered through the protection privilege, who also received titles in the military rank system but generally started at higher rank. The time when these differences would be made most visible was at major court assemblies, when those with civil titles would line up in order of rank on one side of the hall and those with military titles on the other, with imperial clansmen between them, facing the throne.[3]

As part of the New Policies overhaul of the government, Wang Anshi added a specialized training program in law and proposed bringing other specialized training programs such as medicine and mathematics under the Directorate of Education. Part of the motivation for this reform was to raise the standards and the prestige of specialized learning and attract better qualified men to it. His plan, however, was never fully implemented.[4]

The ambitious school system that Cai Jing proposed early in Huizong's reign drew from ideas Wang Anshi had articulated, but extended them more systematically. Technical training would be offered by schools that would fall under the control of the Directorate of Education, rather than the government organ that would employ the graduates. The School of Mathematics can be used as an example. It prepared men to do the calculations needed above all for calendar-making and astronomical predictions. The school was removed from the supervision of the Astrological/Astronomical Service and organized on the model of the Three Halls system used by the Imperial Academy and the Biyong Academy. It enrolled 210 students, who, like the students in the Imperial Academy and the Biyong Academy, had to take monthly and yearly tests, which were used to weed out underperforming students, so that less than half of the students who started the program made it to the third level. At the new school, students' training was to include the study of at least one minor classic, probably in the hope that a better classical education would give professional mathematicians more standing within the civil service.[5] Study was organized into subjects, which included calendar making, astronomy, and "three formula" calculations. All read the *Mathematical Canons*, written in the Tang dynasty but recently revised and reissued by the Song government. The exams they took included questions on the meaning of texts as well as actual calculations, such as predicting the dates and degrees of solar and lunar eclipses, or predicting the weather for the next three days.[6]

In the assessment of the modern scholar Yu Hui, no other monarch in world history can compare to Huizong in the range of court arts that flourished under his supervision—not only painting but also garden design, architecture, music, poetry, drama, books, and printing.[7] A ruler with no aptitude or interest in the arts or natural sciences could delegate supervision of his technical officials to eunuch palace servants. But that was not Huizong's approach. Huizong seems to have been comfortable working with masters and experts of many sorts, including ones who tended more to the side of craft than science.

This chapter does not try to cover all the fields of cultural production at Huizong's court that employed experts, but only three in which the evidence is strong that Huizong took a personal interest in the work: medicine, architecture, and painting. It is widely believed that fine ceramics were produced for Huizong's court, but there is no record of Huizong involving himself in glazes, designs, or any other issue related to the production of ceramics. The same is true for textiles, metalwork, jade-carving, and other crafts.

Evidence of Huizong's involvement with experts ranges from prefaces he wrote for books produced by these experts to amusing anecdotes about Huizong's interaction with them. Huizong's handling of medicine and his handling of painting have something in common—he set up schools to train experts in both of them. Also in both cases we have products produced by court specialists—paintings and medical books. We do not have any of the buildings built by Huizong's master builders, but architecture and painting overlap in that court painters were regularly assigned to decorate the walls of new palace and temple buildings.

Physicians

During the Northern Song period the throne was a major patron of medical learning. The early emperors all took an interest in medical treatment. Taizu and Renzong both practiced moxibustion and acupuncture themselves, and Zhenzong mixed together medications to treat his officials. These emperors also sponsored the publication of key medical books. Taizu had a materia medica *(Bencao)* published in 974 and wrote a preface for it. Taizong wrote the preface for the first government-sponsored formulary issued in 986, a huge book one thousand chapters long (a condensed one hundred-chapter version was issued six years later). Renzong commissioned a manual on acupuncture and moxibustion in 1023, assigning the job to the chief steward of the Palace Medical Service. As part of that project, two full-size bronze models of human beings were made with holes at the acupuncture points to use in training.[8]

The physicians who compiled these books held court medical appointments. Occupants of these positions were sometimes referred to as "medical workers/artisans" *(yigong)* and like other technical officials held low ranks, with their titles in the military rank system. Still, perhaps because they treated the emperor when he was ill, emperors could show them personal favor. Renzong, for instance, handsomely rewarded the doctor whose acupuncture cured him of some ailment.[9]

In 1044 Renzong set up an office devoted to medical education at the Imperial Medical Service. In 1060 its enrollment was set at 120 students. Their course of study focused on a variety of medical texts, both old and new, some emphasizing theory, others practice. Under Shenzong as part of the New Policies reform of the government school system, the Medical School was reorganized along the line of the Three Halls system and enrollment increased to three hundred students, with two hundred in the Outer Hall, of whom sixty would be promoted to the Inner Hall and of them forty to the Upper Hall. Students were promoted on the basis not just of written tests but also the success rate of their treatment of ill government students.[10]

Huizong honored these precedents in many ways, by expanding the medical education system, sponsoring the compilation of new medical texts, and by writing (or claiming to write) medical books himself. In 1103 the Medical School was made independent of the Imperial Medical Service and put, like the other specialized schools of law, mathematics, painting, and calligraphy, under the Directorate of Education. A memorial proposing the Medical School stressed that it was important to attract better educated men to the study of medicine. The school's three hundred students were divided into halls as they had been earlier. Four erudites and three hall masters offered instruction in three subjects: internal medicine, acupuncture/moxibustion therapy, and external medicine, which in turn were divided into nine specialties such as pediatrics, ophthalmology, and acupuncture/moxibustion. The texts assigned were largely government-sponsored editions of medical classics.[11] Like the other government schools, examinations were used both to admit students and to advance them. Given four times a year, the progress exams tested not only knowledge of the key texts but also clinical skills. Students needed to diagnose hypothetical cases and explain how they would treat them.[12]

Soon after Huizong's Medical School was opened, numinous mushrooms were found growing by its buildings. Wang Anzhong, in his congratulatory memorial, cites ancient precedent for the ruler involving himself with medicine:

The Yellow Emperor, in writing the books of prescriptions, was truly doing the work of a sage. When [King] Cheng of Zhou cured the epidemics, he was extending the generosity of the ruler in substantial ways. Over the ages, some [of this knowledge] has been obscured in deep recesses, the techniques lost among the craftsmen. [In other words, medical knowledge has survived as technical craft rather than sagely wisdom.] Now encountering a brilliant era, the ancient origins [of medicine] have been investigated, the teachers who transmit the Dao have been increased, and the learning of the classics and rituals has been advanced.[13]

Huizong made other efforts as well to raise the status of court physicians. In 1117 he had a new set of rank titles issued just for physicians, with the top one being the Grand Master of Health and Peace. He also

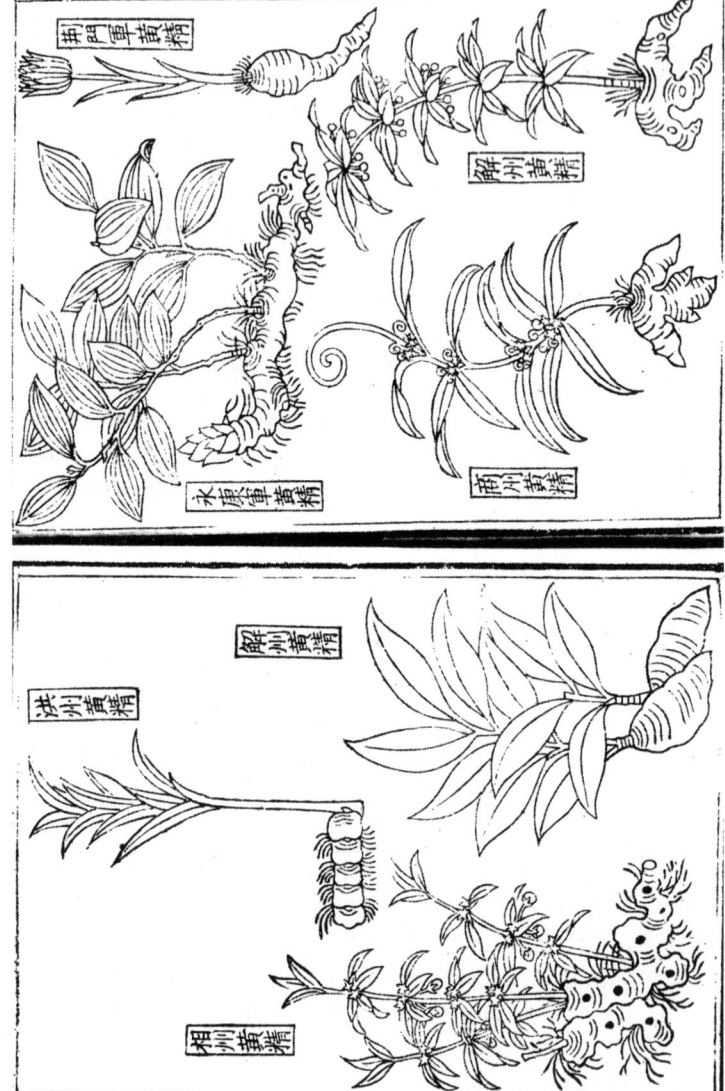

Fig. 7.1. Pages from the *Revised Material Medica of the Zhenghe Period, Classified and Verified from the Classics and Histories*. These pages show pictures of Yellow Essence (*Polygonatum*) from different prefectures. (CXBC 6.3b–4a)

used the term "scholar-physician" to refer to the best type of physician, well-grounded in learning.[14]

Some physicians gained appointments at Huizong's court by submitting medical books. Zhu Gong had passed the civil service examinations in 1088 but later retired and took up medical study, eventually writing a book on treatment of Cold Damage disorders titled *Book for Saving Lives as at Nanyang*. The book was well received and as a consequence in 1114 Zhu Gong was appointed as professor of the Medical School. Similarly, Kou Zongshi earned an appointment to an office that handled drug purchases by submitting an innovative medical book to the throne titled *Dilations on Materia Medica*. Out of the huge materia medica, he selected 472 drugs important for clinical practice for extended discussion. He took particular aim at alchemy and drugs taken to attain longevity, saying that they had caused many deaths.[15] Joseph Needham is particularly impressed by Kou Zongshi's mineralogy and discussion of fossils. In an example of the common ground shared by medicine and Daoism, Kou's book was incorporated into the Daoist canon then being compiled under Huizong's patronage.[16]

Huizong put some of his court doctors to work compiling medical texts. Early on Huizong appointed a group of medical scholars to revise a huge manuscript on materia medica originally produced by a medical scholar working privately. The revision, finished in 1108, was titled the *Materia Medica of the Daguan Period, Classified and Verified from the Classics and Histories;* it detailed 1,744 drugs, giving information on how they should be processed and prescriptions that employed them, both of which were innovative features. The illustrations were designed to allow identification of plants and recognition of differences in form when the plant grew in different locations and climates (see Figure 7.1). In 1116 Huizong had a team of his medical officials, led by Cao Xiaozhong, revise the book and reprint it, now titled *Revised Materia Medica of the Zhenghe Period, Classified and Verified from the Classics and Histories*. The names and offices of the twelve medical officials who worked on the revision have been preserved, giving a sense of the scale of the work.[17]

Another influential medical work Huizong commissioned was the *Comprehensive Manual for Sagely Benefaction of the Zhenghe Period*. Begun in 1111, it was not finished till around 1122. Huizong got personally involved in the work on this book, which eventually reached two hundred chapters and included more than twenty thousand prescriptions or formulas, along with information on such treatments as diet, exercise, acupuncture, moxibustion, incantations, and amulets. Compared to earlier formularies, this book used fewer infusions and more powders, ointments, pallets, and boluses. In his preface, Huizong said that he had "ordered those in the empire with technical skills to present their [knowledge] to the throne" and was including their contributions in the appendix.[18]

In 1118, when Huizong was deeply absorbed in Divine Empyrean Daoism, he issued under his own name a ten-chapter theoretical treatise on medicine, the *Classic of Sagely Benefaction*. Asaf Goldschmidt describes it as the first book in a thousand years to discuss the principles of classical medical theory. It discusses microcosm and macrocosm, the visceral system of functions, circulation tracts, diet, techniques for prolonging one's life, and drug therapy. Central to this book is the theory of the Five Circulatory Phases and the Six Seasonal Influences *(wu yun liu qi)*. This theory, in Goldschmidt's words, "provides a pattern that relates the Yin-yang and Five Phases modalities to the changes of the seasons and the sixty-year-based Chinese calendar. According to this doctrine, as long as all the seasonal changes and characteristics appear at their proper time, corresponding changes in the body should occur. However, when climatic factors appear off-schedule, for example a heat wave in the middle of winter or a snowstorm in summer, then these untimely changes promote diseases."[19] Even if Huizong drafted parts of *Sagely Benefaction* himself, he would surely have discussed issues in it with his medical staff (and may have been happy for them to submit drafts of some chapters or sections). One of the officials at the Medical School, Wu Ti, wrote a commentary to explicate this text, suggesting the possibility that he might have taught it at the school.[20]

Huizong was by no means the only nonprofessional to write on medicine in Song times. Even in fields where many practitioners were not literati, some men of letters gained expert knowledge in the theoretical texts of the field. This was especially true in music, medicine, and astronomy. Polymaths, who could write intelligently on a wide range of practical and theoretical issues, were much admired. In the late eleventh century both Su Shi and Shen Gua wrote on medical matters, as did several less well known literati.[21]

Builders

Huizong rarely criticized his predecessors—but he did disparage earlier Song emperors' taste in architecture. Less than six weeks after he took the throne, Huizong told his councilors that he thought the palace compound was too ornate. "The palace is excessively ornamented," Huizong complained. "The walls, ceiling, beams, and pillars resemble jewelry with their gold paint and 'feathers and fur' embellishments." The worst of all was Jade Void Hall, built only a few years earlier, which he considered "an extreme case of over-the-top decoration."[22] Zeng Bu, who recorded the conversation, agreed that Jade Void Hall should never have been built. However, he praised the painting in some of the halls at the northern suburb temple complex, another project completed during Zhezong's reign. Huizong countered that restraint characterized some of the halls for serving tea, but others were overly ornamented.[23] The next day, two of the leading eunuchs in the palace, Hao Sui and Liu Youduan, were assigned out of the palace because their management of painting and calligraphy production in the Rear Garden workshops had led to excesses.[24]

Huizong soon had many opportunities to construct buildings more to his taste. Like his predecessors, he presided over a steady stream of building projects. During the early years of his reign he made regular use of the talents of Li Jie, the official who had overseen the construction of his princely mansion in the 1090s. During Huizong's first year on the throne, Li Jie submitted the revision of the official architectural manual which he been working on since 1097. This book, the *Building Standards (Yingzao fashi)*, was designed to help officials who had to supervise stone masons, carpenters, surveyors, and the other craftsmen.[25] It provides 193 illustrations as well as detailed discussions of everything from formulas for paint to making tiles in kilns and sawing beams. In contrast to the books on medicine just discussed, this book is overwhelmingly technical rather than theoretical, and uses the jargon of carpenters and other craftsmen. It would have been especially useful to the six officials in the Palace Building Directorate, where Li Jie had served for eight years. According to the *Song History*, that office was responsible for the construction and upkeep of "buildings, city walls, bridges, boats, and carriages," managing "all craftsmen of earth and wood work," storing materials and tools, supervising training programs, scheduling projects, and keeping accounts.[26]

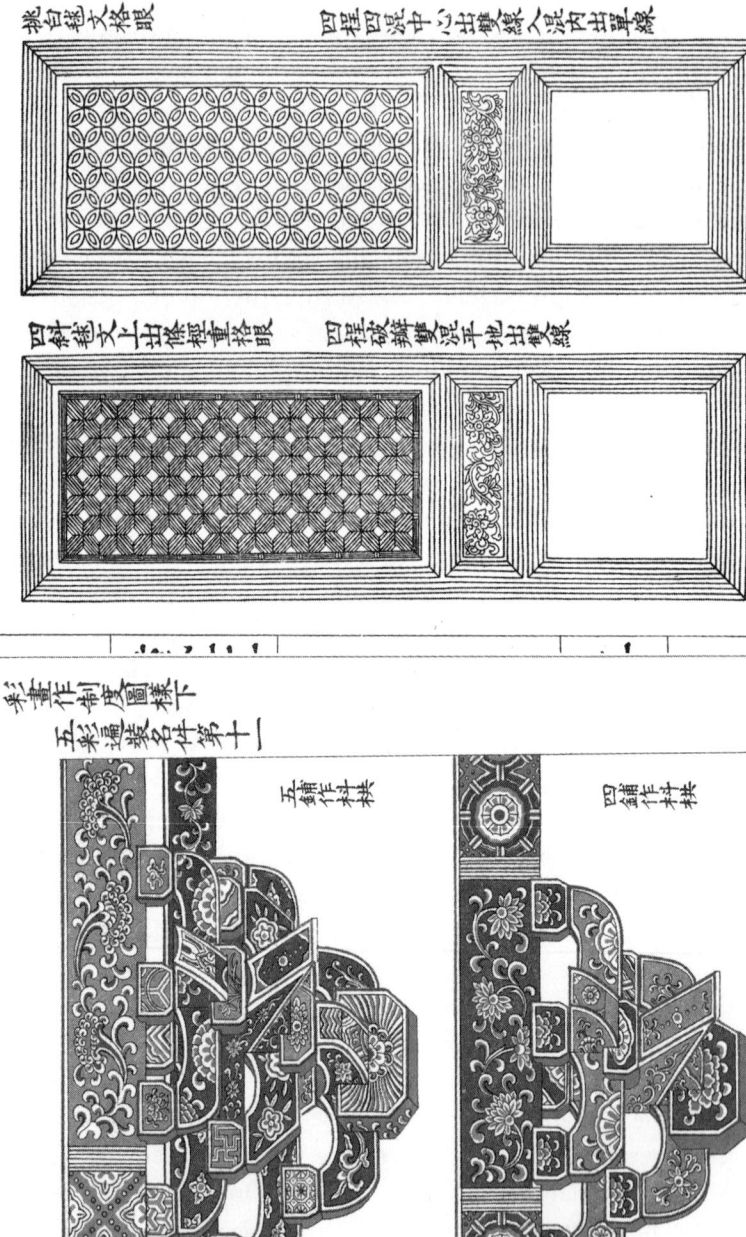

桃台毬文格眼　　　四程四混中心出雙線入混內出單線

四斜毬文上出條重格眼　　四程破瓣雙混平地出雙線

彩畫作制度圖樣下
五彩徧裝名件第十一

五鋪作枓栱

四鋪作枓栱

Fig. 7.2. Two pages from *Building Standards*, showing elaborately decorated roof supports, left, and two sample designs for doors, right. (YZFS 34.2a, 12.5a)

In terms of the scale of projects, the *Building Standards* provides instructions for eight grades of buildings, ranging from relatively small buildings with three columns across, to huge ones with ten or twelve columns on a side. The outer dimensions of these buildings ranged up to 150 feet or more on a side.[27] The book illustrates a great many designs that could be carved into stone steps, railings, column bases, and the like. Moreover, the wooden gates, doors, and windows could be made with a wide variety of designs. The elaborate brackets visible under the eaves of the roof would normally be painted, either in solid colors or patterns of flowers, mythical creatures, geometrical designs, or various combinations of elements, examples of which were provided (see Figure 7.2). Everything could be scaled up or down, as measures were relative rather than absolute.

Because the *Building Standards* specifies how much output to expect of workers, it indirectly provides evidence of the organization and degree of division of labor in government-sponsored construction projects. The labor unit was the "job" (*gong*), probably originating in the practice of drafting people for unpaid labor service. For porters, one job could involve carrying a load weighing sixty catties (*jin*) a distance of thirty *li* (about fifteen kilometers) and then returning. For those digging wells, it meant digging sixty feet. For carpenters, it could mean hewing a wooden column fifteen feet tall and one foot one inch in diameter. But some tasks were so labor-intensive that they had to be specified in terms of the number of jobs that would be credited for completing a task. For those decorating a pillar foundation stone with surface carving, the number of jobs depended on the size of the stone and the depth of the relief carving. A carver got credit for fifty jobs for carving a 3.5-foot stone base with decoration of protruding water, land, clouds, and dragons. However, he would get credit for only forty jobs if the decoration was of flowers, and only thirty if the design did not protrude.[28]

Li Jie's privately written funerary biography traces the promotions in rank that he received with the completion of each building project. He probably started at the lowest rank of 9b. With the completion of the mansions for Huizong and his four brothers in the late 1090s, his rank rose to 8b, two steps up from the bottom. By that point he had been working in the Palace Building Directorate for eight years and had received the commission to revise the *Building Standards*. After he submitted it he had to retire to mourn his mother who had just passed away, but in 1102 he returned to the Palace Building Directorate as vice director. The next year he asked for a provincial assignment to be able to take better care of his father, but within a few months was called back to take charge of the construction of the Biyong Academy. When it was completed he was made director of palace buildings and served in that post for the next five years. After completing work on the Department of State Affairs buildings, he was promoted to rank 8a. When he finished the renovation of Dragon Virtue Palace/Temple (Huizong's old princely mansion), he was promoted to rank 7b. With the work on the complex for the imperial clan members who were descended from Shenzong's brothers (that is, Huizong's first cousins), he reached rank 7a. When the rebuilding of Vermilion Bird Gate was done, he was granted the privilege of wearing the robes of officials of rank 5, and for work on Spectacular Dragon Gate and the Temple of the Nine Completions to hold the Nine Cauldrons, he was moved up to rank 6b. The next project was the Kaifeng prefectural office complex, which brought promotion to rank 6a. Adding new structures to the Supreme Shrine in 1106 brought the privilege of wearing the robes of rank 3 officials. After he completed a Buddhist temple dedicated to Huizong's deceased mother, he reached rank 5b. When Li Jie asked for leave because his father was ill, Huizong sent a court physician with him as well as a gift of a million cash. In 1107 or 1108 his father died and Li Jie had to retire from office once again. In 1110, when Huizong saw Li Jie's brother at an audience, he asked about him, and on learning that he had taken a prefectural post, sent a messenger to summon him back. Before the messenger arrived, however, Li Jie had died.[29]

It is easy to imagine that Huizong enjoyed his interactions with the multitalented Li Jie. An avid book collector, Li Jie had copied in his own hand several thousand books. He also was skilled at both calligraphy and painting. Somewhere along the way he found time to write books on horses, the game of Liubo, the musical instrument the pipa, the ancient seal script, as well as history and geography. Li Jie's biographer portrays Huizong as taking a personal interest in him. Li Jie wrote a *Record of the Rebuilding of Vermilion Bird Gate* in small seal script, which he presented to Huizong. Huizong esteemed it so much that he ordered it carved on stone and placed at the base of the gate. When Huizong heard that Li Jie was good at painting, he sent someone to let him know he would like to see something by him, and Li Jie sent a painting of five horses, which Huizong praised.[30]

Other sources also suggest that Huizong closely involved himself in buildings he commissioned. Deng Chun, writing in 1167, reported that Huizong went himself to inspect the murals his painters did at Dragon Virtue Palace/Temple early in his reign, and was disappointed to find only one painting fully satisfactory.[31] The Biyong Academy was a larger project as it involved four lecture halls and one hundred residence halls housing thirty students each, for a total of 1,872 room-units.[32] In a stone inscription erected after the construction was completed, Huizong is described as reviewing the plans with Li Jie but then calling for some changes. His words were quoted: "In ancient times schools always had sacrifices to the Former Teacher [i.e., Confucius]. Here we are gathering several thousand scholars from every region. We ought to enlarge the image hall [for the sacrifices] and put it in front, move the library to the rear, and lay out the lecture mats in the four corners. The rest can be as you designed."[33] In 1105, when a proposal to build a Bright Hall was made, Huizong specifically asked that Li Jie come to the audience to discuss the proposed plan. At the audience, Huizong stressed to Li Jie that the construction should use high-grade materials and be done in a way designed to last.[34]

Li Jie came from an official family, as his father, grandfather, and great-grandfather had all held office. Even though he did not take the civil service examinations (entering instead through the protection privilege extended to his father), Li Jie held regular civil service positions, not the lower-ranked technical posts like the experts in medicine, astronomy, and painting. He seems to have become a specialist by accident, by doing well when he was appointed to an entry level post in the Palace Building Directorate. As a consequence, he spent most of his career there, moving step by step from the lowest post to the highest one. In the preface to the *Building Standards* he said that he had acquired knowledge of construction techniques by talking to master carpenters and other craftsmen. Before Huizong came to the throne, after fifteen years in office he had risen only two steps, but under Huizong, who clearly appreciated him, in the next seven or eight years he rose six steps.

Huizong continued to have buildings built after Li Jie's death in 1110, but we know nothing about who designed them. Li Jie was not considered important enough to be given a biography in the *Song History*, and little would be known about him had the *Building Standards* and his funerary biography not survived. For all we know, one of Li Jie's subordinates in the Palace Building Directorate may have succeeded to his post and designed the many buildings Huizong had built during the next fifteen years of his reign.

The Painting School

Huizong was continuing a long tradition in employing court painters. Zhang Yanyuan's *Celebrated Painters of All the Dynasties* written in 847 praised the work of many painters active at the Tang court, including the horse painter Han Gan, the highly versatile figure painter Wu Daozi, and Zhang Xuan, who was best known for his paintings of palace women.[35] Even after the breakup of the Tang dynasty, some of the successor states attracted and employed highly capable painters, especially the state of Shu in Sichuan, and the Later Tang, with its capital at modern Nanjing. When these states were absorbed into Song in the 960s and 970s, their artists were brought to Kaifeng, where they formed the nucleus of the Song court painting establishment. By 998, the Painting Bureau had three painters in attendance, six apprentice painters, four assistant painters, and forty students.[36]

Several types of sources offer glimpses of Huizong's relationships with court painters. These range from government documents on the curriculum adopted for the Painting School from early in his reign, to the catalogue of his huge painting collection, compiled after he had been on the throne two decades, to anecdotes recorded decades or centuries later about the exacting standards to which he held his court painters, and to a handful of surviving paintings done by painters at his court. Taken together, these sources provide persuasive evidence that Huizong put thought and effort into upgrading the work of court painters and did not hesitate to deal with painters in person rather than through intermediaries.

It should be remembered that, even before Huizong came to the throne, he had both studied painting and begun to collect paintings. Knowing how to paint and appreciating fine paintings surely influenced what he wanted his court painters to do. Before long Huizong decided that he needed to upgrade the skills of court painters. According to Deng Chun, Huizong's disappointment in the work of painters recruited from across the country to do paintings on the walls of a new temple building early in his reign motivated him to reform painters' training.[37] He decided that he needed two types of painters, one able to accurately capture a likeness, the other also capable of combining poetry and painting and infusing ideas into painting.

Painters had been trained at court before Huizong's time, but not in a systematic way.[38] As part of the overhaul of the education system, in 1104 the Painting School was put under the Directorate of Education. It offered a three-year training program with instruction in six subjects: religious art, figures, landscape, birds and animals, flowers and bamboo, and architecture. The students had to be literate and were given instruction in etymology from the ancient dictionaries including the *Shuowen* and *Erya*, giving them a foundation in calligraphy. On the basis of a preliminary exam on their understanding of these subjects, sixty students would be selected and divided into two groups of thirty each: those who would combine scholarship and painting, and those who would do miscellaneous painting, requiring less mastery of literary traditions. None of the other technical schools had two tracks (and they also admitted larger classes). Those in the scholar group would have to study one major and one minor classic plus the *Analects* or the *Mencius*. The others could study one of the minor classics or books on philology.[39] In judging students, the highest grade was given to those able to "catch the feelings, form, and color of the subject in an entirely natural manner, with the tone of the brush lofty but simple, all without imitating earlier masters." Second best were those who "in imitating old masters are able to go beyond the sense of antiquity, whose forms and colors correspond to the subject, and whose application of color and design are ingenious." The lowest grade went to those who could "make accurate copies of paintings." Students who pursued the scholar track would get titles in the civil rank hierarchy, while those in the miscellaneous track would continue as before to get titles in the military rank system.[40]

Huizong set high standards for his court painters and painting students. Deng Chun, who reported that candidates came in a steady stream to study in the Painting School and take its exams, claimed that many were rejected because they could not attain a satisfactory level of "form-likeness." Those who were too free were said to lack technique.[41]

Perhaps he was referring specifically to the students in the "miscellaneous track," as there is ample evidence that the examinations for the students studying on the literati painting track were designed to weed out students who could not convey ideas.

Exams for students in the literati track involved creating a painting that captured a poetic couplet, an ability that went way beyond draftsmanship. Deng Chun wrote:

One examination topic consisted of the poetic couplet: "No passenger crosses the river in the wilderness. / A lonely skiff all day cross-wise." Most painters depicted an empty boat tied to the shore, perhaps with an egret resting on it or crows nesting on its awning. One, however, took a different approach and depicted a boatman lying in the back of his boat, playing a flute. He showed a boatman, but a boatman with nothing to do because there were no passengers. Another topic was "The disordered mountains hide an ancient temple." The highest scorer depicted desolate mountains filling the sheet, above which stood out a Buddhist banner which conveyed the meaning of "hidden." The others showed the top of a pagoda or a corner ornament. Some even showed temple halls, failing entirely to convey the meaning of "hidden."[42]

Deng Chun elsewhere cited the example of the line, "In the dream of the butterfly, the house is ten thousand *li* away." The painter Zhan Dechun was ranked highest for a painting of Su Wu dozing while herding sheep.[43]

Another author, Yu Cheng, in a work with a preface dated 1200, gave further examples of test assignments and stressed the fundamental similarity of the painting test and the civil service exams, as both selected for exceptional talent. According to Yu, for the topic "A tavern in a bamboo grove by a bridge," Huizong was most impressed by the painter who did not draw a tavern but hinted at its existence by showing a pole with a flag with the word for "wine" just barely visible above a bamboo grove.[44] Another topic posed to the candidates was "The scent of trampled flowers follows the hoofs of the returning horse." Conveying scent visually is not easy, but, according to Yu Cheng, one painter found a way to illustrate it perfectly by painting some butterflies following the horse and fluttering around its hoofs.[45] Another

Southern Song author, Yu Wenbao, referred to an exam with the couplet, "Above the tender greens on the branch, one dot of red./ To move men, spring's colors need not be abundant."[46] The painter ranked best depicted a woman leaning against a railing atop a building surrounded by green bamboo. A Ming author, giving only the first line of the couplet, reported a different winner. The one judged best ignored the allusion to a woman and painted the sea with a myriad ripples and a round red sun.[47]

The last example appeared for the first time in a book written several centuries after Huizong's time, so one cannot exclude the possibility that by then people had dreamed up some new assignments and clever ways to respond to them. The overall idea behind Huizong's tests for literati painters is, however, clear: the painter should create images that worked indirectly, by suggestion, much as poets composed poems. Each time the painter ranked highest had, in Ronald Egan's words, "transferred to his art the ideal that had long been valued as the highest achievement in poetry: capturing meaning that lies beyond the words."[48] It is also worth noting that the paintings that were made in response to these assignments were mostly landscapes, probably the sorts of "small scenes" that survive in large numbers from the Song but are generally dated to the Southern Song.[49] Although it would not have been difficult to find couplets that could inspire bird-and-flower paintings, as there are plenty of poems that mention birds and flowers, there is no evidence that that was done. Perhaps Huizong did not think court traditions of bird-and-flower painting were in as much need of new directions.

Huizong may have participated in judging the paintings done in response to these assignments, but he also recruited established literati painters to serve as professors at the school. According to Cai Tao, the first to hold the post was Song Zifang. Deng Chun claimed that "At that time Zifang's brushwork and use of ink were the most outstanding of his generation; hence everyone said that he was the appropriate choice." Another person appointed to the post was Mi Fu, perhaps on the recommendation of Cai Jing or Wang Shen.[50] Mi Fu, a rather eccentric personality, had an established reputation as a painter and calligrapher as well as a collector and connoisseur of both painting and calligraphy. Mi Fu made it known that he wanted a post at Huizong's court. At different times he wrote to Jiang Zhiqi and Deng Xunwu, both on the Council of State, asking for their help. Mi Fu's letters to both of them survive, the one to Jiang Zhiqi amusing in offering him language he could use in his recommendation to Huizong, such as "[Mi Fu] relies on his own talents and has nothing to do with factions. He is old now and hampered by his qualifications. If it were his misfortune to die one day without having the opportunity to enrich His Majesty's enterprise and thus embellish His Majesty's magnanimity, this official would consider it a pity."[51]

No anecdotes survive depicting Mi Fu interacting with students at the school, but there are some humorous anecdotes of his meetings with Huizong. The following, recorded by a contemporary named He Wei, can serve as an example.

> When Mi Fu was professor at the Calligraphy School, one day the emperor visited the Rear Garden. It was springtime, and everything was beautiful, and the honor guard was neatly arranged. A messenger summoned Mi Fu. After he arrived, a scroll in a black silk wrapper was taken out and Huizong said, "I know that you are able to write large characters. Do some on this scroll for me." Mi Fu expressed his gratitude, then immediately took the silk, licked the brush, and unrolled the scroll. His divine rhymes were attractively done. The twenty large characters read:
>
> > With my eyes I look at the nine sources of light shine.
> > The clouds pace and rise like steam, then there is thunder.
> > I cannot tell if heaven is close or far.
> > I personally see the arrival of jade augustness.
>
> Very pleased, the emperor conferred a generous reward.[52]

Mi Fu held the school position less than a year, but we do not know if it was he who found the duties unrewarding or Huizong who found Mi Fu unsatisfactory.

In 1110, after Cai Jing was dismissed as grand councilor the second time, Huizong placed each of the technical schools under the government agency that needed its graduates rather than the Directorate of Education. This reorganization does not seem to have signaled a lessened commitment on Huizong's part to the training of painting students, which continued. In 1113, when Cai Jing returned as grand councilor, the schools of medicine and mathematics were again put under the Directorate of Education, but not the Painting School. Shimada Hidemasa argues that the Painting School was never reestablished because Huizong had achieved what he wanted in terms of stronger literary educations for his painters and after 1110 was content to work directly with the painters in the Painting Bureau.[53]

Court Painters

If the numbers of painting students were maintained at the level of sixty at a time, with twenty graduating each year from 1104 to 1110, there would not have been enough vacancies in the court Painting Bureau to absorb all of them, so we must assume that some of those who entered the program had to find employment elsewhere.

For those who were offered court painting positions, perhaps especially those who had gone through the literati track, Huizong made gestures to raise their status. He ruled that specially favored court painters were eligible to wear the fish pendant attached to their belt. He also saw to it that, when all officials lined up according to rank, court painters stood ahead of lute players and such craftsmen as jade carvers. Another symbolic gesture was calling the compensation calligraphers and painters received "salary," the same term used for the compensation given civil servants, rather than "food money," the term used for craftsmen who were treated more like servants. On the other hand, it was required that one of the "miscellaneous" (nonliterati) painters be on call at Sagacious Thoughts Hall in case the emperor felt a need for his services, something less commonly required of civil servants.[54]

We know the names of more than fifty painters who worked at Huizong's court.[55] The records often say where they came from, what sort of paintings they specialized in, or whom they took as their teachers or models. Among painters' specialties, landscape and figure or religious paintings were most common, followed by bird, flower, and animal painting. Some painters were even more specialized, concentrating on dragons, bamboo, architectural paintings, children, or ghosts. The painter mentioned most frequently as a model or teacher was the landscape specialist during Shenzong's and Zhezong's period, Guo Xi.

Liu Yi was one of the more accomplished painters at Huizong's court. He had been given the job of painting a hundred monkeys on the corridor to the rooms occupied by one of Huizong's favorite consorts, Liu Mingda. To Liu Yi's dismay, he never got a personal interview with Huizong, reportedly because he stuttered.[56] By implication, Huizong must have met and talked with most of his painters.

Huizong considered making copies to be good training for his court artists and he had paintings from his collection regularly shown to them. Painters who had painted for Huizong told Deng Chun that "every ten days two cases of paintings from the palace collection would be brought out and the emperor would order a high-ranking palace functionary to take them to the bureau to show to the painters." To see that they were not damaged, guards remained present. As a result of these opportunities, Deng Chun concluded, "artists of that time developed a fine mastery, enabling them to comply with the emperor's wishes."[57]

There are scattered stories, undoubtedly amusing to those who heard them, that Huizong was a very tough critic of his court artists' work. Deng Chun is the original source for three such stories. As mentioned above, Huizong inspected the work his painters were doing at Dragon Virtue Palace/Temple. According to Deng Chun, he found only one painting he could praise. He later explained to an attendant why he had richly rewarded this painter: "Few are skillful enough to paint the tea rose, for its flowers, stamens, and leaves differ with the seasons and time of day. The rose in this painting is exactly like one at noon on a spring day."[58] The Huizong depicted in this anecdote is something of a show-off, demonstrating his exceptional powers of critical discrimination.

Stories of this sort were not new. Guo Ruoxu, writing in the 1080s, recorded a story of a rustic who pointed out to an artist that his painting of fighting oxen was flawed because oxen do not stick up their tails when they are fighting. Shen Gua, in a book written about 1090, tells of a connoisseur who praised the accuracy of a picture of a cat under peonies because both the cat and the peonies were portrayed at midday—evidenced by the narrow slit of the pupil in the cat's eyes, and the wide open, dry petals of the peony. As James Cahill points out, the anecdotes about Huizong's insistence on getting the details right mark "perhaps the last moment in the history of Chinese painting when such a criterion of literal truthfulness could be seriously advanced: the literati critics' dismissal of form-likeness, once their doctrines had come to prevail, relegated concern for representational accuracy to the philistines."[59]

What did Huizong accomplish by taking a personal interest in the work of court artists? Did the influx of resources and attention lead to a spurt in artistic creativity? Or, just the opposite, did his insistence on accuracy have a deleterious effect, as artists were rewarded not for experimenting but for being careful? Michael Sullivan sees Huizong as imposing "a dictatorship of form and taste upon his academicians as rigid as that of Le Brun over the artists working for Louis XIV." To him, "the imposition of a rigid orthodoxy laid the foundation for a decorative, painstaking 'palace style' which was to govern court taste until modern times." Other art historians, by contrast, give Huizong credit for the successful combination of poetry and painting that continued to flourish among court painters long after his day.[60]

To pursue these issues it is necessary to identify paintings by Huizong's court painters. So far, art historians have not identified very many. One reason is that Song court painters did not routinely sign and date their works. Although we have the names of several dozen painters who worked at Huizong's court, it is difficult to link them to surviving paintings, most of which are neither signed nor dated. Then, since Huizong did not list his own court artists in the catalogue of his painting collection, we have no painting titles linked to names as we do for eleventh-century court painters in the catalogue. The many anonymous paintings generally taken to be the product of the Song court are dated only roughly by style. The problem here is that Huizong's period was one of stylistic transition, falling between the classic Northern Song—monumental landscapes, large hanging scrolls or screens of birds and flowers—and the classic Southern Song—small, intimate scenes and poetic album leaves. In landscape, for instance, not only did some artists still paint large central mountains, but painters like Zhao Lingrang, Liang Shimin, and Li Anzhong were painting much more intimate scenes, including riverscapes without any mountains at all. Anonymous paintings of this sort are usually identified as "Southern Song" by art historians, but some could well have originated at Huizong's court. The same is true of bird-and-flower paintings. Although we know that Huizong was fond of the genre and that his court produced hundreds if not thousands of small bird-and-flower pictures, most anonymous Song bird-and-flower album leaves are loosely classified as "Southern Song."[61] Still, there are some very fine works that art historians do attribute to Huizong's court and can be used to assess what Huizong was able to accomplish through his court painters.

Another challenge is to understand how politics impinged on court painting production. A basic question here is who is addressing whom. Is the emperor the agent, using the painter to communicate to an audience? Or is the emperor the intended audience? In earlier eras, when most court paintings were done on walls or screens, the question of audience was simple: paintings were meant to be seen by those who lived in or spent time in a hall. Walls in temples, audience halls, and the women's quarters were decorated with different subject matter. Some pictures were meant simply to be decorative, but others clearly were intended to convey ideas. Just as Buddhas and bodhisattvas were painted on the walls of temples, the walls of the more public palace halls often had portraits of acclaimed figures or narrative paintings of morally uplifting stories. By contrast, paintings done on scrolls, fans, and album leaves were portable and kept rolled up or stored in boxes much of the time. Since they were not on constant display, questions of audience are more complex.

When a painting does not have a helpful inscription, inferring agency, audience, and meaning is more an art than a science. Many scholars have vigorously debated the agent, intended audience, and message of the Song masterpiece, *Peace Reigns over the River*, believed by some to have been made at Huizong's court, but quite possibly the product of another reign.[62] In my view, not all paintings carried political meanings beyond the obvious message that the court was able to attract and cultivate men capable of producing beautiful objects. Uninscribed landscapes and bird-and-flower paintings could demonstrate Huizong's elegant taste and artistic sophistication without carrying more specific meanings. This was of course also true of many of the items of fine craftsmanship made for the court—such as textiles, ceramics, jade-carving, and jewelry. These objects added to the splendor of the court without saying much about the politics of the court.

Of the paintings that carried political meaning, it is useful to distinguish ones made to flatter the ruler from those intended as a form of propaganda, to influence a broader audience. Chinese courts—like courts elsewhere—were places where flattery was raised to a high art.

Many court paintings that others have seen as forms of political propaganda I think are better thought of as panegyric. This involves a shift in understood agency—from seeing the active agent as the emperor who is addressing a wider audience whom he wants to persuade of his merits—to seeing the emperor as the intended audience, and the agent as either the painter himself or someone who told him what to paint, such as a high-ranking official, eunuch supervisor, or a palace woman. It was a diversification strategy for them to flatter the emperor not only in writing but also in pictures.

Here I examine five of the paintings with the best claim to having been made at Huizong's court—a figure painting, two bird-and-flower paintings, and two landscapes—to show the success of Huizong's efforts to upgrade the work of his court painters and explore issues of meaning, agency, and purpose. Huizong used the resources of the court and his own talent and interest in painting to bring court painting to a new high. At the same time, paintings made at his court were quite varied. Some had explicit political meaning—usually made clear through an inscription. Others, I believe, were intended to convey Huizong's artistic sophistication and refinement, but do not carry political meanings in any narrow sense. While many were given away, even more remained in the palace where very few people ever saw them.

A good candidate for a painting made to flatter the ruler is *Literary Gathering* (Plates 3 and 4), a painting thought to have been done by one or more of Huizong's court artists and graced with inscriptions by both Huizong and Cai Jing.[63] This painting is reminiscent of several other Song court paintings, each of which has a balustrade that cuts through the painting, marking the foreground as palace garden space.[64] It focuses on a large banquet table, elaborately set with cups, plates, bowls, flowers, and food. Eight men in the clothes of literati are seated around the table, assisted by servants; two others are having a conversation nearby. Close to the viewer, servants are preparing tea. Although *Literary Gathering* has suffered extensive damage, its technical polish is still evident. The leaves of the trees are all individually drawn, and coarse brushstrokes give a rough texture to the tree trunks. The figures are well drawn, observed from several angles, and meticulously rendered, with shading on many of the men's clothes and individual hairs drawn in one by one on their beards.

One feature that makes this painting stand out from the other paintings of palace gardens is the inscription of two poems. In the upper right, Huizong inscribes the title *Literary Gathering* and adds a quatrain:

> Learned scholars and our glorious land are the same past
>   and present.
> Poets wield brushes and compose verses drunk and sober.
> Many new scholars have joined the literary company.
> We rejoice at meeting these great minds in painting.

In this poem Huizong evokes the glory of elegant literary gatherings, states that in the past and present alike scholars have gotten together to chant poetry and drink, alludes to the pleasure in having so many talents within reach, and praises the painting for letting us see such literary elegance. In the upper left is Cai Jing's response, which uses the same rhyme words. He compares Huizong's ability to attract talented men to the eighteen scholars who were recruited by Tang Taizong, a well-known story.[65] Cai Jing goes on to imply that their own time surpasses the Tang because Huizong has attracted many more than just eighteen scholars:

> Times have changed since the Tang dynasty,
> And great scholars of the past have now departed.
> How amusing that the Eighteen Scholars of those years
> Must wait to see who is more commendable![66]

From the inscriptions we know that Huizong and Cai Jing looked at the painting together and considered its meaning. Chinese figure and narrative paintings often allude to stories that carry Confucian moral messages, and they assign that sort of meaning here.[67] Quite plausibly Cai Jing uses the painting to flatter Huizong; one can imagine that the former suggested the subject to either a painter or someone supervising court painters in order to use it in this way.

Bird-and-flower paintings did not usually carry the same sorts of meanings as figure paintings. The introduction to these paintings in Huizong's painting catalogue lays emphasis on how varied and rich both birds and flowers are, and how people enjoy viewing them. It brings up the large number of birds and flowers mentioned in the

Book of Songs and that since then poets have been able to lodge meaning by referring to a faded flower or the silence or chirping of a bird, and that the most subtle of painters are able to achieve comparable effects.[68]

Two interesting bird-and-flower paintings made at Huizong's court are *Two Birds on a Blossoming Wax Plum* and *Pheasant on a Hibiscus Branch* (Plates 5 and 6). Although in the past art historians treated these two paintings as works by Huizong, it is now recognized that Huizong claims only to have written the poem and done the calligraphy, making it likely that court artists did the painting.[69] These, thus, are examples of Huizong's collaboration with court artists. Both paintings could well have been made to present to someone as a gift.

The two paintings have identical inscriptions: "Both composed and inscribed by the emperor in Harmony Revealed Hall," followed by Huizong's cipher (two graphs that taken together mean "the one man in all under heaven" *[tianxia yiren]*). To add to the similarities, both of the surviving paintings are of nearly identical size, varying by less than two centimeters in each dimension. And in both cases the composition seems to have been planned to leave a large open space for the poem, written in four lines of five characters in Slender Gold calligraphy. Even their subject matter and composition are similar. Both show one large and one small plant, with a bird or birds on the larger plant and insects nearby. In each the objects are arranged in a balanced way over the plane of the painting, with little attempt to depict depth or natural setting.

The poem on *Pheasant on a Hibiscus Branch* can be translated as follows:

> His autumn strength wards off the fearsome frost,
> With lofty cap, the brocade-feathered fowl;
> His knowledge complete, perfect in the Five Virtues,
> In ease and rest, he surpasses the ducks and widgeons.[70]

As Charles Hartman notes, the poem makes this painting an appropriate gift to a high official, perhaps on the occasion of a promotion. The poem implies that the recipient is to other men as the pheasant is to other birds: eminent, with a lofty cap (like officials wear), at ease among the more common folk (ducks and widgeons).[71]

The painting itself is finely crafted. It shows a brightly colored pheasant turning its head to look at two butterflies. The butterflies have been attracted to the blooming hibiscus and the smaller chrysanthemum below it. Movement is captured by showing the two butterflies from different angles, one seen mostly from above, the other more from the side with its rear wings raised. Physical presence is also conveyed by the way the pheasant weighs down one of the branches of the hibiscus. The key elements in the painting, the bird and butterflies, are painted in a meticulous, closely observed style. The patterns and colors of the bird's feathers are carefully delineated, down to the red tips on the tail feathers. This emphasis on the detail of the feathers can be seen as almost taxonomic, as though part of the motivation was to record the visual properties that distinguished each species.[72] In contrast, the leaves are done in a simple wash, with relatively little variation in tone, and there is no attempt to convey the rest of the setting, not even a hint of the ground plane.

Two Birds on a Blossoming Wax Plum is a less flashy painting; not only are the birds much less colorful, but instead of butterflies that catch one's attention, there are inconspicuous bees or wasps buzzing around the bush. The season is different, winter or early spring, not fall, and there are two small birds, not one large one. Moreover in *Two Birds*, no element of the picture is cut off; the entire wax plum bush and the small lily growing at its base are shown. The inscription for this painting can be translated as follows:

> Mountain birds, proud and unfettered,
> Plum blossoms' pollen, soft and light.
> The painting will be our covenant,
> Until a thousand autumns show upon our hoary heads.[73]

The two small birds depicted are called in Chinese "white heads," which is also a common term for those who have grown old. As the poem refers to the hoary heads of those who have been together a thousand autumns, the theme of this picture must be married love, with the two birds representing the couple who will remain together until their hair turns white. This painting would have made a good gift to present to a relative getting married or perhaps one whose long marriage was worth celebrating.[74]

What about the landscape paintings made by Huizong's court painters? Art historians have often interpreted court landscapes as carrying positive messages about the court or the dynasty, such as representing the grandeur and majesty of the emperor or the peace and prosperity of the era. Often, to support this interpretation, they cite a passage in an essay on landscape painting by the eleventh-century court painter Guo Xi. He described great mountains as dominating the nearby hills like a chief and added, "The general appearance is of a great lord glorious on the throne and a hundred princes hastening to pay him court, without any effect of arrogance or withdrawal [on either part]."[75] From this passage, scholars have inferred that a dominant central mountain represents the emperor. Some also see more specific messages. Alfreda Murck, for instance, describes Guo Xi's famous *Early Spring* as "an elegant metaphor for the success of the New Policies." To her it depicts "a dynamic, harmonious society and an ideal socio-political hierarchy. Court literary conventions prompt one to read in the composition a declaration that nature is flourishing in the warmth of spring just as the body politic is thriving under the beneficent, well-managed rule of the emperor."[76]

The two landscape paintings with the best claim to have been done by Huizong's court painters are Wang Ximeng's *Thousand Li of Rivers and Mountains*, in the Palace Museum, Beijing (Plates 7 and 8) and Li Tang's *Wind in the Pines amid Ten Thousand Valleys*, in the National Palace Museum, Taipei (Figure 7.3). Neither carries an inscription that articulates a political meaning or purpose.

Wang Ximeng's painting has a colophon written by Cai Jing in 1113 (this chapter's epigraph). It records that the artist was eighteen when he did the painting. The year before, when he was a student in the court Painting School, Huizong had recognized his exceptional talent and given him personal instruction, after which his painting greatly improved.[77] The most striking features of this painting are its brilliant colors and its size and scale. This painting is brighter than any other extant blue-green painting of the period, with thick mineral pigments. The painting also is huge, almost twelve meters long and half a meter tall. It depicts not merely mountains and rivers, but a succession of mountain ranges with their own paths, bridges, waterfalls, and so on. The land forms are highly varied and the recessions are convincing, features it owes to developments in landscape painting during the eleventh century.

Fig. 7.3. Li Tang, *Wind in the Pines amid Ten Thousand Valleys*, hanging scroll, ink and color on silk, 188.7 × 139.8 cm. (National Palace Museum, Taiwan, Republic of China)

Why was the painting done in bright blue and green? Some modern scholars have suggested that blue and green pigments in Song landscapes carried references to the realm of Daoist immortals.[78] In this case, however, the vast territory seems decidedly earthlike. It is not a remote region where only solitary scholars and Daoist recluses stray. Nor do any of the figures announce themselves as gods or immortals. Rather it is a world where houses and boats dot the landscape, and people catch fish, grind grain, and tend farms.

Other scholars have seen the use of blue and green as a gesture of respect for the past, homage to Tang use of those colors.[79] Wang Ximeng's painting borrows from Tang painting practices not only its colors, but other features such as the carefully drawn-in waves on the water, and perhaps the decision to feature people traveling through the landscape on foot, on horseback, and in boats. Its compositional methods, however, are entirely Song; mountains and trees are not outlined, the hills are volumetric, and the lighting effects are dramatic.

Certainly Huizong was familiar with Tang blue-and-green landscape paintings and could have shown them to his protégé. The catalogue of his painting collection included paintings by Li Sixun and Li Zhaodao, Tang painters known to have painted blue-and-green landscapes. At the end of the entry for Li Sixun, the cataloguer remarks that "People today who paint mountains in color often model themselves on him," but gives the practice no further meaning. Perhaps association with the two Lis was reason enough for painters to choose this style. The Lis were members of the Tang imperial clan during the period when Empress Wu persecuted the clan, and they survived into the reign of Emperor Xuanzong. Their ties to both Xuanzong and to the Tang imperial establishment probably gave them positive associations to Huizong. Huizong also surely knew of blue-green landscapes by his older contemporaries Wang Shen and Zhao Lingrang. Surviving examples of their blue-and-green landscapes are much more restrained than Wang Ximeng's, with a quite different sensibility and scale (see Figure 1.3).

Does Wang Ximeng's painting carry a political message? Murck sees it as a good example of how a landscape could depict mountains in ways that celebrate the hierarchy and stability of the state. She describes the painting as a "superb visualization of [Guo Xi's and Guo Si's] concept 'a great lord glorious on his throne and a hundred princes hastening to pay him court.'"[80] But in this painting there is no single dominant mountain but rather a succession of more or less equal ones.

To me, there is no need to identify a specific message in this painting. I think Huizong was satisfied with Wang Ximeng's work because the painting demonstrated that the court could cultivate painters capable of spectacular paintings, ones that showed mastery of illusionistic technique and grand imaginative powers.

Li Tang's *Wind in the Pines amid Ten Thousand Valleys* is dated by the artist to 1124 (see Figure 7.3).[81] It is a large painting, 189 by 140 centimeters, possibly originally made for a screen. Although the silk has darkened, traces of green paint can still be seen. It depicts a group of tall pine trees in the foreground, growing from rocks much like those in the hills and mountains behind them. Mists separate nearer hills from further ones. No people appear in the painting, nor much sign that people had ever intruded.

Art historians who discuss this painting tend to describe it very positively, either for leading the way toward the Southern Song style of landscape, especially through its use of "axe cut" brushwork to depict rocks, or for its adherence to the Northern Song dominant central mountain motif.[82] Wen C. Fong emphasizes both features, first comparing the painting to earlier large dominant central mountains by Fan Kuan and Guo Xi, then linking it to new trends:

> Li's landscape represents an intensive new realism with a narrowed focus, marking the beginning of the Southern Song "retreat toward the object." Whereas Fan Kuan's monumental landscape opens into the viewer's space, inviting him to step into an infinitely expanding world of nature, Li creates a world in which perfectly executed mountains and trees are framed by the four borders of the picture. Instead of Guo Xi's emotion-laden representation of a dynamic and changing nature, Li Tang's vision, reflecting that of Emperor Huizong, is harmonious and controlled. Replacing the immeasurable vastness of the earlier Northern Song landscapes with a more limited and realistic view, somber and restrained, Li's work prefigures the more intimate landscapes of the Southern Song.[83]

Richard Barnhart takes a somewhat different stance, seeing in this painting a departure from the "imperial image of landscape." Instead of seeing Huizong's vision in the painting, he finds in it evidence that

Huizong must have allowed court painters like Li Tang "considerable freedom to experiment with styles and techniques."[84]

These five paintings taken together demonstrate not only the technical skill and polish that Huizong's painters were capable of but also their creativity. They were doing new and creative things, including coupling poetry and painting. Huizong does not seem to have insisted that his painters all paint alike, or that all of their works carry political meanings. This should not be surprising. Since Huizong was fond of paintings that conveyed poetic sentiments, he should have been open to paintings that expressed as diverse a range of ideas and feelings as found in poetry.

Although three of the five paintings discussed here would seem to have been given away, the actual proportion of court paintings given away surely was much smaller. This can be seen from all the paintings that remained in the palace. Even though Guo Xi was one of Shenzong's favorite painters, the emperor rarely seems to have made gifts of Guo Xi paintings. When Guo Xi's son Guo Si was granted an audience in 1117, Huizong spoke of Shenzong's love of Guo Xi's paintings and mentioned that they still filled palace halls.[85] Similarly, from his painting catalogue we know that there were thousands of bird-and-flower paintings by earlier court artists still in the palace during Huizong's reign, never having been given away.[86] Many paintings, it would seem, were made not for any utilitarian reason but just to have.

⟿ WHAT DO WE LEARN about Huizong from his interactions with specialists and experts?

Although Huizong had many other demands on his time, he did not neglect this side of presiding over the court—indeed, he seems to have enjoyed working with masters and artists. He had enough confidence in his own critical acumen to direct his builders and painters to do things the way he proposed. He recruited a few exceptional men like Mi Fu and Li Jie to work at his court. He reorganized training in medicine, painting, calligraphy, and mathematics in the hope of attracting more highly educated men to these fields. In one case at least, Wang Ximeng's, he personally supervised a student's training. He pushed his court painters to master a highly descriptive style, probably knowing such technical virtuosity was not easily matched by artists working outside the court. Yet he also rewarded those able to paint in a poetic, allusive way.

Some of the works made by Huizong's masters and experts are still extant, including several medical books, the *Building Standards*, and a sizable body of court paintings. Huizong wrote a preface for one of the medical books, but we do not have anything Huizong wrote himself about the paintings of his court painters. We can make inferences from the extant paintings themselves, and consider the inscriptions on them by Huizong or Cai Jing when they exist. The sources that most color understanding of Huizong as a patron of artists, unfortunately, are the least reliable—the anecdotes recorded after his death, sometimes centuries after. Here I have tried to highlight the earliest ones, those written by Deng Chun, whose grandfather had served on Huizong's Council of State. But it is important to keep in mind that stories often get improved over time—even a few years is long enough for a story to develop new twists. These anecdotes let us see what people were saying about Huizong but are not necessarily true to the facts. Huizong undoubtedly did take an interest in the work of his painters, but he may not have said the words attributed to him in an anecdote.

Huizong found the works of his experts so interesting that he tried his own hand at them, not only writing a medical treatise but also painting pictures and doing calligraphy. To Huizong it would seem that so long as one was at heart a man of letters, expertise was entirely commendable. Even if we suspect that he may have passed off as his own work things done by his court experts, we should not lose sight of the fact that he wanted to be viewed as expert in these fields. Chapter 8 turns to what we can learn from Huizong's personal practice of the literati arts.

 *8*

Crafting an Image as an Artist

At the beginning of the Daguan period [1107] a banquet was held in the capital on the Lantern Festival. At the time, [the northwest territories of] Huang and Shan had been recovered, which Huizong referred to in a verse written for his officials. Its first couplet read: "At midnight the *sheng* pipes and singing connect everyone from the sea to the highest peaks; in the spring breezes the fire of the lanterns extends beyond Huangzhong." None of the couplets written by those who stepped forward to continue [the emperor's poem] were as good.

—*Hong Mai's observation, published in 1197*

*H*UIZONG WAS A REMARKABLY accomplished painter, poet, and calligrapher. Among the pieces of calligraphy attributed to Huizong in the collection of the Palace Museums in Taipei and Beijing are several undated transcriptions of poems that he apparently wrote himself.[1] Most of them are written out in slightly large calligraphy in standard script on a single sheet of paper. One stands out as different because it is much larger: the characters on it are about 12 centimeters tall, written out two per line on a handscroll 263 centimeters long (Figure 8.1). Sometimes this work is called *Two Poems*, on the understanding that the two quatrains are independent of each other, other times simply *Poem:*

Luxuriant and fragrant, the blue-black calyxes slant
  sideways,
Their radiant vigor fills the courtyard.
Soaked by beads of dew, they are limp as drunkards;
The scattered dew shines like melting snow.

Among the red and blue [painters' pigments], it is hard to
  put down the brush;

219

Fig. 8.1. Huizong, *Two Poems,* handscroll, ink on silk, 27.2 × 263.8 cm. (National Palace Museum, Taiwan, Republic of China)

> Only through creativity does one's merit remain behind.
> Dancing butterflies are confused by fragrant pathways;
> Fluttering about, they chase the evening breeze.[2]

This striking scroll is two art forms in one: it is poetry and it is a work of calligraphic art. Moreover, the second quatrain makes reference to a third art—painting—and comments on artistic creativity. The lasting power of products of the creative brush that it cites strikes a chord, as this scroll is one of a small group of works by Huizong that have survived in original form for about nine hundred years.

Whereas the emphasis in Chapter 7 was on Huizong's supervision of the cultural production of court artists working under him, in this chapter it is on his presentation of himself as an artist. There was no hard line between supervising others and doing things himself, especially since many of the artistic acts he performed were collaborative in one sense or another. Still, we should not miss the political meaning of Huizong's claiming credit for works of art. Performing as a man of letters was a central element in Huizong's performance of the role of emperor.

The idea that a single person could master the "Three Perfections"— poetry, calligraphy, and painting—dated back to the Tang period.[3] Mastering two of these arts was not all that rare. In the Tang period Wang Wei achieved eminence as a poet and as a painter. Among the cultural leaders of the generation before Huizong were several multi-talented literati, such as Su Shi and Huang Tingjian, admired for both their poetry and their calligraphy, and Mi Fu, known for both painting and calligraphy. Yet it remained uncommon for any single person to attain mastery of all three. Li Yu, ruler of the short-lived Later Tang dynasty in the tenth century, is a rare example and seems

to have served as a model for Huizong. The *Xuanhe Calligraphy Catalogue* drew attention to Li Yu's development of a distinctive tremulous "gold inlaid knife" calligraphy style: "His strokes were slender and stiff, with overflowing style-spirit, yet his calligraphy was very rarely seductive, resembling more closely the style of a poor hermit, a needy student, or a ragged hunched-shouldered pauper; it had no trace of the airs of the rich and high-ranking."[4] The entry in the *Painting Catalogue* stresses the connection between Li Yu's calligraphy and his painting:

> Mr. Li was a talented writer and good at both calligraphy and painting. In calligraphy he worked with a tremulous brush; its turning and curving resembled the intense strength of wintry pines and frost-covered bamboo. This style was known as "the gold-inlaid knife." His painting also was pure, lively, and distinctive, with a style all his own. His calligraphy and his painting were so much in the same mode that Tang Xiya, who began by studying Mr. Li's gold inlaid knife brushwork, later painted bamboo with the same sort of tremulous, struggling shapes as in his calligraphy. Mr. Li was also skilled at doing ink bamboo, and the two of them influenced each other.[5]

Huizong's Slender Gold Calligraphy

Like most calligraphers, Huizong could and did write in all the common scripts. Examples survive in cursive *(cao)*, running *(xing)*, and regular *(kai)* scripts. More than once he copied a text in ten scripts, which must have included clerical, seal, and other less common scripts.[6] What makes Huizong exceptional as a calligrapher, however, is not his versatility, but that by 1104, when he was twenty-one years old, he had developed a highly distinctive style of regular script, commonly dubbed "Slender Gold." He continued writing in this style throughout his reign, but some evolution can be observed. During Huizong's first five or six years on the throne, his Slender Gold calligraphy used exceptionally thin and stiff strokes, but by 1112 it had evolved in the direction of greater variation in the thickness of strokes and greater fluency.[7]

Two Poems is an excellent example of the mature Slender Gold style. There is a general angularity to the characters, with sharply chiseled corners rather than rounded ones. The upward slant common to characters in regular script is kept to a minimal level. Horizontal strokes end with pronounced stops; that is, they reveal rather than hide that the brush was brought back in the reverse direction (bottom character, fourth column from the right). *Na* strokes (strokes that sweep down and right) have a distinctive hitch in them (top characters, fifth and sixth columns from the right). *Pie* strokes (vertical strokes on the left of characters that slant slightly left) often begin with a curved corner (last column, far left, bottom character). Another very distinctive feature is the upward hooks at the end of strokes, which are lengthened and often curl, whether they are hooking to the left (first column, far right, top character) or the right (far left column, both characters). When this piece of calligraphy was exhibited abroad in 1961–1962 as part of the international exhibition of Chinese art treasures from the National Palace Museum, the cataloguers remarked that "the characters are composed of taut, attenuated lines, swelling and thinning gracefully." "The result," they wrote, "has a special reedy strength and considerable beauty, although it verges on preciousness."[8]

What was Huizong trying to convey by making his standard script so distinctive? In surviving texts, Huizong never explains his intentions, nor do his contemporaries raise them as an issue. Huizong, like everyone else, would have begun his education in calligraphy by copying the works of earlier masters, and historians of calligraphy usually begin their analyses of Huizong's style by identifying his models. Cai Tao, the only contemporary to discuss Huizong's calligraphic style, reported that in his youth Huizong was influenced by the styles of his teacher Wu Yuanyu and kinsman Zhao Lingrang, who in turn had modeled their calligraphy on the Tang calligrapher

Xue Ji and Huang Tingjian, respectively. Modern scholars have pursued these possible sources in various directions.[9] One can also point out similarities in overall approach between the Slender Gold style of calligraphy and the highly exacting style of painting birds and flowers that Huizong sometimes used. Tseng Yuho describes Huizong's calligraphy as "a painter's calligraphy." Yet even if we can detect in Huizong's calligraphy traces of the models he copied in his youth and his practice of painting, what is most striking about his calligraphy is its originality.[10]

Thin and angular was not the only way to make one's calligraphy stand out. Su Shi, for instance, wrote characters that were plump and rounded, diametrically opposed to Huizong's angular and sharp-edged ones.[11] Huizong chose to go toward the pole of order, precision, and control. By perfecting a distinctive but highly disciplined style, Huizong was presenting himself as a person who appreciated elegance and beauty but was also methodical and in control.[12]

Even as a young man, Huizong was confident enough in the impression he made through his calligraphy to let it represent him. In 1104 he wrote the characters for the name plaques for the Personal Destiny halls at the prefectural Daoist Honoring Calm temples all over the country. That same year he began having compositions he wrote inscribed on stone in his Slender Gold calligraphy and placed where they could be widely viewed, some near government offices, others at government schools or temples. In 1107 he also let his Slender Gold calligraphy be used on newly minted coins (Figure 11.2).[13]

Huizong also made gifts of his calligraphy to officials beginning early in his reign. He gave Tong Guan a transcription of the *Thousand Character Essay* in Slender Gold calligraphy in 1104 (Figure 11.3). Wang Anzhong and Wang Fu received copies of that text in cursive script (Figure 11.1). Sometimes an entire group of officials was so favored. In 1122 at the celebration of the newly constructed Palace Library, Huizong made gifts of his calligraphy in running and draft script to fifty-six officials. Wang Fu, who had handled much of the arrangements, was given twenty-three pieces of Huizong's calligraphy on that occasion, much more than anyone else. Over the years, top officials such as Cai Jing, Wang Fu, Wu Juhou, and Liu Zhengfu ended up with so much of Huizong's calligraphy that they built special pavilions to hold it.[14]

Huizong frequently put his distinctive Slender Gold calligraphy on paintings, both paintings that were done by court painters and paintings he claimed to have painted himself (see Plates 5, 6, 10, 11, and 12). In all of these cases, the calligraphy is prominent, attracting the eye almost as much as the painting.

Huizong's pursuit of the art of calligraphy can be placed in the tradition of emperor-calligraphers. The catalogue of Huizong's calligraphy, the *Xuanhe Calligraphy Catalogue*, places emperor-calligraphers at the beginning of the book. It credits the Tang emperors, especially Taizong and Xuanzong, with advancing the art of calligraphy through their own example and their patronage of the best calligraphers of their day. Some early Song emperors, especially Taizong and Renzong, were also enthusiastic calligraphers and like Huizong made many gifts of their writing. As a calligrapher Huizong pursued originality to a level they did not—to them mastering the classic Two Wang style was accomplishment enough.[15] But Huizong could look on a fondness for practicing calligraphy as an established dynastic tradition.

What if we set aside the fact that Huizong was an emperor and look only at the work attributed to him? How good was he? The range of scholarly opinion is quite broad. Yu Hui, curator of painting at the Palace Museum in Beijing, ranks him as an especially creative calligrapher, and argues that if he had not been emperor he would have merited being classed as one of the four great calligraphers of the Song.[16] Others find his calligraphy too precise for their taste.

Huizong's officials, ready to flatter him in other ways, did not attempt to imitate his Slender Gold style. Huizong reportedly trained some palace women and eunuchs to write in his style, to help with paperwork, but he did not encourage his officials to adopt it. They probably did not take it up on their own because they sensed that he wanted his calligraphy to be distinctive. The only person to prominently take up Huizong's calligraphy style was the Jin emperor Zhangzong (r. 1189–1208) nearly a century later. But even if later Song emperors did not perpetuate the Slender Gold style, they did follow Huizong's lead in prominently embracing the art of calligraphy. Huizong's son Gaozong even wrote a treatise on calligraphy and undertook to write out in his own hand six of the Confucian classics so that they could be carved on stone and placed at the Imperial Academy.[17]

Huizong as a Painter

Skill in painting was part of the public persona that Huizong presented at court. Although Huizong's paintings are not as strikingly distinctive as his Slender Gold calligraphy, they are highly polished and aesthetically appealing. The simple fact that so many survive makes Huizong stand out among emperors, not only of the Song period, but across the dynasties. All Song emperors made at least minor efforts at poetry and calligraphy, as did most literati. Emperors could convey a disinterest in these arts but could not refuse to participate in such long-sanctioned rituals as poetry compositions at the banquets to honor new examination graduates. Painting was another matter. It was entirely optional for both literati and emperors. Huizong could have represented himself as a patron of painting without also painting himself; his collecting of old paintings and supervision of court painters would have been enough to earn him a place in the history of the art. But Huizong took pride in his skill in painting and occasionally showed his works to others. At a party in 1115, Deng Chun reported, Huizong showed his guests a painting he had recently completed of a pair of ducks by the banks of a pond, for which he had written a preface. In Deng's words, "All those present at the banquet gathered around to look at it. Each viewed the painting with awe and praised it as the most exquisite and sublime in the realm."[18] At the opening of the newly built Palace Library in 1122, the same occasion when Huizong made gifts of this calligraphy to fifty-six officials, he showed those present both original paintings he had made and a copy he had done of an old painting in his collection. He also gave a painting he did himself to each of the fifty-six.[19]

Huizong was remarkably successful in his self-presentation as a painter. Most of those who commented on Huizong's paintings in Song times declared him an artist of exceptional talent. Wang An-zhong declared to Huizong that a screen he painted "truly surpasses anything ancient or modern."[20] Only a few years after Huizong's death, Zhang Zheng described Huizong as naturally gifted and turning to painting in his leisure. "His bird-and-flower paintings are as beautiful as those of Xu Xi and Huang Quan and his sons." Zhang Zheng mentioned seeing a set of twelve paintings with an inscription by Huizong that recounted how he had come across Song Di's *Eight Views of the Xiao and Xiang Rivers* and was inspired by it to paint a series of twelve views. Zhang Zheng also reported seeing an exquisite set of depictions of village scenes, plants, and animals by Huizong. In addition, a dealer once showed him twelve landscape hanging scrolls, each about five feet high, and each with a four character title written by Huizong.[21]

An even fuller account of Huizong as a painter was written in 1167 by Deng Chun, whose grandfather had served as an official in Huizong's court. The opening sentence in his *Painting Continued* reads: "Emperor Huizong was endowed by heaven with intelligence and sagacity, and his art reached the sublime level. No court painter was his equal." Although remarking elsewhere that many paintings signed by Huizong were done by court painters, he had only superlatives for Huizong's own paintings. He referred to several specific paintings, including one of twenty cranes in various postures. Another depicted mountain ranges that looked like masses of jade brushed by the wind, the sort of place where immortals lived. The painting "makes the viewer wish to enter and climb up to the fairy islands that drift mysteriously, floating beyond the earth, the real with the unreal seeming to mingle."[22] Other Southern Song sources attribute to Huizong paintings of puppies, kittens, apes, mynahs, magpies, egrets, pigeons, ducks, sparrows, rabbits, and horses.[23] In the fourteenth century Tang Hou, in his *Mirror of Painting*, placed Huizong's birds and flowers, mountains and rocks, and figure paintings all in the sublime class. "Among the emperors of preceding dynasties who were capable of painting, only Huizong can be said to have attained his own concepts." He described a painting of the Tang emperor Xuanzong riding on Night-Shining White—one of his three famous horses—crossing the Plank Road. "The horse is frightened and hesitates to approach [the bridge]. Two people are picking melons at a remote distance, and several riders gradually approach from the rear. This is an amazing scene." Tang Hou was equally impressed by a painting titled *Dreaming of Traveling to the Heavenly Palace*, his description reminding one of Huizong's vision after the sacrifices to heaven in 1113. "Walls, palaces, military camps, music and dance, court ladies, deities, sky, clouds, birds, dragons and horses, all the beings in the world are included. The painting technique is so complete and detailed that it provokes the viewer into thinking of traveling through heaven in his mind and forgetting about the mundane world. It is an amazing painting."[24]

Extant paintings should, in theory, offer even better evidence of Huizong's mastery of the art of painting. But which paintings should be considered? The most common reasons paintings have been ascribed to Huizong are that they bear one or more of his seals and usually also his cipher.[25] These paintings can be problematic, given the presence of forgeries, copies, and misattributions. Scholars largely concur that the paintings with his seals include ones by his hand alone, ones he did in collaboration with court artists, ones done by court artists at his behest, later copies of paintings from his court, and later imitations and forgeries. Some attributions can be rejected because the seals or signatures are unconvincing, others because the paintings are not of the period. No modern art historian accepts more than a fraction of the paintings ascribed at one time or another to Huizong, but not all accept the same set.[26] The ones I consider good sources for Huizong as a painter are listed in Table 8.1.

The long handscroll, *Birds and Butterflies in an Autumn Garden* (Figure 8.2) is more ambitious in composition than the other bird paintings, showing several different plants growing from the ground, plus four birds and two butterflies.[27] One magpie is walking, seen in full profile, the other is pecking at the ground, seen at something of an angle (though the head, again, is in profile, as is true in all Huizong's bird paintings). The patterns created by the stems of the grass, the leaves of the bamboo, and the clustering of the chrysanthemum flowers, all show an inventiveness in composition beyond that of any other Huizong painting. The attention to the distinguishing traits of the birds, however, is just as well done as any other, down to the overlay of white feathers over black on the belly of the magpie and the holes in the beak. This painting seems an especially good candidate for imagining Huizong working together with a court painter, who might, for instance, have filled in the plants after Huizong had done the birds.

A very different brush technique is used to paint the birds in *Finches and Bamboo* (Plate 9), which can be seen as an up-to-date small scene composition, with the viewer up close to the objects. The birds have little color, but the bamboo leaves are a bright light green, with the winter damage still evident on their tips but new sprouts emerging as well. The feathers on the breasts of the birds are painted in with a fine brush, and their eyes are dotted with lacquer. The large rock on the right is an element not found in any of Huizong's other bird-and-flower paintings,

Table 8.1. Major extant Huizong paintings

Subject	Format	Location	Poem by Huizong?	Illustrated
Bird-and-flower				
Five-Colored Parakeet	Handscroll	Museum of Fine Arts, Boston	yes	Plate 10
Cranes of Good Omen	Handscroll	Liaoning Provincial Museum	yes	Plate 12
Birds and Butterflies in an Autumn Garden	Handscroll	Private collection	no	Figure 8.2
Two Birds on a Blossoming Wax-Plum Tree	Hanging scroll	National Palace Museum, Taipei	yes	Plate 5
Pheasant on a Hibiscus Branch	Hanging scroll	Palace Museum, Beijing	yes	Plate 6
Finches and Bamboo	Handscroll	Metropolitan Museum, New York	no	Plate 9
Autumn Evening by a Pond	Handscroll	National Palace Museum, Taipei	no	National Palace Museum 1995:365–368
Landscape				
Streams and Mountains in Autumn Hues	Hanging scroll	National Palace Museum, Taipei	no	National Palace Museum 2000:212
Returning Fishing Boats	Handscroll	Palace Museum, Beijing	no	Figure 8.3
Other				
Listening to the Qin	Hanging scroll	Palace Museum, Beijing	yes	Plate 13
Auspicious Dragon Rock	Handscroll	Palace Museum, Beijing	yes	Plate 11

Fig. 8.2. Huizong, *Birds and Butterflies in an Autumn Garden*, handscroll, ink and color on silk, detail. (East Asian Art Photographic Archive, Department of Art and Archaeology, Princeton University)

Fig. 8.3. Huizong, *Returning Fishing Boats on a Snowy River*, handscroll, ink on silk, 30.3 × 190.8 cm., detail. (Palace Museum, Beijing)

and serves to ground the delicacy of the birds in a massive solidity. Art historian Wen C. Fong, who thinks this painting dates from late in Huizong's reign, sees in it "the enchanted vision of a sequestered ruler in retreat from a troubled world." He detects in it both the influence of Huizong's Daoism and his calligraphic sensibility.[28]

As a bird-and-flower painter, Huizong built on the achievements of tenth- and eleventh-century court artists. Hundreds of works by these artists are included in Huizong's painting catalogue.[29] Huang Quan and his son Huang Jucai each were represented by more than three hundred paintings, and Xu Xi and Yi Yuanji by more than two hundred. Huizong may well have taken paintings by these artists as models for his own bird-and-flower painting. In the catalogue, the exuberance of nature is given as a reason to paint birds and flowers. The great variety of plants, "each with its own shape and color," beautifies the change of seasons and brightens the world. The "three hundred and sixty" species of birds vary not only in their appearance but also in their calls and manner of pecking. The fact that the *Book of Songs* mentions many birds and animals is further reason for painters to try to capture their appearance.[30] Huizong admired artists' ability to capture the spirit of birds as living, moving things, and at the same time get the details right—for instance, when painting cranes to "accurately depict every detail: the shape of the head, the hue of the down, the length of the beak, the thinness of the legs, and the position of the knees."[31]

Although a majority of the well-accepted paintings attributed to Huizong depict birds and flowers in color, early critics also refer to his monochrome paintings. Deng Chun mentioned ink flower, bird, and insect paintings, and Tang Hou claimed that Huizong's monochrome flowers and rocks were even better than his colored works. Several monochrome bird-and-flower paintings with Huizong attributions have survived, each showing rather different techniques.[32] None of them have convincing inscriptions in Slender Gold calligraphy, leaving them more doubtful in my mind, though others accept some of them.

Two monochrome landscape paintings are regularly attributed to Huizong, one a hanging scroll in the National Palace Museum in Taipei, the other a handscroll in the Palace Museum in Beijing.[33] The latter, *Returning Fishing Boats on a Snowy River* (Figure 8.3), is reminiscent of the landscape handscroll by Wang Shen now in the Palace

Museum, which in turn draws on the landscape tradition associated with Guo Xi.[34] Although much of the modeling of the mountains is done with washes, Huizong has added fine detail for the trees, rocks, and boats. Cai Jing, in his 1110 colophon on this handscroll, refers to four pictures, perhaps one for each season (the other three presumably lost). He also praises Huizong's ability to capture the creative forces of the cosmos:

> I, your subject, have examined the painting, *Returning Fishing Boats on a Snowy River,* made by Your Majesty. There are no waves on the water extending into the distance; the long sky is uniform in color; the mountain range glistens. A traveler on foot all alone; the oar slapping in the stream; the sail at the horizon: through these the meaning of a fishing boat returning on a snowy river is fully captured. In heaven and earth, the vital forces vary in the four seasons. The growth of the myriad things in the cosmos occurs in accordance with their vital force; with heat or cold, dark or light, the living breath flourishes or decays. The creatures that fly, run, or slither are in continuous transformation in ways no one can exhaustively comprehend. Your Majesty, with paint and marvelous brush technique, captures the visual appearance of the four seasons and the conditions of the myriad creatures. Within these four pictures, your divine intelligence is on a par with the creative powers of the cosmos.[35]

Although by 1110 Huizong must have been used to Cai Jing's flattery, he still may have drawn encouragement from Cai Jing's response to this painting.

As a creative artist, Huizong was particularly innovative in his combination of poetry and painting in a single work. Huizong required students in his painting academy who wished to pursue the literati track to create paintings that would subtly capture a poetic couplet. Huizong also wrote poems to go with paintings. The catalogue of paintings in the Southern Song imperial collection lists nine paintings that Huizong inscribed with his own poems, and records each poem. Two of these poems match the poems on extant paintings discussed in Chapter 7 as works by court artists (Plates 6 and 7). Here are two of the remaining seven:

Apricot Blossoms and Parrots

Together they fly up into the piled clouds,
They make their sturdy nest in the apricot branches.
Perched so high, they are proud of themselves.
The wasp and butterfly cannot compare.

Peach, Bamboo, and Warbler

Leaving the valley, they call one after the other beautifully.
Flitting to the highest branches, none loftier in ambition.
Therefore they learn under the shadow of peach and
    bamboo,
To keep away from the overgrown thicket.[36]

These poems do not announce that the author is an emperor. The focus seems in all cases on plants, birds, and insects, parts of the natural world that all poets were free to describe or allude to. All of the poems include flattering references to the recipient, who has a fine name, excellent qualities, aims high, has lofty ambition, and so on. The paintings probably depicted the birds and plants, especially flowers, that are mentioned in the poems.

Huizong as a Poet

Besides the seven poems translated in this chapter, there are five in Chapter 5 on Huizong's Daoism, seven in Chapter 6 about auspicious signs, five in Chapter 10 on court and palace culture, and two in Chapter 17 on Huizong's time in captivity. These twenty-six constitute about 6 percent of all the extant poems attributed to Huizong. In recent years, the editors of the *Complete Song Poems* gathered together 414 poems by Huizong, of which 296 are classed as palace poems (*gong ci*), a set which had circulated separately from at least the Southern Song period. Another sixty are Daoist hymns, preserved in the Daoist canon. Of those remaining, twenty-five have survived because an author, usually one writing in the century after Huizong's reign, quoted a poem by him. For instance, Cai Tao recorded five poems Huizong wrote to mourn Zhezong during his first year on the throne.[37] Twenty-three of the poems survived because a later author up through the

Qing period recorded an artwork that he believed to be by Huizong which had a poem on it (and which may well have included poems made up by a forger). Eight of the poems in the *Complete Song Poems* are from such works extant today.

If this seems like a lot of poetry, we need to keep in mind that much more poetry survives from the Song than the Tang—the *Complete Song Poems* has nearly 270,000 poems, among them more than 2000 poems by Su Shi. In addition, authorship meant different things when the author was the emperor. Just as Huizong's officials regularly drafted edicts issued in his name, literary officials could have supplied ideas, images, and language for poems he treated as his own. Still, a distinction should be drawn between edicts and poems in that there is a large body of edicts attributed to each of the Song emperors but the number of poems attributed to them varies widely. Neither Shenzong nor Zhezong, whom Huizong made so many efforts to honor, seem to have had a desire to be known as a poet, and few poems are attributed to them.

At the same time, it should be kept in mind that the extant poems are only a fraction of the number Huizong wrote (or had someone ghostwrite for him). Wang Anzhong matched fourteen poems by Huizong, none of which survives independently.[38] A grandson of Cai Jing showed Wang Mingqing poems that Cai Jing and Huizong wrote to each other, and explicitly said that they were only 1 or 2 percent of the poems that the two had written. An early collected works of Huizong, covering up to 1110, had 370 poems. In the posthumous collected works put together from scattered materials, there were 195 *shi* poems, in addition to 200 palace poems.[39] Huizong's son Gaozong, who commissioned this collection, explicitly said that most of Huizong's writings had been lost: "His various styles of poetry, worthy to be in print, filled cabinets. . . . But alas, most of them were lost during the calamity."[40] Cai Tiao, who accompanied Huizong into captivity, said Huizong wrote more than a thousand poems during his exile.[41] To give some basis for comparison, the Tang emperor with the largest number of extant poems, Tang Taizong, has 108. At the other extreme, the Qing emperor Qianlong claimed 43,630, making it clear that in his case ghostwriters must have been heavily involved.[42]

The largest body of extant poems credited to Huizong are the 296 palace poems. These are all heptameter quatrains, without titles or prefaces. Earlier poems in this tradition focus on palace ladies and often touch on their frustrations. By contrast, as Ronald Egan convincingly argues, Huizong's palace poems convey satisfaction with life in the palace and have nothing of the note of complaint of earlier poems in this tradition. Some of his palace poems do not refer to palace ladies; others look on them as just one more attractive element the scene.[43] Here are two examples:

> A row of crimson Banners flickers in the morning sun,
> Ten thousand horses neigh in the wind, the road back
>   stretches afar,
> Knowing the wily western barbarian has come to swear
>   allegiance,
> I personally approach Crimson Tower to receive the
>   surrendered king.[44]

> The sun is warm, the wind soothing deep inside the
>   palace,
> Amid high blossoms and tall bamboo leisurely birds chirp.
> Palace ladies, hand in hand, approach the crimson pen,
> Delighted to watch the patterned ducks' impulse for
>   water play.[45]

Huizong is also credited with a small group of thirteen song lyrics (*ci*), some written after his abdication. In line with poetic practice of the period, these songs seem more personal than the palace poems just given. One of the most moving of the songs attributed to Huizong is this song written at the Lantern Festival when he was in mourning for one of his favorite consorts, Liu Mingjie, who died in 1121:

> Words catch in my throat—
> The lanterns bring back this day in other years—
> Strolling here, there, pointing to the moon, on and on,
>   talking.
> We wanted the moon full forever,
> Not so quickly dented.
> This year, flower lanterns displayed in rows
> Beautiful as before, but oh how different!
> To this lady, here, I can't explain.
> I dare not raise my head,
> Ashamed to see the moon of former times.[46]

What did Huizong's officials think of his poetry? An emperor showing poems to his officials was inviting acclaim if not adulation. Since
flattering the emperor was a standard feature of court life, it is difficult
to tell what recipients of Huizong's poetry thought of him as a poet. For
instance, to what degree should we believe Cai Tao who began his *Talks
on Poetry* with enthusiastic appreciation of Huizong's poetic talents:

> The current emperor is endowed by heaven with intelligence and
> sagacity in both the literary and the military arts. Even in minor
> matters of the arts everyone in the realm looks up to him as though
> he were the sun and moon or the starry dipper. If a piece written
> by him appears in the morning, by evening it has been passed ev-
> erywhere within the four seas. When he first took the throne he
> wrote five songs to mourn the deceased emperor Zhezong. [The
> text of these poems follows.] Both the Chinese and the non-
> Chinese competed to recite these poems, all nations in unison.
> Furthermore, in writing poems collaboratively with his ministers,
> his brilliance exceeds anything done before him.[47]

Cai Tao then recorded some of the poems Huizong wrote for his officials, ending with an exchange of poems using identical rhymes between
Cai Jing and Huizong after a major sacrifice in 1120. Cai Jing, as portrayed by Cai Tao, also had remarkable poetic talent, as he was able to
promptly match Huizong's poems, coming up with marvelous images
on the spot.

Authors would have had more freedom to express less enthusiastic
opinions of Huizong as a poet after his death, but it is difficult to find
authors who belittled his poetry. Hong Mai, in the epigraph to this
chapter, refers to an occasion when Huizong began a poem with a couplet for his councilors to complete. In Hong Mai's opinion, none of
their couplets could really equal his.[48]

Huizong's poems could be evaluated in terms of the long tradition
of emperor poets. Jack Chen, in a study of Tang Taizong as a poet, has
argued that, within the culture of poetry at court, poetry written by
the ruler had its own tradition and genealogy. In his words, "The imperial poet was not free to choose his poetic voice or subjecthood; the
fact of his sovereignty determined what he could say and how he said
it." An emperor, he argues, can never completely take on the persona

of literatus—he is always simultaneously creating the imperial persona, even if an enhanced imperial persona that incorporates elements associated with literati. He sees in nearly all of Taizong's poems something imperial.[49]

Huizong's poems do not seem to lend themselves to the sort of reading that Tang Taizong's do. The poems selected for translation here are ones that can be read as reflecting on Huizong's experience as emperor, but most of his poems, if attributed to someone else, would have easily passed as the work of a literatus or a Daoist. Naturally, no one at his court would forget that he was the emperor when reading a poem he wrote, but Huizong doesn't seem to be trying to find poetic ways to evoke memories of earlier emperors.

It should not be surprising that in his poems Huizong crafts a representation of himself very different from the one that Tang Taizong crafted. The Tang dynasty was still quite new when Taizong took the throne, and the circumstances of his accession (forcing his father to abdicate after killing his elder brother) meant that Taizong had to work to get people to accept his legitimacy. He had to try very hard to appear a good emperor. Huizong, by contrast, was the eighth Song emperor—there was no need to buttress the legitimacy of the dynasty or make a show of commitment to Confucian views of the ruler's moral obligations. Huizong could present himself as a very different sort of emperor, one who is comfortable on the throne. In many of his poems, including the palace poems and poems on auspicious phenomena, Huizong conveys satisfaction with life, an appreciation of the beauty around him, a confidence that all is turning out well. In the Daoist poems there is in addition awe and wonder at the larger cosmic forces at work. Perhaps to Huizong this was the persona appropriate to a ruler who was heir to a long line of eminent ancestors.

WHAT SORT OF A PERSONA was Huizong crafting through his poetry, painting, and calligraphy? Huizong wanted to be taken as the consummate amateur, the man who excels at the arts of painting, calligraphy, and poetry, in full command of contemporary artistic styles even though able to devote only his rare leisure time to the practice of those arts. I suspect that Huizong showed his works to officials because he believed that he had attained a level of skill and artistry that few literati could surpass.

Because many other emperors practiced the arts of poetry and calligraphy, it is Huizong's practice of painting that most makes him stand out. Even if he were not the emperor, his paintings would draw notice. He developed remarkable mastery of the techniques of court bird-and-flower painting, producing paintings that remain highly appealing. Huizong's personal practice of painting reinforced the standards he set for court painters and thus helped shape the direction of Song court painting till the end of the dynasty. His celebration of close observation, of getting the details right, continued to inspire court painters in the Southern Song, and probably painters outside the court as well. His marriage of poetry and painting in so many of his works, whether done entirely on his own or collaboratively, set a model many would later follow. Several Southern Song emperors starting with Huizong's son Gaozong added their calligraphy and poetry to paintings by court artists, perhaps at times writing poetic lines as subjects for painters. Southern Song court painters, too, frequently coupled poems and pictures in directions Huizong laid down.[50]

Huizong often made gifts of his poems, paintings, and calligraphy. Because these artworks were believed to come from deep within the individual, when Huizong conferred them on his subjects he was making a gift of himself. Huizong gave Liu Hunkang poems, hand-copied scriptures, and paintings of deities. Huizong was just as openhanded to other men he was on close terms with, such as Cai Jing and Wang Anzhong. Occasionally he made gifts to larger groups, which was much easier to do with poems that could be conferred on all officials present, than with paintings or calligraphies. Those who received gifts of paintings or calligraphies undoubtedly showed them to others, so that Huizong's reputation as a brilliant artist spread widely.

The usual way to approach Huizong's painting is to consider it together with his training of court artists and his collecting of both old masterpieces and recent works by Song artists. Huizong's insistence on close observation is then seen to explain his own carefully crafted paintings. The stories about his assessing painters based on their ability to convey a poetic couplet in a subtle way are treated as especially revealing evidence. Sometimes Huizong comes across almost as a court painter himself. Often Huizong's calligraphy gets at least brief mention but rarely is his poetry considered at any length.

In this book I have tried to bring out other connections by considering Huizong the artist after Huizong the patron. Huizong's practice of the three literati arts surely enhanced each other. The sort of control of the brush needed for Slender Gold calligraphy would make it easier to add fine details in paintings; Huizong's love of poetry and experience coming up with imagistic lines should have helped him compose paintings that would seem poetic, not to mention help him join poems and paintings in single artworks. It is true that there were many occasions when Huizong composed a poem without also painting a picture and times when he did not write much on a painting. But Huizong clearly saw the capacity of these arts to enhance each other and exploited this capacity in novel ways. In the process he crafted a persona of his choosing—the emperor who finds pleasure and contentment in the world around him and has the talent to convey it in subtle and nuanced ways.

Even if Huizong at times seems to be presenting himself as a highly cultivated literatus, he never forgot that he was the emperor and that the vast resources of the throne were at his disposal. Chapter 9 looks at some of the largest projects he undertook, ones that were possible only because he had so many officials and other subordinates he could assign to a task.

III

ANTICIPATING GREAT THINGS, 1107–1120

9

Pursuing the Monumental

> The Bright Hall in antiquity was magnificent, but among my
> predecessors down to Shenzong, despite thorough
> deliberations, nothing ever got completed.
>
> —*Huizong thanking Cai Jing for his contribution to the*
> *building of the Bright Hall*

$\mathcal{E}$ARLY IN HIS REIGN Huizong came to realize how satisfy-
ing it was to initiate a project and see it through to completion. He
liked to watch the progress of buildings under construction, to talk to
scholars he had set to work on research projects, and to offer guidance
to his court painters. By the time he had been on the throne seven or
eight years, he had acquired the confidence to take on grander and
more ambitious projects. For the next dozen years, he frequently set
out to accomplish great things.

This chapter looks at six grand projects which Huizong set in motion. Two are book projects, one a painting project, one a collecting
and cataloguing project, and two are construction projects. Seen one
way, they reflect the broad range of Huizong's cultural, religious, and
artistic passions. Seen another, they show Huizong's distinctive style
of engagement. Although all of these projects were ambitious, they
were designed with different audiences in mind, ranging from Daoist
masters to Confucian ritualists and art collectors.

A New Ritual Code

The Confucian ritual classics give great cosmological significance to
the rituals that the ruler performs. The "Li Yun" chapter in the *Book of*
Rites, for instance, asserts that "Ritual forms a great instrument in the
hands of a ruler. It is by ritual that he resolves what is doubtful and

243

brings to light what is obscure; that he conducts his intercourse with spiritual beings, examines all statutory arrangements, and distinguishes benevolence from righteousness; it is by them, in short, that government is rightly ordered and his own tranquility secured."[1]

The ritual classics, however, are not very useful to those trying to orchestrate the sacrifices the monarch must make to his ancestors, heaven, and other deities. Consequently, over the centuries Confucian ritualists in government employ charged with organizing state rituals prepared much more concrete ritual instructions. By Song times there was an enormous body of literature of this sort, much of it in conflict. On some issues, discrepancies in the classics led to disagreements. In other cases, the larger meaning of the rite was in question. Some practices were condemned as not really ancient, others because they were antiquated. Intellectual positions on the different ritual classics—especial the *Rites of Zhou*—could also shape the stances taken by Confucian ritualists. During the New Policies period, Wang Anshi had favored the *Rites of Zhou* because it offered a model of the activist state that regulated all elements in people's lives. Citing the *Rites of Zhou*, thus, could be a way of showing support for the New Policies.

When Huizong first became emperor, he did not have the leisure to think through all of these ritual issues before officiating at any rite. When deciding the level at which he would mourn Zhezong and how Zhezong's tablet should be accommodated in the Supreme Shrine, he could listen to opposing arguments but could not delay making a decision. He took somewhat more time to consider the arguments for and against joint sacrifices to heaven and earth at the Suburban Altars, but did not consider all of the implications for the state cult. When in doubt Huizong would ask what his father had thought about an issue.

After Huizong had been on the throne nearly seven years, he decided to tackle the entire state ritual program. On the first day of 1107, he announced the establishment of the Agency for Deliberating on Ritual. The agency, with seven officials, was to do research into ancient ritual texts and propose revisions to court rituals, attempting where reasonable to return rituals to more ancient forms.[2] No earlier Song emperor had taken on this task. Early in the dynasty the court had made modest adaptations to the 150-chapter *Rituals of the Kaiyuan Period* from the Tang period (extant today) to issue a *Rituals of the Kai-*

bao Period (not extant).[3] From time to time, revisions of ritual practice were issued, but not a complete code.

The size and comprehensiveness of the *Rituals of the Kaiyuan Period* probably made replacing it seem too daunting a task. That work outlined the steps in about 150 separate rituals, such as offerings to Confucius at the Imperial Academy, worship of deities that took charge of rain, thunder, and wind, and the installation of an empress. For each rite, the code provides specific guidance for the responsible officials. It begins with the things that needed to be done in advance: any preliminary abstentions, the collection of the necessary equipment, the preparation of the food offerings, and selection of the day of the rite. The time participants would need to arrive on the day of the rite and where they would stand are clearly stated. The wording of prayers is also given. After describing the steps in the ritual itself, the *Rituals of the Kaiyuan Period* gives instructions for returning people and things to their normal locations. This huge ritual compendium gave Huizong's officials a place to start.

As the Agency for Deliberating on Ritual began its work, Huizong promised to personally review each of the recommendations they submitted. As a guide to the sort of manual he wanted, he sent them a ten-chapter work he had done himself on the capping ritual, telling them that they could use it as a model.[4] (Capping was a ritual that marked adulthood for males.) The final product of their work, completed in 1113, survives in almost complete form (200 of 220 chapters are extant). The first twenty-four chapters provide specifications relevant to many rituals, such as the arrangement of orchestras, the literary forms for use in announcements, ritual garments, honor guards, and lists of officials to participate as observers at various rituals. The largest section, Chapters 25–135, covers auspicious rituals. These are the sacrifices the emperor or someone standing in for him performed not only at the Suburban Altars, the Supreme Shrine, the Temple of Spectacular Numina, and the imperial tombs, but also lesser sacrifices to the Lords of the Five Directions, the "hundred deities" of each of the four directions, and the sun and the moon. Instructions are also given for the rituals local officials would perform to pray for rain or make offerings to Confucius, as well as rituals that all officials would perform for their own ancestors in their own homes or family shrines. Chapters 136–156 are for guest rituals, which included the New Year and Winter Solstice assemblies, other lesser assemblies, and the reception of foreign envoys. Army rituals took up only eight chapters (156–164) and included receiving surrendered kings, sending off armies, victory announcements, and hunting expeditions. Celebratory rituals came next (Chapters 165–206) and ranged from celebrations of the emperor's birthday and various seasonal banquets to weddings and cappings differentiated by rank (from the emperor, to the heir apparent, to other princes and princesses, imperial clansmen, down to ordinary people). The last fourteen chapters cover funeral rituals, from sending death announcements and offering condolences to preparing the body and putting on mourning garments, from the imperial level to ordinary people.

The body of this *New Forms for the Five Categories of Rites of the Zhenghe Period* is preceded by Huizong's guide to capping and a prefatory chapter of correspondence between Huizong and the compilers which allows us to reconstruct many of the considerations that went into putting the huge book together. In the preface Huizong wrote for the finished compilation, he claimed that he was completing a project that his father had hoped to undertake. Knowing the value of rites for achieving order and aspiring to the achievements of the Three Ancient Dynasties, Shenzong had his officials debate the protocols and garments for the Suburban Sacrifices but their discussions were never collected together. Thus Huizong, ever conscious of the need to continue his father's legacy, had set up the Agency for Deliberating on Ritual.[5]

The prefatory chapter of the *New Forms of the Five Categories of Rites of the Zhenghe Period* includes a long series of queries and responses exchanged between the agency and Huizong, and others have been preserved in the *Song Collected Documents*. One of Huizong's early notes (1108/8) acknowledged that change over time was to be expected in ritual but cautioned that some of the accumulated practices were not sufficiently rooted in ancient principles to be preserved. He then went on to object to two elements in the material his officials had submitted. They had put the capping ritual first, which he thought neither matched the classics nor Sui and Tang practice. The five categories of the rites are auspicious, guest, military, celebratory, and inauspicious. The auspicious rituals begin with the service to heaven and the gods, not with capping. The recent practice of classing capping with auspicious rituals loses the hierarchy of the ancient kings' rituals, since service to the gods ranks higher than service to man. Huizong also went on to argue a much more idiosyncratic position: he objected to capping coming before weddings, because cappings "complete" a person and weddings join people, and "one first marries and later is capped." He suspected that, even though the classic *Etiquette and Ritual* listed cappings before weddings, that order must reflect mistaken theories of scholars, not the true teachings of the ancient kings.[6]

The officials in the Agency for Deliberating on Ritual did not enter into a debate with Huizong on these issues but simply adopted his views. They classified both weddings and cappings as celebratory rituals, and put weddings before cappings. In neither the educated class nor the imperial family was capping widely practiced in Huizong's day.[7] In the imperial family, most people married relatively young, which may have been the basis for Huizong's argument that people could not be said to be completed before they were married. When Huizong had his eldest son capped in 1114, it was the first time the ceremony was performed in the Song palace.[8]

In 1110, as they were trying to complete their draft of the ritual manual, the Agency for Deliberating on Ritual submitted issue after issue to Huizong, and he approved their analysis and proposed solution most of the time. Topics they brought up ranged widely: Should the measurement stick based on the length of Huizong's fingers be promulgated to standardize measurements beyond music? Should the clothing prefectural officials wear when presiding at ceremonies be specified and illustrations distributed? Should the presentation of silk be eliminated from more minor rituals to conform more closely to the *Rites of Zhou?* What sort of clothing should be depicted on the statue of Confucius at the Directorate of Education? Should all of his seventy-two disciples have their names listed? If so, with what titles? What sorts of sacrificial vessels, in what numbers, should be used at different sacrifices? Which gods should have their name tablets in gold-painted wood and which in red-lacquered wood? Is it necessary to set up an orchestra for all sacrifices? Should the sequence of the five categories of rites follow the *Rites of Zhou*, which put inauspicious rites second, or the *Kaiyuan* and *Kaibao Rituals*, which put them last? Should local officials practice abstention before presiding at rituals?[9]

On some occasions, it was Huizong who initiated a discussion. One issue on which he felt strongly was intrusion of Buddhist rituals into the state cult. On 1110/8/3 Huizong raised the issue of the rituals on the fifteenth day of the seventh month (referred to as the Yulanpen Festival by the Buddhists and the Middle Prime Festival by the Daoists) and the ways Buddhist practice had entered the Temple of Spectacular Numina with its statues of the prior Song dynasty emperors:

> Every year, at the Middle Prime festival, both literati and commoners bend bamboo to make multi-story buildings and fold paper to make figures of resident monks, which they call Yulanpen. The Buddhists say that they are solemnly presenting these offerings to the deceased to get them released from purgatory and reborn in the heavenly realms. It is all right to let this practice continue among the populace at large since it is an expression of filial virtue. However, the practice does not belong in the two Temples of Spectacular Numina, where the spirits of my ancestors abide; there vulgar customs should not be permitted, nor should we falsely give credence to the unfounded teachings of the golden barbarian [the Buddha]. It may well be that the Buddhist canon has textual sources for this practice, but is there any evidence for it in Confucian writings? Moreover, on this day, at the place setting for each of the imperial ancestors and ancestresses, people set out *mazhulian* leaves with melon flowers. Please consider whether these items are suitable or not for the ancestral temple. Report back with detailed discussion.

> Further, the Buddha was a scholar from the western regions who attained the Dao. Since Emperor Ming [of the Later Han dynasty, r. 57–75] dreamed of him, his teachings have flowed into China and he has been looked on as a man of eminence. Now, on the death-day anniversaries of the imperial ancestors and ancestresses in the Eastern and Western Temples of Spectacular Numina, people conduct Buddhist Water and Land Retreats; they decorate the place with curtains and awnings and with banners inscribed, "bath house of emperor-title." The monks and their attendants issue orders: "Do not violate the Buddha's edicts; descend to this ritual space." Isn't this a very demeaning way to address the spirits of the ancestors in heaven? Not to mention the fact

that the Buddha is not authorized to issue edicts. Is there any verifiable source for these practices? In your report cite specific facts.

Next, with regard to dogs, in the Daoist religion dogs are referred to as contemptible and people today rarely eat them. Yet,
every year at the seasonal sacrifices, they are prepared in a ritual
manner and placed in cauldrons and raised dishes. What authority is there for this in the ritual classics? Do research on this and
report back in detail.[10]

These imperial queries elicited a lengthy response. First, the agency
officials tried to explain the Sanskrit meaning of the term Yulanpen,
and told the story of Mulian saving his mother who had descended into
the realm of the hungry ghosts.[11] They agreed that while this festival
was acceptable as a popular custom, it did not belong in the solemn
precincts of the Eastern and Western Temples of Spectacular Numina.
They also condemned as disrespectful Buddhist monks holding Water
and Land Retreats and issuing commands using language that should
come only from emperors. They cited a ruling of 1106 which had employed the language of the Daoist ritual of the Golden Registers, which
seems to imply that Daoist ceremonies would be acceptable on the day
of the Middle Prime. On the issue of the use of dog meat at the Supreme Shrine, they proposed discontinuing it on the classical principle
that one should serve the dead as one serves the living, and people don't
generally eat dog meat. This allowed them to ignore references to it as
one of the five sacrificial meats in ancient texts. Within a couple of days
Huizong responded that the first and third items should be eliminated,
as they proposed, but more research was needed on the second item.[12]

While officials were discussing these issues abstractly, they were
also preparing the protocols for the installation of Empress Zheng,
which took place in 1110/10. Among the documents they prepared
were four volumes (*ce*) on steps to be followed, one volume of music,
and two volumes of pictures of the clothing to be worn.[13]

In 1110 a preliminary *Rituals of the Daguan Period* was issued, but the
agency continued to consider ritual issues. During the next couple of
years many of the issues raised concerned rituals that had some connection to ordinary people. There were lengthy discussions of the
plowing ritual, the sericulture ritual, ceremonies to honor elders, and
local rites to the god of the soil.[14]

In most of the discussions between Huizong and the Agency for Deliberating on Ritual, the sources cited could all be thought of as Confucian, above all classical texts. For all that Huizong talked down relying on the accumulated practices of the Sui and Tang, or automatic acceptance of anything in the *Rituals of the Kaiyuan Period*, that book also gets cited quite often.[15] As David McMullen has pointed out, the *Rituals of the Kaiyuan Period* is resolutely Confucian, and does not refer to the Buddhist and Daoist rites that were also performed at the Tang court.[16] By contrast, the *New Forms of the Five Categories of Rites of the Zhenghe Period* includes many elements that would have been recognized at the time as Daoist. Two chapters are devoted to the offerings made to the Nine Cauldrons in Nine Completion Temple and one each to the Grand Unity Temple and Power of Yang Temple.[17] There are a variety of occasions when announcements are made not only to heaven and earth, the imperial ancestral shrines, and the altar of soil and grain, but also to "Daoist temples" *(gongguan)*. For instance, after a new empress is installed, announcements are made to these Daoist temples: Central Grand Unity, Beseeching the Spirits, Sweet Springs, Highest Clarity Accumulated Auspices, Power of Yang, and Nine Completions.[18] As we might expect, no visits to Buddhist temples are mentioned. Chapter 8 of *New Forms* explains how these announcements would be performed at Daoist temples. The position of each dish of food is specified, along with all of the movements of the person presiding.[19]

Provisions for Daoist ceremonies also found their way into the opening chapters of the *New Forms*, which cover basic elements of the rituals, such as spirit tablets, sacrificial vessels, music, vehicles, honor guards, and so on. In Chapter 4, there is a subsection on prayer strips that describes "green verses," the common term for Daoist prayer strips. It specifies that at Daoist temples *(gongguan)* one would use green verses strips a foot one inch long and one inch wide (in Chinese measurements), "connected together with a red silk cord and tied with red silk cloth."[20] This chapter also has instructions on the color of silk offerings, and lists several Daoist temples where silk is offered, including the Temple of Spectacular Numina (blue), Highest Clarity Accumulated Auspices Temple, Accumulated Felicities Temple (both green), Sweet Spring Temple (red), Nine Completions Temple (yellow), Protecting the Spirits Temple (five directions), Central Grand

Unity Temple (different colors for each season). Chapter 5, on sacrificial vessels, has a section on which vessels should be used when the offering is being made at a Daoist temple, along with the sorts of vegetarian food they should contain, ranging from rice and millet to dried peaches and persimmons, dumplings and noodles, and bamboo shoots and scallions.[21]

Despite these Daoist elements, the *New Forms* remains focused on the state cult, above all the rituals that officials played a role in preparing. It does not include Daoist ceremonies performed by Daoist priests in their own temples, even when the court was a patron of the temple. In the case of the Yulanpen festival, Huizong wanted to remove Buddhist elements from veneration of imperial ancestors, which he claimed for the state cult. By contrast, he wanted to acknowledge the place that Daoism had gained in the state cult.

After the final version of the *New Forms* was issued in 1113 (renamed to reflect the new reign period that began in 1111, Zhenghe), Huizong had many occasions to put its provisions into practice. At this time his children were coming of age, giving him many occasions to draw on the new ritual forms for their cappings and weddings.

In contrast to the *Rituals of the Kaiyuan Period*, the *New Forms* included specifications for the weddings, funerals, and ancestral rites common people should perform. To spread knowledge of these forms, Huizong approved having an abridged version of *New Forms* printed and circulated.[22]

Court ritual always had a political side. Officials could try to advance their careers by proposing revisions in the ritual program, and they could try to discredit their opponents by criticizing their positions on ritual issues. One scholar argues that Cai Jing used the state cult rituals to elevate Huizong's authority, on which his own power depended.[23] In that context it is worth noting that Cai Jing was out of office during most of the period when the *New Forms* was compiled. It seems to have been Huizong who was the major force behind the effort to revise the code. Another way officials could make political use of court rituals was to use them to keep the ruler occupied. As Joseph McDermott puts it, "as the central figure in imperial politics, the emperor is to follow the script written by his officials in order to fulfill his dynastic obligations to heaven, the empire, and his family. The great number of rituals assigned to him, the preparation periods requiring

fasting and isolation, and the rehearsals all combined to keep him busy
as the ritual, rather than the administrative, head of state."[24] Not all
rulers became the captives of the rituals their officials formulated, and
the more politically adept of them could turn ritual to their own purposes, by using the dictates of ritual to accomplish their own goals. A
ruler like Huizong who wanted a more magnificent court, with more
pomp and pageantry, could get around some of the Confucian calls for
austerity by making use of ritual occasions.

A New Daoist Canon

Around the time that the work on the ritual code was being completed, Huizong took on an even more ambitious textual project: compiling a new Daoist canon. Establishing a canon is a project with major
consequences. It involves not merely selecting texts to be preserved
but also putting them in some sort of order. Because books included
in canons are much more likely to survive than ones omitted, the formation of canons can shape the direction of the religion for centuries
to come.

The first true Daoist canon had been compiled under Emperor
Xuanzong in the Tang. That canon came to 3,477 *juan*. The wars of the
ninth and tenth centuries led to the destruction and scattering of most
copies, so in the early Song period Zhenzong commissioned a new
canon, which when completed in 1017 came to 4,350 *juan*. Rather than
have it printed, as the Buddhist canon had been a few decades earlier,
Zhenzong authorized making handwritten copies which were distributed to major Daoist centers.[25]

Huizong initiated the canon project in late 1113. He wrote out in his
own hand a general call for the collection of Daoist texts. He began by
arguing that even if, as Laozi says, the true Dao cannot be conveyed in
words, still the textual tradition of Daoism has great value and needs
to be preserved:

> The Dao cannot be transmitted through words; what can be put
> in words are clues to the Dao. The Dao is wondrous and without
> form, too deep to be plumbed. Without words, though, it cannot
> be made prominent. Therefore the Dao is recorded in words, al-
> lowing its wondrous principles to be preserved. The ancient sages

perceived the Dao through words, established the teaching on the basis of the Dao, which myriad generations have relied on in perpetuity. For my part, I have embodied it and carried it out, respected and illuminated it, and extended it through government action. Although its books may all exist, sometimes the transmission has been interrupted. It will be a great blow to my intention to honor the Dao and establish its teachings if the books of the Great Mystery and Emptiness and Profundity, and the texts of the jade strips are destroyed or lost or fall into cut-off places beyond the ability to reach through searches.[26] I am thus ordering that officials, Daoist priests and laymen, scholars and commoners all submit any Daoist books they possess—in whatever numbers— to be forwarded by the express couriers. I am expecting the circuit intendants and prefects to search widely. Any who dare to hinder or not carry out this order will be charged with opposing an edict and will not have their penalty reduced in subsequent amnesties. On the other hand, there will be rewards for officials who are thorough in gathering books as well as private collectors who forward scriptures and other Daoist teachings. Those who have large numbers that they fail to submit should be reported to the Department of State Affairs.[27]

When completed, the new canon came to 5,387 *juan* and was given the name *Longevity Daoist Canon of the Zhenghe Period*. The blocks were carved in Fuzhou (Fujian), then sent to the capital, where the actual printing took place.[28] Since Huizong's canon was 20 percent larger than Zhenzong's, the compilers must have added many titles not in the earlier one.

Daoist priests who worked on the canon project came from more than one tradition within Daoism and often traveled a considerable distance to participate. One of them was Xu Zhichang, who held court Daoist positions during Huizong's reign. Familiar with both Daoist and Confucian texts, he had a reputation as a writer. Another was Li Derou, a learned priest who was also a skilled painter. The thirteenth-century hagiography of a third Daoist master who participated in this project, Liu Yuandao, mentions the series of official appointments he was given and also says he participated in Daoist rituals at the palace and sometimes was summoned to discuss Daoism with Huizong, who conferred on him generous gifts.[29] Perhaps the most interesting man to work on the canon was Yuan Miaozong, who for thirty years had been traveling across the country to meet other Daoist masters and learn about their Daoist methods. He was particularly interested in healing through the use of talismans. His ten-chapter work, *Secret Essentials on the Totality of the Perfected for Assisting the State and Saving the People, in the Most High Tradition*, is considered one of the foundation texts of the Heart of Heaven tradition. In the preface he wrote to this scripture, dated 1116, he praised Huizong's efforts to collect Daoist texts and described his own participation in the project and his submission of the fruits of his searches for secret practices associated with the writing of therapeutic talismans.[30]

Because Huizong's canon was the first to be printed, it played a large part in the preservation of Daoist texts, especially texts written in Northern Song times. When the next Daoist canon was compiled in the early Ming period, copies of Huizong's canon were still in circulation, allowing books in it to be included in that canon, still extant today.

Visual Documentation of Auspicious Signs

Besides setting Confucian ritual scholars and Daoist priests to work on book projects, Huizong came up with a project to employ his court painters. He would have them document in pictures the auspicious occurrences of his reign.[31] There were already many written texts documenting these omens, both reports and congratulations, but there were visual elements that words failed to fully capture.

At first, Huizong seems to have had pictures made in an ad hoc manner.[32] In his second decade Huizong made several attempts to be more systematic. The *Song History* reports that when Bai Shizhong served as a ritual official, he was commissioned to edit a compendium of memorials on auspicious phenomena and "have pictures made for those that cannot be adequately conveyed in words." The resulting work was titled *Records of Auspicious Responses of the Zhenghe Period*. Deng Chun, in his *Painting Continued* of 1167, refers to paintings Huizong made of unusual phenomena deemed to be of good omen, such as a red crow, numinous mushrooms, sweet dew, white birds and animals, doubled-stemmed bamboo, parrots, and ten-thousand-year rocks. He states that these pictures were made up into "thousands" of albums of fifteen leaves each and implies that Huizong did all the painting himself. "Nothing done in ancient or modern times exceeded this in beauty." He mentions the name *Album for the Imperial Gaze of the Xuanhe [Hall or Reign Period]*.[33] Wang Yinglin, a century later, mentions a one-*juan* work illustrating fifteen types of auspicious images, each with a preface and poem by Huizong. Tang Hou, writing some decades later than Wang Yinglin, claimed that hundreds of albums of thirty pictures each were made and concluded that court painters must have done much of the work.[34] Could all of these reports be true? It could be that after one set of pictures was completed, auspicious phenomena continued to be reported, leading to the decision to commission another set.

Three extant paintings apparently resulted from one of these projects to document auspicious signs at Huizong's court. All of these are presented as work by Huizong himself: *Five-Colored Parakeet, Auspicious Dragon Rock*, and *Cranes of Good Omen* (Plates 10, 11, and 12).[35] The size of these short handscrolls (possibly originally very large album leaves) varies from 51 to 54 centimeters tall and 125 to 138 centimeters wide. All have a prose account of the phenomenon being documented, a poem, and a picture, though the order is not consistent. In the two that have fully legible inscriptions, Huizong claimed not merely to have composed the poem but also to have painted the picture and done the calligraphy.

The arrival of cranes was celebrated as an auspicious event many times during Huizong's reign, so the picture of cranes near the roof of a palace gate fits well with other evidence. The other two extant paintings show a broader interpretation of what is auspicious. From Huizong's inscription on *Five-Colored Parakeet*, one gets the impression that the parakeet was a palace pet, cherished at least in part for its ability to speak:

The five-colored parakeet came from the far south (Lingbiao). Reared in the imperial enclosure, he has become docile and is lovable. He flits and sings as he pleases, moving to and fro in the garden. Now in mid-spring the apricots are in full bloom and he flies to the top of them. He is noble and placid, and possesses a dignity peculiarly his own. As I gaze upon him, he seems to present a sight superior to a picture. Therefore I compose this verse:

Heaven produced the parakeet, this anomalous bird,
From far away he came as tribute deep into the imperial
    precinct,
His body has all five colors, making him far from ordinary.
Blessed is he uttering many a word, the tone most beautiful.
When flying high, to be envied is he, noble among the
    feathered creatures.
When walking about, contented is he, fed with choice grain.
His yellow breast and purple feet are truly elegant.
Thus I compose a new verse and sing as I stroll.[36]

The *Five-Colored Parakeet* shows the highly colored bird in profile, perched on the twig of a flowering shrub or tree, against a blank background of unpainted silk. Judged as an example of Song court bird-and-flower painting, it is a very high-quality painting. The distinguishing features of the bird have been closely observed and are meticulously conveyed. The sharp edge of the beak is drawn with a precise, thin line; the eyes were made to shine by the application of a dot of lacquer. The texture of the feathers is conveyed by layers of semitransparent red, yellow, and green wash. The scaly texture of the claws is shown using outline and fill. The parakeet is perched on one of two multi-twig branches, each with buds and open blossoms but no leaves. The twigs of the branches extend in many directions, giving a sense of depth to the picture. Probably the closely observed style in which this painting is done should be linked to its function. That is, making the auspicious omen look so real gave it reality.[37]

Auspicious Dragon Rock shows a deeply faceted rock pierced by several holes against a blank background. The only indication of the size of the rock is the plant growing on it, suggesting that it must have been at least several feet tall. The painter used shading to suggest the effects of light on a very uneven surface. Since rocks are immobile, the artist could well have sat by the rock, sketching what he observed. The rock has two characters inscribed on it—"auspicious dragon." The inscription to *Auspicious Dragon Rock* describes the location of the rock but does not specify precisely what makes it auspicious:

The auspicious dragon rock stands to the south of Circling Blue
Pond and to the west of Fragrant Continent Bridge, like a mighty

ocean facing them. Its force is bounding and roiling, like a serpentine dragon emerging to give form to an auspicious response. Its rare shape and ingenious manner cannot be adequately conveyed even with the most marvelous words, so I have personally painted it on silk and added a poem to record it.

> Its beautiful undulation, a configuration like a dragon.
> Its power thrusting, an auspicious sign, unique for its
>   vigor.
> When clouds merge beautiful colors, it borrows from them.
> When water moistens the pure brightness, it becomes even
>   more variegated.
> Like a constant band of dark smoke, one might think it was
>   shaking its mane.
> Every time it ascends the empyrean's rain it towers aloft.
> Therefore I avail myself of colors and a brush to depict its
>   form.
> The depths that resulted from its fusing are not easy to
>   exhaust.[38]

The third painting, *Cranes of Good Omen*, depicts eighteen cranes flying above the main front gate to the palace, with two more cranes perched on the roof ornaments. Clouds surround the gate. Above the clouds the sky is painted an azure blue, something quite unusual in a Chinese painting. The lines of the tiles and the brackets of the eaves are all drawn with a ruler, a standard technique in architectural painting. The cranes, although small, are carefully depicted, the black and red feathers of their heads, necks, and tails scrupulously indicated. Their heads are all seen in profile, but the wings of those in flight are seen from above. They are flying in several directions, suggesting that they were circling around above the roof. This impression of action is countered by an equally strong impression of elegant patterning. The cranes are distributed fairly evenly over the sky in a two-dimensional pattern, with none blocking the view of another, rather like the sort of pattern one might find on a textile or lacquer box.

The inscription on *Cranes of Good Omen* instructs us to view it as a visual record of an extraordinary event witnessed by thousands of residents of the capital:

On the evening of the day after the First Prime festival in 1112, auspicious clouds suddenly formed in masses and descended about Duan Gate, illuminating it. The people all raised their heads to gaze at them. Suddenly a group of cranes appeared flying and calling in the sky. Two came to perch atop the "owl-tail" ridge-ornaments of the gate, completely at ease and self-composed. The others all wheeled about in the sky, as if responding to some rhythm. Residents of the capital walking about all bowed in reverence, gazing from afar. They sighed at length over the unusual sight. For some time the cranes did not disperse. Then they circled about and flew off, separating at the northwest quarter of the city. Moved by this auspicious event, I wrote the following poem to record the facts:

> At the break of day, multihued rainbows caress the
>   roof's ridge.
> The immortal birds, proclaiming good auspices,
>   suddenly arrive in favorable response.
> Wafting about, originally denizens of the Three Immortal
>   Isles,
> Pair after pair, they go on presenting their thousand-year-
>   old forms.
> They seem to be imitating the blue *luan* phoenix that
>   roosted atop the jeweled halls.
> Could they possibly be the same as the red geese that
>   congregated at Heaven's Pond?
> Lingering they call and cry at the Cinnabar Tower,
> Thus causing the ever-busy common folk to know of
>   their presence.[39]

In this poem Huizong suggests that the cranes are comparable to the auspicious bird mentioned in the classics, the *luan* phoenix, which responded to music, and also to the red geese that Emperor Wu of the Han caught during an expedition to the ocean. Huizong also stresses the connection between cranes and immortality, linking them to the mythical Penglai mountains and referring to their ability to live a thousand years. To Peter Sturman, the meticulous fashion in which the cranes and building are painted makes the auspicious event somehow more real. Maggie Bickford sees it slightly differently, interpreting the paintings as practical objects, designed to be efficacious.[40]

With only three surviving paintings, this visual record might not seem an especially monumental project, but if in fact thousands were made, as Deng Chun and Tang Hou claimed, it too can be taken as evidence that Huizong was not deterred by the challenge of huge undertakings. As a court art project, the pictures of auspicious phenomena would seem to fall to the side of art created to be stored away. There are no anecdotes about Huizong showing these paintings to his guests or groups of officials, even a small selection of them. Although one can imagine these paintings as bolstering the legitimacy of the Song house and its current emperor, they would not have performed that function through their visual imagery if few people in fact saw them. Perhaps it was enough that people knew they were being made. Or perhaps their real audience was Huizong, who certainly saw not only the ones he painted himself but also ones others did for him.[41]

Collections of Cultural Treasures

The collections of antiquities, paintings, and calligraphy that Huizong put together and catalogued certainly also deserve to be characterized as "monumental." Rulers before Huizong had collected treasures of many sorts, but Huizong's ambition as a collector was unprecedented. He not only put together large, comprehensive, up-to-date collections of books, paintings, calligraphies, and antiquities, but he also had them carefully catalogued.[42] Huizong knew that fine collections of culturally valued objects could add to the luster of his court. He had to go about collecting with care, however, given the many advances in art criticism and connoisseurship in the eleventh century. For his collections to be a source of prestige, they had to meet up-to-date standards.

The Song founders initiated the palace collections by confiscating the collections of the states that they defeated. In the eleventh century, however, it was private collectors who were the most active. Knowledgeable collectors sought not only books but also calligraphies, paintings, rubbings of inscriptions, ancient vessels, ancient jades, and even inkstones. They refined connoisseurial standards by articulating criteria for judging the artistic merit of works and assessing their authenticity.

In his own collecting, Huizong built on their accomplishments but carried them to a new, more imperial level. Huizong willingly used the resources of the throne to make the palace collections the preeminent ones in the land.

Huizong did not just collect on a large scale: he also catalogued his collections. Huizong used the resources at his disposal—the highly educated men who served in his literary organs—to prepare catalogues rich in information. In 1117 it was decided to catalogue the books in the imperial library for the first time in seventy-five years. When complete, the catalogue, which does not survive, was about a third bigger than the previous catalogue, listing altogether 73,877 rolls/chapters of books. The catalogues of antiquities, calligraphies, and paintings all do survive. Each of them is a selective list of the best objects in the collection. The thirty-chapter antiquities catalogue, *Antiquities Illustrated*, records 840 pieces, each depicted in a drawing. Annotations supply its measurements, a rubbing and a transcription of any inscriptions, and a discussion that dated the object by dynasty, classified it by type, and discussed its decoration and purpose. Altogether fifty-nine types of antiquities are distinguished, from cauldrons used in sacrificial ceremonies, to other ritual vessels such as goblets and tureens, to musical instruments such as bells, and mirrors. A large share of the sacrificial vessels have inscriptions, which adds to their interest and was probably a reason why they were selected for illustration in the catalogue (see Figure 9.1).

The *Xuanhe Calligraphy Catalogue* lists 1,220 works by 247 artists. Each calligrapher is given a brief biography and the items by him in the collection are listed by title. For the pre-Song period, the *Calligraphy Catalogue* includes works by most of those avidly sought by Song collectors, such as Wang Xizhi and Wang Xianzhi, and it has a generally strong showing for the entire pre-Tang period, with another 67 artists and 112 items. Nearly half the collection was made up of Tang works, with 122 artists represented. The Tang calligrapher best represented was Huaisu, with 101 pieces. Next was Ouyang Xun with 40, Yan Zhenqing with 28, Emperor Xuanzong with 25, and Zhang Xu with 24. In terms of script types, the catalogue heavily favored cursive and running (semicursive) scripts, each of which accounted for more than a third of the items listed. Seal and clerical script, by contrast, made up a very minor portion of the catalogued collection.[43] From the

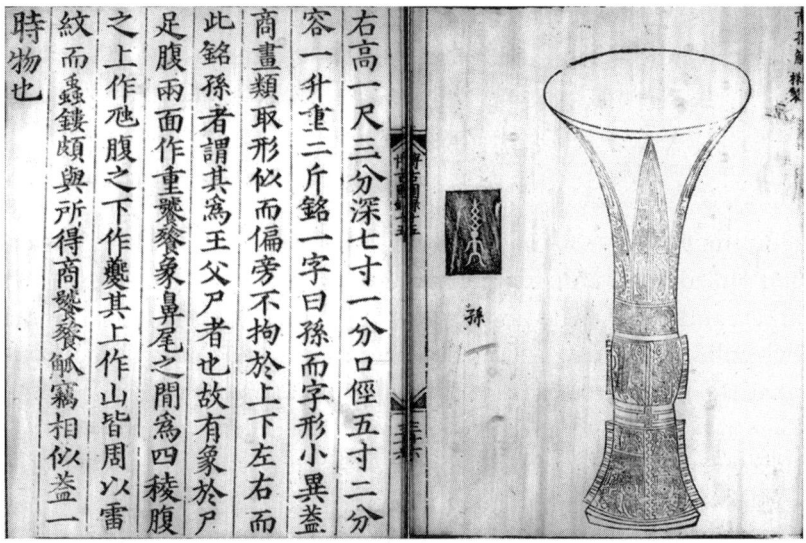

時物也 紋而蟲鏤頗與所得商饕餮瓿甕相似蓋一 之上作虺腹之下作夔其上作山皆以雷 足腹兩面作重饕餮象鼻尾之間爲四稜腹 此銘孫者謂其爲王父尸者也故有象於尸 商畫類取形似而偏旁不拘於上下左右而 容一升重二斤銘一字曰孫而字形小異蓋 右高一尺三分深七寸一分口徑五寸二分

Fig. 9.1. Entry in *Antiquities Illustrated.* The entry for a Shang dynasty *gu* wine cup gives the dimensions of the cup (1.3 ft. tall) and reads the inscribed character as *sun,* "grandchild," which it describes as slightly unusual, reflecting the tendency in early writing to be more picture-like. It identifies some of the imagery as an animal mask *(taotie),* snakes, dragons, and mountains, and compares it to another vessel with similar decoration. (BGT 1528 ed. 15.36a–b)

catalogue, it is clear that Huizong made enormous strides in updating the Song imperial calligraphy collection. Many works that had been in private hands in the late eleventh century had been acquired for the imperial collection.

The *Xuanhe Painting Catalogue* is similarly a select list, with biographies of artists and titles of works, but it includes five times as many items. It lists 6,397 paintings, each assigned to a painter, the painters categorized by the type of painting they specialized in: religious, figure, architecture, northern border people, dragons and fish, landscapes, animals, bird-and-flower, ink bamboo and small scenes, and vegetation, in that order. Five Dynasties and Song painters are well-represented, especially ones who worked in bird-and-flower, religious, and landscape painting. Fourteen artists have more than a hundred paintings listed. Some of these are Song court painters, such as Huang Jucai and Wu Yuanyu, but there are also many paintings by artists who never served at court, whose works must have been acquired by the court by gift or purchase. These would include such masters as the landscapists Fan Kuan and Li Cheng, and the literati painter Li Gonglin.

How did Huizong acquire objects for his collection? Some were offered to him as gifts, probably with an expectation of political or financial rewards. According to Mi Fu's funerary biography, after he was appointed professor of Huizong's Calligraphy School, he offered Huizong choice works of calligraphy and painting from his collection and Huizong rewarded him generously with gold, which encouraged others to submit their possessions. Certainly not every piece in Mi Fu's collection entered Huizong's collection, but a dozen or more apparently did. Objects once in the collection of Huizong's uncle Wang Shen also entered the palace collection. Wang Shen, for instance, was the owner of Sun Guoting's *Treatise on Calligraphy* as well as two pieces of Yan Zhenqing's calligraphy, all three of which are recorded in the *Xuanhe Calligraphy Catalogue*.[44] Another collector who presented objects from his collection to Huizong is Liu Fengshi, son of the notable collector of antiquities Liu Chang. In the case of antiquities, local officials would forward to the court pieces that had been unearthed in their jurisdictions, especially if they seemed especially fine or historically interesting. Huizong also made use of agents to seek out and acquire works for him. According to one account, the eunuch Tong Guan was sent south to search for artworks soon after Huizong took the throne. Other eunuchs were sent to Luoyang late in his reign, ready to spend liberally to obtain old paintings.[45]

Huizong's ritual reform project indirectly encouraged the acquisition of ancient vessels. In 1108/11, Huizong approved the request of Xue Ang, then serving in the Agency for Deliberating on Ritual, that "counties and prefectures be ordered to inquire about scholar-officials or commoners who have ancient vessels, then send someone to their homes to make drawings of them to be sent to the Agency for Deliberating on Ritual." In many cases, rather than just submit a picture, the vessels themselves were presented. In 1113/7 Huizong announced that more than five hundred ancient vessels had been found.[46]

Once art objects and ancient vessels arrived in the palace, Huizong assigned talented and erudite men to work with them. Three men who had passed the civil service examinations in 1100, Huizong's first year on the throne, worked with his collections: Liu Bing, Huang Bosi, and Zhai Ruwen. Others who worked at one time or another include Mi

Fu, Dong You, and a scholar named Gou. The eunuch Liang Shicheng also was entrusted with curatorial tasks. Liu Bing's *Song History* biography reports that he was summoned to examine ancient vessels whenever they arrived at Huizong's court.[47] Dong You and Huang Bosi both wrote notes on antiquities, paintings, and calligraphies that they worked with while serving in the Palace Library. Because of Huang Bosi's reputation for learning, we are told, Huizong summoned him to lecture to him on old documents and objects. When ancient vessels arrived, Huang Bosi took the lead in examining them.[48] After Zhai Ruwen was appointed to the Agency for Deliberating on Ritual, Huizong gave him an audience. He afterward told Cai Jing that Zhai Ruwen's knowledge of ancient vessels was profound and had him moved to the Palace Library. Zhai Ruwen was interested in books, paintings, calligraphy, and antiquities. He collected rubbings and old paintings and was skilled himself at several arts: calligraphy, painting, and even sculpture, sometimes redoing temple statues that he considered of poor quality.[49]

Any painting or calligraphy that Huizong acquired posed connoisseurial challenges. Those working with Huizong's collections had to determine if a work was authentic, identify and date it, and make a judgment on its quality. For the catalogue, they had to write up notes that dealt with these issues. Often these notes reveal the influence of Su Shi's writings on the connections among poetry, calligraphy, and painting.[50] Although Huizong's ban on the Yuanyou faction led him to ban publication of Su Shi's writings, Huizong did not champion the opposite of everything Su Shi had advocated. To Huizong, ideas about poetry and painting were the common property of the art-loving cultural leaders of the Kaifeng of his youth—men such as Wang Shen, Mi Fu, Zhao Lingrang, Li Gonglin, and Cai Jing—and did not need to be rejected just because Su Shi had written about them.

At the same time, Huizong's cataloguers drew attention to the great art produced by people close to the throne. Huizong's painting and calligraphy catalogues depict a cultural realm where the court plays the leading role but fully appreciates the enormous talents of its subjects. Men of letters are prominent among those subjects, but there is room also for Buddhist and Daoist clergy, imperial clansmen, court painters, and even court eunuchs. The exuberant treatment of Cai Jing as a calligrapher is discussed in Chapter 10. Also featured as calligraphers are

Wang Anshi, Cai Bian, and Liŭ Zhengfu (a member of Huizong's Council of State from 1110 to 1117).[51]

One reason, perhaps, that the cataloguers adopted the theory of the superiority of literati painting is that they could then use it to promote the art of imperial relatives. In fact, five of the twelve painters profiled in the section on ink bamboo and small scenes were Huizong's relatives: one was a prince (Shenzong's brother), one was that prince's wife, two were imperial clansmen, and one was an imperial son-in-law.[52] One of the fullest explications of literati painting is in the entry for the clansman Zhao Lingbi. The author contrasts ordinary painters who belabor their work and exceptional literati painters who "put their efforts into free expression, resulting in an abundance of meaning. The more they abbreviate, the more they capture the essence."[53]

Even less expected than the inclusion of so many imperial relatives as painters is the inclusion of nine eunuchs, including the eunuch general Tong Guan. Huizong, having grown up among eunuchs, perhaps having even learned something about painting or painting connoisseurship from palace eunuchs, did not share most literati's antipathy toward them. Some of the eunuch painters are described as amateurs, much like the imperial relatives. A few, however, seem closer to professional painters. This would seem to be the case with Jia Xiang, who was placed in charge of the painters when Harmony Preserved Hall was built and decorated. A eunuch who was himself a master painter (and whose water dragons, we are told, were realistic enough to give people goose bumps) would obviously make a good supervisor of painters.[54]

Whom did Huizong leave out of the painting and calligraphy catalogues? There are no glaring omissions from the painting catalogue, but the calligraphy catalogue pointedly left out Su Shi and Huang Tingjian. Both were recognized as major calligraphers in their lifetime, and their reputations had not diminished in the decade or two since their deaths. It would have been easy to find a few of Su Shi's memorials to transfer into Harmony Preserved Hall or the Palace Library if Huizong had wanted him in his calligraphy collection. But he did not. Even though both Su Shi and Huang Tingjian had been dead for more than a decade, Huizong still found their fame among the educated class sufficiently annoying that he was willing to risk discrediting his other selections by conspicuously excluding them. Here he went too far, setting himself an unattainable goal. Still, his ambition is worth noticing.

The Bright Hall

Huizong loved to build—schools, temples, offices, residences, gate towers—he commissioned them all. Of all of these, the one that perhaps best deserves the adjective "monumental" is Lis Bright Hall, not because it was the largest, but because it was seen as most fully embodying "antiquity." The classics refer in awed language to the wonders of the Bright Hall and its cosmic importance. It was said to have a round roof, symbolizing heaven, and a square foundation, symbolizing earth. The *Discussions of the White Tiger Hall* from the second century CE sums up much of the Bright Hall lore: "The Son of Heaven establishes the Bright Hall in order to communicate with the spirits, move heaven and earth, correct the four seasons, produce instruction and transformation, give a foundation to those of virtuous power, honor those who have the Dao, make eminent those who are capable, and reward those of good conduct."[55] Confucian ritual experts over the centuries tried to disentangle the contradictions in the sources on the Bright Hall and determine which were the earliest or most valid.[56] In the early Song, Nie Chongyi in his *Illustrations of the Three Ritual Classics* favored a plan with five rooms, with one room in the center and the others in the four corners, but he also included an alternative diagram with nine rooms, a version which he saw as a Qin deviation (see Figure 9.2). Chen Xiangdao (1053–1093), in his 150-*juan Book of Ritual (Lishu)* provides a more complex diagram, showing not merely five rooms, but also ancestral shrines, side rooms, windows, and doors. His nine rooms are arranged as a three-by-three grid (Figure 9.3).[57]

Probably because of all the difficulties in deciding what a Bright Hall should look like, it was rarely constructed. The two best documented cases are those of Wang Mang in the first century CE, who had a Bright Hall built in the years leading to his proclamation of a new dynasty, and Empress Wu, who built hers in the late seventh century after she had announced her own dynasty, which gave the Bright Hall the dubious distinction of connection to the two best-known usurpers in Chinese history.[58] Both of these halls were quite large.

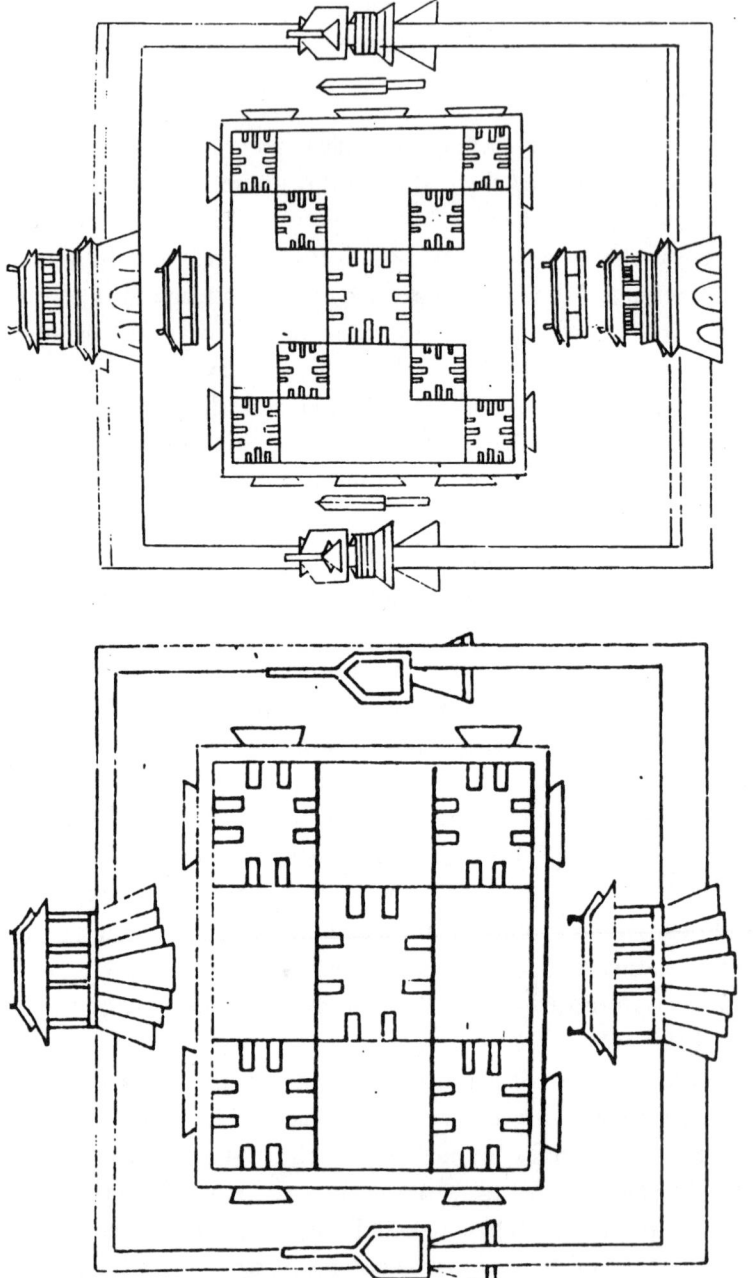

Fig. 9.2. Five-room and nine-room layouts for the Bright Hall in Nie Chongyi's *Illustrations of the Three Ritual Classics.* (SLTJZ 4.2a, 24a)

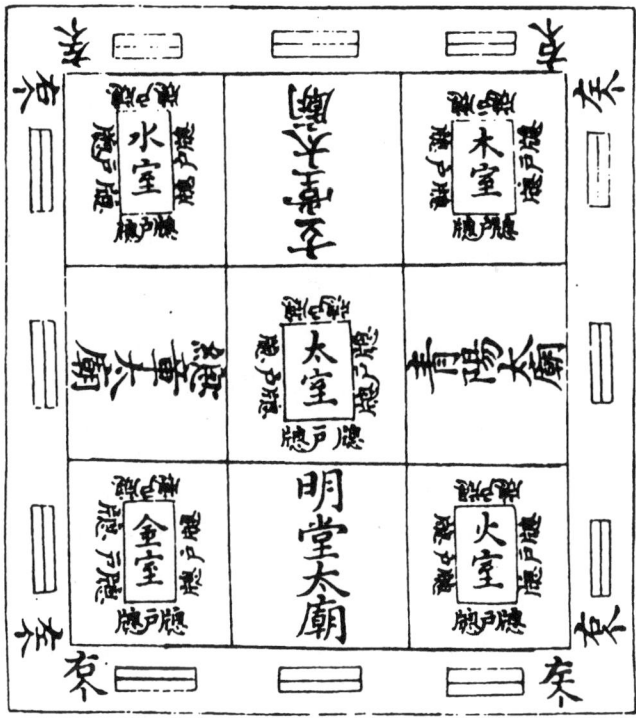

Fig. 9.3. Layout for the Bright Hall in Chen Xiangdao's *Book of Ritual.* (LS 89.1b)

Wang Mang's, which has been excavated, was square, about forty-two meters on each side, and oriented to face due south. It had three stories, with the top story a single round room. The middle level seems to have had nine rooms, the bottom level probably had twelve. Empress Wu's Bright Hall was larger, 300 *chi* ("feet") on each side and 294 *chi* tall. The ground floor represented the four seasons, each of the buildings facing one of the four different directions and decorated in the matching color according to Five Phases cosmology. The middle floor was divided into twelve units. The highest story was round, its roof was made of wood carved and lacquered to resemble glazed tiles. At the top was a gilded iron phoenix ten Chinese feet tall, but after it was damaged by wind it was replaced by a "flaming pearl" held up by dragons. Her Bright Hall continued to be used under Emperor Xuanzong, and the rituals performed in it are specified in the *Rituals of the Kaiyuan Period.* In it, all of the divinities given offerings at the Suburban Altar were also made offerings at the Bright Hall, along with the imperial ancestors.[59]

No Song emperor before Huizong built a Bright Hall, but Renzong and his successors all performed Bright Hall ceremonies in Grand Celebration Hall, marking out five rooms. Some of Renzong's officials thought that Bright Hall sacrifices should be made only to the highest divinity, heaven (equated with Lord of Highest Heaven), and the emperor's own father. Renzong, though, wanted the rituals at the Bright Hall to be as comprehensive as at the Suburban Sacrifice, which included the spirits of both heaven and earth, the sun, moon, rivers, and seas, plus the five lords. He also wanted all of his three predecessors on the Song throne to receive offerings as corollaries.[60] James Liu sees Renzong's position as appropriate for a ruler with absolutist aspirations, wanting to control all the spiritual forces under a single roof.[61] Nevertheless, Shenzong, hardly less absolutist than Renzong, came out strongly for limiting the Bright Hall rites to heaven and his own father, a stance Huizong later adopted out of filial respect.

Cai Jing was the one to raise the issue of the Bright Hall to Huizong. In 1105 he asked Huizong to consider the plan of an official named Yao Shunren who had been thinking about the Bright Hall for twenty years. Huizong was receptive and told Cai Jing that Shenzong had wanted to build a Bright Hall. He also said that a diagram had been prepared which still was extant in the palace, but that many details had not been settled. Cai Jing responded by telling him that Yao Shunren had drawn up two alternative plans, one with each room facing south, the other with the four rooms each facing a different direction, with the ruler going to a different one each season. Huizong chose the latter, and assigned the architect Li Jie to work with Yao Shunren to come up with a detailed plan.[62]

When Yao Shunren reported back, he began by praising all the steps Huizong had already taken to restore the institutions of antiquity, especially the school system and the Biyong Academy. He also tried to entice Huizong by evoking how splendid the ceremonies at the Bright Hall would be, with the procession of the imperial carriage and honor guard, resplendent with pennants flying and drums and flutes resounding, and envoys from all directions standing in their appropriate positions. He described how he envisioned the Bright Hall complex, with a two-story central room, four gates each with a room, four corners without walls, and a roof of thatch. "Evaluated in terms of its connection to antiquity, it is based on the examination of texts. In terms of ritual, it is not disruptive. It is neither extravagant nor penny-pinching." Building it would involve "reaching back a thousand years to antiquity." Huizong concurred on the need to recover the true ancient form: "We should not model ourselves on the degenerated forms used in Han and Tang times, but go back to the system of the Three Ancient Dynasties," and he authorized gathering the lumber. Nevertheless, the project was canceled a few months later when the appearance of a comet was taken as a negative omen and Cai Jing was dismissed.[63]

The first sign that the Bright Hall plans would be revived occurred in 1114/6 when an official in Yuanling county (Hunan) reported that twenty-seven large cedar trees had floated down the river after a flood, trees large enough to provide the pillars and beams for a Bright Hall. By this point, Yao Shunren and Li Jie both had passed away, but their plans were still extant. Huizong had a model made and placed in Promoting Governance Hall for his officials to inspect and discuss.[64] Wang Anzhong wrote on behalf of the officials to congratulate Huizong on the model of the Bright Hall and the calligraphy Huizong did for the name plaque for the central Great Room. He explicitly contrasted Huizong's design with those of the Han and Tang periods which had not been as firmly rooted in the classics. Not long afterward, heaven confirmed approval of the project. Those selecting stones at Yingyang for use in the construction of the Bright Hall found a stone with the word "Bright" *(ming)* on it, a discovery considered so auspicious that it was celebrated with new procession flags. Wang Anzhong, in his congratulatory memorial, not only interpreted this inscribed stone as a positive response to the construction project but even likened it to the famous ancient cases of mysterious inscribed objects, the River Diagram and Luo Document.[65]

Once the decision was made to go forward with the Bright Hall, Cai Jing was given general charge of the construction, assisted by three of his sons, Cai You, Cai Tiao, and Cai Shu. The eunuch Liang Shicheng served as the construction manager. After receiving this assignment, Cai Jing submitted a detailed plan specifying the dimensions of each element in the complex. The overall dimensions were 171 by 189 Chinese feet, making it considerably smaller than Empress Wu's Bright

Hall. An important innovation was the location of Huizong's Bright Hall inside the Palace City at a site selected on geomantic principles. To make room for it, the Palace Library was moved south of the Palace City. The *Song History* records that ten thousand workers were drafted for the project, which should probably be taken simply to mean a large number, or more than the author of some document approved.[66]

Once construction was started, Huizong kept an eye on its progress and periodically issued hand-drafted edicts about it. In one he stressed how rulers building Bright Halls had failed again and again to come up to the standard of antiquity. "Some violated the classics and followed custom; others were misled by the diverse theories and lost the main idea." Huizong also explained what he had learned from the *Rites of Zhou*'s "Examining Artisans," such as how the structure could have five rooms (*shi*) and twelve chambers (*tang*).[67] Other hand-drafted edicts refer to complaints about how the project was being managed. One dated 1115/5/11 insisted that all costs come from government funds so that the project would not become a burden on the people. Transportation of goods should be paid for, not treated as a labor service obligation. A few weeks later Huizong put on notice officials who acted corruptly in recruiting workers or gathering materials: they faced loss of official status and exile to the far south.[68]

Cai You submitted nine memorials in the tenth month of 1115 on the design of the Bright Hall. One discussed roofs. Earlier practice had ranged from thatch to tile to wood lacquered to look like tile. To give due consideration to ancient precedents and modern needs, he proposed using plain unglazed tile for the main building but glazed tile for the gates, which would also have owl-tail ornaments.[69] In another memorial he urged eliminating the use of bells hanging from the corner eaves because the practice was not ancient. He also rejected the decorative flaming pearl used at the top of Empress Wu's Bright Hall. On the matter of color, he proposed yellow for the roof ridge and owl-tail ornament, and red for the walls because yellow is the color of the earth and red the color of the dynasty (from its association with fire in the Five Phases scheme). The longest discussion concerned the classical associations of various trees, with Cai You coming to the conclusion that catalpa and pine should be planted in the Bright Hall compound.[70]

Since the *New Forms of the Five Categories of Rites of the Zhenghe Period* had been issued before the Bright Hall was built, its specification for Bright Hall rites had assumed that they were being held in Grand Celebration Hall, and thus did not fit the new space.[71] Thus new ritual instructions had to be drawn up. The Agency for Instituting Rituals asked for guidance on such issues as the direction the emperor should face, how many people should accompany him as an honor guard, and the colors of the banners and pennants they would carry. The agency also proposed announcing major amnesties at the Bright Hall and having imperial brush edicts announced there before passing them to the Secretariat-Chancellery for distribution. Other issues raised concerned the use of jade tablets, the music to be performed, the garments the emperor should wear, and the containers for food offerings. The agency proposed setting a large number of vessels with food before the tablets for both Highest Heaven and Shenzong, including quite a few of the vessels listed in the *Rites of Zhou*, such as the oxen beaker, sheep beaker, pig beaker, mountain beaker, elephant beaker, and sacrificial animal beaker.[72] Many of these vessels were probably cast for this purpose, modeled on ancient vessels in Huizong's collections (see Figure 9.4). Before the completion of the Bright Hall, Huizong personally wrote out the names for each of the five rooms and their five gates, to be used for their name plaques.[73]

On 1117/4/23, Huizong drafted an edict himself that announced the completion of the Bright Hall. He took pride in its basis in investigation of the ritual classics and claimed that it came close to the model of the Three Dynasties. On the important issue of which divinities and ancestors would receive offerings in the Bright Hall, he took the more austere position: offerings there should be offered exclusively to Highest Heaven and Shenzong, as Shenzong had also ruled. All of the other offerings should be moved to Grand Celebration Hall or Cultured Virtue Hall.[74] A few days later Huizong announced that Daoist masters would participate in Bright Hall ceremonies. Huizong also involved himself with the music to be used in the ceremonies at the Bright Hall. The Music Bureau had located a set of stone chimes made at Shenzong's request which they thought could be used for music in the Bright Hall, an idea that Huizong approved. On 1117/8/12 Huizong showed his officials nine songs he had written for the Bright Hall rites and asked the academicians to write the remaining three.[75]

Fig. 9.4. Mountain beaker made at Huizong's court. The 1121 inscription on this vessel identifies it as a "mountain *zun*," one of the vessels called for in the *Rites of Zhou*, and declares that the emperor made it on the basis of studying antiquity. Height 29 cm., weight 5.4 kg. (Palace Museum, Beijing)

A rehearsal of the rites took place on 1117/8/24 and the first ceremony twelve days later. A few weeks after that Huizong imitated ancient practice by going to the Bright Hall on the first day of the tenth month to announce the next year's calendar. He also began going there on the first day of each month to announce the schedule of government business for the month. Many of these announcements have been preserved, and give an interesting glimpse of what an emperor's schedule looked like, much of it consisting of astronomical information and the schedule of sacrifices. In the twelfth month Huizong approved a request to post these monthly announcements of policies where people could read them and print them for people outside the capital.[76]

The next year (1118/4/27) Huizong issued an edict pledging to perform the Bright Hall rites himself each winter but also stating that the rites should be done on a relatively modest scale. Because the Bright Hall is within the Palace City, he explained, there was no need for an honor guard. "In the days of the former kings, the major rituals were simple." What really matters are the "internal feelings," not the material objects. In 1119/8 a full set of specifications for ceremonies for the ceremonies in the Bright Hall were issued, coming to 1,206 volumes (*ce*), and Huizong approved having wood blocks cut to print and distribute them.[77]

The Northeast Marchmount

As the details of the Bright Hall were being settled, Huizong took on another grand project, a new royal park, known as the Northeast Marchmount (Genyue).[78] The park can be seen as the second phase in Huizong's enhancing of the royal palaces. Because Kaifeng was not a planned city the way the Tang capitals Chang'an and Luoyang had been, the space set aside for the palace was much more cramped— amounting to only ten percent of the space for palace buildings in the Tang capitals.[79] After Huizong had been on the throne a decade, he began trying to expand the palace grounds. He had a wine brewery, two army barracks, two Buddhist temples, and workshops for imperial tailors moved from the region just north of the Palace City. Then he "moved" Extended Blessings Palace from the west side of the palace complex to the newly cleared space. This was a substantial increase in the footprint of the palace complex, even if the statement that it doubled the size is an exaggeration. Hong Mai described the newly constructed Extended Blessings as the most extravagant palace project done in Northern Song times. It had seven halls and thirty pavilions, the largest 120 feet wide.[80] An artificial mountain with a pavilion on top was 110 feet tall. Hong Mai attributed the frivolity to the way the work was assigned: Cai Jing arranged for five leading eunuchs each to take responsibility for one part of the complex (they are identified as Tong Guan, Yang Jian, Jia Xiang, Lan Congxi, and He Xin). Each had considerable leeway to decorate the buildings in the styles he preferred, and they competed against each other to make the most exquisite buildings.[81]

In the space that had been occupied by the former Extended Blessings Palace, on the west side of the palace complex, Huizong built a new complex, called Harmony Preserved Hall. This was the site of the 1119 banquet discussed in Chapter 10. Decorated in an understated style with unpainted wooden beams and rafters, its buildings had a total of seventy-five room-units. It had pavilions for storing books, antiques, paintings, calligraphy, and musical instruments. Huizong wrote a record of it that listed the names of the structures, praised the craftsmanship, and referred to the collections stored there.[82]

Even though Extended Blessings Palace contained extensive gardens, by 1117 Huizong had decided to create a separate park further to the northeast, just within the wall of the old city and adjoining the recently built Daoist temple, Highest Clarity Precious Registers Temple (see Map 1). This was a time when Huizong was deeply absorbed in Daoism, and his interest in Daoist paradises seems to have shaped his development of this park.

There was a long tradition in China of both large imperial parks and of gardens that represented paradises. Probably the most famous was the huge cosmic park (four hundred *li* in circumference) created by Emperor Wu of the Han and celebrated in many Han literary works. This Shanglin Park was said to have 3,000 species of plants and valuable exotic stones, including a coral tree with 462 branches. Edward Schafer remarks that this park "had indeed become a cosmic mandala—a replica of 'Under Heaven,' the holy domain of the Son of Heaven." Lothar Ledderose stresses the magic involved: making gardens like this drew on "the magical belief that by artificially making a replica of something one wields power over the real object."[83] Sui and Tang rulers also built large parks. The Sui imperial park to the west of the palace in Luoyang was 229 *li* in circumference, which the Tang emperors reduced to 71 *li*.[84]

Huizong's park was small in comparison: it had a circumference of "more than ten *li*" (i.e., about six kilometers around, or no more than 2.25 square kilometers, making it 20 percent smaller than the Qing

Summer Palace, which is 2.9 square kilometers, and 30 percent smaller than New York's Central Park, which is 3.4 square kilometers). A forty-six-foot-tall stone, named Divine Conveyance Rock, was just one of many named rocks in the park, all admired for their unusual shape and the way they represented the forces of nature. Behind this rock was an artificial mountain made of piled stones and dirt.[85] There were also streams, pools, waterfalls, and grottos, all given names, some of which carried Daoist overtones, such as "Propitiating the Perfected Ones Ledge" or "Eight Immortals Lodge." Paths led through the park and over its hills, sometimes on steps carved into rocks and wooden planks fastened to cliffs. Water was brought to the top so that it flowed down into pools. The park was stocked with rare plants and a great variety of birds and animals, including gibbons from Sichuan and hundreds of deer. One of the buildings, called Thrice Lovely, housed an image of Huizong's recently deceased consort Liu Mingjie, whom Lin Lingsu had revealed was Peaceful Consort of Nine-Splendored Jade Truth. Perhaps this building functioned as a shrine for her.[86]

Huizong wrote an account of the Northeast Marchmount that was inscribed on a huge stele placed near the entrance of the park. This rather long text begins on a very general level with a discussion of the geographical locations of the capitals since the Zhou dynasty. Huizong then discussed earlier parks: "The park of King Wen was seventy *li* square; in it they built the Numinous Tower, which the common people came to see.[87] When they created the Numinous Pond, fishes jumped in it.[88] [In the Daoist heavens], high above there is the Golden Tower and the mountain of the Jade Capital; from it the Great Lord of the Divine Empyrean came down to extend broad love.[89] And in the sea there are the three islands of Penglai, which the lords treat as their capital and where the Transcendents and sages dwell."[90]

Huizong next discussed ways the park re-created the great mountains and bodies of water of the realm and the plants from all over growing there, such as loquat, orange, tangerine, lichee, magnolia, and jasmine. Even though the Northeast Marchmount was known above all as a garden, with rare plants and animals as well as unusual stones, it had many buildings as well, all of which needed to have distinctive names. Huizong mentioned more than thirty structures, such as Hall of Flowers with Green Perianths, Receiving Mist Kiosk, Kunlun Clouds Kiosk, and Documents Lodge.[91] The names of the halls were part of the overall aesthetic package. That is, giving a poetic name, or a name with poetic overtones, to a building helped frame how an observer responded to it. Moreover, for every building with a name, there had to be a name plaque, and its calligraphy contributed to the visual interest of the garden. Who did the calligraphy on the name plaques in this garden has not been recorded, but it would not be exceptional if Huizong did some himself and called on Cai Jing to do others.

The most massive element in the garden was Longevity Mountain:

To the south [of the Hall of Dragons' Song] is the jagged and cragged Longevity Mountain. Its two peaks are erect side-by-side; its aligned cliff walls are like screens. From it, a waterfall descends into the Wild Goose Pool. The pool water is clear and fresh, wavy and ripply. Wild ducks and wild geese float and dive on the surface of the water. Those roosting and resting among the rocks are beyond reckoning in number. The kiosk atop the mountain is called "Honk-Honk." Directly to the north is the Scarlet Empyrean Loft, where peaks and ridges rise prominently in thousands of folds and in myriad layers, for who knows how many tens of *li*. Yet in square area they encompass not even several tens of *li*. To the west, then, is grown ginseng, hill-thistle, boxthorn, chrysanthemum, yellow-germ, and hemlock-parsley, which blanket the mountains and pervade the embankments. The center [of this area] is designated the Drug Shanty. Moreover, grain, hemp, pulse, wheat, millet, beans, rice, and sorghum [are grown there]. The homes constructed [in this area] resemble farmhouses; thus it is known as West Village.[92]

Huizong's building of a rocky mound with structures at the top is reminiscent of the Han Emperor Wu's Jianzhang Palace, which had replicas of the islands of the immortals, Penglai, Fangzhang, and Yingzhou. The platform at the top, where he hoped to meet immortals, was two hundred Chinese feet high. In Sui times, Emperor Yang similarly built a garden with these three island mountains. At the top they had structures whose names let us recognize that their purpose was to allow contact with Daoist Transcendents: "Lookout for Reaching the Perfected," "Platform for Assembling the Spirits," and "Place for Gathering the Immortals."[93] Huizong was probably conscious of these precedents.

Huizong was not exceptional in liking unusual rocks; in the eleventh century both Su Shi and Mi Fu were known for their fondness for striking rocks.[94] Many Song paintings depict rocks in garden settings, including *Literary Gathering* (Plate 3), discussed in Chapter 7, and *Auspicious Dragon Rock* (Plate 11), discussed earlier in this chapter. Huizong's love of strange rocks is mentioned in a few anecdotes, and he is said to have had a catalogue of his rocks compiled, which unfortunately is not extant.[95] A monk named Zuxiu who left a record of his visit to the Northeast Marchmount says that Huizong gave the rocks in the Northeast Marchmount park names such as "Ascendant Dragon of the Dawning Sun," "Seated Dragon Gazing at Clouds," "Jade Dragon with Raised Head," "Venerable Pine of Myriad Longevity," "Perched in Roseate Clouds and Stroking the Triaster [Stars]," "Embouching the Sun and Spewing the Moon," "Arrayed in the Clouds and Reaching to the Dipper," "Thunder Gate and Lunar Den." These names were incised into the rocks.[96]

Literary men at Huizong's court knew it fell to them to extol and glorify the park. Wang Anzhong wrote two poems on it, as did several other poets of the time. Once Huizong assigned Cao Zu and his colleague Li Zhi the task of writing rhapsodies *(fu)* on the new park. They both wrote at length, Cao Zu composing his in the form of a dialogue between a resident of the city and a visitor who asks questions about the garden. The last question concerns the viability of plants brought from the south. The local resident attributes the success of the transplants to the ruler's looking on the land within the four seas as one family and his unifying the *qi* of all under heaven.[97]

On another occasion, Cao Zu and Li Zhi were instructed to write one hundred quatrains on the Northeast Marchmount and its sights. Here is one:

Honk-Honk Pavilion

As the sage ruler does not shoot living things,
By the banks of the pond the flock of geese take off and
    honk at will.

> Yet they form lines as they enter the cloudy sky,
> Just like a proper set of brothers.[98]

These poems were perhaps intended to counter the association of imperial gardens with royal indulgence. Already in Han times, as Schafer notes, "the moralizing writers of Han liked to use the idea of the imperial park and the activities characteristic of it as symbols of folly and frivolity, metaphors of extravagance and waste."[99] The two poets assigned to write rhapsodies on the Northeast Marchmount, by contrast, identified it with divine response to sage rule.

⌒ Do THE SIX PROJECTS discussed in this chapter have much in common? Their diversity reflects the broad range of Huizong's intellectual, artistic, and religious interests. What they share is their ambition—they are all monumental in intent. Huizong wanted tangible accomplishments, concrete evidence that he had surpassed his predecessors in one way or another. Huizong used his reign names in the titles of the books—The Zhenghe ritual code, medical books, Daoist canon, book catalogue, and album of auspicious pictures, and the Xuanhe catalogues of his antiquities, paintings, and calligraphy. Thus these works would be forever associated with his reign.

Looking at these projects together brings to the fore the ways Huizong organized large projects, the ways he tried to manage the interpretation of his projects, and the ways his interests in Daoism found expression in projects not in any narrow sense Daoist.

In thinking about the politics of these projects, it should be kept in mind that they all involved substantial allocation of resources, either from state coffers or the Privy Purse. Ritual could be costly but was rarely discussed in terms of cost—rulings on disputed ritual issues never explicitly favor the less expensive alternative. Revising the ritual code took up the time of a substantial number of scholars, and working on the code could have been an assignment many officials sought, if for no other reason than it kept them in the capital working on what was essentially a literary project.[100] The Bright Hall and the Northeast Marchmount were both costly projects which provided opportunities for those handling the assembly of materials or workers to benefit financially, as Huizong indicated in his hand-drafted edicts denouncing illegal profiteering. Thus, there would always be officials who would be in favor of new projects because they saw possibilities to benefit personally.

Did Huizong's officials encourage him to busy himself revising the ritual code or building a Bright Hall to keep him away from things they wanted to handle themselves? Much of the work on the ritual code was done while Cai Jing was out of office. The decision to go forward with the Bright Hall was made in 1115, a time when Huizong was pursuing Daoist projects and Cai Jing was attending court every third day. One could imagine that Cai Jing supported the idea of the Bright Hall as something that would appeal to Huizong yet keep him engaged on the Confucian side of governing. What better than the Bright Hall to distract someone like Huizong, with his love of building, pageantry, and interest in cosmic forces? But we could also turn this around. Could Huizong have been making use of the highly approved "antiquity" of the Bright Hall to keep Cai Jing and his sons busy with a "Confucian" construction project, to keep them away from his Daoist projects and let him turn to Daoist masters for expertise there?

Of course, we do not have to assume that only one side was trying to use the other: both Huizong and Cai Jing could have had motivations for the building of the Bright Hall other than the desire to recover antiquity in a more authentic way, and both could have been trying to manipulate the other at the same time. There could well have been other actors involved, such as Liang Shicheng, the eunuch who was so often given charge of construction projects and who most likely benefited financially whenever large projects were undertaken.

Building the Northeast Marchmount was seemingly the most costly project. What made it so expensive was that most of the rocks, trees, and other plants were transported long distances. In 1118 Huizong received a report that those procuring things for the palace used a variety of ploys to profit themselves, such as not paying the market price or keeping some of the items for themselves. The author wanted to require receipts for all purchases, with date, prices, and quantities all specified. In response, Huizong issued a hand-drafted edict that began, "I rule over the many lands and have the wealth of all within the four seas. With the entire realm supplying me, what could I lack?" He then went on to say that he had from time to time given cash, ordination certificates, or silks to the various authorities to purchase things such as interesting stones and plants. Some were intended for offerings at the ancestral temples, or to give to leading officials or relatives, so they were not all for himself. Corruption of any sort connected to procuring these items would be treated as a serious crime, not eligible for pardon, he declared.[101] Huizong's stern warning against corruption would seem to have had little effect. The man in overall charge, Zhu Mian, was perceived as not only personally corrupt but also indifferent to the hardships he imposed on people.[102] Thus, the way the plants and rocks were collected has always tainted this park and made it a symbol of Huizong's inordinate profligacy.

Huizong naturally had tried to frame this park quite differently. To publicize the court's view of these projects, Huizong wrote or claimed to write edicts, inscriptions, and essays. Two of the justifications he offered are worth brief discussion. One is to continue Shenzong's legacy. This glossed the efforts as filial, a motivation that Confucian scholars could not dismiss as trivial, making use of this justification politically astute. Huizong claimed that Shenzong had wanted to prepare a new ritual code, for instance. The other reason was to recover or reattain antiquity. Antiquity was such a broadly shared value in his day that this was not a controversial claim. Collecting antiquities and building the Bright Hall were both presented as ways to get closer to the perfection of antiquity.

In order for people to understand his rationales, Huizong had his essays engraved on stone where relevant people would be able to read them—often near the government building most directly concerned. Huizong's preface for the *New Forms* was carved into stone placed at the Court of Imperial Sacrifices.[103] His account of the Northeast Marchmount was inscribed on a stele placed at its entrance. Printing was also used to get the court's interpretation out. An abbreviated edition of *New Forms* was printed for distribution throughout the country. The entire Daoist canon was printed. The large catalogue of Huizong's antiquities was also printed and probably the intention was to publish the others as well.[104] So too was a collection of pronouncements made at the Bright Hall, and the 1,206 volumes of specifications for the rituals performed there.

All six of these projects offer testimony of Huizong's determination to integrate Daoism into the life of his court. He had Daoism introduced into the state cult rites in many small ways, such as making announcements at Daoist temples. Prominent among the paintings in Huizong's collections were paintings of Daoist divinities and immortals; in addition, several Daoist priests were among the artists included.[105] The Bright Hall was explicitly mentioned in several of the ancient classics, which kept it part of the learning of Confucian ritualists. Still, its spirit was not that far from the Daoism of Huizong's day. In a hand-drafted edict of 1116/4/29, Huizong argued that the Daoist Jade Emperor is none other than the Lord of Highest Heaven of the state cult.

> The Dao cannot be named and yet it hides in the unnamed. If to name it is to possess it, then it can be named in a way that enlarges it or in a way that diminishes it. Therefore, since antiquity, it has not been possible to dispense with naming it. When named with respect to strength, it is called the Dao. When named with respect to transcending form, it is called heaven. When named in terms of gods and their responsiveness, it is called Lord (*di*). The three emerge together but have different names. Although my virtue does not merit it, the highest rank has been conferred on me. Morning and night when thinking of the enormity of the Dao and its marvelous minute interpenetrations into the mysterious, profound beyond understanding, I tremble with awe, fearing that I will not be able to embody and sustain its laws. Through eternity the Jade Emperor and the Lord of Highest Heaven have controlled the myriad transformations. Although their names are different their substance is the same. Nevertheless, in the past commentators have discussed them separately. Because they could not grasp their unity, their subtleties were not fully expressed. Now we are building a Bright Hall in order to make offerings and associated offerings and yet the name and substance are not in accord, which makes my heart skip a beat and puts me in trepidation, fearful that I have no way to succeed to heaven's blessings and the mandate of the honored lord. I have circumspectly selected days to fast and purify myself so that I can reverently confer this honored title: Supreme Opening Heaven, Grasping the Talisman, Directing the Calendar, Containing the True, Embodying the Dao, Highest Heaven, Jade Emperor, Lord on High. I order

that when the authorities prepare for the rituals, offering the jade treasure and jade strips, they will do it in accord with my ideas.[106]

Huizong also associated the Northeast Marchmount with Daoism. In the essay Huizong wrote on the first day of 1122 to commemorate the completion of the park, he suggests connections between the pressure of work, the appeal of Daoism, and his need for the park:

When there is time after all the myriad affairs [of state], I take a leisurely walk here, where rank and wealth are irrelevant. Then I ascend the mountains and visit the pools. Going deep in and searching out the narrow passages, [seeing] the green and red signs of new growth and the splendid pavilions that soar up makes me happy and content and in tune with the gods. Thus I forget about the commotion and confusion of everyday life and want to float up to the clouds where bliss is lasting. When on a clear night I spread out a *jiao* offering and intone the prayers, the [incense] smoke rises like clouds to the grottos, and torches illuminate the half empty [space]. Jade belt ornaments tinkle as I walk down the path; suddenly thunder and lightning shake the doors of the pavilions. Then there is [the return to regular life], the carriage and the formal hat, coming and going, dealing with people, tasting sweet and sour [food], inspecting the incense and pouring libations, and yet [something remains], a drop, a kernel, the piles under the bed. Then in a moment, I fly up to mount the clouds, silent without a sound.

Now, it is true that heaven without people has nothing to work with; people without heaven cannot develop. I occupy the most honored position as ruler with ten thousand chariots and dwell within nine layers of walls. Still, here I can find pleasure among the mountains and trees, invigorate my internal organs, and bring clarity to my ears and eyes.[107]

The projects discussed in this chapter range from the fully public— such as the books produced and the Bright Hall where the officials in the capital participated in ceremonies—to the semipublic, Huizong's collections of paintings, calligraphies, and antiquities, which he showed not only to court painters but also to occasional guests, to the Northeast Marchmount, which his highest officials all seem to have visited, to the more private, such as the pictures of auspicious phenomena, probably shown only to a very restricted audience. Chapter 10 turns to the pleasurable side of life in the palace, again from the more public side to the more private, from court poetry writing to Huizong's relations with his consorts and children.

10

Finding Pleasure in Court and Palace Life

> With the aid of heaven, I now have exactly fifty sons and daughters. The time is nearing for them, in order of age, to be set up and houses built for them.
>
> *—From an edict Huizong drafted himself on 1116/2/26*

> Huizong called for attendants to bring the tea equipment, then with his own hands he poured the hot water and whisked the tea. Before long the white foam in the teacup resembled scattered stars and the moon. The emperor turned to us and said, "This is tea I made myself."
>
> *—From the account of an 1120 party in Extended Blessing Palace*

IN THE SONG IMAGINATION, paradise resembled a royal court where guests were entertained by lovely young women performing on musical instruments, dancing, and serving the finest food and drink. This meant also, of course, that when people thought about the leisure time of the emperor, they imagined him surrounded by endless temptations and able to fulfill any wish. In most people's imagination, it took a fierce determination for a ruler not to let the easy availability of sensual pleasures divert him from his weighty political responsibilities, and all too many rulers did not pass this test.

What sorts of entertainments diverted Huizong and his guests? Like rulers other places Huizong sponsored entertainments involving music, song, food, wine, and games. Composing poetry was a common amusement, but one that was considered relatively noble and culturally uplifting. Women entertainers could perform for his guests, by playing instruments, singing, or dancing, but his own consorts and daughters did not participate in these entertainments. Huizong himself had ample opportunities to enjoy the pleasures of feminine company as well as the pleasures of seeing his dozens of children grow up.

Poetry in the Culture of Huizong's Court

Over the centuries, quite a few Chinese rulers have been esteemed for making their courts centers of poetry and related arts. Particularly notable were Emperor Wu in the Han, who brought poets to his court, Emperor Wu of the Liang, who was a patron of both literature and Buddhism, Emperor Xuanzong in the Tang period, who was a patron not only of poets but also of painters and musicians, and Li Yu of the Later Tang, who gained a reputation as a poet, calligrapher, and painter, as well as a patron of those arts.[1] Huizong embraced this facet of emperorship; he seems to have been genuinely fond of poetry and to have enjoyed its performative side.

Huizong promoted poetry at his court in diverse ways. From time to time he appointed officials above all for their talent as poets. Jiang Han, Chao Duanli, and Chao Chongzhi, after being recommended by Cai Jing, all received appointments in the Music Bureau, where part of their duties was to write song lyrics (*ci*).[2] Huizong was a patron of this literary genre through the Music Bureau, especially after the introduction of a new form of banquet music in 1113 and a search for old songs that had been lost. Other men known as song writers who worked at the Music Bureau in this period include Zhou Bangyan, Tian Wei, Wan Siyong, and Xu Shen. Zhou Bangyan had served during both Shenzong's and Zhezong's reigns, seemingly quite comfortable with the reform program. He served in the provinces during much of Huizong's reign, but in 1116 returned to the capital. In recognition of his standing as one of the leading song writers of the day, in 1117 he was appointed head of the Music Bureau, a post he held only a few months.[3]

Another leading poet of the day recruited by Huizong was Chen Yuyi, known above all for his *shi* poetry. In 1122 Chen Yuyi was recommended to Huizong by Ge Shengzhong, a high official at the Imperial Academy, where Chen Yuyi was a student. Ge Shengzhong, impressed with Chen Yuyi's poetic talent, sent Huizong a set of five poems the student had written on the topic of monochrome plum blossom paintings. Huizong, liking the poems, summoned Chen Yuyi for an audience and eventually assigned him to literary posts, mostly in the Palace Library. Huizong is said to have especially appreciated a couplet of his that compared the painter's ability to capture the essence of the flower without concentrating on its external appearance to discernment of a famed judge of horses who did not even notice their color or sex.[4]

Even officials not viewed principally as poets were encouraged by Huizong to write poetry at court. We saw some of their poems on celebration of auspicious omens in Chapter 6. At banquets and other occasions when the emperor spent time with his high officials, he often had them write poetry. He might assign a topic, a tune, and/or a rhyme word and expect those in attendance to compose a poem or song. At one banquet, he asked two of his leading officials to write poems. Wang Anzhong complied with a two-hundred-line poem (five words per line) and Feng Xizai submitted one eighty-eight lines long (seven words per line). Reportedly, Huizong was greatly pleased with Wang Anzhong's poem and had copies of it made to distribute to his top officials.[5]

Xing Junchen, an official good at writing humorous and satirical poems, was once asked to write a song with the rhyme word *gao* (tall) to the tune "Lin Jiang xian" (Immortal by the bank of the Yangzi River), then asked to compose one on a Chen dynasty cypress tree using Chen as the rhyme word. The third assignment was to discuss the excellence of a poem submitted by the high-ranking eunuch Liang Shicheng using the rhyme word *shi* (poem).[6] Writing poems in response to assignments was a common pastime among men of letters, so men at Huizong's court would have been familiar with the practice.[7] When it was the emperor initiating the activity, however, the social dynamic was undoubtedly different.

One such exchange took place in 1107 after Huizong wrote a poem for Cai Jing to commemorate a new studio he had named the Pavilion of the Joyous Meeting of Ruler and Subjects. Many officials responded with matching poems, which were collected together into a book. Wang Zao, then a young official eager to get noticed, on seeing the book of poems wrote three poems using the same rhymes, which soon got passed around and helped him secure an appointment in the Palace Library. This was considered much to Wang Zao's credit and reported in his biography.[8]

Huizong kept many of the poems Cai Jing wrote for him, treating them as calligraphy, so the list of Cai Jing's calligraphies in the *Xuanhe Calligraphy Catalogue* provides titles of many poems he had written for Huizong. These included a poem to wish Huizong a long life while visiting the Northeast Marchmount, a few on Daoist themes, some on the change of seasons, or birds and plants, and some on auspicious phenomena, such as sweet dew. One was on an old painting of horses.[9] Another source showing the range of occasions on which officials wrote poems for Huizong is Wang Anzhong's collected works, which includes many poems he wrote in response to Huizong's poems.[10] They are listed below:

Occasions of Poems by Huizong that Wang Anzhong Matched

On heaven's response
Banquet at Sagacious Thoughts Hall (100-line)
Receiving oranges at a banquet at Sagacious Thoughts Hall on
    1125/9/23 (100-line)
Banquet at the Northeast Marchmount park
At the Northeast Marchmount (two)
On the first full moon of the year
A visit to the Imperial Academy and the Palace Library
On the Palace Library
On the Gathering Flowers Garden (two)
On white lotuses
At the banquet held on the third day of the third month
On a visit to a pond
On the screen that the emperor had painted in Great
    Brightness Hall
A banquet at Duo Edifice
On auspicious snow
On enjoying snow
On enjoying snow in 1125 (done on the spot)
On enjoying the snow at the completion of the sacrifices at the
    Suburban Altar[11]

Since all of these poems were written in response to poems by Huizong, Huizong was clearly quite active as a poet himself and willing to let his officials read his poems on a wide range of subjects.

Two of the shorter poems with prefaces can serve as examples of Wang Anzhong's efforts:

> Your subject recently, as an official in attendance, was by imperial order allowed to view the screen in Great Brightness Hall which Your Majesty painted. The depiction of forms is marvelous, as rich as all creation, with lush plants and birds in flight. The ideas behind the living things are complete in all ways. It must be that Your Majesty's filial piety pours out from your sincere heart, and that heaven operates through your brush and ink. This screen truly surpasses anything ancient or modern. The spirits surely appreciate Your Majesty's work.
>
> After respectfully reading what Your Majesty wrote, I was allowed to present a poem to match it. Mediocre as I am, I earnestly try my best in response to the honor granted me, but will surely only annoy and defile the exalted one. I know that this is inadequate.
>
>> By the gem-like gate tower, spirits roam freely, driving the wind.
>> On the folding screen, the filial feelings of the one who personally painted it are expressed.
>> The bird from Yue, blue-green, darts by outside the eaves of the palace.
>> The fruit from Min, red, hangs down among the palace buildings.
>> Nearby, at the steps, shadows retain tiny fragments of gold.
>> In the distance, the forest glows jade green.
>> For ten thousand years the imperial ancestral portrait hall is honored to the utmost,
>> Making even more apparent the merits of the dynasty's rulers.[12]

Second example:

> I was graciously allowed to see Your Majesty's poem, "Viewing the Lanterns," and was given permission to match it. I have heard that in the city the elders are all saying that there never has been a first full moon as splendid as this year's. It would seem that customs

are improving now that the entire realm has had successive years of good harvests. Moreover, since the beginning of spring, rain has fallen and the gentle wind conforms to the seasonal pattern, letting boats get through on the rivers. What better time to return to the palace gates and courtyards so divinely beautiful, with the tower of Duan Gate, the new cauldrons, and the five gates displaying the lanterns, which really begin here. I venture to select from folk songs to continue Your Majesty's rhymes, defiling your sagacious glance. Knowing that this is inadequate, I tremble.

> By the old city wall, the merging clouds open to show the
>   blue sky.
> The Bian River in spring lets loose the Luo River.
> Silky peaks, a thousand strong, invite the disk-like moon.
> Beaded curtains for ten *li*—the flickering light of the
>   lotus lanterns.
> At the Five Gates' Duan gate tower [the central gate]
>   one celebrates the first full moon festival.
> Sequentially, it is the second year of the Harmony
>   Revealed period [1120].
> In this sagely era, I have personally experienced favor as
>   one of [His Majesty's] closest ministers,
> Day after day he has offered me the goblet, treating me
>   as part of his group of worthies.[13]

A contemporary described the occasion of this poem more fully:

When Wang Anzhong was promoted from Hanlin recipient of edicts to assistant director of the right, it was the time of the Lantern Festival, and he attended a banquet at Virtue Revealed Gate. Huizong commanded a poem on the topic of the Five Entrances of Duan Gate Tower. Wang Anzhong improvised in response to the command, intoning [the poem given above]. . . . The emperor was pleased with it and moved the banquet to Spectacular Dragon Gate, where he personally mixed together cabbage soup for him.[14]

Several anecdotes attest to Huizong's fondness for humorous poetry. Once he summoned Cao Zu, a popular poet of the time. When Huizong asked if he were Cao Zu, he responded in rhyme:

> I am the only Cao Zu.
> Idle chatter is all I can do.
> In calligraphy I'm not up to Yang Qiu,
> But my love of money surpasses Zhang Bu.

Huizong, we are told, laughed out loud, apparently appreciating the reference to two of his close associates.[15]

Cao Zu had failed the civil service examinations six times, but Huizong appointed him as a literary official and occasionally gave him assignments. On one occasion when he was given a time limit of a single day, the poem he produced was so good that Huizong granted him a civil service degree.[16]

Often Huizong's poetic interactions with officials were not assignments but rather reciprocal gifts—the recipient of the first poem returning the favor by composing one to match it. Many of Huizong's poetic exchanges with Cai Jing and Wang Anzhong were of this sort. Sometimes Huizong's gifts of poems are mentioned in historical sources but the poems themselves are not quoted. For instance, the *Song History* treatise on ritual mentions that in 1115 at a court banquet, Huizong conferred a poem he had written on Cai Jing, but does not quote it.[17] Wang Mingqing reported that while visiting a grandson of Cai Jing he saw manuscripts of poems Cai Jing and Huizong had written for each other on various occasions, such as the completion of court ceremonies or visits to gardens or parks. In one case Huizong sent Cai Jing an eight-line, seven-character regulated verse; Cai Jing wrote four poems with the same rhyme words, which sparked Huizong to do yet another two poems. Here is Huizong's first poem, one of the matches Cai Jing wrote, and two more by Huizong:

> On the thirteenth day of the eleventh month of 1119, prompted by fasting in preparation for the Suburban Sacrifice to heaven, I wrote this poem to give to the grand preceptor:
>
>> In gratitude to the source,[18] the smoke from the fine offerings rises from [the shrine] south of the capital.
>> In advance we purify the shrine and strictly observe the overnight fast.
>> The rosy clouds begin to disperse as the sky clears.

Gentle breezes suddenly reverse as the sun rises over the water.
One hundred thousand soldiers stand frozen in their ranks.
The paired tiles along the nine avenues seem eaves of jade.
Majesty and harmony manifest themselves among the elders.
With the performance of the felicities bestowed equally, the
    entire world benefits.

Cai Jing employed Huizong's rhyme words in this response:

In dragon robe and scarlet shoes, at the central staircase
    he faces south.
By the great carriage, the phoenix calls and the imperial
    guards are solemn.
The jade carriage quickly turns and the conjunction of the
    sun and moon is set.
As the golden crow [the sun] begins to rise, the white
    clouds brighten.
By the Five Gates [to the palace] the early morning
    breezes make the flags and banners flutter.
The ten thousand horsemen in their splendor enter,
    [their faces shaded by] their hat brims.
We have already seen the divine light shine in response
    to the [the ruler's] merit.
The crane letter [imperial edict] extends benevolence
    and the myriad countries benefit.

Huizong continued the poetic exchanges:

In the enclosure for abstention at the pure shrine, I wrote a poem
for the grand preceptor, who then submitted to me one that matches
the rhymes. Once the sacrificial ritual was completed, based on
things that struck him, he submitted more poems using the same
rhymes. Now I also, using the original rhymes, confer another on
the grand preceptor. I am not trying to make this extra bother, but
in good times for a ruler and minister to continue each other's
poems is yet another sign of how flourishing the times are.

The holy drums and yellow pennants lead the way south.
The purple altar and blue jade disk testify to our solemnity.

The endless procession [lit. jade and feathers] under the
   rosy clouds,
The brilliant divine light caresses the scene as the sun rises.
With joy the imperial carriage returns to the phoenix
   precincts [the palace].
Deliberately left behind, the carriage canopies emerge
   from the dragon eaves.
Serving heaven with this ritual invites blessings for our
   people.
With the rain breaking up now, all of creation should
   receive benefits.

Huizong did a second poem as well:

Three times the grand preceptor presented a poem to match the
one I conferred on him that used the rhyme word *xian* 暹 ("the
sun rises"), since I had wanted him to demonstrate that the stricter
his use of rhymes, the more skillfully he writes. Here is yet another
poem using the same rhymes for the grand preceptor:

When heaven is in position to welcome Yang and turns the
   Dipper south,[19]
The thousand officials stand mountain-like, fully
   reverential.
They participate in the pleasure of making the offerings of
   jade as the sacrificial smoke begins to reach them.
They compete to attend the returning carriage after the sun
   has risen.
On the way back in the snow I ask, "Whose poem will be
   the best?"[20]
I ponder which of the officials [is best] while walking under
   the eaves.
The ritual completed, poems wishing happiness pile up.
Propitious is the auspicious grain that brings benefits to the
   myriad homes.[21]

   Poems written at court, and also sometimes ones written by men
hoping for appointments at court, often seem to go rather far in ap-

plauding the emperor, the government, and the signs that all was right in the world. China is, of course, not the only place where rulers were praised in elegant language; panegyrics were considered an art form in imperial Rome and its successors in both the west and the east.[22] In China the tradition dates back to the earliest surviving literature, as many of the poems in the *Book of Songs* were hymns extolling the rulers and the royal ancestors. A major theme of Han and Tang rhapsodies was the glory of the state and its rulers. When court officials matched an emperor's poem, their praise of the sovereign and his responses to their praise were central to the creation of "the imaginary space of the court."[23] The poets were also in the process crafting representations of themselves as loyal and awed subjects.

In China, not all panegyric poetry was simple flattery; there was also a tradition of conveying indirect criticism in poems laden with praise.[24] Did Cai Jing or Wang Anzhong ever write poems intended to get Huizong to rethink an issue? The closest I have found is a poem not explicitly intended for Huizong. When Cai You was leaving the capital to take part in the Yanjing military campaign, his father, Cai Jing, who did not approve of the campaign, wrote a poem to him that was critical of the decision to abandon the long-established treaty with Liao. This poem eventually reached Huizong, who reportedly suggested a change of wording but did not comment on the implicit criticism.[25]

At least once, Huizong received a set of poems whose criticism was not concealed. The author, an Imperial Academy student named Deng Su, wrote eleven quatrains and a lengthy preface on the Flower and Rock Network, the agency that had provoked a lot of criticism for the way it had been gathering materials for the Northeast Marchmount. This one is the third in the series:

> Prefects and magistrates make plans to compete with each
>   other to show their loyalty,
> Vowing to take the flowers and rocks till the land is swept
>   clean.
> They know that the strength of subjects can be exhausted
> But the favor of the ruler is hard to repay in full.

Huizong could easily recognize the satire in Deng Su's poems, and this time was not amused. Deng Su was soon sent home.[26]

By bringing poets to court, supporting research into song tunes, showing his officials poems that he wrote, and encouraging them to compose poems in response, Huizong could lay claim to being a patron of poetry. At the same time, of course, Huizong had prohibited the printing of some of the most popular poets' works, most notably those of Su Shi and Huang Tingjian. In the case of painting theory, Huizong did not reject ideas that Su Shi had championed, and in his support of poetry, too, Huizong took no steps to align himself at the opposite end of the spectrum from Su Shi. During Huizong's reign, *ci* lyrics continued to evolve in directions that Su Shi had influenced, including tendencies toward elevating the language to make it more refined and using song lyrics to convey personal feelings that had earlier been expressed in *shi* poetry.[27]

What did Huizong gain from encouraging poetry-writing at his court? Above all, he got to associate himself with the long history of imperial patronage of poetry. Rulers from Zhou times on wanted men of talent at court, and poetic talent was the talent most prized. More recently, in the early Song Taizong and Zhenzong had been enthusiastic poets and left behind significant bodies of poetry. The quality of the poetry produced at court was something people talked about. Near the end of Zhezong's reign, after a banquet celebrating the birth of a son, the emperor and his councilors discussed the mediocre quality of the poems produced on that occasion, and considered who might be able to raise the literary standards of the court.[28] Huizong, who liked poetry, wanted his court to be considered one where poetic talent was on display.

Banquets and Garden Parties

Many of the occasions when Wang Anzhong and other officials wrote poems to match Huizong's were banquets or parties of one sort or another. These occasions were a central element in the culture of Huizong's court. Some banquets were regularly scheduled events that were orchestrated by ritual officials. These would include the banquet at New Year, when the ambassadors from Liao, Xi Xia, and Koryŏ would be honored guests; the spring and fall banquets; and the banquets on Huizong's birthday. Music was a central feature of all these banquets, and many of the musicians were women. The court orches-

tra played tunes for each of the rounds of drinks and food and between performances of other entertainers, which included skits, poetic recitations, boy and girl dance troupes, and solo performances
on the *qin*.[29]

Sometimes the skits at parties involved political satire. Hong Mai
summarizes three skits that were performed in front of Huizong and
got him to laugh or rethink an issue. One made fun of Cai Jing's rejec-
tion of anyone with a connection to the Yuanyou period, including a
monk whose ordination certificate was dated Yuanyou three (1088).
Another made fun of the elevation of Wang Anshi to the Confucian
temple by having Confucius's disciples Yan Hui and Mencius defer to
him, giving him the most honored seat, making Confucius uncomfortable. A third touched on the charitable ventures. It involved a Buddhist
monk discussing how illness, growing old, and death no longer awak-
ened religion sentiments because the new charitable organizations that
provided medical treatment, care for the aged, and burial of the impov-
erished had removed much of the inevitability of suffering.[30]

Besides scheduled entertainments, Huizong would from time to
time decide to hold a party for a more select group of guests. Huizong
had devoted considerable energy to beautifying the palace and its gardens, and also to collecting rare and valuable artworks and antiquities,
and he enjoyed occasionally inviting his councilors and other favored
individuals to enjoy them with him.

Most of the banquets and garden parties that Huizong arranged
have left no trace in the historical record—or only a brief reference,
such as the note that on 1107/3/3 Huizong held a banquet for his officials from Cai Jing on down at Golden Brilliance Lake Park, which
was in the western suburbs (see Map 1).[31] Fortunately, records have
been preserved of several parties, written by one of the guests but
meant undoubtedly above all for Huizong's eyes.

The first occasion recorded in this way took place in 1112 to celebrate Cai Jing's return to the capital. In the account Cai Jing wrote of
this occasion, the idea for the party came to Huizong when he was
thinking of a poem in the *Book of Songs* in which King Xuan feasts a
returning noble. He would revive the ancient practice by opening up
Grand Clarity Edifice in the Rear Garden. The guest list included
Huizong's two brothers, plus all of the councilors at that time (He
Zhizhong, Cai Jing, Zheng Shen, Wu Juhou, Liu Zhengfu, Hou Meng,

Deng Xunren), plus Zheng Juzhong, Deng Xunwu, and the generals Gao Qiu and Tong Guan.[32] Preparation was assigned to a group of high-ranking eunuchs (Tan Zhen, Yang Jian, Jia Xiang, and Liang Shicheng). Three days in advance, Huizong himself inspected the site and gave instructions on where different items should be placed and where the musicians and dancers should perform. Particularly fine wine and tableware were taken from the storerooms for the occasion. The guests were to wear the belts Huizong had recently conferred on them. On this occasion, rather than the usual court musicians, Huizong decided to use a group of young female musicians whom the councilors had not previously seen perform. Probably to disprove any charges that he let his pursuit of pleasure interfere with government business, on the day of the party Huizong held his normal morning audience in Hanging Hem Hall.

Once the guests had arrived, the first order of business was to insist that they sit to watch the entertainment, which began with a demonstration of military skills, then a polo game played by palace ladies on horseback. With its completion, the guests passed through the gate into the Rear Garden toward their final destination, Grand Clarity Edifice, at which point Huizong suggested a detour to Harmony Revealed Hall, where paintings, calligraphy, and ancient vessels were set out on black lacquered tables for them to inspect. One of the side buildings was named "Porphyry Orchid." By it were "stones formed into a mountain with craggy peaks protruding here and there" and "springs flowed from carved stones into a pool."[33] Later they were led to a place where four hundred boy and girl musicians were lined up. Huizong's third son Kai, then ten years old, stood in attendance, "as serious as an adult." After three rounds of wine, Huizong told his guests to enjoy themselves and not worry about etiquette. Then he offered them newly arrived tea specially prepared using spring water. The musicians and dancers performed next. Cai Jing claimed that since Grand Clarity had first been used for banquets in Zhenzong's time, there had never been an occasion that surpassed theirs in the quality of the music, the food and drink, as well as the feelings of closeness between ruler and ministers.[34]

Cai Jing also wrote an essay on a banquet held in the fourth month of 1115, which also involved demonstrations of horse-riding skills. Only a summary of it survives, but it is worth quoting:

In the fourth month of 1115 a banquet was held for the councilors in Harmony Revealed Hall. First the imperial party went to Promoting Governance Hall, where they watched more than five hundred young men shoot while riding horseback, their strength and accuracy exceptional. Next the guests were instructed to sit. Palace women entered and lined up before the hall, with drums and rattles sounding; their horses leapt and the arrows flew. They slashed with willow branches and struck the embroidered ball. Using their saddles they pulled "divine arm" bows, in an utterly amazing way, putting the guards to shame. Huizong said, "Even though this is not women's work, the girls are able to do it, so it must be that everyone in the realm can be taught it." Cai Jing and the others came forward and said, "The men can pull the bow forcefully, and the women can shoot while riding. How lucky the world is that we do not forget danger while at peace!"[35]

Another party described at length in an essay by Cai Jing took place in 1119. Cai Jing mentions no special reason for the party, but it was largely a family affair. Huizong invited several of his own relatives—his two brothers, his third son Kai, and another more distantly related prince, Zhao Zhonghu, who was a major art collector.[36] In addition, he invited Cai Jing and several of his sons and grandsons, including the one who the year before had married Huizong's fifth daughter. Other guests included Feng Xizai, Wang Fu, and Tong Guan, then all on the Council of State. The first major activity on this occasion was a tour of the cultural treasures Huizong had collected. A series of studios in Preserving Harmony had objects laid out for viewing, and Huizong personally acted as tour guide, pointing to each item and commenting on it. The first two held Confucian and Daoist books, respectively. The rest, all with "antiquity" in their names (Investigating Antiquity, Pursuing Antiquity, Honoring Antiquity, and so on) contained the writings of the previous Song emperors, ancient bronze vessels and inscribed stones, and masterpieces of early paintings and calligraphies, many of which Cai Jing claimed never to have seen before. Cai Jing depicts Huizong as interacting with his guests as a man of education and a connoisseur of cultural relics:

> At the Hall of Complete Truth, the emperor gave us tea, personally holding the kettle and pouring it into the cups. The tea

foamed up, and the foam got in the emperor's face. This made us, his subjects, uncomfortable and we said to him, "Your Majesty is neglecting the distinction between ruler and subject, and treating us subjects as equals, boiling tea for us. We are in trepidation. How dare we sip?" We lowered our heads and bowed. The emperor said, "Let's take a break."

We went out to Jasper Forest Hall. A palace servant, Feng Hao, came to inform us that the emperor wanted us to write poems to inscribe on the wall of the hall, and that the brushes and ink had all been prepared. I wrote:

> With jewel-like magnificence it is as dense as a forest.
> The junipers and bamboo have grown into each other, so
>   that it is shady at noon.
> We mere mortals have been graciously permitted to wander
>   freely,
> Unaware that our bodies are deep in the five-colored clouds
>   [of the immortals].

After a while, we took our seats and female musicians began to play. Lichees, oranges, and tangerines were placed around for us, and the eunuch Wenhao was told to peel and separate them for us. We were given five rounds of wine.[37]

A fourth party of this sort took place in the last month of 1120, after Cai Jing had retired from the Council of State. It was held in Extended Blessings, the huge palace complex that had been built in 1113, extending the Palace City to the north.[38] On this occasion, Huizong invited some of his sons and the current councilors to a party, and as a special favor also invited the Hanlin academicians Li Bangyan and Yuwen Cuizhong. Once again the guests moved from site to site over the course of the day. They began at Sagacious Thoughts Hall, where music was performed and Huizong told the guests that there should be no formality. They should eat and drink whatever pleased them and feel free to take home any leftovers. After the meal, they retired to the Eastern Chamber for a rest, then in the evening gathered at Spectacular Dragon Gate, the central gate on the north side of the Palace City, where they could see lanterns hanging for the Lantern Festival in the streets outside the palace. "From Jade Splendor Pavilion we viewed the lantern display in the city. The glittering gold and shining turquoise made us feel as though we were in the clouds. On an open stage below, an opera was being performed. City folk moved about, some got drunk, some were jesting, some singing songs of praise [of the ruler]. All this showed the ruler and his subjects sharing their joys. It was an exuberant expression of a time of great peace."[39]

The next destination was Joined Calm Hall, where there were eight galleries lined up across from each other, each one devoted to one of Huizong's enthusiasms: lutes, chimes, chess, calligraphy, painting, tea, medicine, scriptures, and incense. The guests were invited to look carefully at the objects on display. Another repast was spread out for them on small tables nearby. After they had satisfied themselves there, the group moved on to Peace Achieved Hall, where lanterns were hung. Huizong ordered tea, then tended the stove himself and even whisked the tea. When some women came out to dance and sing, Huizong told the two Hanlin academicians, Li Bangyan and Yuwen Cuizhong, that they were the first academicians to have been invited to such an occasion.[40]

It is worth noting Huizong's personal preparation of tea for his guests at these parties. Tea clearly had a place in the culture of Huizong's court, as it did in literati culture of the time. Huizong had opinions of how tea should be prepared and liked to make it himself.[41] Huizong has long been credited with a brief treatise on tea, dated to the Daguan period (1107–1110), the earliest version of which dates back to the *Shuofu*, compiled in the fourteenth century. After an introduction extolling the wonders of tea, the treatise covers twenty steps from selecting the site to plant the tea, through picking, steaming, grinding into cakes, making discriminating choices among types of tea, pouring water, selecting cups, and so on. A few passages are enough to show the approach Huizong takes:

> *How to judge quality:* Teas vary as much in appearance as do the faces of men. If the consistency of caked tea is not dense enough, the surface of the cake will be wrinkled and lack luster, whereas it should be both glossy and close-knit. Caked tea processed on the day it was picked has a light purple color; if the processing has taken longer, it will be darker. When caked tea is powdered ready for infusion, the powder will look whitish but turn yellow when

infused. There are also fine tea pastes with a greenish color; the powder, though grey, becomes white upon infusion. However, teas may *look* ordinary and nevertheless be remarkably good, so one should not go too much by appearances. . . . Unfortunately tea merchants have many artifices for making tea look much better than it really is.

White tea: White tea is different from all others and deemed the finest. With wide-spreading branches and thin shiny leaves, the trees grow wild on forested cliffs. Their product is very sparse, however, and there is nothing one can do about it. Four or five families on the Beiyuan tea estate have some trees of this kind, but only a couple of them come into leaf, so no more than two or three bagfuls can be gathered each year. Both shoots and leaves are small; steaming and firing them is rather difficult; for if the temperature is not exactly right, they will taste like ordinary tea. Thus, a high order of skill is needed and the drying must be carefully done. If everything is exactly as it should be, the product of such trees will excel all others.

Cups: The best kinds of tea bowls are very dark blue—almost black. They should be relatively deep so that the surface of the liquid will attain a milky color, and also rather wide to allow for whipping with a bamboo whisk.

Whisk: This should be made of flexible bamboo; the handle should be heavy, the brush-like slivers light, their tips sharp as swords. Then, when the whisk is used, there are not likely to be too many bubbles.[42]

How should we understand Huizong's penchant for entertaining his councilors? The great gap in the status of the emperor and all those around him meant that no relationship could be a simple friendship. Still, emperors were human beings, and not surprisingly sometimes sought relationships with men who would do the things friends do—share food or drink, chat idly, visit each others' homes, show off recent acquisitions, and the like. Officials rarely acknowledged that an emperor needed people he could treat as friends and were suspicious of men who got close to the emperor, looking on them as favorites, likely to abuse their power. It is therefore difficult to find any royal companions who are portrayed positively in surviving sources. But if we try to think of the situation from the emperor's point of view, it seems only natural to crave not merely the companionship of the palace women and consorts, but also the companionship of men who shared some of their interests and seemed to appreciate them as people, not just defer to them as subordinates (though of course they would have had to do that as well).

In Europe, kings had nobles who could join them in many activities, including many related by blood or marriage—brothers, cousins, brothers-in-law, and so on. They could ride together, enjoy meals or music together, and chat relatively informally. Men of rank attended them through the day, even when they were dressing or eating. Some of this service was provided in China by eunuchs, such as helping with clothing, fetching food or drink, listening to ideas or complaints, and providing escorts. Huizong did have two brothers and did invite them to informal banquets, but there is no mention of anything like going out to ride with them. In his second year on the throne, the censor Jiang Gongwang submitted a memorial saying he had heard a rumor that someone had entered the Rear Garden of the palace with a falcon. The censor claimed not to believe the rumor, but he still went on at length on the reasons Huizong should not involve himself with anything as cruel and dangerous as hunting.[43] If Huizong ever did go hunting, no record of it has been preserved. It should not be surprising, then, that Huizong occasionally turned to his councilors for companionship. He might even have selected men for court positions because he considered them good companions (Cai You, Wang Fu, and Wang Anzhong all seem possibilities in this regard).

Consorts and Children

The more private spaces in the palace were also sites for pleasure—the pleasures of feminine company and family life. An emperor's family was potentially quite large because, in addition to an empress, he was expected to have multiple consorts, each with one of twenty-three titles that indicated her rank. And he could easily acquire more consorts by promoting any of the thousands of palace ladies.[44]

One rationale for having so many potential mates was the need for male heirs. Many Song emperors needed all the help they could get to secure an heir. That was not the case with Huizong. Huizong was an

exceptional emperor in many ways, but none more so than in the number of children he had—sixty-five during his time on the throne.[45] No
other Song emperor had more than twenty-six children. Even if one
compares emperors of earlier and later dynasties, not one matches
Huizong in fecundity. The emperor who came closest to Huizong was
Xuanzong in the Tang who had sixty children; next was Ming Taizu
with forty-two. The two Qing emperors who each reigned sixty years,
Kangxi and Qianlong, had thirty-five and twenty-seven children respectively. All of these emperors reigned longer than Huizong. Thus,
considered in terms of the number of children born per year on the
throne, Huizong is even more of an outlier.[46]

How did Huizong manage to beget so many children? Clearly he
did not have the fertility problems that plagued several other Song
emperors. An equally important element is that he was not in any sense
monogamous: he was able and willing to get several women pregnant
more or less at the same time. Most of his years on the throne he had
children born to more than one woman. Huizong himself may well
have attributed his great success in producing heirs to his medical
knowledge and Daoist practices. The Yellow Emperor—esteemed in
both the medical and Daoist traditions—was in esoteric sexual treatises also the master of sexual arts.[47]

It is also worth noting that Huizong was a man who liked women.
Sources ranging from the *Song History* and other standard sources, to
anecdotes, legends, and gossip, present Huizong as a romantic man
who enjoyed spending time with his consorts and who could become
deeply attached to particular ones. Huizong did not depose any of his
empresses, like his great-grandfather and elder brother had done, and
most of the time treated his consorts with kindness and generosity.

Perhaps the best way to see Huizong's consorts and children from
his perspective is by tracing how his family changed over time. When
Huizong took the throne, he already had a wife, Princess Wang. She
was from an official family in Kaifeng, but not an especially prominent
one. The two had been married only half a year, but she was already
pregnant and gave birth to their first son, Prince Huan (the future
Qinzong) in the fourth month of 1100.[48] By that time she had already
been raised to the status of empress. Sometime within the next year
she gave birth to a daughter, but the exact date is not known, as the
only dates given for princesses are the day when they got their first

title, which could well be several months after they were born. After the birth of her daughter in 1101, Empress Wang had no more children.

The biography of Empress Wang in the *Song History* hints that Huizong was never very attached to her. "The empress was respectful and restrained. The two consorts Zheng and Wang were at the time competing for favor; the empress treated them in an even-handed way."[49] Huizong had known these women for a few years, as they had been servants of his legal mother, Empress Dowager Xiang, and she had assigned them to look after him when he visited. When he took the throne, she gave them to him as consorts. Consort Zheng was given the title Talented One late in 1100, perhaps after she had given birth to her first child, a girl. Talented One was at the bottom of the ranks of consorts, but was higher than the numerous untitled palace ladies. The following year, pregnant again, she was promoted to Beautiful One. The next month, she gave birth to a son who lived only one day. Her rival, Consort Wang, gave birth to Huizong's third son in late 1101. By then her title was also Beautiful One.[50] Thus, by the end of 1101 Huizong had four children, two boys and two girls.

Of these first three women, Consort Zheng seems to have especially pleased Huizong. We are told that she liked to read, that she was a good enough writer to draft state papers, and that Huizong appreciated her talent. She was promoted rapidly to Worthy Consort in 1102 and reached the highest rank of Noble Consort in 1104. Huizong, we are told, wrote songs for Consort Zheng which "the whole world sang."[51]

During his third year on the throne, 1102, three more children were born in the palace, all girls. Huizong's third daughter was born to Consort Yang, about whom little is known other than she received her first title in the second month of 1102 and in later years received a series of promotions.[52] Huizong's fourth daughter was born to Consort Zheng, her third child in three years. His fifth daughter was born to sixteen *sui* Consort Liu Mingda, who had entered the palace in the fourth month of 1100 when she was fourteen *sui* as a palace lady (*yushi*). She attracted Huizong's attention, and by the end of 1102 had her first title and her first child. She became one of Huizong's favorites, bearing five more children over the next nine years. Thus, by the end of 1102, Huizong had five consorts who were mothers and seven children: five girls and two boys, all infants or toddlers.

In 1103 no new women became mothers: another girl was born to Consort Zheng and a boy to Consort Wang, perhaps helping Wang in her competition with Zheng, as Zheng had three daughters, but Wang had two sons. By the end of 1103 Huizong still had five consorts who were mothers but two more children, bringing the total to three boys and six girls.

Subsequent years followed similar patterns. About a quarter of Huizong's children did not survive to adulthood, some dying soon after birth, others living for several years or longer; still, their survival rate is better than that of the children of earlier Song emperors (only two of Zhezong's five children outlived him, and only ten of Shenzong's twenty-four children were alive at his death). Thus, in most years the total number of living children in the palace increased. For example, at the end of 1107 Huizong had eighteen living children, just as he would have in 1108 (as one child was born and another died), but in 1109 the total reached twenty-two, as five were born and only one died. By the end of that year, after completing nearly ten years on the throne, eight of Huizong's consorts were mothers. Six years later, at the end of 1115, Huizong had thirty-four living children, and ten consorts who were mothers. After another five years, at the end of 1120, he had thirty-nine living children, and nine or more consorts who were mothers (beginning in 1118 there are children born whose mother is not listed in extant sources, so the total number of mothers is incomplete). At the end of his reign in late 1125, Huizong had forty-seven living children and at least eight consorts who were mothers.

On the whole, Huizong's consorts got along well, at least in comparison to the consorts of earlier emperors. The biography of Empress Wang refers to an unpleasant episode when one of the high-ranking eunuchs spread false rumors about her. Huizong assigned an official in the Ministry of Justice to look into the matter but he found that there was not one iota of evidence against her. We are told that Huizong was touched when she next saw him and said nothing about the affair.[53]

Huizong outlived several of his consorts. Empress Wang was the first to die, at twenty-five *sui* in 1108. Because of her high rank, the funeral and burial were major rituals. Huizong was repeatedly asked to appoint a new empress, but he delayed until 1110, when he promoted Consort Zheng, whom he had known since his years as a prince and who by then had given birth to seven children, five of whom were living, all girls. Generally empresses were chosen from families in the civil or military elite, as Empress Wang had been. By promoting from within Huizong was elevating a woman he loved and the mother of many of his children, but one with no important relatives. Still, the ceremonies associated with raising her to empress were quite elaborate. The *Song History* describes them as follows:

> In 1110, the Noble Consort Zheng was appointed as empress. The Agency for Deliberating on Ritual specified the steps to be performed. The appointment commissioner approaches the carriage. The emperor proceeds to Cultured Virtue Hall, wearing the Extending to Heaven hat and scarlet gauze robes. The hundred officials wear court dress. The yellow banner and decorated staffs are displayed. The orchestra is set out in the ancient way. The appointment commissioner exits from the gate of the hall, and according to recent practice does not climb into the carriage. Solemn Purity Hall is made the temporary hall for receiving the appointment. On the day of the ceremony, the empress wears sacrificial dress. A palace attendant serves to receive the appointment documents and jewels and transfer them to the empress. When she has received them, the empress submits a memorial to thank the emperor, and the lined-up titled ladies from within and without the palace offer congratulations. The group of officials enters the hall to congratulate the emperor, and at the eastern gate to the inner hall they submit written congratulations to the empress.[54]

The account goes on to specify the musical compositions played during each phase of the ceremony.

Even before she became empress, Zheng does not seem to have been inclined toward jealousy, since two of the women who served her, Wei and Qiao, served Huizong as well, bearing him children beginning in 1104 and 1107. These two women themselves became sworn sisters and each promised not to forget the other if she rose in favor.[55]

Huizong may have chosen Zheng as his empress, but he was very attached to other women as well, notably Consort Liu Mingda. As seen above, she had joined the palace service at fourteen *sui* in 1100 and borne her first child in 1103. She died ten years later at twenty-seven *sui*, after bearing six children altogether, three boys and three girls, only one of whom had died. Huizong was so distraught when she died that he not only wrote poems in her memory, but he had her posthumously promoted to empress, an exceptional (and costly) step.[56] Even three or four years later, Huizong's grief was still keen. Cai Tao reported that he asked the Daoist master Wang Laozhi about her and was told that she had the title Highest Truth Purple Void Primal Lord, and he carried messages back and forth between them.[57] The even more influential Daoist master Lin Lingsu was also said to help Huizong get in touch with this beloved consort. He did this at night, first setting out a Daoist *jiao* offering, then summoning her with a "flying" talisman. He reported to Huizong that his consort was at that time banqueting with the Queen Mother of the West, but when she heard Huizong's summons she immediately set out. When she appeared before Huizong, she looked just as she had during her lifetime and told Huizong, "Your handmaiden formerly served the chief of the Transcendent Officers, but because in the Divine Empyrean I committed an offense, I was dispatched to the human world. Now that I have paid back my karmic burden, I have returned to my former duties." The two went on to chat about other members of the family until she left.[58]

The girl the first Consort Liu had "adopted," known as Consort Liu Mingjie, next caught Huizong's fancy, and the histories report that he let her tend to him from morning to night. She was exceptionally good-looking, skilled in applying makeup, and dressed stylishly. When Lin Lingsu saw her, he identified her as the Peaceful Consort of Nine-Splendored Jade Truth and had a statue of her placed to the left of the statue of the Lord of the Divine Empyrean. After this woman, the second Consort Liu, died in 1121, Huizong fell into deep grief and would weep with whoever came to console him. One of the consorts who had borne six children, Consort Cui, did not seem to him to be in grief, which annoyed him so much that he had her demoted to commoner. In the edict dismissing her, however, she was accused of occult practices and other nefarious acts.[59]

Altogether Huizong had children by at least thirteen consorts (and from 1118 on had eleven children by unidentified women, perhaps including the thirteen consorts, but quite likely including some of the seven women who received titles but do not have children listed; see Appendix B).[60] Two of the mothers had only a single child, but at the other extreme, Empress Zheng had six children, as did Consort Liu

Plate 1. Portrait of Huizong (anon.), hanging scroll, ink and color on silk,
118.2 × 106.7 cm. (National Palace Museum, Taiwan, Republic of China)

Plate 2. Imperial Honor Guard (anon.), detail, ink and color on silk, 51.4 × 1,481 cm. (National Museum of China)

Plate 3. Literary Gathering (traditionally attributed to Huizong), with inscriptions by Huizong and Cai Jing, hanging scroll, ink and color on silk, 184.4 × 123.9 cm. (National Palace Museum, Taiwan, Republic of China)

Plate 4. Detail of *Literary Gathering.* (National Palace Museum, Taiwan, Republic of China)

山禽矜逸態

梅粉弄輕柔

已有丹青約

千秋指白頭

宣和殿御製并書

Plate 5. Two Birds in a Blossoming Wax-Plum Tree (traditionally attributed to Huizong), with inscriptions by Huizong, hanging scroll, ink and color on silk, 83.3 × 53.3 cm. (National Palace Museum, Taiwan, Republic of China)

Plate 6. Pheasant on a Hibiscus Branch (traditionally attributed to Huizong), with inscriptions by Huizong, hanging scroll, ink and color on silk, 81.5 × 53.6 cm. (Palace Museum, Beijing)

Plate 7. Wang Ximeng, *A Thousand* Li *of Rivers and Mountains*, section of a handscroll dated 1113, ink and color on silk, 51.5 × 1191.5 cm. (Palace Museum, Beijing)

Plate 8. Closing section of Wang Ximeng's *A Thousand Li of Rivers and Mountains*, with Cai Jing's colophon. (Palace Museum, Beijing)

Plate 9. Huizong, *Finches and Bamboo*, handscroll, ink and color on silk, 33.7 × 55.4 cm. (The Metropolitan Museum of Art, John M. Crawford Jr. Collection, Purchase, Douglas Dillon Gift, 1981 [1981.278])

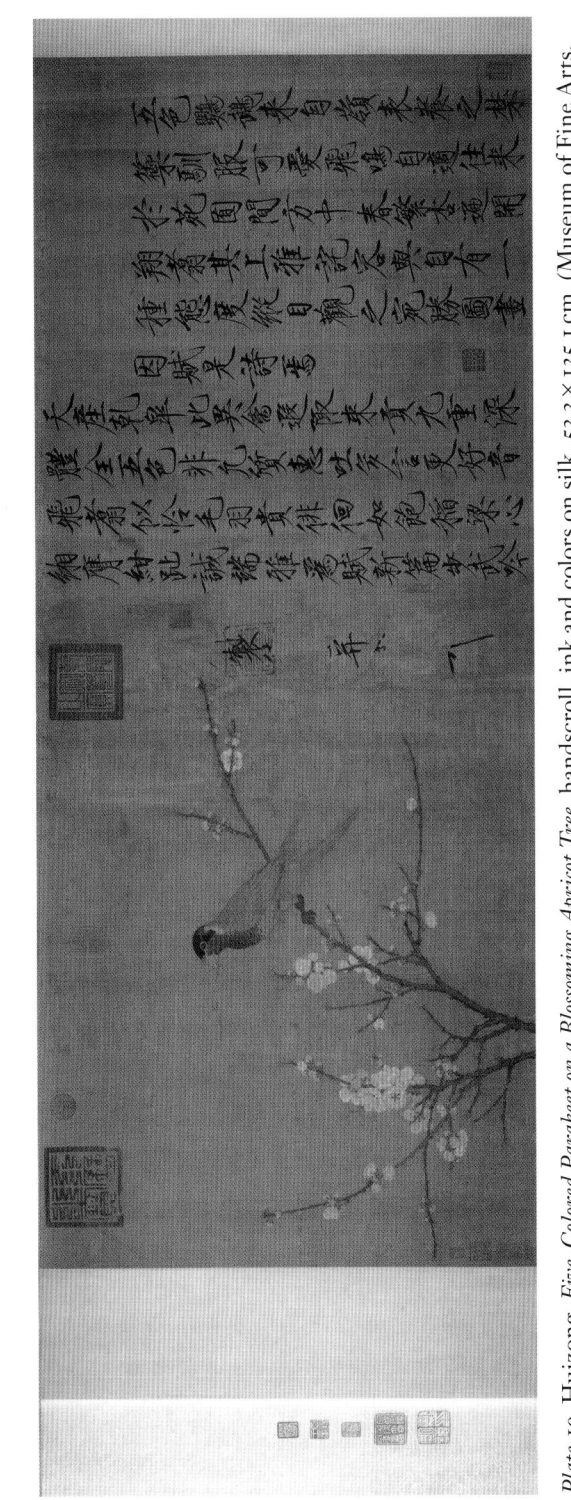

Plate 10. Huizong, *Five-Colored Parakeet on a Blossoming Apricot Tree*, handscroll, ink and colors on silk, 53.3 × 125.1 cm. (Museum of Fine Arts, Boston, Marie Antoinette Evans Fund [33.364]. Photograph © 2013 Museum of Fine Arts, Boston.)

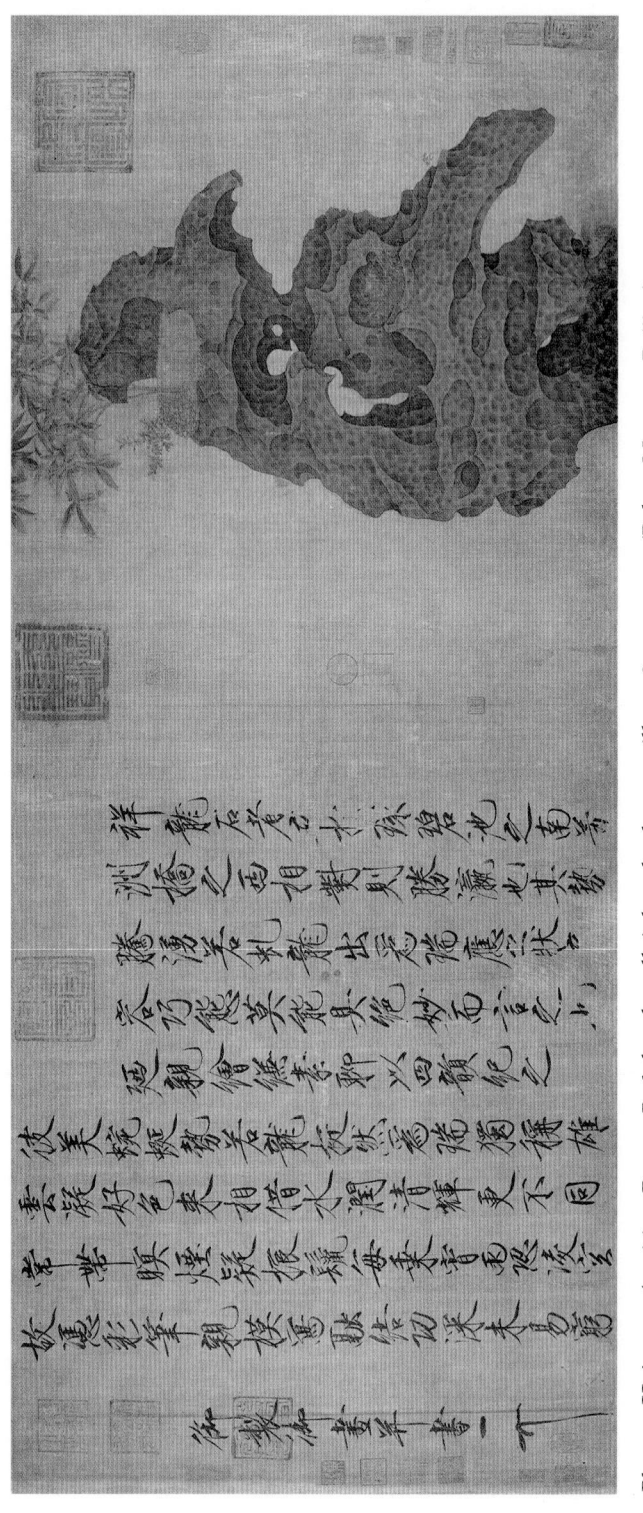

Plate 11. Huizong, *Auspicious Dragon Rock*, handscroll, ink and colors on silk, 53.8 × 127.5 cm. (Palace Museum, Beijing)

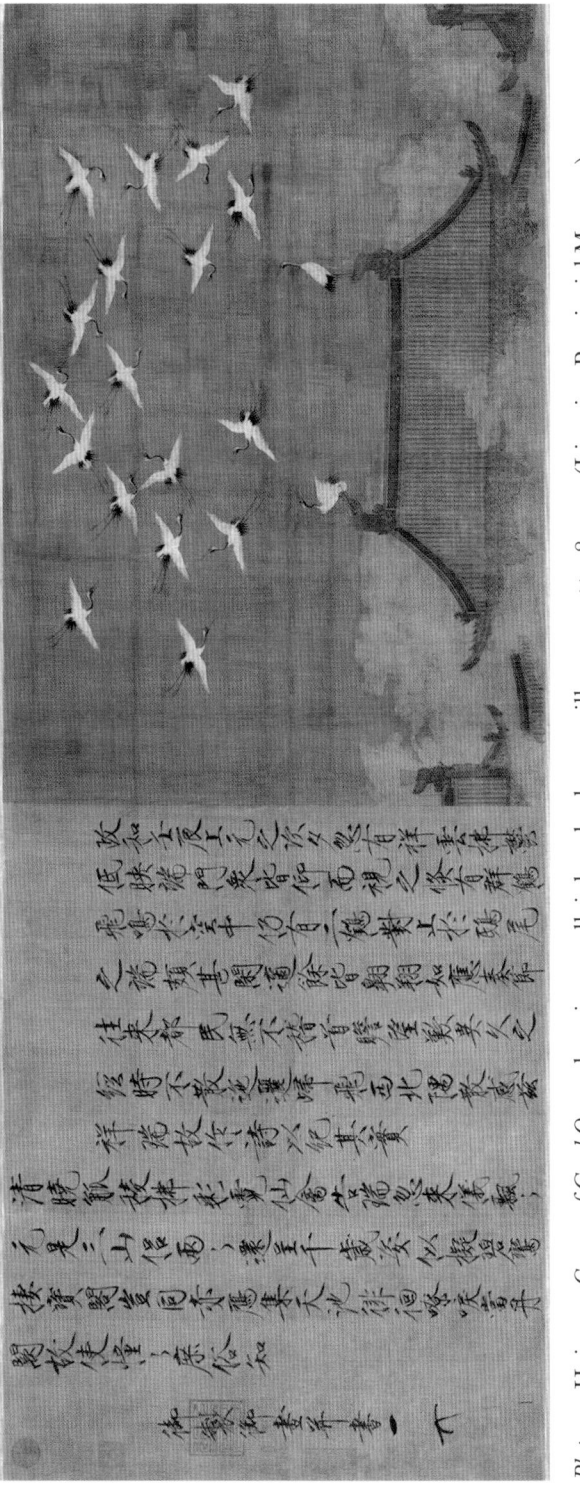

Plate 12. Huizong, *Cranes of Good Omen*, hanging scroll, ink and colors on silk, 1112.51 × 138.2 cm. (Liaoning Provincial Museum)

吟徵調宮商竈下桐
松間疑有入松風
仰窺低審含情客
以聽無絃一弄中
臣京謹題

聽琴圖

Plate 13. Huizong, *Listening to the Qin*, hanging scroll, ink and colors on silk, 110.2 × 51.3 cm. Inscriptions by Huizong of the title and Cai Jing of the poem. Huizong's cipher is in the lower left. (Palace Museum, Beijing)

Plate 14. Boat Race on Golden Brilliance Lake (anon., Southern Song), album leaf, ink and color on silk, 28.5 × 28.6 cm. (Tianjin Museum)

Plate 15. The Return of the Coffins (anon., Southern Song), handscroll, ink and color on silk, 26.7 × 142.2 cm., detail (Shanghai Museum)

Mingda and Consort Cui, and two had seven (Consort Qiao and the second Consort Wang), and one had eight (the first Consort Wang). Huizong was quite capable of maintaining an interest in women for years, including ones who had been pregnant several times already. We know the birthdates of seven of these women. From this partial evidence, Huizong did not begin to lose interest in his consorts until they were in their thirties; two of the women he had several children by had their last child at thirty-two.

Besides the twenty consorts recorded in surviving official sources, Huizong had at least 123 other women with titles. We know their names, ages, and ranks because the Jurchens, after seizing the Song capital, Kaifeng, treated these women like booty and made an inventory of them in 1127. The inventory listed 504 palace women, for whom no details were listed, and 143 consorts, who were listed by name, title, and age.[61] The five of highest rank (also referred to as his wives, with ranks of Empress, Noble Consort, Pure Consort, Virtuous Consort, and Worthy Consort), ranged in age from thirty-four to forty-two, and all were mothers of children. The next thirteen (referred to as concubines) held fourteen different titles and ranged in age from nineteen to thirty-nine. Several of them were also mothers of Huizong's children. The remaining 107, none of whom had borne children, held the lowest titles and ranged in age from sixteen to twenty-four.[62]

Huizong alludes to his palace ladies and the pleasure they brought him in quite a few of his palace poems. As Ronald Egan has shown, in Huizong's poems the palace ladies are not only lovely but also talented and contented. These three can serve as examples:

> Rock piles and circling streams surpass the palace in
>   Paradise,
> The fragrances and beauties of the scene change every-
>   where you look.
> Jade pendants tinkling, incomparably delightful,
> Their elegant songs and comely dances have endless appeal.

> Goddess-like in her loveliness, with skin of jade,
> A pampered disposition, she is used to having fun.
> If she doesn't go to the garden for a flower-picking contest,
> She'll join some companions in a game of pitch-pot.

> Peaches form her fragrant cheeks, jade her skin,
> Fluttering skeins of cloud is the trailing hem of her robe.
> Rare and gorgeous sewing, she can do it all.
> But all she cares to exert herself at is reading.[63]

Although these poems do not explore the complexities of life as a palace woman, they do give us insight into Huizong's understanding of how women could add to the delight of the palace.

The many sons and daughters born to Huizong all required attention at various times of their lives. Early on, wet nurses had to be found for them. Their illnesses required attention. Once they were four or five, they needed to start their educations, probably under women in the palace. When the boys got a few years older, they would begin studying with outside male teachers. When girls reached fifteen *sui*, they were generally married out, which required not only finding suitable husbands but also building houses for them and preparing other elements of their dowries. Mansions also had to be built for the boys so that that they could move out of the palace, but they often stayed a few years longer than their sisters, to seventeen or eighteen. The oldest of Huizong's children naturally went through these processes first and probably as a consequence we know more about their educations, marriages, and houses. A few examples should suffice.

The two oldest surviving sons were Prince Huan and Prince Kai, born about a year and a half apart in 1100 and 1101. Huan would become the heir apparent but Kai was the more artistically inclined and was said to be Huizong's favorite. In 1107 Huizong issued an edict in his own hand saying that he had been blessed with many sons (by that point he had nine living), and that it was time to send the oldest two to outside teachers. In 1111, when they were eleven and twelve *sui*, they began to study in the same hall used by Renzong years earlier, Nurturing Goodness Hall. Huizong's ministers were invited to welcome them formally to the school.[64] Reports of their studies mention learning the *Analects*, *Mencius*, a morality book, the *Laozi* with Huizong's commentary, and the histories of the Former and Later Han dynasties.[65] One of those who tutored the five older princes was Ge Cizhong, the elder brother of Ge Shengzhong, mentioned in earlier chapters for his work at the Imperial Academy. Ge Cizhong spent seven years as their tutor, Huizong deciding that he should make tutoring them a

full-time position, rather than a concurrent one. His biographer reported that once when he was chatting casually with Huizong the
emperor commented on how well Kai was progressing and showed him
the request Kai had written asking to go to an outside teacher, pointing particularly to how well the large characters were formed. The
biographer also related that during Ge Cizhong's seven years serving
as the princes' teacher, he had explained the classics in several hundred
thousand words, selected thousands of examples of excellent words and
deeds from the histories and other literature, and used the princes'
questions as a basis for deeper discussion.[66]

At some point Huizong also decided that his daughters should be
given educations, and the palace paid for teachers for them. We know
about this because, after the Jurchen invasion, when the palace was trying desperately to cut costs, an official complained that teachers were
being paid to teach both consorts and princesses. He argued that teachers were needed only for the princes, not their sisters or mothers.[67]

The next big events concerning Huizong's sons were the capping of
the eldest prince in 1114, his formal installation as heir apparent in
1115, and his marriage in 1116. Huizong called on his officials to nominate young women to marry the crown prince. The young woman
chosen was already connected to the imperial family: her father, Zhu
Bocai, was the elder brother of the deceased Consort Dowager Zhu,
the mother of Zhezong. For the wedding itself, a gold-decorated carriage
was used to bring the bride to the palace.[68]

For each of these ceremonies, Huizong called for adhering to the
rituals specified in the *New Forms of the Five Categories of Rites of the
Zhenghe Period*. During the compilation of this ritual manual Huizong
had taken particular interest in the capping ritual and a ten-chapter
book on issues related to capping was issued under his name. It includes discussion of such questions as the time of year the ceremony
should be held, the type of hats to use, who should perform various
steps, and the use of music during the ceremony.[69]

Each of these three ceremonies—the capping, appointment as heir
apparent, and wedding—was a grand affair. Cai Tao reported that in
the past the imperial family had not done anything public to mark
princes' coming of age. Yet for the capping of Huan, Huizong went to
Cultured Virtue Hall where the ranked officials were standing in attendance, and he instructed the designated officials to carry out the

"three placings" (placing the three different kinds of hat on his head). After that was done, he conferred on Huan his polite name. According to Cai Tao, the crown prince objected to riding in the gold-decorated carriage to report his new status at the Supreme Shrine and instead rode a horse. Cai Tao added that it was the first time in anyone's memory that those clearing the road had used the phrase, "Imperial Heir Apparent." By his calculation, for more than a century residents of the capital had not seen an heir apparent on the streets.[70]

On more than one occasion, Huizong returned to his good fortune in having so many children. The first epigraph of this chapter has him referring to the blessing of having fifty children (accurate only if deceased children are counted; only thirty-four or thirty-five were then living). Huizong was aware of the expense of building houses for them all. He did not want to confiscate the land of urban residents, who might thereby lose their businesses, so proposed moving one of the military camps from inside of the city to outside it so that the part of the city it had occupied could be used to build homes for the princes and princesses. According to Cai Tao, the vacated place was outside the north gate of the old city wall (Spectacular Dragon Gate; see Map 1). Tong Guan, then a high-ranking general, took charge of the construction of Kai's mansion. The group of mansions had a common gate which led into a road off of which the mansions were lined up east to west.[71]

When the crown prince had his first son in 1117/10, it was the first case in the history of the Song dynasty that an emperor had lived to see a primary-line grandson born.[72] After the birth of Huizong's first grandchild, the next big event in his family must have been Kai competing in the civil service examinations and placing at the top. Huizong thought it would not look right for him to be ranked number one, so reversed the order of the top two candidates. Appropriately, his teachers shared in the honor.[73]

Although Huizong does not seem to have hesitated to designate his eldest son—and his only son by either empress—as heir apparent, their relationship seems to have been strained. Cai Tao reports that Cai Jing was worried about it. Other signs of difficulty include the crown prince's derision of the Daoist priest Lin Lingsu, whom his father favored so strongly, and rumors that he did not get along with some of the highest-ranking eunuchs.[74]

Beginning in 1115 marriages of the princesses took place in rapid succession. As in the case of the cappings of his sons, Huizong ruled that his daughters' weddings should follow the *New Forms of the Five Categories of Rites of the Zhenghe Period*. His eldest daughter married first, in 1115 at age fifteen *sui* to Zeng Yin, from a prominent family and already an examination graduate although he was only a year older than her.[75] Zeng Yin benefited from this marriage not only because he got a house and other material benefits, but also titles and other privileges of officialdom. Most other marriages fell into this pattern, with the princess about fifteen *sui* and her husband not much older.

The marriage of a princess that probably attracted the most interest was that between Huizong's fifth daughter and Cai Jing's son Tiao, who seems to have been several years younger than her.[76] Once the decision for them to wed was made, Cai Jing tried to use it as a reason to retire, citing an edict from early in Huizong's reign that marriage relatives should not serve on the Council of State. Huizong rejected his request. Two days before the wedding, Huizong conferred promotions in rank on eleven members of the Cai family. Also, the month after the wedding took place, Huizong visited the new couple and gave his son-in-law another promotion in rank.[77]

As his children married one after the other, Huizong quickly became a grandfather many times over. After 1120, his own consorts bore fewer children, but Huizong's total progeny continued to increase as his sons began having children. By the time the Jurchen were recording the members of the imperial family in early 1127, eight of his sons had already married, and seven of them had already had children, forty-six altogether. His daughters must also have had children, but no record was made of them.[78]

The most tragic event in the inner quarters during Huizong's reign occurred in late 1118 when lightning started a fire in the palace, destroying some five thousand room-units of buildings, mostly halls where palace ladies lived, many of whom lost their lives.[79]

Gossip about Huizong's Love Life

Beginning in Huizong's lifetime and continuing all through the Southern Song (not to mention later), people told stories about Huizong and the women of his palace. Several authors repeat or allude to an occasion when Huizong let his guests at a party meet the Consort Liu Mingda. The fullest account, recorded by Wang Mingqing, cites Cai Jing's own account of the occasion. At one point, Huizong gave guests a poetic couplet to match, "At the elegant banquet, drinking wine adds to our high spirits. / Within Jade Truth Gallery one can see the Peaceful Consort." Cai Jing's matching couplet was based on the assumption that they were about to meet the consort. However, when they entered the hall, they discovered instead a portrait of her. Cai Jing immediately wrote a new poem, after which Huizong said he would let him see the consort after all. Cai Jing described her this way:

> The consort was plainly made up and wore no pearl or jade ornaments. Her appearance was as refined as an immortal. I came forward and bowed twice, expressing my apologies. The consort bowed in response, and I bowed again. She had her attendants help me up. The emperor took a large cup in his hand and offered us wine, telling the consort, "You should encourage the Grand Preceptor to drink."
>
> I responded, "Every polite gesture must be repaid. I wonder if I could offer her a drink?" Then I took the bottle of wine and handed it to the attendant to present.
>
> After we sat, the young maids and the drummers were dismissed, and the imperial attendants played soft music and sang such old tunes as "The Prince of Lanling," and "Yangzhou." There were several rounds of toasting.[80]

This story was frequently told because letting even elderly relatives by marriage like Cai Jing see an imperial consort was thought a bit risqué.

Another oft-repeated story depicts Huizong sneaking out of the palace at night in order to visit the courtesan Li Shishi.[81] Beginning probably late in the Song, these stories were linked together in a work of historical fiction called *Unrecorded Events of the Harmony Revealed Era*.[82] The book begins with a conventional analysis of the rise and fall of dynasties, associated with the alteration of yang and yin. Palace women, a force of yin, are linked to decline. The ancient Xia dynasty had declined because King Jie was infatuated with Meixi, the Shang dynasty because King Zhou was similarly taken with Daji, the Western Zhou declined after King You was captivated by Baosi. Other examples are a king of Chu, a king of Chen, the second Sui emperor, and finally Xuanzong of Tang, infatuated with Yang Guifei. The reader is warned that Huizong was similarly amorous.

Despite this preface, the *Unrecorded Events* does not in fact give women or Huizong's weakness for them much of the blame for the fall of the dynasty. Huizong is depicted as making numerous bad decisions, but because he was manipulated by favored officials or duped by Daoists, not because he was under the sway of crafty women.

After a brief review of the earlier Song emperors, the *Unrecorded Events of the Harmony Revealed Era* goes through Huizong's reign year by year. Nothing is said of his relations with any women until 1117, when he is said to have missed Consort Liu Mingda so much that he asked the Daoist master Lin Lingsu if he could arrange for him to meet her, and he arranged it so that Huizong saw her in a dream.[83] Under the year 1120, the story of Cai Jing getting to see Consort Liu is recounted.[84] Not until 1123 is there any evidence that Huizong let his interest in women go to any unusual lengths. Beginning in that year we get a probably totally fictional account of his infatuation with the aforementioned courtesan Li Shishi and the problems he had sneaking in and out of the palace to see her. The story of Huizong's visits to Li Shishi is told with broad humor. Huizong is shown as captivated by her beauty, but she is depicted as beautiful only on the surface; underneath she is more interested in money than affection and is loyal to no man. By secretly visiting her, Huizong is stooping to act like an ordinary city resident. He not only ends up competing with another man over a woman, but finds himself the subject of rebuke by his officials. In no sense does Huizong come across as a man so deeply in love that he loses his sense of proportion; rather he seems not quite intelligent enough to see when he is being set up by others or the consequences of his acts. This episode provides one among many examples of Huizong's foolishness, needed to make his later fate not undeserved.

At one point Li Shishi explains why she does not expect that Huizong will visit again, given the many attractions in the palace:

He's the Son of Heaven and already has not only an empress, but three first rank consorts, twenty-seven second-rank consorts, eighty-one third-rank consorts, three thousand palace ladies, and eight hundred other assorted beauties. And when night falls, he rides his dragon coach and phoenix chariot through the thirty-six palaces and twenty-four gardens of the harem, where the number of jade-immortal maidens is countless. Not only that, but they cater to him under candle and lamplight, beauties perfectly made up and correctly robed, soothing him with sweet music and eager to serve him with their charms. Why should he have the slightest interest in me? He's just bored for the moment with the palace and happened to show up here.[85]

Note that it is not Huizong who claims to have an essentially unlimited supply of women, but an outsider who has never been to the palace.

The story of Huizong's affair with Li Shishi seems a good example of what people who never entered the palace might imagine of an emperor. In their minds, as they imagined Huizong, the extreme luxuriance of his life and the plethora of women available to him did not lead to contentment but to a certain restlessness and a desire not to let his officials control him.

☙ DID A COUPLE of decades on the throne dull Huizong's appreciation of the pleasures of the palace? Probably not. Although he could always choose a new or younger woman, he did not come to treat his consorts as interchangeable or expendable: when his consort Liu Mingjie died in 1121, he was overcome with grief. Poetry, too, retained its attraction and he continued to write poetry throughout his life. We know nothing of what he liked to eat, but his love of tea is well documented. Although as emperor he could ask for any tea grown in the country, he did not lose his enthusiasm for trying new ones and perfecting ways of brewing it.

Besides his consorts and children, Huizong had many other relatives he saw from time to time. Two of his brothers—the only two to live past 1106—were frequent guests in the palace. There was some unpleasantness early in his reign with his younger brother Si, the brother who had hoped to succeed to the throne himself. In 1100, 1101, and 1102 Huizong's officials urged him to make every effort not to let himself become estranged from this brother, who had offended in some way, and Huizong did seem to be making a real effort to improve their relationship.[86] In 1104, however, a more serious incident occurred. Officials reported that despite Huizong's overlooking his minor misbehavior, the prince was still unruly and wayward. Recently he and his subordinates had cut a hole in the rear wall of his compound and gone out "without hat or belt." They walked around the market, ate and drank with imperial clansmen, and had purchased a clanswoman to be a concubine. Although the councilors knew that Huizong preferred to forgive the prince, they wanted to punish those who had helped him in his escapades, such as those who had accompanied him on his walks, who had made the hole in his wall, who had invited people to eat with him, and those responsible for the management of his establishment. Huizong agreed with this plan and had the case sent to the Kaifeng authorities.[87]

In addition to close relatives, Huizong had some contact with the thousands of imperial clansmen who came to the palace to stand in line during major assemblies. Because clansmen normally had concubines in addition to wives, the number of clansmen had increased dramatically over the course of the eleventh century. Clansmen the same generation as Huizong (the fifth generation) numbered 3,488, and there were members of the fourth and sixth alive as well. Supporting them had become a major government expense.[88] Huizong undoubtedly recognized a fair number of clansmen, especially ones who were regular in attending court. He took note of clansmen talented in the arts, and his painting catalogue included paintings by thirteen of them. The two clansmen Huizong is known to have been on familiar terms with—Zhao Lingrang and Zhao Zhonghu—were both prominent art collectors.[89] In 1114 Huizong hosted a banquet for clansmen, the first recorded since Renzong's reign. At the banquet, Huizong expressed pleasure in the educational attainments of clansmen but regretted that more than a hundred listed in the clan genealogy did not hold office titles. He gave promotions to those who already had rank and titles to those without them.[90]

Should Huizong's family life be linked to any other facet of history? Does it help explain, or provide nuance, to anything discussed in other chapters? As emperor, Huizong was regularly expected to appear in public, to preside over all sorts of rituals, major and minor. Even small audiences with his Council of State had a layer of ritual. What he said and what he did was made part of the record. Time with his consorts and young children was, however, not on the record. Possibly with them he could simply be himself (assuming that after a few years as emperor he still had a sense of his true self). Thus when thinking of other pressures on Huizong it can be useful to keep in mind that in the inner quarters of the palace there were many young children ready to greet Huizong whenever he wanted their company.

Huizong's family also becomes particularly relevant in the last two chapters in this book when his brothers and sons were called on to help the dynasty in its crisis and subsequently accompanied him into captivity. During Huizong's last eight years, his closest male relatives were his main companions.

This chapter has looked into some of the ways Huizong interacted informally with his councilors. It is now time to turn to the serious work they did together governing the country.

⟲ *11*

Working with Councilors

> Cai Jing's loyalty is as strong as metal and stone, and he is
> devoted to bringing security to the dynasty. For eight years
> he assisted me in governing, his virtues constant. Yet perverse
> people revile the upright ones, hoping to injure them. They
> recklessly spread baseless gossip as a way to trap them in
> unexpected disasters. I now see what is going on and can
> clearly recognize the false accusations.
>
> —*From Huizong's hand-drafted edict of 1112,*
> *reappointing Cai Jing to office*

*I*N CHINA, the ruler–minister relationship was considered
one of the building blocks of the social and political order. In Confucian thought, it was one of the five cardinal relations (the others were
father–son, husband–wife, elder brother–younger brother, and friend
to friend). The ruler–minister relationship should be reciprocal and
based on loyalty, trust, and respect. The minister should want what
was best for his ruler and thus might have to tell the ruler things he
did not want to hear. The ruler needed to be an excellent judge of
character to select the right men as ministers. He also should be even-
handed in dealing with subordinates and immune to flattery so that he
would not come under the sway of sycophants. These themes were repeated in every age. The Confucian philosopher Xunzi in the late
Warring States period strongly urged rulers to concentrate on selecting a worthy minister, who then takes care of the details and chooses
the lower level administrators. Tang Taizong, in his "On How to Be
an Emperor," urged his heirs to seek worthy men, accept remonstrance, and get rid of flatterers. Ouyang Xiu, in the mid-eleventh
century, wrote two essays on the difficulty of being an emperor which
stressed how hard it was to know whom to trust and how to make the
best use of advice.[1]

Ideas about the ruler–minister relationship were conveyed not just in discursive texts of these sorts, but also by historical examples. There were many famous ruler–minister pairs in history: the Han founder and Zhang Liang; Liu Bei and Zhuge Liang during the Three Kingdoms period; the second Tang ruler Taizong and Wei Zheng, to name just a few.[2] In Song times, literati told all sorts of stories about the notable councilors of the recent past and their own day, some undoubtedly based on personal knowledge, but many based mainly on rumor. To most Song literati, it would seem, the central figures in history were the men who vied for the most powerful posts and the central events were the ways they maneuvered around each other and managed the emperors, who not infrequently were themselves adept at playing ministers off against each other.

All of the men on Huizong's Council of State stood in the position of subject/minister to him, but the top two grand councilors (the senior and junior grand councilors) were thought of as his chief ministers, the ones who served as intermediaries between him and the larger body of officials, who would meet with him the most often and discuss policy with him the most candidly. Although about twenty men held these posts at one time or another during his reign, the one who held it the longest was Cai Jing.

Cai Jing and the Council of State

Huizong met with many officials. Heads of ministries, censors and remonstrance officials, and others in the central government could request audiences and present their ideas to Huizong in person. He also regularly met with officials who were about to go off for provincial assignments or were returning from one. It is not rare for the biographies of officials to record their conversations with Huizong as high points of their careers. For instance, during an audience with one of his former tutors, Xu Ji, Huizong said that since Xu Ji had spent a lot of time outside the capital, he should tell him about the problems of the poor. Xu Ji in response talked about problems with the way the tea and salt monopolies were administered.[3] Another example is Zhang Gen, who served in a variety of regional posts and had done work with Huizong's charitable ventures. His biographer relates several face-to-face conversations with Huizong.[4] Guo Si, a civil official who passed the civil service examinations the year Huizong was born (1082), vividly described an occasion in 1117 when at an audience Huizong realized that Guo Si was the son of the famous painter Guo Xi and began discussing with him how highly Shenzong had thought of Guo Xi and how many of his paintings were still in the palace.[5]

Yet even if Huizong dealt with many officials whom he knew by name or face, the ones that mattered most were those who met almost daily with him—the members of the Council of State. Like earlier emperors, Huizong was repeatedly told that if he got the right men in these crucial positions, the job of emperor would be simple: he could rule successfully without having to exert himself. The Council of State generally consisted of five to seven men, including the senior and junior grand councilors, the top one or two men in the Secretariat-Chancellery, the Department of State Affairs, and the Bureau of Military Affairs. Men appointed to these posts needed to be experienced, respected for their intelligence, insight, and political skills, and willing to cooperate so that deliberations on issues could be productive. Rarely did it turn out to be easy to put such groups together. Even when a vacancy was filled with someone recommended by the other councilors, after a couple years of working together, councilors tended to get on each other's nerves. As friction mounted, the work of the council suffered; one member would oppose an idea in large part because a rival had advocated it. Emperors often responded to discord among councilors by replacing one or more of them; another common tactic was to encourage the senior grand councilor to take charge more forcefully. Although the scholar-official elite regularly objected when one minister seemed to monopolize power for years at a time, emperors found it easier to get decisions made and implemented when they had a single chief minister with leadership ability. Of course, what looked like leadership to the emperor could seem like domination from the other side.

Forty-seven men served on the Council of State during Huizong's reign, thirty-nine of them after Huizong had sided with the reformers in 1102. Thirteen of them at some point reached junior or senior grand councilor. Some of the forty-seven were on the council only a matter of months, but others were there for years, usually moving from one post to another. Sometimes a position was left vacant for lengthy periods, especially junior grand councilor and assistant director of the

Bureau of Military Affairs. But there still were normally at least five men on the council at any time. Table 11.1 lists the more notable members of Huizong's Councils of State.

When Huizong came to the throne at seventeen, he inherited Zhezong's Council of State. When he began replacing its members, he

Table 11.1. Huizong's major councilors, in order of age

Name	Date of birth	Dates on council	Total years on council	Years as senior or junior grand councilor
Zeng Bu	1035	1100/1–1102/6	3	2
Wu Juhou	1037	1103/4–1107/1		
		1110/8–1113/1	6	0
Han Zhongyan	1038	1100/2–1102/5	2	2
Zhao Tingzhi	1040	1102/6–1105/6		
		1106/2–1107/3	4	1
Zhang Shangying	1043	1102/8–1103/8		
		1110/2–1111/8	3	1
He Zhizhong	1044	1105/2–1116/8	12	7
Cai Jing	1046	1102/6–1106/2		
		1107/1–1109/6		
		1112/5–1120/6		
		1124/12–1125/4	14	14
Tong Guan	1054	1116/11–1123/7		
		1124/8–1125/12	8	0
Hou Meng	1054	1110/2–1117/10	8	0
Zhang Kangguo	1056	1104/9–1109/3	5	0
Deng Xunwu	1057	1104/9–1107/5		
		1116/5–1121/1	0	
Zheng Juzhong	1059	1107/10–1110/10		
		1113/5–1117/8		
		1121/5–1123/5	9	2
Yu Shen	n.d.	1108/9–1110/5		
		1112/6–1120/11	10	3
Xue Ang	n.d.	1109/4–1110/6		
		1113/4–1118/9	7	0
Liu Zhengfu	1062	1109/4–1116/12	8	0
Bai Shizhong	n.d.	1116/11–1125/12	9	2
Wang Anzhong	1076	1119/11–1123/1	3	0
Cai You	1077	1123/6–1125/12	3	0
Wang Fu	1079	1118/1–1124/11	7	3
Zhang Bangchang	1081	1119/3–1125/12	6	0
Yuwen Cuizhong	n.d.	1124/9–1125/12	1	0

Sources: SDCNB 15–19; Zhuge Yibing 2000:307–315.

chose men a generation older than he was, especially favoring those who had served under Shenzong. Once Huizong had decided to side with the reformers, he never turned back to the anti-reformers for councilors. For much of this time Cai Jing was the dominant councilor. Yet there were nevertheless three major shake-ups of his administrations, because Huizong dismissed Cai Jing three times (1106/2, 1109/6, and 1120/6).[6] Those who replaced Cai Jing were critics of him but still reformers. As a consequence, elements of the New Policies that had been introduced during Shenzong's reign and reinstated during Zhezong's personal rule—such as the Hired Service System, the mutual security groups, the revised civil service examination curricula, and the state trade policy—were largely retained throughout Huizong's reign. By contrast, policies introduced by Cai Jing as extensions of the reform program, such as the expansion of the school system, the charitable programs, the ten-*qian* coin, and residential centers for imperial clansmen outside the capital, were curtailed or even abolished each time Cai Jing was dismissed.[7]

The first time Huizong dismissed Cai Jing (1106/2–1107/1), he kept him out of office only eleven months. The second time, he was out almost three years. Cai Jing's second absence had two stages: the first lasting about a year while Cai Jing remained in the capital (from 1109/6 to 1110/6), and the second lasting nearly two years when he was sent to Hangzhou and his critics were freer to speak out against him (1110/6–1112/5). During that second period Huizong received so many indictments of Cai Jing that he wrote out several edicts in his own hand in an effort to get officials to tone down their language.[8] Once back in office in 1112/5, Cai Jing, well into his sixties, had a special dispensation to attend court only every third day, then from 1117, every fifth day, with the understanding that he would work from home most of the time. In that period Huizong seems to have seen Cai Jing as indispensable. To retire at seventy-five *sui* in 1120, it was not enough for Cai Jing to plead illness—he had to refuse to get out of bed.[9] Finally, in 1124, when relations with the Jurchen reached a critical point, Huizong did not turn to a young man with fresh ideas but insisted on bringing back the by then nearly blind Cai Jing. This did not prove to be a good solution, and he was dismissed again after only a few months.

Most surviving accounts of Cai Jing are based on indictments of him and offer little insight into what he meant to Huizong.[10] One exception is the sketch of Cai Jing's accomplishments included in Huizong's calligraphy catalogue, which reflects Huizong's views. This *Xuanhe Calligraphy Catalogue* draws attention to Cai Jing's efficiency and problem-solving skills. Concerning Cai Jing's service during Huizong's reign, the narrator uses extremely laudatory terms: "Since he was first appointed Hanlin recipient of edicts [in 1102], he has served as grand councilor three times. Reverently, brilliantly, he has managed the country's affairs. He is a true minister, admired by the people." The narrator draws particular attention to Cai Jing's ability to make complex tasks look easy. "When deciding major affairs and initiating major policies, the tasks that others cannot solve he gets done easily while pleasantly chatting." It also says that he excelled at the sort of writing required of a civil servant: "His edicts and memorials are to the point, detailed, clear, elegant, and refined. When writing on imperial order he moves his brush promptly and never has to add a dot or do a second draft."[11] Cai Jing is credited with a major role in reinstating the New Policies and praised for helping with Huizong's key initiatives, including the casting of the Nine Cauldrons, the building of the Bright Hall, the new protocols for music and ritual, and the reform of the civil service recruitment system to allow promotion through the schools. In this sketch Cai Jing is explicitly compared to Wang Anshi:

> Think of how Shenzong, when first devoting himself to seeking good government, advanced Wang Anshi, made him grand councilor, and with him devised ways to achieve good order, brilliantly forming the institutions for a king. Wang's great accomplishments extended everywhere in the realm and he was treated in an unprecedentedly magnanimous way. When I began to rely on my good assistant to reinstate my predecessor's plans, I employed the right man. Therefore I have not dared treat my trusted assistant in a way inferior to how Shenzong treated Wang Anshi. Consequently, for twenty years, the world has been at peace, and not one man or animal has failed to benefit. Even children and servants know that Cai Jing is the grand councilor who brought this great peace.[12]

Huizong, in this passage, likens his relationship with Cai Jing to his father's with Wang Anshi. Wang Anshi was certainly castigated by political opponents; perhaps Huizong saw the vociferous criticism of Cai Jing as a badge of honor, a sign that he was as fearless as Wang Anshi.

Cai Jing was, of course, never Huizong's only councilor. Serving with him were a series of experienced reformers. Wu Juhou offers a good example because his funerary biography has been preserved (not true for most of the councilors).[13] Born in 1037, Wu Juhou began his career in 1063 after he passed the examinations; like many others, he began at the entry-level as a county registrar. In 1075, when there was a famine in the southeast, he was chosen to manage the relief efforts. From then on, he occupied a series of fiscal posts, alternating between the central government and the provinces. After a stint in the capital Shenzong put him in charge of the granaries in Hebei West circuit. When he was brought back, Shenzong treated him well, giving him, for instance, scarlet robes and the "silver fish" robe ornament. The emperor next sent him out as an assistant fiscal intendant, where he was credited with efficient management of the salt monopoly, then brought back to the central government and given other signs of favor, including a note written by Shenzong saying that, of all the officials handling finance at court or in the provinces, there was not a one better than Wu Juhou. Shenzong was delighted when Wu Juhou submitted a memorial arguing that revenues could be raised to supply the armies in the northwest by casting two million iron coins. After Shenzong's death, Wu Juhou was out of office for a decade, undoubtedly because he had been enthusiastic in his implementation of the New Policies, but when Zhezong was ruling on his own, he brought Wu Juhou back to serve in fiscal posts, then appointed him governor of Kaifeng prefecture, where he acquired a reputation for lowering the crime rate.

After Huizong took the throne, Wu Juhou was again appointed governor of Kaifeng, then minister of revenue. He was one of the twenty-seven men Cai Jing selected to serve on the Advisory Office during its two-year existence (mid-1102 to mid-1104), and it fell to him to write the proposal for charity clinics. It was his idea to reduce the proportion of copper in bronze coins to make possible the minting of an additional 159,000 strings of cash.[14]

At sixty-seven *sui* in 1103/4 Wu Juhou was appointed to the Council of State, then moved from one post on it to another for nearly three years. In 1107, because he had reached the retirement age of seventy, he was allowed to retire from the council with full honors. In 1109, however, "The emperor, thinking that men who had served during [Shenzong's] Yuanfeng period should not be left without offices for long," appointed Wu Juhou as a prefect, then in the eighth month of 1110 (when Cai Jing was in retirement), brought him back to serve on the Council of State, within the year moving him to director of the Bureau of Military Affairs. "In casual conversation he would bring up to the emperor the need to honor the worthy men of the past, and hold firmly to his goals." Whenever there was a matter of importance, Huizong would send a palace attendant to his house to ask his views, which then were frequently implemented. "After deliberations on important issues such as preparing defenses and selecting generals, the emperor always gladly took his advice." Huizong, because the circuit fiscal officials so often came up short, rewarded Wu Juhou with a hand-drafted note which read: "The fiscal officials do not focus on their responsibilities but make their main business requesting things from the court. In the past, when you were in charge of the area east of the capital, you never reported shortages, which undoubtedly reflects how much more talented you are."

A mark of honor mentioned in Wu Juhou's funerary biography was Huizong's interest in his poetry. Huizong was impressed by the poetry he did at court, we are told, and would sometimes respond with a poem of his own using the same rhymes. When Huizong asked him to show him poems that he had done outside of court, Wu Juhou submitted several hundred.[15] Huizong gave him so many pieces of calligraphy that Wu Juhou built a special pavilion for them at his house in Yuzhang (Jiangxi province). Huizong also favored him by writing out in seal script its name, "Pavilion of Honoring the Worthy," which the palace then copied onto a board with the characters filled in with metal; Wu Juhou himself, in addition, had the calligraphy carved into stone. Ge Shengzhong, the author of Wu Juhou's funerary biography, also noted his devotion to Huizong: "On each of Huizong's birthdays and his Personal Destiny *renxu* days, Wu would always ritually purify himself, then summon an expert (*fangshi*) to perform an offering service at the pavilion and pray for the emperor's hundreds of thousands of years of longevity. The cost he never charged to government accounts."

In 1113, after serving a second term of two years and four months on the Council of State, Wu Juhou requested to retire on grounds of illness and old age. Huizong made every effort to dissuade him. When he finally had to grant him retirement, we are told, Huizong repeatedly sent attendants to ask him what he needed, and at his farewell audience Huizong asked him to submit one memorial each month. Later that year when he learned that Wu Juhou had died, Huizong canceled audience for the day and personally wrote out the seal script title for his funerary stele and also called upon Ge Shengzhong to compose the funerary biography.[16]

Several themes that appear in Wu Juhou's biography are also central in accounts of other councilors. Huizong made generous gifts to most of his councilors. Earlier emperors had done this as well, but Huizong set a new high. He seems to have given pieces of his calligraphy to most of his councilors and quite commonly would write out the name plaque for a hall at their home.[17] When an official had a special need, such as the death of a parent, Huizong made substantial gifts; for instance, after their mothers died he gave four hundred lengths of silk to Feng Xizai, then a Hanlin academician, and Yao You, a former minister of rites. In 1116, when Liu Zhengfu was retiring due to ill health, Huizong made gifts to him of ink stones and brushes, paintings, medicine, incense, and tea. From the memorials of thanks that Wang Anzhong wrote, we know that among the gifts he received from Huizong were clothing, a gold belt, a saddled horse, a Daoist scripture, medicine, various varieties of tea, as well as calligraphy and paintings Huizong had done himself. In 1116, after Huizong had had new ritual bronzes cast for imperial rituals, he had sets of bronze vessels cast for each of his councilors for them to use for their own ancestral rites.[18] Another common gift was a belt, often of gold, but in rare cases of jade, an item generally reserved for royalty. Jade belts were given to Cai Jing, He Zhizhong, Zheng Juzhong, Wang Fu, Cai You, and Tong Guan. Cai Jing even once received a retinue of two hundred men to accompany him when he was traveling on horseback.[19]

Among the most valuable gifts Huizong conferred on officials were houses, which he granted Cai Jing, Deng Xunwu, He Zhizhong, Zheng Juzhong, Yu Shen, Hou Ming, Xue Ang, Bai Shizhong, Wang Fu, the eunuch Liang Shicheng, and the general Gao Qiu. These houses were all in Kaifeng and presumably would revert to the government on their deaths. Cai Jing's house, granted to him in 1110, was probably the largest; one of its halls—named the Six Cranes Hall, was said to be forty-nine Chinese feet tall. Cai Jing was also given a home in Suzhou.[20]

Cai Jing had a propensity for alienating people. Quite a few councilors turned against him after serving with him for a while. When Cai Jing became grand councilor, we are told in Zhang Shangying's *Song History* biography, Zhang Shangying was lavish in his praise, which led to his own appointment on the Council of State. Before long, however, Zhang Shangying and Cai Jing were regularly disagreeing. After only twelve months on the council, Zhang Shangying was sent out to serve as a prefect. Cai Jing was so adamantly against him that he had him put on the 1104 list of banned Yuanyou partisans. A little later Liu Kui, on the Council of State as second in command of the Bureau of Military Affairs, became a harsh critic of Cai Jing. Shi Gongbi, too, had been considered a member of Cai Jing's faction and in 1107 had helped pave the way for Cai Jing's return, but by 1109 was writing denunciations of him.[21]

Wu Juhou was one of only two councilors to avoid falling out with Cai Jing. The other was one of Huizong's tutors as a prince, He Zhizhong. He Zhizhong managed to spend more than ten years on the council (including several when he formally outranked Cai Jing) without turning against him. Wu Juhou and He Zhizhong were credited with keeping Cai Jing's policies and appointees largely in place during his second absence in 1109–1112, as well as with orchestrating Zhang Shangying's fall in 1111. Another long-term supporter of Cai Jing was Zheng Juzhong, but in his case by 1118 observers were detecting a rift between him and Cai Jing.[22]

Why did people turn so vehemently against Cai Jing? First, it should be remembered that enmity was a favorite topic of gossip and so is well represented in surviving sources, probably skewing our understanding of what went on. After all, the sources often refer to "Cai Jing's faction," so there must have been people working with him. Just being so favored by Huizong undoubtedly raised suspicion of Cai Jing in many people's eyes. Cai Jing's personality undoubtedly also played a role.[23] The vague quality of many of the criticisms of him suggest that people found him too self-centered, too indifferent to other people's ideas, interests, or feelings. He does seem to have had a cruel streak. After he won out over Zeng Bu in 1102, not only did he have him put on the blacklist, but he also saw to it that although he was already sixty-seven *sui*, he was forced into almost constant movement for the last five years of his life as he was steadily demoted and transferred. Just as troubling, Cai Jing went after Zeng Bu's sons, accusing them of corruption and having them interrogated under torture.[24]

As noted above, the funerary biography of Wu Juhou mentions that Huizong asked to see the poems he had written outside of court. Huizong's interest in his councilors as men of talent comes through in several other cases as well, none more than Cai Jing. Part of the intimacy between Cai Jing and Huizong probably came from working together on poetry, painting, and calligraphy. Huizong claimed to have admired Cai Jing's poetry and calligraphy even before he took the throne and in 1119 was able to recall a poem Cai Jing had composed two decades earlier. Huizong had Cai Jing's calligraphy displayed along with his own on several stone steles. From time to time, Huizong called on Cai Jing to add his calligraphy to a painting Huizong had made, a form of collaboration relatively new to artistic practice in the late Northern Song. Four surviving paintings involved such collaboration with Cai Jing: *Literary Gathering* (Plate 3), *Listening to the Qin* (Plate 13), *Returning Fishing Boats on a Snowy River* (Figure 8.3), and *White Hawk*.[25]

Huizong's appreciation of Cai Jing's calligraphy only got stronger over time. In Huizong's calligraphy catalogue, Cai Jing's calligraphy is described as combining discipline and freedom: "His characters are stern but not restricted; they are relaxed but do not violate the rules." Examples of Cai Jing's large-character calligraphy are said to include the "uncountable" inscribed plaques he had done for the government.[26] At the 1119 banquet, discussed in Chapter 10, Huizong showed his guests where he had stored Cai Jing's calligraphy. As Cai Jing relates: "Then His Majesty pointed to the studio, saying it was where every one of the memorials in my hand had been stored. He ordered someone to open the case. In it was a red divider, and behind the divider a small box, and in the box was something covered in silk. That turned out to be the appointment paper I had written for the Pure Consort Miss Liu. I said to the emperor, 'My calligraphy is poor and my prose is bad. I had no idea you would have kept it.'"[27]

Huizong also honored Cai Jing by visiting his house. In the ninth month of 1119 Huizong visited Cai Jing's house for the fourth time that year and the sixth time since it had been built. On this occasion, he first visited Precious Registers Daoist temple where numinous mushrooms had been sighted, then traveled by boat along Spectacular Dragon River to Cai Jing's house, bringing one of his consorts with him as well as Tong Guan. According to Cai Jing's account, Huizong kept telling him not to make a fuss, and said that because they were now relatives through marriage (through the marriage of their children), they should talk informally. Huizong personally prepared tea and handed the cups to those present. He also told his host that he should take off his hat and robe, which Cai Jing successfully refused, saying it was something a subject could not bear to do—"a crime worth ten thousand deaths." Telling him to set aside ruler–minister ritual, Huizong took an olive and handed it to Cai Jing. Huizong passed a cup of wine to Tong Guan as well. The consort cut up pieces of fruit and handed them out. Cai Jing brought up a matter that had been discussed in court that day, which Huizong told him not to worry about. Huizong asked for some paper, then wrote out an edict dismissing charges against one official and reassigning another, apparently the actions Cai Jing had wanted him to take.[28]

It was not until 1118 that Huizong began to appoint men of his own generation to the Council of State. He started with Wang Fu (b. 1079) in 1118, the next year added Wang Anzhong (b. 1076) and Zhang Bangchang (b. 1081), and in 1123 Cai Jing's eldest son Cai You (b. 1077).

Wang Fu passed the civil service examination in the Honoring Calm period (1102–1106), and served in a series of central government positions including Hanlin academician. By 1116 Huizong had given him a house.[29] He reached the Council of State two years later, where he served for six years, the last three of them as grand councilor. The surviving biographical sources are if anything harsher on Wang Fu than on Cai Jing, probably because he was a strong supporter of the alliance with Jin. The only explanation these sources offer concerning why Huizong may have wanted him around was that he was good-looking, astute at figuring out what others wanted, and willing to amuse Huizong by performing amateur theatricals.[30]

Wang Fu had been willing to work with Cai Jing, but once the latter retired in 1120/6 and Wang Fu took his place as the leading councilor, he systematically dismantled most of Cai Jing's programs, including the Biyong Academy, the medical and mathematics schools, the charitable programs, and so on. In addition, he curtailed some of the fiscal measures.[31] Some critics charged that he was personally corrupt, that he had reorganized palace procurement in a way that allowed him to profiteer. He was also accused of openly selling offices.[32] He retained Huizong's confidence, however. A piece of calligraphy that Huizong conferred on him in 1122 is still extant (Figure 11.1).

After Cai Jing retired in 1120, his eldest son Cai You rose in power and in 1123 gained a place on the Council of State. Cai You held palace posts from early in Huizong's reign and at the beginning seems to have been as much a companion as a bureaucrat, joining Huizong in amusements.[33] He gradually got more deeply involved in government matters, especially Huizong's pet projects, such as the music reform, the Bright Hall, the Palace Library, the burial of consort Liu Mingda as an empress, and the many Daoist initiatives.[34] Although Cai You's rise certainly owed much to his father's power, as he rose, he and his father became estranged. Each maintained his own house (both of them gifts from Huizong). Observers suspected that Cai You resented his father deferring retirement so long.[35] Cai You was much more strongly in favor of the alliance with Jin than his father.

Policymaking and the Issue of Currency

The purpose of the Council of State was to deliberate on important issues and formulate recommendations to the emperor. Most of the time emperors accepted recommendations that had the full support of the council. If an emperor rejected too many of their proposals, the grand councilor would feel obligated to offer his resignation, which the emperor might by that point want.

Once Huizong had decided to side with the reformers in 1102, there was considerable consistency in the policies followed at his court. The measures implemented by Huizong and Cai Jing that have attracted the most scholarly attention are the ones that can be seen as succeeding, especially the schools and charities.[36] Here, to extend the analysis of the working relationship between Huizong and Cai Jing, let me look at a measure that has to be considered a failure: the introduction of ten-*qian* coins. Huizong deserves part of the blame for its failure because he allowed the measure to be abruptly canceled and just as abruptly reintroduced as Cai Jing came and went.

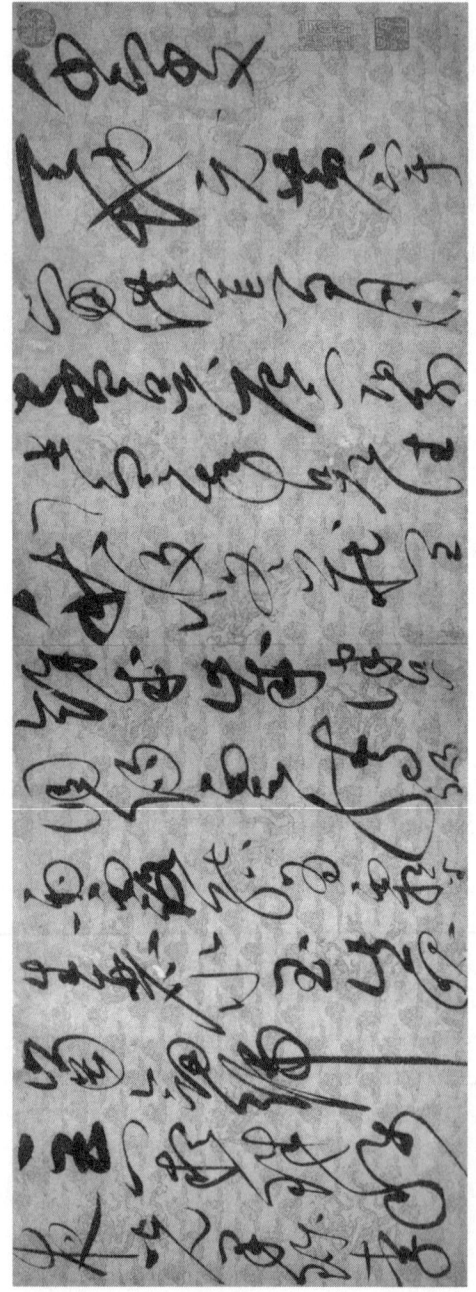

Fig. 11.1. Huizong's transcription of the *Thousand Character Essay* in cursive script, on decorated paper, given to Wang Fu in 1122, 31.5 × 1172 cm., opening section. (Liaoning Provincial Museum)

From the beginning of the dynasty, the government had had problems maintaining an adequate supply of bronze coins, which needed to expand along with the economy if economic growth was to continue. The standard coin was worth one *qian* (elsewhere translated as "cash"), but two-*qian* coins had also been introduced during Shenzong's reign. For larger transactions, people used strings of cash, nominally one thousand cash, but due to the shortage of cash, the government allowed short strings of 770 coins for tax payment. The government took other measures to ease the shortage of copper as well: it opened new mines, reduced the proportion of copper in the coins, permitted taxes to be paid in silver, issued iron coins for use in the northern border area and Sichuan, outlawed melting down coins, circulated vouchers in connection with the grain trade and the tea and salt monopolies that along with ordination certificates could be traded, and in time issued paper money. At the peak in 1085, the government was issuing six million strings of copper cash a year (7.5 times what it issued in 997). Money was not minted in one place and distributed around the country, but rather minted in more than two dozen places and circulated locally. Minting so many coins during the New Policies period seems to have seriously depleted supplies of copper, and after Shenzong's reign production of coins fell, leading to a serious unmet demand for more currency by the end of the eleventh century. Another reason coins were in short supply is that both ordinary people and the government set aside significant amounts as a way to store wealth.[37]

When Cai Jing became grand councilor in 1102, he promoted the idea of casting higher denomination coins, both a large bronze coin that would be worth ten *qian* as well as tin-iron alloy coins that would be worth three *qian*.[38] Both measures would allow the government to expand the supply of currency without requiring new sources of copper. Since the use of a variety of forms of paper currency was expanding, though still largely limited to Sichuan, it was not unreasonable to suppose people would accept another form of fiat currency, that is, currency that did not have the intrinsic value assigned to it. Moreover, in the early 1040s when currency was short near the border, the government had cast ten-*qian* coins to cover military expenses.[39]

As a first step, in 1103 certain prefectures were told to have their mints switch to casting five-*qian* coins and others ten-*qian* coins. The quota for the year was set at three hundred thousand strings of bronze coins and two million strings of iron coins (still way below the peak of six million in 1085).[40] The government had not tried to suppress private casting of one-*qian* counts, as there was not much profit in it. To discourage counterfeiting of the new high-denomination coins, private casters were to be recruited to work in the new mints and counterfeiting severely punished. It was also decided that some places should cast tin alloy coins. Some of the old two-*qian* coins were collected and recast as ten-*qian* coins. Each coin was to weigh three times as much as the one-*qian* coins. In the first month of 1104, the distribution of the newly minted coins was divided up this way: of the six hundred thousand strings, half would go to the Board of Revenue, two hundred thousand would go to the Privy Treasury, and one hundred thousand would go to the Yuanfeng Treasury, the so-called grand councilor's treasury. In 1105 ten-*qian* coins were issued with the inscription in Huizong's calligraphy. A string of these coins was to weigh 14 catties 7 ounces and use 9 catties 7 ounces 2 *qian* of copper, 4 catties 12 ounces 6 *qian* of lead, 1 catty 9 ounces 2 *qian* of tin, and 1 catty 5 ounces of casting waste.[41]

At this time, Zhao Tingzhi, then junior grand councilor, opposed Cai Jing on many issues, the ten-*qian* coins among them. His primary objection was that the new coins made counterfeiting too tempting. Steps also had to be taken to deter counterfeiting paper currency, but for some unknown reason, the problem does not seem to have been as extreme with paper money. Cai Jing's response to the counterfeiting was to put more effort into enforcement, but the problem did not go away. In the two Zhe circuits counterfeiting was so prevalent that one-*qian* coins became scarce, making ordinary trading difficult. Another complaint about the ten-*qian* coins was that they led to price inflation.[42]

In 1106/1, after a comet led Huizong to rethink many policies (but before Cai Jing was off the Council of State), many places were ordered to cease casting ten-*qian* coins. Once Cai Jing was off the Council of State the next month, more places were gradually added to the list until the casting of ten-*qian* coins was fully abolished. People were told to convert any ten-*qian* coins they had. In exchange they would get newly issued paper money. The coins removed from circulation were deposited in the Yuanfeng and Chongning treasuries. Reportedly, counterfeited coins could be traded in for their weight in copper.[43]

The arguments against the high-denomination coins were laid out in a memorial submitted by the censor Shen Ji:

> Anyone who advocates ten-*qian* coins does not understand that he is inviting crime. Why would the riffraff shrink from casting these coins when they can easily make a several-fold profit? Even if the policy is put in place gradually, the forces at work cannot be stopped. It is not only the urban lower class who have taken up counterfeiting; often the wealthy and scholar-officials engage in it as well. Before much time went by, the small coins disappeared in the southeast.
>
> When coins have a low value, the price of goods will increase [i.e., price inflation]. When the price of goods goes up, it hurts the poor the most. When they suffer hunger and cold, banditry increases. The people are on edge, each day expecting the court to change the rules. How can this be a long-term plan?[44]

At an audience in the fifth month of 1106, Huizong questioned the remonstrance official Zhan Piyuan about his views on the ten-*qian* coins. Huizong said, "Circulating the ten-*qian* coins was originally intended to be a convenience for the people. Now to the contrary it is causing them such harm. If you hadn't explained it to me, I would not have understood this. It would not be difficult to directly convert the ten-*qian* coins into three-*qian* coins, but won't those from distant places who have saved them up by the tens of thousands feel bitter if the coins are sharply reduced in value?" Zhan Piyuan answered, "Your Majesty, if you want to make changes in institutions, then 'when the grass is cut, the wildlife gets killed.' If this troubles you, keep in mind that five [people] will be better off for each one who is not." Huizong then brought up people's complaints when Wang Anshi introduced profit-oriented policies and the likelihood that this policy would be viewed the same way. Zhan objected that Cai Jing should not be put in the same class as Wang Anshi, who had stayed away from the tea and salt monopolies.[45]

Although in this conversation Huizong seems to have rejected the ten-*qian* coin, he let Cai Jing persuade him to reintroduce it when he returned to office a few months later. In 1107/2 Cai had imperial-calligraphy ten-*qian* coins cast, using the metal from melted-down

Fig. 11.2. Size comparison of one-, two-, and ten-*qian* coins issued in the Daguan period (1107–1110), with the inscriptions in Huizong's Slender Gold calligraphy. (Photo by author)

counterfeit coins (see Figure 11.2). To deter counterfeiting he made an example of Zhang Yan, who had counterfeited strings of cash in the tens of millions. This case ended up implicating many members of the southeastern local elite in 1107.[46]

When Cai Jing was dismissed a second time (in 1109/6), the issue of the ten-*qian* coins came up again. A lengthy memorial by Zhou Xingji probably dates to this period. Zhou Xingji was a disciple of Cheng Yi who had spent more time in teaching positions than in substantive posts. He argued that although the government seemed to be gaining financial resources by issuing the larger denomination coins, in fact it did not:

> From my calculations, ever since the government started issuing ten-*qian* coins, for each one that the government issues, private casters issue ten. Although the profit from these coins doubled, prices went up 200 percent. . . . If counterfeiting is not stopped, then prices will continue to rise and legal enforcement will become more burdensome. Goods come from the people and money comes from the government. Taxes in kind cover about 40 percent [of the government's needs] and 60 percent is purchased. Food and equipment, whatever is needed, must all be purchased on the market. If what the people produce costs more, and what the government issues is worth less, there is no possibility of balancing the government budget.

Zhou Xingji proposed that the government buy back the ten-*qian* coins in the five circuits near the capital, compensating owners with ordination certificates, honorary official titles, salt vouchers, and paper money. Once all of the ten-*qian* coins were collected, the government could reissue them as three-*qian* coins. This would lead to price stability and an end to counterfeiting, Zhou Xingji argued. The government did issue a very large number of ordination certificates in 1110 (thirty thousand), which not surprisingly brought its own problems as they declined in value.[47]

The new grand councilor, Zhang Shangying, in 1110/7 proposed his own solution. He asked to borrow silk, gold, silver, and salt vouchers from the Privy Purse and the Bureau of Military Affairs to buy up all the ten-*qian* coins in the country, giving people six months to trade theirs in. Those turning them in would not get their face value, but 30 or 40 percent of it. By using the Privy Purse, Zhang Shangying was asking Huizong to bear much of the burden of the failed fiscal policy.[48] Once the coins had all been collected, the counterfeited ones could be melted down for casting one-*qian* coins and the genuine ones could be circulated as three-*qian* coins. The issue must have been debated for a while, as Huizong did not announce the new policy until 1111/5. In that hand-drafted edict, Huizong underlined the importance of stable currency to both the people and the government. Recent poor policy decisions had led to prices rising rapidly, forcing some people into bankruptcy and tempting others to take up counterfeiting. After discussing the issue with a wide range of people, he had decided to revise the currency. The government and the Privy Purse would together issue several ten millions of strings of coins to buy up the ten-*qian* coins, paying three *qian* a piece for them.[49]

Zhang Shangying was lavish in his praise of Huizong for drawing on the Privy Purse but also admitted that things had not gone perfectly smoothly:

> Your Majesty has acted heroically, determined to remedy the problem of inflation [lit., "money losing value and goods becoming more expensive"]. On the day you announced that you would spend several million strings worth of currency and treasure from the Privy Purse to fund converting the ten-*qian* coins to three-*qian* ones, a sigh of relief went up inside and outside the capital, the multitudes speaking as one. A search through the historical record, from the time of the ancient sage rulers on, will find no act equal to this. Yet disreputable people in the palace have secretly spread rumors, saying, "Before long the policy will be reversed, so

you can hold onto [your ten-*qian* coins] and wait." Reprobates outside the palace, trying to impress people, tell them, "When [the coin] equals three *qian*, you are the one to loose; the seven *qian* is taken by the palace." Because people hear such talk and think it makes sense, even though the order for the conversion was issued fifty days ago, it still has not been widely obeyed. I would like Your Majesty to remain resolute in your decision, so that the correct understanding finally takes hold, the wicked become conscience-stricken, and resentment gradually abates.[50]

In other words, Zhang Shangying labeled Huizong's use of the Privy Purse as an unprecedentedly magnanimous gesture but conceded that people still resented having to turn in their coins at a loss and many were biding their time to see if policy would be altered again.[51]

When Cai Jing returned as grand councilor in 1112, he reestablished casting supervisory offices and tin-alloy coins. But he did not reintroduce the ten-*qian* coins. In fact, a county magistrate was banished after he submitted a memorial saying that the ten-*qian* coins should be reinstated because they had been an excellent means of enriching the state while offering convenience to the people. In 1113, at an audience with Huizong, the court official, Yuwen Cuizhong, said that officials having difficulty maintaining supplies of one-*qian* coins were proposing that the ten-*qian* coins be issued again. Huizong replied, "How would they dare! Even though we converted the ten-*qian* coins to three-*qian* ones, inflation persists. How could we issue ten-*qian* coins again? The ancients had a saying, 'Even when profit tilts one hundred to one, do not change the law. When the [chance for] profit is slight and the [risk of] harm is heavy, it is better to do nothing.'"[52]

What do we learn about Huizong as a supervisor from this saga? Coinage was not an issue that he identified himself with; he did only a few hand-drafted edicts on the subject.[53] People identified the original idea with Cai Jing and the counterarguments with several other officials (Zhao Tingzhi, Zhang Shangying, Shen Ji, etc.). In the sources that survive, Huizong's contribution seems to have been limited to approving proposals. Nevertheless, there are a few records of conversations between Huizong and his officials that reveal that he was familiar with what was going on and cared what the public thought of the measures taken.

What Huizong personally contributed to these policy choices was his willingness to let Cai Jing's measures be overturned when he was dismissed and restored when he returned. Given the animosity of so many people toward Cai Jing, it may have been difficult to do otherwise. Huizong did not ask Zhao Tingzhi or Zhang Shangying to carefully consider the drawbacks of canceling policies too quickly. Nor, when he brought Cai Jing back in 1107, did he ask him to reconsider whether all the measures canceled really needed to be restored. Perhaps Huizong took too seriously the injunction to rulers to choose the minister, then leave things to him.

Trusted Eunuchs

In Huizong's day, it was accepted as historical fact that eunuchs could gain so much power that they threatened the dynasty. In both the late Han and late Tang periods, eunuchs at court gained control over access to the emperor, forcing civil officials to ally themselves with eunuchs if they wanted a say in government. Song officials often spoke contemptuously of eunuchs, viewing them as hardly more than slaves. Emperors, who interacted more with them, were less inclined to reject them categorically, finding some of them to be useful and dependable. To prevent eunuch domination at their courts, the Song founders had restricted the number of eunuchs and limited their responsibilities. Their numbers seem to have nevertheless gradually increased, and one thirteenth-century author claimed that the number of eunuchs reached more than a thousand during Huizong's reign.[54]

Two eunuchs gained Huizong's highest respect and trust. Tong Guan rose to the top of the military command structure and Liang Shicheng acquired responsibility for the smooth running of the palace paperwork and also Huizong's collections.

Liang Shicheng started in the palace as an assistant to Jia Xiang in the Calligraphy Bureau. After Jia Xiang's death, Liang Shicheng was put in charge of the document storehouse attached to Sagacious Thoughts Hall, giving him responsibility for documents from and to the emperor, among them Huizong's imperial brush edicts. Cai Tao wrote that at the Outer Document Storehouse, "clerks like Yang Qiu and others manage things, with Zhang Bu and others checking them and three or four junior eunuchs carrying them back and forth and placing seals for transmission to the outside." (Yang Qiu and Zhang Bu appeared in Chapter 10 as Huizong's close associates in a humorous poem.) Liang Shicheng so impressed Huizong that he awarded him a *jinshi* degree in the civil service examinations in 1109. Liang Shicheng and Cai Jing were among the men who would evaluate calligraphy when it arrived at the palace. Late in his career, Liang Shicheng was appointed supervisor of the Palace Library. One of the steps he took in this capacity was to recommend that rubbings of inscriptions be collected. He also was involved in many of Huizong's building projects, including the Bright Hall and the Northeast Marchmount. In an essay Huizong wrote commemorating the completion of the Northeast Marchmount, he praised Liang Shicheng for his organizational ability: "Liang Shicheng is broad, refined, faithful, attentive to detail, and skillful. He can put together a group of talented individuals and assign them each separate tasks."[55]

Tong Guan played a more public role than Liang Shicheng and as a consequence more is known about his career. Eunuchs who served in the military had a long tradition in Northern Song times.[56] Huizong's first encounter with him, however, seems to have been in his capacity as a palace servant. At any rate, in 1102, soon after taking the throne, Huizong sent Tong Guan to Hangzhou to supervise the acquisition of old books and paintings for the palace. Thereafter Tong Guan was more commonly engaged in military matters focused on the western and northwestern borders. Tong Guan knew that Liao was Song's chief adversary, and in 1111 he took the opportunity to learn more about Liao by traveling there as part of a mission.[57] After his return from Liao, Tong Guan's rank and influence steadily rose. In 1112/2 he was given the highest military title, Defender-in-Chief. Cai Jing was not comfortable with Tong Guan's rise and tried to get Huizong to reconsider the favor he showed him. One source says that in 1111, when Tong Guan was sent on the mission to Liao, Cai Jing, then in retirement in Hangzhou, felt so strongly that Tong Guan was the wrong man that he wrote to Huizong, expressing doubts about Tong Guan's capability, but Huizong responded that the Liao ruler had asked to meet him because of the reputation he earned through the western campaigns. In 1116/2 Tong Guan was the first eunuch to be made a member of the Council of State as assistant director of the Bureau of Military Affairs, and he remained a member of the Council of

State till 1123 with steady advances in rank and title. Anecdotes report that Cai Jing complained frequently to Huizong about giving such honors to a eunuch, but Huizong discounted his remarks. Apparently Tong Guan enjoyed going out on campaign, however, since he did not use this court appointment to remain permanently in the capital. In 1119, he was with the army during the battles against Xi Xia.[58]

Huizong treated Tong Guan as he would have a civil or military official. In 1104, after Tong Guan achieved his first notable victory in the Qingtang war, Huizong conferred on him a sample of his calligraphy, a transcription of the *Thousand Character Essay* in his own distinctive Slender Gold calligraphy, a piece of calligraphy that still exists in the collection of the Shanghai Museum (see Figure 11.3).[59] Like other leading eunuchs, Tong Guan sometimes supervised major construction projects. Tong Guan is listed among the five senior eunuchs who each took responsibility for building a part of Extended Blessings Palace, completed in 1113. Not long afterward he was given charge of construction of the mansion for one of Huizong's sons.[60]

Huizong also apparently liked Tong Guan's paintings. In Huizong's painting catalogue, Tong Guan is one of ten Song eunuchs given entries. Tong Guan's reports that he learned about painting from his father (perhaps a eunuch adoptive father), who collected paintings of contemporaries such as Cui Bo, Yi Yuanji, and Guo Xi. Tong Guan, we are told, painted to amuse himself, "making mountains, forests, springs, and stones, following his own inclinations and stopping when the inspiration left him." His painting style is described in terms usually associated with literati painters: "In general, his compositions are relaxed and his brushwork simple, but the paintings are full of ideas and very natural, seemingly the result of practice and not from trying to please people."[61]

Like others who enjoyed Huizong's favor for lengthy periods, Tong Guan and Liang Shicheng aroused bitter resentment, and Huizong heard a variety of charges against them and other eunuchs. Zhai Ruwen, an official who had worked with Huizong's antiquities, reportedly told Huizong that Liang Shicheng was forcing ordinary people to sell their fields and graveyards in order to expand a park. Liang Shicheng was so annoyed that he persuaded the grand councilor to send Zhai Ruwen out to serve as a prefect. Zhou Wuzhong in 1120 reported to Huizong a major famine in the Huainan region, which he

Fig. 11.3. Huizong's transcription of the *Thousand Character Essay* in Slender Gold calligraphy, given to Tong Guan in 1104, closing section. (Shanghai Museum)

blamed on the local allies of the eunuchs. Around the same time an Imperial Academy student named Zhu Mengshuo submitted a series of memorials that expressed his views that "the palace is overly extravagant and eunuch attendants bring disorder to the government." Corrupt eunuchs, he charged, expropriated people's land for gardens and sold offices through an open system of bribery.[62]

None of these denunciations seems to have persuaded Huizong that his trust in Liang Shicheng and Tong Guan was misplaced. After all, earlier Song emperors had received similar warnings to be on their guard against eunuchs.[63] Huizong maintained his confidence in Tong Guan and Liang Shicheng to the very end of his reign.

Perhaps the most detached assessment of the power of eunuchs in the later years of Huizong's reign was written by Cai Tao, well-positioned to have noticed what was happening, though it should be recognized that putting blame on eunuchs deflected some of the blame from his father. Cai Tao saw eunuchs as gaining increasing power over the course of Huizong's reign. Early on, civil officials did not have much contact with them, but from about 1113 or 1114, Huizong brought more of the policymaking into the inner reaches of the palace and issued more orders through imperial brush edicts, giving eunuchs control over the flow of documents. In Cai Tao's view, Tong Guan had gradually gained full control of the military, and Liang Shicheng came to do things chief ministers traditionally did, so that those two eunuchs between them controlled both the civil and military sides of the government. Even grand councilors paid court to Liang Shicheng. Cai Tao also mentions officials who allied with other eunuchs, including He Xin and Wang Reng. Wang Anzhong and Wang Fu, he noted, treated Liang Shicheng with special deference. Officials had to go through eunuchs to get audiences with Huizong, and the different bureaus ended up competing with each other for the favor of eunuchs. After Cai Jing retired in 1120, Cai Tao reports, he was saddened by these turns of events. Huizong, too, saw that things had gotten out of hand, and had Feng Hao and other eunuchs executed for unspecified offences. Unfortunately, in Cai Tao's opinion, frightening the eunuchs led them to pursue more dissolute lives rather than more circumspect ones.[64]

How GOOD was Huizong at selecting councilors and managing his Council of State? Probably about average. Extant historical sources depict Huizong as an enthusiastic participant in almost anything that can be classed as cultural. He took an interest in the work of experts employed by the court in many fields, such as physicians and painters. He asked officials to show him poems and paintings they had done outside of court.

Huizong's involvement in the nitty-gritty of governing is rarely depicted as equally absorbing to him. He is not shown as negligent—he does not cancel audiences or ignore memorials. He tried to understand the issues referred to him, even ones as technically complex as the potential pitfalls of issuing currency. He treated his councilors with courtesy and good humor. Although many officials saw dangers in powerful grand councilors, Huizong saw comparable drawbacks to collective leadership. Rather, he took to heart the traditional Confucian advice to select a minister, then trust him. Like other Song emperors, he preferred a grand councilor able to persuade others to fall into line behind him. Outsiders may well have worried that a grand councilor like Cai Jing, able to dominate the other councilors, might dominate the emperor as well. Huizong, however, showed no wariness in that regard. Cai Jing remained deferential to Huizong even when the emperor was making every effort to tell him not to stand on ceremony. Huizong and Cai Jing did not always see eye to eye on every issue. But Huizong never doubted Cai Jing's motives the way so many other people did.

From Huizong's perspective, a grand councilor who could handle most matters on his own meant that Huizong had time and mental energy to think about other things. During his second decade on the throne, Daoist scriptures, masters, and heavens were some of the concerns that Huizong wished to pursue. They are the subject of Chapter 12.

12

Accepting Divine Revelations,
1110–1119

We have reached a high point with a benevolent sage on the throne who has received the precious mandate from heaven and promulgates the ultimate Dao. Recently he has established Precious Registers Temple in the capital, where he set up an ordination platform close to the palace. To aid those in need among the populace, talismans and drugs are dispensed, which benefits thousands of people every day. Eight or nine out to ten of them turn toward the true [religion]. [The emperor] is also searching for lost holy scriptures, extending [the search] to the farthest reaches and leaving out nothing. Work on editing this canon is ongoing and it will be carved into woodblocks [for printing], and thus transmitted forever. The realm will be suffused in the pure and the ancient and the people will show concern for their life spans. This can be called a time of completion for the Dao and its emanations, an era of great peace that will last a myriad generations.

—From the preface dated 1116 written by Yuan Miaozong for Secret Essentials on the Totality of the Perfected for Assisting the State and Saving the People, in the Most High Tradition

*F*ROM THE BEGINNING of his reign Huizong was a devout Daoist. He read standard Daoist scriptures, participated in Daoist rituals, painted Daoist icons, interacted with Daoist masters, and funded the construction of Daoist temples. Over time, his involvement with Daoism deepened and widened. By 1113, he was taking an interest in seers such as Wang Laozhi and Wang Zixi. That year and the next he reported visions of deities after both the sacrifice to heaven and the sacrifice to earth. He also began a major search for Daoist texts in preparation for the compilation of a new Daoist canon. By 1116 he had met the Daoist priest Lin Lingsu and responded positively to his revelations about the highest realm of heaven, the Divine Empyrean. Huizong became convinced that the highest gods wanted him to act on their behalf. Over the next several years, Huizong issued a flurry of edicts that elevated Daoism and strengthened its ties to the government. Many of these projects required substantial outlays of funds, which Huizong freely provided.

A variety of questions can be asked of emperors involved with Daoism. There are the motivations of the emperors—which could range from personal desire for long life to a hope of establishing a Daoist utopia on earth. There are also questions about the Daoist masters who worked with these emperors. Did one have the emperor's ear, or did several compete to influence him? Were the Daoist masters pursuing agendas different than their imperial patrons? If so, were their agendas ones that most Daoist clergy of the time would support, or were they suspected of pursuing personal advantage and power? What about the balance of power between the emperor and his Daoist advisors? Were the Daoist masters able to manipulate their imperial patrons? Or were their positions vulnerable because the emperor could at any time redirect his favor to a rival? Were the main rivals other Daoists, or people who did not share Daoist goals, perhaps grand councilors or court favorites?

It is not often that historians can give definitive answers to questions of these sorts. Among Huizong's contemporaries, some thought Lin Lingsu had the upper hand and was skilled at manipulating Huizong, others saw Huizong as making his own decisions to pursue Daoist goals for commendable Daoist reasons, such as leading his subjects to Daoist deliverance. Inner-court politics played a role, and Lin Lingsu did lose favor, but we will never know for sure what combination of circumstances were involved—Lin Lingsu's failure to perform miracles, backbiting by other favorites, pleas by Cai Jing not to alienate Buddhists, or court officials bringing up cost issues—and perhaps Huizong himself would not have been able to sort out all of the factors that went into his decisions.

Seers, Dreams, and Visions

Huizong never seems to have doubted that some individuals have exceptional powers. Just as some are extraordinary in their ability to play music or catch a likeness with a brush, others have uncanny abilities to foretell the future or communicate with the dead.

In his second decade on the throne, Huizong was particularly impressed by two seers both surnamed Wang. Wang Laozhi was an ascetic who ate only one meal a day and wore only a single garment winter or summer. Many literati visited him to have him write characters for them, which were interpreted as cryptic prognostications. In the ninth month of 1113, Wang Laozhi was summoned to the palace and given the title Master of the Cavern Tenuity. The following year an even grander title was conferred on him, adding the phrase "Illuminated Perfected One Who Observes the Marvelous." Huizong had Cai Jing house him in the southern garden of the house Huizong had given him. Once, according to Cai Tao, Huizong asked Wang Laozhi about his consort Liu Mingda who had recently died. As mentioned in Chapter 10, Wang Laozhi told him she was the Highest Truth Purple Void Primal Lord. For some time he carried messages between her and Huizong. One of the other consorts, who also missed Consort Liu, asked Wang Laozhi whether the Primal Lord still remembered her, and the next day he brought a letter from her discussing things the two consorts had talked about the previous autumn.[1]

After Wang Laozhi departed in 1114, another clairvoyant, Wang Zixi, took his place, both at Cai Jing's house and at court. A Daoist priest, Wang Zixi claimed to have received the *Secret Book of the Great Cavern* from the immortal Xu Xun.[2] Wang Zixi possessed some unusual abilities, such as the ability to see stars in the daytime. During a drought, when Huizong prayed for rain, he would send a messenger to Wang Zixi to get him to write a prayer for rain on a plain piece of paper. Once when this occurred, Wang Zixi suddenly wrote a small talisman with a note to the left: "Burn this talisman, put the ashes in hot water, and wash with it." The palace messenger was afraid to take it, but Wang Zixi insisted. This talisman water turned out to be an effective cure for the pink-eye then afflicting a favored consort. Through uncanny prescience of this sort, Wang Zixi developed a reputation for being able to foresee events. In 1116 he told Huizong to move the Nine Cauldrons from the temple where they had been installed a decade earlier to the palace, advice that Huizong followed, building a new hall to house them. Cai Jing, however, grew tired of Wang Zixi and complained to Huizong about having to house him, whereupon

Huizong had Wang Zixi sent instead to the Daoist temple he had just built, Highest Clarity Precious Registers Temple.[3]

Besides turning to Daoist masters to gain understanding of Daoist realms, Huizong also took his own dreams seriously. Cai Tao believed that a dream the emperor had early in 1111 while recovering from a long illness marked a turning point in Huizong's commitment to Daoism. In the dream Huizong was not yet emperor and responded to a summons to a Daoist temple. "Two Daoist masters acted as ushers and brought him to an altar where the exalted one told Huizong: 'It is your destiny to promote my religion.' Huizong bowed twice and accepted the command." When he woke up Huizong made a record of the dream and sent it to Cai Jing, still a confidante of Huizong's even though he had been dismissed as grand councilor and was living in Hangzhou.[4]

This dream gave Huizong the confidence to bring Daoism more fully into state ritual. In 1113 Huizong amended the ritual procedures for the winter sacrifice to have one hundred Daoist masters lead the procession to the altar and stand in two files at its base. The priests of Jade Void Hall (the main hall of a new Daoist temple in the palace complex) were among those chosen to participate.[5] Something else made this performance of the rite particularly memorable: on his way to the altar Huizong had a vision of heavenly Perfected Ones descending from heaven. He wrote out in his own hand an edict that referred to this vision.[6] He also wrote a fuller account of his experience: "I turned my head and gazed toward the east when suddenly I saw a palace with terraces, multistoried buildings, and double pavilions, only partly visible." He told Cai You to look east, and he saw it as well. Soon huge people appeared:

> In the middle there seemed to be a phoenix carriage densely surrounded by a thousand or more attendants. A moment later sunlight pierced the space and the people all became fully visible. Some were walking, some hurrying, some were in profile, some faced straight ahead, some turned to look at others, some turned their heads, some resembled Daoists holding strips, some resembled youths with their hair in coils, some wore court dress, some had the hats of Daoist priests or scholar-officials, their dress yellow, green, purple, or red, some light yellow or apricot yellow,

some red-black or pale blue, some seemed embroidered, some painted. There also was a green carriage [drawn by] what did not seem to be horses, but rather dragons or tigers, with several thousand people crowding around it. The clouds gradually parted, making [the finest detail, such as] the seams in the clothes and eyes and eyebrows all distinctly visible. The banners and streamers floated and twisted. The people also were light-footed, turning slightly south from the east. From the southeast [the scene] gradually became indistinct and quickly disappeared.[7]

Huizong added that several of those near him, including soldiers, all said that they saw the same scene. Huizong knew of no close historical precedents, but the vision did remind him of his dream two years earlier. Three months after this vision, Huizong ordered that the day it occurred (the fifth day of the eleventh month) be made a holiday to be celebrated in the same way as the holidays for the emperor's birthday and the birthday of Laozi.[8]

The following summer, on the way back from the sacrifice to earth, Huizong reported another vision, this time after the offerings had been completed:

The feathered guards, the carriage drivers and military men, along with those assisting with the ceremonies, all turned to look up at the sky, where the clouds opened up and a bolt of lightning pierced through. There creatures resembling ghosts, holding spears and lances, with bird-like beaks and animal faces, were lined up in the sky. Those who saw them were terrified, and both the people and the horses stepped back. The tradition is, "At the round mound on the earth, if one plays the music six times, the heavenly spirits descend"; and, "at the square mound in the marshes, if one plays the music eight times, the earth spirits emerge."[9] Because I performed the sacrifice reverently, last winter [heavenly] officials were seen to the left of the road, and this summer ghosts stood in the air. Thus it is not an empty saying that heavenly gods come down and earthly spirits rise up.[10]

Later in this essay, Huizong gave the credit for this spiritual response to the merit of his father and elder brother, Shenzong and Zhezong.

What are we to make of these accounts? Daoist scriptures often provide exuberant descriptions of the courts and retinues of Daoist gods that could have provided inspiration for both the dream and the visions. Moreover, visualizing deities was a central practice within Daoism, one which Huizong may have mastered. Could Huizong have been purposely visualizing Daoist deities, using Daoist techniques? What about all those who confirmed for him that they too saw them? Were they telling him what he wanted to hear, or was something staged that everyone in fact saw? In another book Cai Tao credited the winter sighting of heavenly spirits and summer emergence of earthy spirits to Wang Laozhi, but whether he meant that he summoned spirits on those occasions, put ideas in Huizong's head, or staged a performance is left ambiguous.[11] And it is difficult to exclude entirely the possibility that Huizong wanted so strongly to achieve what the classics said could be achieved at the sacrifices that he staged the scenes himself. Some modern scholars take the fabricated nature of these visions for granted.[12]

Stepped-Up Patronage

Early in his second decade on the throne, Huizong initiated a huge project to compile a new Daoist canon, discussed in Chapter 9. In 1114, while it was underway, Huizong ordered each of the twenty-six circuits to send ten Daoist masters to the capital where they were to receive advanced training in the new liturgies for the Rites of the Golden Register.[13] That must have made the capital an exciting place for Daoist masters, who would have opportunities to learn from each other and promote new teachings.

Huizong also undertook Daoist construction projects. In 1113 he decided that there ought to be a Daoist temple within the Palace City itself. The temple he built, called Jade Clarity Harmonious Yang Temple, had three main halls and six side halls and measured 142 room-units in size altogether. A long list of deities were enshrined in its halls, from the Three Clarities and the Jade Emperor to the Grand Unity, the Four Saints and the Five Sacred Mountains, to Huizong's Personal Destiny god. When the halls were ready in 1114, Cai Jing led the procession to have the statues installed. That year and the next, protocols were issued for ceremonies at this temple for occasions such as Laozi's birthday and Huizong's birthday.[14]

During the years 1113–1116, Huizong had another Daoist temple built in the capital outside the northeast corner of the palace. Called Highest Clarity Precious Registers Temple, it took up more than one hundred *mu* (on the order of six hectares) of land and included several hundred room-units. Its beams and pillars were not painted but left natural. Its central hall, called Incipient Clarity, enshrined the High Perfected Ones. The western hall, called Heaven's Auspicious Signs, housed Huizong's Personal Destiny star god. East of that were lodging for the novices and spaces for ceremonies. Closer to the street were two dispensaries open to the public, one offering prescription drugs, and the other talisman-water. Huizong wrote a commemorative essay on these dispensaries, testifying to his equal commitment to two forms of healing: use of drugs that drew on long-established traditions of pharmacology and the use of Daoist talisman-water. He also went from time to time to inspect how his court painters were doing painting the murals for the temple.[15]

Lin Lingsu's Revelations

Huizong enjoyed talking with eminent Daoist masters. Sometimes he asked for demonstrations of their ritual prowess, sometimes he engaged them in conversations about Daoist ideas, and often he assigned them places to stay in Kaifeng's leading Daoist temples to make it easier to summon them for repeat visits.[16]

The Daoist master who did the most to draw Huizong deeply into new currents in Daoism was Lin Lingsu.[17] Southern Song and Yuan sources on Lin Lingsu range from the very hostile to the hagiographic. At the negative end are two Buddhist histories and an account by Lu You based on what was passed down to him from his grandfather and father.[18] In between are the standard historical sources, which reflect the Confucian tendency to dismiss much of Daoism as silly or superstitious.[19] The Daoist perspective naturally differed. To Daoists, a ruler who could secure blessings for his subjects through Daoist rituals was doing what rulers should do. Not surprisingly, the most positive account of Lin Lingsu, and by far the longest, is in a 1294 set of hagiographies, the *Comprehensive Mirror of Transcendents Who Embodied the Dao through the Ages.*[20] Although the hagiography often differs on basic points with other accounts, it has the advantage of providing a Daoist interpretation of Lin Lingsu's career. At the same time, it makes obvious efforts to "improve" the record by having Lin Lingsu and the gods he summons warn Huizong that he must reform, rid himself of sycophants, and curb his spending. There would seem to be little doubt that these were inserted after the fall of the Northern Song both to show Lin Lingsu's prescience and to absolve Daoists of any guilt for the debacle of the Jurchen invasion.

Lin Lingsu is said to have come originally from Wenzhou (Zhejiang) and to have traveled widely in south and west China where he learned Thunder Rites.[21] According to the hagiography, when Lin Lingsu was in Sichuan, he became a follower of a Daoist priest who gave him a nineteen-chapter treatise called *Jade Book of the Heavenly Altar of the Divine Empyrean*. This book, in partially incomprehensible celestial seal script, taught Lin the secrets of capturing evil spirits, curing illnesses, warding off the plague, and making rain. Once he had received this jade book, his "every act was effective." Not only did he attain profound understanding, but also the ability to summon spirits and demons, write talismans, control thunder and lightning, and cure illnesses. Lin Lingsu reportedly wrote several works, including one on Thunder Rites, only one of which, a long hymn, seems to be extant.[22]

Lin Lingsu may have arrived in the capital as early as 1113, but he did not come to much notice until 1115 or 1116, when the court Daoist, Xu Zhichang, recommended him to Huizong.[23] At Lin Lingsu's first audience, Huizong asked him what techniques he possessed, and he rather immodestly claimed to comprehend the heavens, the world of men, and the subterranean regions. Huizong gave Lin Lingsu a title, a place to stay (at Penetrating Truth Temple), and assigned him to work on the Daoist canon. In the hagiography, another factor in Lin Lingsu's gaining Huizong's respect was his poetic talent. Huizong provided an opening line, "The myriad countries enter through the five-fold Gate of Virtue Revealed." Lin Lingsu's matching line, "The single bureau of the Divine Empyrean controls all the heavens," was judged the best.[24]

At one audience, Lin Lingsu revealed to Huizong his place in the hierarchy of the gods. The Divine Empyrean was the highest of nine celestial regions and far superior to those that governed the other Daoist orders. The eldest son of the Lord on High (Shangdi) was the

Divine Empyrean Jade Clarity Monarch, given the title Great Lord of Long Life, and he had responsibility for governing the south.[25] In plainer language, Huizong was not an ordinary mortal but an incarnation of the son of a high god. When the god descended to the earth to be incarnated as the ruler of China, he delegated much of his responsibility to his younger brother, the Sovereign of Green Florescence. Lin Lingsu revealed that he himself had a lower place in the celestial hierarchy, as did many of Huizong's top officials and even one of his favorite consorts. This revelation is recorded in several secular sources and a surviving text in the Daoist Canon, *Formulary for the Transmission of Scriptures according to the Patriarchs of the Most Exalted Divine Empyrean.*[26]

What did it mean, declaring that the emperor was an incarnation of a high god? It was not like the deification of Augustus during the Roman empire. No one was required or urged to make offerings at temples to Huizong. There was talk of adding statues of the Great Lord of Long Life at Divine Empyrean temples, and offerings may have been put in front of them, but no one refers to making sacrifices or offerings to Huizong. No one, including Huizong, seems to have thought that any special powers came with his connection to a high god.[27]

No Divine Empyrean text can be firmly dated to before the time of Lin Lingsu, and therefore some scholars hypothesize that he was the actual founder of the teaching. Still, like many before him, Lin Lingsu attributed the teaching to his deceased teacher.[28] Divine Empyrean texts from the Southern Song are relatively abundant, and provide a coherent body of doctrines and rituals. This teaching deliberately borrowed ideas and rituals from other strands of Daoism, both Highest Clarity and Numinous Treasure.[29] Liturgy occupied a central place. The salvation of humankind could be achieved by performing a full cycle of recitations to break the circle of life and death and make possible rebirth in the Great Peace heaven. Thunder Rites were absorbed into the teaching; adepts learned to interiorize the cosmic and apotropaic power of thunder and lightning.

Huizong not only accepted Lin Lingsu's revelations, but also showered him with titles and honors. From time to time Huizong called on Lin Lingsu to perform rituals. We are told, for instance, that after Huizong asked him to deal with some odd occurrences in the palace, Lin apotropaically buried a nine-foot-long iron strip, after which no more disturbances occurred. Hong Mai recorded a ceremony Lin Lingsu performed to bring rain after a long dry spell. It involved Lin Lingsu going to Highest Clarity Precious Registers Temple and performing the Pace of Yu while wielding a sword and reciting invocations. Lu You records that Lin Lingsu delighted Huizong when he used talisman-water to cure the blind, lame, and deaf (in Lu You's view he must first have recruited unreliable types to pretend to be disabled).[30]

Besides conducting rituals, Huizong had Lin Lingsu give monthly sermons at Precious Registers Temple, attended by many officials, imperial relatives, and students from government schools. Many in the audience had no prior experience with Daoist practice. One of the Buddhist sources describes Lin Lingsu as cracking jokes during his lectures, leading to unseemly laughter. Sometimes Huizong would attend himself, and take a subordinate position, treating Lin Lingsu as his teacher. Besides preaching on the Daoist classics, Lin Lingsu also described the "descent of the King of Jade Clarity Divine Empyrean to be born on earth." Reportedly, several dozen cranes then appeared in response. At these gatherings Huizong showered largess on the Daoist clergy present, leading skeptics to charge that the urban poor would put on Daoist robes to attend the sermons just for the free meals provided.[31]

On 1117/1/14 Huizong announced his new understanding of Daoism and its schools. He described the five established schools of Daoism, which were centered on the Venerable Celestials, Laozi, Zhuangzi, and Zhang Daoling. "As for the Divine Transformations of Highest Clarity Penetrating Perfection and Attaining Numinosity in Response to the Descent of the Perfected Ones and Saints, it should not be classed as one of these five schools, as it constitutes the highest Dao. Its teacher is the Master of Doctrine and Emperor Lord of the Dao."[32] With this last phrase, Huizong put himself at the head of the Daoist religion. In his first decade on the throne, Huizong had deferred to Liu Hunkang in all matters Daoist; with this edict Huizong not only revealed himself to be an incarnation of a deity, but he also declared that he was in charge of the religion.

Huizong particularly appreciated Lin Lingsu's ability to summon gods and spirits. Two such occasions are recorded in standard historical sources and a few more in Lin Lingsu's hagiography. In the second month of 1117, Lin Lingsu announced that the Sovereign of Green

Florescence had descended to earth. Huizong assembled a thousand or more Daoist priests at Precious Registers Temple to hear Lin Lingsu tell of this great event. An official of the Daoist Registry, Fu Xilie, who had formerly studied with Liu Hunkang, made a record of the event.[33] According to Fu Xilie's account, in the middle of the night fireballs appeared in the air, moving all around, scattering then coming back together again, amid sounds of thunder and music. The room became as bright as day and those who looked up saw images resembling painted icons, then two divinities arrived on clouds. One wore scarlet robes and a jade hat, the other green robes, identifying them as the Sovereign Lord of the Dao and the Sovereign of Green Florescence. At the head of a throng of followers dressed in red was someone who, Fu Xilie said, looked just like Zhang Xubai, one of the Daoist masters whom Huizong regularly invited to court.[34]

Less than three months later, on 1117/4/2, Huizong issued a hand-drafted edict making explicit the meaning of the recent revelation. As the eldest son of the Lord on High, he had received an order to correct vulgar errors: "The Lord on High wants me to serve as men's ruler in order to return the world to the correct doctrine, and I have accepted this charge. I ordered that my younger brother, Sovereign of Green Florescence, take responsibility for my precincts of the Supreme Empyrean. Morning and night I am in trepidation, aware that our teaching is not yet pervasive."[35] Huizong concluded his edict with a note to his ministers that they should not use his Daoist title (Master of the Doctrine, Lord of the Dao) in normal government correspondence; it was strictly to be used in his Daoist petitions to the gods.

Huizong's confidence in Lin Lingsu was strengthened by another visitation of celestial gods in the twelfth month of 1117. The *Song History* records simply that gods came down to Kunning Hall and that a stone was carved to record the event. One stele with this record is still extant. About seven feet tall, the stele is visually striking because of the "dragon-emblem cloud-seal" script used for the poem by Lin Lingsu at the top (see Figure 12.1). In the lower part, Huizong recounts his experiences in his distinctive Slender Gold calligraphy. The gods descended on the night of a full moon amid flashes of light, music, and fragrances. Then a four-line poem written in dragon-emblem cloud-seal script appeared on a table, its ink still wet. It was written by Chu Hui, the divine official whom Lin Lingsu incarnated. This was

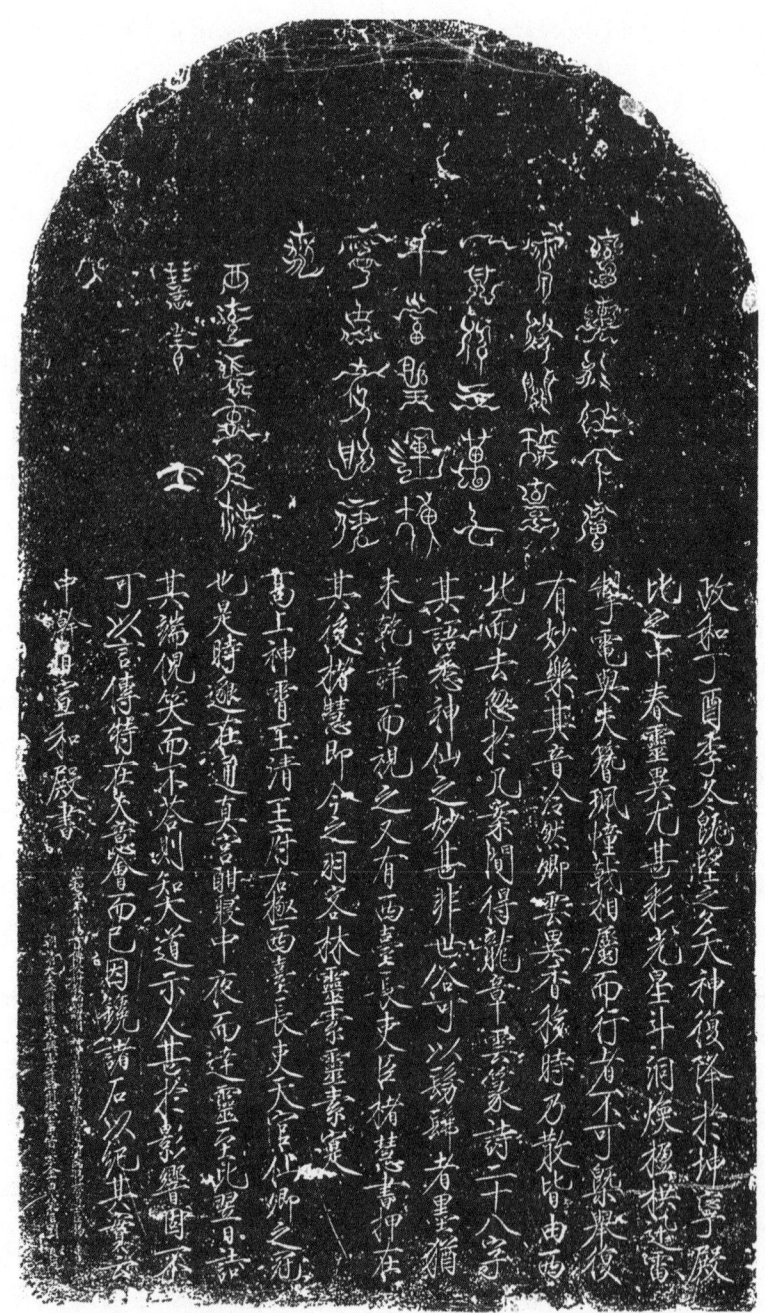

Fig. 12.1. Rubbing of the 1117 stele commemorating the descent of celestial gods. (After Yao Sheng 1965:147)

miraculous because Lin Lingsu was at the time sound asleep in his temple lodgings. When Huizong questioned Lin Lingsu the next day, he merely smiled, which to Huizong was further proof that the Dao cannot be fully expressed in words.[36]

Lin Lingsu's hagiography records several other examples of his ability to summon deities. Once after Lin Lingsu had redecorated a hall at a temple, Huizong asked to see Zhenwu, the martial god of the north. The scene is described this way:

The emperor said, "I would like to see an image of the saintly Zhenwu." Lin Lingsu said, "Please allow me and Xujing [Zhang Jixian] to petition the Celestial Masters."[37] They stayed overnight in the hall, fasting. At precisely noon, black clouds concealed the sun, then huge bolts of lightning illuminated a green tortoise and a large snake blocking the entrance to the hall. The emperor, offering incense and bowing, said, "I wish to see the Perfected Lord descend." With another peal of thunder, the tortoise and snake disappeared. However, an enormous foot was visible blocking the way down from the hall. The emperor offered more incense and bows, saying, "I humbly would like the Mysterious Primal Holy Ancestor, in response to transformations, to descend out of compassion. Just a glimpse would be my great fortune." A moment later [Zhenwu] revealed himself. He was more than ten feet tall, dignified and awesome. His hair was disheveled and his black robe reached the floor. He wore golden armor, large sleeves, a jade belt, and at his waist a sword. His feet were bare. Around his head was a halo. He remained there, flying about, for two hours, which enabled the emperor to sketch his appearance and then summon a court painter to complete the painting. As soon as [the painting] was done, [Zhenwu] disappeared.[38]

The next day Cai Jing suggested comparing the painting just made of Zhenwu to the one that had been made under similar circumstances during Taizong's reign and kept sealed up ever since. The two, we are told, turned out to be identical.[39]

Lin Lingsu's hagiography also recounts a time when he summoned the ghost of one of Huizong's deceased consorts, Liu Mingda.[40] On another occasion, Huizong mentioned that Emperor Wu in the Han had successfully asked for the Queen Mother of the West to come down, and asked if Lin Lingsu could do the same for him. Before long she descended with ranks of her jade maidens.[41]

Lin Lingsu attracted many followers and also some imitators, but definitely did not win over everyone. Some contemporaries saw him as domineering, calling him a Daoist grand councilor. Cai You's biography in the *Song History* reports that he supported Lin Lingsu, "joining with [his] followers to prove the spiritual occurrences." He also sometimes tried to outdo him, for instance reporting to Huizong all sorts of exceptional phenomena, such as pearly stars, rings around the moon, dragons and phoenixes, and celestial documents in cloud-seal script.[42]

What should we think of Lin Lingsu? He was of course not the first religious professional to flatter a ruler or speak of him as divine. Among Buddhists, the concept of "expedient means" provided a rationale for gaining a ruler's support through displays of magic or flattering references to him as a living Buddha. Daoists in the service of Tang emperors undoubtedly often catered to the ruler's predilections in hope of gaining support. And when several clerics gained access to a ruler, rivalry for influence frequently resulted, just as it did among civil officials. Within the Chinese context, revealing to Huizong that he was the incarnation of a high god was going a bit far, but was not outside the bounds of the religious culture of the day. The idea of some sort of divine origin of emperors had been a part of imperial rhetoric from the beginning of the imperial period. Dynastic histories regularly told of unusual signs connected to the birth of the founding emperor, such as his mother dreaming of a dragon during pregnancy.

The historical sources on Zhenzong's discovery of a divine ancestor in the early eleventh century make it seem that Zhenzong and his top officials were in control of the situation, conscious of their political motivations. The sources on Huizong's discovery of his own divine status do not portray him as in charge, just waiting for someone like Lin Lingsu to appear and reveal what he wanted revealed. Rather they make Lin Lingsu the active party, and portray him as having enormous power to sway Huizong. Either scenario has a certain plausibility: Huizong, as a believer, could indeed have fundamentally changed his outlook after encountering Lin Lingsu and hearing of his new revelations. At the same time, Huizong had been searching for exceptional Daoist masters since early in his reign. Thus, it is not easy to exclude the possibility that Huizong had been waiting for a Daoist who would proclaim a grander place for him in Daoist cosmology. Edward Davis suggests that it was Huizong's "inflated ideological needs" that led him to prefer Lin Lingsu over the many other Daoists who made their way to Kaifeng at that time. Cai Tao reported that Huizong had been frustrated that despite promoting Daoism for a decade, not many of his subjects had followed his lead, making Lin Lingsu attractive to him.[43]

State Support for the Divine Empyrean

During the years 1116–1119, Huizong lavishly used imperial resources to fulfill his understanding of his Daoist mission. Once Lin Lingsu convinced Huizong of the Divine Empyrean Heavens, Huizong, full of fervor, wanted to spread the word of what he had learned. Although Huizong was clearly a Daoist from the beginning of his reign, it was not until he met Lin Lingsu that he put much effort into evangelism, into trying to convince others of his beliefs. For three or four years, Huizong made promoting the teachings of the Divine Empyrean a top priority.

How could Huizong bring others to a true understanding of Daoism? To reach scholar-officials, Huizong would stress the common origins of Daoism and Confucianism and depict his goal as a larger synthesis that would accommodate the truths of both the Confucian classics and the Daoist revelations. There was at best a blurry line between the state cult and Daoist ideas and rituals, and Huizong wanted to make that line even blurrier. On 1118/8/20, when Huizong issued an edict establishing Daoist schools, he asserted the common origins and purposes of Daoism and Confucianism: "The Dao is everywhere; it is in the Confucian scholar's administering of the state; it is in the literati's cultivating of themselves. Before there was differentiation, the separate paths all returned to the early sages, and the later sages fit together well. Since the Han, they have split and become different, and the learning of the Yellow Emperor and Laozi is no longer one with the learning of Yao, Shun, the Duke of Zhou, and Confucius." Huizong would try to bring them into harmony. Later that year, when Huizong addressed his subjects to explain the benefits he saw in promoting Divine Empyrean Daoism, he decided to make his words as widely available as possible by having them inscribed on stones erected at the prefectural Divine Empyrean temples (discussed below). In this inscription Huizong starts by assuring his subjects that they will all receive blessings from the Daoist divinities if his reform is successful. He wanted them to know that "the Great Lord of Long Life and the Sovereign of Green Florescence embody the marvels of the Dao, stand above the myriad things, control the Divine Empyrean, and supervise the myriad countries."[44]

Besides mass appeals, Huizong also directed efforts at the officials he saw regularly. He gave Wang Anzhong a work titled *The Wondrous Scripture on the Grand Unity's Preservation of the Embryo and the Jade Infant's Divine Transformation, Spoken by the Perfected King of the Divine Empyrean of the Highest Jade Clarity*. This scripture does not survive but in his thank-you note Wang Anzhong described it as relating the descent of the Great Lord of Long Life to rule the sacred land of China. The scripture, he said, revealed the concealed names of the many heavens, the secret sayings of the myriad sages, and the hidden messages of the Great Vehicle, and had resulted in all sorts of positive omens. In 1119/11 Cai Jing recommended that this scripture be printed.[45]

A large number of Huizong's officials were willing to be persuaded by Huizong, or at least make a show of it. On 1118/10/21 Huizong presided when eight hundred people received the transmission of Divine Empyrean registers at Precious Registers Temple. Cai Tao stated that all of his brothers and nephews received the "Secret Registers of the Divine Empyrean," and that he had been under pressure to do so as well, but had successfully resisted.[46]

Huizong did not restrict himself to words in his efforts to convey to his subjects the power and beauty of the Divine Empyrean; he also established temples. The Daoist temple that Huizong had built in the Palace City in 1113, originally named Jade Clarity Harmonious Yang Temple, was renamed Jade Clarity Divine Empyrean Temple. At the huge Precious Registers Temple, finished in 1116/2, Huizong established a Divine Empyrean Precious Registers ordination platform. There was also a Divine Empyrean Hall at this temple with a fine set of processional paraphernalia and images of the main deities. A new set of the Nine Cauldrons, called the Nine Divine Empyrean Cauldrons, were cast and placed in this temple in 1117.[47]

Soon Huizong wanted Divine Empyrean temples everywhere in the country. On 1117/2/13 he ordered the renaming of all of the Heavenly Calm Longevity Daoist temples dedicated to the celebration of his birthday and Personal Destiny days, giving them the new name Divine Empyrean Jade Clarity Longevity temples. Small prefectures with no Heavenly Calm Daoist temples could convert other Daoist temples to Divine Empyrean temples, and if they had no Daoist temples at all, converting a Buddhist temple was an acceptable alternative. Huizong justified converting Buddhist temples on the grounds that he did not want to impose labor burdens on the common people by requiring them to build new temples. Whatever the origin of a temple, images of the Great Lord of Long Life and his brother the Sovereign of Green Florescence were to be installed in it.[48]

In many cases, rather than convert a Daoist temple, the local officials seized a Buddhist temple instead.[49] A Buddhist account of these actions claims that the Buddhist temples selected for conversion were the larger ones. Undoubtedly some local officials, trying to show their zeal, converted Buddhist temples unnecessarily. In an edict of 1117, Huizong denied rumors that he was in the process of abolishing Buddhism, saying that no more than one Buddhist temple should be converted in a prefecture and that anyone who passed the slander that he was persecuting Buddhism would be heavily fined.[50]

All through 1118 Huizong kept track of the progress being made on the Divine Empyrean temples. On 1118/12/20 he called for adding images of Zhuangzi and Liezi to the images in the temples. The temples were first granted the privilege of ordaining one novice each year and granting one priest purple robes, then given exclusive authority to ordain Daoist priests. In 1119/6 Huizong gave the Divine Empyrean temples responsibility for charity clinics, in a sense expanding the charitable ventures begun early in his reign. The edict asserts: "Talismans, registers, incantations, and prayers are indeed efficacious for curing illness and vanquishing virulent plagues. Up until now, residents of the capital using these means have surely benefited from them. I have always desired to extend access to them to the entire realm as a way to aid the people." Huizong then ordered that prefectural governments create small Humane Aid Pavilions in a corner of the local Divine Empyrean temple, where three to five practitioners should dispense talisman-water from dawn until noon. "They must be concentrated and purified to remove evil and dispel plagues."[51]

Some prefects dragged their feet on establishing Divine Empyrean temples. At least, that seems the inference to be made from Huizong's edict of 1118/2/20, in which he complained that many officials had not taken the task seriously, that they were satisfied with sham temples, and also that when Daoist priests objected, they treated them harshly. He ordered that the circuit intendants investigate the temples under their jurisdiction.[52]

In a few cases descriptions of these temples survive. Wang Zao described the conversion of a two-century-old Buddhist temple in Jin-shan (Zhejiang province). After the year-long makeover, it had three halls, two platforms, a library, and residential quarters. Huizong wrote out the title plaques for ten of its buildings. Lu You noted that Divine Empyrean temples typically had twenty-two immortals depicted on their eastern and western walls, plus images of the main deities at their altars. In addition, each temple received a set of twenty-four items of processional paraphernalia, such as halberds, brocade canopies, jew-eled shades, beaded streamers, and huge fans with images of cranes. These were displayed on racks along the walls of the hall.[53] The local history of Guiji, written in 1201, begins its description of the Divine Empyrean temple there by noting that it had a red-lacquered pavilion to protect the stele inscribed with Huizong's edict. The grounds of the large temple complex were maintained by imperial soldiers. The main hall had statues of the two main deities, the Great Lord of Long Life and the Sovereign of Green Florescence, each with two attendant Perfected Ones. There were paintings of immortals on its walls and a full set of twenty-four items of processional paraphernalia. Other buildings included a pavilion for the distribution of talisman-water, a lecture hall called the Hall for the Daoist Era, and a scripture hall called the Room of the Cloud-Emblem Treasures. On five specified festivals, including Huizong's birthday, the holidays declared to cel-ebrate Huizong's visions at the summer and winter sacrifices of 1113–1114, as well as the day the Sovereign of Green Florescence descended to earth, up to 1,200 people would participate in the ceremonies, using imperial incense and green and red prayer strips sent from the capital.[54]

A Divine Empyrean ritual text records protocols for the services on Huizong's birthday and the holiday celebrating the descent of the Sov-ereign of Green Florescence.[55] The Daoist priest recites the incantation one thousand times, swallows twenty-one talismans, burns incense to the Three Clarities, the Ten Exalted Perfected Ones, the Lord on High, the Master of Religion and Lord of the Dao [the last referring to Huizong], and bows nine times. He next faces south to bow nine times to several deities including the Great Lord of Long Life, then facing east bows nine times to the Sovereign of Green Florescence and other deities, and so on. According to the *Song History*'s treatise on ritual, on these holidays officials were given five days off, the prefectural governments held offering ceremonies (*jiao*), and the populace held parties, which in the capital included lighting lanterns.[56]

While establishing these temples, Huizong also committed himself to an ambitious plan to establish Daoist schools and examinations. The schools were not aimed narrowly at training experts in Divine Empyrean teachings or Thunder Rites, but rather at producing Daoist masters with broad educations. Huizong's first step was to establish a Daoist school in the capital, the first since Tang times. In 1118 he went further and had Daoist schools incorporated into the local government school system. He assigned the task of drafting rules for the Daoist schools to Cai You. Prefectural schools were told to appoint a Daoist professor to teach the Daoist curriculum. Students could pass up from the local Daoist schools to the Imperial Academy and its Three Halls system. At some schools, critics charged, a significant number of students switched to the Daoist curriculum, presumably because it offered favorable opportunities for advancement.[57]

The texts to be studied in the Daoist schools were announced in late 1118. The major classics were the *Inner Classic of the Yellow Emperor* and the *Laozi*; the minor ones were *Zhuangzi* and *Liezi*. It is undoubtedly significant that one of the major classics was concerned above all with health and medical treatment, since Daoist masters at local temples were also responsible for the clinics located there. Two professors (*boshi*) were appointed to teach each of these four classics, at both the Imperial Academy and the Biyong Academy. They also taught Huizong's treatise on medical theory, the *Classic of Sagely Benefaction*. Students majoring in Daoist texts also had to study two Confucian classics, the *Book of Changes* and the *Mencius*.[58]

Creating Daoist schools and a Daoist curriculum is reminiscent of Huizong's efforts to enhance the status of court painters and calligraphers by reform of their training. Until Huizong's time, Daoist priests serving in the government were treated in much the way technical specialists were treated. That is, their overall rank was low and they were eligible for only a narrow track of specialized jobs. Huizong, in 1118, decreed that Daoist officials should be treated as comparable to ·civil officials and opened many new opportunities for them. A new hierarchy of ranks and duty assignments followed.[59]

Work on the Daoist canon had not been completed when Huizong learned of the Divine Empyrean. This canon included texts from all the Daoist traditions and was not in any narrow sense a vehicle for promoting Divine Empyrean traditions. As Michel Strickmann points out, however, the text placed first in the canon is clearly connected to Lin Lingsu's teachings. This sixty-one-chapter expansion of the *Book of Salvation* devotes a chapter to the Great Lord of Long Life, who dwells in the empyrean and is attended by a retinue of Perfected Ones.[60]

As the work on the canon was completed, Lin Lingsu and other Daoist experts in the capital were given two further projects to work on, a *History of the Dao* and an *Institutes of the Dao*, the first covering the period before the Song, the latter the Song period. The history was modeled on the dynastic histories, and had chronological chapters, treatises, and biographies. The twelve treatises dealt with such subjects as garments, talismans and registers, regulations, and alchemy. Its annals started with the Three Clarities and covered rulers who had attained the Dao. Liu Dong, Zhang Pu, Cai You, and Lin Lingsu were among those involved in compiling the *History of the Dao*, which was finished in 1121.[61] Neither of these books survived into the Southern Song, and quite possibly neither was ever printed.

Besides commissioning Daoist scholars to write and edit books, Huizong did some writing himself—or at least claimed he did. The hymns he wrote are discussed in Chapter 5. Huizong also authored a subcommentary to the commentary written by Emperor Zhenzong on the *Book of Salvation*. A few texts in the surviving (Ming dynasty) Daoist canon have prefaces purportedly written by Huizong. One of the most interesting is for *Talismans and Diagrams of the Book of Salvation*. In Judith Boltz's words, "Designed to introduce the rudiments of the Shenxiao [Divine Empyrean] reenactment of the Lingbao [Numinous Treasure] revelation, the treatise supplies the essential diagrams, talismanic inscriptions, sacred recitations, and lengthy registers of the celestial bureaucracy."[62] Strickmann sees it as a work of the period, perhaps by Wang Wenqing. In his words, "It was in any case intended as an interpretation of the dramatic events of Huizong's reign, when the celestial lord was present in person among men revealing his long-hidden scripture and diffusing the perfect rule of the Dao." The talismans have obvious visual interest, especially to someone as devoted to calligraphy as Huizong (see Figure 12.2).[63]

The most substantial Daoist texts by Huizong still extant are his commentaries to early Daoist philosophical texts: the *Laozi*, *Liezi*, and *Ascension to the West*.[64] (Huizong also wrote a commentary for the *Zhuangzi* that does not survive.) *Ascension to the West*, written in the fourth or fifth century, claims to be the teachings that Laozi conferred on the keeper of the pass when he departed China going west. In Huizong's preface to his commentary on it, he explained his interest:

Fig. 12.2. "Talisman for Summoning the Nine Transformations of Great Obscurity," from *Talismans and Diagrams of the Book of Salvation*. (LBFT; DZ 3:82C)

The central point of the scripture is the attainment of the One. The ascent into heaven, on the other hand, appears quite irrelevant. This is because the major intention of the text is to urge later generations of the world to reach the realm of the marvelous ground, of free and easy wandering, of spontaneous realization. How good the text is at leading to salvation can be clearly seen from this!

At myriad occasions of leisure I myself have traversed the Great Clarity in spirit and roamed around the pointers to the Dao and the virtue. Every time I noted down their meanings, collating and ordering my notes in the two scrolls below. Once written down they cannot but be transmitted further. Intention combating with will—thus theories are produced.[65]

In 1118/8/12 Huizong issued a hand-drafted edict that called for his commentary on the *Laozi* to be carved onto stone at the capital Divine Empyrean temple. Since few people have been able to understand Laozi's subtle and far-reaching ideas, writes Huizong, "When I have had leisure from the myriad tasks, I have read his book, marveled at the reasoning, and made annotations."[66] Subcommentaries were written by contemporaries to Huizong's commentaries on the *Liezi* and *Laozi*. A prominent Daoist official at Huizong's court, Fan Zhixu, wrote a subcommentary for his work on the *Liezi*.[67] Two were done for his commentary on the *Laozi*, one by a low-ranking official, the other a student at the Imperial Academy, suggesting that it may have been taught at government schools.

Huizong was not the first emperor to write a commentary on the *Laozi*: Emperor Wu of the Liang and Emperor Xuanzong in the Tang both preceded him.[68] Moreover, many eleventh-century Song scholars generally thought of as Confucians also had written commentaries on the *Laozi*, including Sima Guang, Su Che, Wang Anshi, and Lu Dian.[69] Huizong's commentary on the *Laozi* cites a range of authorities, including Confucius and Mencius, but draws most heavily on the *Zhuangzi* and the *Book of Changes*. It is not in any obvious way connected narrowly to Divine Empyrean teachings. Liu Ts'un-yan, who studied the commentary in depth, finds in it evidence that Huizong looked on the *Laozi* as a guidebook for rulers on how to govern.[70] Other scholars have identified Buddhist influence in it.[71] There are also passages in which Huizong seems to reveal something of his experience at court.

His commentary to the line in chapter 20, "Between yea and nay, how much difference is there?" reads as follows: "There may be little distinction between 'yea' and 'nay,' and little difference between 'good' and 'evil,' for such discriminations are found only in the mind of a selfish, bigoted person, while in the vista of a broad-minded gentleman they merge into one. However, a sage in looking after worldly affairs discusses and argues with [his] ministers at court with such vehemence that, in stamping out the evil and praising the good, he spares no effort to assure that what is right is being done. [For Laozi said] 'What others fear, one must also fear."[72]

With Lin Lingsu's urging, Huizong began to place curbs on Buddhism. The Daoist Registry reported in 1118/4 that it had reviewed over six thousand volumes of Buddhist texts for slander of Daoists or Confucians and found nine that deserved to be destroyed, keeping only one copy for evidence. Lin Lingsu wrote a treatise detailing the slanders in the condemned works, which was printed and circulated. Anti-Buddhist measures went a step further in the first month of 1119 when Huizong issued a hand-drafted edict forbidding Buddhist temples and monasteries to increase their land or buildings. This edict also aimed to erase the foreignness of Buddhism through a process of renaming and disguising. Buddhist monks were renamed "scholars of virtue" (*deshi*, to correspond to Daoist priests who were called *daoshi*). They were to wear Daoist-style robes, use their original surnames, and salute with raised fists, not joined palms—in other words, they were to make themselves visually indistinguishable from Daoist clergy. Buddhas, bodhisattvas, and arhats were given new names—Shakyamuni was to be called the Golden Immortal of Great Enlightenment and Mañjuśrī the Calm Great Master of Peaceful Graciousness. Temples could retain the old statues of these renamed deities, but had to put the robes and caps of Daoist divinities over them. The anti-Buddhist tenor of these measures was evident to everyone, and in response to charges that this was persecution of Buddhism, Huizong issued an edict explicitly stating that Buddhist rituals and teachings should not be interfered with. A Buddhist history claims that officials who objected to these measures were cruelly punished and monks who objected were expelled from their temples.[73]

Huizong was not Lin Lingsu's only supporter. Lu You reported that "shameless scholar-officials day after day gathered at his door." Lin Lingsu's hagiography reports that he had good relations with Zhang

Jixian, the patriarch of Celestial Masters tradition, and describes him collaborating at times with Liu Dong and Wang Wenqing.[74] Still, it is clear that not everyone was enthralled with the Divine Empyrean or swayed by Lin Lingsu's sermons. Even if eight hundred of Huizong's top officials were willing to accept Divine Empyrean registers in 1118, others resisted. Liu Dong spoke up against Lin Lingsu's proposal to establish a new Divine Empyrean musical scale and also his proposal to build an altar 150 feet tall, nearly twice as tall as the Suburban Altar used for sacrifices to heaven.[75]

Unhappiness with the 1119 policies to erase the foreignness of Buddhism was especially pervasive. According to a Buddhist source, Cai Jing tried several times to convince Huizong that he was going too far. He argued, for instance, that "The Buddhist images in the realm were not all made for the monks. Sons make them for their fathers, subjects for their rulers, as a way to pray for blessings and express their gratitude." Interfering with this practice could be politically destabilizing, he argued.[76] One of the top officials in the Central Buddhist Registry, himself a monk, submitted a memorial comparing Huizong's action to earlier cases of anti-Buddhist measures. He pointed out that those who had taken such measures regularly came to bad ends and their policies had always been reversed by their successors. He also brought up the fact that the Song founders, Taizu and Taizong, had supported a large Buddhist translation project. He did not mince words: "Doesn't Your Majesty remember that [Emperor] Taiwu [of the Northern Wei] was killed at the hand of a eunuch, or that [Emperor] Wu of [Northern] Zhou was shackled in prison, or that [Emperor] Wu of the Tang suffered the retribution of losing the throne through an early death? These events are all verifiable. How can Your Majesty err by following these depraved rulers and reversing the precedents of your predecessors [on the Song throne]?" This memorial, the Buddhist source tells us, angered Huizong so much that he banished the author.[77]

Supporters of Buddhism circulated texts ridiculing the Divine Empyrean, and even Huizong's former grand councilor Zhang Shangying wrote a text defending Buddhism. Complaints were made about presumptuous Daoists and overzealous officials who forced people to vacate their homes on short notice so that they could build Divine Empyrean temples there. Many Daoists, too, resented Lin Lingsu's political power. Lin Lingsu was ruthless in his efforts to discredit other Daoists in whom Huizong showed interest, such as Wang Zixi and Wang Cai. Cai Tao, in his account of Li Derou, says the latter was sent away from the capital because he had made fun of the Divine Empyrean affair.[78]

Patience with Lin Lingsu also grew thin among some of those close to Huizong. Tong Guan reportedly could not stand him. The heir apparent, Prince Huan, then in his late teens, was the most direct, calling him a fraud who used tricks like paper cranes to create the visions with which he dazzled Huizong. In one account the heir apparent arranged a contest between Lin Lingsu, twelve foreign Buddhist monks, and two monks from the Buddhist establishment at Mount Wutai, hoping to show Lin's shallowness.[79]

Crucial to Huizong's support of Lin Lingsu was the latter's effective performance of Thunder Rites. But in time he proved fallible. One source reports that Lin Lingsu failed to end a drought until he got help from Wang Wenqing. Then in 1119, some sources report, he failed to curb a major flood that was threatening Kaifeng. Lin Lingsu reportedly had his disciples perform a Pacing the Void ceremony on the city walls, but to no effect. According to a Buddhist account, Lin Lingsu unsuccessfully tried for several days to curb the flood and had to run away to escape an infuriated crowd.[80]

In the eleventh month of 1119 Lin Lingsu was packed off to his hometown, Wenzhou. A Buddhist source says he was executed on the way there, but most others record that he died the following year after arriving home. In 1120/1 the Daoist schools were abolished, having been established less than two years. In 1120/9 Buddhist temples, deities, and clergy got their original names back. In 1121 Buddhist temples that had been converted to Divine Empyrean temples were given permission to convert back.[81]

Even if Huizong lost confidence in Lin Lingsu, he did not waver in his belief in Daoism and the Divine Empyrean. Huizong turned to other proponents of the teaching, most notably Wang Wenqing, another Divine Empyrean Daoist priest. Ceremonies to confer Divine Empyrean registers continued. In 1121/10 at a ceremony at Precious Registers Temple, Huizong personally conferred on Wang Fu two sets of registers. The Divine Empyrean temple network was also left in place, even if some temples were changed back to Buddhist temples. Huizong sent two Daoist officials with his envoy to Koryŏ in 1123 or 1124 who performed Divine Empyrean ceremonies on the voyage.[82]

Huizong's preoccupation with Divine Empryean Daoism did not turn him against other Daoist teachings. In 1118 he had the Dragon Virtue Palace / Temple renovated as the Northern Grand Unity Temple, to add to the set that included the Eastern, Western, and Central Grand Unity Temples, built in earlier years by Taizong, Renzong, and Shenzong. The chief Daoist priest there, Zhang Xubai, had been a favorite of Huizong's for years and had always stayed clear of politics. Several halls were added specifically for him. The temple had four large halls and more than ten small ones, all beautifully decorated. In 1119 when Cai Jing was ill, Huizong held a Daoist service at the temple. According to Cai Jing's thank-you note, Huizong not only composed the prayers himself, but also burned the prayers with his own hands.[83]

   SHOULD WE GIVE Huizong's patronage of Divine Empyrean Daoism a political reading? And if so, of what sort? One could speculate that Huizong was attracted to the political potential of Daoist cosmology and wanted to make use of it to strengthen the powers of the throne. How could one do more to elevate the ruler than have Daoist masters declare him an incarnation of a high god? To support such an interpretation, one could point to the autocratic tendencies of the Song throne noted by an earlier generation of Song historians. One could also bring up comparative examples, such as the Roman emperors who were treated as gods.

A somewhat different political interpretation would be phrased in terms of Huizong's perception of a need to renew the legitimacy of the throne. Did Huizong perceive a loss of support for the Zhao family as rulers? Was there noticeable unrest in the country by 1116 when he began to promote Lin Lingsu's teachings? Did he think it would help to show that the high gods were on the dynasty's side? Although today we know that Huizong's court would be brought down a decade later, I see no sign that anyone was able to foresee that in 1116 or 1118.

Yet another sort of political reading would focus on inner-court politics. Perhaps tactical reasons were behind Huizong's support of the Divine Empyrean. Did Huizong bring Lin Lingsu to court to give himself room to maneuver, to act independently of both precedent and entrenched advisors like Cai Jing?

If given any of these political readings, Huizong's Daoist measures would have to be judged failures. That is, the political benefits did not outweigh the political costs, since financial outlays were substantial and Divine Empyrean teachings hardly helped unite the educated class or even those serving in office. Huizong's Daoist initiatives in this later phase ran up expenses far beyond his many earlier projects. A hierarchy of Daoist offices was created and those appointed to them given salaries, adding substantially to the numbers of officials on state payrolls. Processional equipment was given to hundreds of prefectural Divine Empyrean temples across the country. After learning of his place in the celestial hierarchy, Huizong seems to have lost a sense of restraint. Thinking of Daoist heavens, realms filled with abundance of all sorts, seems to have chased out any thought of limited resources.

On the whole, I find a religious reading of Huizong's actions more persuasive than these political ones. Such a reading of Huizong's Daoist measures would start with the assumption that Huizong was motivated above all by religious convictions. As an ardent Daoist, Huizong was open to new Daoist dispensations and tried to act on Daoist principles, which places him among the many millions of his contemporaries who found Daoist rituals and ideas compelling. As Shin-yi Chao puts it, "Utilizing political power to realize a Daoist utopia was part of Daoist tradition."[84] From a Daoist point of view, Huizong's goals were the right ones, even if sometimes he did not pursue them in the most effective ways.

What exactly were Huizong's religious goals? He lays them out in many of his edicts, so we do not need to speculate in this regard. The first, and most explicit, goal is to spread knowledge of the Dao to the benefit of all who as a result become practicing Daoists. Huizong repeatedly states the benefits his people will attain once they fully recognize Daoist truths. We can probably assume that many of the measures to give financial support to Daoist temples and clergy were seen as aiding in the larger goal of bringing more people to Daoism. Linked to this is an expansion of Daoism to encompass much that had been thought of as Confucian or Buddhist. Huizong argues that Confucianism and Daoism share the same root in the religion of ancient China and should be united again. His brief effort to relabel Buddhism as a part of Daoism can be conceived in this way as well. His simultaneous construction of the Bright Hall fits this side of Huizong's agenda. In a sense, Huizong wanted a Three-in-One religion, but with Daoism clearly in the dominant position.

A second religious goal was to align the state and the religion to make both stronger. There was nothing in the Daoist tradition that denigrated entanglement with the government; rather, close ties between the religion and the government were seen as an ideal way to advance the religion. In the plan Lin Lingsu and Huizong worked out, church and state shared the same head—Huizong himself. But the interlacing of church and state was pursued in other ways as well. The imperial declaration of the truth of the Divine Empyrean realm was to be introduced down to the prefectural level with the conversion of local Daoist temples associated with Huizong's birthday (or in their absence, other temples) to Divine Empyrean temples. Government-run Daoist schools and Daoist examinations also are measures that unite church and state. Many of the measures that can be considered supportive of Daoism can also be seen to enhance state control of Daoism as well. A good example here would be the collection of Daoist texts and the compilation and printing of a new Daoist canon. The power to select texts and impose a hierarchy on them is a very real power. The canon project was widely welcomed by Daoist clerics, who seem to have been satisfied with its broad inclusivity, but the potential to suppress some teachings and promote others was real. Seeing Huizong as moved by his religious experiences does not mean that we have to deny that his actions could have political consequences.

What impact did Huizong's Daoist initiatives have on the history of Daoism? Historians of Daoism are divided on this question. Imperial patronage sometimes fosters popular practice, but not always.[85] Twenty years ago Strickmann presented a paper calling the early twelfth century a period of renaissance for Daoism. He saw Huizong's reign as the "beginning of another great wave of Daoist revelation, comparable in some sense to the fourth-century movements" and argued that "in the same way that fourth-century scriptures provided the substance of Daoist practice throughout China's Middle Ages, the re-establishment and revivification of the religion during Huizong's reign is responsible for much in the shape and complexion of Daoism in modern times." One reason Strickmann placed so much importance on Huizong's patronage is the importance he gave to the textual traditions of Daoism, and Huizong's expansion of the Daoist canon and printing of it had an undeniable impact on the survival of Daoist texts. Other contemporary scholars of Daoism draw attention to the impact of Divine Empy-

rean ritual practices. According to Kristopher Schipper and Franciscus Verellen, Divine Empyrean rituals for the salvation of the souls of
the dead became part of standard Daoist practice, and through Divine
Empyrean texts "a vast number of demon-quelling spirits" were integrated into the Daoist canon. Boltz referred to its "immense impact on
the liturgical tradition of Daoism as we know it today," in part by
stimulating the development of rival schools of practice. Davis draws
attention to Huizong's efforts to combine classical and Daoist ritual,
concluding that the major effect of Huizong's religious policy was
"to create the atmosphere in which classical and Daoist ritual could be
performed enthusiastically, and without a sense of contradiction, by
members of the bureaucratic elite."[86]

On the other hand, Divine Empyrean Daoism by no means became
the dominant strand of Daoist teachings in subsequent centuries. The
historian of Daoism Ren Jiyu sees a reaction against Huizong's emphasis
on ritual-oriented Daoism, which he suspects helped other strands like
the more ethically oriented Complete Truth Daoism gain strength in
the mid-twelfth century. Tang Daijian goes further. He sees the Northern Song government's patronage of Daoism as corrupting the religion. In his view, giving temples land and tax exemptions created a
religious elite that relied on imperial favor and lived on a grand scale,
in time evoking a reaction.[87]

In almost exactly the same period that Lin Lingsu encouraged
Huizong to think about the Daoist salvation of all his subjects, other
officials, notably Tong Guan and Wang Fu, got his attention with talk
of military glory. Huizong had shown occasional interest in military
policy earlier in his reign, but the opportunities that presented themselves after 1115 seemed heaven sent and not to be passed up.

13

Allying with Jin

China's old territory has long been in the hands of the
barbarians. Today heaven gives signs that Your Majesty will
achieve great things. If we do not take advantage of the
opportunity, I fear we will regret it.

*—Wang Fu's argument in favor of making an alliance
with Jin in 1119*

$\mathcal{H}$UIZONG'S CONFIDENCE contributed to the worst decision he ever made—to ally with the Jurchen Jin dynasty against Song's
immediate northern neighbor, the Kitan state of Liao. For more than
a century, peace on the northern border had been maintained through
yearly payments from Song to Liao that many on the Song side viewed
as humiliating and Liao considered tribute. Allying with Jin meant
repudiating those agreements. The goal was to recover the so-called
Sixteen Prefectures. These prefectures in northern Shanxi and Hebei
had substantial Chinese populations and had been part of the Tang
empire but were absorbed into Liao in 938, before the founding of the
Song dynasty. The rallying cry of the war party since the early decades of the dynasty had been the need to recover the Sixteen Prefectures of Yan and Yun, Yan referring to the area around Yanjing (today's
Beijing) and Yun the area around Datong.

From the beginning of the Song, the northern border had been a
matter of vital interest. Debates at court about how to respond to a
military threat, provocation, or opportunity were frequently conten-
tious, given the enormous cost of war, the ignominy of defeat, and the
differing interests, knowledge, and ambitions of the key players, including the emperor, grand councilors, military strategists, and generals. The Song government devoted more than half its fiscal resources
to maintaining huge armies of six hundred thousand to a million professional soldiers. The best-trained and best-supplied armies were the

imperial armies stationed near the capital and in strategic areas. Armies in the field were supervised by civil officials appointed as military commissioners or by trusted eunuchs appointed as army supervisors. Supply was handled by fiscal intendants who reported to the central government, not the field commanders. Intelligence was largely the responsibility of the eunuch-dominated Capital Security Office, which maintained agents in the capital, the provinces, and the armies.[1]

Huizong had several sources of information about military affairs and border issues. The top two officials at the Bureau of Military Affairs, generally civil officials with no battlefield experience, were members of the Council of State and met regularly with Huizong. The emperor also met envoys from Song's neighbors at least twice a year.[2] He undoubtedly learned more from his own envoys on their return from trips. For someone like Huizong, whose travels outside the capital were limited to formal ritual duties and never took him very far, his envoys' reports on what they saw on their months-long journeys across the borders would have made engrossing reading.[3]

Balance of Power in the North

It was not merely pride that made the Song want to reclaim the Sixteen Prefectures from Liao. Defending the north China plain was much more difficult when Song did not hold the strategic passes and other defense bastions along the line of the Great Wall. Song tried digging trenches and planting trees along the new border to make it more difficult for horsemen to enter Song territory, but these measures did not eliminate Liao's geographic advantage.[4] Moreover, the loss of this territory exacerbated Song shortages of horses, since it was among the best horse-raising regions. When coupled with the loss of northwest territory to the Xi Xia, Song had enormous difficulties supplying its cavalry with adequate mounts. The Northern Song was able to maintain herds only a fraction as large as the Tang had, and despite large purchases of horses from Tibetan traders in the Qingtang region, in 1061 only a fifth of the sixty thousand Song cavalrymen could be provided with mounts. The Song would never be able to recover the Sixteen Prefectures without finding a better way to acquire horses.[5]

The rulers of the Liao were Kitans, a nomadic, pastoral people originally from the eastern slopes of the Khingan Mountains that separate Mongolia and Manchuria. They had been in regular contact with the Tang and with other sedentary societies, such as the Bohai in southern Manchuria and beyond it Korea. The early Liao rulers took advantage of the chaotic situation in north China after the collapse of the Tang to expand into territories settled largely by Chinese. In 947 the Kitan ruler led his army all the way to Kaifeng, took up residence in the imperial palace, and announced the name Liao for his dynasty. After three months, when the temperatures began to get too warm for him, he departed, taking as much treasure—human and material—as he could transport. The baggage train stretched for miles as he conveyed thousands of families of artisans, hundreds of families of officials, and the contents of the imperial library and storehouses.[6] Even after Liao forces withdrew, they still dominated the area and treated the warlord left in Kaifeng as a puppet.

The Song founders made concerted efforts to push the Kitans out of north China. In 979 Taizong attacked Yanjing, the Liao's Southern Capital, but Liao cavalry forces bested the Song army. Facing the imminent defeat of his forces, Taizong fled the battlefield without even informing his generals. In the rout, the Kitans captured huge quantities of Song weapons and armor. In 986 Taizong made a second try. He sent three large armies to attack simultaneously on three different fronts. Liao defeated each army, and Song had little choice but to resume diplomatic relations.[7]

In 1004 the Liao launched a major campaign into China, bypassing well-defended cities in order to get to Kaifeng quickly. The third Song emperor, Zhenzong, gave in to the demand of his grand councilor and personally led the imperial armies to repel the Kitan. The two armies met at Shanyuan, about a hundred fifty kilometers northeast of Kaifeng. Zhenzong put up a show of resistance, then opened negotiations to try to forestall military action. Unwilling to give in to Kitan demands for territory or a princess to marry the Liao heir, the Chinese negotiators came up with the idea of offering the Kitans money to go away. The payment offered—two hundred thousand bolts of silk and one hundred thousand ounces of silver—seemed immense to the Kitans, especially after they understood it was to be annual. In the final version of the treaty, it was also agreed that neither side would add to their fortifications along the common border, and that the two emperors would address the other as "emperor," adding kinship terms based on their respective ages and generations ("elder brother," "uncle," and so on). Although there were other confrontations between Song and Liao over the course of the next century, the basic framework created by the Treaty of Shanyuan set the tone for their relationship.[8]

The Song's northwest border took a little longer to get settled. The Tanguts (who spoke a language related to Tibetan) had established themselves in large parts of northwestern Shaanxi and Gansu, the crossroads of trade between China and Central Asia (see Map 2). In 1038 the Tangut ruler took the title Emperor for himself, an affront to Song. Renzong's court officials expressed a wide range of opinions on the best course for Song to follow, depending not merely on how hawkish they were, but also their best guesses of what was going on in the Xi Xia and Liao courts.[9] Three-way negotiations ended with the Song increasing its subsidy to the Liao and providing one to the Xi Xia as well. Each year Xi Xia was to get 130,000 bolts of silk, 50,000 ounces of silver, and 20,000 catties of tea. However, the Song did not use the title Emperor for their rulers, referring to them simply as the ruler of Xi Xia. From this time on there was a three-way balance of power in the north that proved relatively stable.

At the Song court, to counter arguments for aggressive policies, peace advocates would bring up the cost of war. Although the pro-war irredentists saw these agreements as humiliating, a stain on national honor, the pro-peace accommodationists could justly point out that they were much less costly than war. During the reigns of the first three emperors, the size of the Song armed forces was rapidly expanded, from about 370,000 at the end of Taizu's reign, to 650,000 at the end of Taizong's, to almost a million by the end of Zhenzong's. By that time the military was consuming three-quarters of the tax revenues. Annual spending on defense in Hebei alone was about forty times the amount of the subsidy to the Liao.[10] By contrast, even counting the expenses of the exchange of embassies, the cost of maintaining peaceful relations with the Liao would not have consumed more than 2 or 3 percent of the state's annual revenues.[11]

From our modern perspective, it is apparent that the payments to the Liao and Xi Xia did not damage the overall Chinese economy. Even after the tribute to Liao was raised to 500,000 units of silver and silk in 1042, it did not result in an increase in Liao's bullion holdings since Song exports to Liao normally exceeded their imports by a large margin, which meant that the silver sent to Liao found its way back to China as payment for Chinese goods. Some today even argue that Song's many successes owe much to the pragmatic decision to buy peace.[12] At the time, however, it seemed only common sense that payments to Liao and Xi Xia helped them and harmed Song.

Shenzong came to the throne in 1067 determined to solve the fiscal and military problems that had kept his predecessors from pushing back the Kitans and Tanguts. He rejected Sima Guang's argument that the Chinese by nature and livelihood would never be a match for the war-loving barbarians, but did see the wisdom of Wang Anshi's prudent contention that state reserves had to be built up before beginning military action. Shenzong and Wang Anshi made progress on the crucial issue of good horses. From 1074 on, the Tea-Horse Agency each year acquired ten thousand horses from Tibet in exchange for tea grown in nearby Sichuan. By 1081 Shenzong was ready to act. He drew on the resources assembled for over a decade to initiate the largest military expedition of the eleventh century, an attempt to gain territory in the west at the expense of the Xi Xia. Even though he authorized nearly 400,000 porters to support about 300,000 combat troops, problems of supply ultimately doomed the Song campaign, which made modest territorial gains at enormous cost. After this failure, Shenzong lost his taste for war.[13]

During the regency of Empress Dowager Gao, advocates of peace dominated at court, and no new initiatives were undertaken. To the contrary, in exchange for a hundred Chinese captured during the wars, Song returned to Xi Xia four of the six towns it had captured.[14] This did not satisfy the Xi Xia rulers, however; they took advantage of the dominance of peace advocates at court to encroach on Song territory and redraw the borders in their favor. Once Gao died and Zhezong set about returning to his father's agenda, he was swayed by the returned reformers to look on the anti-reformers as cowardly appeasers. From 1097 through 1099, Song forces in the northwest strengthened fortifications, fought battles, and offered inducements to Tibetan leaders to become Song clients. The Xi Xia, responding to these provocations, in 1098/10 mobilized a reported hundred thousand troops to try to recover one of the lost towns. This time the Song armies soundly defeated the Xi Xia forces and captured their generals. In 1099/9 Xi Xia sent an emissary to Kaifeng to sue for peace.[15]

During the first twenty years of Huizong's reign, military affairs were matters of concern—raising enough horses and maintaining troop strength were constant worries—but the dynasty was never in any real sense threatened. Huizong seems to have generally adopted a middle course, showing little of his father's irredentist ambitions, but not rejecting out of hand proposals to enhance Song positions along the borders when the costs or dangers appeared manageable. In the southwest, Song authority was extended as loosely affiliated non-Han chiefdoms, called "bridle and halter" territories, were converted into counties and prefectures. From time to time prefects and circuit intendants had to mobilize troops to capture bandits or quell uprisings, but they were generally able to deal with them without having to call on the assistance of the centrally controlled armies.[16]

After Cai Jing was appointed grand councilor in 1102/7, his brother Cai Bian was appointed director of the Bureau of Military Affairs and the Qingtang initiative was reopened. A multiethnic army with Tong Guan as army supervisor proved successful, and by 1103/7 Song forces had recaptured two prefectures. Cai Jing, we are told, reported to Huizong every time a prefecture was recovered, showing him its location on a map and explaining its significance by saying, "this place connects to the western regions," or "this place connects to Qinghai," and so on. By the end of 1104, Song could claim full recovery of Qingtang with its more than seven hundred thousand people.[17] When Xi Xia responded with attacks on Song forts and walled cities, Song retaliated by attacking Xi Xia territory. Finally when the Xi Xia walled city of Yinzhou fell, Xi Xia sued for peace. In the end, Xi Xia recognized Song sovereignty in the Qingtang region, but Song returned Yinzhou.[18]

Even after peace was reached with Xi Xia, the Tibetans in Qingtang remained a quandary. In 1108 Huizong authorized a second campaign and put Tong Guan in command. Once there, Tong Guan made use of Tibetans who had not turned against the Song to both persuade and intimidate other Tibetans to return to the fold, making possible a major victory. The victorious general Liu Zhongwu was brought to court for an audience with Huizong, who after crediting him for much of the victory, asked him how many sons he had, and when Liu Zhongwu told him nine, Huizong had all of them assigned military posts.[19]

Huizong consulted a range of officials on the wisdom of these campaigns. During one audience, he asked Qian Ji, an official responsible for the provisioning of the army, whether to push further into Xi Xia territory. Qian warned him not to underestimate the Xi Xia, since the Tanguts were natural soldiers and did not require as much food as Song soldiers. When Huizong asked about a possible target, Qian described it as a salt marsh, of no use to anyone. Others gave Huizong more optimistic estimates, telling him that it would be possible to take a couple more prefectures from Xi Xia.[20] In 1106 Huizong was incensed when Feng Xie argued in a memorial that the military campaigns had accomplished nothing other than exhaust the soldiers and throw the nation into turmoil. Huizong declared that by recovering these territories he had been fulfilling the ambitions of Shenzong and Zhezong. Feng Xie's proposal to switch the region to the "bridle and halter" client arrangement, in his view, equaled abandoning it.[21]

After several years of peace, hostilities between Song and Xi Xia resumed in 1114. Between 1114 and 1119 the two fought a dozen or so battles, each side winning some of them. In the assessment of the modern scholar Li Huarui, Song was the overall victor, and in 1119/6 Xi Xia sued for peace, bringing to an end Song expansion in this area. A very different assessment is given by Ari Levine, who views the entire campaign as a Song defeat. He sees Tong Guan as "sacrificing hundreds of thousands of soldiers to briefly recapture a barren stretch of land."[22] According to the *Song History*, Tong Guan was quick to report victories but concealed the extent of losses. Perhaps for that reason, at Huizong's court the entire campaign was classified as a victory, and Wang Anzhong was assigned the task of commemorating it. As he summed it up, in the Qingtang Tibetan areas, Song gained two hundred thousand tribesmen and set up four prefectures, one military prefecture, one fortress, six walled cities, and twenty-two forts or stockades. From Xi Xia, Song gained territory extending several thousand *li*, seven walled cities, twenty-nine forts or stockades, destroyed walls of eight of their cities, and gained sovereignty over twenty thousand tribesmen. In 1119/7, in recognition of his military achievements, Tong Guan was promoted to the lofty office of Grand Mentor.[23]

By 1120, when Wang Fu became grand councilor, Huizong was no longer a neophyte in diplomatic or military matters. He had read and responded to thousands of memorials on matters ranging from ways to increase the supply of horses or improve the morale of soldiers, to intelligence reports about the situations on the borders. He had developed a comfortable relationship with Tong Guan, whom he trusted to run the Bureau of Military Affairs and to command armies in the field. He believed that there had been no major foreign policy or military failures during his watch, but to the contrary his armies had made significant gains in both the northwest and the southwest. He knew that some of his top officials thought the armies were underfunded, but he also knew that lack of funds had not in fact kept them from functioning effectively. Huizong was ready to consider more ambitious initiatives.

New Opportunities

In 1115, the year that Huizong built the Daoist Precious Registers Temple, appointed his eldest son as heir apparent, and revived the plan to build a Bright Hall, he learned that the balance of power in the north was shifting. The news came from a Liao official who wanted to defect. He described the turmoil caused by the Jurchen uprising and proposed ways Song could take advantage of the situation.[24]

The Song had had no reason to concern themselves with the Jurchen, who lived in the eastern reaches of the Liao empire around the Sungari River, their economy based on fishing, hunting, animal husbandry, and some farming. Liao claimed overlordship, as it did over other non-Kitan ethnic groups in the region. The Jurchen's area was well suited to raising horses, and by the mid-eleventh century the Jurchen there were supplying the Kitans about ten thousand horses per year. During the mid- to late eleventh century, the Wanyan clan gradually built a coalition of Jurchen clans, and under the leadership of Aguda (1068–1123) began challenging Liao authority. In 1115 their repudiation of Liao overlordship was made explicit by the proclamation of their own dynasty, which they named Jin (Golden).[25]

The defector, later known as Zhao Liangsi, would become one of Huizong's most trusted envoys.[26] He was from an ethnically Chinese family that had served as officials under Liao for generations. He thus brought to the Song an intimate knowledge of both the Liao government and the Yanjing area. Song treaties with Liao prohibited subjects crossing the border, so when he wanted to defect in 1115, he had to take precautions to keep his actions secret. He first sent someone to approach the prefect of a Song border prefecture with his proposal for attacking Liao with Jurchen help.

When this proposal reached the court, Huizong assigned the task of evaluating it to Cai Jing and Tong Guan. Tong Guan, who had been to Liao as a member of the 1111 mission to congratulate the Liao emperor on his birthday, was definitely interested. After ten days, Cai Jing and Tong Guan reported back, recommending that secret arrangements be made to help Zhao Liangsi cross the border. Those proved successful and Huizong received him in Extended Felicity Hall on 1115/4/18. Zhao Liangsi described for Huizong the turmoil at the Liao court and the success of the Jurchen under Aguda in attacking county and prefectural seats. Now was the time for the Song to reclaim China's old territory, he argued. "Those who act first will rule; those who act later will be ruled by others." Zhao Liangsi assured Huizong that the people of the Yan area (around modern Beijing) would welcome a Song army, as their territory had formerly been part of China. He also reported that it was possible to get in contact with the Jurchen by ship from the Shandong peninsula to the Liaodong peninsula. Huizong was impressed with Zhao Liangsi, gave him an official post, and conferred on him the imperial surname. Tong Guan became a major patron of Zhao Liangsi and was instrumental in having him later sent as an envoy to Jin.[27]

Tong Guan favored taking advantage of Liao weakness, but Huizong was yet to be convinced. He sent the eunuch general Tan Zhen to the northeast to investigate the armies there and assess how ready they were for war. What Tan Zhen learned discouraged him. Some of the local commanders said that Liao was still formidable or their own troops unfit, others that the country did not need more land.[28] Huizong asked the prefect of Zhending to report in more detail, and he submitted a long memorial making many points. First, the Han Chinese are not disloyal to Liao, and indeed most of the civil officials are Han Chinese. Second, the northeast does not have the grain and fodder for a military operation, and its reserves would be depleted within a single year of war. Third, the soldiers are too used to peace and not adequately disciplined. As a consequence of this report, on 1116/8/2 Huizong issued an order to commanders on the northern border not to provoke any sort of incident. Six months later (1117/2/27) Huizong issued another edict to the same effect.[29]

Wang Fu's biography in the *Song History* reports that after Zhao Liangsi's plan was introduced at court, most of the senior officials posed objections, but Wang Fu argued, "although North and South have gotten along for a hundred years, we have suffered repeated humiliations for several reigns. The best military strategy is to compound weaknesses and to attack when the other side is blinded. If we do not take [the region] now, the Jurchen will get stronger and the old territories of the Central Plain will never be ours again." When Huizong turned the matter over to Tong Guan, Wang Fu offered Tong Guan his support. Huizong himself, however, had not yet decided to break with Liao.[30]

Zhao Liangsi's reports of Aguda's successes were on the mark. After largely slaughtering the first army he faced, Aguda went on to set siege to a Liao prefectural seat, which fell in less than a month. In later encounters, Aguda was often able to capture Liao weapons, horses, and carts as well as convince Liao generals to switch sides. Several non-Kitan tribes under the Liao renounced Liao suzerainty and joined the Jurchen advance. The Liao emperor Tianzuo tried to negotiate a settlement with Aguda, offering to recognize the Jurchen as a vassal state, but Aguda took this as a sign of weakness and continued his advance. In 1115/8 Tianzuo mobilized one hundred thousand Kitan and Chinese troops and personally led a massive expedition against Aguda. When this campaign failed, many Kitan leaders began to wonder if it was time for new leadership. Tianzuo consequently had to divide his attention between controlling internal challenges and suppressing the Jurchen. In the resulting factional struggles among Liao leaders, the losers tended to join the Jurchen.[31]

At this time, 1117–1118, Huizong was absorbed in Divine Empyrean Daoism and Lin Lingsu was giving sermons and calling down spirits. Huizong had ordered all prefectures to convert a temple into a Divine Empyrean Jade Clarity Temple. When prefects along the border and in Shandong began submitting memorials reporting rumors of Liao defeats, Huizong had to wonder whether the high gods were responding to his pious devotion.[32]

One group of refugees from Liao set sail for Korea but were blown off course and landed by mistake on the coast of Shandong. The local prefect, after learning from them the extent of Jurchen advances, submitted a report to the court. Huizong had Cai Jing and Tong Guan discuss the situation, then ordered the prefect to sail to Liaodong on the pretense of a horse-buying mission but actually to try to make contact with Aguda. Early in 1118, when Huizong heard that their ship had failed even to land, he instructed Tong Guan to organize a secret

mission himself. To help smooth the way, Huizong wrote out an imperial brush rescript for the envoys to use if any officials tried to interfere. In the fourth month of 1118, the envoys set off from Kaifeng with
an interpreter, eighty soldiers, and seven officers. Five months later
they departed by ship from Dengzhou in Shandong.[33] This was the
first of more than a dozen missions that reached the Jurchens.

While waiting for his envoys to return, Huizong was getting mixed
opinions from his officials. A spy who had seen the Liao emperor reportedly told Huizong that Tianzuo had the physiognomy of a ruler
who loses his country. Intrigued, Huizong sent three court painters on
the next mission to Liao. They painted the landscape on the journey
and the Liao ruler's likeness. When they presented the paintings to
Huizong on their return, they asserted that, from just looking at the
Liao ruler, they could tell that his days were numbered.[34]

At about this time, Tong Guan, in a memorial that has not been
preserved, proposed taking advantage of the disorder in Liao to regain
Yan and Yun. He argued that the army should be divided, first surrounding Yan and Ji in the east, and then bringing the heaviest forces
to take Yun in the west. Huizong wanted Cai Jing's opinion of Tong
Guan's proposal and several times sent a eunuch to ask Cai Jing what
he thought of it. It was not until Huizong kept Cai Jing after an audience and asked him directly, however, that Cai Jing was willing to express his opinion. He told Huizong that he did not have confidence in
Tong Guan and that invading another country is much too momentous an undertaking to entrust to him. When Huizong brought up
Tong Guan's earlier successes on the northwestern border, Cai Jing
disputed how much of the credit for those victories should go to Tong
Guan.[35]

An Yaochen, a scholar with no official standing, submitted a long
memorial that countered Tong Guan's proposal even more bluntly. He
began by warning Huizong of the dangers of listening to only one side
of an issue and making it difficult for dissenters to be heard. He cited
numerous cases in the course of history where sending troops to the
borders had proved disastrous and argued for preserving the arrangements earlier Song emperors had negotiated. An Yaochen went on at
length about the dangers of letting eunuchs gain political power, then
criticized Tong Guan by name, accusing him of all sorts of malfea-
sance. Huizong rewarded An Yaochen for presenting his opinion so
courageously, but did not change his opinion of Tong Guan.[36]

Although Huizong wanted secrecy for the mission to the Jurchens (after all, to the Liao they were rebels), the overall policy of exploiting the Liao's predicament was openly debated at court and Huizong heard a range of opinion. Tong Guan and Wang Fu were both sold on the prospects of recovering territory from Liao. Other senior officials raised objections, however, including Cai Jing, Zheng Juzhong, Deng Xunwu, Liu Zhengfu, and the general Chong Shidao.[37] Zheng Juzhong, for instance, insisted that war is enormously costly, that the Song was much better off paying subsidies to Liao than running up the sorts of expenses that the Han dynasty incurred in fighting the Xiongnu. Deng Xunwu, who also stressing the dangers of war, suggested to Huizong that he take the reports submitted the previous year by each circuit on its soldiers and grain supplies and keep it by his seat to read from time to time. Moreover, he should ask himself which he would rather have as a neighbor, the strong Jurchen or the weak Kitan.[38]

Huizong did not find it easy to get the Council of State to agree to break the treaty with Liao and making one with Jin. A few years later, in 1126–1127, a servant of Cai Jing's reported what he knew about how the decision to go ahead was finally reached. His account begins with the arrival of emissaries from Jin on 1119/11:

When the Jin envoys arrived, Tong Guan was appointed to receive them and Zhao Liangsi, and they met at Cai Jing's private home. All the attendants were excused, and I alone watched the door. From there I could only overhear the Jin envoys speak of "striking the drums from both sides" [attacking from two sides]. But even after the envoys had left, Cai Jing still had not made up his mind. This made Tong Guan irritated with Cai Jing and he criticized him in front of the emperor. Cai Jing, alarmed, sent me to go to see [Tong Guan]. I said [to Tong Guan], "The Grand Preceptor [i.e., Cai Jing] and you, sir, know each other well. Recently he heard that you have not supported him in front of the emperor. In all matters, if there is something that you disagree with, you merely have to inform him. There is no need for you to be indirect."

Tong Guan rose and said to me: "I am an insignificant palace servant [eunuch] who only because of the Grand Preceptor's support hold the office I do today. How would I dare forget what I owe him? Please reply to him that he shouldn't believe the stories people tell or let them make us suspicious of each other." As I was leaving, Tong Guan called to me, "Another request: Ask the Grand Preceptor who was working to get him his current position while he was sitting quietly in Hangzhou. I have already fully repaid the Grand Preceptor."

When I returned, I reported everything Tong Guan had said. Although Cai Jing knew Tong Guan was displeased with him, this was a matter on which he really could not go along with him. He could not help but worry.

A second crucial encounter occurred during a meeting Huizong convened of the Council of State without Cai Jing present:

One day [officials from] both the Bureau of Military Affairs and the Secretariat-Chancellery were at court. Cai Jing was not in attendance.[39] Huizong abruptly said, "There is a matter I want us to discuss. What is the situation in the north really like?" Zheng Juzhong replied that the time was not yet ripe for action.[40] Huizong then turned to look at Yu Shen. Yu Shen answered that his opinion was the same as Cai Jing's, and that he had previously made known his views on the matter, reiterating that it was a matter that should not be decided lightly. Next Huizong asked Bai Shizhong, but while Bai was hesitating, Wang Fu interrupted, "China's old territory has long been in the hands of the barbarians. Today heaven gives signs that Your Majesty will achieve great things. If we do not take advantage of the opportunity, I fear we will regret it." He continued in this vein with dozens of words, all seemingly sensible. Huizong smiled and said, "Everyone else says it cannot be done. Only you say it is possible, which makes it difficult to carry out. Let's postpone [a decision] for a while." However, in his mind he was already siding with Wang Fu.

Cai Jing was present at the next important meeting:

A few days later [Huizong] gave a banquet for the grand councilors. When everyone was mellow with wine, he told them to board a boat. Huizong abruptly took a piece of paper and passed it on to Tong Guan. It said to tell Cai Jing and the others to discuss the matter. If they thought it could be approved, they should sign their names. Cai Jing and the others were shocked. They asked Tong Guan to report back to Huizong that they wanted to discuss the matter with him in person and were not willing to sign their names. Wang Anzhong said, "I was born and raised in the north. I heard that the people of Yan strongly desire to be reincorporated. If we act now, the directives could be settled. I will sign my name." The others remained silent.

Wang Fu was appointed grand councilor and the emperor conferred on him a jade belt. He dismissed the other officials and it was through discussions with Tong Guan, Wang Fu, and Wang Anzhong that the emperor decided to carry out the plan. It was really Tong Guan who had brought about that day' s decision. However, if it had not been for Wang Fu and Wang Anzhong, his plans would not have come to fruition.[41]

The long-standing Song desire to acquire the Sixteen Prefectures certainly contributed to Huizong's conclusion that the imminent collapse of the Liao was an opportunity not to be missed. The modern scholar Zhang Tianyou argues that in these circumstances conspiring with Jin to attack Liao "was not Huizong's blind ambition, but the continuation of long-standing state policy." Not long afterwards, in 1120/6, Cai Jing retired, quite possibly because Huizong was tired of his resistance to the new alliance.[42]

During the next few years it was Tong Guan and Wang Fu who played the leading roles in assessing intelligence reports and proposing courses of action. The two did not work as a team the whole time. To put himself in a position to manage the initiative, Wang Fu established the Frontier Defense Office. By heading it, he was able to compete with Tong Guan in directing the campaign to recover the Yan-Yun region.[43]

Negotiations through Envoys

The first party of Song envoys, led by the military officer Ma Zheng (see Table 13.1), left Kaifeng in 1118/4, landed on the coast of Liaodong in 1118/i9, and returned to Kaifeng in 1119/1, after more than eight months away.[44]

Table 13.1. Principal envoys

Envoy	Mission
From Song to Jin	
Gao Yaoshi	Ethnic Chinese from Liao whose boat was driven to Chinese shore and told about rise of Jurchen. Sent on 1118 mission that failed to get off the boat.
Huyan Qing	Military officer good at languages. Sent with 1118 Song mission as an interpreter; kept for six months by Aguda.
Ma Zheng	Military officer recommended by Tong Guan; had studied at the imperial military academy and received a military *jinshi*. He served on three missions, from 1118 to 1122.
Zhao Liangsi	Ethnic Chinese; former Liao official who defected to Song in 1115. Served on eight missions from 1120 to 1123. Protégé of Tong Guan. The official report he submitted on his mission in 1122–1123 is extensively quoted in surviving sources.
Ma Kuo	Son of Ma Zheng; 1118 military *jinshi*. First accompanied his father, but after 1122 his father no longer served as an envoy and Ma Kuo was himself the envoy. Served on seven missions, 1120–1125, some of which were from Tong Guan to the Jurchen general Nianhan. Held as a hostage by Jin for several months. His autobiography is extensively quoted in surviving sources, and describes both the Jurchen and conversations between the envoys and the emperors.
Zhou Wuzhong	Song official; sent on three missions in 1122–1123 to Yanjing.
Lu Yi	Song official; sent on 1123 mission to Yanjing.
From Jin to Song	
Li Shanqing	Bohai native; sent to Kaifeng in 1119.
Gao Sui	Bohai native; sent to Kaifeng in 1120, 1121.
Xicisalu	Jurchen; sent to Kaifeng in both 1120 and 1121. In 1121 detained for two months in Shandong. Also called Helu or Xilu.
Gao Qingyi	Bohai native who had served under Liao; sent to Kaifeng in 1122.
Li Jing	Sent to Kaifeng in 1122 and 1123.
Saluwu	Jurchen; sent to Kaifeng in 1122 and twice in 1123.

Because the returning Song envoys brought Aguda's envoys with them, Huizong would have heard from his own envoys and from the Jin envoys at the same time. His envoys had adventures to report. When their boat landed in Liaodong, their goods were seized and they were tied up. After their captors decided to take them to see Aguda, they spent nearly three weeks crossing a dozen prefectures, traveling more than fifteen hundred kilometers before meeting key Jurchen leaders, including Aguda and his nephew Nianhan.[45] Aguda was sufficiently satisfied with these meetings that he sent his own emissaries back with them, two Jurchen and Li Shanqing, a Bohai literate in Chinese. They carried an official proposal that if a joint campaign were launched against Liao, Song and Jin would each retain whatever territory it captured. The envoys also carried presents, including pearls, gold, furs, ginseng, and pine nuts, all considered local products of their homeland.[46] Huizong had the Jin emissaries engage in direct discussions with Cai Jing and Tong Guan, and kept them in the capital for more than ten days. This was the first of numerous exchanges of diplomats that led to an alliance referred to in Chinese as the alliance made by crossing the sea, that is, by boat from Shandong.[47] While these envoys were traveling back and forth between Song and Jin, Liao envoys were at work as well. In fact, Liao sent six missions to the Jin court in 1118 alone, their frequency a sign of the desperation they felt as Jin consolidated its control over the eastern part of Liao territory. Aguda did not accept any of the Liao offers but made his own counterproposal: cede three of the five Liao circuits, send members of the ruling houses as hostages, grant Jin superiority in diplomatic relations, and pay an annual subsidy. Liao not surprisingly refused since accepting these demands would be tantamount to surrender.[48]

The mission Huizong dispatched to carry his reply did not get a quick start. First, the lead envoy died in Shandong before the party set sail. After a delay, the mission proceeded without a lead envoy. When they met Aguda, he took umbrage at the language of the message, since it took the form of an edict and thus addressed him as Huizong's inferior, something the Song envoy had done only after consulting Aguda's envoy, who had implied it did not matter. Aguda evidently already had experts on interstate diplomacy who had explained such niceties to him. The absence of a lead envoy too was judged an insult by Aguda.[49]

Aguda kept the Song envoy Huyan Qing for six months before letting him return, probably a ploy to delay treaty negotiations with Song while negotiations with Liao were in progress. The Jurchen were then winning one battle after another against the Liao and had no reason to settle prematurely with either side. Just before releasing Huyan, Aguda underlined to him that Jin could easily conquer Liao on its own. If Song wanted to maintain friendly relations with Jin, it would have to treat Jin with respect.[50] When Huyan Qing finally reached Kaifeng in 1120/2/16, he passed on these messages and the news that Liao and Jin had not concluded a treaty.

Huizong's court then began to step up its diplomatic efforts. For the third mission, Zhao Liangsi, the former Liao official who had defected in 1115, was made the lead envoy. Huizong gave him an imperial brush edict instructing him to seek an oral agreement with Aguda for a joint attack on Liao and recovery of Yanjing.[51] Zhao left Kaifeng in 1120/3/6, Shandong on 1120/3/26, saw Aguda in the fourth and fifth months, and was back in Kaifeng 1120/9/4, six months after he departed.

Zhao Liangsi's account of this trip survives. In it he reports that soon after their first meeting, Aguda took him along on his attack of the Liao Supreme Capital. By midday, Jin commanders were standing on the walls of the city. Zhao Liangsi was deeply impressed by Jin military capability, and perhaps for this reason he agreed to Song paying a substantial price for the return of territory. From Zhao Liangsi's testimony, Aguda was a persistent negotiator, quick to point out how much Jin had accomplished and what Song needed to do to make an alliance with it. Aguda agreed orally that Yan was originally Chinese territory and would be returned to the Song on the condition that Song participate in the defeat of Liao by capturing Yanjing and also that Song make annual payments of five hundred thousand units of silver and silk to Jin, in essence sending them what they used to send to Liao. Zhao Liangsi tried to bring up the fact that the Liao Western Capital (Datong) was also originally Chinese and touched on other parts of the Sixteen Prefectures, including the prefectures of Ping and Luan, near Yanjing, with Aguda acting as though Song would get the Western Capital but making no commitment on Ping and Luan.[52]

Zhao Liangsi's original charge from Huizong had been to try to get the Yanjing area back. In bringing up the Datong area, he seems to have been exploring a perceived opportunity, since the rationale of letting Song take Yanjing because it was ethnically Chinese and previously part of Chinese dynasties applied just as strongly to Datong. As time went on Aguda had both more former Liao officials to advise him and his armies had conquered more on their own, so it is not surprising that Aguda later realized he had no need to let territory his armies conquered go to Song. But Song expectations had been raised once Aguda let Datong be put on the table, leading to a long series of frustrating but ultimately doomed negotiations between Song and Jin.[53]

When Zhao Liangsi arrived back in Kaifeng in 1120/9, the Jurchen emissaries with him carried a state letter, the first formal written agreement between Song and Jin. It made no reference to the Western Capital but otherwise matched Zhao Liangsi's record of their oral agreements. Huizong was apparently sufficiently satisfied with Zhao Liangsi's performance that from then on he had him serve as envoy on most of the missions he sent to the Jin. Huizong met the new Jin envoy Xicisalu in Promoting Governance Hall and had Tong Guan feast him and his colleagues in his home. Huizong passed on the message that his most urgent concern was for Jin to take the Western Capital. The envoys responded that their army could be relied on to achieve that goal. Huizong had a state letter written, ratifying the terms proposed. The state letters used reciprocal language. Aguda's letter begins "the emperor of the Great Jin respectfully sends this letter to the emperor of the Great Song," and Huizong's letter begins "the emperor of the Great Song respectfully sends this letter to the emperor of the Great Jin."[54]

Ma Zheng, who had been the envoy on the first mission, was one of the envoys who carried these documents back to Jin in 1120/9/20, arriving about two months later, 1120/11/29. His charge was to reassure Jin that Song would commit troops to the defeat of Liao and to keep alive the issue of the Western Capital region.[55] Tong Guan, in accord with the agreement with Jin, began preparing the army for an attack on Yanjing.

꙳ How DID HUIZONG reach a decision about the best course to take as the Liao began to falter? He consulted widely. One group of his advisors, mostly the older ones, were cautious, afraid that things might go wrong. The younger ones, Wang Fu and Cai You in particular, were straining at the bit, eager to make the best of the opportunity. Tong Guan, in age closer to first group, was the only one who had ever fought a battle, and he sided with those who wanted to take action.

Neither Huizong nor any of his councilors had much information to go on. There were some written and oral reports of the Chinese envoys such as Zhao Liangsi and Ma Zheng. The main check on the story they told would have been the documents sent by Jin and what could be learned by interviewing the Jin envoys who came to Kaifeng. Much thus rested on individual talents and acumen of the envoys. They needed not only to be able to articulate their ruler's positions and monitor the written language of agreements, but also had to win the respect and goodwill of those with whom they were negotiating and learn as much as possible about their military situation. Ma Zheng's son, Ma Kuo, who accompanied his father's missions and would later serve in higher capacities, wrote a record of his experiences which shows the many ways the envoys were tested.[56] According to him, Aguda took a group of warriors out hunting and brought the envoys along. The general Nianhan, through an interpreter, asked Ma Kuo, "I have heard that men of the southern court are capable only of writing and know nothing of the military arts. Is this so?" Ma Kuo explained that there were both military and civil officials, but many individuals were skilled in both arts. When Ma Kuo admitted that he had a military degree, Nianhan gave him his bow and asked him to demonstrate shooting from a galloping horse, sarcastically saying he wanted to learn the techniques of the southerners. Ma Kuo whipped his horse and shot successfully. When Aguda heard this, he too wanted Ma Kuo to give him a demonstration.[57] Ma Kuo was doubtless a skilled archer, but recording this story served purposes beyond self-promotion—it helped convince Huizong and others at his court reading reports of the mission that the Chinese envoys knew how to hold their own even when toughened warriors tried to belittle them or placed them in demeaning situations.

Over the next three years, Huizong received envoys from Jin six times. The normal protocol involved two formal audiences, the first within a couple of days of their arrival, the last, just before their departure. The formality of these audiences meant that after the envoys stated their mission and presented their documents, Huizong had a eunuch orally pass on his greetings and general comments. Huizong usually directed that they see Wang Fu in his private home to discuss specific issues. Huizong, however, did not hold himself aloof from the details. Sometimes he had more private audiences with the Chinese envoys who had been to Jin and had been traveling with the Jin envoys. Several times he wrote out some of the documents to transmit to Jin in his own hand to lend them weight and honor the recipients. In addition, he regularly gave the Chinese envoys letters in his own hand explaining to them how to handle the negotiations, such as when they could accept a compromise.

It is worth noting that Aguda negotiated in person much of the time but Huizong seems to have usually kept his contact with the envoys to more ritualized audiences, sending them to Tong Guan or Wang Fu for substantive discussions. To some extent, of course, this reflects the difference in their political roles. Aguda was a military leader whose political power derived very largely from his personal relations with subordinates. Huizong presided over a huge bureaucracy and his ritual elevation was a central element in maintaining the hierarchical structure of the system. But it is certainly possible that personality differences entered into the matter as well. Aguda, who thrived on military confrontation, seems to have similarly enjoyed the gamesmanship of negotiation; he would try out different ploys in an effort to win the most for his side. Huizong had no taste for this sort of high-stakes game.[58]

IV

Confronting Failure, 1121–1135

14

Adjusting to Military Setbacks,
1121–1125

> In 1122, because of the opening of the northern border,
> expenditures were extraordinary. All the treasuries, both
> Privy Purse and government, were empty, much to Huizong's
> dismay.
>
> —*Cai Tao's later recollection*

GRAND AMBITIONS had marked Huizong's second decade
on the throne. He constructed magnificent palaces, gardens, and temples. He put teams of scholars to work sifting through earlier writings
to compile new, up-to-date compendia on ritual, medicine, and geography. He assembled great collections of art and antiquities and assigned erudite men to study and catalogue them. He took state support
for Daoism to a new high, integrating Daoist masters into the government hierarchy. He began arranging marriages and housing for his
wealth of offspring. His officials found one occasion after another to
congratulate him.

When did Huizong begin to have premonitions that all might not
work out as planned? Cai Tao argues persuasively that it was early in
1121 when he had to pull back the troops that were scheduled to attack
Yanjing and reassign them to suppress a rebellion in the south.[1]

Fang La's Uprising

In the twelfth month of 1120, Huizong learned that a rebel had formed
an army in one of the richest parts of the country and had captured
several cities, including the major city of Hangzhou (see Map 1). The
news was kept from Huizong for days if not weeks because at each level
of administration officials wanted to be able to present their superiors

with an laudable victory, not a dangerous new problem, so first tried to handle the matter themselves before informing higher levels.[2] When Huizong finally did hear of the revolt, the news must have been devastating. By then, the rebellion had expanded way beyond its original base in Muzhou into most of the surrounding prefectures. Many local government officials had fled once they heard the rebels were approaching rather than put up a fight.

On 1120/12/21 Huizong authorized the eunuch general Tan Zhen to lead crack imperial troops intended for the assault on Yanjing to suppress the rebels. Three days after dispatching Tan Zhen, Huizong issued an edict offering free pardon to those who surrendered:

> People in the two circuits of Zhe have been used to peace and have witnessed no warfare in almost two hundred years. Recently, however, violent bandits have taken advantage of the strategic mountainous area to start an uprising. We sympathize with the many innocent people who may have been forced to follow them, with the officials and inhabitants of the two areas who may have been unwillingly involved, and with those soldiers who have run away after defeat. All these cases are subject to pardon, but they have had no way to explain their situations. Therefore it is hoped that Tan Zhen will take a suitable opportunity to declare my kind intention. All the people mentioned above, relatives of the bandits, and those followers now in the group who surrender to the government or give information about the movements of the bandits leading to their capture, will be exempted from punishments and their records not held against them. Even small contributions will be given generous rewards. We hope that by proclaiming an amnesty to rebels and stopping senseless slaughter, peace will be restored in the south.[3]

While issuing amnesties and dispatching troops, Huizong also tried to learn more about what was going on. One of those he asked for his assessment was Chen Gou, the fiscal intendant of the Huainan region. According to him, "When Fang La first rose in Qingxi, he had less than a thousand men, but now by forcing people to join, he has more than ten thousand. Shi Sheng of Suzhou and Lu Xinger of Guian [other bandits] have joined forces with him. In the southeast, the soldiers are weak and life simple; educated men do not practice the military arts and cannot destroy the bandits [by themselves]. I would request that you send the capital armies, the Ding and Li lancemen, and move quickly before even more ignorant people get caught up in this."[4] With advice like this and continuing reports of rebel advances, Huizong decided on 1121/1/7 to send a second capital army under Tong Guan, who would also serve as overall commander. The troops he led included non-Chinese units and brought the total troop strength to 150,000. Since the rebellion was centered so far from the capital, Huizong gave Tong Guan the authority to issue imperial brush edicts on his own, which relieved him of the need to seek approval before changing his plans.[5]

Who was Fang La? What had allowed him to gain so much territory so quickly? There has been much debate about him—was he a Manichaean? Did he own a lacquer plantation or just work on one? Reportedly Fang La had been drafted to serve as a village tax collector, a duty no one ever wanted, especially when, as in his case, they had to make up shortfalls from their personal resources.[6] At some point he started attracting the poor to his cause.

By the time Fang La's uprising came to the attention of the court, it had avowed anti-dynastic elements to it. On 1120/11/1 Fang La gave himself the title Sacred Lord and announced his reign period—Perpetual Happiness. He exploited resentment of the exactions that the transportation of flowers and rocks for Huizong's gardens had imposed on the region. One Southern Song author reports that Fang La harangued his followers, complaining about the wealth sent to the Liao and Xia and the extravagance of the emperor who indulged in "music, women, dogs, horses, buildings, sacrifices, weapons and armor, and plants and stones for the imperial gardens," all funded through the toil of the people in the southeast.[7] Whether this is what he actually said, or what someone writing after the fall of the Northern Song thought he would have said, is impossible to determine.

At an early stage Fang La and his followers occupied a huge cave with many tunnels. Like bandits, they would go out to plunder the countryside or kill officials, then return to their cave. The county officials did poorly against them, falling into their ambushes. They had wooden fortifications built and trenches dug, but Fang La's band burned the fortifications and captured the county seat. When the prefectural seat fell on 1120/12/4, the rebels killed as many officials and soldiers as they could lay their hands on. The rebels quickly took surrounding towns, making their way toward Hangzhou, which they took on 1120/12/29 after the prefect fled. The city was set ablaze and burned for six days; 30 percent of the population, we are told, died in the flames.[8]

Once the imperial army arrived, it proved fully able to suppress the rebels. Tong Guan arrived in Zhenjiang on 1/21, only fourteen days after the order to take his army south, suggesting they traveled largely by water.[9] One of Tong Guan's first measures was to abolish the Flower and Rock Network and the imperial manufactories, which had caused much resentment and proved good rallying cries for the rebels.[10] An imperial brush edict was issued, probably by Tong Guan, offering sizable rewards to anyone who would help with suppressing the rebels. Whoever killed or captured Fang La himself would get ten thousand ounces of silver, rolls of silk, and strings of cash, not to mention five hundred ounces of gold. There were also lesser rewards for capturing his top officers. If one of the rebels turned in Fang La, dead or alive, his own involvement would be forgiven and he would get the reward.[11]

Tong Guan, then over sixty, had overall command of the imperial army, but field command was in the hand of younger men, including Wang Bing, Yao Pingzhong, He Guan, and Liu Guangshi, all of whom would later play major roles in the wars against Liao and Jin. In their first major engagement, lasting six days, the government claimed to have killed twenty thousand bandits. On 2/18 Hangzhou was recovered. Often, it seems, when the imperial army approached, the rebels would leave the city they had occupied and move on to another one. Still, gradually, more and more of them were killed or captured. On 3/27 Muzhou was recovered. On 1121/4/24 the imperial armies converged on the rebels' home base. Approaching from the rear, they "found the cliffs of the ridge perilous, and the pathway dangerous, and several tens of thousands of rebels defending them. Liu Zhen, with his best soldiers, advanced along a back trail and took the key ridge by surprise, killing over six hundred rebels." It took them till dawn to force their way in. Soon they were setting fire to the houses. "Twenty thousand bandits resisted their attack from all sides until evening. The rebels were cut down until their blood reddened the earth." The army claimed to have killed thousands of rebels and freed tens of thousands of civilians who had been forced to join the rebels. The next day Fang

La was captured in his cave along with his chief officials and relatives, about three months after Tong Guan had arrived in the region. Fang La was brought to the capital in the seventh month and presented at court as a captive. The following month he was executed.[12] Other followers, however, remained active in nearby areas, requiring the imperial armies to remain in the area for fifteen months altogether.

The destruction caused by the Fang La rebellion and its suppression was enormous; Song sources use round but gigantic numbers such as one million adherents and two million civilians losing their lives, which is surely just a guess. Six prefectures and fifty-two counties suffered from the rebels' looting and burning.[13] When the rebels set fire to towns, the losses were huge. When imperial troops fought the rebels, they regularly killed many more than they captured. For instance, when Liu Guangshi took Longyou, his troops killed 2,209 rebels and captured 50. One reason for the heavy casualties in battle was that the rebels were not well armed or trained. One official reported that the rebels did not have many weapons and often fought with bare fists, trying to scare their opponents by painting their faces to look like monsters.[14]

Although there were many cases of local officials who fled when the rebels attacked, there were also many stories of determined resistance and men who refused to budge even though they knew that they faced certain death.[15] Li Gang, who was in the region when the rebellion started, wrote to each of the members of the Council of State in the first month of 1121. He offered his observations of the behavior of the rebels and the sorts of military strategies that would work. He insisted on the need for well-trained soldiers brought in from outside, as local soldiers were not effective. Although many of the rebels had been captured and forced to join Fang La's army, this did not mean they posed no threat. He thought poor farmers forced to join often found the bandit life exhilarating, as they were able to get everything they wanted simply by stealing it.[16]

Strains in the Alliance

The timing of the Fang La rebellion could hardly have been worse. While Song armies were busy in the southeast, Jurchen armies took Ping, Luan, and Ying prefectures just east of Yanjing as well as the

Liao Western Capital (Datong).[17] Aguda was no longer willing to discuss turning these prefectures over to Song. Aguda sent his envoy Xicisalu to carry his formal message, but when that mission arrived in Shandong in 1121/2, it was detained there for two months, a stalling tactic necessitated by the fact that Tong Guan was in the south fighting the Fang La rebels. Not until Xicisalu angrily threatened to walk to Kaifeng did Huizong give permission for Ma Zheng to bring the Jin envoys to Kaifeng.[18]

The message the envoys carried put Huizong in an awkward position, given that Tong Guan and his best troops were in the south suppressing the rebellion. Aguda reiterated his promise to return the Yan area, but not if Jin captured it themselves without Song help. The same would be true of the Liao Western Capital as well. Huizong tried to resist the new terms, and in the state letter he sent back with the Jin envoys insisted Yan should be ceded to Song. Apparently reflecting a new coolness on Huizong's part toward the alliance with Jin, this time the Song did not send its own envoy, but merely let the Jin envoys carry the Song state letter.

While Tong Guan's army was mopping up the last of the rebels, Jin was destroying Liao. According to Cai Tao, Huizong's court first heard that the Liao emperor Tianzuo had led one hundred thousand troops to Yanjing, then later heard that he was in flight in the other direction. In fact, by 1122 the Liao ruling families were at war among themselves. One of Tianzuo's consorts charged that key leaders were planning to force Tianzuo to abdicate in favor of one of his sons. As a result, Tianzuo had several close relatives and officers executed. Soon key figures went over to the Jin out of fear that they would also be targets of Tianzuo's suspicions. In 1122/1 the Liao Central Capital (see Map 2) fell to Jin forces.[19]

With the loss of three of its capitals and the flight of its emperor, by 1122 the Liao was no longer a centrally controlled state. In 1122/3 Liao officials in the Southern Capital (Yanjing), out of contact with Tianzuo, declared a member of the imperial family, Yelü Chun, to be their emperor and tried unsuccessfully to negotiate an accommodation with Aguda. Based on reports from its spies, the Song court began to worry that Liao armies might try to take Song territory as they were pushed out of their own. Consequently the Song court encouraged commanders along the border to step up military preparations.[20]

Despite the fact that Huizong had concluded the alliance with Jin, Huizong still received memorials trying to get him to give up the idea of attacking Yan. One of the longest and most persuasive was by Yuwen Xuzhong, then the pacification commissioner in charge of the armies in Hebei, Hedong, and Shaanxi. He argued that one never should begin a campaign before fully assessing the assets and liabilities on each side. This memorial annoyed Wang Fu so much that he transferred Yuwen Xuzhong to a literary post, but he kept submitting memorials against military action anyway.[21]

While part of the Jin army was pursuing Tianzuo, Song was getting ready to act on its commitment to join Jin in the attack on Yanjing, the Liao Southern Capital. Yanjing was a major city, surrounded by a nine- or ten-meter-high wall about twenty kilometers in circumference, not as big as Kaifeng, but still substantial. It was the central city of a region with ten prefectures and thirty-two counties, with a total population on the order of 1.2 million people, most of whom were ethnically Chinese.[22] On 1122/4/10, Huizong reviewed the hundred thousand troops Tong Guan was taking to Yanjing from a suburban park. Huizong gave Tong Guan a rescript in his own hand, setting out the three alternatives he should pursue. The best would be if the local people welcomed the Song army and asked to have the old borders restored. The next best would be if the local pretender, Yelü Chun, asked to be a vassal. The least desirable alternative would be for the Song army to suppress resistance on the part of the local people, then return intact. Huizong also issued an edict directed to the people of Yan which condemned Liao, promised tax relief to those who submitted, and threatened death to those who resisted. Another edict made similar offers to Yelü Chun.[23]

Within two weeks, 1122/4/23, Tong Guan was at Gaoyang Pass and the Pacification Commission posted placards calling on the people of Yan to surrender. The placard began: "The regions of You and Yan were originally part of our territory which abruptly fell [to the enemy] and have been lost for about two hundred years. In the past the Han Chinese and the frontier people have been at odds and there has been disorder on both sides of the border. Your old ruler [Tianzuo] is still alive but a new ruler [Yelü Chun] has usurped his position." The placard went on to promise that those who submitted could keep their positions and land and that Kitans as well as Han Chinese would be treated well.[24]

Because Huizong was not entirely confident in Tong Guan's ability to manage the invasion, on 1122/5/9 he ordered Cai You to go to Yanjing to supervise him. He noted in the rescript that because Tong Guan was getting old, he was prone to stupid mistakes, which he would try to cover up, but since this border matter was so critical to the dynasty, it was important to have someone reliable to keep an eye on the situation. Cai Jing and Cai You had been at odds over other matters for some time, and when Cai You departed, his father wrote a poem to see him off that indirectly questioned the entire campaign. The poem eventually reached Huizong, who suggested a slight modification in the wording.[25]

For his part, Tong Guan pursued several strategies simultaneously. One plan was to spark an insurrection within Yanjing to throw out the Kitan and invite in the Song. He found a willing organizer in Li Chuwen, the son of a former Liao high official, and had Zhao Liangsi deliver a letter to him giving him authorization to operate within Yan. This effort, however, failed within a month, and Li Chuwen was executed by Yelü Chun's forces.[26] At the same time Tong Guan was pursuing diplomatic channels. He sent Ma Kuo into the Yan area to scout out the situation, find local Chinese who would aid the Song, and serve as an intermediary to Yelü Chun. Yelü Chun's officials told Ma Kuo that Song had violated its treaty with Liao, but Ma Kuo rejoined that Yelü Chun was a usurper and that Tianzuo was still emperor. Probably in an attempt to sway Ma Kuo, the Yan officials had him kneel while they unrolled two portraits, one of the Song emperor Zhenzong, the other of his successor Renzong, portraits that had been sent by Song decades earlier. Yelü Chun also had an interpreter read the oath letters of the two states.[27]

In the end, Tong Guan had to rely on his generals. Unfortunately, they did not all support the venture. The septuagenarian Chong Shidao likened what they were doing to someone who does not aid his neighbor during an attack of bandits, but rather joins in the looting. Late in the fifth month (1122/5/26 and 5/29) Yelü Chun's army under Dashilinya attacked Song forces under Chong Shidao. The *Documents on the Treaties with the North during Three Reigns*, in a passage that defies credulity, states that a major reason why the Song armies were badly defeated was that Chong Shidao had ordered his troops not to kill anyone from Yan, but just to wait for their surrender. In giving this order he was obeying Tong Guan who believed that the people of Yan wanted to be part of China and would not fight the advancing Song army unless provoked. In all likelihood, this is a myth made up by those disgusted at the Song defeat. Whatever the truth of the matter, when the Yan forces attacked him at Baogou, Chong Shidao ordered a retreat.[28]

By the time Cai You arrived at the Song army encampment in the sixth month, Tong Guan had retreated to Hejian, in Song territory, and people from the Yan region began streaming across the borders, saying Liao no longer had a ruler and fearing further conflict. About this time Yelü Chun died and his widow took over leadership of the Yan forces in the name of the heir.[29]

At court Wang Fu persuaded the wavering Huizong that the Song should mount another offensive. Huizong wrote out in his own hand an edict approving the proposal. This time two hundred thousand soldiers would be mobilized from across the country. Several new generals were appointed, including Liu Yanqing and Liu Guangshi, both of whom had served under Tong Guan in earlier campaigns. Tong Guan was soon able to report that their raids into the Yan region had met with success and that they had captured large quantities of supplies and soldiers.[30]

Huizong himself was busy entertaining envoys from Jin who arrived in Kaifeng on 1122/9/11 after first meeting with Tong Guan at his camp. The lead envoy, a Bohai named Gao Qingyi, was familiar with Chinese diplomatic protocol and made sure that the Jin envoys were treated with honors beyond anything Liao envoys had customarily received. Huizong let them ascend the steps in Promoting Governance Hall to present the state letter. Not only did they visit Wang Fu's home for discussions, as had become customary, but several times high ranking officials were sent to dine with them. The envoys were showered with gifts and taken for tours of the Bright Hall, Dragon Virtue Palace, and other palace buildings. When it was time for them to depart, Huizong even wrote out both the state letter and its appendix in his own hand. The Jin envoys, for their part, proved not the most gracious of guests. At the farewell audience, Huizong said that there was no real ruler left in Yanjing, and the only remaining problem was the army. "How can the state of Jin tolerate this? It would be good if they were quickly caught," Huizong commented. The Jin envoys retorted that there was a contradiction between the claims Song made of repeated victories over the Kitan and the evidence that they could not subdue this one army without the help of Jin.[31]

After seven days, on 1122/9/18, Zhao Liangsi, Ma Zheng, and Ma Kuo were sent to accompany Gao Qingyi and his colleagues back to Jin. The state letter they carried reported the Song's recent victories over the Kitan and the plan that Song would attack Yanjing from the prefectures of Zhuo and Yi while Jin attacked from Gubeikou. In addition, the letter warned Jin not to trust Xi Xia, which had been aiding the Kitans.[32] Although the original understanding of a joint attack on Liao had been that Jin would attack Datong and Song would attack Yanjing, by this point Huizong was talking of a joint attack on Yanjing, clearly concerned that they would not be able to take the well-fortified city unaided. This was one of the most serious mistakes that Huizong made, since it exposed Song military inadequacies and removed the main incentive for Jin to let Song take the Yanjing area.

While these diplomatic efforts were underway, Song armies were making some progress in taking over areas south of Yanjing. In the ninth month, both Yi and Zhuo prefectures submitted to Song without fighting (in Yi, the local people first slaughtered resident Kitans). Guo Yaoshi, the Bohai commander of Yelü Chun's Ever-Victorious Army in Zhuo, switched his allegiance to the Song.[33]

In the tenth month, 1122/10/9, envoys from Yelü Chun's widow arrived at the Song camp and met with Tong Guan and Cai You. They delivered the message that she was willing to become a vassal, claiming that she wished to spare her people. Tong Guan wanted the land to go to Song, not be left in the hands of a vassal, but the envoy replied that submission was tantamount to returning the land and they would make a better neighbor than Jin. Tong Guan kept the envoys with him but sent the state letter on to Kaifeng.[34] Song agreements with Jin had of course prohibited either side from making its own peace agreement with Liao, but Huizong had told Tong Guan that making Yelü Chun a vassal was the second-best alternative, which meant he had to consider this offer.

When the memorial of submission from the widow arrived in the capital on 10/13, it was treated at court as cause for celebration, and officials congratulated Huizong in Hanging Hem Hall. Huizong issued hand-drafted edicts conferring tax relief on the residents of the newly acquired territory, renaming the prefectures and counties, and promising to recruit its capable men for government service.[35]

Even though in Kaifeng the court was celebrating the submission of Yanjing, Yelü Chun's widow had not received the status she wanted and had not opened the gates to the city. At the front, the Song armies were getting ready to set siege. On 1122/10/19 the combined armies of Liu Yanqing, He Guan, Guo Yaoshi, Liu Guangshi, and others met at Zhuo prefecture. Guo Yaoshi, as a recent turncoat with good knowledge of Yanjing's defenses, was able to advise how best to attack the city. His plan involved getting soldiers dressed as civilians to infiltrate the city by joining the throngs at the early morning market outside one of the gates, then entering and making their way to the other gates, which they would then open for the Song soldiers. This part went well, and the Song soldiers, once in control of the gates, ordered the people to surrender and to rise up against the Kitans. At one point, Yelü Chun's widow ascended one of the gates to observe the fighting. Guo Yaoshi sent someone to urge her to surrender, but she replied that she had heard that the Song soldiers were killing Kitans and looting homes, which made her soldiers determined to fight to the death. She stayed in the palace as Song and Liao soldiers fought hand to hand on the streets from morning to night. After the Song soldiers were exhausted, the widow opened the gates of the palace and sent out her fresh troops. Relief troops expected by the Song commanders did not arrive in time, and the Yan forces quickly gained the upper hand. The Chinese residents of Yanjing, fearing reprisals for having fought on the side of the Song, begged Guo Yaoshi to stay, but he escaped with only four hundred of his original five thousand troops.[36]

Over the next several days, the situation went from bad to worse. On 1122/10/25, the Kitan general Xiao Gan led his troops out of Yanjing to confront the Song forces. To convince Liu Yanqing and his army that all those who had entered the city had been killed, he displayed the armor and horses of Guo Yaoshi and other commanders. On 10/27 the Pacification Commission, under Cai You, worried that Zhuo prefecture might fall, sent two thousand troops to defend it. On 10/28, Liu Yanqing reported that he was withdrawing his army. The next day he burned his camp and his troops retreated in disorder.[37]

Military Embarrassment

News of the rout would not have reached Huizong for several days. In the meantime, Zhao Liangsi and Ma Kuo had arrived once more at Aguda's camp. When they met Aguda on 1122/11/1, he already knew of the Song defeats and was no longer willing to hand over all the territory previously promised to Song. He now consented to turn over only Yanjing and the six prefectures between it and Song territory. The Song envoys tried to insist that it should still get Datong as well as Ping, Luan, and Ying prefectures east of Yanjing, but to no avail. The Jin negotiators moreover now said they should only get the Han Chinese residents of the region; other ethnic groups, including Kitan, Bohai, and Xi, would become subjects of Jin and presumably be moved to Jin lands.[38] They also said that the Jin army should be free to cross through the region, which Zhao Liangsi saw as a fundamental infringement of Song sovereignty.

Both Zhao Liangsi and Ma Kuo left accounts of this crucial meeting.[39] Ma Kuo's version is not very flattering to Zhao Liangsi. After traveling by night for several days, they met with Aguda, his son Wolibu, and a translator in a tent:

> Aguda said, "Last time, when I sent Xicisalu Dadiwu to discuss dividing and returning the Yan territory, your court did not send a return envoy. That was breaking the agreement. Your current envoy does not want to honor the treaty made by "crossing the sea." I know that the [Song] Zhao emperor has a sincere heart and would not bear to break off our good relations. Once Yanjing is pacified, we can provisionally discuss whether or not to give it to you. Now the Western Capital has already been pacified and can be returned to your court. We should send troops to handle the transfer and demarcation." At that time, because Guo Yaoshi had already surrendered [to Song] and Liu Yanqing had already brought force against Yan, he brought up the idea of ceding Yunzhong [i.e., Datong].
>
> Zhao Liangsi was flustered and at a loss for words. He replied, "We discussed demarcating and returning Yan territory. Until Yanjing is acquired, we do not want the Western Capital [Datong]."

Wolibu said, "Yanjing is not finished, and we already said we would engage in provisional discussions about it afterwards. The Western Capital is finished and we have assigned it to your court. But you say you do not want it. Do you want us to impose it on you?"

The next day we were summoned to discuss matters again. [The Jin negotiator Pujienu] Xiangwen said, "The emperor [Aguda] has commanded that we cancel what we talked about yesterday concerning the Western Capital, since it was your court that broke the "crossing the seas" treaty. However, to give the [Song] Zhao emperor face, he will magnanimously grant him Yanjing and the six prefectures with their twenty-four counties. If you court's army enters Yan first, then our army will borrow the road to return home. But we still want the official money and goods belonging to Yan. If your country is not able to enter Yan, wait for our country to take it and give it to you."

At this time, the Jurchen had heard that Yang Keshi, Gao Yijian, and Guo Yaoshi had already entered Yan, which is why they spoke this way. They were establishing the basis for later conflict. Zhao Liangsi said, "The money and goods can be granted. However I fear it may be difficult to accept your borrowing the road."

Xiangwen said, "We can send someone back with you to the southern court to discuss the matter." Then he rose.

When Liangsi came back he looked pleased and composed a poem, . . .

The next day we went to the palace to take our leave. Xiangwen said, "We have already appointed Li Jing as envoy, Wang Yongchang as vice envoy, and Saluwu as negotiator. We wish to keep one of you two state letter envoys here to accompany our army into Yan and to guard the passes. When we borrow the road, we will deal with each other."

Liangsi started to sweat and could not reply. I touched his ear and said, "Since you are a man of Yan, the Jurchen are not afraid of you. If we cannot avoid it, I can request to stay. We should be calm in our hearts."

Liangsi hesitated, then answered, "There is no precedent for retaining an envoy."

Xiangwen said, "This is the emperor's idea."

That evening Aguda summoned us and to say goodbye. "Which of you two envoys will stay?" Liangsi answered that [the demand] was unprecedented. Aguda said, "Armies on the march do not follow precedents."

I answered, "If it must be, then let me stay. The principal envoy should return to report. I request to remain."

Subsequently we said our farewells. The next day Liangsi and Li Jing and the others left for the capital with the letters.[40]

Zhao Liangsi arrived back in Kaifeng with the Jin envoys on 1122/11/21, not long after news of the debacle at Yanjing. Huizong could not afford to let the envoys linger, and turned them around quickly. When he sent them back, besides a conciliatory state letter, he gave Zhao Liangsi two letters in his own hand about how to conduct the negotiations. The first brought up the fact that the tax revenue of the three prefectures of Ying, Ping, and Luan was not high and the harvest was undependable, so the payment of one hundred thousand units in silver and silk that Jin wanted would exceed the income from the prefectures. Huizong also proposed explaining that Song wanted to take the Western Capital to help defend against the Kitan ruler. The second letter went over the items that had previously been settled and reiterated his desire to preserve each of them, expressing a willingness to enhance the silk and silver payments if Ping and Luan prefectures were turned over to Song, and ending by saying that his letter could be shown to the Jurchen as evidence if necessary.[41]

In 1122/12/6, before the envoys reached Aguda, Jin forces moved on Yanjing, taking their hostage Ma Kuo with him. Despite the efforts of Yelü Chun's widow to rally resistance, the commanders and senior officials surrendered both the pass and the city itself to Jin without fighting. Thus, it was not Jin military superiority that allowed it to take Yanjing where the Song had failed, but the preference of the local officials, most of them ethnically Chinese, to surrender to Jin rather than to Song. Aguda sent Ma Kuo to inform Tong Guan of the Jin victory, giving him an escort of five hundred horsemen and a farewell gift of five saddled horses. The confidence of Wang Anzhong and others that the Chinese ethnicity of the local population would guarantee their support for Song had proved unfounded. Aguda kept most of the officials in their posts and assigned them the task of convincing the remaining Liao cities to submit. Yelü Chun's widow fled to Tianzuo's court, a journey that took ten months. When she arrived there, Tianzuo had her killed in a fit of rage.[42]

Zhao Liangsi and another Song envoy, Zhou Wuzhong, finally met Aguda on 12/15 and attempted to negotiate the return of the Yan-Yun region. Aguda refused and in the state letter sent back to Kaifeng accused Song of reneging on its agreement to attack Yanjing. Jin increased its demands to include not only the subsidy that Song had formerly paid to Liao, but the tax revenue of the Yan region. By now Aguda was no longer interested in any give-and-take. If Song wanted Ying, Ping, and Luan, he would not give them Yanjing.[43]

On the first day of 1123, the Jin envoy Li Jing arrived in Kaifeng with Aguda's new demands. Huizong met with them in Promoting Governance Hall a few days later. Huizong conveyed to them his pleasure with the success of the alliance and instructed them to see Wang Fu to negotiate the remaining issues such as the tax revenues from the Yan region. Out of Huizong's presence, the negotiations were tough, with each side arguing its position vigorously, just as they had at the Jin headquarters. The Jin envoys asserted that, because Jin had taken Yanjing on its own, it was reasonable to add the tax revenues to what Song would pay Jin. Wang Fu countered that the original agreement had made no mention of tax revenues. However, Wang Fu was willing to make concessions for the sake of keeping the alliance alive, and brought up the practical matter that silver and silk were easier to transport than tax revenue in grain and coinage. The Jurchen had no objection to receiving the tax revenue converted to silver and silk.[44]

Ma Kuo, in his own account, reported that after the Song envoys returned together with Li Jing and the other Jin envoys, Tong Guan questioned him, saying his account of the negotiations did not match Zhao Liangsi's. Ma Kuo was next sent to discuss matters with Wang Fu. Ma Kuo stressed to Wang Fu that, even though getting back this territory had been a long-term dynastic goal, because the Song failed to enter Yanjing before the Jin, they now faced a difficult situation and had to rethink the long-term consequences of their decisions. Ma Kuo outlined three possible courses of action. The best would be if they got all the territory, up to the easily defended passes, then even if they had to double their annual payments, they would benefit. But if the Jurchen would not cede Ping, Luan, and Ying prefectures, they could only increase payments a little, since they would have to build new fortifications to be prepared for a possible invasion. To accept the current Jin offer, which involved turning over only six prefectures but handing over all of the old tax revenue of the area, he saw as a clearly inferior strategy that dealt only with the current situation. To seek territory without considering the fiscal implications, he argued, was no strategy at all. Wang Fu, however, said the court had already decided on the strategy he placed lowest.[45]

In the first month of 1123, Wang Anzhong, one of the original proponents of the effort to take the Yan-Yun region, gave up his appointment on the Council of State to go to the front as prefect of Yanjing and pacification commissioner for Hebei and Hedong. Wang Anzhong, well known for his literary talent, had no battlefield experience. Guo Yaoshi was appointed as his deputy, but in fact ran the offices.[46]

The Jurchen now kept finding problems with the Song offers. Huizong thought he was honoring the Jurchen by writing out the state letter and appendix in his own hand, but the Jurchen became suspicious when they observed that the calligraphic style differed from earlier documents.[47] Huizong gave Zhao Liangsi, Ma Kuo, and Zhou Wuzhong an imperial brush instruction to make every effort to get the region past the mountains, but if that was unsuccessful to move to a new stage in the discussions. The draft of the treaty Jin offered mentioned only Yanjing and the prefectures of Zhuo, Yi, Tan, Shun, Jing, and Ji, directly surrounding Yanjing. The Jurchen finally agreed to cede Datong but only if Song would repay their military expenses. This agreement was added as an appendix to the official letter, and stated that Jin was handing over Datong as an act of generosity. The draft also stated that the two sides would not use kinship terms in addressing each other (which was a departure from Song–Liao practice). Song accepted the Jin draft, doing little more to it than add a preamble on the importance of observing mutual trust. The Jin version of the treaty added language not in the Song version, however, asserting that the Song had not fulfilled its commitment to attack the Liao.[48]

This treaty has been preserved in both Song and Jin sources. The oath-letter issued by Huizong begins by noting that the "great and holy august emperor of the Great Jin" had taken complete possession of the Liao and was now conferring on Song the territories of Yan that had been absorbed by Liao during the Five Dynasties. These were explicitly listed as Yanjing plus the prefectures of Zhuo, Yi, Tan, Shun, Jing, and Ji, and to include their subordinate counties and populations. The two hundred thousand ounces of silver and three hundred thousand bolts of silk that Song had previously paid to Liao it would now pay to Jin. In addition, they would pay one million strings of cash from the land tax of Yanjing, equal to about one-fifth to one-sixth of the revenue of the area. Neither side would send spies or retain fugitives from the other or in any way incite trouble along the border. If they needed to pursue a bandit across the border, they would first send written notice. Roads between the two areas, however, would be open.[49]

The treaty of 1123 was largely dictated by the Jin. Still, there was no reason for Huizong to feel aggrieved. The Song had invested extensively in diplomacy and more modestly in military mobilization, and in return had incurred both new fiscal responsibilities and new territory. After it was signed, Huizong's court probably still thought that what they had gained was more than adequate compensation for what they had spent. After all, ever since Taizong's failure to take Yanjing in 979 the Song had dreamed of regaining the Yanjing area. That goal had finally been achieved.

In the third month, Huizong received the Jin envoys in Promoting Governance Hall. Later, because they made repeated requests for a garden or "flower" party, Huizong arranged one. When they were taking their leave, they explicitly asked how much of a special reward Jin would be given, and when Huizong replied two hundred thousand, they tried to get him to increase it, but Huizong did not relent. After they were gone, Huizong talked to Zhao Liangsi and Ma Kuo about them, saying that their demands seemed never to end. Zhao Liangsi agreed that they were rapacious, thinking only of their own advantage. Ma Kuo added, "It has reached this point because our army has not been awe-inspiring." Huizong, we are told, said that the damage caused by the Jurchens' greed and violence was worse even than that of the infamous Huang Chao, who had rampaged across much of China in the final decades of the Tang dynasty. Huizong added that he would not have begrudged increasing the payment to a million if that would have pacified them. On the lighter side, Huizong mentioned that he had heard that Ma Kuo had literary talent, and Zhao Liangsi responded by telling him that Ma Kuo had a military *jinshi*, to which Ma Kuo responded in the appropriately humble way, saying he had benefited

from the educational institutions that Huizong had established. Huizong that evening rewarded Ma Kuo with an imperial brush edict
raising his official rank.[50]

On 1123/4/17, Tong Guan and Cai You entered Yanjing with the
Song army. Residents who had not fled or been moved out by the Jur-
chen lined the road holding lighted incense to welcome the new rulers.
Five days later, on 4/22, Tong Guan submitted a memorial announcing
the recovery of the territory, casting the events of the past several
years as a series of Song victories.[51] During the six months that the
Jurchen had occupied the city, they had thoroughly looted it, so to the
Chinese it seemed they were getting an empty city. After two days,
Tong Guan and Cai You departed for Kaifeng with their armies.

To celebrate the recovery of Yan, Huizong issued a general amnesty.
On 1123/5/7 officials gathered in Cultured Virtue Hall to offer their
congratulations and on 5/8 Huizong wrote in his own hand an edict
celebrating the return of the Yan-Yun region "in fulfillment of our
ancestors' long-standing ambitions," and rewarding all of the grand
councilors. On 1123/5/9 Wang Fu, for his part in leading the effort to
recover Yanjing, was promoted to the level Cai Jing had reached before
he retired. A few days later he was given a new house, bigger than the
one he had been given seven years earlier. When it was ready, Huizong
personally did the calligraphy for the name plaques on seven of the
buildings that made it up.[52]

On 1123/5/29, when Tong Guan and Cai You arrived back in Kaifeng, Huizong went to Spectacular Dragon Gate (in the center of the
north wall of the Old City) to watch the triumphal procession.[53] Tong
Guan and Cai You brought with them the turncoat general Guo Yaoshi,
whom Huizong treated as an honored guest, apparently hoping that a
non-Chinese general would be able to defend the northern border much
the way foreign generals had served the Tang. He gave Guo Yaoshi a
house and some serving women. Besides asking his leading officials to
entertain him, he invited him to visit some of the gardens in the palace, as well as Golden Brilliance Lake, where he arranged boat races to
entertain him (see Plate 14). When Guo Yaoshi expressed his appreciation, Huizong asked if he could assign him a task, and Guo Yaoshi
responded, "I am a man of the distant barbarian regions. Today I have
received the greatest favor in the world. I have already sworn to serve
to my death, even if Your Majesty sends me to walk through boiling

water or fire or face bare blades, I would willingly let my flesh and bones be ground up. Whatever the assignment, I will do it even if it costs my life." Huizong then brought up the one assignment Guo Yaoshi felt compelled to refuse: "Tianzuo is not finished. Could you take him for me, to eliminate the expectations of the people of Yan [for a revival of Liao]?" When Guo Yaoshi tearfully pleaded not to be asked to attack his former lord, Huizong instead rewarded him for his loyalty, wanting to win him over.[54]

On 1123/6/1 the retired Cai Jing submitted a memorial to congratulate Huizong on the conquest of Liao, an achievement unprecedented in the dynasty and an augury that great peace had finally arrived. He referred to Shenzong's frustrated military ambitions, Huizong's own promotion of the civil over the military, and concluded that heaven must have helped bring about these victories.[55]

On 1123/7/16 Tong Guan officially retired, reportedly because Huizong had not been pleased with him and Cai You after their return from Yan.[56] That same day, Wang Fu proposed a new, more elaborate title for Huizong, with references to both his activities promoting Daoism and his combination of military and civil achievements. Huizong wrote out in his own hand his response:

> I have succeeded to the most honored of positions; its title draws from the Three Kings and Five Lords [of ancient times], thereby commanding the armies of the nine regions. Far and near, all are my subjects. Heaven has given evidence of its approval in the orderliness of the four seasons and the appearance of auspicious omens. We have raised armies; Yan and Suo have submitted; all is united under heaven. This is due to the spirits of my ancestors and the blessings of the ancestral temples and altars of the soil. My father Shenzong passed on to me his plans and his many achievements; but how does my virtue come up to his? And yet you high officials maintain that the titles used for the Yellow Emperor of Yan and Yu of Tang are not good enough and want to add on to them overly pretty words of this declining age. This shames me deeply. Your request is not permitted.

Although the request was denied three times, and others, including Prince Kai, students from the Imperial Academy, and elders reiterated the request, Huizong never relented.[57] Still, it would seem that many people of the time thought he would enjoy the flattery.

In the ninth month (1123/9) Wang Fu reported to Huizong that auspicious mushrooms had been found growing in his home. In pondering its significance, he recalled that in prior year he had been given portraits of the Great Lord of Long Life and the Peaceful Consort of Nine-Splendored Jade Truth (the gods that had incarnated themselves as Huizong and Consort Liu Mingjie). He was therefore familiar with their appearance, and saw that the unusual fungus resembled them, which had to be an auspicious sign for the entire country. Huizong responded both by visiting Wang Fu's home to view the fungus himself and by giving him a hand-drafted edict. In it, after praising Wang Fu's virtue, Huizong touted his help in recovering Yan: "Since the Zhenghe period [1111–1117], the corner by the sea has been pacified and the spirits have responded. In all aspects of undertaking this great task and deciding on doubtful issues, you proved superbly capable. At that time, no one at court could decide on the plan to pacify the enemy; only you had the brilliance of foresight to help me decide." Even the plants were now responding to his virtue. Other sources, however, say that on this visit Huizong discovered the palatial luxury of Wang Fu's home, on a par with the palace gardens, and began to have doubts about his probity. Huizong got drunk that night and Wang Fu wanted him to stay overnight, leading to an incident when Wang Fu told the emperor's escort to go home without him and they refused unless they could see the emperor and he personally dismissed them.[58]

The New Territories

Absorbing the new northern prefectures strained the resources of the Song government. Chinese living in those parts of the Sixteen Prefectures not ceded to Song, worried about the Jurchens as their new rulers, were fleeing into Hebei, a region that had suffered from shifts in the course of the Yellow River and had little in the way of surplus resources.[59] The local authorities had difficulty feeding and controlling them. Many men joined self-defense militias, and the largest, labeled the Righteous Army, claimed to have one hundred thousand men. Banditry became so serious a problem that merchants were unwilling to travel into the area. On 1124/1/29 Ma Kuo was sent to Yanjing to discuss with Wang Anzhong how the new territories should be admin-istered and how to win over the local residents and help them recover from the war. But Jin was a menacing presence. In 1124/3 Jin sent an envoy to Yanjing to ask for two million piculs of grain that they said Zhao Liangsi had promised. Tan Zhen, the eunuch general in com-mand, refused the request, saying there had never been a formal writ-ten agreement.[60] Since famine had struck the area and Song soldiers there were not getting enough to eat, some even starving to death, Tan Zhen probably had no choice.[61]

The costs of the campaigns to take Yan and Yun and manage the refugees were enormous. Feeding nine thousand border troops and the fifty thousand soldiers in Guo Yaoshi's Ever-Victorious Army re-quired more than one hundred thousand piculs of grain a month.[62] The population in the capital and Henan and Hedong had already been overtaxed, so a new surcharge was added to the taxes imposed on other regions, called a service exemption fee and levied as twenty strings of cash per adult male. Even officials, imperial clansmen, and priests had to pay. The new tax raised twenty million strings of cash but created a lot of ill-will.[63] The epigraph to this chapter is from Cai Tao's lengthy description of the impact of this new tax on his father and on Huizong:

In 1122, because of the opening of the northern border, expendi-tures were exceptional. All the treasuries, both Privy Purse and government, were empty, much to Huizong's dismay. At the time Wang Fu was worried by the losses, so he took the advice of an old clerk to institute a service exemption fee throughout the coun-try. The service that one was being exempt from was the military service in Yan, which everyone should have contributed to, but they were now being allowed to give money instead. Once the hand-drafted edict was issued, tears appeared in Cai Jing's eyes, and one day when he saw Huizong, he said, "The present high of-ficials are not serving Your Majesty, who is wise and benevolent and nurtures the multitudes, extending benefits to the furthest reaches of the realm. Our earlier policies may have taken the trea-sures of the earth [mining] and gone after large merchants, but they never reached the farmers' fields. Today the high officials are raising money by grabbing food out of the mouths and rice bowls of poor peasants. Please do not do this." Huizong then regretted the decision and quickly ordered a revision, but it was of no help. From then on he was like a wooden puppet [without emotion, manipulated by others], and grew accustomed to transfers of land. There had been nothing this [draconian], not only in earlier reigns, but also earlier in Huizong's reign. At this time, the revenue from the service exemption fee came to sixty-two million strings of cash, which the court saved for emergencies. By the spring of 1125, it had been all used up except for six million strings. The authorities did not know how it had been spent. This is what Wang Fu secretly used for his own pleasures.[64]

Attributing the shortfall to Wang Fu is clearly hyperbolic; he could hardly have spent more than fifty million strings of cash for his own pleasure. Much more likely, it was sending the army to Yanjing and dealing with the refugees that exhausted the government's reserves. War is enormously expensive.

The Song government, however, was not in a position to cut back on its military posture. More horses were desperately needed, and the government set up a schedule of bonuses for officials who increased the number of horses raised in their jurisdictions. Because of friction between Tan Zhen and the Jurchens, Tong Guan was called back from retirement and sent to replace Tan Zhen at Yanjing in 1124/8.[65]

Realignments were occurring at court as well. After Li Bangyan and Cai You criticized him, Wang Fu was dismissed in 1124/11. Yuwen Cuizhong submitted a memorial on the huge fiscal burden of all the recent military campaigns and the impact this had had on the common people, who were being taxed without limit. Huizong's many edicts expressing his sympathy for the people had become empty texts, he argued. It was essential to make drastic cuts to spending to get it back to the level during earlier reigns. In response, Huizong appointed a budget commission headed by Cai You, Bai Shizhong, and Li Bangyan to try to identify waste in government spending. Tong Guan argued that the only real way to cut the budget was to reduce the number of people on the payroll, which had steadily increased.[66]

The next month, on Zhu Mian's advice, Cai Jing was brought back after four and a half years of retirement. He was to come to court every fifth day. This arrangement did not last long, however. Since he was nearly blind, he had to have his son Cai Tao handle business for him, and Li Bangyan and Bai Shizhong were uncomfortable with the power Cai Tao gained. In 1125/3 they convinced Huizong to dismiss Cai Jing. Huizong sent Tong Guan and Cai You to tell him to quit. Although he was already eighty *sui* and in poor health, Cai Jing did not readily agree. Tong Guan retained his high position through all of this. In fact, in the sixth month of 1125, he was promoted to prince, in accord with Shenzong's instructions that whoever recovered Yan should be enfiefed as a prince *(wang)*.[67]

The budget commission did not report until after Cai Jing had once more retired. Then, during the fourth through eleventh months of 1125, they issued a long series of proposals for cutting personnel and eliminating various fees, privileges, and wasteful practices. For instance, circuits and prefectures were told not to spend so much at the annual party to celebrate Huizong's birthday. At one point the commission complained about the way provincial officials would ignore new rulings, even ones that were identified as imperial brush edicts. The central government could prohibit all sorts of corrupt practices, but had limited means to enforce compliance to its rules at the local level.[68]

By this point, Jin had a new emperor. Early in 1124, when Song learned that Aguda had died a few months earlier, Huizong suspended court for five days and put on mourning garments. Aguda was succeeded by his brother Wuqimai, known as Jin Taizong (r. 1123–1135). Under Taizong, Jin was already proving a prickly ally. He was outraged when in late 1123 the Song accepted the offer of a former Liao official, Zhang Jue, to switch from Jin to Song, bringing the border prefecture of Ping and two others with him. Song was happy to get more prefectures and awarded Zhang Jue both money and titles, conveniently ignoring the provision in their treaty with Jin that prohibited either side giving sanctuary to the other's subjects. Jin, infuriated, took Ping prefecture back by force and demanded that Wang Anzhong, then in charge at Yanjing, turn over Zhang Jue's head, which he eventually did.[69] This step prevented a major break with Jin but made former Liao subjects wary of putting their trust in Song protection.

In the first month of 1125 Huizong sent a mission to congratulate the new Jin emperor Taizong on his accession. The report by the Song envoy Xu Kangzong is the only envoy's report to survive from

Huizong's reign. Xu Kangzong began by reporting that protocols established for such missions to Liao were followed closely. Besides the envoy and deputy envoy, the mission included eighty people, including a doctor, two interpreters, forty-five soldiers, and a variety of clerks, porters, grooms, and the like.[70] To carry their luggage, they had three carts, ten camels, and twelve horses. Gifts ranged from tea and fruit to three horses fitted out with saddles decorated with gold and silver and bridles and whips adorned with ivory and tortoise shell. The party left near the end of the first month of 1125 and returned in the eighth month, traveling 1,150 *li* inside Song borders, in 22 stages, and 3,120 *li*, in 39 stages, beyond Song borders.

Xu Kangzong described both the natural and cultural geography of the regions they traversed. He found Chinese spoken quite widely and used by Kitans, Jurchens, Xis, and Koreans to communicate with each other. He also saw many reminders of the recent wars. In the Yanjing area there had been a drought, and even though available supplies were channeled toward maintaining Guo Yaoshi's Ever-Victorious Army, the soldiers looked emaciated; in fact, 70–80 percent of them had died of starvation because relief supplies had arrived too late. As the mission got deeper into Jin territory, the density of population declined rapidly. One time, well into Jin territory, a Jin official prepared tents to receive and entertain the visitors. Sixty to seventy dancers performed to the music played by musicians employing a wide range of instruments. Xu Kangzong found the food strange and had a hard time with soups of mutton hearts or blood. Once when a host eating with him started bragging about the strength of the Jin, how it was unrivaled in the world, Xu Kangzong responded by saying Song was not weak, but to the contrary had a two-hundred-year history, a vast size, and a several-million-man army. Xu Kangzong did admit being impressed, however, when he finally reached the Jin court and saw the splendid halls that craftsmen had been building there. In the hall where the Jin emperor Taizong sat, the furnishings were luxurious, with golden goblets and ivory spoons.[71]

By the time Xu Kangzong returned and Huizong read his report, the evidence that the Jurchens were preparing for war with Song was unmistakable. All during 1125, Ma Kuo repeatedly sent reports to Tong Guan that his spies were sure that Jin was preparing to invade.[72] Tong Guan did what he could to prepare, but was reluctant to pass on such bad news to Huizong.

The Jurchens were now a more formidable foe than they had been when they first rose against Liao a decade earlier. During the wars against Liao, they had learned how to seize cities and fight infantry armies. Aguda's son Wolibu and his nephew Nianhan had learned not to be intimidated by the size of their opponent's forces and had mastered ways to manipulate and deceive the other party during negotiations, increasing their demands whenever they sensed their enemies wished to settle. Song had reason to be wary.

In the eleventh month of 1125 Huizong performed the major state sacrifice to heaven at the Suburban Altar. By early the next month, the court was receiving secret memorials from officials near the border that the Jin army had entered Song territory, but the councilors did not pass on the news to Huizong, in part wanting to spare him until all the rituals were complete.[73] Early the next month (1125/12/8), Li Ye, an administrative assistant of the fiscal intendant in Shaanxi, volunteered to go as an envoy to Jin and asked for thirty thousand ounces of gold in the hope that he could convince the Jurchens to withdraw. Huizong did not have that much gold ready, so he took two gold urns used in the ancestral cult, together weighing about ten thousand ounces, and had them melted down and made into bars.[74] Before Li Ye returned, however, things took a turn for the worse.

༄ DOES HUIZONG DESERVE the blame for the Fang La rebellion? Traditional historians certainly thought so. The outbreak of a rebellion proved that Huizong did significant damage to the state through his extravagances: people were so oppressed that they rose in revolt. Economic hardship undoubtedly helped the rebels recruit new followers, even if we should not believe the exact words that Southern Song sources put into the mouth of Fang La. How much of that hardship was new and how much was the result of recent government policies is more difficult to determine, but it probably should be granted that government policies had aggravated the situation.

Once Huizong was informed of the gravity of Fang La's revolt, he did not hesitate to send large armies under two of his most experienced generals. The rebellion itself was speedily put down. Its importance lies primarily in delaying the Song advance on Yanjing by more than a year, which gave Jin time to nearly complete its conquest of Liao. Had the Song army arrived a year earlier, Jin would have placed higher value on Song contributions to the war effort.

Even after Huizong saw that things were not going well, he did not give up. He persisted in doing what was in his power—reading memorials, soliciting the advice of those he trusted, meeting in person with his envoys, and writing out personal instructions to envoys to guide them through negotiations. Moreover, he used imperial resources as needed, even having gold sacrificial vessels melted down to use as bullion. He entertained his new allies lavishly and authorized a huge military force. It was not Huizong's refusal to get involved that led to the unraveling of the grand plans to expand the realm.

Did Huizong's decision to ally with Jin contribute to the destruction of Liao? Probably not. Song played very little role in the destruction of Liao; Jin was able to accomplish that itself, in no small part by getting Liao forces to change sides. The most one could argue is that Jin gained confidence because of its alliance with Song.[75] If the Song had instead cooperated with Liao to help it put down the Jurchen rebellion, possibly Liao might have managed to survive, but that outcome was not assured.

Distance made it difficult for Huizong and his councilors to manage both war and diplomacy from Kaifeng. Intelligence was often spotty. Sometimes the negotiations took place in Kaifeng, and the Song court could make sure that the agreement was satisfactory to them, but just as often the negotiations took place at the other court and Song envoys would have to make at least tentative decisions when new issues were raised. Military action, too, was very difficult to control hundreds of kilometers from the capital. It could not be assumed that a commander's report was a full and accurate account of what had taken place. All of these difficulties would continue to plague Huizong over the next couple of years.

Were there possibilities of saving the day later on, after the original agreement with Jin had been signed? Every time Song conceded to a new demand made by Jin, Jin seems to have raised its expectations of what it could get from Song. If Song had taken Yanjing, or even another of Liao's well-fortified cities, Jin generals might have hesitated before deciding to plunge so quickly into a massive campaign in north China.

15

Abdicating the Throne, 1125–1126

> I was formerly lord over all the land within the four seas and looked after the myriad people, but because my virtue was slight and I did not make the right choices, war has broken out and no one is safe.
>
> —*From Huizong's prayer of 1125/12/24*

On 1125/12/16 Tong Guan arrived in the capital, bringing with him news that the Jurchens had invaded. Tong Guan had learned this in Taiyuan, where Ma Kuo and his scouts brought him news of the invasion of the Jurchen armies into Hedong and Hebei under the generals Nianhan and Wolibu. Tong Guan was in Taiyuan because Jin had told him to meet them there so that they could turn over territories to him in the Datong region per earlier agreements. When he learned of the Jin army incursions, Tong Guan sent two emissaries to ask Nianhan for an explanation and was informed that the Jurchens were invading the Song because of the Zhang Jue affair and that only if Song ceded Hedong and Hebei and made the Yellow River the new boundary would Song be allowed to survive.[1] This was a declaration of war and Tong Guan, despite the pleas of the commander of the Taiyuan garrison, left immediately for Kaifeng to inform the court and to coordinate the Song response. Later Tong Guan's critics would call this act cowardly, but as he himself argued as the Song's highest general, and over seventy, his job was overall command, not the defense of a single city.[2] Sending an urgent message would not do because the councilors often did not show Huizong disturbing messages. Tong Guan had to see him in person.

The territory north of Taiyuan fell fairly quickly, but Taiyuan itself settled in for a long siege. In the east, defense was entrusted to the

421

Bohai general who had switched from the Liao to the Song, Guo Yaoshi, the man Huizong had entertained so lavishly two years earlier. The army Guo Yaoshi commanded, called the Ever-Victorious Army, had originally fought for the Liao and was made up of both Chinese and Bohai troops. Unfortunately for the Song, when Wolibu's troops defeated Guo Yaoshi's in a battle, rather than retreat, Guo Yaoshi decided to switch sides once again. Soon he was using his troops against the armies of other Song commanders. The next day, 1125/12/10, Yanjing fell, less than three years after Jin had turned it over to Song.[3]

On 12/19 Huizong issued a call for men in the Hebei and Yanjing areas to volunteer to help with the defense, promising opportunities for all with talent. He suspended the collection of plants and the manufacture of goods for the palace and ordered that funds set aside for those projects be redirected to Liang Fangping, the eunuch commander of the army defending Liyang, some one hundred kilometers northeast of the capital, who had been assigned the task of keeping the Jurchens from crossing the Yellow River. The experienced general He Guan, then in the capital, disagreed with this strategy. He told the grand councilor Bai Shizhong that it would be impossible for Liang Fangping to hold back the Jurchens, who had mobilized their entire country for this attack, and that it was dangerous to move troops needed for the defense of the capital so far away.[4]

The Decision to Abdicate

Discussions of what to do in this crisis were intense, both in open court sessions and in the corridors and offices where officials gathered. Among the ideas discussed at court at this time was giving over responsibility for safeguarding the capital to the heir apparent, Huizong's eldest son Huan, then twenty-five, while Huizong and a small group of senior officials would set up another base in a safer place, perhaps in the south, perhaps in Chang'an, the capital during the Han and Tang dynasties. Although some considered this running away, others saw it as prudent. When the Tang dynasty was threatened by the rebellion of An Lushan, Xuanzong and his court evacuated the capital, heading west into Sichuan, and as a consequence when the capital fell, the dynasty did not fall with it. Moreover, there was reason to think the Jurchens would rather raid deep into China than take over large stretches

of Chinese territory permanently. In the tenth century, when the Kitan had invaded and captured Kaifeng, they left after a few months,
taking their loot with them. Since no non-Chinese group had ever
held territory south of the Yangzi River, that part of the country
promised the greatest security. Preliminary steps were taken for a
transfer to the southeast, including the appointment of officials to
manage the move.[5] As a further step in that direction, on 1125/12/20,
Huizong wrote out an imperial brush edict, using a draft text supplied
by a Hanlin academician, appointing the heir apparent as governor of
the capital.[6]

Two envoys from Jin arrived just when the bad news was sinking in,
but the councilors did not dare bring them to court to see Huizong.
Instead the councilors Bai Shizong, Li Bangyan, and Cai You met with
them in the offices of the Department of State Affairs. The envoys, in
loud voices, announced that their emperor had invaded by two routes,
using the classical term for a just war, *diaomin fazui*, "to bring comfort
to the common people and chastise the guilty." When the Song officials asked what might be done, the envoys, again in booming voices,
told them that the only alternative was to give up the land and call
themselves subjects of Jin, or in other words, surrender.[7] This encounter convinced the ministers that they could procrastinate no longer.

Huizong, wanting to do something, issued a memorial placing the
blame for the disaster on himself. According to Yuwen Cuizhong, it
was his brother Yuwen Xuzhong who nudged Huizong to take this action and who drafted the edict. Xuzhong had been serving under Tong
Guan and had just returned to the capital with him. Although he had
served as an advisor to Tong Guan, he had not been a supporter of the
policy of allying with Jin and had submitted numerous criticisms of it,
which had earned him the enmity of Wang Fu.[8] Huizong's conversation
with Xuzhong is recorded in some detail:

> On this day the emperor summoned [Yuwen] Cuizhong's younger
> brother Xuzhong to the inner hall to discuss matters with the
> Council of State. A report had just arrived that Nianhan's army
> had set siege to Taiyuan. The emperor looked at Xuzhong and
> said, "Wang Fu did not use your idea to enfief the Kitan as a fron-
> tier barrier. Now the Jin army is advancing along two routes.
> What do you think can be done about the situation?"

Xuzhong said, "Despite the ferocity of the bandit soldiers, if an urgent call to arms is issued to summon soldiers from each of the circuits to come to our aid, it will unite the people. Let us rely on the accumulated goodwill built up by your ancestors. Your Majesty should be resolute and not dither. There is nothing to worry about. Under the current circumstances, it would be best to first issue an edict taking the blame on yourself, then root out evil practices. That way, you will gain people's support and heaven's favor will return. Then the generals can take up the resistance."

The emperor issued directives and told Yuwen Xuzong to draft the edict. Xuzhong said, "I did a draft last night, before I had your order, planning to present it today." The emperor told him to spread it out for him to read. . . . After Huizong read it, he said, "Each one of these can be put into effect right away. Now is not the time to hold back on reversing mistakes." Xuzhong bowed again, tears streaming down [his face].

Because the officials still had qualms, [Yuwen] Cuizhong pleaded to issue a yellow traced version of the edict. The emperor then issued an urgent summons for the department clerks and the people of the various courts to assemble in the executive office of the Department of State Affairs to make copies, add the seals and signatures, and send them out to be posted around the capital.[9]

This edict adopted the language of Huizong's critics: everything they have said about him, he now said about himself.

Two cycles of twelve years have passed since I, succeeding to my highly virtuous ancestors, was placed above the literati and common people. Despite the caution in my heart, my errors have been visible to the world. Mediocre myself, I inherited a flourishing dynasty. But the avenues for criticism were blocked, so that on a day-to-day basis I heard only sycophants. Favorites gained power and the greedy could do as they pleased. Wise and able scholars were caught in the proscription on factions and for years have not been able to influence political affairs. Taxes and impositions have exhausted the people's resources; military and labor service have worn out the army and levies. Many of the projects undertaken proved of no benefit. Extravagance became the fashion, depleting the sources of wealth. Yet profit-seekers still keep making demands. Even though the clothing and rations for the army have not yet been secured, those with more than enough to eat still enjoy the benefits of their wealth and rank. Ominous portents did not bring me to my senses. Nor did I recognize the resentment of the multitudes. The fault is all mine, but my regrets are too late.

Huizong then promised to do away with all government abuses. He admitted that in the past he had not been fair to those who offered honest criticism, but promised that this time would be different.

From today on, let heaven and earth bear me witness, in order to preserve the country there will be no more reversals. Given the current crisis, it is essential to communicate openly, without circumlocutions. We need all men of wisdom and courage to develop strategies to solve this calamity. I hope that the relief armies coming from the four regions will devise ways to repel the enemies at the two borders. May they remember the accumulated virtues of the kind and wise [rulers of the past] who looked after the world for over a hundred years.

Huizong then called for the prefectures to dispatch armies and men with military talent to volunteer their services. He promised to read all proposals himself and not to punish those whose plans did not work. Huizong also wrote in his own hand edicts abolishing many of his initiatives, including revisions of bureaucratic organization, the Music Bureau, the land set aside for Divine Empyrean temples, the system of Daoist offices, and the collection of flowers and rocks for gardens. Any funds that these agencies had were to be turned over to the general government treasury for military uses. The staff at the Northeast Marchmount, the Extended Blessings Palace, and Precious Registers Temple were all dismissed, as well ones at other parks that predated Huizong. The agency building homes for Huizong's sons was abolished and they would have to share homes.[10]

The next day, 1125/12/22, military commanders were given new assignments. Yuwen Xuzhong was appointed to supervise the defense in the Hebei and Hedong region. Yao Gu and Chong Shidao were summoned to bring their armies from the west to help defend the capital.

To prepare for a possible siege, rewards were offered to get people to bring grain into the city walls. At the same time, Li Ye was sent as an envoy to Jin in the hope of negotiating a truce before the capital was attacked.[11]

As these measures were being taken, some officials were beginning to discuss among themselves the possibility that the best course would be for Huizong to abdicate. This was a subject that required meeting Huizong face to face. One official who came to this conclusion was Li Gang, a 1112 civil service degree-holder who had served in capital posts until 1119 when he was transferred to a minor post in the far south because his memorial on the great flood of Kaifeng attributed it to letting yin forces gain too much strength. He had been brought back in 1125, however, and made vice minister of the Court of Imperial Sacrifices. Li Gang called on a friend, Wu Min, who had a higher office with better access to Huizong. Wu Min is elsewhere described as one of those in Cai You's faction who helped keep Huizong entertained.[12] According to Li Gang's record of their conversations, he told Wu Min that appointing the heir apparent as governor of the capital was an inadequate response: "Unless the throne is passed and the heroes of the empire summoned to join in national defense, how can the crisis be overcome?" He urged Wu Min to ask for an emergency audience, to discuss the matter frankly with the emperor, even at the risk of angering him. Wu Min asked about a regency, but Li Gang said it wouldn't do.

Wu Min did not get to see Huizong on 12/21 and had to wait until the next day:

> In attendance were the grand councilors Bai Shizhong, Li Bang-yan, the directors of the Bureau of Military Affairs Cai You and Tong Guan, and the vice councilors Zhang Bangchang, Zhao Ye, Yuwen Cuizhong, and Cai Mao. The pacification commissioner Yuwen Xuzhong and the military commissioner Wang Fan also participated.
>
> First the councilors were summoned to report, then they stepped back. Then Wang Fan came forward to report, then he stepped back. Then Wu Min came forward to report and said, "I would like to request some space." Huizong looked at the group of officials and they stepped back a little. Min then said: "The Jin ban-

dits have broken the treaty and violated order. How are you going to deal with it?"[13]

When Huizong asked Wu Min his idea, he responded,

> "I have heard that Your Majesty has already decided to take a trip. Is this so?" When Huizong did not reply, Min continued, "The way I figure it, now that the people in the capital have heard that the barbarians have invaded, they are shaken up. Some want to run away, some want to defend the city, some want to take this as an opportunity to return [from their posts to the court]. If these three types of people simultaneously try to [pursue their different strategies] for defense, the country will certainly collapse."
>
> Huizong said, "But what can we do?"
>
> Min said, "Since the barbarians entered, I have been praying privately at the imperial ancestral altars. In the past I had a dream, but I don't know if you would permit me to describe it to you or not."
>
> Huizong said, "Don't hold back."
>
> Min said, "In my dream, to the north of a river was a golden Buddha with a spiral topknot, so tall it reached up to the sky. To the south of the river was an iron basket covering a jade statue, which people called Mengzi. To the south of Mengzi was another river, and on its south was a steep mountain slope. I was on this. People called it Taishang (Supreme Upper) mountain. I explicated it for myself this way; north of the river is Hebei, south of the river is Jiangnan.[14] The Buddha is the Jin [=golden] people. What Taishang means, Your Majesty ought to know without my being explicit.[15] As for Mengzi, I discussed it with the secretariat drafter Xi Yi, who explained to me that the characters *meng zi* mean the first son."[16]
>
> When Huizong nodded, Min said, "Since Your Majesty understands its meaning, I will risk a myriad deaths [by speaking my mind]. Your Majesty has settled on a plan to take a trip. If by any chance those guarding are not firm and the travelers do not get to their destination [implied: you are captured or killed] , then what?"
>
> Huizong said, "That is exactly my worry."

Min said, "If Your Majesty grants those guarding full power to control those under them, then the defense will definitely be stronger, and if it is strong, then the travelers will reach their destination." Huizong was beginning to be swayed. Min continued, "Given that you understand the matter I just explained and are able to adopt my policy, I would venture to ensure your unlimited longevity. You have set up the Divine Empyrean for some years. The Great Lord of Long Life means the sage of unlimited longevity. But if the Great Lord of Long Life does not have the Lord of Green Florescence by his side, then how can the Great Lord of Long Life attain sagely unlimited longevity? The Lord of Green Florescence refers to the heir apparent."

Huizong was very pleased.[17]

Wu Min seems to have taken Huizong as someone who truly believed in the significance of dreams and turned to them when difficult decisions had to be made. He not only promised Huizong a long life himself, but assured him that he was preserving the Song intact:

Min said, "If Your Majesty is able to make this decision, then the central plains will be Chinese for the next several centuries. If you are not able to take this step, then the central plains for the next several centuries will be barbarian. The fate of the central plains for the next several centuries depends on you today." He also said, "Your Majesty, decide quickly. As I see it, you should not take more than three days. After three days, the situation of the defenders will be unsettled and incentives will not work. Once the barbarians arrive, this step [abdication] will no longer be of use."[18]

Huizong, knowing the Jin forces were expected in about ten days, agreed to Wu Min's proposal. Wu Min then recommended Li Gang and Huizong agreed to give him an audience the next day. The audience continued with the other grand councilors bringing up other matters. Finally Huizong dismissed everyone but Wu Min and Li Bangyan. Li had previously objected to the idea of abdication, but Huizong now told him to stop hesitating and also to appoint Wu Min to the Council of State. Then he turned to practical matters.

Huizong said, "I don't want to be called Senior Emperor; just use a single title like Lord of the Dao." He also said, "What day would do?"

Min said, "I submitted to you that the plan wouldn't work if three days passed."

Huizong then calculated cyclical characters for the days and said, "Tomorrow will be good. You and Li Bangyan should come together." Huizong said, "Which would be more convenient, living in the palace or outside it?"

Bangyan said, "I fear that living in the palace in the end will not be convenient."

Huizong said, "Is there no need to claim illness?"

Min said, "Your majesty, with the utmost sincerity, is making a major policy decision. [An excuse] is not needed."

Huizong said, "Let me think about it some more."[19]

The next day, according to another source, Li Bangyan and the other grand councilors finally showed Huizong the communication Tong Guan had received from Jin that used extremely derogatory language in referring to Huizong, much like the language both Huizong and Jin used in referring to Tianzuo when they were trying to conquer Liao. Rather than submit it immediately to Huizong, after he got back to Kaifeng Tong Guan conferred with the other high officials on how to handle it. After the edict was issued calling for criticism and proposals, Li Bangyan said the message from Jin should be submitted as a wake-up call to Huizong.[20] If Li Bangyan already knew Huizong was contemplating abdication, this letter would have helped push him over the edge. After he read it, we are told, Huizong wept but said nothing. Finally he told his grand councilors to come back that evening.[21] Meanwhile, he continued to make plans with Wu Min for his abdication. He gave Wu Min an audience in Jade Splendor Pavilion.

After the grand councilors finished their reports and stepped back, Huizong called for Li Bangyan and Wu Min. He said, "The plan is set. Today is good." He took out a document and put it down. Min picked it up respectfully. It was Huizong's own list, in his own hand, of what needed to be done, for instance that he would live outside at the Dragon Virtue Palace, and the empress at the Western Garden of Gathered Views, that [his son Kai] the Prince of Yun would no longer be in charge of the capital security office, that Wu Min would be appointed vice director of the chancellery, that eunuchs who accompanied him to Dragon Virtue Palace would be executed if they exceeded their authority, and the like. Huizong had dealt thoroughly with everything himself.

Huizong said, "I must use the excuse of illness. I am afraid of disorder breaking out."

Min said, "That would also be fine."

Huizong said, "Just call me Lord of the Dao."

Min said, "I request to call you the Senior Emperor."

Huizong said, "You shouldn't be a stickler for ancient ways." He also said, "Who will draft the edict?"

Li Bangyan said, "Academician Wu Min."

Huizong said, "Very good. I want you to say, 'Internally I am not able to manage governmental affairs, externally I am not able to repel the barbarians.' Also say, 'I by this act am first accepting heaven's will, second bringing peace to the ancestral temples, and third serving the people.' He also said, "My intention lies in planning for the benefit of the central plains for several centuries, as you said yesterday." Min's tears were flowing as he accepted the edict and withdrew to wait at the base of the veranda.

The councilors then reported on other matters. Huizong said to Cai You, "I used to have a resolute nature. I didn't expect minor enemies to dare . . ." He grasped Cai You's hand and suddenly his *qi* was blocked and he lost consciousness, falling off the throne. The nearby officials quickly called to his attendants to lift him, and they got him to the eastern chamber of Preserving Harmony Hall. After the group of officials discussed what to do, medicines were brought and he suddenly revived a little. He raised his arm, looking for paper and ink. With his left hand he wrote, "I have lost half my body. How can I deal with great matters?" The high officials said nothing. Huizong again wrote, "Why don't you gentlemen say anything?" Those around him looked at each other, but no one spoke. So he wrote himself: "The heir apparent should ascend the throne as emperor. I will be the Lord of the Daoist Teaching and retire to live in Dragon Virtue Palace/Temple." He also wrote to Wu Min, "I selected you myself. Don't abandon me today. Let me call on you to draft the edict."[22]

At that point the heir apparent and Wu Min were summoned. Wu Min submitted the draft requested, and Huizong edited it, changing some of the pronouns so that in the middle he shifted from the imperial "I" to an ordinary "I." Bai Shizhong was still resisting, however, so at the end of the sheet, Huizong wrote several times, "Vice councilor, take care of it," until Bai Shizhong finally took it.

It proved more difficult to get the heir apparent Prince Huan to play his assigned role:

The heir apparent wouldn't accept the mandate. Tong Guan and Li Bangyan held the imperial robes, but the heir apparent rose and pushed them off, not daring to accept them. Huizong also with his left hand wrote, "If you do not accept, you are unfilial."

The heir said, "If I accept, then I am unfilial."

Huizong again wrote summoning the empress. When she arrived, she told the heir, "The emperor is old. He and I wish to entrust our lives to you." He still insistently declined. Huizong then instructed the eunuchs to carry the heir to Blessed Tranquility Hall and put him on the throne. The heir was definitely unwilling to walk, so the eunuchs forcibly carried him. The heir struggled with them, almost losing his breath. After he recovered they resumed carrying him to the western chamber of Blessed Tranquility Hall, where the grand councilors met and congratulated him. He was then carried into Blessed Tranquility, where he still resisted mounting the throne. At that time, the hundred officials had been summoned to assemble in Hanging Hem Hall, but once he was there, because the sun was fading and the hour late, the general view was not to delay, and the new emperor took the throne.[23]

Other sources record Prince Huan's resistance in just as convincing terms: Qinzong (as he can be termed from this point on) was not performing the ritual of declining three times to show his modesty, but genuinely dreaded taking over in the middle of a crisis.[24]

Huizong's edict abdicating the throne on 1125/12/25 was credited to Wu Min from early on, but apparently Huizong copied it out in his own hand (his left hand?). It does not include the specific phrases Huizong proposed, but the spirit is similar. It reads:

> Despite my lack of virtue, I have been depending on the spirits of heaven and earth to protect the ancestral altars, and the country has been a peace for twenty-six years. For a long time I have been longing to turn over this heavy burden inherited from my sagely [forebears]; day and night I worry, unable to feel at ease, working and fretting till I became ill. Because of these worries about the ten thousand things, I have made up my mind to take this major step. The heir apparent Huan is endowed with intelligence, and day after day, month after month, has acquired a reputation throughout the realm for filial piety, friendliness, warmth, and cultivation. Heir apparent for ten years, his education and training has reached the sages' classics. It is appropriate to follow tradition and entrust him with the altars of the grain and soil. This fulfils the hopes of both heaven and the people; I would not dare do this for personal reasons. Heir apparent Huan should ascend the throne as emperor. Both military and civil affairs should be put into his hands. I will use the title Lord of the Dao and live in my former palace. I will devote myself to the Dao. I am gladly relieving myself of this heavy burden and entrusting to him the sacrificial vessels. I rely on the loyalty and goodness of the civil and military personnel to come together to achieve long-lasting good order.[25]

Huizong made up his mind to abdicate rather suddenly, and probably had not thought through all of the consequences for himself or those associated with him. By choosing to be addressed by a Daoist title and to live in a palace that had been converted to a Daoist temple, he was signaling that he was entering a phase of his life where his religious devotions would be more central to his identity and occupy more of his time.[26] Probably he assumed that, once others had taken care of the crisis, he would lead a quiet but comfortable life in an elegant temple garden, with plenty of books, priests, and other company to make life enjoyable.

In these stressful circumstances, at least according to one account, Huizong turned to his faith in Daoism. Yue Ke wrote that, on the night before he abdicated, Huizong went to the Daoist temple within the

Palace City, to its Jade Void Hall, which was where he regularly made offerings to Daoist divinities. "There he made a hundred bows and secretly prayed to lengthen the dynasty by sacrificing himself. When the night reached the fifth watch, he burnt the prayer. The palace ladies and eunuchs only heard the sound of praying but didn't know what it was about." About three months later, he showed Li Gang a copy of the prayer. In it he wrote:

> Because I worry about the ancestral temples, the temples of the soil and grain, and all the people, I have already transferred the Great Seal to my heir in order to conform to heaven's desires above and to stop the armies below, in the hope that those near return and those far off become obedient, the world becomes peaceful, the dynasty has unlimited blessings, and those inside and outside enjoy the pleasures of peace.
>
> If in this way the enemy soldiers put down their weapons, after there is general peace, I will with all my heart observe the Dao and happily live in reclusion. May heaven be my witness, I do not dare to lie. Once the situation is settled, it will be a great sin to covet my old responsibilities . . .
>
> When [the ancient sage kings] Yao of Tang and Shun of Yu took the blame on themselves, things suddenly flourished. Let heaven grant me the heart of such sages![27]

Although many sources report simply that Huizong collapsed, the fullest version depicts him faking a stroke in order to make it easier for his councilors to accept his decision. As there is no sign that he had difficulty speaking or walking in the days that followed, it seems unlikely that he actually had a stroke (and impressive that he could write legibly with his left hand). At the time it was apparently widely thought that Huizong's officials had forced him to abdicate. According to the biography of Li Xijing, who was one of the officials assigned to Huizong after his abdication, a year after the abdication Huizong told him that the common view that the abdication was the work of Wu Min was wrong. It was his own idea, Huizong told Li Xijing, and if he had not been willing to do it, no one would have dared to bring it up. Huizong also said that others thought he was afraid of heaven's wrath and therefore abdicated, like Ruizong in the Tang, but that also was incorrect. In fact, he had been thinking of abdicating for some time.[28]

Why did some officials want Huizong to abdicate and others resist? Those close to Huizong definitely fared much worse after his abdication. Although some may have realized that they would lose power, there is no evidence that any of them foresaw the extent of the political revenge that would be unleashed by the change in administration.

Those who favored his abdication could have done so for at least two reasons. The first would be that they did not think Huizong had the personal qualities to handle the crisis. Wu Min seems to have thought that he would be easily swayed by arguments phrased in terms of Divine Empyrean Daoism. It would seem his reading of Huizong was of someone with his head off in Daoist mysteries. Since he is described as one of the coterie around Cai You who spent time with Huizong, he may have been right. But it is also likely that men like Li Gang and Wu Min thought they were more capable of handling the crisis than Huizong, and thought that a new, younger emperor would be more likely to go along with them than one who had been on the throne a quarter century. They may also have thought that the armies, officials, and the people at large would be easier to rally behind the throne with a new emperor on it, one who deserved no blame for the crisis.

The Trip South

Li Gang told Wu Min that if Huizong abdicated, Jin would withdraw its armies. Wu Min told Huizong that if he abdicated, the central plains would remain part of China for centuries to come. Their arguments were persuasive, but their predictions proved wrong.

Song envoys reached Wolibu's camp to request a truce on 12/29, just four days after the abdication. Guo Yaoshi urged Wolibu to turn them down and to continue south, assuring him that Kaifeng was a much richer prize than Yanjing.[29] Bypassing major walled cities that would have slowed them, the Jurchen forces moved quickly toward the Yellow River.

The first day of the new year, 1126, Qinzong went to the Bright Hall to receive the congratulations of his officials and promulgate a new reign name, Jingkang (Secure and Vigorous). The very next day the seven thousand troops guarding the north side of the Yellow River and the thirty thousand guarding the south side failed to stem the Jurchens' advance. Although the Song had burned the pontoon bridge before retreating, by seizing every available boat, the Jurchen army was able to cross in six days.[30]

Preparations for a siege entered high gear. On 1126/1/2 Qinzong announced that Huizong would leave the capital to visit the shrine to Laozi at Bozhou (Anhui). Around this time six to seven thousand of the women who had served as palace ladies under Huizong were dismissed, including all the female musicians. On 1/4, at night, with the situation critical, Huizong and his party left the capital by boat. With him were Empress Zheng and most of his children and about a hundred attendants. Three of the officials who had served Huizong the longest and in the most personal capacities accompanied him: Tong Guan, Cai You, and Zhu Mian.[31] Tong Guan was perhaps the most experienced military commander, but it is very unlikely that those around Qinzong would have wanted him to lead the defense even if he had volunteered to stay. For these three to leave with Huizong expedited the transition to a new administration.

Some officials, such as Cai Xiao and Bai Shizhong, urged Qinzong to withdraw to Chang'an, the capital of the Han and Tang dynasties, arguing that he could raise an army there to defeat Jin. Huizong also saw the sense of that plan, and Qinzong seemed attracted to it as well. Other advisors urged Qinzong to stay, including Huizong's youngest brother Ssi, the king of Yue. Even leaving to lead an army in emulation of Emperor Zhenzong in 1004 would be unwise, his uncle argued. No place was better fortified than the capital, but defending it required a determined populace. To reassure his subjects, Qinzong should instead appear before them at Harmony Revealed Gate to give visible evidence that he was still with them. Another who pleaded with Qinzong to stay was Li Gang, who had become a close advisor. Impressed with Li Gang's passion, Qinzong put him in charge of defense of the capital even though he had no military experience. The old Music Bureau buildings were made his headquarters, and he was given ten thousand strings of cash, ten thousand ounces of gold, and ten thousand bolts of silk for expenses, as well as a sizable staff.[32]

Qinzong could not devote all of his attention to defense matters because people were clamoring to punish those whom they considered responsible for the crisis. Once Qinzong took the throne, the anti-reform faction expected to get their turn, as they had when Empress Dowager Gao took over on Shenzong's death. Just days after the accession, the Imperial Academy student Chen Dong called for the execution of Huizong's leading officials, including ones no longer in office, such as the eighty-plus Cai Jing, relatively inactive since 1120. Chen Dong labeled them the "Six Traitors," a label that stuck (the list included Cai Jing, Wang Fu, Zhu Mian, and the eunuchs Tong Guan, Liang Shicheng, and Li Yan).[33] Also in Qinzong's first week on the throne another official submitted a memorial blaming problems for the last several decades on Cai Jing's policy of employing only his own partisans and allowing no dissension at court. He called for Cai Jing's execution. In response to calls like these, the property of Wang Fu was confiscated.[34]

Although there were complaints that the walls and towers had not been kept in good repair, Kaifeng had enough troops and supplies to withstand a siege. Altogether about ninety-six thousand troops were available to defend the city. Li Gang positioned twelve thousand troops armed with crossbows and catapults on each of the four walls. Another ten thousand were assigned to defend the Yanfeng granary with its four hundred thousand piculs of stored grain and beans. He also put ten thousand soldiers at Morning Sun Gate on the eastern wall of the New City. He held about twenty-eight thousand soldiers in reserve.[35]

Wolibu's army arrived on 1126/1/7 (Nianhan's army had been held up trying to take Taiyuan). That same day Li Ye returned from his month-long mission to report that the Jin could not be defeated; he urged the court to sue for peace. Qinzong promptly sent envoys to negotiate with Wolibu even though Li Gang thought that the Song could hold out. Qinzong told the envoy to offer money rather than land, as much as 3.5 million. He also had him make an immediate gift of ten thousand ounces of gold. By 1/10 the envoys had given tentative agreement to an increase in the annual tribute of two million strings of cash and a special indemnity of five million ounces of gold, fifty million of silver, two million lengths of silk, as well as ten thousand horses, oxen, and mules and one thousand camels. In addition, the three prefectures of Taiyuan, Zhongshan, and Hejian would be turned over to the Jin and an imperial prince and a grand councilor would serve as hostages.[36] On hearing these terms, Li Bangyan urged Qinzong to accept while Li Gang argued that such appeasement would make the Jin more dangerous in the future. Qinzong tried to get the indemnity reduced but otherwise promptly accepted Jin terms. Zhang Bangchang and Prince Gou were sent to serve as the hostages. Finally, on 1/15, Wolibu agreed to the relatively token change in the amount of the annual payments, and the treaty was signed. Four days later Chong Shidao and his armies arrived from the west. Not all of the court officials were happy to see a settlement; on 1126/1/27 Li Gang submitted a memorial arguing that although the Jin army was very strong, they did not have more than thirty thousand crack troops, since more than half of their troops were not Jurchens, but of Xi, Kitan, or Bohai ethnicity. The relief armies that had just arrived, by contrast, had two hundred thousand men.[37]

Although relieved that they would not have to endure a long siege, the capital was thrown into an uproar trying to raise the truly huge sum of gold and silver, equal to 180 times the annual payments that Song had been paying to Liao. The government treasuries had large quantities of copper cash, but the Jurchen wanted gold and silver, in much shorter supply. Everyone who had received gifts of gold or silver from the throne, including all the princes, Daoist officials, court musicians and artists, and so on, were to turn it over at the Yuanfeng Treasury. All palaces and imperially sponsored temples, as well as the Kaifeng prefectural offices were to turn over any gold and silver they had to the main treasury. Huge sums were confiscated from Wang Fu's house—more than seven thousand bolts of cloth and ten million strings of cash—but a third of that was looted by people who forced their way in during the inventory. By 1126/1/20, the besieged Song court sent to the Jin camp more than three hundred thousand ounces of gold and twelve million ounces of silver.[38] When that still was not enough, the government ordered any families owning gold or silver to turn it in to one of several collecting points. They would be compensated later at the rate of 20 strings of cash for each ounce of gold and 1.5 strings for each ounce of silver. Informing on those who concealed their gold or silver was rewarded at a rate of two-tenths of the concealed gold and one-tenth of the concealed silver. On 1/26, the court sent the equivalent of another five hundred ounces of gold and eight million ounces of silver, with much of it made up of jewelry and utensils collected from the populace. There was reason to rush; on 1/27 it was reported that the Jurchens were excavating the tombs of imperial consorts, princes, and princesses.[39] Finally, on 2/10 the last of the gold and silver was delivered to the Jurchen army camp and the following day, the Jurchens departed, unexpectedly taking a prince (Huizong's fifth son, Prince Shu) with them. The pressure on Kaifeng was relieved, but not the pressure on the Song, since these negotiations made no mention of the second Jurchen army still surrounding Taiyuan, which occasionally struck further south toward Luoyang.

Qinzong's advisors included both hawks and doves, both those who believed the best hope lay in showing Jin that the Song could not be pushed around, and those who thought it would be possible to reach a stable peace with the Jurchens through negotiation and adherence to treaties. The appeasers had held sway as long as the Jurchens were at the gates of Kaifeng, but after the Jurchens withdrew in the second month of 1126, the proponents of standing up to the Jurchens gained dominance at court. The day after the Jurchens withdrew from Kaifeng, Yang Shi, the chancellor of the Imperial Academy, reproached the court for so readily turning over to the Jurchens three northeastern prefectures. The relief armies that had not been in place when the Jurchens first appeared were now in place, so the balance of power had changed. Moreover, because the Jin had violated the treaty by taking Prince Shu with them, Song had no obligation to fulfill its part of the bargain and turn over the three prefectures. Rather, the Song should go on the offensive. Yang Shi also advocated executing the general Yao Gu for failing to relieve the siege at Taiyuan. Li Gang took similar tough stands and advocated that the Song send troops to "accompany" the Jin troops on their return home, meant to both harass them and keep them from pillaging the countryside. Qinzong authorized one hundred thousand troops, instructing the generals to keep their eyes open for chances to attack. "The Jin are returning home heavily laden, their many carts fully loaded, and they have countless captive women, adding to their high opinion of themselves. If we attack them, we will surely be successful. Our generals and soldiers are eager to fight."[40]

In the meantime, when Nianhan, still besieging Taiyuan, heard of the indemnity Wolibu had received to leave Kaifeng, he demanded an indemnity for his troops, which the commander of Taiyuan refused. Nianhan then sent part of his army on raids south, giving the Song court, in their own minds, further reason to abrogate the agreement with Jin. Qinzong appointed Chong Shidao's younger brother Shizhong to defend Zhongshan and Hejian in Hebei. When Wolibu arrived and found Chong Shizhong ready to defend the region, he continued north with his army.[41] For a while it seemed like putting up a fight might work.

A Forced Return

During the month when Kaifeng was most threatened, Huizong and his party were making their way southeast. The first stages were rough; Huizong rode on a boat carrying bricks and tiles, even on a mule, before his party was able to requisition government boats. They had not brought enough provisions, which they had to secure from local people. Still, by 1/15 Huizong and his party had reached Zhenjiang on the far side of the Yangzi River.[42]

The men who had served in high posts under Huizong but had not accompanied him south became the targets of the first purges. On 1/24 Wang Fu was stripped of his posts and sent into exile. When he was a few dozen *li* from Kaifeng, he was executed and his head was sent back to the capital in a box. Because Qinzong did not think it looked right to be executing high officials so soon after taking the throne, he had the word spread that bandits had killed Wang Fu. Before long, however, the high-ranking eunuch Li Yan was sentenced to death and his property confiscated.[43]

By the time Huizong had been gone three weeks and negotiations with the Jurchens were in progress, calls for his return began to be voiced. The prime motive behind these calls was the desire to punish Huizong's leading officials, several of whom were in his entourage. Some of the more paranoid critics spread rumors of a separatist plot on the part of the "mobile palace." Chen Dong, the Imperial Academy student who had coined the term "Six Traitors," submitted a memorial that catalogued Liang Shicheng's crimes, which led to the eunuch's demotion and suicide. In the memorial Chen Dong also accused Cai You, Tong Guan, and Zhu Mian of kidnapping Huizong and taking him south against his will. Chen Dong wanted them brought back to be punished. In his view it was particularly dangerous to let the mobile palace get to the southeast, since Cai Jing's faction was strong in that region and might try to establish an independent state there. He insisted that Qinzong should write out an edict in his own hand and send it to Huizong, "inviting" him to return to the capital. Chen Dong argued against those who said the Jurchen posed a greater threat. "Inner troubles" of evil officials are more serious than outer ones of barbarian enemies, he asserted. He claimed forcing Huizong back would not be unfilial since the physical separation between Qinzong and his father made it difficult for Qinzong to serve Huizong in the way expected of a filial son.[44]

A week or so later, Chen Dong organized large numbers of university students and general residents of the capital to put pressure on Qinzong, upset that he had dismissed Li Gang and the general Chong Shidao.[45] Reportedly tens of thousands of people assembled outside the gate of the palace and knelt. They soon were beating palace eunuchs who came out to talk to them, killing a dozen or more before soldiers were able to establish order. Qinzong agreed to reappoint Li Gang and Chong Shidao, and Li Gang mounted the gate tower to try to calm the crowd.[46]

Qinzong had not proven a very decisive ruler so far, and Chen Gongfu thought part of his problem was qualms about his filial responsibilities to his father. In the memorial he submitted on 2/14, he brought up the passage in the *Analects* 19.18 that presents the ability to maintain a father's government as the height of filial piety, but argued nevertheless that Qinzong should dismiss those officials who had served under Huizong, including the ones who had urged him to abdicate like Wu Min and Li Bangyan. Moreover, although it was appropriate while he was a prince to decline responsibility, as emperor he should take the lead to show toughness.[47] Chen Gongfu argued that Huizong himself at the end had come to recognize that those around him were evil. Thus Qinzong, by getting rid of ministers who had served Huizong, would be doing what Huizong would have done. Qinzong undoubtedly could see through this—emperors for centuries had routinely taken on the blame when anything went wrong, from comets to solar eclipses, droughts to uprisings, but their officials did not normally act as though they really meant everything they said. Moreover, it was more than a week after he had issued the edict of repentance that Huizong himself selected the officials to accompany him on his trip south. Still, by arguing that Huizong had come to his senses at the end, Chen Gongfu was giving Qinzong a way to claim that demoting, banishing, and executing Huizong's leading officials was a filial act.

Memorials impeaching Huizong's leading officials kept pouring in, and one after the other they were demoted. Prime targets were Cai Jing, Cai You, and other Cai relatives. But even less obvious targets like Yuwen Xuzhong and Wang Anzhong were demoted and banished. At the same time, honors were restored to leading anti-reformers, including the long-dead Sima Guang.[48]

Our main evidence of what Huizong's party was doing during the first month or two it was away comes from the writings of those bitterly opposed to Huizong's administration, who wanted the group brought back so that the ringleaders could be punished. How much to credit their accusations, therefore, is uncertain. Wang Zao wrote that the mobile court issued its own orders, made its own appointments, and redirected the relief armies, all causing confusion in command. Besides, the mobile court was expensive, using up six thousand strings of cash a day, and some of the scoundrels associated with it were proposing that palaces be built and parks be purchased, all very costly.[49]

In the midst of all this overhaul of the administration, on 3/1 Qinzong sent an official who had served under Huizong, Song Huan, to deliver a letter to Huizong asking him to return.[50] Qinzong's court, however, was not in full agreement on how much force to use to get Huizong back and on how real the rumors were that he or those around him were setting up an alternative government far from Kaifeng. The best evidence we have of the sorts of discussions that were taking place among officials in the capital is a long memorial that the mid-rank official Wang Zao sent to the grand councilors. Since he was not addressing Qinzong, he could use franker language in discussing what many clearly felt was the threat of the "mobile palace." Wang Zao did not conceal his disdain for Huizong. If, when the barbarians had first invaded, Huizong out of shame and fear had worked with Qinzong "to wipe away the humiliation to the dynasty, and soothe the hearts of the army and people," then it would be appropriate for Qinzong to invite Huizong back into the palace and consult with him morning and evening. Since Huizong had left when the siege was imminent, however, without even saying when he would return, Qinzong had no obligation to discuss policies with him. And Wang Zao was even angrier at the entourage who had accompanied Huizong, who had left for their own safety.[51] That these men had gone unpunished,

Wang Zao claimed, weakened the credibility of Qinzong's court. He recommended sending a current grand councilor to invite Huizong back, but also proposed dealing directly with the military and civilian personnel attached to the mobile court. He suggested offering rewards to those who cooperated and threatening death to those who did not. If Qinzong's sincerity did not move Huizong, an even tougher approach was warranted: "If scoundrels still dare to obstruct things, then identify the worst among the officials of the mobile palace, from the commissioner on down, and replace them. Once those treacherous conspirators are gone, and the retired emperor hears upright words every day, he will not tarry any longer." Wang Zao did not discount the possibility that everything would be fine once Qinzong and Huizong were together again, but wanted to convince Qinzong that he had to remember his other responsibilities and make sure that only one court was issuing orders. Two days after Wang Zao wrote this memorial, Qinzong sent another letter to Huizong, again asking him to return. He had one of his own brothers carry it, perhaps to remind Huizong that this was a family matter.[52]

As the capital recovered from the threat of a siege, tension between the two courts abated a little. On 1126/3/15 Huizong sent a letter to Qinzong, saying that the recent visit of Qinzong's envoy Song Huan had helped clarify matters and smooth relations. To try to reduce the paranoia of so many of the officials at Qinzong's court, Chen Gongfu submitted another memorial expressing his doubts about the rumors of separatist traitors seizing control of Huizong. To reassure Qinzong that he would not go down in history as an unfilial usurper, Chen Gongfu argued that there was no grounds for comparing Qinzong's relationship to Huizong to the Tang case of Suzong and Xuanzong, an analogy others must have been citing. He had only taken the Great Seal after his father had repeatedly instructed him to, not at all like Suzong who set himself on the throne while his father was elsewhere. "Even a thousand or ten thousand years from now, no one will doubt [your motivations]."[53] Chen Gongfu tried to convince Qinzong not to worry that Huizong would be upset with him for demoting and executing so many of his top officials. "These acts were all done with the dynasty in mind and were in accord with popular opinion, and were a way to follow through on the retired emperor's edict." Moreover, he argued, Huizong is a kind person and the father–son relationship a natural one: "Is the retired emperor closer to you or closer to his officials? In my opinion, no one is closer to him than Your Majesty." Chen Gongfu worried, though, that Qinzong had not selected an adequately diplomatic official to carry his message to Huizong, and wanted someone else sent. "Should by any chance the retired emperor harbor the slightest suspicion, [the envoy] could immediately in an appropriate way earnestly and fully describe Your Majesty's true filial sincerity and item by item explain that there is no difference between his edict of last year and the intentions behind your recent actions."

Chen Gongfu urged a grand show when Huizong returned to the capital:

> The ritual of welcoming him should be done on a grand scale. Your Majesty should take the imperial carriage and go in person to welcome him at the suburbs. The empress, consorts, princesses, and imperial relatives, down to the ministers, officials, scholars, commoners, and elders, should all come to meet him, so that he sees the contrast between the fluster of his past departure and the honor of his present return, and how this was possible only because Your Majesty bore the heavy burden entrusted to you, ameliorating the difficulties caused by the invasion, stabilizing the capital, restoring the administration, and gladdening the people.

Should these courtesies not be enough to win over Huizong, once Huizong was back, Qinzong could control who talked to him. "You should select from among your officials scholars of probity known for their virtuous behavior, scholarship, filiality, and integrity to act as advisors to the retired emperor. They should attend him every day, joining him when he is at leisure, leading his sagely mind toward metaphysical truths so that he frees himself from the burden of worldly affairs."[54]

Another person who worried about the danger of aggravating the friction between the two courts was Li Gang. At an audience with Qinzong, he objected to plans to send Nie Shan with soldiers to arrest key officials in Huizong's entourage such as Tong Guan, Cai You, and Gao Qiu. He also brought up the example of Suzong and Xuanzong to make his case, reminding Qinzong that Suzong had not gone after

Xuanzong's former officials out of concern for how Xuanzong would have taken it.[55] This was an apt comparison because Tang contemporaries had been as quick to blame the An Lushan rebellion on the former powerful chief minister Li Linfu as Song contemporaries were to blame the Jurchen invasion on Cai Jing and Tong Guan. When Qinzong asked what alternative he had, Li Gang suggested demoting and transferring Huizong's top officials first to gradually reduce their power and get them away from Huizong.

Perhaps seeing in Li Gang the sort of diplomatic emissary Chen Gongfu had recommended, Qinzong next sent Li Gang to convey messages to both his legal mother Empress Zheng and his father Huizong. Li Gang called first on the empress. She had not gone as far south as Huizong had, and she agreed to return to Kaifeng. The mood in Kaifeng was so paranoid at this point that rumors spread that Qinzong wanted to bring her back so that they could rule jointly. One official submitted a memorial on 3/11 to object to this rumored plan, largely on the grounds that letting women gain power had so often in the past created problems. The next day officials urged that when she returned she not be allowed into the palace. When Li Gang arrived at the empress's boat, he did his best to make the new decision not to let her into the palace seem less hostile than it really was. He tried to soften the new order that she live outside the palace by telling her that given Qinzong's "sagely filiality," nothing would come between the two, no matter where she lived. Still, when the empress did in fact return to Kaifeng on 3/19, the imperial guard was ready to prevent her from entering the palace. She, however, made no effort to do so.[56]

When Li Gang reached Huizong, according to his own account, he "fully reported on Qinzong's sagely filiality and affection, of his intention 'to use the empire to take care of him,'" alluding to a passage in *Mencius* 5A.4 about the way Shun treated his father. Huizong's tears streamed down, we are told, as he acknowledged that Qinzong was a filial son. The two men then talked about everything that had happened since Huizong left the capital, with Li Gang trying to convince Huizong that Qinzong had made reasonable decisions, and Huizong similarly explaining why he had taken several steps that had raised suspicions about his intentions. For instance, Huizong said he had cut off the transmission of documents between the mobile palace and Qinzong's court during the siege because he thought, if messages were intercepted, the Jurchens would learn his location. In response to thirty-odd questions posed by Huizong, Li Gang explained such measures as the new posthumous honors granted to Sima Guang.

The most persuasive part of Li Gang's message encouraged Huizong to think of Qinzong as eager to win his approval:

> The emperor [Qinzong] is benevolent, filial, and cautious; his only concern has been that he fail to do as you would want him to. Every time he receives an inquiry from you, he becomes so anxious and frightened that meals cannot be served. Let me compare it to an ordinary family where the esteemed father has left and entrusted the family business to a son. Then fierce bandits rob and plunder and the son must decide what measures to take. While awaiting the father's return, the son cannot help but worry. The esteemed father ought to praise and comfort the son for coming up with a plan to preserve the fields and gardens, and not make a fuss over the details. Now, it was just when the current emperor had begun to reign and Your Majesty left on a trip that the enemy invaded. To save the dynasty, he had no choice but to make minor changes in the government. Today the dynasty is no longer endangered and the four directions are calm. If Your Majesty now returns, in my view it would be a great comfort to His Majesty. There is no need to ask about the minor details.[57]

Li Gang was trying to convince Huizong that if he came back, he would be treated like a father who had returned from a business trip and be put back at the center of things. Certainly no one at Qinzong's court intended anything of the sort. It is not clear from Li Gang's account whether Li Gang saw himself as deceiving Huizong toward a higher end, or saw himself as saving Huizong's face in a way Huizong would know was a polite fiction. Two days later, before Li Gang returned to Kaifeng, Huizong gave him a personal note which read, "You have assisted the emperor in defending the dynasty. Anyone able to bring peace between a father and son so that all suspicion is resolved deserves to have his name passed down in the histories for ten thousand generations."[58]

Li Gang continued to play a conciliatory role after returning to Kaifeng. For instance, on 3/27 he argued with the court official, Geng Nanzhong, when the latter proposed dismissing all of Huizong's eunuch servants. He was not entirely successful in this effort, however; when Huizong was finally welcomed back to Kaifeng in the early summer, ten of the eunuchs with him were prevented from entering Kaifeng. Another official prevented from entering with Huizong was Cai You.[59]

When Huizong returned, the people who lined the roads to watch him got to see that he was wearing the brightly colored robes and hat of a Daoist priest. He moved into Dragon Virtue Palace, his chosen residence. From this point on, the volume of records in which Huizong figures plummets. Once he was under the control of Qinzong's court, officials stopped submitting memorials on the subject of how to manage him. Over the next several weeks, Qinzong, on the urging of his officials, gradually tightened control over Huizong and those around him. Beginning on 4/8, officials were assigned to Dragon Virtue Temple and required to make daily reports on Huizong's activities. At one point they were given orders to question everyone who visited Huizong and confiscate any gifts he made to them. Qinzong's visits to Huizong were rare, and Huizong was apparently invited to the palace only once, on 5/13.[60]

Qinzong's court continued to purge the ranks of officials with ties to Huizong, with apparently little resistance from the many officials who had risen under the patronage of these men. People who had gained office through the Daoist rank system, or as relatives of such men, were dismissed. Relatives, even relatives through marriage, of Cai Jing, Wang Fu, Wang Anzhong, Zhu Mian, and the like were dismissed. In the fifth month each of the sons and grandsons of Cai Jing was banished to a different place. In the sixth month Bai Shizhong and Li Bangyan were dismissed, in the seventh Wang Anzhong, in the eighth Wu Min.[61] In the seventh month Cai Jing was banished. On the way south merchants reportedly refused to sell him food. Ill and over eighty, he died within ten days on his way to his site of banishment. On the same day, it was ruled that no future amnesties would lighten the exiles of twenty-three of Cai Jing's sons and grandsons. From then through the tenth month the key officials who had accompanied Huizong were executed: Tong Guan, Zhao Liangsi, Cai You, Cai Xiao, and Zhu Mian.[62] In the ninth month Tong Guan's head was displayed in the Kaifeng marketplace with a placard in large characters listing his crimes.[63]

⌒ How DID THE WORLD LOOK to Huizong in the summer and fall of 1126, in the months after he had returned to Kaifeng? Huizong lived in Dragon Virtue Temple, well north of the Palace City, and had no say in the operation of the government. He could hardly have missed the hostility of many of Qinzong's top officials toward him. During the summer and fall, Huizong heard of the banishment or death of one after another of his former officials. It is difficult to imagine that he was able to detach himself entirely from these acts of vengeance, even if he was attempting to reach higher truths through a religious life. Later, when both he and Qinzong were prisoners of the Jurchens, he told his son-in-law Cai Tiao that he thought too many people had been executed during Qinzong's reign, that some of the misfortunes that they later suffered were retribution for the taking of so many lives.[64]

The military situation would have had to worry Huizong all summer and fall. The siege of Taiyuan continued, both sides determined to win despite heavy bombardments and food shortages. Song generals proved unable either to relieve the siege of Taiyuan or prevent the steady advance of Jin forces. Aguda's nephew Nianhan had retained command of the western army in charge of the siege of Taiyuan and campaigns elsewhere in Hedong (Shanxi), and Aguda's son Wolibu again took charge of the eastern army, which began advancing again in Hebei and set siege to Zhending. In the fifth month, the Song general Chong Shizhong led his army from Jingjing in Hebei into Hedong to come to the aid of the defenders of Taiyuan. He was ambushed, but organized a "fight to the death" with all of his troops shooting their crossbows all morning at the Jin troops. Chong Shizhong himself suffered four wounds and died in this battle. The Song court next sent Li Gang to lead the effort to relieve Taiyuan on 6/25, but he had no more success.[65] In the seventh month Chong Shizhong's elder brother Shidao was given charge, but Jin troops began pushing south and east, preceded by streams of Chinese refugees.

In the last month of autumn, 1126/9/3, Jin finally took Taiyuan after a siege of 260 days and the starvation of much of the population.[66] Zhending ran out of supplies and fell about a month later on 10/6. That month Huizong told associates that he was convinced that the Jurchens would return and proposed that he go to Luoyang to organize an army there. Wu Min convinced Qinzong to reject this idea.[67]

Although Huizong and Qinzong had little contact with each other after Huizong's return, Qinzong could not avoid visiting him on his birthday in the tenth month. The occasion did not go well. First, someone stepped on Qinzong's toes. Then, Qinzong refused the glass of wine Huizong offered him, bringing Huizong to tears. After this meeting, Qinzong had placards posted outside the Dragon Virtue Palace / Temple offering rewards to anyone who turned in people passing rumors about the two palaces. From this point on, we are told, there was no real communication between the two palaces.[68] Huizong had become a prisoner.

16

Losing Everything, 1126–1127

> On that day [1127/2/9], at Virtue Revealed Gate, a yellow
> notice was posted listing the sequence of the transfers to Jin.
> There were also the responses of Sun, Jie, and other officials.
> Only then did the populace understand that Jin wanted to put
> someone with a different surname on the throne. They
> looked at each other, wept and wailed, thoroughly dejected.
> Everyone then regretted the decisions not to let Huizong
> travel east or Qinzong move the capital.
>
> —*From Zhao Shenzhi's* Surviving Accounts

$\mathcal{B}$Y THE FIRST MONTH OF WINTER, 1126/10, Song's situation was perilous. With Jin forces in easy striking distance of the capital, Kaifeng residents fled in large numbers.[1] The Song court once again had to summon armies from other parts of the country to defend the capital. It also made gestures to mend its relations with the civil service, since officials who rose during Huizong's reign were uncertain where they stood after a summer and fall of purges. An edict of 10/18 assured officials that capable men would not be dismissed even if they had once been recommended by Cai Jing, Wang Fu, Tong Guan, or Liang Shicheng. As the situation worsened, Chong Shidao urged Qinzong to relocate the court to Chang'an. Qinzong recalled him for consultation, but the seventy-six-year-old Chong Shidao died of illness on his way back. Envoys from Jin insinuated that they would be willing to call off the invasion for the right inducement, and the Song court quickly sent one hundred thousand bolts of silk as rewards for their soldiers. Once Jin received the goods, of course, different conditions were announced.[2]

Early in the eleventh month officials at court bitterly argued over whether to reverse themselves and grant the Jurchens the three

449

prefectures north of the Yellow River that they demanded and which the court had refused to turn over all summer and fall. Fan Zongyin and seventy other officials were in favor of ceding them; He Zhuo, Qin Gui, and thirty-five others were opposed. Qinzong went with the majority. He sent his nineteen-year-old brother Prince Gou and the official Wang Yun to serve as "envoys to cede land and sue for peace." The day before they left, however, Jin forces were crossing the Yellow River (1126/11/15). Unaware of the rapid movement of the Jin army, Prince Gou and Wang Yun missed the Jin army and ended up behind their lines in Hebei.[3]

The Fall of Kaifeng

Once he got to the suburbs of Kaifeng, Nianhan made an offer: he would withdraw if the Yellow River were made the border between the two countries. Soon Qinzong was sending envoys to agree to this proposal, but he also took the precaution of bringing those who lived outside the city walls into Kaifeng and closing the gates.[4] On 11/25, the first Jin cavalry arrived outside the walls of Kaifeng. Inside the city almost anyone willing to fight was put to work, including a certain Guo Jing who gained the confidence of the high official Sun Fu for his plans to recruit 7,777 soldiers and use magical techniques to make his soldiers invisible. Some of the fiercest critics of Huizong's administration, including Hu Shunzhi and Sun Di, now agreed that Qinzong should depart (euphemistically called moving the capital).[5] Whether or not the plan would have succeeded the year before, at this late date most considered it unworkable.

By 11/30 the armies of both Wolibu and Nianhan were camped outside Kaifeng with an estimated one hundred thousand troops altogether.[6] Nianhan chose for his camp the Green Enclosure complex south of Kaifeng used when the Song emperors performed the Suburban Sacrifices. Wolibu's camp was at a Buddhist temple complex northeast of the city called Liu Family Temple. During the earlier invasion, Nianhan's army had been held up at Taiyuan, so this time, with both armies at the city's gates, the situation was much graver. Moreover, the city's resources were less ample, given what had been turned over to the Jurchen the year before. Still, this time the court was determined to fight the enemy rather than appease them.

In preparation for attacking the city walls, the Jurchens set Chinese they had seized to moving stones and cutting trees for siege machines.[7] Fortunately, Song armies from other parts of the country began arriving, the largest Zhang Shuye's thirty thousand troops from the southern circuits. Real combat began in the intercalary month between the eleventh and twelfth months of 1126. Song concentrated on defending its walls, using many recently recruited civilians, and only rarely sent out sorties to disrupt Jin preparation of siege equipment. Both sides initially tried fire to strengthen their positions. The Jurchens set fire to eleven of the twelve gates to the city, and the Song sent out troops to burn the Jurchen stockades. Catapults were widely employed to rain stones on the other side. To keep its catapults supplied, on 1126/i11/8, residents were told to take the stones from Huizong's Northeast Marchmount garden for launching at the attackers.[8] According to Shi Maoliang's account of the weapons and tactics used by both sides in the siege of Kaifeng, Song soldiers shot the Jurchen siege towers with incendiary arrows. If they caught fire, the Song would shoot kindling material such as straw or hay packed in bamboo, to help the fire spread. The Jurchens would counter this the best they could by daubing thin mud over the structures. Once Jin soldiers had to leave the siege tower, the Song forces would shoot arrows at them.[9]

As combat moved from one gate to another, both sides dispatched a stream of envoys. Jin urged Qinzong to come in person, saying that if he came immediately he would be treated with courtesy, something he could not expect after the city fell. A few days later, Jin offered to reopen negotiations if Qinzong would send as hostages his father Huizong, the heir apparent Prince Chen, an uncle, and a brother. To this Qinzong responded, "How can I send my own father as a hostage!" He did however try to send Huizong's brother Ssi, the prince of Yue.[10]

Battles for the walls grew fiercer as negotiations stalled. On 1126/i11/25, with snow swirling about, the grand councilor He Zhuo and commissioner of military affairs Sun Fu called on Guo Jing and his 7,777 troops to save the day.[11] The doors of Transformation Revealed Gate in the southern wall were opened, and his army surged out to engage the Jin forces, followed by several thousand Kaifeng residents hoping to help them. Rumors spread that Guo Jing achieved great victories, whereas in fact his troops were mowed down. Jin forces soon put up scaling ladders and scaled the walls. The heavy snow was only one further example of the extreme weather the capital had been experiencing that year. Nianhan reportedly told one of his subordinates, "Having snow this bad is the equivalent of getting twenty thousand fresh soldiers."[12]

When the outer walls of Kaifeng fell, large numbers of the soldiers died in the final onslaught, and others fled the city along with tens of thousands of residents. The Jurchens set fire to the gate towers and defense works along the wall and soon much of the city was aflame. Fleeing Song soldiers began looting, and some even killed their officers. Near several of the gates, Jurchen soldiers entered the city and began both killing and looting. People panicked. The well-to-do changed into poor people's clothes and hid. Reportedly thousands committed suicide by jumping in the rivers or wells or hanging themselves, especially women. Qinzong climbed Eastern Splendor Gate (on the east side of the Palace City) and ordered weapons distributed to the populace, but people were losing the will to fight.[13]

Once he heard that the outer walls had fallen, Huizong had his guards bring him to the more secure Palace City. When the eunuch palace guards would not let his party enter, they found a way in through a water gate but got lost because the snow obscured everything. Qinzong, on learning of this, sent two hundred armored attendants to lead them into Extended Blessings Palace, the palace built at the rear of the Palace City in 1113, where Empress Zheng had already settled.[14]

On the morning after the Jurchens took the outer walls, Qinzong appeared at Virtue Revealed Gate to speak to the soldiers and people. He asked them what they wanted to do, given the current situation, saying no one would be blamed for the failure to hold the walls. People began shouting questions and ideas so informally that some used the ordinary pronouns "you" and "I" instead of "Your Majesty" and "your subject." Some thanked him for staying in the city and not abandoning them. A group of several hundred soldiers willing to try to break out climbed on the roof of a nearby building and shouted that Qinzong should immediately leave, that the city was no longer the place for him. Qinzong said it would be necessary to first prepare food and money to take, and issued orders to begin preparations. Back in the palace, however, court officials, including Mei Zhili, advised against rash action, and Qinzong put it off. The next day Jin sent a Song official into Kaifeng to tell Qinzong not to attempt to leave since Jin controlled everything within 250 kilometers. The idea of breaking out was then abandoned.[15]

Even after the Jurchens had occupied the walls, there were plenty of people—both soldiers and residents—willing to fight hand to hand with the invaders, something the Jin commanders preferred to avoid if possible. So they began negotiating with the Song court to get it to turn over everything they wanted from the city in exchange for a promise not to let their soldiers loose on the population. Qinzong sent his brother Kai (Huizong's third son) and He Zhuo as envoys/hostages to Jin. Jin offered assurances that they wanted only territory, not the destruction of the dynasty. Their first demand was that Huizong come to their camp as a hostage, along with a long series of other people, including relatives of officials in Hebei and Hedong, who would serve as guarantors that those officials would not resist turning over their prefectures. In addition, they wanted relatives of a long list of officials who had been involved in Song policymaking, from Cai Jing to Li Gang, Wu Min, and more minor figures. The official letter, preserved in Jin sources, put particular emphasis on the need for Huizong and his grandson, the heir apparent Prince Chen.[16] When He Zhuo protested that he could not carry such a message, Nianhan said, in effect, that Qinzong had a choice—he could turn over either his father or his wife and daughters. Song sources describe Qinzong as offering to go himself rather than hand over Huizong. The official letter that Qinzong sent read, "Concerning your desire for the senior emperor and the heir apparent to depart for the suburbs, now that the city has fallen, the power over life and death belongs to your court, so how could I resist? However, between a father and son there are things their hearts cannot bear to do. What if I go myself to your headquarters to ask for sympathy and beg for our lives?" While sending this letter, however, he also sent a messenger appointing Prince Gou as Grand Marshal of Hebei and asking him to mobilize an army.[17]

Prince Gou had been stranded north of the enemy lines in Hebei. Like several of his elder brothers, he had been drawn into the conflict. During the first invasion, in the first month of 1126, when Jin had demanded a prince as a hostage to maintain negotiations, he had volunteered to go and ended up spending more than ten days in Wolibu's camp. In the eleventh month, as Jin forces were advancing south again, he was sent to make an offer to Wolibu. Only partway there, however, local people opposed to appeasement blocked the road and killed the Song envoy with him. In the meantime, Jin forces had crossed the Yellow River and he could not return to Kaifeng. With Qinzong's authorization, he now began working with local officials and the general Zong Ze to organize an army to fight the Jurchens from the rear, suppress bandits, and if possible relieve Kaifeng.[18]

On 1126/iii/28, princes and high officials went to the Jin camp to request negotiations. Placards were posted around Kaifeng saying that elders and ordinary people should go to the Jin camp and offer gold, silk, meat, and wine as rewards for their soldiers. People responded, and soon the streets were crowded with people carrying signs giving their names, wards, and the objects they were offering to Jin in thanks for their sparing the population. The city itself, however, was descending into disorder. The markets were by now selling human flesh without hiding the fact. Song soldiers, whose rations had run out, were escaping from their camps and seizing what they could find in the city. To try to get the situation under control the court allowed those who caught such thieves to execute them, leading to even more deaths. By the next day, young men in the city had organized themselves into patrols, which brought robbery under control.[19]

On 1126/iii/30, Qinzong went himself to Wolibu's camp, accompanied by his two uncles (Huizong's brothers Wu and Ssi) and four hundred other men, imperial clansmen and officials, all of whom, according to Jin sources, "called themselves subjects of Jin." Neither Wolibu nor Nianhan would see Qinzong that day, and the next they sent messengers to demand a formal letter of surrender from him. Sun Di promptly drafted one, which he had to revise several times before the Jin commanders accepted it. For instance, Song was not allowed to refer to two emperors, one of Great Jin and one of Great Song; only the Jin could be said to have an emperor. When Qinzong did finally meet with both Wolibu and Nianhan, he asked the Jin commanders to withdraw their troops, volunteering to submit treasures for generations and present gold and silk from the imperial treasuries. "Is there a person or object that is not already mine?" was Nianhan's rebuke.[20]

In the city, people lined up by Southern Infusion Gate (the gate in the center of the southern wall of the New City), waiting for Qinzong's return. When a yellow flag appeared, it signaled a message from

Qinzong, who told his subjects that a peace agreement had been reached, though the figure of Song payments had not yet been decided, and that he would return the next day. People lined up again the next day, waiting in the snow for much of the day. When they finally sighted the yellow canopy of his carriage in the late afternoon, they began shouting and running through the streets.[21]

The next day, after Qinzong had returned to Kaifeng, Jin informed Qinzong of their basic demand: ten million bolts each of silk and satin, five million bars of gold (each bar fifty ounces), and ten million bars of silver.[22] This was impossibly high—fifty times the gold demanded after the first invasion at the beginning of the year and ten times the silver. Moreover, the Song authorities had not been able to raise the sums demanded then and had not had time to replenish government storehouses. Jin also sent a letter to Prince Gou, demanding his return, but Qinzong sent a secret message reiterating the need for him to raise troops.[23]

Jin officials entered Kaifeng and opened the Song government storehouses, which were found to have even more bolts of plain silk than demanded, but only a tiny fraction of the gold and silver. Song officials were assigned responsibilities for searching specific quadrants of the city and confiscating all gold and silver. Every few days, the Jurchens demanded something else for the Song government to deliver to them. For instance, on 12/5 Jin demanded ten thousand horses. Ranking officials were allowed to keep one horse, but all others were seized, over seven thousand altogether.[24] The next day, 12/6, Jin demanded weapons, many of which people had taken after soldiers abandoned them. Qinzong issued an order that all weapons in Kaifeng, both government and private, be turned over to the Jin authorities. A few days later, on 12/10, all the money in the storehouses was distributed to the Jin soldiers as their rewards. On 12/13, a call was issued for twenty painters, fifty wine-makers, and three thousand bottles of wine. Ten days later Jin demanded a long list of books and documents by name, including Sima Guang's *Comprehensive Mirror* and calligraphy by Su Shi and Huang Tingjian. In some cases, the Kaifeng prefectural authorities had to buy the works from bookshops to fulfill the orders. A few days after that, the books from the Directorate of Education were taken (though as an insult, ones by Wang Anshi were discarded). As the scholars in Jin employ discovered that they were missing a title, they added it to their requisition lists.[25] Just before the Lantern Festival, Jin demanded all the lanterns usually used not only by the palace, but also by temples and shops, then held their own ceremony outside the walls of the city. Not long afterward, they demanded the full set of procession paraphernalia, then took such objects as the Nine Cauldrons, the bells and other instruments used for the Music of Great Brilliance, consorts' headgear, the blocks for printing books, including those for the Buddhist and Daoist canons, and maps, diagrams, and pictures of all sorts. From time to time, the Jurchen commander requisitioned specific craftsmen or specialists, such as physicians, musicians, astronomers, weapons makers, masons, gardeners, jade carvers, clerks, painters, storytellers, professors, Buddhist monks, and so on. Lists of objects taken from the palace are often staggering: 25,000 ancient bronze vessels, 1,000 ox carts, 1,000 parasols, 28,700 pills from the imperial pharmacy, 1,000,000 *jin* of silk thread, 1,800 bolts of a certain type of silk made in Hebei.[26]

The crucial element in the Jin demands, however, was for gold and silver. If the Song court did not want the Jurchen soldiers to be set loose to pillage the city, they were repeatedly warned, they had to fill the quota as quickly as possible. Court officials knew that the quantity of gold and silver demanded was impossibly high, but were divided on how to cope with that fact. Some urged going to the Jurchens and pleading with them to lower the quota on the grounds that it was impossible to fill, but the view that prevailed was to do as thorough a search as possible and then present the Jurchens with the results, a strategy that had worked eleven months earlier. On 12/14 the goods in pawnshops and silk, gold, and silver shops were all confiscated.[27] On 12/24, placards were posted in the marketplaces detailing the demands. They reported that the government treasuries had had enough plain silk, but not enough gold, silver, or satin. Valuables in the homes of officials and the members of the imperial family, from Huizong and the heir apparent on down, had already been confiscated; thus it was time to search the homes of rich families. Specified officials were given charge of different sectors of the city. Compliance was encouraged by rewarding informers. Those who informed on people concealing wealth, including servants informing on their masters, would get one-tenth of anything discovered. Many officials were deprived of their ranks when it was discovered that they had concealed some of their belongings.[28]

A week later, on 1127/1/8, the quota for satin had been filled, but little progress had been made on the gold and silver. Because they had only been able to collect 1 percent of the gold and 10 percent of the silver, He Zhuo went to the Jin camp to ask to have the quota reduced, but Nianhan refused. After this point, the searches and confiscations had to be done more violently, with people tied up and beaten to try to get them to reveal where they had concealed their treasures. On 1/9 a list was made of people from the highest officials on down who had not contributed silk or silver, and in the renewed searches even many officials were forced to wear wooden collars for failing to turn over sums demanded.[29]

Although the city had fallen, the Jurchen forces kept the gates closed, enforcing, in a sense, a reverse siege to keep up the pressure on the city until all its demands were met. Food and firewood, therefore, were in very short supply. On 12/21 the court allowed government office buildings to be demolished for firewood; the next day, after a snow fall aggravated the situation, approval was given for people to enter Northeast Marchmount Park to chop down the rare trees planted there. A few days later, with another snowfall, people were also allowed to break up the hundred-odd buildings in the garden for fuel. So many rushed there that people were trampled to death. Fire also continued to add to the destruction of the city. On 12/25 a fire that started at the Heavenly Calm Temple spread to destroy more than five hundred houses. That same day placards were posted in the city informing families who had had members abducted by Jin soldiers to go to the eastern and western pagoda temples to file reports so that ransoms could be arranged. When twenty to thirty thousand people showed up at the Western Pagoda Temple, the officials were overwhelmed and had no way to deal with them all.[30]

New Year's Day, 1127/1/1, could not be celebrated with the usual festivities. Qinzong paid a visit to Huizong at Extended Blessings Palace, but rather than hold the usual New Year's audience, he told his officials and the clergy to go to the Jin camp to offer their congratulations, an admission that they were the real rulers. Nianhan, however, told them such a mass visit was unnecessary; it would be enough to have a group of Qinzong's brothers come to offer their greetings. In return, he had his own sons call on Qinzong.[31]

Not long after this inauspicious start to the year, the Jurchen commanders pressured Qinzong to return to their camp. Some officials thought Qinzong should refuse, but He Zhuo urged him to go. Before leaving, Qinzong visited Huizong and Empress Zheng and the three of them drank together, without Qinzong telling them his decision to go to the Jin camp the next day. Before leaving, Qinzong told Sun Fu that in case of his own death, he should recruit two to three hundred men to break out of the city, taking with them Huizong and the heir apparent. More publicly, Qinzong named his eldest son, the heir apparent Prince Chen, as regent. Recognizing that a boy only a little over nine years old would need help, he appointed Sun Fu and Xie Kejia to assist him.[32]

Why did Qinzong appoint his young son regent rather than one of his many adult brothers? One possibility is that the officials he assigned to "assist" the prince were calling the shots and wanted to have a free hand. Another is that Qinzong feared that if something happened to him while one of his brothers or uncles was in charge, that person would end up succeeding to the throne rather than his own son Prince Chen. Serving as emperor had been a heavy burden on Qinzong from the first day, but he apparently preferred to see the throne go to one of his own descendants than to a brother.

Qinzong's Departure

On 1127/1/10, when Qinzong proceeded through the city to leave by Southern Infusion Gate, he reassured the people lining the road that he would return the next day. He left with a large retinue, but Jin allowed only eleven of the officials accompanying him to enter their camp, including his brother Kai. Guards locked Qinzong in a side room by himself, not even providing him with quilts or food. His request to meet with either Wolibu or Nianhan was denied, but an envoy arrived to press him to agree to make the Yellow River the boundary; to consent to the marriage of a princess to a Jurchen prince; to turn over two thousand items of court paraphernalia, five hundred commoner women, and five hundred female musicians; and to send a long list of named individuals. The next day the Jin authorities specified that the princess they wanted was Cai Jing's daughter-in-law, Princess Fujin. This princess, Huizong's fifth daughter, had married Cai Tiao more than eight years earlier in 1118, when she was sixteen *sui*. Huizong had visited them in their new home in 1119, and their first son was given a title in 1122.[33]

The Jurchens forced Qinzong to write in his own hand an edict urging faster collection of the gold and silver. Soon the city was posted with placards saying that Qinzong would not be allowed to return until the quota of gold and silver had been met. Still, every day officials and city dwellers would gather at the southern gate to wait for Qinzong's return. On 1127/1/13, a Song official returned from Green Enclosure, reporting in tears that Qinzong had not eaten in the three days since he left. With him were Jurchen envoys who wanted to inspect the princesses.[34]

Song officials tried every means they could to collect gold and silver. There was a steady line of soldiers and people from Virtue Revealed Gate to Southern Infusion Gate carrying objects from the palaces used by Huizong and the princes. On 1/13 commoners were organized into mutual security units of five families to aid in the collection of gold and silver, with more pressure put on ordinary poor families. Placards were posted with word from Qinzong that everything had to be delivered by 1/15 for him to be released. On 1/14 Huizong added his consent to an order that all of the sacrificial vessels used in the ancestral sacrifices at the Supreme Shrine or the homes of princes be handed over.[35] On 1/18, Buddhist and Daoist clergy were asked to pray for the early return of the emperor, and all along the route from the palace to the southern gate of the New City stood people holding incense and praying. By 1/19 Kaifeng prefecture had delivered 160,000 ounces of gold and six million ounces of silver.[36]

Life in the city kept getting more and more difficult as the price of food rose to three hundred cash for a peck of grain, six thousand cash for a catty of pork, eight thousand for lamb, ten thousand for beef or horsemeat, if it could be found. Because people could not leave the city, bodies were piled everywhere, mostly of people who had died of starvation, frozen to death, or succumbed to the epidemics raging through the city. Even those who did not die often contracted beriberi from the limited diet.[37] On 1/23 the Song government began selling rationed grain and firewood at about 10 to 20 percent of the market price. The demand was so great that at first only the strongest, mostly soldiers, were able to get to the front to buy the grain, so soldiers had to be banned from the markets and alternate days designated for men and women to make sure that the weak were not deprived of the chance to purchase food. The situation was not much better in the surrounding prefectures, which the Jurchens regularly raided for their own food. In addition, the Jurchen soldiers with time on their hands dug up graves, large and small, to get the grave goods buried in them.[38]

After more than ten days in captivity, on 1/22, Qinzong had to countersign a new agreement worked out by Nianhan and Wolibu, which had several significant provisions. Huizong would not have to go north, but six hostages, including the heir apparent, Prince Gou, and a grand councilor, would have to serve as hostages until all agreements had been fulfilled. All the treasures in the palaces would be turned over to Jin. Two princesses, eight clanswomen, 2,500 palace ladies, 1,500 female musicians, and 3,000 craftsmen would be turned over. The annual payments would be increased to five million units of silk and silver (ten times what Song used to pay Liao). If the sum required for rewarding the soldiers (the one million bars of gold and five million bars of silver) was not turned over within ten days, the quota would be filled by the sale of women. Each princess or consort of a prince would be assessed at one thousand bars of gold, each close clansmen's daughter at five hundred bars, each distant clansmen's daughter at two hundred bars, wives of close clansmen at five hundred bars of silver, distant clansmen's wives at two hundred silver bars, and daughters of nobles at one hundred silver bars. To make sure Song did not just send the old and ugly, the Jurchen authorities reserved the right to select the women they wanted.[39]

The Song had no choice but to fill most of the quota through women, over five thousand all told, ranging from princesses and imperial consorts to low-status performers and prostitutes. Within days, all the women of the entertainment quarters were rounded up, along with all the women who had been palace ladies during Huizong's reign and later dismissed, even if they had already been married. On 1/28, the private courtesans in the homes of Cai Jing, Tong Guan, and Wang Fu were taken, but so were their wives and daughters, including Cai Tiao's wife Princess Fujin. The princess had been tied up and when she was delivered to the Jurchen camp she "no longer looked human." When the women were delivered, the Jurchen soldiers, in order of rank, got to take their pick; Nianhan took several dozen, senior generals several, and other officers one or two. More than a thousand were rejected and sent back because they were not in good enough health. The Song had to send substitutes.[40]

While their houses were being ransacked and their daughters seized, the populace of Kaifeng remained remarkably loyal to the Song imperial family. Every day, we are told, hundreds of thousands would line the Imperial Way, showing their solidarity with Qinzong and waiting for his return. People became excited when a notice was posted that Qinzong would be able to return after attending a polo match, which could not be scheduled until the weather cleared. Temples throughout the city held services to pray for sunshine. Finally the skies cleared, but still there was no news of Qinzong. Then, when the polo match finally took place on 1127/2/5 and Qinzong asked to go home, Nianhan replied, "Where would you go?" leaving Qinzong speechless.[41]

The next day, 1127/2/6, Jin held a ceremony formally deposing Qinzong, described in a Jin source in this way:

> At dawn on the sixth, the two commanders ordered the Song ruler to enter the Green Enclosure camp. The Song officials all accompanied him. The Jin soldiers, who waved that the imperial guards should leave, dismounted their horses on arrival at the camp. [Qinzong] was ordered to kneel to hear the edict demoting him to commoner. The minister [Nianhan] ordered [the Jin officials] Xiao Qing and Liu Si to take off the younger ruler's hat and robe. The loyal Song official Li Ruoshui held on to the imperial garment and cursed the commanders. He was dragged out by the soldiers.[42]

A Song source quotes Li Ruoshui as shouting: "These bandits are acting outrageously! This is the true emperor of the great dynasty! You dead dogs cannot violate ritual!" The account goes on: "He held the emperor in his left hand and pointed to Nianhan with his right, cursing him. Several guards hit his face till it was bleeding and pushed him aside. Then when he saw the emperor without his imperial garments, he collapsed."[43] Jin sources, by contrast, stress the humiliation rather than the resistance and continue the story by saying that soldiers dragged Li Ruoshui out and made Qinzong write out an order to those left in command in Kaifeng telling them that Huizong had only till the next day to lead all of the palace residents and imperial clansmen out of the city and recommend someone of another family line to be enthroned. For his part, Li Ruoshui was taken outside the city and beaten to death.[44]

Green Enclosure

Historical sources contain only brief references to Huizong during the three-and-a-half weeks after Qinzong entered the Jurchen camp on 1/10. Occasionally in Qinzong's absence the grand councilors got Huizong to support measures, especially ones that involved the imperial family or clan or the ancestral cult. But there is no reason to think that he was regularly consulted, or even that his opinion was given much consideration. This can be seen when Qinzong's councilors forced him to take the fateful step of leading all of the imperial family and clan out of Kaifeng. Several accounts of how this happened have been preserved.[45] Huizong's son-in-law Cai Tiao wrote in his *Annals of the Young and Old* that on 1127/2/6 two officials returned from the Jurchen camp and conveyed the message that "unless everyone from the Senior Emperor on down exited that afternoon, soldiers would be released on all sides to enter and kill people." Then "Sun Fu and Wang Shiyong and the others then went directly to see Huizong and begged him to proceed with all the princes and consorts to the headquarters to plead their case. When Huizong did not respond, Fan Qiong pressured him. Huizong, with tears streaming down, was given no choice, so climbed into a bamboo sedan chair and left. From the palace to Southern Infusion Gate, the common people filled the Imperial Way, blocking them and weeping."[46] Another author tells largely the same story but adds his suspicion that the officials worried more about the impact on their own families of having soldiers set loose, and therefore used sweet words to entice Huizong to leave the city before people in the city were aware what was happening.[47]

A fuller account is given by Cao Xun, one of the officials who had been assigned by Qinzong's court to attend Huizong:

> On the morning of 2/7, it was secretly reported that Li Shi, Zhou Xun, Wu Jian, and Mo Chou had come with a message from Qinzong. They were let in immediately [to see Huizong]. Li Shi reported: "The emperor ordered us to pay our respects to Your Majesty. Jin is strongly insisting that Your Majesty depart for the

suburbs. Although we were able to decline before, they are again demanding that you go to the office at Southern Infusion Gate to present a report begging for the return of the emperor. Once your report reaches the camp, His Majesty will be able to return to the palace. The Jin desire is to do our dynasty a favor; there is nothing else behind their request." Li Shi also secretly reported, "I was told to say, 'Dad, Mom, please come quickly; don't delay. I am worried that we will miss the chance.'"

Huizong thought for a while, then said, "Has there been any change in the situation at the army headquarters? Do not hide anything from me. Your present ranks and salaries you owe to me. Don't mislead me about major matters for a small profit. If something has happened, I could still make a plan to deal with it. But dying uselessly will do no good."

Li Shi and the others responded, "If we have been untruthful, we would gladly suffer ten thousand deaths."

Huizong clearly suspected that he was not being told the whole truth and kept pressing the messengers:

"First the court kept me from going south, and then during the siege, those in charge have not kept me informed, and now this has come to pass. The matter you bring up today should not be decided without careful thought. Do not conceal anything from me."

Li Shi responded, "I would not dare misinform you."

Huizong then sent an attendant to fetch Empress Zheng. At the time she was outside Dawn Radiance Gate, dealing with matters of bedding and cooking. She invited Huizong to join her, and they talked. After a short while, Huizong asked for his Daoist robes, preparing to leave. [The official] Jiang Yaochen and others came forward and said, "Although they say that they are inviting your carriage only to the center of the gate, we are afraid that the enemy is trying to deceive you and there might be danger. You ought to give the matter more thought. This place will do; probably you should not move."

Huizong replied, "Just now in the palace the empress got word from the emperor ordering us to go temporarily to the front of the gate. If true, how can I not go?" When the palace ladies and attendants all wailed, Huizong asked, "Even if they have bad intentions, at least we can bring the matter to a close. I would not object to being held hostage if the emperor thereby is able to return to preserve the dynasty. But I do resent the repayment I am getting for yielding my position in a ritual manner and retiring to a Daoist temple, keeping out of court politics, and never resisting the commands I was given or exceeding my station. What shame this brings my ancestors!" He looked at those attending him and said, "Those who want to come with me may." Everyone cried and followed him. He also took the imperial sword he normally wore and gave it to [the eunuch attendant] Ding Fu to wear, then climbed into a sedan chair together with Empress Zheng. They left Extended Blessings Palace, exiting through Dawn Radiance Gate.

When they got to Southern Infusion Gate, guards opened both doors. Huizong said, "This must be the Jin representatives here to meet us." They were about to go to the building on the west side when [Jin] soldiers surrounded them and made them exit through the gate. Huizong stamped his feet in the sedan chair and exclaimed, "Something has indeed happened, just as I expected." He called Ding Fu to get the sword back from him, but the Jin guard had found it on Ding when he went through the gate and confiscated it.[48]

When they got to Wolibu's camp, Huizong was able to keep only three servants with him. Before long messengers arrived asking Huizong to produce documents on the Zhang Jue affair. Huizong gave his version of the events and complained, "Your country made this into a pretext and now the disaster has reached the point where my city has fallen and my country is lost. What document would there be? Besides, we have already sent you any documents we had. Whether I live or die depends on fate. You do not need to make this a pretext." After that, the Jurchen dealt mainly with Qinzong.

At the same time that Huizong was being told he had to leave within hours, the Jurchens sent more than a hundred eunuchs into the palace to help make arrangements for moving the consorts and princesses. These eunuchs, of course, had worked in the palace until the Jurchens had confiscated them and they knew the women there. Soon Huizong's and Qinzong's consorts, young children, palace ladies, maids, and wet nurses were leaving the palace. Many of the wet nurses and palace maids had to walk, since most palace vehicles had been removed by the Jurchens earlier. The imperial party reached Southern Infusion Gate about noon. According to one witness, residents of the capital, who had seen numerous processions of captives leave the city in the round-ups of women and specialists, did not realize that Huizong and the princes and princesses were the victims this time.[49] When the party got to the gate, ten thousand cavalry were waiting there ready to guard the exodus as the party moved toward the camps at Green Enclosure or Liu Family Temple. At the gate, the soldiers would open the sedan chairs and have the eunuchs identify the occupants. One baby son of Huizong had been taken by his wet nurse to hide among the common people, but the Jurchens had good enough records to discover that he was missing and gave Xu Bingzhe one day to find him and turn him over.[50]

After they were checked off, the empresses, princes, and princesses were sent off on carts and sedan chairs, but the rest of the consorts and palace ladies were picked up by Jin soldiers, who put them on their horses and galloped off with them.[51]

Shen Liang, a student at the Imperial Academy, heard from a guard that on arrival at Green Enclosure Huizong had a meeting with Nian-han and Wolibu. Nianhan took the ruler's position facing south and had Huizong face east and Wolibu face west. The guard overheard Huizong say in a harsh voice,

> You say your former emperor did us a great favor. I say, to the contrary, that we did you a great favor. If Liao attacked us, it would be understandable. Last year when you raised an army, I turned over the throne to my heir and later we used the city's resources to reward your army, after which you left. Now you raised an army claiming my successor was not trustworthy. Do you remember the oath letter? You are not speaking on your own here, but saying what Xiao Qing and Wang Rui et al. [i.e., former Liao officials] tell you to say. You should summon Xiao Qing et al. and have them try to prove this to me face to face. I am not afraid to die.[52]

Shen Liang reports that Nianhan said nothing in reply, but a Jin source quotes further reproaches:

The two marshals said, "You didn't approve a marriage alliance with us, but now you are all captives.[53] How do you have the face to confront anyone?"

Huizong replied, "Your uncle and I were each rulers of a state. Every state experiences ups and downs. Moreover, all human beings have wives and children. I suggest that you two think through the implications of this."

Nianhan responded, "Captives have always been made slaves. Because our former ruler had a good relationship with you, however, you may keep your wives and children. The others are no longer yours."[54]

The close family members Huizong was allowed to keep with him were five consorts, including the empress, twenty-eight sons, sixteen grandsons, and seven sons-in-law.

Shen Liang also tells us that that evening Huizong got to meet Qinzong, who did not look good after twenty-seven days in the camp. They grasped each other and cried together, and Huizong told his son, "If you had listened to the old man, we would have avoided this disaster." Shen explained, "He must have been referring to the fact that he had earlier wanted them both to depart, but He Zhuo had strenuously objected, so they did not go." A Jin source recorded that at this meeting Huizong maintained his composure and tried to buoy up Qinzong, saying, "Heaven has discarded us. How shall we deal with heaven?"[55]

People in Kaifeng did not learn that Jin was planning to set up an emperor of another family until 2/9. According to the Imperial Academy student Ding Teqi, both literati and commoners now all regretted that Huizong had not been allowed to move east and Qinzong had not moved his capital.[56] At least the heir apparent and his mother Empress Zhu were still in Kaifeng. Sun Fu tried to fulfill his promise to Qinzong to spirit the heir away, but did not have enough time to find anyone willing to undertake the risky mission. On 2/11, after both Qinzong and Huizong were forced to write letters to Xu Bingzhe requesting that Prince Chen and his mother be sent, they also were brought to the Jurchen camp.[57]

Beginning on 1127/2/13, members of the imperial clan, including Huizong's sons and daughters who had previously moved out of the palace, along with their spouses and children, were rounded up and moved to the Jurchen camps. Since the dynasty had been founded over 160 years earlier, descendants of Taizu and Taizong and their brother numbered in the thousands. During Huizong's reign, the clan included members of the fourth, fifth, sixth, seventh, and eighth generations. Total numbers would have been well over ten thousand: the sixth generation alone (whose members were born over the long period from 1059 to 1144) had 5,155 members born to it. During Huizong's reign clan members outside the mourning circle (that is, beyond second cousins) were encouraged to move out of Kaifeng to secondary clan centers established in Luoyang and the Southern Capital, so that the Jurchens were not able to capture all members of the imperial clan. Still, they did take thousands.[58] The Jurchens had copies of the *Jade Registers* listing all members of the imperial clan and used it to check which princes, princesses, or clansmen were missing, then order officials in the capital to track down those in hiding. A deadline of 2/25 was established for them to be turned over to the Jin authorities, and the Kaifeng prefectural government did a vigorous search "as though they were thieves." Officers went around the city calling out, "Do not hide Zhao family members. If you have hidden any, produce them immediately or suffer the consequences."[59]

Huizong and Qinzong, however much they mourned their fate, were treated much better than the princesses, palace ladies, and other younger women taken prisoner. Shock and terror were used to get them to accept their fate. A couple days before the main group arrived, three women who had resisted Wolibu had been stabbed with iron poles and left to bleed to death in front of his tent. When the huge group of women were brought there on 2/7, the guards pointed out these three to them as a warning. Princess Fujin, who had arrived at the Jin camp a week earlier, was assigned the task of calming the frightened women, then getting them to change into entertainers' clothes to serve at a party Nianhan was hosting for his generals. At the feast, Nianhan ordered the palace women to sit among his generals and serve them wine. Three who resisted were executed and another committed suicide. A few days later, on 2/14, the palace ladies and female slaves were moved to a newly built camp at Green Enclosure along with the wives and daughters of the imperial clan. Two days later, an order was issued that the women given to Jurchen soldiers should start wearing their hair in Jurchen fashion and let doctors abort their fetuses if they were pregnant. The next day, the Jurchen command made its selection from the women collected, choosing 3,000 women for the basic tribute and 1,400 to be given as rewards to the soldiers. Wolibu and Nianhan each took 100 serving women.[60]

No source describes conditions in these camps, but they cannot have been very good because a great many people died there. The *Record of the Song Captives*, by a Jin author identified as Kegong, states that of the more than sixteen thousand people taken as captives into the Jin camps, two thousand died during their two-to-four-month stay there. Among them was Huizong's eleven-year-old son Prince Ying who died a week after arriving. On 2/30 Qinzong sent in an order that food and clothing be sent from the palace for the captives.[61]

On 1127/2/18, Wolibu hosted a feast for Nianhan and other leading Jurchens and forced Huizong, Qinzong, and their empresses to attend, probably as part of the entertainment for his men. Wine was served by fifty-two of the confiscated women—twenty consorts and princesses and thirty-two singing girls. Huizong, Qinzong, and their empresses, mortified at seeing them, wanted to leave but were not permitted. After the meal, Wolibu told Huizong that Nianhan's son Sheyema liked Huizong's daughter Princess Fujin, and he wanted Huizong to give her to him.[62] Huizong replied, "Fujin is already married. In China this is very shameful; one does not take two husbands. We are not like your esteemed country in having no taboo against it." To this Nianhan replied, "Recently we ordered the distribution of the prisoners. How can you resist this command? Let each guest take two of them." Huizong protested, "Everywhere on earth people all have daughters and daughters-in-law." Nianhan railed at him and sent him out. Empress Zheng, who saw the wife of her nephew among those serving, knelt and beseeched Nianhan, "My family was not involved in the government. Please let her go." Nianhan nodded and her nephew's wife was released.[63]

Such clemency was definitely the exception. On 2/20, the fiancée of one of Huizong's sons committed suicide. Three of Huizong's daughters died in Wolibu's camp between 2/25 and 3/7, probably either because they resisted rape or committed suicide.[64]

Jin made no attempt to oust or replace the Song officials who ran the government in Kaifeng, but they tried to make them understand who their real masters were. They sent in soldiers to thoroughly search the palaces, assigning former eunuchs to show searchers where treasures were kept. During these searches twenty-five of Huizong's seals were found in Extended Blessings and Dragon Virtue palaces, including both jade and gold ones.[65] Jin also pressed the Song court officials to select someone from another family to be installed as emperor. Leading officials submitted memorial after memorial pleading that the Zhao line be continued, perhaps with a descendant of Shenzong or more distant clansman. Weary of their foot-dragging, the Jin commanders threatened once again to turn their soldiers loose unless the grand councilors promptly came up with a name that the officials, elders, and clergy could agree was a man of virtue, worthy of the throne. They seem to have assumed that this method, reminiscent of methods of selecting rulers among the northern tribes since the time of the Xiongnu, would result in a ruler who would command authority. The Jurchen leaders seemed to find it difficult to comprehend why the Chinese elite would cling to the Song imperial house after it suffered such a devastating defeat, especially since they were giving them the opportunity to select someone else in their place. Under this sort of intense pressure, the Song officials finally nominate a grand councilor, Zhang Bangchang, who was not in Kaifeng to refuse.[66]

The Jurchen commanders were getting ready to pack up and leave, but the full quota of gold and silver still had not been filled. When Nianhan's soldiers discovered that some of the palace women had jewelry with them, he drew the conclusion that the confiscation of gold and silver had not been thorough enough and ordered it renewed. It was suggested that Jin could check if anyone still had precious metals by offering to sell food to the starving inhabitants for gold or silver. When people did come to buy it, even at exorbitant rates, they took this as proof that the Song officials assigned the task of collecting the gold and silver had lied when they said that the city had been stripped of treasure. Four officials were taken to Southern Infusion Gate on 2/24 where they were required to take off their clothes and lie face down. They were then beaten over a hundred strokes. Another four officials were beaten to death with the large cudgel while kneeling, then beheaded.[67]

Huizong ended up spending nearly two months in the Jurchen camp, giving him plenty of time to contemplate the fate of defeated rulers. He was an admirer of the poetry, painting, and calligraphy of the defeated ruler of the Southern Tang, Li Yu (937–978), who had been brought as a captive to Kaifeng in the early decades of the Song dynasty and went on to produce some of his best poetry after he lost his throne. Then there was the more recent example of the Liao imperial family. Tianzuo had not stayed in his capital, but the Jin had gone to great lengths to hunt him down, and he did not live long in captivity. His sons, daughters, and other family members had been made slaves, a fact Huizong's captors did not let him forget.

Still, Huizong did not give up hope. According to Cao Xun, after Huizong had been in the Jurchen camp more than twenty days, he wrote a letter to Nianhan, relating the history of the treaty between Song and Jin, his decision to abdicate, his trip south, his return, and his subsequent quiet life in a Daoist temple. "Although I did not interfere in government matters at all, treacherous officials drove a wedge between me and my son, and even when your great army came south, I was not informed." He accepted blame for the failure of his son to adhere to the treaty, and offered to trade places with Qinzong: "I would be willing to take the place of my heir and undertake the long journey to serve at your court, but I wish that my son could be given a small commandery in the malarial regions of the far south so that he could carry on the sacrifices to our ancestors and live out his natural years." The next day a messenger brought his letter back, telling Huizong not to worry but also that everything depended on the instructions of their emperor. Huizong also wrote a prayer confessing his mistakes, which he burnt at midnight.[68]

After having devoted over three months to stripping Kaifeng of its assets, by the third month of 1127 the Jurchens were nearly ready to leave. On 1127/3/4 a commander was dispatched with 1,050 carts of books and ritual implements. On 3/7 the former grand councilor Zhang Bangchang was installed as emperor of a puppet regime given the name Chu. Places outsides the city walls were more thoroughly searched. Last minute searches of a temple turned up paintings and calligraphies owned by Zhu Mian's family. On 3/12 and 3/13 the temples devoted to the Song imperial ancestors were looted—the soldiers even took the clothing off the statues of imperial ancestors. On 3/15, however, the Jurchens agreed to a request from Zhang Bangchang not to dig up the Song emperor's tombs.[69] On 3/16 Huizong, Qinzong, and their empresses were given ordinary people's clothing to wear and

Huizong was ordered not to wear his Daoist robes. Some of the specialists taken from Kaifeng were released on 3/21, and on 3/24 about three thousand women and children were let back into the city, along with the bodies of three princesses and eleven officials. On 3/23 Qinzong wrote to his former officials, asking them to send three thousand strings of cash from the Left Treasury so he could prepare food for the upcoming trip. Perhaps in response, the Jurchens gave Huizong three thousand ounces of silver and assorted supplies for the trip.[70]

On 1127/3/23, the Jin declared that the gold and silver quota would be considered filled, with much of the total made up through women. The document submitted by the Kaifeng prefecture gave the breakdown. Altogether, 247,600 ounces of gold and 7,728,000 ounces of silver were collected, a little less than the year before. At 50 ounces to the bar, this equaled 49,520 bars of gold and 1,545,600 bars of silver. Another 607,700 bars of gold and 2,583,100 bars of silver were credited in exchange for 11,635 women, of whom 129 were princesses and high-ranking consorts, 451 low-ranking consorts or women of the close branches of the imperial clan, 1,241 more distant clanswomen, 1,083 palace ladies and palace entertainers, 2,091 wives of close clansmen, 2,007 wives of distant clansmen, 1,314 women of the entertainment quarters, and 3,319 women of the families of officials or nobles.[71]

⮑ How SHOULD WE LOOK on the Jurchen invasion and siege of Kaifeng? These were traumatic events to all those who lived through them and a source of ignominy even to those living in relative safety in more distant parts of the country. Educated men of the day, beginning with eye witnesses and continuing for several generations, searched for explanations for the events. Some collected as much evidence as possible, others attempted moral or political analyses. Since scholars generally saw themselves as potential advisors to the throne, they did not focus on technical military mistakes, such as particular battles that might have been won if troops had been deployed in a different fashion or armed with different weapons, but with the decisions made at court. The general strategy adopted at court—trying to negotiate a peace agreement—had failed, from which fact many inferred that the opponents of appeasement must have been correct. But the aggressive stance taken by Qinzong's court once the Jurchen departed in 1126 had not worked either. Moreover, since most battles between Song and Jin ended in Song defeat, it is difficult to be confident that Song could have turned back the enemy simply by engaging the enemy more times.

A common assumption in much of this literature is that Huizong brought on this disaster by his love of luxury. One of the main charges made against men close to him, such as Cai Jing, Cai You, Wang Fu, Liang Shicheng, and Tong Guan, is that they aided and abetted him in these inclinations. It is certainly true that military expenses began to overwhelm government revenues, probably beginning in early 1121 when an army was dispatched to suppress the Fang La rebellion. But court expenses were a relatively small part of the overall finances of the government. Moreover, the enormous list of gold, silver, silk and other valuables that were removed from the palace and government treasuries to pay the huge indemnities in 1126 and 1127 is evidence enough that the palace was not down to its last string of cash.

Did Huizong's extravagance undermine popular support for the dynasty? Certainly the officials Qinzong put in charge had little sympathy for him, even if they could not say anything disrespectful in their memorials. Yet, given that people were dying of starvation and freezing to death, I am more impressed by the loyalty of the populace of Kaifeng to the dynasty than its occasional outbursts of fury. It is true that Kaifeng residents jumped at the chance to cut down the trees and demolish the buildings at the Northeast Marchmount, but then they had already broken up other government buildings for firewood. Not only did people wait out in the snow for Qinzong to return, but they showed in many small ways their grief at the capture of Huizong, his sons and daughters, and all those who worked in his palace. After all, the issue that most inflamed the literati critics of Huizong—his exclusion of a couple hundred leading figures from office—was not relevant to the commoners in the city, who seem on the whole to have appreciated the splendor of his reign and the ways it enlivened life in the city.[72] Huizong's charitable ventures seem to have earned him some gratitude among the poor. We are told that when the city was turned upside down in the search for gold and silver, the paupers living in one of the poorhouses were able to collect together two ounces of gold and seventy of silver to contribute.[73]

What of other explanations of this disaster? From the Jin point of view, Song brought on its own demise by not fulfilling its end of the agreements negotiated between the two. Bad faith, however, was never

a peculiarly Song failing. Both the early negotiations for the joint attack on Liao and the later negotiations to get the Jin to return north
were marked by continual changes in the terms of the bargains, generally by Jin as the party in a better bargaining position. It made sense
for Jin when issuing propaganda in Chinese to claim it was attacking
Song to punish it for its treaty violations, because interstate language
of the period did not have a vocabulary to justify waging war to gain
plunder. From their behavior, however, it seems likely that men like
Aguda, Nianhan, and Wolibu spoke differently when discussing their
goals among themselves.

Many literati writers assumed one reason Song armies went down to
defeat was that eunuchs commanded them. Tong Guan was a eunuch,
and he led the original failed campaign to take Yanjing. However, men
from families with long military backgrounds, such as Chong Shidao
and Yao Youzhong, did not have much more success, nor did literati
like Li Gang. There are undoubtedly many elements that contributed
to the poor showing of the Song armies, but it is important not to assume that these battles were the Song's to win or lose. The Jurchens
had clearly put together an awesome military machine, perhaps one
more on the order of the subsequent Mongol armies than usually recognized. Much of the failure of the Song to fend off the Jurchens should
be credited to the military genius of Aguda, Wuqimai, Nianhan, and
Wolibu, rather than blamed on the ineptitude of Tong Guan, Chong
Shidao, and Li Gang. Herbert Franke observes that Song military
leadership suffered from "the tendency to organize warfare in detail
from the palace, that is, from a distance and disregarding the situation
in the field."[74] Other weaknesses contributed as well. Intelligence was
woefully inadequate. Despite the numerous envoys sent to the Jin court,
Song failed to realize how different Liao and Jin were as allies and enemies. The political culture of Huizong's and Qinzong's courts also did
not help matters. Once Qinzong invited in anti-reformers, their desire
for revenge against their political opponents was so ferocious that much
more attention was devoted to demoting, banishing, and executing
Huizong's officials than to rethinking defense, on the oft-stated grounds
that internal problems were a much more serious threat than anything
an outside barbarian could do. Thus, no leader emerged to unite the
political elite behind a defense plan. Given the intensity of factional
hatred, it might in fact have been better if Huizong had not abdicated,

but kept in place a stable if dictatorial group of ministers. They could have carried out a much more orderly transfer of the capital than Huizong's son Gaozong would be able to manage a year and a half later, and might well have been able to preserve more of the dynasty's accumulated wealth, or at least kept it out of the hands of the Jurchens.

None of this should be taken as an effort to absolve Huizong of guilt. He was clearly not the ruler China needed in a military crisis of this magnitude. Many of the decisions he made, such as the honors and rewards he heaped on the turncoat general Guo Yaoshi, came back to haunt him. Huizong had nothing of the love of confrontation that Aguda and Nianhan had, and when everything seemed to be unraveling around him, he had an intense desire to flee and let others take responsibility. He was brilliant at one central component of rulership—the creation of imperial majesty and splendor. Perhaps aware that he would make a poor crisis manager, he took the primary option open to him within the Chinese political system of abdicating in favor of the heir apparent. Unfortunately, even though Qinzong was then in his mid-twenties, the prime age for military daring, he did not prove any more effective in the crisis than Huizong.

Looking at the situation purely from Huizong's perspective, perhaps the most fateful decision was to obey Qinzong and return to Kaifeng in 1126/4. Had he remained in the south, he could either have stayed out of the way of those organizing resistance or given them whatever help they requested. In none of the surviving sources, however, does Huizong say that he made a terrible mistake by complying, or that Qinzong was wrong to require his return. Perhaps he felt that the tragic consequences were so obvious to everyone that to mention them would seem to be placing blame on others, something he made an effort not to do.

17

Enduring Captivity,
1127–1135

> When you see Prince Gou, let him know how much I think of
> him and the bitterness and grief we are enduring. No one
> knows when we will see each other again. He should restore
> order to the Central Plain as soon as possible and quickly
> rescue his parents.
>
> —*Huizong's instructions to Cao Xun before sending him to try to*
> *escape and carry a message to Huizong's one son not in captivity*

*D*URING THE FIRST FORTY-FIVE YEARS of his life, Huizong
rarely left Kaifeng; indeed for weeks at a time he did not even leave the
Palace City. The last eight years of Huizong's life, therefore, marked a
radical break with everything that had come before. He not only was
forced to leave Kaifeng, but was taken progressively further and further
from civilization as he knew it. He did not mix much with ordinary
people, but he did endure hardship.

Just before the fourteen thousand captives were to begin the journey north, Nianhan summoned Huizong. When Huizong in purple
Daoist robes and Daoist headgear got down from his sedan chair,
Nianhan came out of his tent to meet him. Seven weeks earlier, when
Huizong had first met Nianhan at Green Enclosure, he had defiantly
expressed his exasperation at the behavior of the conquerors. By this
point, however, Huizong knew that trying to intimidate his captors
would get him nowhere. Recognizing that his best hope lay in trying
to evoke Nianhan's sympathy, he told him: "I am at fault and deserve
to be taken north. But I dare to beg that you let the princesses who
have already married stay here. It would be a great favor." Nianhan did
not reply. Later Empress Zheng entered and said to Nianhan, "I am at
fault, and it is right that I follow the senior emperor on the trip north.

But my relatives have never participated in the government. I dare to beg that they be left here." This time Nianhan nodded his approval, so her relatives were sent back that day.[1]

The next day, on 3/28, the Jin soldiers finally came down off the walls of Kaifeng, which they had occupied for nearly four months. Knowing that the two emperors, the imperial family, and the thousands of other captives were about to depart, the newly enthroned Zhang Bangchang, accompanied by officials and Imperial Academy students, went to the Gate of Southern Infusion to take leave of Qinzong and Huizong "from a distance." For their part, Huizong, Qinzong, the two empresses, the princes, consorts, princesses, and sons-in-law also made a ritual of saying goodbye by prostrating themselves facing the direction of the palace and the ancestral shrines. Huizong lay on the ground face down, so grief stricken that his son Prince Qi had to help him up.[2]

Huizong and Qinzong were not the first (nor would they be the last) Chinese emperors to be taken as prisoners to their conqueror's lands. Huizong must surely have seen the resemblance of his situation to that of the ruler of the Later Jin whose state was conquered by the Kitans in 947. The Kitans plundered the capital thoroughly, demanding, as the Jurchens were later to do, all palace ladies, eunuchs, workmen, musical instruments, documents, weapons, armor, and silk. The ruler and a sizable group of relatives, eunuchs, and officials were moved several times, and eventually given lands to till so that they could support themselves. The deposed ruler lived on in captivity seventeen years until 964.[3] Huizong could hope that his fate would be no worse.

Convoys

Transport of the nearly fifteen thousand captives was organized into seven separate convoys. The first convoy was composed of more than 2,200 clansmen and male nobles and over 3,400 clanswomen and female nobles.[4] The second convoy was much smaller, with 35 people, all women and children, among them the mother and wife of Prince Gou (Consorts Wei and Xing), two princes, two princesses, two princes' daughters, and the wives and concubines of another of Huizong's sons. It was under Nianhan's son Sheyema and other generals. The third convoy, under Nianhan's son Xiebao, had 37 women, including the wives and concubines of Qinzong and two princesses. The fourth convoy had Huizong, his consorts, his two brothers, nineteen of his sons, plus grandsons, sons-in-law, and enough maids to bring the total to more than 1,940 people. Wolibu's younger brother Eluguan was in charge. The fifth convoy again was all women, consisting of 103 princesses and consorts of princes plus 142 serving women. Wolibu took charge of this one. The sixth convoy was huge, made up of 3,180 women and 3,412 commoners drafted for their special skills, including doctors, craftsmen, entertainers, and the like. The seventh convoy, under Nianhan's command, had Qinzong and his sons and daughters, plus 12 officials including Sun Fu, He Zhuo, and Qin Gui, and 144 serving women.[5] For a summary, see Table 17.1.

The first six convoys took the easiest route to Yanjing, through the relatively flat plains of Hebei (see Map 3). The seventh convoy retraced the route of Nianhan's army through Shanxi as far as Taiyuan before turning east toward Beijing.

Conditions on the march north were difficult, and many did not survive. Of the 6,592 in the sixth convoy, 1,892 (28 percent) failed to make it Yanjing, some dying on the way, others, especially young children, abandoned along the road when they could not keep up. According to the *Record of the Bian Capital*, by Tao Xuangan, those transported were grouped into troops of 500 and driven like cattle by several dozen mounted soldiers. Most were city dwellers not used to walking long distances, and if they fell behind they were beaten or killed, so that bodies littered the fields they passed. According to the Imperial Academy student Ding Teqi, on the march Qinzong rode a horse, with a hundred mounted soldiers surrounding him. Huizong's two brothers, Wu and Ssi, the princes of Yan and Yue, had to ride in an oxcart. The other clan members in the party had to walk. Huizong occasionally rode a horse, but most of the time seems to have been in an oxcart pulled by five oxen, driven by two Jurchen who did not speak Chinese.[6]

After the first day on the road, when they set up camp, Huizong and the Jurchen commanders slept in two felt tents and the rest of the people in his party were in forty-eight cloth tents set up in a circle around them. The other parties followed similar strategies, undoubtedly for security reasons. In the case of Qinzong and his son Prince Chen, when they slept their hands and feet were tied to prevent escape.

Table 17.1. Captives taken north in 1127/4

	Convoy							Total
	1	2	3	4	5	6	7	
Princes, princesses, and their spouses	5	34	2	42	103		3	189
Consorts and palace ladies of Huizong		1		651				652
Consorts and palace ladies of Qinzong			35					35
Imperial clansmen	5,600+							5,600+
Others				1,247	142	6,592	156	8,135
Total	5,605+	35	37	1,940+	245	6,592	159	14,613+

Sources: SFJ 244–250 and KFFZ 92–122.

478

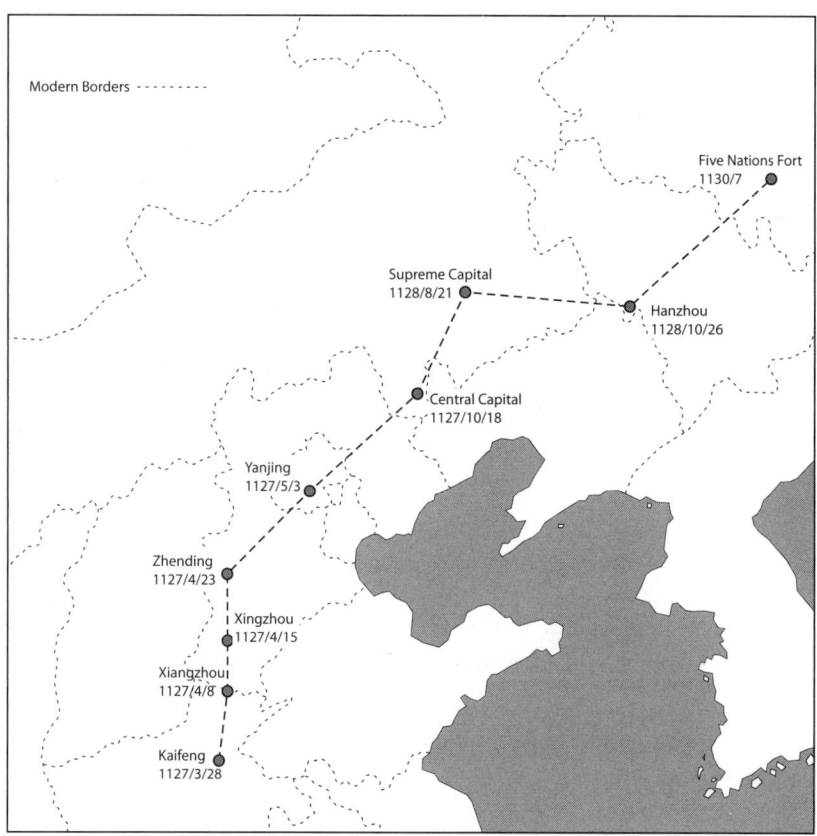

Map 3. Huizong's route in captivity

According to Cao Xun, the Jurchen generally erected a wooden barrier around the camp, with gaps between the planks that allowed people to peer through. Peddlers would come up to it to sell food, and the Jurchen often used these peddlers to spread rumors to the captives, in the hope that if they thought they might soon be rescued they would not try to escape.[7]

While traveling, the captives were expected to prepare their own food. According to Cao Xun, each evening after camp was set up, rice was distributed on a per capita basis but people had to supply their own firewood and water to cook. Since they were not allowed out of the camp, they soon learned to pick up what water and wood they could while they were traveling and save it for the evening. Sometimes, in the vicinity of cities, peddlers came with other food. No food was brought for the oxen, which also were not given much rest or chance to graze, as a result of which 40 to 50 percent of them had died within a month before reaching Zhending. Those that died were slaughtered and used for food. Once when Cao Xun was buying food for two ounces of silver, the peddlers refused the money when they learned the food was for Huizong.[8]

Several first-person accounts survive of the experiences of these convoys. One is by the Chinese interpreter assigned to the second convoy, which included Prince Gou's mother and wife. Later the third convoy joined up with them, which had two of Qinzong's consorts and his baby daughter. This group's destination was the Supreme Capital, which they reached on 5/23. The text records in rather matter-of-fact manner the hardships the members of this party endured. For instance,

> 1127/3/29. Because the two consorts Xiang and Zhu and the two princesses had fallen off their horses and hurt their fetuses [miscarried], they could no longer ride on horseback.[9]
>
> 1127/4/2. We left early. At a halting place, Consort Zhu turned to the side to relieve herself, and [the Jin soldier] Guolu forced [raped] her. He also would take opportunities to try to get into [Qinzong's] Empress Zhu's vehicle. The [Jurchen] prince's younger brother whipped him.[10]
>
> 4/4. We crossed the river and went north. The commander, Great Prince Gaitian, met us. When he saw Guolu riding on the same horse with Princess Huanhuan, he killed Guolu and threw his body in the river. Gaitian wanted to help Huanhuan leave, but our prince told him of the edict ordering them to bring [the captives] to the capital, so he accompanied us.[11]
>
> 4/11, noon. . . . The commander Shaohe prepared a meal for the two [Jurchen] princes. Since Consort Zhu and Consort Zhu Shen were good at songs, he made them compose some new songs. After he repeatedly insisted, Consort Zhu composed this song, "Formerly I lived in heaven above, in pearly palaces and jade towers. Now I live among the grass and brambles, my blue robe soaked in tears. My body is bent and my will humbled. I hate the difficult snow. Not until I arrive at the springs below will my grief end." Consort Zhu Shen matched the song: "When young

I was rich and high ranking, dressed in fine gauzes. Grown up, I entered the palace to attend the one on the throne. Now I am cast down in a foreign land. My fate is not timely, my will is not strong." In both cases they composed the songs but did not sing them.[12]

4/18. Arrived at Yanjing. The [Jurchen] prince, his younger brother Gaitian, and Atiji did not go to the prefectural office but lodged at Pity and Loyalty Shrine. The people of Yan had been clamoring to see the Song captives for a month, since they heard they were coming. When they arrived, all the relatives of the [Jurchen] princes, down to distant relatives through marriage, all gathered, as though to view rare treasures. They greeted the consorts with their hugging ritual, showing great respect, but since the Chinese women were not used to it, it alarmed them.[13]

4/28. Crossed the Great Wall and arrived at the border of Qianzhou. Desert stretched for ten thousand *li*, with no sign of human habitation.

5/1. We arrived at a temple and tied up the horses. The [Jurchen] prince and the consorts and princesses all washed their hands and burnt incense. The consorts and princesses had me write prayers for them, expressing their wishes to return to their native land. The prince ridiculed their stupidity but did not prevent them from doing it.[14]

5/8. We crossed the Liangyuwo River. These two days [there was so much rain that] it was like we were traveling through water. Although the consorts and princesses were in chairs on the backs of camels or horses, they still got soaked through all layers of their clothes. The sufferings in hell cannot be worse than this.[15]

The original destination of the other convoys was Yanjing. Several of those who accompanied Huizong at least part of the way left accounts of their experiences. Cao Xun only accompanied Huizong as far as Yanjing, but his description of that part of the journey is relatively full.[16] Cai Tiao, who stayed with Huizong for many years, did not write as much detail on particular incidents, but offers the fullest accounts of the ways Huizong spent his time.[17] Another account was written by Zhao Zizhi who traveled to Yanjing with the clansmen but got free a year later in 1128/4.[18] For day-to-day listing of events, the fullest source is the anonymous *Shenyin yu*, apparently by a Song subject often in the company of Huizong.[19] The account below draws primarily from these four sources.

Before his convoy departed, Huizong was taken to Wolibu's camp at Liu Family Temple. Wolibu had Huizong, Empress Zheng, and the princes and princesses sit and drink with him. Using a translator, he tried to cheer up Huizong, telling him that dynastic transitions were to be expected and that even Yao and Shun had abdicated their thrones in favor of worthy people. He also told him he was being treated better than the Liao ruler, as he was being allowed to keep his children, while all of Tianzuo's children had been distributed to the soldiers as rewards. Huizong expressed his thanks, but brought up his idea that he could substitute for his son, arguing that he alone should bear the responsibility for everything that had gone wrong. "The fault is mine. Please let Jingkang [Qinzong] stay with some small commandery as a fief. The princes, princesses, and their wives and husbands do not participate in government. I beg you to let them go." Wolibu said that the Jin emperor had rejected the idea, but he could bring it up again after they reached Yanjing and tried to assure Huizong that "from now on there will be peace and happiness." Wolibu also asked that one of Huizong's consorts named Wang be given the status of princess and married to a younger son of Nianhan, which Huizong approved. Although Wolibu did not see Huizong in the coming days, he had his people send him food every day, including chicken, rabbit, fish, wine, and fruit. Traveling by cart, however, made Huizong queasy and he had no appetite for meat or wine.[20]

During the invasion several months earlier the Jurchen armies had passed through this territory, but they had not in any real sense pacified it. Not only were forces under Prince Gou trying to hold territory, but roving bandits had become a major problem. On 1127/4/2 because of such disturbances the convoy stopped for two days. The captives were continually hopeful that Song forces would come to rescue them and one of Huizong's consorts made a garment for him to wear if he thought there was a chance to escape.[21]

On 4/5 the convoy crossed the Yellow River. Two days later, when a soldier had raped one of the consorts, all Huizong could do was advise them not to get separated from the others. On the 4/8, the convoy reached the suburbs of Xiangzhou, where one of the divisions with tribute women was also camping. They learned that because it had rained for several days and the ox carts they were traveling in were soaked through, some of the women had sought shelter in the tents occupied by the Jurchen guards, which were set up in a circle around them, but this proved a flawed strategy, since "most were raped to death."[22]

On 4/15 the convoy arrived outside Xingzhou. Despite several days of storms, they kept going, even though carts were breaking up and horses falling. The death toll from violence also was mounting. Part of the difficulty of the trip was the devastation the captives saw around them. In many places bodies still lay unburied. The captives often got injured when their carts overturned, and women were frequently raped. On 4/16, Huizong's brother Wu, the prince of Yan, died, reportedly of starvation. Huizong had him laid out in a horse trough, which was so short his feet stuck out. His request that the body be sent back for burial was refused and it was cremated. Huizong took the cinerary casket on the rest of the journey. At the end of the day, when the convoy stopped, Huizong spoke mournfully to his brother's ashes, saying, "We will be together on this trip." Prince Wu's wife, in a different party, was not allowed to join them for the funeral.[23]

On 4/23, Huizong's party reached Zhending and for the first time entered a city. Huizong and Wolibu entered on horseback, the public knowing who they were because of the lead flag of the procession read, "The Senior [Retired] Emperor." According to Cao Xun, the Jurchen guards did not interfere when the local people wailed at the sight.[24] The next day, undoubtedly for the Jurchens' own amusement, Wolibu brought Huizong and Empress Zheng to a polo game. An attendant asked Huizong to commemorate the occasion in a poem. Huizong replied that he had not been in the mood for poetry since Kaifeng fell, but in the end acquiesced and turned out a poem designed to appeal to his hosts, who after hearing it translated expressed their appreciation. It read:

> In satin jackets and on strong horses
> The two teams hold themselves apart.
> When the hundred mounts gallop,
> The ball flies like a shooting star.
> To win the very first prize

Strike it right across the goal;
Do not sweep it from the side
For then the ball will go astray.[25]

Huizong's party stayed in Zhending for three days, changing horses and carts. They learned that Consort Wei and her party had been through eleven days earlier. One day, Wolibu hosted another banquet, inviting not only Huizong but also his sons and letting Empress Zheng and the princesses and consorts have a meal together in another room.

On 4/25 Wolibu had Huizong attend a hunt. There he encountered two turncoat generals, Guo Yaoshi and Zhang Linghui. According to Cao Xun,

After the meal, a horse and a purple umbrella were sent to invite Huizong and he and Wolibu went together to the field to view the hunt. After a while the horses all had foxes and rabbits hanging on them. Suddenly, two people came and stood in front of Huizong's horse. Wolibu pointed to them and said, "These are your former subjects Guo Yaoshi and Zhang Linghui."

After this introduction, the two men both bowed twice. Linghui then withdrew, but Guo Yaoshi knelt in front of the horse and said, "In the past I was Your Majesty's subject. I fought to the death at Yanjing several times but did not have the strength to prevail and so surrendered to Jin. I failed to repay Your Majesty's generosity." As he talked, tears streamed down and he bowed again.

Huizong said to him, "Things worked out this way both because of heaven and the actions of human beings. But that day, you were just one death short [i.e., you would have wanted to die yourself as well]."

Wolibu said, "Yaoshi is quite loyal to the southern court [i.e., Song]."

Huizong said, "Without ever having resisted a large army, Yaoshi was credited with great accomplishments and overly rewarded, leading to this disaster."

Wolibu said, "He first was not loyal to Tianzuo, then did not contribute to the southern court."

"So true," said Huizong.[26]

Although the Jurchen had been able to cross Hebei to get to Kaifeng six months earlier, they had not stopped to attack the major walled cities, but had gone around them. Part of the agreement Qinzong made with Jin was to cede all of this territory to them, but not all prefectural commanders were willing to surrender without a fight. Among the prefectures holding out was Zhongshan. On 4/27, Huizong and Wolibu set out without the others for Zhongshan. On arrival the next day, Huizong tried to convince the Song commander to surrender, telling him, "I am the Lord of the Dao emperor, now on my way to an audience with the emperor of Jin. It would be right for you to surrender." When the commander refused to obey, a Jurchen officer killed him and the city surrendered.[27]

Sometime before reaching Yanjing, Huizong decided to see if he could get a message to his son Prince Gou. He took apart the collar of a jacket and wrote an eight-word message on the piece of silk: "Please take immediate action to rescue your parents," then signed it and sewed it back inside. Apparently the convoy with Prince Gou's wife and mother was camped in the same location at the time because Huizong next went to Prince Gou's wife to get some token, and she supplied a hairpin that he had given her. A note from Prince Gou's mother Consort Wei was also added. Huizong asked Cao Xun to carry it for him, and he agreed to look for an opportunity to slip away. As seen in the epigraph to this chapter, before sending him off, Huizong enjoined him not to let their suffering on the march north be forgotten. He expressed a hope of being rescued but added that recovering the Central Plain and preserving the ancestral shrines were more important than rescuing him. He also made a comment on how things had come to this pass: "[The Song founder] Taizu made an agreement which was kept in the Supreme Shrine, swearing not to execute high officials or employ eunuchs. Violations of this would be inauspicious. Therefore through seven emperors there was no change in the policy. I always think that during the Jingkang era [when Qinzong ruled], the executions went too far. Even if this is not the sole cause of the current calamity, warning should be taken from it." Huizong also told Cao Xun to remind Prince Gou of the example of Emperor Guangwu, who had succeeded in restoring the Han dynasty in the first century AD. Prince Gou's wife told Cao Xun to tell her husband that his mother had maintained her devotions to the Four Saints and to ask him to sponsor Daoist offering ceremonies on her behalf. Cao Xun succeeded on this trip, arriving at the Song Southern Capital in southern Henan in the seventh month and showing the imperial garment to Prince Gou, who by this point had been enthroned and can be called by his posthumous name, Gaozong. Cao Xun proposed that the new court recruit a group of daring navy men to try to rescue Huizong via a sea route, but this idea was rejected as impractical and Cao Xun was given no assignments for the next nine years.[28]

Besides Cao Xun, another member of the imperial party to escape was Huizong's eighteenth son, Zhen, then seventeen *sui*. After hiding for some time among commoners, he was able to get word to Ma Kuo, at that time leading Chinese resistance forces in Hebei. Ma Kuo made the prince the nominal head of his group. He also carried a letter from him to his brother Gaozong, asking for help in fighting Jin. When Ma Kuo and the letter arrived in the third month of 1128, Gaozong was in Yangzhou. His councilors were afraid the prince might be an imposter, but Gaozong assured them that he could recognize his brother from the handwriting of the letter. Still, the presence of another prince who could conceivably enter Kaifeng worried Gaozong's court, and no real aid was provided. Before long the encampment where Prince Zhen was staying was attacked by Jin forces. Prince Zhen was apparently taken captive and forced to rejoin the imperial captives.[29]

Yanjing

On 4/30, after nearly a month on the road, Wolibu sent Huizong and some other members of the convoy ahead to Yanjing, where they arrived on 5/13. Wolibu followed a few days later with the rest of the group, and the whole party, nine hundred-odd, were settled in Extended Longevity Temple where they were treated comparatively well. There they learned what had happened to the other groups: Twenty-plus people with Consort Wei had passed by on their way to the Supreme Capital, while thirty-odd with Empress Zhu were staying at Pity and Loyalty Shrine. The convoy that began with more than 5,600 clansmen had arrived on 4/27. However, because of the long journey, exposure to the elements and inadequate food, many had perished, and women and children unable to ride horses had been abandoned on the road, so that less than 3,000 had reached Yanjing; moreover, in the next couple of weeks about half of them died. On 5/19 they heard that convoys that started with 3,000 tribute women, 3,000 families of craftsmen, and 2,500 carts of goods would arrive. After they were checked in, half of them were sent to the Supreme Capital. Of the remaining, the palace women and eunuchs were given to Jurchen officers. The craftsmen were set free and expected to make their own living, and the nonpalace women were largely sold into prostitution.[30]

Cai Tiao and Cao Xun record many incidents to demonstrate that Huizong had sympathy for captives whose plight was worse than his. According to Cai Tiao, by the time the captives had reached Yanjing, more than half the people in the imperial party were sick. Huizong had all the clothes taken out and ordered Li Zongyan to trade them for drugs, which he then prepared and distributed. These medications reportedly cured 80 to 90 percent of the people. When Huizong heard that many of the clansmen staying in a separate temple lacked adequate food and clothing, he asked Jiang E to make a list of them all, with their ranks indicated. He then had him distribute the silk he had received from the Jin generals to the clansmen for them to use to make winter clothes.[31]

Back in Song territory, there were further developments. Zhang Bangchang had never wanted to be made emperor, and once the Jurchen left, he invited into the palace the only person remaining in Kaifeng with some claim to represent the Song imperial family, Zhezong's former empress Meng who had been deposed by him and sent to a Daoist nunnery. Empress Meng did what was needed to make Prince Gou's succession legitimate by naming him as the successor. Gaozong did not think it advisable to enter Kaifeng, so he was formally enthroned on 5/1 at the Song's Southern Capital in southern Henan.

There is more than one version of how Huizong learned of this event. According to Zhao Zizhi, he heard on 6/2 when Wolibu and Nianhan's younger son Xiebao invited Huizong and the imperial relatives to yet another polo and archery party.[32] Xiebao personally participated in the ball game and knelt and offered Huizong and Empress Zheng a cup of wine, observing the rituals of a son-in-law, implying that he had married one of Huizong's daughters. Wolibu, apparently in a generous mood, sent Huizong a copy of an amnesty Gaozong had issued that had made its way to Yanjing. Huizong then summoned the consorts to celebrate, "pleasure animating his dragon countenance."[33]

This version could perhaps be consistent with another account, which has the Song official Sima Pu finding a copy of the amnesty, but being discovered by Jin authorities when he tried to get it to Huizong. Cai Tao reported yet another version, that Huizong discovered the amnesty after he sent out a servant to buy some incense, and the yellow paper package he came back with turned out to be a copy of the amnesty. Hong Hao also claimed to have gotten word to Huizong and Qinzong of Gaozong's enthronement through a merchant.[34] It is of course possible that several people tried to get word to Huizong, but not possible that they were all first, even if they wanted to think they were.

A few days later two of Huizong's sons arrived back from the Supreme Capital, bringing with them wives given to them by Jin, both from the defeated Kitan palace, one a Kitan princess, the other a former consort.[35] Since most of Huizong's consorts, palace ladies, daughters, and daughters-in-law had already been distributed to Jurchen (and others would continue to be for the next couple of years), the receipt of these new brides marks a shift in the gender composition of the people with whom Huizong lived. For most of his life, while living in the palace, Huizong had been surrounded by many more women than men. As his sons grew up they moved out, but his numerous consorts stayed with him through the years. With the numbers of his consorts severely curtailed, and his daughters and daughters-in-law largely gone, Huizong lived with a group of men he had known for years but relatively few women who were close to him. With time, as his sons and grandsons were given new wives to replace those confiscated, something close to a one-to-one ratio would be established, but Huizong's ties would be much stronger to the males than to the females.

Cai Tiao reported that Huizong wrote more than a thousand poems during his exile.[36] One surviving poem is explicitly linked to his period in Yanjing as it was inscribed on the wall of a Buddhist temple there.

> With nine generations the great enterprise suddenly stops.
> I was crazy not to listen to my upright officials' advice.
> Willingly I travel ten thousand *li* as a surrendered captive.
> Just think how in my former country I was saddened when
>   the jade halls grew cool in autumn.[37]

Another lyric was annotated as having been written on the trip
north. Its second stanza refers directly to Huizong's experiences:

> To convey an exile's manifold sorrows, shall I entrust
> This pair of swallows
> Who know not the human tongue?
> Horizon so remote, land so far away—
> Beyond a myriad streams and a thousand mountains—
> Where, pray, are my old palaces?
> How can I help longing?
> Only in dreams have I gone back sometimes.
> Illusions!
> Even dreams
> Do not recur of late.[38]

On 1127/6/10, Wolibu arranged for the princesses and consorts
staying at Pity and Loyalty Shrine to call on Huizong and the others
lodging at Extended Longevity before they had to depart. Not long
afterwards, Wolibu died. Qinzong's party, which had taken a longer
route, did not arrive for another month. When they got there they
were put at Pity and Loyalty Shrine.[39]

Relations between the captives and their captors sometimes grew
friendly, despite language difficulties. Nianhan's son Sheyema got
along well with Huizong's son Ting, and on 7/12 Sheyema consented
to Ting's request to reunite all the princesses and princesses with Qinzong, Huizong, and their empresses at Vast Heaven Temple. According to Zhao Zizhi, the princes lined up on the east and the sons-in-law
lined up on the west. Huizong sat on the left and Qinzong sat on the
right, with Qinzong's son the heir apparent to his south, facing west.
The reunion lasted from the morning till noon and involved five rounds
of wine. A few days later, when Empress Zheng was ill, Sheyema led
the princes to Extended Longevity Temple to inquire about her health.
Moreover, he let the heir apparent, Prince Ting, and a third prince
move to Extended Longevity Temple, which left Qinzong relatively
isolated.[40]

Song forces, now with Gaozong to unite them, were proving stronger than Jin had expected, and the Jurchen decided to move Huizong
and Qinzong further north after they had spent four months in Yanjing.

When on 9/13 they left from the eastern gate of Yanjing, residents knelt by the side of the road to see them off, both "Southerners" (that is, people recently transported from Kaifeng) and natives of the Yan region once subjects of Liao. As a form of protest, for several days afterwards, the populace reportedly boycotted the markets.[41]

Alien Lands

Yanjing had always been an essentially Chinese city. From the time Huizong arrived at the Jin Central Capital on 1127/10/18, however, he was in the steppe zone, occupied by herders since early times (see Maps 2 and 3). At the Central Capital, Huizong and Qinzong were lodged in separate sections of the Assisting the State Monastery. Because of the paucity of supplies in the area, food for the imperial party, over a thousand people altogether, had to be shipped from Yanjing once every two months and was never sufficient. That spring two sons and one daughter were born to Huizong's consorts within a span of two months, but all died in quick succession, perhaps by infanticide. It seems likely that these births were the results of rape, given that they would have been conceived during the march north, and one source explicitly says that they were not Huizong's offspring.[42]

According to Cai Tiao, at this stage of his captivity Huizong sometimes fell into depression, showing no interest in food and sleeping poorly. Books, however, came to offer him a way to both pass the time and cope intellectually and emotionally with his change in circumstances. Cai Tiao reported that Huizong especially liked reading histories and complained that it was difficult to find books to read in the north. Once when he heard someone had books for sale, he traded clothing to buy them. One of the princes got a copy of the ancient classic, the *Spring and Autumn Annals*, which had been out of political favor during Huizong's reign and which he had earlier thought was dangerous because of all the accounts it contains of people killing their rulers or fathers. Cai Tiao urged Huizong to read it, and the next time he saw him, Huizong expressed regret that he had put off reading it so long, as he now had a much deeper understanding of Confucius. From then on, he read it constantly, trying to understand the principles behind the rise and fall of states and the behavior of rulers and officials. He even compiled a book of extracts he made from it. Once at a party for Qinzong's birthday, Huizong wrote Qinzong a poem full of allusions to the *Spring and Autumn Annals*. Another time when Huizong heard that someone had a copy of Wang Anshi's diary for sale, he purchased it.[43]

Fresh from reading so much history, Huizong once told Cai Tiao that he could not think of another case in history of a reversal of fortunes as great as his. His history reading, however, also gave him hope that the dynasty would be revived by Gaozong and he began to try to think of ways to contribute to it. He drafted a memorial to send to the Jurchen authorities and asked Cai Tiao and Qin Gui, also with them, to help him polish it. Cai Tiao assured Huizong that he was a better writer than either of them. The memorial, which eventually reached Nianhan, began with polite acknowledgments of the commanders' kindness and broadmindedness and apologies for not having written earlier. Huizong then spoke of the responsibility of great leaders to look after the people of their realms. The heart of his argument, however, concerned the relationship between the Chinese and their northern neighbors. In both the Han and the Tang dynasties the two sides collaborated with each other and refrained from pushing each other to the limit. For instance, Tang Taizong, after conquering as far west as Gaocheng, involved the Turks in the defense of the north, and at the end of the dynasty the Turks were still there to avenge the humiliations that the Tang suffered. An example of a non-Chinese who had the upper hand was Maodun, the Xiongnu ruler during Han times. He once had Han Gaozu surrounded so that his food was cut off for seven days. However, because he kept his people's long-run interest in mind, he did not capture Gaozu, but rather let him return to continue the ancestral line and provide the Xiongnu with money and silk year after year. Later, the Han came to the rescue of the Xiongnu royal line when it ran into problems. In both of these cases, Huizong argued, the rulers had protected their interests by aiding the other side. Their models were much more worthy of emulation than that of the tenth century Liao ruler Yelü Deguang, who marched into Kaifeng in the tenth century to punish the Shi family for breaking its agreement but was not able to hold the territory.[44] Huizong then went on to give his version of recent events:

> When the former [Jin] emperor [Aguda] raised his army in Liaodong, I did not hesitate to send people by sea, relying on lower

officials. I received the former emperor's promise to treat me as his brother and let me take the Yan-Yun region. But it happened that a crazy person from Yun [Zhang Jue] organized people against the government. My officials and generals were timid and couldn't make up their minds. Listening to them, I was misled by incorrect views. When I first offended your country, I was deeply aware of my own fault, so abdicated in favor of my heir. Conscious of my offense, I have no cause for complaint. Recently I have heard that one of my sons has been enthroned. This is not the result of my son's worthiness but the deep legacy of the virtue of my ancestors, which people do not easily forget.

I am wondering whether you want to model yourself on Tang Taizong and Maodun Shanyu and get a reputation for saving a dynasty on the point of extinction. You would then benefit from yearly payments of money, jade, and silk, protect your country, and give life to its people, and serve as a model for ten thousand generations. Or do you want to copy Yelü Deguang [of Liao] and kill to the last person but end up with others gaining possession [of what you conquered]? If the latter, there is nothing I can say. If the former, I would like to send an emissary to bring a letter to my son to explain my plan that my sons and grandsons forever offer tribute [to Jin]. Wouldn't this be of benefit for ten thousand generations?[45]

Huizong's memorial ended with a final historical example, this one from the Warring States period on the importance of rulers listening to the advice of those around them. This petition reached Nianhan, but apparently not the Jin emperor Taizong.

After less than a year in the Central Capital, Huizong and Qinzong and the rest of their party were moved further north, this time to the main Jurchen capital, the Supreme Capital near modern Harbin (Heilongjiang province). They arrived there 1128/8/21 and a few days later were presented as offerings at a sacrificial ceremony at the shrine dedicated to Aguda. As they were led in, five white flags identified the different members of the group as "the two captive Song emperors," "the captive mothers and wives of the rebellious slave Zhao family," and so on.

As Winston Lo has demonstrated, this ceremony was not based on Jurchen custom, but cobbled together by Jin China experts to evoke ancient Chinese rituals of surrender.⁴⁶ It is described in one source as follows:

> At dawn, several thousand enemy soldiers loudly entered the camp and forced [the Song party] to go to the temple, where they had to remove their clothes outside the gate to the temple. The two emperors and empresses took off only their outer garments, the rest all had to bare their upper bodies and wrap a sheep skin around their waists. They were linked with a felt cord tied to their hands. The two emperors led the way into the curtained hall, along with the sheep to be sacrificed. In the hall was a tent of purple curtains, with precious vessels laid out on a hundred mats. Various barbarian tunes were played. The enemy chief [Jin emperor Taizong] with his wife and concubines, his officials and slaves, knelt in the barbarian fashion [i.e., on one knee]. Everyone from the [former Song] emperors and empresses on down knelt in the barbarian fashion. The enemy chief personally took two sheep to be offered in the hall. The enemy soldiers then pressed [the Song party] to go to the imperial stockade, and the enemy chief ascended Bright Origin Hall, his wife and concubines and the various leaders in attendance at his sides. Everyone from the two emperors on down knelt. The ruler proclaimed four amnesties and the two emperors were given ranks and clothes, then waited with the princes in a small tent outside the hall. The empresses and consorts then entered the palace, were granted favors, then after a while it was announced that empresses Zheng and Zhu would return to their places. At the completion of the ceremony, they changed into barbarian clothes and came out.⁴⁷

After the ceremony, the women, still partly naked, were divided up. Three hundred women from Consorts Wei and Xing on down were assigned to the palace laundry to work as palace slaves. Others were given to particular men. When princes or others wanted the slaves, however, they could generally have them.

After Empress Zhu returned from this ceremony, she tried to hang herself; when she was revived, she killed herself by throwing herself into a pool of water. The next day Huizong and Qinzong were given humiliating titles: Lord of Confused Virtue and Lord of Double

Confusion respectively. The following day twenty doctors were assigned to evaluate the imperial women, aborting any who were pregnant and treating those who were ill, in preparation for their entry into the palace.[48]

Only two months later, on 1128/10/26, Huizong, Qinzong, and the others were forced to move north again to Hanzhou, a journey that took two months (see Map 3). In Hanzhou Huizong was reunited with 904 members of the imperial clan, who had been moved there earlier. These men and women had been through a lot. When Huizong's group left Yanjing the year before, the clansmen had remained, subsisting on only one pint of rice a day. Abortive revolts in the Yan region had finally led to their transfer further north, where they were given land and expected to support themselves through farming.[49] After asking them about their experiences, Huizong made gifts to them of firewood and food and helped them get organized. Because many of them had started quarreling with each other, he appointed some of them to take charge and tried to establish rules, based on kinship position. By this point the officials who had accompanied Huizong were also very short of clothes, and Huizong submitted a memorial requesting that some be issued to them. Empress Zheng also contributed ten bolts of cloth for this purpose.[50]

While in Hanzhou Huizong was required to express his thanks for the titles given to six of his daughters who had stayed in the Supreme Capital and borne sons for the Wanyan imperial clan, as well as for the gift of ten bolts of silk he had received as a consequence.[51] The three memorials of thanks that survive are evidence that after all those years of reading effusive memorials from his officials, Huizong was fully capable of turning out satisfactorily flattering ones himself. But he did try to take advantage of the situation to gently remind the Jin ruler of his plight:

> Your great deeds are difficult to repay. I touch myself and know that I am fortunate. But I venture to note that my whole family, all ten thousand fingers [i.e., a thousand people], have been banished for several years. I know this is because of the vastness of my guilt, and I constantly devote myself to reflecting on its causes. May the spirits bear witness, how would I dare do anything unexpected? [i.e., I am no threat] In heaven and earth, I have no pri-

vate hopes and so have become satisfied with my stupid lot. Unexpected waves took me thousands of *li*, upsetting all my plans. Fortunately I have been preserved in my old age, and have just managed to avoid being eaten by the fish and crabs. This is because of the great kindness of Your Majesty . . . [52]

While living in Hanzhou, Huizong's favorite son Kai died.[53] After a year and a half, the captives were transferred again, since even Hanzhou, it seems, was not far enough north to calm the fears of the Jin rulers. In 1130/7, the imperial party was moved to Five Nations Fort by boat. En route, five hundred clansmen and three hundred palace attendants were sent to other destinations. Huizong begged the Jurchen guards not to separate them, but to no avail. When they had to part, Huizong spoke with tears streaming down his face, "You gentlemen have accompanied me, and we have shared our sorrows and joys. But other people are in charge, so what can we do?" As a consequence, only six kinsmen of Qinzong's generation from this group were still with the two emperors when they reached Five Nations Fort. In 1131 the clansmen were moved to the Supreme Capital, by which time their numbers were down to five hundred-odd. Other captives, deemed surplus, in 1130 were traded to the Tanguts, Mongols, and Tartars for horses at a rate of ten slaves for one horse.[54]

Not long after arriving in Five Nations Fort, Empress Zheng died, age fifty-two. Huizong lived on in Five Nations Fort another four years. Cai Tiao reported that Huizong maintained ancestral sacrifices under these trying circumstances, that he would often gaze south and ask those around him where the Song imperial tombs were located. He observed the death day anniversaries of former Song emperors and empresses, and would fast with tears in his eyes. He would also not taste any fresh foods without first making offerings of them on his altar. He also continued to pay attention to the education of his children and would often make them stay after they paid their daily visits. He even continued to work with them on writing poetic couplets.[55]

Since Cai Tiao does talk about the importance of reading and composing poetry to Huizong during his years in captivity, it is perhaps significant that he says very little about some of the other interests Huizong had cultivated in earlier years. It is to be expected that Huizong could no longer take any interest in architecture or gardens, but what about painting and calligraphy, which could be done with paper, brushes, and ink alone? Huizong's calligraphy continued to be prized—Zhang Duanyi reported that the Jin emperors made small gifts to him while he was in captivity in order to get his memorials of thanks, which the northerners collected and published as a volume that circulated for several decades.[56] However, there are no anecdotes by Cai Tiao or others saying that Huizong turned to calligraphy or painting to while away the time or bring pleasure to his companions. These activities required more material goods than composing poetry— even calligraphy requires paper and good brushes—so perhaps after years of being able to practice under ideal material conditions, practicing them under diminished circumstances had little if any appeal to Huizong.

Nor is there evidence that Huizong found solace in his Daoist beliefs or devotions. Although sources mention his offering a prayer to Daoist divinities just before he abdicated and another prayer early in his captivity, nothing else is said of Daoist devotional activities. Huizong is described at times as wearing Daoist clerical garb, and is sometimes quoted as expressing detached sentiments that could be associated with Daoism, but that is about as far as the evidence goes to indicate that Daoism remained an important part of his life. However, he did continue to report to others his dreams and find in them significant meanings.[57]

Could it be that Huizong's faith in the cosmological underpinnings of his Daoist faith were shaken? Over the years he had often found auspicious signs that portended well for the dynasty, his reign, and his longevity—the clearing of the Yellow River, the arrival of dancing cranes, the discovery of auspicious mushrooms, and so on. If he now felt that no previous emperor had fallen as low as he had, it would be hard to think these phenomena had been interpreted correctly.

Life seems to have been quiet in Five Nations Fort, at least until the middle of 1132 or 1133, when one of Huizong's sons and one of his sons-in-law (his fifteenth son E, Prince of Yi, then twenty-three *sui*, and Liu Wenyan, the husband of his sixteenth daughter) accused Huizong of plotting to overthrow the Jin. The conspiracy was supposed to involve Huizong's eighteenth son, Zhen, the Prince of Xin, then twenty-two, and other associates. Huizong called a meeting of all the relatives and accompanying officials to discuss the crisis. Cai Tiao claimed credit for talking them into holding firm. The Jin sent an investigator, and Huizong deputed another son and another son-in-law to argue his case. When the Jin investigator wanted Huizong himself to come, he sent Qinzong, his son Zhen, his son-in-law Cai Tiao, and the eunuch Wang Ruochong to argue for him, and also allowed the local officials to question him. After the investigator decided the accusation was false, he asked Huizong to deal with the accusers, but he declined and the investigator had them executed.[58] Huizong must have been quite worried while this case was being investigated because he burned the thousand-odd poems that he had written since leaving Kaifeng. Afterwards Huizong told Cai Tiao, "Learning that my son E and the others had made the wild accusations has given me true understanding of the phrase, 'followers may rebel and close relatives may become estranged.' I tried to look to myself for a solution, but did not know what to do. If I do not cleanse my heart and root out worries, then how can I preserve my life, keep harm at bay, and make regrets and cares rare?"[59]

News from the south would have been very difficult to come by in Five Nations Fort. Gaozong and his envoys made many attempts to get in contact with Huizong and Qinzong, but Jin frequently did not even let the envoys sent by Gaozong return to Song, much less let them travel north to see the hostages. In an 1131 memorial of thanks to the Jurchen for a gift of two sets of clothing, Huizong, after effusively praising the generosity of the rulers, added, "I have traveled ten thousand *li* from home, and have not yet received a single letter." Cai Tiao reports how happy Huizong was when people arrived with news from the south.[60]

At the beginning of 1135, by which time Huizong had been in Five Nations Fort four years, his old adversary, Jin Taizong (Wuqimai) died, age sixty-one. He was succeeded not by his own son but by a grandson of Aguda's, a man relatively well versed in Chinese, known as Xizong (r. 1135–1150). Xizong soon released Consort Wei and six other women from the palace laundry and sent them to Five Nations Fort. A few months later, 1135/4/21, Huizong died in Five Nations Fort. He had asked to be buried in Song territory, but the request was rejected. Song officials still in Yanjing put on mourning clothes for him, and Hong Hao, a long-detained Song emissary, had Daoist services performed for him. The end of this generation of leaders came two years later in 1137 when Nianhan was executed, a victim of Jin political in-fighting.[61]

Another ending came in 1142/5, after Gaozong reached a peace agreement with Jin and negotiated the return of his mother Consort Wei and the coffins of Huizong, Empress Zheng, and Gaozong's own first wife Empress Xing. When the entourage reached Yanjing, Hong Hao led former subjects of Song out of the city to meet them on the road and express their grief.[62] Qinzong was also treated somewhat more leniently from this point on and moved south to the new Jin Supreme Capital. To Gaozong, getting his mother back and the coffin of his father was important as an act of filial piety, and he had it celebrated in a painting still extant (see Plate 15).

Gaozong also kept the memory of his father alive through the local temples that had been designated for celebrations of his birthday, which continued to make offerings on Huizong's birthday and Personal Destiny days. After learning of his father's death, Gaozong had their name changed to Repaying Favor and Extending Filial Piety and offerings at them continued. Incense continued to be offered to Huizong at many of these temples even after Gaozong's death.[63]

The Fate of Huizong's Family

Practically every one of Huizong's relatives that the Jurchen invaders was able to find—including all of the Song imperial clansmen in or near Kaifeng, all of his daughters who had married, along with their husbands—were transported north at the same time he was. A great many died of abuse or neglect over the next couple of years, especially the clansmen, who were of little use to the Jurchen. By 1128/7, when the clansmen and women were moved from Yanjing to Hanzhou, only 900 of the original 5,600 were still living, and three years after that, when they were moved to the Supreme Capital, their numbers were down to five hundred-odd.[64]

Huizong's immediate relatives fared somewhat better. Of his sons, twenty-six were living in 1127, and of them twenty-five were taken captive, that is, all but Gaozong. None of the very youngest, six *sui* or younger, survived the trip. And even those in their teens and twenties had a hard time. Only sixteen sons survived to Five Nations Fort, which was the harshest of the five locations. Three of them died the first year there, another two in the next two years (one a suicide), bringing the total down to eleven during Huizong's lifetime. These survivors, however, were given wives in Five Nations Fort City and had children there. Qinzong lived until 1161, never ransomed by his younger brother Gaozong. Like his father, he had children in captivity, and as late as 1195 there were still descendants of Huizong under the control of Jin.[65]

Huizong had little contact with his daughters after they were taken out of the Kaifeng palace in 1127. Of Huizong's daughters, twenty-two were living in 1127, but three soon died at Wolibu's camp outside Kaifeng. Several were given to Jurchen officers before leaving Kaifeng, while others, especially the youngest, were taken to Yanjing and made palace slaves, though eventually six were promoted to titled palace women or consorts. Fujin, the princess married to Cai Tiao and initially requested by the Jin commanders for a marriage alliance, died in the camp of the Jurchen general Wushi in 1128. One of Huizong's daughters ran away from Nianhan's camp in 1137 and once caught was banished to Five Nations Fort, where she died within the year.[66]

Thirty-four of the wives, fiancées, and concubines of Huizong's sons were also taken captive. Most were given to Jurchen officers, though some became palace slaves or consorts. Because they were scattered, good records were not kept of how long they lived, though there are detailed lists of whose camp they entered.

In 1127 Huizong already had fifteen grandsons and twenty-nine granddaughters through his sons, most very young. Their survival rate was very poor. Only two of the boys seem to have made it to Five Nations Fort. The girls who survived were made palace slaves or palace women.[67]

Of Huizong's own consorts, five were ranked by the Jurchen as wives, including Empress Zheng. These were women thirty-five or older that did not interest the Jurchen as mates. All eventually made it to Five Nations Fort, with Empress Zheng dying soon after arrival in 1130. In addition, 31 higher consorts, 41 intermediate level consorts, and 67 lower-ranked consorts were taken captive, along with 504 palace ladies. Like the princesses, many of these women were given to Jurchen officers before leaving Kaifeng. At Yanjing, five of them were returned to Huizong, with the remaining women given to Jurchen officers or made palace slaves. After becoming captives, consorts of

Huizong bore him another fourteen children.[68] With the Song already reestablished in the South and with Huizong and his family so remotely located, the Jurchen do not seem to have worried that Huizong was adding to potential claimants to the Song throne.

Outside his own wives and children, Huizong's closest relatives were his two brothers Wu and Ssi, both of whom played important roles in the negotiations with the Jurchens in Kaifeng. Their families were taken captive, but at least their married daughters were spared. Ssi and his wife both died in Hanzhou. Two of Ssi's sons made it to Five Nations Fort and one of his daughters entered the Jin palace. Other women, such as Ssi's concubines and daughters-in-law, died en route or became palace slaves. As already mentioned, Wu died on the road before even getting to Yanjing. His wife, two sons, three daughters, one granddaughter, and one grandson made it to Five Nations Fort. His concubines became palace slaves and one of his daughters or granddaughters became a Jin palace lady.[69]

⟫ How MUCH DID Huizong and the others transported north suffer? Surviving historical sources generally observe a degree of reticence about the physical details of the captives' conditions, particularly with regard to the two emperors and their empresses. Cai Tiao, who may have anticipated that his writing would have to pass through Jin authorities to survive, said nothing negative on these matters. Cao Xun, writing in the south while Huizong and Qinzong were still alive, may not have wanted to alarm people or enter into the controversy over how best Gaozong's court should deal with Jin. By contrast, works that are clearly fictional elaborations of somewhat later date, such as *A Personal Account by Southern Leftovers (Nanjin jiwen)* and *Unrecorded Events of the Virtue Revealed Era (Xuanhe yishi)*, repeatedly say the two emperors had only one meal a day of coarse food, barely enough clothes to avoid freezing, were often forced to live in cramped, damp rooms, and the like. These narratives draw extensively on surviving historical works and undoubtedly also draw on some that do not survive, so it is impossible to determine for sure whether these details were invented by the storytellers or drawn from sources no longer extant, but I suspect they are mostly inventions.[70]

In 1126, while in Kaifeng, Qinzong as emperor outranked his father Huizong and Huizong had to obey his orders. After they were both made captive, Huizong's seniority in the family structure seems to have taken precedence over their recent political rank and most authors treat Huizong as the head of any group of captives that included him.

Huizong was able to maintain some dignity during captivity. Until the move to Hanzhou there were plenty of eunuchs in the imperial party, so surely there would have been people to attend Huizong as servants. There were still a few after that, as twice Jurchen nobles sent requests for eunuchs. The first, from a prince, requested two capable, talented, and lively servants. Huizong felt he had no choice but to obey, but, in the letter he sent back, stressed how much they had been through since leaving Kaifeng. The second request, from the wife of a Jurchen official, he declined on the grounds that he had only one or two left himself. His sons-in-law, all of whom naturally had had official titles, seem to have formed a small court for him. Cai Tiao refers to them as the "accompanying officials" and their place of residence as the "temporary palace." Cai Tiao praised the respectful way Huizong treated this group, "never once calling them by name."[71] At least in the case of Cai Tiao, Huizong had an extremely devoted follower.

Were everyday items such as clothing adequate? A Jin source contains the memorials of thanks that Huizong and Qinzong wrote in 1131 after each of them received two sets of clothes. If this is all the clothing the entire group received, it would not have been adequate, especially given the extreme cold in Five Nations Fort. On the other hand, the edict conferring the clothes, which survives only in fragmentary form, seems also to mention the gift of ten bars of silver.[72]

The hardest evidence of the physical conditions of the captives is their death rates, and these suggest that conditions varied greatly according to status. The death rate among the imperial clansmen was so high that one cannot help but suspect that the Jin authorities were trying to kill them off. What had motivated the Kaifeng officials to plunder the city for the Jurchen had been the promise not to kill the residents—if Jin had taken out the clansmen and systematically slaughtered them in the suburbs of Kaifeng, compliance on the part of the residents of the city would not have been so easy to achieve. But once the clansmen were far from Kaifeng, they were a burden, not an asset. Women, at least those young enough to appeal to soldiers, had their uses and they survived in greater numbers than men, though generally in demeaned positions where suicide may have been the greatest danger to their survival.

During his long detention in the north, Hong Hao learned something about the daily conditions of the captives. His son Mai, on the basis of what he learned from his father, described the captives as being treated as slaves, regardless of rank:

> Everyone, sons of emperors and grandsons of princes, families of officials and literati, were made slaves and required to work. Each person was given five pecks of coarse millet a month, which they had to husk themselves, producing one peck and eight pints to be used for food. Each year they were given five pieces of hemp cloth to sew into clothes. Beyond this they received not one penny of cash nor one piece of cloth. Men who could not sew had their bodies exposed all year long. Enemies who had sympathy for them gave them kitchen jobs. Although for a while they would get warm from the fire, when they went out to get firewood and then returned to sit by the fire, their skin and flesh would fall off and they would die within days. [The Jurchen] only liked those with skills such as doctors or embroiders. On ordinary days when sitting they could cushion themselves on the ground with worn out mats or rush pads. When guests arrived, bamboo mats would be rolled out and those able to make music would be summoned to play. When the wine was gone and the guests left, [the captives /slaves] would go back to what they had been doing, as before sitting in a circle embroidering. [The captors] did not care whether they lived or died, looking on them like no more than grass or weeds.[73]

Hong Hao's description may well apply to the clansmen who died in large numbers, and perhaps other groups such as the palace ladies and female entertainers sold into slavery after arrival in Yanjing, but it probably doesn't apply to the smaller group of consorts, sons, and their wives and children who lived with Huizong. Huizong and Qinzong both lived into their fifties, which suggests that they generally had adequate basic living conditions. On the other hand, fewer than half of Huizong's sons taken into captivity outlived him, many dying in their teens and twenties, when they should have been at their most robust. Most of the time they seem to have been living with him, which makes it unlikely that conditions which affected them would not also have been shared by Huizong and Qinzong. Perhaps Huizong and Qinzong had strong constitutions and survived diseases that spread through their compounds and claimed many lives. The sons who did survive the first couple of years at Five Nations Fort generally went on to have children who survived, again suggesting that conditions, if not comfortable, were at least adequate to sustain life.

Afterword

$\mathcal{W}$HAT MAKES HUIZONG an engaging character? He was smart and well read—he was able to engage specialists in fields as diverse as Confucian rituals, Daoist heavens, music, and pharmacology. He was generous to a fault, happily making gifts to those he dealt with, sometimes trying to surprise them, such as when he had new quarters built at Accumulating Auspicious Temple for the use of Liu Hunkang. He made many small gestures to show his respect and appreciation for those around them, from mixing up tea for them to inquiring about their relatives. He found many people he liked among the eunuchs and palace ladies who attended him. He had enormous energy, at least during his first two decades on the throne, because he would tirelessly involve himself in the details of numerous projects and also find time for his rapidly expanding family. He was artistically talented and willing to let others see his efforts as a poet, calligrapher, and painter. When fate dealt him severe blows, he handled his plight with some grace and dignity, showing concern for those whose fate was worse than his and avoiding as best he could placing blame on others. If at times he became bitter or depressed, that was only human.

How should we evaluate him as an emperor? In this book I have tried to look at Huizong's world through his eyes and keep in mind what he knew at the time. Before the end of 1120, when he learned of the Fang La uprising, Huizong had no inkling that his reign might end badly, or that outlays he made for a new park would seem ludicrous six or seven years later when the government had difficulty getting adequate food to its soldiers at the front. To the contrary, he was gambling on the sort of military victory Song had not had for more than a century, one that would let it expand its territories into areas occupied primarily by Chinese. Did Huizong and his officials make less provision for the possibility of war than earlier Song emperors had? Shenzong spent a long time building up resources in order to undertake a military campaign, but found war so expensive that after a relatively limited engagement in the northwest, he pulled back. It is unlikely that Shenzong or Zhezong had reserves large enough to easily handle the sort of military catastrophe that engulfed Huizong and Qinzong.

As an emperor, Huizong deserves credit for thinking big and supporting worthy causes of many sorts. The nationwide school system and the charitable assistance for the sick and homeless were quite remarkable for their time. The book compilation and printing projects are also meritorious efforts. Not only was the huge Daoist canon compiled, but so were several medical books, the *New Forms of the Five Categories of Rites of the Zhenghe Period*, and even a collection of rubbings of calligraphy. Some major projects may seem less noble, but they contributed to the majesty of the throne. These include his reform of court music, his formation of great collections of masterpieces of art and antiquities, and his construction of exquisite temples, palaces, and gardens.

What of Huizong's flaws? He was undoubtedly vain—there is perhaps no other way to account for the extreme to which he carried his love of auspicious signs. Vanity probably also explains his confidence that his literary and calligraphic skills were of such a high order that everyone should have a chance to see them on the stones he had erected in every prefecture.

Overconfidence was another flaw. It contributed to his miscalculation of what would happen when he banned prominent men from service in his government. Belief that he could ignore other people's animus toward Cai Jing also reflects overconfidence. The decision to ally with Jin can similarly be attributed to overconfidence—when confronted with officials who disagreed on how prepared Song was for war in the north, Huizong hesitated but then sided not with the worriers but with the visionaries who thought a major feat was well within the realm of possibility.

Huizong's energy and passion—admirable in many situations—also created problems for him, perhaps especially his strong faith in Daoism. I do not see Huizong as either deluded or cynical in his support for Daoism, but in the period 1117–1119 he did let himself abandon whatever inclination he had had toward prudence.

Traditional Chinese historians looked on Huizong differently. They drew a moral from his reign: rulers risk their countries and their lives when they indulge their desires or immerse themselves in religion. The *Song History*, compiled by the Yuan government two centuries after Huizong's time, has been particularly influential in this regard. At the end of the annals covering Huizong's reign, the historians first make the point that the Jurchen invasion was not inevitable. It might not have happened had a different brother of Zhezong had been placed on the throne in 1100. There were also possibilities for alternative outcomes later: if the Song court had refused Zhang Jue's offer to defect from Jin in 1123, "then, Jin, despite its strength, would have had no grievance and would not have invaded Song." Other rulers who had lost their thrones had been stupid or cruel, or had been victims of military coups, none of which was true of Huizong. Rather, he had been misled. Cai Jing had biased him against the conservatives, "so that he sent away upright scholars and kept nefarious sycophants by his side." Cai Jing also tempted him with finery so that he indulged himself. Added to this, Huizong put too much faith in Daoism, which led both to overspending and a failure to supervise the military adequately. "The ruler and his minister took their ease and talked boastfully, losing the country out of negligence." Especially disastrous was putting Tong Guan in charge of the armies. The final judgment of the historians is harsh: "Since antiquity, rulers who find pleasure in material things and let their will weaken, who give way to their desires and lose a sense of proportion, generally come to bad ends—but Huizong's is the most extreme case."[1]

Twelfth- and thirteenth-century intellectual trends that rejected the New Policies and found heroes in the anti-reformers underlie this negative evaluation of Huizong. It has also been reinforced by popular fiction, especially the Ming novel *Water Margin*, set in Huizong's reign. In the late sixteenth century, when the Wanli emperor was a boy and Zhang Juzheng was tutoring him, Zhang Juzheng compiled an illustrated book about the good and bad actions of rulers of earlier dynasties, titled *The Emperor's Mirror, Illustrated and Discussed*. Of the seventy-two examples of wise actions, sixteen were from the Song, five taken by Taizu, two by Taizong, and nine by Renzong. Of the thirty-six examples of unwise actions, three were from the Song, all three by Huizong. The first of these was holding Daoist ceremonies at which Huizong placed himself below Lin Lingsu. After quoting from the *Song History*, Zhang Juzheng adds his comment: "Huizong was the ruler over millions of subjects, but he set aside the correct [Confucian teachings] and followed the deviant [Daoism], and showed deference to a strange teaching, mingling with commoners, personally accepting a Daoist title, and willingly letting himself be deceived. Since antiquity, his is the most extreme case of a ruler absorbed in Daoism. Where were his Three Clarities Celestial Worthies when he was taken into captivity and died in Five Nations Fort? Why didn't they save him?" Zhang Juzheng clearly saw Huizong's faith in Daoism as both delusional and ruinous. The second example given of an unwise action was setting up the "flower and rock network" to collect plants and stones in the southeast for transportation to the capital to be used in Huizong's new park, the Northeast Marchmount, a project that led to widespread corruption and other abuses. Zhang Juzheng ends his comments on this case by claiming that stones and rocks have no utility and that Huizong's endless love of them had led to unrest, invasion, his own death in the wilds, and the scattering of his relatives. Royal magnificence, to Zhang Juzheng, had no utility. The third unwise action was Huizong's employment of the "Six Traitors" (Cai Jing, Tong Guan, Wang Fu, Li Yan, Zhu Mian, and Liang Shicheng). In his commentary, Zhang Juzheng declares that loyal officials urge their rulers to be frugal and restrained, even when the ruler does not want to hear their message. Those who tell the ruler what he wants to hear and encourage lack of restraint are treacherous and can do boundless harm.[2] Any one of these three faults would have been enough to bring Huizong to a bad end in Zhang Juzheng's understanding of the workings of history.

   The Emperor's Mirror was a primer, written for a child emperor, but it proved very popular and went through many editions. In the seventeenth century, Wang Fuzhi wrote a more serious, scholarly evaluation of Huizong's reign in his *On the Song Dynasty* (which, however, did not circulate in his own day).[3] Wang Fuzhi was primarily concerned with the choices scholars and officials made, especially well-known Confucian scholars such as Yang Shi and Li Gang, but he did not question the received wisdom that Huizong was a mediocre ruler, referring to him as "frivolous," "obtuse," and "in a dream world." He pointed out that Huizong was not as extravagant as some earlier rulers, such as Emperor Yang of the Sui dynasty, and Cai Jing was not as bad as some other chief ministers, such as Li Linfu of the Tang dynasty, yet the disaster that befell Huizong was much worse.[4] Perhaps the most interesting observation that Wang Fuzhi made was the theatrical or make-believe quality of much that went on at Huizong's court. He described Cai Jing as play-acting when he presented himself as a follower of Wang Anshi. Even the alliance with Jin and the destruction of Liao he saw as a kind of game played by Huizong and Cai You.[5]

How valid is the charge that Huizong lost the throne above all because he lacked restraint and indulged his desires? Certainly, Huizong did find pleasure in material things, especially artworks, ancient bronzes, gardens, and palace buildings. Huizong's collections must have been costly, but no numbers are available and many objects were undoubtedly presented to the emperor as gifts rather than acquired by purchase. In terms of building, Huizong did more to add to the palace complex than any of the previous Song emperors, but the resulting palace compound was still much smaller than the Tang palace in Chang'an—and the Tang also had a spacious palace compound in Luoyang, as well as large hunting parks. As Huizong became absorbed in Divine Empyrean Daoism from 1117 to 1119, he does seem to have taken on projects without considering costs, but it is not until 1120, with the dismissal of Cai Jing and escalating military outlays, that the high officials became aware of looming deficits. Even then, when the Jurchen held Kaifeng for ransom, government treasuries still were found to have large stores of bronze coins as well as silver, gold, and silk.

To put these issues in perspective, it is also worth noting that the trope of the ruler who loses his throne because of his personal indulgence was an ancient one.[6] In the classical *Zuo Commentary*, even an interest in fashionable dress was thought enough to bring on the destruction of a state.[7] The early Tang historians who compiled the histories of the immediately preceding dynasties saw the falls of Liang,

Chen, and Sui as "due to the dissolute pleasures" of their last emperors, to their "immoderate indulgences and entertainments."[8] They probably inferred that if a ruler loses his throne, that is in and of itself evidence that he failed to restrain himself appropriately. The Tang emperor Taizong, in his own writings, recognizes that "excess was the cause of imperial ruin."[9] In the Confucian tradition, royal austerity was prized, not royal splendor.

One can also consider Song palace expenses in cross-cultural context. The impulse to build, decorate, and collect is very common among monarchs worldwide. Huizong's spending on the dignity of the throne does not seem out of line with spending on royal courts elsewhere. Throughout Eurasia, it would seem, courts tend when conditions permit to use resources in ways that added to their grandeur or magnificence, such as by enlarging palace complexes and adding to palace staff. This provokes both criticisms of irresponsibility and periodic needs to retrench, especially when the court also wants to field armies.[10] All of this is relative, of course. In Europe in the Renaissance and early modern period, the total spending per capita on the court would seem to have been much higher than it was in Song China: The Medici in Florence, with a population of only a million and not much more territory than a Chinese prefecture, built the enormous Pitti Palace and kept large numbers of artists and artisans busy. France in the age of Louis XIV had only twenty million subjects, a fifth the size of Song China in Huizong's day, but managed to support huge establishments at Versailles, Fontainebleau, the Louvre, and so on. Undoubtedly one explanation for this difference is that in Europe, the dynamic fostering opulence involved competition among different kingdoms and principalities for prestige, something not felt the same way in Song China.

Huizong's seeming indifference to cost drew the attention of historians, but none of them went on to explore what this revealed about his character or how he developed it. Despite China's long history of writing biographical accounts of politically important individuals, emperors were treated as the exception. In the dynastic histories, founders' lives are recounted in some detail, but little is said of the early years of their successors. In Huizong's case, we are told his full formal posthumous name (eighteen characters long), his given name, the date of his birth, and that he was Shenzong's eleventh son and born in the palace to a consort surnamed Chen. A list of his successive titles follows. Immediately afterwards comes Zhezong's death and Huizong's succession to the throne. Nothing is said of his life before he took the throne.[11]

The *Song History* annals for each emperor are themselves quite dry and could hardly be read as a biography in any normal sense. Neither do they offer much of a picture of what happened at court. Consider, for instance, these two months in 1107:

> In autumn, in the seventh month, on the day *yiyou*, the first day of the month, the Yi and Luo Rivers overflowed their banks. On the day *wuzi*, [the emperor] issued an edict to gather the adult males of the realm who had slipped off of the tax registers. On the day *renyin*, sacrificial garments were distributed to the prefectures. On the day *yisi* the Worthy Consort Wu died.
>
> In the eighth month, on the day *yimao*, Zeng Bu died. On the day *dingsi*, [the emperor's] son Gou was appointed Duke of Shu. On the day *gengshen*, the minister of revenue Xu Churen was appointed vice director of the Department of State Affairs, and the minister of personnel Lin Shu was given the concurrent appointment of manager of the Bureau of Military Affairs. On the day *jisi*, [the emperor] issued comforting words to the twenty-six prefectures of Hai, Wu, and Chu, and reduced the penalties on criminals one degree, with full pardons to those sentenced to labor service far from home or any lesser punishment.[12]

From other parts of the *Song History*, one could flesh out these accounts a little. One could learn, for instance, that the consort who had died was one of Huizong's step-mothers (the mother of one of his brothers); that the distribution of sacrificial garments had been proposed by the Agency for Deliberating on Ritual; and that the Yi and Luo Rivers had flooded in earlier years as well.[13] To get any deeper into the subject, however, one would have to piece together information from other sources, as I have done in this book.

Why did historians before the twentieth century apparently think it inappropriate to write a biography of an emperor, even an emperor of an earlier dynasty?[14] Is it that once a person became emperor he lost all of his individuality and became a symbol of the state?[15] That might

make sense in some contexts, except that from very early times political crises were blamed on the individual actions of rulers. Surely, a biography could make connections between a ruler's character and his
actions clearer. Another alternative explanation is that concerns about
the security of the throne led to the taboo on writing emperors' biographies. That is, those with power were reluctant to let subjects try to
imagine what it would be like to be the emperor. Placing themselves
imaginatively on the throne might possibly encourage people to think
that they could get to sit on the throne in real life. But this is specula-
tion; I cannot point to any explicit statement along these lines.[16]

This taboo on writing about the lives of rulers struck me as I worked
on this book, probably because the lives of rulers has been a major
genre in Western history writing. In medieval times, many chronicles
were centered on the king and what happened at his court, making the
king's personality and foibles a central part of the political narrative.
In the case of major rulers, often several accounts of their lives were
written within a century of their deaths.[17] Books on European rulers
continue to be popular to this day. Chinese storytellers did sometimes regale their audiences with fanciful accounts of profligate emperors giving in to the vast array of temptations palace life offered
them.[18] Rarely, though, do these imagined rulers come across as complex but flawed individuals of the sort portrayed by Shakespeare. Although Chinese historians and other commentators felt free to condemn Huizong, they did not relate in any detail how he developed
his failings.

The lack of biographies is just one of the aspects of Chinese emperorship that intrigued me as I tried to reconstruct Huizong's life. Another was the constraints on emperors. Consciously or unconsciously I
found myself measuring Huizong and other Song emperors against
emperors of other dynasties.[19] When thinking comparatively across
the Chinese dynasties, Song emperors stand out for their civility.
Huizong and almost all of the other Song emperors come across as
gracious and magnanimous in their dealings with their officials, not
universally true of all of China's emperors. Critics may have thought
Huizong was out of bounds for publicly listing a couple hundred men
he did not want in his government, but he did not summon them to
court to berate them, much less order them beaten or executed. Ill-
tempered and violent emperors are not so rare in other dynasties.[20]

One explanation for this would seem to be Song officials' success in getting emperors to conform to their views of proper imperial conduct. Consider, for instance, officials' efforts to keep emperors from leaving the palace to see more of the world. In earlier chapters I cited a memorial submitted to Huizong in 1101 objecting in strong terms to any plans he might possibly have to go hunting. I also cited a memorial nearly two decades later objecting to Huizong leaving the palace quietly to visit officials in their own homes. In Song times, except for well-established rituals such as the sacrifices to heaven every third year and annual visits to the suburban parks, officials preferred for the emperor to remain inside the Palace City.[21] People from all over came to the palace—the emperor was not cut off from knowledge of the world. Still, an encounter in the audience hall with the emperor seated on the throne was fundamentally unlike an encounter elsewhere. The modern historian Ray Huang, writing about the late Ming, sees "an effort to dehumanize the monarchy" since the bureaucracy "needed only a cloistered sovereign to act as its presiding officer."[22] The situation in the Song bears certain similarities.

It was a cliché for officials and the emperor to say that he lived behind nine layers of walls and could not witness everything that went on in the empire, thus needing his officials to serve as his eyes and ears. But why not let the emperor leave the palace and see more of his realm himself? Did the emperors really need so many walls separating them from their subjects? The idea of keeping the emperor concealed goes back to the Warring States period and was exemplified by the First Emperor of Qin who had elevated walkways built so that he could walk from one palace to another without revealing his location.[23] In earlier dynasties, despite officials' protests, emperors had often left the palace to go hunting, or had traveled to other parts of the country for any of a number of reasons, with leading troops and visiting holy places probably the most common. This type of mobility is a part of ruling in most parts of the world. In Thomas Allsen's words, "the vast majority of the royal houses and aristocracies of Eurasia made some use of the chase in the pursuit and maintenance of their social and political power."[24] The second Tang emperor, Taizong, spent each summer at a detached palace more than one hundred fifty kilometers from the capital.[25] In most of the rest of the world, it would seem, monarchy is strengthened, not weakened, by the ruler and the

ruled encountering each other outside the palace. It is true that many
of the functions of the office of emperor could be filled while remaining in the palace. The emperor was essential to the political system as
the symbol of the state, as the center of a centered polity, at the highest
point of a hierarchical structure, the key officiant in sacred rituals. For
these purposes, no travel was necessary. But just because the ruler did
not need to travel does not mean that travel would have been of no
benefit.

The first three Song emperors did not stay put. Taizu and Taizong
were generals and subjugating the other rival states took much of their
energy. Zhenzong was raised in the palace, but did make several
lengthy trips outside of the capital district—in 1004 to Shanyuan,
nominally at least to lead the troops resisting the Kitan; in 1008 east to
Mount Tai to perform the *feng* and *shan* sacrifices; in 1111 west to Fen-
yin to sacrifice to earth; in 1114 south to Bozhou to visit the shrine to
Laozi there.[26] Subsequent emperors did much less travel, perhaps a
reflection of the growing importance of Confucian learning at court.
In 1047, when Renzong wanted to go out hunting a second time, many
officials submitted memorials opposing his plans till he finally canceled them.[27] From Renzong on, the Song emperors largely stayed in
the capital and its environs. There is no record of Huizong leaving the
vicinity of the capital any time during his reign. The Song officially
had four capitals, one for each of the cardinal directions, but the emperors did not pay regular visits to them. Instead they remained in the
Eastern Capital, Kaifeng, for decades at a time. By contrast, in the
larger society, travel had, if anything, become more common in Song
times. Literati and officials traveled to the capital for schooling, to
take civil service examinations, and if successful to posts anywhere in
the country. They also enjoyed tourism, taking side trips to notable
places, often for the scenery or historical associations.[28] The emperor
was being denied the sorts of experiences that had become common
for the elite of the land.

Why did officials raise an outcry when a ruler proposed going hunting or taking a trip? The rhetoric against hunting and other travel
dates back to Han times.[29] One reason was that travel, and especially
hunting, was a form of recreation, its purpose to amuse the ruler, and
pleasure was in and of itself suspect. Another was that unforeseen
events might occur which those attending the emperor could not fully

control. In other words, the emperor might be accidentally injured or even killed. Moreover, the closer the emperor got to subjects the more difficult it would be to prevent assassination plots.[30] Added to this, the high officials who dealt with emperors probably did not see any advantage in the emperor forming his own opinions. An emperor who traveled might get new ideas and want to change routines in ways they did not approve. The more varied the experience of the emperor, the harder he might be to manage. Allsen argues that Tang officials decried the chase in order to prevent emperors from spending time outside the company of literati, and especially to spend it "in the company of 'undesirables'—military men, frontier officials, and foreigners."[31] The big difference between Tang and Song is not the arguments used against the emperor venturing beyond the capital but the greater success of Song officials in getting the emperor to comply with these geographic restrictions. In the two extant books compiled to educate emperors, Fan Zuyu's *Learning of Emperors* and Zhang Juzheng's *Mirror for Emperors*, the Song emperor held up for emulation above all others was Renzong, who treated his highest officials as though they were his teachers and complied with their admonitions against venturing out of the palace.[32]

Huizong, it is true, found many ways to make life interesting and pleasant without traveling very far. Both his religious and his artistic pursuits kept his world from seeming too small. The imagination of the cosmos in Daoism is anything but narrow and constrained. Huizong designed the Northeast Marchmount to replicate the great sights and botanical diversity of the realm and gathered plant specimens from all over. Modern historians have long faulted the Song for downgrading the military side of rule.[33] Limiting emperors' exposure to generals and armies by keeping them in the palace was another way to keep them focused on the civil and cultural side of sovereignty. Had Huizong made regular trips to inspect his armies and talk to his generals in the field, perhaps he would have had better instincts about how to negotiate with the Jurchen ruler Aguda, and he might have had a better sense of which generals to entrust with which task.

Appendix A:
Reasons for Rejecting
Some Common Stories
about Huizong and His Court

$\mathcal{D}$ECIDING which stories to give credence to is one of the most basic tasks of historians, who are well aware that records are not all equally reliable. In the case of Song China, even state papers can be suspect, especially memorials submitted by remonstrance officials, who were authorized to report things they had heard people talk about, even without any other evidence. Then there are the hundreds of *biji*, books of anecdotes and essays, written by Song literati. Many of the stories recorded in *biji* were based not on personal knowledge, but on stories the authors had heard, perhaps second- or thirdhand, or even read in someone else's *biji*. In Song times, as in other times and places, people loved to be amused, and clever stories could be very amusing. Thus even stories about prominent historical figures could well have been embroidered or even made up. At the same time, many topics can be discussed today only because of the survival of these books, so historians are reluctant to reject them out of hand. Here I have cited Cai Tao's *Tieweishan congtan* many times, thinking that a son of Cai Jing who was often in the palace could quite plausibly know the sort of things about Huizong and his court that Cai Tao records. Another author I have drawn on many times is Wang Mingqing (1127–1214), who seems to have had access to many documents dating back to Huizong's reign, but certainly his anecdotes are not all equally credible. It should also be recognized that material from *biji* not infrequently found its way into the standard historical sources. Thus, a historian today must always be a little skeptical about anything that seems more likely to have been based on rumor rather than on direct knowledge.

There is no foolproof way to decide which stories to accept and which not. Sometimes common sense is enough to reject a story. Sometimes one can conclude that an anecdote was probably made up because of discrepancies between the story and more reliable historical sources— for instance, perhaps the individual involved could not have been where the story placed him. Sometimes the stories seem so fictional that they can be rejected even without contradictory evidence. Of course, even the stories that have been embroidered or made up from whole cloth add to our understanding of the time; they let us see the sorts of stories and rumors they passed around. When the issue is what actually happened, however, rumors are not a good source.

Below, I give my reasons for rejecting six stories, some included in standard historical sources, some found only in *biji*. A couple of the examples are included because the issue touched on is fairly important, others as examples of the sort of fictions that can easily enter the historical record. I have included only examples that some modern scholars have accepted as true.

Huizong's Birthday

There was a rumor, recorded in Yuan times, that Huizong was actually born on the fifth day of the fifth month, but as that was considered an unlucky day, his birth date was moved to the auspicious tenth day of the tenth month.[1] Zhou Mi (1232–1308) recorded this anecdote in two of his books, *Qidong yeyu* and *Guixin zazhi*.[2] No earlier source for it is currently extant.

This rumor is highly implausible since it would have meant altering the seniority among Shenzong's sons, something their mothers would surely have protested. That is, if Huizong had been born in the fifth month of 1082, he would have been older than his brother Bi, born in the seventh month.[3] Surely, if he had been born on an unlucky day, rather than move his birth date by five months, until after his younger brother was born, it would have been moved forward or back one or two days.

Liu Hunkang and the Northeast Marchmount (Genyue)

In the Southern Song, a story circulated that the Daoist master Liu Hunkang advised Huizong to build an artificial mountain in the northeast part of the city so that he would have sons.[4] The earliest extant source for this story is probably the second installment of Wang Mingqing's *Huizhu lu*, dating to 1194.[5] It is short enough to translate in full:

> At the end of the Yuanfu reign period [1098–1100], there were rumors of unnatural occurrences that took place frequently in the palace. A Daoist priest from Mount Mao by the name of Liu Hunkang was noted for his ability in performing exorcism and curing ailments with talisman-water. He was invited into the palace to exorcise demons and had some success. . . .
>
> When Huizong first ascended the throne, he did not yet have many sons. Priest Liu suggested that if the northeast corner of the capital could be elevated to a certain height, the emperor would be blessed with many sons. Thus an artificial hill of several score feet in height was created in the northeast corner and, lo and behold, sons were born one after the other. The emperor was so pleased that he embraced Daoism. An elaborate program of building [Daoist temples] was started. Many retainers of dubious character and motives persuaded the emperor to build the pleasure garden known as the Northeast Marchmount (Genyue).[6]

I reject this story because of its implausibility. It seems unlikely that Huizong was ever worried about being survived by a son. He was married at sixteen and in less than a year his first son was born. At the time he had been on the throne three months. Even on the day of his accession, he most likely knew his wife was pregnant. From that point on, new sons were born at a steady rate. Moreover, the large body of letters that Huizong sent to Liu Hunkang never hint that he is worried about the birth of children, or that he owed Liu Hunkang thanks for telling him how to assure progeny. Nor is there any evidence that work on the Northeast Marchmount and its artificial mountain was started in Huizong's first year on the throne. I suspect that this was a story that got elaborated as it was passed around.

Tong Guan and Cai Jing in Hangzhou

Modern historians often report as fact the story that the time Cai Jing and Tong Guan spent together in Hangzhou formed an important stage in their relationship.[7] The standard historical sources support this story. The *Song History* biography of Tong Guan states, "When Huizong took the throne he established the Bright Gold Agency in Hangzhou and appointed Tong Guan to manage it as a palace servitor, and [while there] he got to know Cai Jing. As Cai Jing advanced, Tong Guan became more powerful."[8] The *Song History* biography of Cai Jing elaborates and put a different twist on who helped whom: "Tong Guan went to the Wu region in his capacity as palace servitor to search for calligraphy, paintings, and other rarities. He stayed in Hangzhou for several months, and Cai Jing traveled with him without cease day and night. Every day Guan sent all the painted screens, fans, and other items they acquired to the palace. Furthermore, he appended descriptions and reports that reached the emperor; and in this way the emperor came to take notice of Cai Jing."[9] A source preserved in the *Documents on the Treaties with the North during Three Reigns* of 1196 goes even further, reporting that while in Hangzhou Tong Guan regaled Cai Jing with stories of the military situation on the frontiers and the battles fought by earlier generals, impressing him with his military acumen so that when it came time to recommend generals to Huizong, Cai Jing readily recommended Tong Guan.[10]

The problem here is that the two individuals, Tong Guan and Cai Jing, were not in Hangzhou at the same time. Tong Guan was appointed to his post in 1102/3, but Cai Jing had already left Hangzhou in 1101/2 to take up a post as prefect of Dingzhou.[11] Moreover, there is ample evidence that Huizong was quite familiar with Cai Jing even before he came to the throne,[12] so would hardly have needed Tong Guan to tell him about him.

Empress Dowager Xiang and the Rehabilitation of the Conservatives

Historians have often assumed that Empress Dowager Xiang was the one most eager to bring back the conservatives once Huizong was on the throne and that only because she died in early 1101 was Huizong able to change course.[13] A close examination of the fullest sources, however, reveals a very different situation. Huizong was not reluctant to bring back conservatives and Xiang was eager to keep at least one reformer.

There seem to be several reasons why this version of the political history of the period has become the established one. Xiang's biography in the *Song History* seems to imply that she should be given credit for bringing back the conservatives. After saying that she had become regent only because Huizong begged her to, it goes on: "The worthy scholar-officials whom Zhang Dun had had banished in the Shaosheng [1094–1097] and Yuanfu [1098–1100] periods began a few at a time to be reemployed."[14] This fits with the tendency to assume that an individual's central character traits do not change in major ways.[15] Then there is the fact that empress regents commonly were the actual power-holders, so that anything that gets decided when a woman was regent gets attributed to her rather than to the child emperor. This would be how historians treat the early years of Renzong's reign when Empress Liu was the regent and the early years of Zhezong's reign when Empress Gao was the regent. In both of those cases, however, the boy emperor sat with the regent behind a screen, and did not have independent meetings with his officials. As discussed in Chapter 2, the members of Huizong's Council of State recommended that Xiang's regency not be on the pattern of those of Liu and Gao, but be more limited, with the councilors first discussing issues with Huizong, then visiting her. The fact that Xiang's mother-in-law Gao had brought back the conservatives while serving as regent may also have led historians to make this assumption. However, just because her mother-in-law was against the New Policies is no reason to assume that Xiang was as well.

The best way to judge how much Xiang contributed to bringing back conservatives is to look at the dates when conservatives were brought back and reformers sent away and how the decisions were made. In the *Changbian*, the *Changbian shibu*, and the *Zenggong yilu*, Huizong is shown to be familiar with the names of most of the conservatives and to propose that specific ones be brought back. Only seven days after taking the throne Huizong asked for a list of men who had previously held important court posts who could be brought back, and when given it went over it item by item with the councilors, picking out ten men for immediate appointment. When the councilors next went to see the empress dowager, she expressed approval of all of Huizong's decisions.[16]

Not only is there no evidence that Xiang ever on her own proposed conservatives to bring back, but, to the contrary, she asserted herself to retain the staunch reformer Cai Jing in the capital. On 4/2 when Huizong met with Zeng Bu, he warned Zeng Bu that Xiang wanted to keep Cai Jing, and when Zeng Bu later went to see her, she in fact was insistent. He warned her that he might resign if she did not give in, but she responded, "What does this have to do with the Bureau of Military Affairs?" (Zeng Bu's position on the Council of State was in his capacity as head of the Bureau of Military Affairs). When Zeng Bu said, "Gentlemen and inferior men cannot abide in the same place," she countered, "During the late emperor's reign you were together." Because Zeng Bu kept obstinately returning to this issue, the empress finally had to tell him it was time for him to leave.[17]

On the first day of the seventh month Xiang formally withdrew from participating in the government. At that point there still were reformers on the Council of State. It was not until two months later, on 1100/9/8, that Huizong finally accepted the leading reformer Zhang Dun's request to retire. Not until the next month was Cai Jing finally sent out of the capital.[18]

Xiang did express some political opinions after giving up the regency, but they were not necessarily pro-conservative opinions. On 1100/9/16, Chen Guan, one of the most outspoken of the conservative censors, submitted a memorial criticizing Xiang's relatives and also charging that she had not in fact given up participating in the government. She became extremely upset and would not eat. Huizong tried to console her by saying he would banish Chen Guan. Her companions suggested that the way to calm her down would be to appoint Cai Jing to a councilor position. Huizong did not appoint him, but the next day he did have Chen Guan assigned a post out of the capital.[19]

The idea that Xiang had restrained Huizong from doing what he had truly wanted to do—revive his father's policies—undoubtedly began during his reign. Even Huizong and Cai Jing contributed to this interpretation of events, probably because they thought consistency made their commitments seem stronger. In the 1107 "imperially composed" record of Harmony Revealed Hall, thought to have been actually written by Cai Jing, all of the wonderful elements in Shenzong's New Policies are listed, one by one, followed by the distorted criticisms of them by the anti-reformers. After Shenzong's death, when the screen was lowered so Gao could govern, "the cliques of evil men helped each other to rise to the highest posts" and overturned all of Shenzong's admirable policies. When Huizong himself came to the throne and he asked his mother to rule with him, the same sort of thing happened again, with those who gained power rejecting all of the established policies out of a desire for retaliation, even "saying it is unfilial to follow one's father's mistakes." Once Huizong was ruling on his own, however, in every single order or ruling he had adhered to the precedents set by Shenzong, or so we are told.[20] Thus, if even Cai Jing and Huizong told the story this way, it is not surprising that most of those who followed did as well.

Cai Jing and the Alliance with Jin

It is not uncommon to find modern historians who portray Cai Jing as a strong supporter of the alliance with Jin.[21] When the historical record is examined more closely, it is evident that one should make a distinction between Cai Jing's early support for learning more about what was happening in Liao and how Song might benefit from the situation, and his later strong reservations about committing to military action. Moreover, it should be kept in mind that Cai Jing retired in 1120/6 and was not involved much in court affairs for the next 4.5 years, the period when the treaty was negotiated and signed.

Contemporaries did often make statements to the effect that Cai Jing was ultimately responsible for everything that went wrong, above all in memorials of indictment. An Yaochen, in a long memorial submitted in 1118, much of which was directed against Tong Guan, says people both inside and outside the court all say Tong Guan and Cai Jing "have together advocated a northern expedition."[22] Not long after Huizong abdicated, Sun Di submitted a memorial that decried Cai Jing's iniquity; it states that he led the way to the breach in the border and incited the military action.[23] In Qinzong's edict demoting Cai Jing in 1126/3, undoubtedly reflecting views like Sun's, Cai Jing is charged with having advocated pacifying Yan.[24] The *Dongdu shilue*, probably basing itself on charges of this sort states: "Cai Jing led the way to advocate the Yanshan campaign."[25] Thus it is not surprising that many modern historians make similar statements. But this is a case where exaggerated claims in memorials of indictment have been too easily accepted as simple fact.

It is true that in 1115 Cai Jing supported the decision to bring the defector Zhao Liangsi to court to learn what he had to say about current conditions in Liao, and that he supported finding out more after meeting him. But that does not mean that he was eager for war. The edicts in 1116 and 1117 warning commanders along the northern borders not to try to create an incident could well reflect Cai Jing's caution.[26] The possibility that Huizong was overriding Cai Jing's strong support for starting a war seems less likely. Moreover, once Cai Jing had learned more about the Jurchen and what was happening in Liao, he, like most of the other senior councilors, saw serious drawbacks to an alliance that would commit Song to military action.[27] Several instances of his reluctance are recorded. After Tong Guan submitted a proposal to take advantage of the disorder in Liao to regain Yan, Huizong wanted Cai Jing's opinion on it and several times sent a eunuch to ask Cai Jing what he thought of it, without getting a response. It wasn't until Huizong kept Cai Jing after an audience and asked him directly, however, that Cai Jing was willing to express his opinion. He told Huizong that he did not have confidence in Tong Guan and that invading another country is much too momentous an undertaking to entrust to him. When Huizong brought up Tong Guan's earlier successes on the northwestern border, Cai Jing disputed how much of the credit for those victories should go to Tong Guan.[28]

A second instance occurred in early 1119. Cai Jing was asked to entertain the envoys from Jin, but still was not convinced in the desirability of the new alliance. Tong Guan, we are told, was mad at Cai Jing and criticized him in front of the emperor. Cai Jing "knew Tong Guan was angry at him, but this was a matter on which he really could not go along with him."[29] Not long afterward, Cai Jing and most of the other councilors resisted Huizong's pressure for them to sign a statement supporting the alliance. The author of the *biji* that recorded this, Zhou Hui (1127–1198+), notes that "it was through discussions with Tong Guan, Wang Fu, and Wang Anzhong that the emperor decided to carry out the plan. It was really Tong Guan who had brought about that day's decision. However, if it had not been for Wang Fu and Wang Anzhong, his plans would not have come to fruition."[30] He does not include Cai Jing in this list. Zhou Hui traces this account to a servant of Cai Jing who had personally heard the conversations. One can also point to observers of the period who are more nuanced about what they blamed on Cai Jing. Cheng Yu wrote, "Although the alliance with Jin began with Tong Guan and was put in place by Wang Fu and Cai You, the decline in the border defenses is the fault of Cai Jing."[31]

Cai Tao also wrote of Cai Jing's deep misgivings about the decision to take military action. Although it was common in the early Southern

Song for people after the events to claim that their own relatives had been against allying with Jin, Cai Tao provides credible instances of Cai Jing's efforts to change Huizong's mind. He reports that in the summer of 1122, after Cai Jing had retired, Huizong summoned him to an audience, during which Cai Jing begged him to stop the campaign. Later, when the situation worsened, Huizong told the eunuch Liang Shicheng that Cai Jing was the only one who consistently had argued against the northern campaign.[32]

Huizong Leaving the Palace at Night to Visit Li Shishi

A romantic relationship between Huizong and the courtesan Li Shishi appears in several works of fiction, *Xuanhe yishi*, *Shuihu zhuan* (chapter 72), and a story devoted to her *(Li Shishi waizhuan)*. None of these three can be dated precisely, but parts of the stories were undoubtedly already circulating in the Southern Song. Connections between Li Shishi and Huizong are also referred to in three Southern Song or early Yuan collections of anecdotes: Guo Tuan's *Kuiche zhi* of about 1165, Zhang Duanyi's *Guier ji* of 1248, and Zhou Mi's *Haoran zhai yetan* of about half a century later.[33] *Kuiche zhi* refers to Li Shishi as frequently entering the palace and one time getting involved with Lin Lingsu while there.[34] In the *Guierji* account the poet Zhou Bangyan (1056–1121) was visiting the courtesan Li Shishi when it was announced that Huizong was about to arrive. With no time to escape, Zhou Bangyan hid under the bed. Later he wrote a song drawing on what he heard. When Huizong learned this, he asked Cai Jing to get the poet appointed out of the capital. He relented, however, on hearing another song Zhou Bangyan had written.[35] Zhou Mi gives a shorter version of the same story.[36]

That Li Shishi was a prominent Kaifeng courtesan is not in doubt. She is mentioned in several Song sources, including *Dreams of Splendor of the Eastern Capital*, and *Mozhuang manlu*. That Huizong might have left the palace quietly is also not implausible. In 1119 Cai Jing mentioned in a thank-you memorial that Huizong had taken a light sedan chair to visit his home seven times that year.[37] Reading Cai Jing's memorial in the official gazette prompted an official named Cao Fu to submit a memorial saying that Huizong should not be leaving the palace without all the usual pomp and protection.[38] Criticizing rulers for leaving the confines of the palace to amuse themselves was an established tradition since Han times.[39] But Cao Fu did not say that Huizong had been visiting the entertainment quarters.

Several modern scholars have written on the issue of the historical validity of the Li Shishi-Huizong-Zhou Bangyan triangle. Wang Guowei decades ago rejected the idea that Huizong would have arrived when Zhou Bangyan was visiting, putting his emphasis on the dates. Could a courtesan who was the subject of poems written in the 1070s and 1080s still be attractive to Huizong thirty or more years later, especially if she were a couple of decades older than him? Wang Guowei's article stimulated other scholars to defend the triangle, by asserting that some of the references to Shishi in poetry could be to other women with that name, or Li Shishi could have been very young when she first became an entertainer, and so on.[40]

To me, the strongest reason to treat these stories as fiction is the nature of the material itself. It reads so much like fictional material that I would want very strong evidence to the contrary to think of it as based on fact. One passage was already cited in Chapter 10 (on Li Shishi saying an emperor would not be interested in her since he had so many beautiful women at his disposal). Let me cite one more:

> This was the queen of all the poets and carousers in two capitals and proprietor of the finest gentlemen's establishment in Bianjing. Her name was Li Shishi and all she cared for was the heads and tails of coins. She was so sharp, she could shuffle the very clouds and mist! Scions of the famous houses were completely undone by her, and if a country boy should cross her path, she had him looking for an early grave. Those who fell for her charms ended by begging from door to door. Huizong's eyes were riveted on her. Shakyamuni Lord Buddha himself would have been so captivated he would have fallen off his lotus! How much less a chance had a crazed fool like Huizong?[41]

For those who might grant that *Xuanhe yishi* has much fictional material but think a *biji* like *Guier ji* should be assumed to be factual unless proven otherwise, let me provide a translation of it as well:

> Zhou Bangyan was visiting the courtesan Li Shishi in her boudoir one day when it was announced that Emperor Huizong was on his way there. Too late to leave, Zhou hid himself under the bed. The emperor brought an orange with him, saying that it was among

the tribute recently arrived from Jiangnan. Unwittingly, Zhou overheard every intimate word between the emperor and the courtesan during the remainder of the evening. Zhou later composed a poem to the tune "Youth's carousal," which runs as follows:

> The ping knife with a blade none sharper,
> The Wu salt is like snow, only whiter,
> With her slender fingers, she peeled the orange.
> Waiting for the quilts to be warmed,
> Watching the smoke curling up from the incense burner,
> She sits facing me, toying with the pipe-organ. "Where
>   are you going to
> spend the night?" she asks, ever so softly.
> "The third watch has been sounded atop the city wall.
> And few people are out on the street—
> It's slippery and the frost is heavy.
> You'd better stay.

A few days later, when the courtesan sang this song to amuse the emperor, the latter asked who the author of the lyric was. Upon being told it was Zhou Bangyan, the emperor was infuriated. The next day, he summoned Cai Jing, the grand councilor, and told him that a certain tax official of Kaifeng, Zhou Bangyan by name, was delinquent in his duty and he demanded to know why the prefect of Kaifeng had not done anything about it. Not knowing what to make of the inquiry, Cai promised to make a thorough investigation of the matter and report back.

When Cai Jing summoned the prefect and told him about the imperial inquiry, the latter replied that among all the tax officials, Zhou was the first to fill his quota. "But his imperial majesty thinks otherwise," Cai told him. "We have to comply with his wishes." Thus, by imperial order, Zhou Bangyan was banished from the capital immediately for delinquency of duty.

A couple of days later, the emperor again visited the brothel, but Li Shishi was not home. Upon inquiry, he was told that she had gone to bid farewell to a tax official named Zhou. The emperor had come with the happy thought that he had gotten rid of his rival once and for all; now he was kept waiting. Li Shishi did not come back until the first watch. The emperor was furious at seeing her brows knitted, her eyes brimming with tears and looking haggard. "Where have you been?" he demanded. "I deserve death ten thousand times," she said tearfully. "Learning that Zhou Bangyan was banished from the capital on account of his trespass, I went to bid him farewell with a cup of wine for old time's sake. I had no idea that your majesty would choose to come today."

"Did he write any more poems," he demanded.

"He wrote a poem to the tune of 'The King of Lanling,'" she said.

"Sing it then," the emperor commanded.

"I'll offer your majesty a cup of wine while I sing the song," said the courtesan.

At the end of the song, the emperor was greatly pleased. He promptly appointed Zhou the director of the Music Bureau.[42]

The version in *Guier ji* may not be as elaborated as that in the *Xuanhe yishi*, but it still is quite improbable and has Huizong rapidly changing his mind depending on the quality of the poetry Zhou Bangyan writes. This shouts fiction to me.

I fully realize that I have not identified all problematic stories about Huizong and his top officials. Even accounts written by people close to the events are not always to be trusted. In 1144, Gaozong complained that the private histories then in circulation often contained errors: "Private records from the Jingkang period [1126–1127] are extremely unreliable. Huizong wanted to follow the example of Yao [who had abdicated]. When he abdicated the throne to Qinzong, it truly came from his inspired decision and yet all the private records have Cai You or Wu Min as the ones behind it. Huizong once told the grand councilors, 'If it had not been my idea, who would have dared propose it?' It would have been [treated as treason], leading to the extermination of one's kin."[43] If people of the time had difficulty distinguishing the more reliable accounts, it is not surprising that we may be misled nearly nine centuries later.

Appendix B:
Huizong's Consorts
and Their Children

Year	Sons born that year	Living sons	Daughters born that year	Living daughters	Total children	Total living children	Living mothers
1100	1	1	1	1	2	2	2
1101	2	2	1	2	5	4	3
1102	0	2	3	5	8	7	5
1103	1	3	1	6	10	9	5
1104	2	4	0	5	12	9	6
1105	0	4	3	6	15	10	7
1106	1	5	2	8	18	13	7
1107	4	9	2	9	24	18	8
1108	1	10	0	8	25	18	7
1109	2	12	3	10	30	22	8
1110	2	14	3	12	35	26	10
1111	2	16	0	11	37	27	10
1112	3	18	1	11	41	29	10
1113	0	17	3	14	44	31	9
1114	2	18	0	13	46	31	9
1115	2	20	1	14	49	34	10
1116	0	19	2	16	51	35	9
1117	0	19	0	15	51	34	9
1118	2	21	1	16	54	37	9+
1119	0	21	2	18	56	39	9+
1120	1	22	0	17	57	39	9+
1121	1	23	2	19	60	42	8+
1122	1	24	0	19	61	43	8+
1123	1	25	0	19	62	44	8+
1124	0	25	1	20	63	45	8+
1125	0	25	2	22	65	47	8+
Total born during reign	31		34		65		

Note: Daughters are assigned a birth six months before the date they received their first title. The living sons and daughters are the number alive at the end of that year. The number of total mothers is a minimum after 1118 since after that date some of Huizong's children do not have their mother listed.

Timeline

Note: For a fuller chronology, see Zhang Qifeng 2008:183–251.

1082 1 *sui* (Yuanfeng 5)

    1082/10/10   Huizong is born.

1085 4 *sui* (Yuanfeng 8)

    1085/3/5   Shenzong dies at thirty-eight *sui*. Zhezong becomes emperor. Empress Dowager Gao takes over control of the court.

    1085/5/18   Sima Guang is appointed grand councilor.

    1085/8–12   New Policies are rescinded one after the other.

    1085/10   Shenzong's coffin is buried; Huizong's mother Consort Chen leaves the palace, never to return.

1088 7 *sui* (Yuanyou 3)

    1088/7   Uncle Jun dies.

1091 10 *sui* (Yuanyou 6)

    1091/10/25   A plan for the education of Huizong and his brothers is presented at court.

1092 11 *sui* (Yuanyou 7)

    1092/4   Wedding of Zhezong and Empress Meng takes place.

1093 12 *sui* (Yuanyou 8)

    1093/9/3   Empress Dowager Gao dies.

1094   13 *sui* (Shaosheng 1)

    1094/7/18   Demotion of the Yuanyou partisans begins.

1095   14 *sui* (Shaosheng 2)

    1095   Tutors are appointed for Huizong and his brothers.

1096   15 *sui* (Shaosheng 3)

    1096/3   Huizong's title is raised to Prince of Duan.

    1096/9/29   Accusations of witchcraft lead to demotion of Empress Meng who enters a Daoist convent.

    1096/9   Uncle Hao dies.

1097   16 *sui* (Shaosheng 4)

1098   17 *sui* (Yuanfu 1)

    1098/3/20   Huizong moves into new mansion.

    1098/10   Huizong makes the second offering at the Suburban Altar.

1099   18 *sui* (Yuanfu 2)

    1099/6   Huizong marries Lady Wang.

    1099/9   Zhezong's Consort Liu is elevated to Empress.

1100   19 *sui* (Yuanfu 3)

    1100/1/1   Zhezong is too ill to hold the New Year audience.

    1100/1/12   Zhezong dies. Huizong is made emperor. Empress Dowager Xiang agrees to co-rule.

    1100/2   Han Zhongyan is brought to court.

    1100/2/10   Huizong's wife Lady Wang is appointed as Empress.

    1100/3/22   There is an eclipse of the sun.

    1100/3/24   An edict calling for frank criticism is issued.

    1100/4/13   Huizong's first son is born (Prince Huan / Qinzong).

    1100/5/19   Cai Bian is dismissed from the Council of State.

    1100/5/10   Former Empress Meng is restored to empress rank.

    1100/5/23   Sima Guang et al. are restored to their old ranks.

    1100/7/1   Empress Dowager Xiang ends co-rule.

    1100/8/6   Construction is started on the Western Temple of Spectacular Numina.

    1100/8/8   Zhezong is buried.

    1100/9/6   Huizong visits his brothers to see auspicious mushrooms and is chastised by Chen Guan and Chen Shixi.

    1100/9/8   Zhang Dun retires from the Council of State.

1100/10/3	Cai Jing is assigned a provincial post.
1100/10/9	Zeng Bu becomes junior grand councilor.
1100	Li Jie submits *Building Standards*.
1100	Huizong summons Liu Hunkang to court.

1101 20 *sui* (Jianzhong jingguo 1)

1101/1/13	Empress Dowager Xiang dies.
1101/7/3	Huizong requests separate lists of those for and against Shenzong's policies.
1101/7/28	Su Shi dies.
1101/11/23	Huizong performs his first Suburban Sacrifice.
1101/12/20	Shenzong is enshrined at Western Temple of Spectacular Numina.

1102 21 *sui* (Chongning 1)

1102/3/17	Tong Guan is sent to Suzhou and Hangzhou to organize palace procurement.
1102/5/6	Han Zhongyan is taken off the Council of State.
1102/5/21	Su Che, Fang Chunli, and fifty-odd others are banned from the capital.
1102/5/24	Empress Dowager Xiang is buried.
1102/5/26	Cai Jing and Zhao Tingzhi are again given court posts.
1102/i6/9	Zeng Bu is dismissed from the Council of State.
1102/7/5	Cai Jing is appointed to the Council of State.
1102/7/11	The Advisory Agency is created.
1102/8/20	Charity clinics are established.
1102/8/22	Cai Jing proposes a major reform of the government school system.
1102/9/6	Poorhouses are set up in capital.
1102/9/13	Memorials written in 1100 are scrutinized to classify authors by degrees of orthodoxy and heterodoxy.
1102/9/15	Zeng Bu, Han Zhongyan, and others are demoted for handling of Empress Dowager Liu.
1102/9/16	117 officials, many long dead, are banned from office.
1102/10/23	Meng loses empress title again.
1102/12/10	Five-*qian* coins are issued.
1102/12/16	Cai Jing issues rules for prefectural and county schools.

1103   22 *sui* (Chongning 2)

    1103/4/19   Portraits of Sima Guang et al. are removed from the
                 Temple of Spectacular Numina.

    1103/4/9   Destruction of the wood blocks for printing Su Shi's
                 collected works is ordered.

    1103/4/27   Burning wood blocks for books by Su Shi, Su Che, Su Xun,
                 Qin Guan, Huang Tingjian, et al. is ordered.

    1103/6/5   Wang is installed as empress.

    1103/8   Zhang Shangying is dismissed, added to list of banned
                 partisans.

    1103/9/5   Imperial clansmen are ordered not to marry their children
                 to Yuanyou partisans.

    1103/9/16   A medical school is established.

    1103/9/17   Prefectures are ordered to establish Chongning temples.

    1103/9/25   Prefectures are ordered to erect Yuanyou ban stele.

1104   23 *sui* (Chongning 3)

    1104/1/6   Those who submitted deviant memorials are banned from
                 entering the capital.

    1104/1/13   Ten-*qian* cash are minted.

    1104/1/17   Quotas for county schools are increased.

    1104/1/29   Casting of Nine Cauldrons is begun.

    1104/2/3   Paupers' graveyards are established.

    1104/4/19   Prefectural Honoring Calm Daoist temples instructed to
                 hold services on Huizong Personal Destiny days.

    1104/6/1   Portraits of reformers are painted on the walls of Shenzong's
                 Portrait Hall at Temple of Spectacular Numina.

    1104/6/3   List of 309 men banned from office or posthumous honors
                 is issued.

    1104/6/11   Schools for calligraphy, painting, and mathematics are
                 established.

    1104/8/3   Cai Jing submits a history of Shenzong's reign.

    1104/9   Tong Guan and Wang Hou are given houses in the capital.

    1104/11/4   Huizong visits the Imperial Academy and Biyong Academy,
                 later commemorated in a stele erected at schools around
                 the country.

    1104/11/17   Announcement is made that civil service recruitment will
                 be entirely through the school system.

    1104/11/26   Suburban Sacrifice to heaven is performed.

    1104   The number of students in government schools reaches
                 210,000.

1104	Song claims recovery of Qingtang territories.
1104	Huizong gives Tong Guan his transcription of the *Thousand Character Essay*.

1105   24 *sui* (Chongning 4)

1105/1/27	Cai Bian is dismissed.
1105/1/28	Tong Guan is given a military command.
1105/i2/16	Tin-alloy coins are issued in four northern circuits.
1105/5/12	Ban on relatives of partisans is removed, the first step in reducing measures against banned partisans.
1105/8	Last of the Nine Cauldrons is cast.
1105/7	Cai Jing initiates discussion of building a Bright Hall.
1105/8/21	A sacrifice is performed for the Nine Cauldrons in Nine Completions Hall.
1105/8/27	Huizong gives the name Music of Great Brilliance to the new music.
1105/9/11	Banished partisans are allowed to move closer in stages, but not to the capital.
1105/9/21	Thirty-five students from the Upper Hall are granted civil service degrees.
1105/12/24	The process of restoring those who had been banned to ranks of men eligible for office begins.
1105	Ten-*qian* coins are issued in Huizong's calligraphy.

1106   25 *sui* (Chongning 5)

1106/1/5	The appearance of a comet leads Huizong to pull back on initiatives.
1106/2/3	Cai Jing is dismissed.
1106/2/14	A collection of Huizong's imperial brush edicts is printed.
1106/3/24	Huizong's brother Si dies.
1106/8/15	Primal Tally Myriad Longevity Temple at Mount Mao is completed.
1106/11/4	Huizong's brother Bi dies.
1106	Mi Fu is appointed professor in the school of painting and calligraphy.

1107   26 *sui* (Daguan 1)

1107/1/7	Cai Jing returns as grand councilor.
1107/1/13	The Agency for Deliberating on Ritual is established.
1107/3/18	Huizong issues an edict on the "Eight Conducts, Eight Offenses" system for promotion through the schools, later carved on stone at many prefectural schools.

1107/3/27	Zhao Tingzhi dies.
1107/5/9	The New Music is promulgated.
1107/7/13	The Yellow River clears at Qianning.
1107/8/2	Zeng Bu dies.

1108 27 *sui* (Daguan 2)

1108/3/10	Liturgy for the Daoist Golden Register Retreat is issued.
1108/3	Mi Fu dies.
1108/4/17	Liu Hunkang dies in Kaifeng.
1108/5/2	Cai Jing is given a jade belt.
1108/9/26	Empress Wang dies.
1108/11	Xue Ang requests that pictures of ancient vessels be collected in order to cast more authentically ancient vessels for use in sacrificial rites.
1108	*Materia Medica of the Daguan Period* is issued.
1108	Tong Guan leads campaign in Qingtang.

1109 28 *sui* (Daguan 3)

1109/6/4	Cai Jing is out of office, until 1112/5.
1109	The *Daguan tie* collection of calligraphy rubbings issued, with titles written out by Cai Jing.

1110 29 *sui* (Daguan 4)

1110/1/4	Casting of ten-*qian* coins is stopped.
1110/8/1	Huizong writes an essay on the Music of Great Brilliance.
1110	Huizong answers dozens of questions from the Agency for Deliberating on Ritual.
1110/10/2	Empress Zheng is appointed.
1110	Architect Li Jie dies.

1111 30 *sui* (Zhenghe 1)

1111/1/9	Thirteen hundred and eighteen unauthorized shrines in the capital are ordered abolished.
1111/3/1	Huizong writes out in his own hand his preface for the new ritual code.
1111/5/7	Ten-*qian* coins are made into three-*qian* coins.
1111/9	Tong Guan accompanies the envoy to Liao.
1111	Huizong shows his sixty Daoist hymns to some officials.
1111	Huizong commissions a collection of pharmacological prescriptions.

	1111	Huizong offers personal instruction to painting student Wang Ximeng.
1112	31 *sui* (Zhenghe 2)	
	1112/1	Cranes appear at Duan Gate, later commemorated in a painting.
	1112/2/1	Cai Jing's titles are restored, and he is given a house in the capital.
	1112/4/8	Huizong entertains officials at Grand Clarity Edifice.
	1112/5/13	Cai Jing begins coming to court every third day.
	1112/12/15	Tong Guan is promoted to Taiwei.
1113	32 *sui* (Zhenghe 3)	
	1113/4/7	Treasured Harmony Hall is completed.
	1113/4/24	A palace hall is converted into Jade Clarity Harmonious Yang Daoist temple.
	1113/4/29	*New Forms of the Five Categories of Rites of the Zhenghe Period* is issued.
	1113/5/30	New banquet music is issued.
	1113/7/22	Consort Liu Mingda dies; later she is posthumously promoted to empress.
	1113/10/18	Ancient vessels and newly cast copies are put on display in Promoting Governance Hall.
	1113/10/20	It is ruled that one hundred Daoist masters should participate in the Suburban Sacrifice and rites at Temple of Spectacular Numina.
	1113/11/5	Huizong has a vision of heavenly spirits on the way to Suburban Sacrifice to heaven.
	1113/12/6	Huizong issues a call for collecting Daoist books.
	1113	Cai Jing writes a colophon on a handscroll by painting student Wang Ximeng.
	1113	Extended Blessings Palace is constructed.
	1113	The Agency for Instituting Ritual is created.
1114	33 *sui* (Zhenghe 4)	
	1114/1/1	Twenty-six ranks for Daoist officials are created.
	1114/2/12	Huizong's eldest son (Prince Huan / Qinzong) is capped.
	1114/4/5	Huizong visits Shangshu sheng.
	1114/6/1	Huizong writes an account of the emergence of spirits on the way to the Suburban Sacrifice to earth.
	1114	Hostilities with Xi Xia begin.

1115   34 *sui* (Zhenghe 5)

    1115/2/5   Prince Huan is appointed heir apparent.

    1115/3/1   Huizong entertains leading officials in an imperial park, and shows them a painting he made.

    1115   The Jurchens declare the Jin dynasty.

    1115/4/18   Zhao Liangsi defects from Liao to Song, and meets Huizong.

    1115/7/10   Construction of the Bright Hall begins.

1116   35 *sui* (Zhenghe 6)

    1116   Highest Clarity Precious Registers Temple is completed.

    1116/2   Tong Guan joins the Council of State as assistant director of the Bureau of Military Affairs.

    1116/6/21   The heir apparent is married.

    1116/8/1   Officials on the northern border are instructed not to incite incidents.

    1116/10   Sets of bronze vessels are given to members of the Council of State.

    1116/11/15   Huizong in an edict mentions that there are more than two hundred thousand students in government schools.

1117   36 *sui* (Zhenghe 7)

    1117/1/14   Daoist schools are established.

    1117/2/6   Lin Lingsu reports on descent of spirits to two thousand monks in Precious Registers Temple.

    1117/4/2   Huizong tells officials not to use his title of Master of Religion Lord of the Dao except in religious contexts.

    1117/6/1   The Bright Hall is completed.

    1117/10/2   Huizong's first grandchild is born.

    1117/11/6   Cai Jing is allowed to come to court only every fifth day.

    1117/12/15   Spirits descend in Kunning Hall.

1118   37 *sui* (Zhonghe 1)

    1118/i9   Song envoys to Jin land in Liaodong.

    1118/2/9   Nine Divine Empyrean cauldrons are cast and are installed at Precious Registers Temple.

    1118/3/26   Prince Kai passes the civil service examination.

    1118/4/19   Buddhist texts that slander the Daoists are identified so that they can be suppressed.

    1118/5/11   Huizong issues in his own name a theoretical treatise on medicine, the *Classic of Sagely Benefaction*.

1118/8/12	Huizong's commentary on the *Laozi* is ordered engraved on stone at the Divine Empyrean temple in the capital.
1118/9/18	Cai Jing's proposal to compile a *History of the Dao* is approved.
1118/10/21	Huizong transmits registers to eight hundred people at Precious Registers Temple.
1118	Huizong's daughter, Princess Fujin, marries Cai Jing's son Tiao.

1119 38 *sui* (Xuanhe 1)

1119/1/10	Huizong visits the home of his daughter married to Cai Tiao.
1119/1/10	The first emissary from Jin arrives.
1119/1/20	Buddhist divinities are renamed.
1119/6/24	Xi Xia sues for peace, hostilities end.
1119/9/1	A banquet is held in Treasured Harmony Hall.
1119/11/19	Huizong writes a poem about the sacrifice to heaven and confers it on Cai Jing, who matches it.
1119/11/29	Lin Lingsu leaves the capital to return to Wenzhou.
1119/12/24	Author of a memorial criticizing Huizong's incognito trips outside the palace is banished.

1120 39 *sui* (Xuanhe 2)

1120/1/23	Daoist schools are abolished.
1120/2/4	Zhao Liangsi is sent as an envoy to Jin.
1120/6/9	Cai Jing retires.
1120/9/7	Buddhist monks are no longer to be called Masters of Virtue.
1120/11/1	Fang La openly rebels in Muzhou.
1120/12	A banquet is held in Extended Blessings Palace.
1120/12	Huizong is informed of Fang La's uprising, first troops dispatched.
1120/ summer	*Xuanhe Painting Catalogue* finished.

1121 40 *sui* (Xuanhe 3)

1121/4/2	Consort Liu Mingjie dies; later posthumously promoted to empress.
1121/1/21	Tong Guan arrives in Muzhou with his army to suppress Fang La's rebellion.
1121/2/18	Hangzhou is recovered from the rebels.
1121/4/25 or 26	Fang La is captured.
1121/8/24	Fang La is executed in the capital.

1122   41 *sui* (Xuanhe 4)

    1122/1/1   Huizong writes an essay to commemorate completion of Northeast Marchmount.

    1122/1/13   Jin captures the Liao Central Capital; Liao ruler flees.

    1122/2/29
    or 3/5
    or 3/2   Huizong visits the new quarters for Palace Library; gives paintings and calligraphy he had done to officials present.

    1122/4/10   Huizong reviews troops before they depart for Yanjing.

    1122/5/23   Tong Guan and his army arrive at Yongzhou in preparation for attacking Yanjing.

    1122/5/29   Song and Liao armies fight at Baigou; Song defeated.

    1122/9   Former Liao general Guo Yaoshi defects to Song.

    1122/10/28   Song armies retreat from Yanjing.

    1122/12/6   With Jin forces about to attack Yanjing, Liao leaders flee; city taken without a fight.

1123   42 *sui* (Xuanhe 5)

    1123/1   Wang Anzhong goes to front as pacification commissioner.

    1123/   Yellow River floods, necessitating relief work.

    1123   Treaty between Song and Jin is signed.

    1123/4/17   Song armies enter Yanjing, already thoroughly looted.

    1123/5/7   Wang Fu is given a jade belt.

    1123/5/21   Jin ruler Aguda dies.

    1123/6   Huizong entertains the turncoat Guo Yaoshi.

    1123/7/8   Tong Guan retires.

    1123/10/29   Wang Anzhong is assigned to write a celebratory account of recovering the Yanyun region.

    1123/11/17   Huizong visits Wang Fu's house.

    1123/11   Jin objects to Song handling of Zhang Jue.

    1123   The revised *Antiquities Illustrated* is completed.

1124   43 *sui* (Xuanhe 6)

    1124/1   Zhang Jue affair continues.

    1124/1/14   The court celebrates the defeat of Liao in Purple Asterism Hall.

    1124/8/1   Tong Guan is called back from retirement and sent to Yanjing.

    1124/10/17   The laws against the writings of Su Shi and Huang Tingjian are reiterated.

1124/11/3	Wang Fu is dismissed as grand councilor.	
1124/12/20	Cai Jing is brought back from retirement.	

1125   44 *sui* (Xuanhe 7)

1125/1	Song sends an envoy to Jin to congratulate the new emperor.
1125/2/8	Five hundred and fifty thousand piculs of grain is sent from the capital to Yanjing.
1125/4/19	Cai Jing is dismissed as grand councilor.
1125/4/19	A tax is imposed on those who do not serve in the military.
1125/6/8	All government departments are ordered to reduce expenditures.
1125/11	Huizong performs his last Suburban Sacrifice.
1125/12/16	Tong Guan arrives with news of the Jurchen invasion; soon news also arrives that Guo Yaoshi has defected to Jin, surrendering Yanjing to them.
1125/12/21	Homes for Huizong's sons are consolidated into ten units.
1125/12/22	Huizong issues an edict taking the blame on himself.
1125/12/23	Huizong abdicates; heir apparent succeeds to the throne.

1126   45 *sui* (Jingkang 1)

1126/1/4	Huizong and a party of his family and top officials leave Kaifeng for Zhenjiang.
1126/1/7	The Jin army arrives at the walls of Kaifeng.
1126/1/10	Tentative agreement is reached for a ransom of Kaifeng.
1126/1–2	Imperial Academy students protest.
1126/2/11	The Jurchen army leaves Kaifeng.
1126/3/1	Qinzong sends a message to Huizong to return to Kaifeng.
1126/4/3	Huizong returns to Kaifeng, lives in Dragon Virtue Palace/Temple.
1126/5/13	Huizong is invited to the palace.
1126/9/3	Taiyuan falls to Jin after a 260-day siege.
1126/11/25	Jin troops arrive at city walls of Kaifeng.
1126/i11	Song forces defend Kaifeng, but Jin forces gain control of the outer wall.
1126/i11/30	Qinzong goes to Wolibu's camp, is told to surrender, and returns the next day, with a demand for huge amounts of gold and silver, silk and satin.

1127   46 *sui* (Jianyan 1)

  1127/1/8   Silk and satin for the ransom are turned over in full.

  1127/1/10   Qinzong returns to the Jin camp after naming eldest son as
                    the heir apparent.

  1127/1   Conditions within Kaifeng become very difficult.

  1127/2/6
  or 7   Huizong is told to lead all of the imperial family members
                    out of the palace to the Jin camp.

  1127/3/7   Zhang Bangchang is installed as puppet emperor.

  1127/3/28   The Jurchens take Huizong and thousands of other
                    captives north as they withdraw.

  1127/5/1   Huizong's son Prince Gou is installed as Song emperor
                    (Gaozong).

  1127/5/13   Huizong arrives in Yanjing, stays there until 9/13.

  1127/10/18   Huizong arrives at the Jin Central Capital.

1128   47 *sui* (Jianyan 2)

  1128/8/21   Huizong arrives at Jin Supreme Capital.

  1128/10/26   Huizong leaves the Supreme Capital for Hanzhou, and
                    arrives two months later.

1129   48 *sui* (Jianyan 3)

  1129   The year is spent in Hanzhou.

1130   49 *sui* (Jianyan 4)

  1130/7   Huizong and his party are moved to Five Nations Fort.

  1130   Empress Zheng dies at the age of fifty-two.

1131   50 *sui* (Shaoxing 1)

  1131   The year is spent in Five Nations Fort.

1132   51 *sui* (Shaoxing 2)

  1132   The year is spent in Five Nations Fort.

1133   52 *sui* (Shaoxing 3)

  1133   The year is spent in Five Nations Fort.

1134   53 *sui* (Shaoxing 4)

  1134   The year is spent in Five Nations Fort.

1135   54 *sui* (Shaoxing 5)

  1135/4/21   Huizong dies.

Notes

1. Growing Up in the Palace, 1082–1099

Epigraph: CBSB 20.707.

1. Huizong is his posthumous name, not what he would have been called in his lifetime. His personal name was Ji, and his family name was Zhao. As a prince he would have been called by a succession of titles, the best-known of which is Prince of Duan, and after becoming emperor by terms equivalent to Your Majesty or Emperor.

2. Since Zhezong was born in the last month of 1076, he was already in his second year (two *sui*) when he was thirty days old. When he died twenty-three years later, he was twenty-five *sui*, but only twenty-three and one month in years. See the section titled Note on Ages, Dates, and Other Conventions at the beginning of this book.

3. DJMHL 1.30.

4. DJMHL 6.173; ZHWLXY 28.1a–6b; 33.3a–6b; 83.2b–6a; 100.4b–8a.

5. See DJMHLZ 1.30–31, 6.167, 10.243; Zhou Baozhu 1992:31. On the length of bays in various types of construction, see Q. Guo 1998:8.

6. THJWZ 4.168–169; Soper 1951:66; LQGZ 54; Bush and Shih 1985:187.

7. CYLY 1.21–22; ZHWLXY, passim.

8. S. Jang 1992; Ogawa 1981.

9. LQGZ 53–54; Bush and Shih 1985:189–190.

10. Ying Yan 1991; Hartwell 1988:42–43.

11. On clerks, see J. Liu 1967b, Umehara 1985:501–548. On technical specialists, see Zhang Bangwei 2005:98–141.

12. On their numbers, see Zhu Ruixi 1994 and Ebrey 2003a.

13. HSSCGY 8.1a–2a.

14. SS 243.8625, 8630.

15. On eunuchs in the Song period, see Zhang Bangwei 1993:263–303; Wang Mingsun 1981; Umehara 1985:163–165.

16. Hartwell 1988:21–26.

17. SHY Zhiguan 34.31b.; CB 341.8210–8211; WCZL 3.142–143; SLYY 4.56. A room-unit is the area between four pillars. As a unit of length, the space between two pillars is called a bay. A building five bays across and four bays deep has twenty room-units.

18. SDJK 13.324.

19. HSSCGY 8.1b; SHY Houfei 3.33a–b.

20. There were later reports that Shenzong's grand councilors conspired to install Shenzong's younger brother Hao instead of his son (CB 351.8409–8412; SS 471.13703). Since Hao would not have needed a regency, if the grand councilors were aware of the empress dowager's antipathy to them and the reforms, this might have been a way to retain power. Given the repeated rewriting of the histories of this period as a result of factional politics, it is difficult to determine if there was any basis for these charges, but I tend not to believe it because of the strong preference for succession by sons.

21. On Tang and Song empress regents, see H. Lee 2010:6–52.

22. CB 252.6169; SSWJL 3.25.

23. SHY Li 29.57a–67a.

24. Sources disagree on the date of her death. SS 243.8631 says she died at thirty-two and implies that she never quit mourning at the tomb. SHY Houfei 1.4b gives her death date as the sixth month of 1089. HSSCGY 8.210 gives the same death date, and says she was thirty-six when she died.

25. Henansheng 1997:532–533. See also the epitaph for one of Huizong's sisters who died just under four (Henansheng 1997:539).

26. Two of Huizong's younger brothers had names pronounced Si, so to keep them straight the younger of them is referred to here as Ssi.

27. Here I refer to Huizong's brothers (and later his sons) by their personal names (*ming*). At the time, and in most of the surviving sources, they were referred to by their frequently changing titles, such as Prince of Wei.

28. CBSB 20.707.

29. SDZLJ 29.153–154. See also SS 19.357; SDZLJ 28.144, 29.152, 155, 30.157–158.

30. SS 121.2841–2842; J. Liu 1985:217.

31. DJMHL 6.34–35; trans. West 1999:34–36. See also Idema and West 1982:31–35.

32. DJMHLZ 10.242–243. See also Ebrey 1999.

33. SSWJ 35.992–993.

34. SS 243.8632–8633.

35. SS 111.2658–2660.

36. Henansheng 1997:539–541, 542–544; SS 246.8720–8721; XHHP 20.565.

37. Henansheng 1997:540, 543–544; SS 246.8721.

38. XHHP 20:304–305, 307–308; XHSP 2.15; SHY Dixi 3.6b–7a. On Jun's interests, see also DDSL 16.5b–6a; SS 246.8721.

39. HZL Houlu 1.53.

40. An allusion to *Analects* 15.1.

41. DX. On this book, see also Guarino 1994, esp. pp. 86–117.

42. CB 467.11154.

43. SHY Dixi 2.14a.

44. YYDRZ 3.26b; CB 493.11711–11712.

45. FXJ 26.308–311; SYXA 5.100; SS 351.11101; SHY Dixi 2.15a. Fu Yi's biographer added that he held himself aloof from the eunuchs who managed the princely establishment, earning him the princes' respect.

46. Egan 1994:104, citing SSJSBM 44.431–432, 46.443.

47. Kaifeng in Song times has been studied by many scholars. For good brief discussions in English, see Kracke 1975; C. Heng 1999:117–135; D. Kuhn 2009:191–205; de Pee 2010. Chinese and Japanese scholarship is very extensive; see esp. Ihara 1991; Zhou Baozhu 1992; Yi Yongwen 2005; and Kubota 2007a. *Dongjing menghua lu*, the principal source used by all scholars, has been the subject of several studies by Stephen H. West. See esp. West 1985, 1987, 1997, 1999, and 2005a.

48. See Kubota 2007a:73–92.

49. D. Kuhn 2009:192.

50. See Hartwell 1967:126n.27; Zhou Baozhu 1992:346; Kubota 2007a:202–204.

51. D. Kuhn 2009:195. On Chang'an's population, see also V. Xiong 2000:196–201.

52. STD 63. On Jōjin see Borgen 1987, 2007.

53. DJMHL 2.14; West 2005b:410. See also Idema and West 1982:15–17.

54. DJMHL 11; TWSCT 4.70; trans. West 2005b:410–411.

55. DJMHL 7.40; trans. West 2005a:313.

56. West 2005a:313–317.

57. C. Heng 1999:162–163. The brick pagoda is one of the few remaining Song relics in Kaifeng today.

58. Soper 1948:24–35.

59. DJMHLZ 3.90–91; Soper 1948:26.

60. SHY Dixi 2:15a.

61. SHY Dixi 2.16b; SS 18.349–350; CB 496.11792.

62. CB 503.11979; SHY Li 1.33a. On the Qingtang campaign, see Smith 2006.

63. TS 10.110; SCBM Jingkang zhong 31.558.

64. HZL Houlu 7.176.

65. On Wang Shen, see Murck 2000:126–156; Barnhart 1983, 1998; Weng Tongwen 1968; T. W. Weng's biography of him in Franke 1976. On the husbands of princesses, see Chaffee 1991:142–143.

66. On Mi Fu, see Ledderose 1979 and Sturman 1997.

67. On Su Shi's trial, see Hartman 1990; Y. Wang 2011. The charge was that Wang Shen had carried on with his concubines while the princess was ill, but it is easy to suspect that the real reason was that once the princess had died, there was no reason not to banish him along with Su Shi; when Su Shi was recalled after Shenzong's death, so was Wang Shen. Empress Dowager Gao, however, still thought that he had not treated her daughter properly, and although she favored Su Shi, she remained cool to Wang Shen. The catalogue of Huizong's painting collection, written three decades later, accepts that Wang Shen had done something offensive, praises Shenzong for showing his impartiality in having him punished, and claims that during his exile Wang Shen reformed himself and devoted himself to painting and calligraphy (XHHP 12.204).

68. Ebrey 2008:104–105.

69. TWSCT 1.5–6. On Cai Tao as an author of a book of anecdotes that frequently mentions his father Cai Jing, see Lamouroux 2008:306–309.

70. See R. Maeda 1970a:244; XHHP 20.306; Chaffee 1999:31, 265, 270–271. The catalogue of Huizong's painting collection included 35 paintings by Wang Shen, 24 by Zhao Lingrang, 189 by Wu Yuanyu, and 241 by Cui Bo (XHHP 12.204, 18.285–286, 19.294–296, 20.306).

71. Murck 2000:142, 146.

72. CBSB 13.523–526.

73. ZGYL 9.221.

74. SHY Dixi 2.11b; ZGYL 7.84, 93.

75. SS 243.8638–8640.

76. Three chapters of this diary survived by being copied into the *Yongle dadian*. They cover the last nine months of Zhezong's reign and the first six of Huizong's. On the diaries Song councilors kept, see Yan Yongcheng 2001. Since Zeng Bu did not live past Huizong's reign, his diary would not have been edited to reflect later views on Huizong's reign the way so much of the rest of the written record was. On Zeng Bu's career, see Liu Zijian 1987:122–134; Luo Jiaxiang 2003a; Xiong Mingqin 2005.

77. ZGYL 7.108–109, 137.

78. ZGYL 8.147, 149.

79. ZGYL 8.152–153, 155–156.

80. ZGYL 8.158, 167; SS 18.158, 111.2657–2660.

81. Two versions of this memorial survive in Zou Hao's collected works, a fairly standard one and a truly inflammatory one that compares Zhezong to the worst tyrants in history. The second is said to have been forged in later years to get Zou Hao removed from office a second time. See DXJ 23.1a–5b (QSW 131:140–143); CBBM 129.2181.

82. SS 345.10957.

83. ZGYL 8.208; FXJ 26.310 (QSW 157:327–329); Chang Bide 1977:1.578; CB 516.12275.

84. ZGYL 8.171, 173–175; HSSCGY 11.2a. Months that are preceded by the letter "i" are intercalary months, inserted when needed because lunar months do not coincide perfectly with solar years. No connection is suggested between the deaths of the two children and Zhezong's own ailments, and maybe there was none.

85. SHY Dixi 2.11b–12a.

86. ZGYL 8.200.

87. On imperial birthday celebrations, see DJMHLZ 9.225–240; DJMHLJZ 9.829–878; ZHWLXY *juan* 165; J. Lam 2005:7–8.

88. ZGYL 8.205–208.

89. ZGYL 9.211–213.

90. On western European court culture in the medieval and early modern periods, see Burke 1992; Duinham 1994; Adamson 1999; Mateer 2000; Vale 2001. Byzantine court culture also makes a good comparison. See Maguire 1997.

2. *Taking the Throne, 1100*

Epigraph: ZGYL 8.212.

1. X. Ji 2005:62–94, Ebrey 2006c.

2. X. Ji 2005:62–63.

3. Mental illness plagued the imperial line in the Southern Song as well, with the case of Guangzong particularly flagrant. See R. Davis 2009:756–773.

4. X. Ji 2005:76–94.

5. On this diary, see note 76 to Chapter 1. The part of the diary on Huizong's first months on the throne is a substantial 84 Chinese double pages, or in the recent typeset edition, 255 pages.

6. ZGYL 8.145–146, 9.214; CB 520.12355.

7. This last sentence is somewhat obscure. Perhaps the empress is trying to indicate that the Prince of Duan was perceptive and attentive to Zhezong.

8. SS 19.357–358 records this conversation in almost identical detail, but the judgment on Huizong at the end of his annals (SS 22.417–418) asserts that "At Zhezong's death, before Huizong was enthroned, [Zhang] Dun said he should not be ruler of the realm because of his frivolousness." In all likelihood the historians here drew on one of the often-embroidered stories that circulated in anecdotal literature. There were, for instance, several stories of fortune-tellers or seers who predicted Huizong's accession, which undoubtedly circulated only after he came to the throne. For these stories, see Zhang Bangwei 2005:226–241.

9. ZGYL 9.212–13. Compare CB 520.12356–12357.

10. ZGYL 9.213.

11. For comparative cases, see Goody 1966. For the Song case, see Ebrey 2006c and Shinno 1993.

12. ZGYL 9.213–214. Compare CB 520.12357. According to a source cited in CB 520.12362, Empress Xiang claimed that Zhezong had told her the Prince of Duan should succeed.

13. TWSCT 1.20.

14. ZGYL 9.214. Compare CB 520.12357–12358.

15. SDZLJ 71.30–31.

16. ZGYL 9.214.

17. ZGYL 9.214–215.

18. ZGYL 9.221. Compare CB 520.12371.

19. ZGYL 9.221.

20. ZGYL 9. 215–216, 247–248, 260. Zhang Bangwei (2005:229) proposes the eunuch Hao Sui as a possible advocate for Huizong.

21. Several, in fact, were talented enough to pass the civil service exams. See, for instance, Zichou (1089–1142), Zisong (*jinshi* 1106), and Zili (*jinshi* 1091, d. 1137). See Chang Bide 1977 4:3381, 8886.

22. On Empress Dowager Xiang, see Ebrey 2011.

23. ZGYL 9.216–217. Compare CB 520.12368–12370.

24. ZGYL 9.217–218. Compare CB 520.12368–12371.

25. ZGYL 9.219, 241.

26. ZGYL 9.238–239, 247–248, 259–260.

27. ZGYL 9.284–285. This number is roughly in the range of those who made up the courts in fourteenth- to sixteenth-century France and Burgundy (Duinham 2003:30–31).

28. ZGYL 9.296, 297, 280.

29. See XTJ 15.238; Zhang Bangwei 2005:265–266.

30. XTJ 15.238.

31. ZGYL 9.292–293, 316; QSW 109:117–118. See also LSZJ 2.291–293; HZL Hou 1.56–61.

32. ZGYL 9.295.

33. The saying is from the "Great Preface" of the *Book of Changes*. See Wilhelm 1967:307.

34. ZGYL 9.295–296.

35. This topic is covered in more detail in Appendix A.

36. On the official gazette, see de Weerdt 2006, 2009; You Biao 2004.

37. See Levine 2006, 2008.

38. On the New Policies, see Smith 2009b. On the factionalism of this era, see also Luo Jiaxiang 1993.

39. Egan 1994:33–38, 46–53; Hartman 1990.

40. Smith 2009b:418. Coins (termed "cash") had holes in their centers through which they could be strung. For larger transactions, the common unit was a string of cash, nominally 1,000 coins but ordinarily considerably less (770 was accepted for tax payment).

41. Forage 1991:17–18.

42. On Song reign names, see Hargett 1987.

43. CB 443.10667–10669; Egan 1994:86–93; Levine 2008:99–103; Levine 2009a:521–529.

44. Egan 1994:93–103; Levine 2009a:518–519.

45. Egan 1994:104–105

46. Once Zhezong and Zeng Bu discussed the friction between the Cai brothers and their tendency to object to people the other one supported. Zeng Bu speculated that their wives probably did not get along, which Zhezong agreed was likely (ZGYL 8.178–179, 198–199; Levine 2008:12–13, 141–143). On the Cai brothers, see also Clark 2001.

47. At European courts, royal favorites regularly aroused enormous resentment, suspicion, and fear. See Elliott and Brockliss 1999; Adamson 1999:19–20; Feros 2000.

48. CB 520.12371; SS 19.358; SHY Zhiguan 76.21a–22b, 67.29a–b, Li 29.68b, 37.14a–b, Houfei 1.17b–18a; SDZLJ 1.3; SCSS 2.23.

49. See Tomota 2002:40.

50. ZGYL 9.218; CB 520.12368. On the factional struggles of Huizong's first two years, see Zhang Bangwei 2002 and Luo Jiaxiang 2003b.

51. ZGYL 9. 228.

52. Zeng Bu had also recommended him to Zhezong (ZGYL 8:155, 198).

53. This Zhu Fu is different from the Zhu Fu who was Huizong's tutor (different characters).

54. ZGYL 9.227–228; CB 520.12378–12379.

55. ZGYL 9.233–234.

56. ZGYL 9.237, 249–250, 252.

57. ZGYL 9.311.

58. ZGYL 9.253.

59. Compare Robinson 2008:27–30.

60. HZL Hou 1.60–61.

61. CBSB 15.573; ZGYL 9.256.

62. XTJ 15.236–237; QSW 111:110–111.

63. CB 520.12377–12378. On the history of this war, see Smith 2006. On the Tibetans of this area, see T. Iwasaki 1986.

64. CB 520.12383.

65. CB 517.12299–12300. On the Annam campaign, see Smith 2009b:465 and Anderson 2008:119–51.

66. CB 518.12317–12322, 12325.

67. CB 520.12381–12382.

68. CBSB 15.577–578; SHY Zhiguan 76.21b–22b, dated 1100/2/26. Interestingly, a briefer version of this list, omitting people's titles, has Su Shi instead of Su Che and omits Zou Hao. See TPZJTL 24.30a–b.

69. QSW 129:3–6.

70. SCZCZY 17.159; SS 346.10982–10983.

71. CBSB 15.581; SDZLJ 155.580; QFJ 1.1a–2a; QSW 109:358.

72. Smith 2006:106–107; SHY Fanyi 6.39a–b; CBSB 15.589, 17.632–633. Another source, SSWJL 5.42–43, credits Zhang Shunmin with persuading Huizong to return the two prefectures.

73. ZGYL 9.260–261.

74. ZGYL 9.263–264; CBSB 15.579–580.

75. ZGYL 9.269–270.

76. ZGYL 9.271.

77. ZGYL 9.277, 279.

78. ZGYL 9.279.

79. ZGYL 9.282–283; CBBM 120.2009; CBSB 15.588–589; QSW 129:7–8. Compare Levine 2008:145.

80. CBBM 120.2009; CBSB 15.592; TPZJTL 24.31b.

81. CBBM 120.2010; CBSB 15.593–594; QSW 129:9–11.

82. ZGYL 9.309–315; CBSB 16.601–602.

83. CBBM 120.2011; CBSB 16.602–603; SS 471.13713. Zhang Dun died four years later at age seventy-one.

84. CBSB 16.606–607; CBBM 129.2168–2169. On 9/18 another official argued that if the empress dowager knew of Cai Jing's role in the demotion of Empress Meng, she would not support him so strongly. CBBM 120.2012; CBSB 16.610.

85. CBSB 16.612; SCZCZY 35.346–349 (QSW 129:48–43).

86. CBBM 120.2013; CBSB 16.613.

87. SS 471.13716; TPZJTL 24.33b; CBSB 16.615–616.

88. SS 345.10965.

89. ZGYL 9.221–223; CB 520.12372.

90. ZGYL 9.219, 226, 236; SHY Li 29.69b.

91. ZGYL 9.240.

92. SHY Li 29.70a; CB 520.12385; ZGYL 9.282.

93. SHY Li 29.78a–79b, Li 37.15b; CBSB 16.604.

3. Trying for Balance, 1101–1102

Epigraph: SCZCZY 11.101–102.

1. CBSB 17.632.

2. CBSB 16.619–620.

3. Zeng Bu seems to have long been sensitive to what was being said about him. Before he became grand councilor, in the sixth month of 1100, he heard

from Gong Yuan that Huizong had told Chen Guan that he suspected Zeng Bu of ties to the eunuch Liu Youduan. Zeng Bu then questioned Gong Guai, Han Zhongyan, Huang Lü, and his own brother Zeng Zhao, trying to find out exactly what was being said about him. ZGYL 9.315; CBSB 16.601.

4. CBSB 17.634–636.

5. CBSB 17.635–637.

6. CBSB 17.639.

7. CBSB 18.645–651.

8. CBSB 18.657–658.

9. SZCZY 11.101–103. For the long tradition of urging rulers not to go hunting, see M. Chang 2007:45–50 and J. Chen 2010:35–37.

10. On kings as scapegoats in many societies, see Quigley 2005.

11. This tradition is analyzed further in Chapter 6.

12. QSW 109:358.

13. On the two eclipses, see SHY Ruiyi 2.3a–4b. On the interpretation of various colored vapors (*qi*) as aurora borealis, see Xu, Pankenier, and Jiang 2000:183–187, 204.

14. See QSW 85:86; 104:208–210; 108:227–230; 120:304–305; 129:25–28; 129:228–229; 131:176.

15. QSW 129:25–28 or SCZCZY 44.464–465.

16. SS 60.1307–1313; NGZML 11.327.

17. On Personal Destiny days, based on the day of one's birth, see Chapter 5.

18. SCZCZY 44.467 or QSW 108:227–228.

19. SCZCZY 44.468.

20. SS 345.10966.

21. QSW 85:86.

22. On the political use of portents by critics of those in power during the Northern Song, see Skonicki 2007. Wang Anshi explicitly rejected the tenets of Han period omenology because of the ways they were used as political ammunition.

23. CBSB 19.687; CBBM 130.2206; trans. Levine 2008:150.

24. SCZCZY 36.360; QSW 93:254–255.

25. QSW 129:37.

26. SHY Li 37.66a–68a.

27. On the history of enshrining portrait statues of the imperial ancestors in Song times, see Ebrey 1997.

28. CB 304.7404, 308.7486; HZL Qian 1.29–30; SHY Li 13.3a–b.

29. CB 363.7a–b, 364.27b–28a; SDZLJ 143.519.

30. SS 109.2623; CBSB 16.604–605.

31. Some sources say that the solicited request was drafted by Cai Jing, some by Han Zhongyan. See YH 100.27b, CBSB 16.604.

32. Since elsewhere we are told that the eastern and western Temples of Spectacular Numina together came to 2,320 room-units, the area occupied by each set of halls was proportional, with about 300 room-units for each emperor and his empresses.

33. YH 100.28a; SCSS 6.100–103.

34. CBSB 16.605; QSW 129:32–35, 48–50, 56–57.

35. SS 19.363, 367; YH 100.28a. Later, the portraits of conservatives were removed.

36. For the pre-Song period, see Wechsler 1985:107–22. For Song practice and debates, see Yamauchi 1986, 2000; Zhu Yi 2009a, 2009b.

37. SS 100.2449–2453; SHY Li 3.26a–b. Compare McDermott 1999.

38. SS 343.10919–10920; SHY Li 28.58a.

39. HCBNBY 26.656–667; CBSB 18.661–663.

40. SS 343.10919. On the equipment needed for these sacrifices in Tang times, see V. Xiong 2000:146–147.

41. SHY Yufu 1.20a, Yue 3.24a–b. The hymns are not extant. On the music performed for these rituals, see J. Lam 2005.

42. HZL Hou 1.61–63. See also CBSB 18.661–663. For the amnesty, see SCSS 5.79–80.

43. Revenue shortfalls seem to have been a common problem of premodern governments. However, when Song is compared to the subsequent Ming dynasty, Song seems to have had a more precarious situation, since the Ming government owned vast tracks of land. See S. Jang 2008:122.

44. For overviews of Song government finance, see H. Wong 1975; Hartwell 1988; Golas n.d.; Wang Shengduo 1995. Lamouroux 2003:104–120 offers a useful overview of recent Chinese scholarship on the topic. For revenue figures, see Wang Shengduo 1995:678–683. On the Privy Treasury, see also Umehara 1976; Bao Weimin 1989; Zhu Hong 1991. Hartwell 1988:71 provides figures for 1093, but they are in the imaginary unit of the silver kilo. Using the conversion rate given on p. 20, it would seem that total revenues in 1093 were 132,586,387 strings of cash (counting taxes in kind, converted). See QSW 95:237–238. On the cost of imperial tombs and the gifts dispensed at the triennial Suburban Sacrifice, see Hartwell 1988:46–50.

45. Zhu Ruixi 1994:64.

46. Hartwell 1988:71.

47. DJMHLZ 1.42–46.; Zhou Baozhu 1992:189; Hartwell 1988:23.

48. DJMHLZ 1.47; Hartwell 1988:70; WXTK 25.244B.

49. Hartwell 1988:28–31.

50. Golas 1988; Hartwell 1988:38 (but see p. 60, where Hartwell says that by 1069 the emperor "supervised the receipt and expenditure of nearly 23% of total government income").

51. Hartwell 1988:38, 43–48, 57, 65.

52. ZGYL 9. 281, 288, 303, 305, 309; SS 19.360.

53. CBSB 16.615, 626; SS 355.11194; QSW 108:341–343.

54. QSW 102:388–389.

55. CBSB 17.642.

56. QSW 129.64–65. Hartwell 1988:36, 55, 70, 72 treats the transfer of regional surpluses to the Privy Purse as routine practice.

57. QSW 129.63–68.

58. CBSB 18.650.

59. Xu Jiang maintains a position on the Council of State from Zhezong's reign till 1104/8, by far the longest tenure, but rarely seems to have taken a stand.

60. Probably one reason many Chinese historians have assumed that the death of the empress dowager explains the shift in policies is the tradition of assuming that a person has distinctive character traits that are revealed over time but do not change in fundamental ways. Thus Chinese biographers select the incidents that

seem fundamentally consistent: the man of courage will be courageous from an early age; examples of early generosity do not get mentioned in the account of a rapacious official. On the Chinese biographical tradition, see Twitchett 1961, 1962, 1992:62–83. In the West, there was a rather different tradition of biographies of rulers dating back at least to Roman times. In the second century CE Plutarch created portraits of complex, inconsistent, and flawed individuals. He attempted to show the human side of major figures, to bring up how chance had shaped their characters, to show formative experiences and turning points, often by paying attention to minor acts and casual phrases. Later European biographers picked up and developed these traditions. On Western traditions of writing biography, see H. Lee 2009.

61. CBBM 130.2197–2198; CBSB 17.639–641. This letter is translated in Ebrey 2008:58–59.

62. For glowing accounts of Chen Guan, see SMCYXL Hou 13.16a–24a; MZLX 7.3a–7b. Chen Guan's fame was undoubtedly enhanced by his appearance as a noble critic in the Ming novel *Shuihu zhuan*, esp. chapters 97, 100, 101, 106, and 108. On the influence of the Learning of the Way on the compilation of the histories of the Song, see Hartman 1998a, 1998b, 2003, and 2006; C. Li and Hartman 2011.

63. QSW 129:62, 38.

64. QSW 129:45–46.

4. Choosing the Reformers, 1102–1108

Epigraph: SS 200.4990–4991.

1. J. Liu 1959:20. See also J. Liu 1962:145.

2. J. Liu 1988:14.

3. Wang Ruilai 1989, 2001, 2004. Other scholars who have made similar arguments include Cheng Minsheng 1999 and Kondō 1999. See also Bol 2001, 2006.

4. Sariti 1970; Wood 1995; Hymes and Schirokauer 1993:43, 45. For a dissenting view, see X. Ji 2005:14–15.

5. Hartman 2006.

6. CBSB 19.676, 683, 686–687; CBBM 130.2205–2206; SS 471.13716–13717.

7. CBBM 131.2219; CBSB 20.700.

8. SSWJL Qian 5.44; SS 472.13722; Hartman 2006:539–540.

9. SZFBNL 11.701–702. This story is credited to the *Dingwei lu*, finished in 1172. See also TS 15.173–174; CBBM 130.2199–2200; CBSB 18.657–660. Part of the story is found in an earlier source, Lü Xizhe's LSZJ 2.294–295.

10. SS 172.13723. See also the edict appointing Cai Jing, SZFBNL 11.700–701.

11. Chaffee 2006.

12. HZL Hou 1.60 dates the decision to depose her a second time to 1102/12. See also SDZLJ 17.87 which dates it to 1102/10.

13. C. Chien 2004:70; Ebrey 2006a:241–248.

14. DYJ 1.2b–4b; SHY Zhiguan 20.37a–b; Chaffee 1999:101.

15. SS 178.4339. Blank ordination certificates were issued by the state and could be traded, giving them monetary value, generally about one to two hundred strings of cash in Huizong's day (K. S. Ch'en 1956).

16. SS 19.364, 131.4331, 182.4444–4445; SHY Shihuo 30.34b, 65.73a; CBSB 20.726. See also C. Chien 2004 and Smith 1991:195–98.

17. CBBM 138.2318; CBSB 25.819–820. SHY Shihuo 1.30b, 4.9a–b dates the introduction of the system to 1105/2/16.

18. See Wang Zengyu 1994 for a concise indictment on these grounds.

19. CBSB 25.831; SS 20.373, 472.13730. For some examples of the charges against Cai Jing, see Levine 2009b:569–570, 581–582.

20. CBSB 26.868–869; SS 351.11094. Shenzong had also asked for criticism in 1075/10 when a comet was taken as an indication of heaven's displeasure. See Smith 2009b:452–453.

21. SZFBNL 11.723–725. Huizong himself had suspicions of another of Cai Jing's sons. He told Zhao Tingzhi that he thought Cai Jing had made his son Cai Xiao a palace guard attendant so that he could keep an eye on Huizong on a daily basis. SZFBNL 11.727.

22. SZFBNL 11.729–730; CBSB 26.878–879, 888–890.

23. SHY Zhiguan 5.12a–b. On the Finance Commission under Shenzong, see Smith 2009b:378–382.

24. CBBM 132.2235; Chaffee 2006:38–39. Wu Juhou and Zhang Shangying are discussed further in Chapter 11. CBBM 132.2234–2240 records the proposals issued by the Advisory Office over the three years of its existence. Levine 2009b:593–596 discusses the revival of the salt and tea monopolies.

25. SS 19.364, 368; SHY Shihuo 60.3b, 68.129a–130a. See also Scogin 1978; Ebrey 1990; von Eschenbach 1994; Goldschmidt 2006:304–308; and Chaffee 2006.

26. SHY Shihuo 168.132b–133a; Chaffee 2006:41.

27. Goldschmidt 2006:299.

28. SHY Shihuo 68.130a; trans. Goldschmidt 2006:300, slightly modified.

29. Goldschmidt 2006:301.

30. D. Kuhn 2009:150–151. See also the original report, Sanmenxiashi 1999.

31. See Levine 2008:142.

32. Records of the conversations that led up to this series of measures are incomplete, largely because after Zeng Bu left the Council of State, he no longer kept an administrative diary. Although the portion of Zeng Bu's administrative diary covering his time as grand councilor does not survive as an independent text, the Southern Song compilers of the main histories had access to it and as a consequence there are many recorded conversations between Huizong and his councilors, especially Zeng Bu, up to the point when Zeng left office in 1102/i6. After Cai Jing replaced him, the histories record many fewer oral conversations, making it more difficult to judge the reasoning behind various political decisions.

33. CBBM 121.2021–2022; CBSB 19.677. Soon other memorials followed, some listing specific men who needed to be dismissed (CBBM 121.2022; CBSB 19.678).

34. CBBM 121.2023–2027; CBSB 19.679–683.

35. SHY Xingfa 6.21a–22a; CBSB 19.682–683.

36. SS 245.10955–10958; SHY Zhiguan 67.38a.

37. Probably referring to the living quarters of Empress Liu and Empress Dowager Xiang.

38. SDZLJ 241.800–801.

39. See Levine 2008:141–143.

40. CBBM 123.2064–2071; CBSB 20.708–713, which lists all those on the list. See also SHY Zhiguan 68.1a–3b, 4b–5a.

41. CBSB 20.718–725.

42. CBSB 20.714–717; SS 19.365; HCBNBY 26.665–666. On discrepancies in the numbers of men on the list, see the commentary in CBSB 20.715–717.

43. SHY Zhiguan 68.6a–b. Later that month when the 538 successful civil service candidates were announced, it was stated that those who had been classified on the basis of their memorials would be moved up or down in the list according to their degree of correctness or deviance (SS 19.376). This is unlikely to have affected many people, as few memorials were written by men who had not yet passed the exams.

44. XZZTJ 88.2251; SHY Zhiguan 68.7a. Another, more minor, restriction was put on kinsmen two years later. In 1105/2 more distant kinsmen of the banned officials within the five grades of kin (such as nephews, first and second cousins, and so on) were made ineligible for appointments as special palace guards, positions reserved for sons and younger brothers of consort families, meritorious military officers, and certain court officials (CBSB 25.831–833).

45. GSJ 35.3a–b.

46. CBSB 22.773–775; SHY Zhiguan 68.9a.

47. SHY Zhiguan 68.10a.

48. CBBM 122.2053–2057; CBSB 24.810–815. For a full analysis of this list, see Vittinghoff 1975.

49. CBBM 122.2058; CBSB 24.817. See also Chen Lesu 1983.

50. CBBM 122.2053; CBSB 24.810.

51. SDZLJ 196.721. SHY Zhiguan 76.25a dates this to the day before, 1104/6/16.

52. JSCB 144.1a–b.

53. YH 163.28b; SDJK 2.37; CBBM 130.2186; CBSB 24.815; SS 105.2549; WXTK 44.415A.

54. On the system of disenrolling officials, then slowly rehabilitating them, see W. Lo 1987:111–112.

55. SS 20.374; SDZLJ 217.829; SHY Xingfa 6.22a; CBBM 122.2060; CBSB 25.846, 853.

56. SHY Xingfa 6.22a–b; CBSB 25.855–858.

57. SHY Zhiguan 76.25a–b.

58. That edict is found in SDZLJ 217.829. Moving banished officials after an amnesty was a standard procedure.

59. SDZLJ 217.829; CBSB 25.861.

60. The SS biography of Liu Kui (SS 351.11109) gives him credit for encouraging Huizong to relax the ban and destroy the steles, but it places that after Cai Jing's dismissal, while other sources place his dismissal on 2/13 (SS 20.375–376).

61. SDZLJ 217.829–830. See also SDZLJ 155.581; CBSB 26.868–869.

62. SDZLJ 196.721–722. In addition, the Secretariat-Chancellery canceled twenty-two orders that had been issued since 1102/3/6 concerning the Yuanyou partisan list (CBSB 26.870).

63. CBSB 26.870–874.

64. SDZLJ 196.722.

65. CBSB 26.880–882, 889, 895.

66. CBSB 28.938–939, 945–946; XZZTJ 90.2328. A few exceptions were later announced, however. In 1111/11, those who had been on the blacklist were not to serve as teachers at government schools, and in 1112/1, those who had been classed as deviant were not to serve as circuit intendants (SS 20.387, 21.389).

67. Shen Songqin 1998:165–171.

68. CBBM 121.2033; CBSB 21.739.

69. NGZML 11.327.

70. This order appears twice, on 1103/4/27 and 1104/1 (CBBM 121.2034, 122.2041; CBSB 21.741, 791). On why these particular authors and books were considered offensive, see Shen Songqin 1998:175–179.

71. CBSB 47.1455–1456; HCBNBY 29.750.

72. SHY Zhiguan 69.13a; NGZML 12.368. See also Egan 2005:134–138.

73. T. Lee 1985:233–246.

74. See Chaffee 1985:77–84; Kracke 1977:6–30; T. Lee 1985:290–292; Kondō 1994. See also CBBM 126.2118–2119; SHY Chongru 2.7b–9a; Zhiguan 28.15a–b; WXTK 46.432C–443C.

75. Kracke 1977:17–18.

76. SS 19.369; SHY Zhiguan 28.15b, Chongru 2.10b; CBSB 21.735–738, 21.743, 21.746, 22.762, 22.767, 23.790, 24.815–816, 24.827, 24.828; Chaffee 2006:58.

77. CBSB 25.827, 833–834.

78. YH 113.8b; CBSB 24.828; T. Lee 1985:66; SS 157.3663; DYJ 24.4b–5a; BQS 109:26b; SZJSZ 17.29a–31b.

79. SHY Chongru 6.10a–b; BQS 109.26b, 28a. See also Ebrey 2006a, which has an illustration.

80. For the classical reference, see ZL 10.24b–26a.

81. WXTK 46.433A–B dates this to 1104, which has been followed by several authors, but CBBM 126.2114 and SHY Chongru 6.10b more plausibly date it to 1107. See also Ebrey 2006a:241–248.

82. SHY Chongru 2.15b–17b; DYJ 1.2b–4b; QSW 142.223–224; CBSB 24.828. On the schools after Cai Jing's return in 1112, see SHY Chongru 2.18a–20b; CBSB 32.1056.

83. SDZLJ 157.591.

84. WXTK 46.433B.

85. ZZYL 130.3127; T. Lee 1985:256. On Zhao, see Chaffee 1990–1992.

86. SDZLJ 150.558, 157.591–592, 124.427, 186.680–681, 217.829–830.

87. SS 159.3731.

88. NGZML 13.383.

89. See Ebrey 2006a and Fang Chengfeng n.d. One of the two on paper was addressed to Cai Jing's grandson Cai Xing and refused his request to decline an office. The other was written to thank the empress and other consorts for their concern about his preparation for the Suburban Sacrifices. For illustrations, see Zhang Guangbin 1984 3:85–104, 185–187.

90. On this see Tokunaga 1998; Wang Yuji 1987; Fang Chengfeng n.d.

91. SS 20.376; SHY Chongru 6.10b–11a; Zhiguan 55.13a–14a.

92. SS 352.11123.

93. See Hayashi 2003:11; Yang Shili 2007.

94. DXZZ 8.73–74; SS 348.11028, 472.13726; SSJSBM 49.497. See also HZL Hou 3.110 for a criticism of Cai Jing manipulating imperial brush edicts starting in 1108.

95. SS 472.13726, 468.13662; Tokunaga 1998.
96. QSW 109:177–178.
97. SS 200.4990–4991.

5. *Placing Faith in Daoism, 1100–1110*

Epigraph: QSW 164:122.

1. An excellent overview of the diversity of Song religion is provided in Von Glahn 2004:130–179. See also Gregory and Ebrey 1993; Hansen 1990; E. Davis 2001; Hymes 2002; H. Liao 2002, 2005, 2007.

2. On the vitality of Song Daoism, see Sun Kekuan 1965; Strickmann 1979; Boltz 1987; Skar 1996–1997, 2000; and E. Davis 2001.

3. On Thunder Rites, see Matsumoto 1979, 2006; Boltz 1993, esp. pp. 272–286; Skar 1996–1997; E. Davis 2001:24–44; Reiter 2007; Li Yuanguo 2007; Capitanio 2008.

4. Boltz 1993; E. Davis 2001; Hymes 2002.

5. See Seidel 1983.

6. On the Tang court's involvement in Daoism, see Barrett 1996 and V. Xiong 1996.

7. Van der Loon 1984:29–38. On Zhenzong and Daoism, see S. Cahill 1980.

8. For brief accounts of Huizong's Daoism, see Ebrey 2000 and Matsumoto 2004.

9. On Mount Mao and Daoism, see Robinet 1997:114–148, 2000:196–224; Schafer 1980; Strickmann 1977.

10. QSW 129:189; MSZ 11.10 (DZ 5.605 A–B). This source dates the needle incident to 1086, an impossible date as Zhezong was still a child and no preparations had yet been made for his marriage to Miss Meng. A more likely date is 1094–1096. A non-Daoist source (HZL Houlu 2.72) reports that Liu Hunkang gained access to Zhezong's palace after his successful therapeutic use of talisman-water (ashes of burnt talismans dissolved in water). It also reports that Huizong consulted Liu Hunkang soon after taking the throne on the issue of securing the birth of male heirs. He gave geomantic advice, we are told, leading to the construction of the massive Northeast Marchmount park in the northeast section of the city, which does not seem likely (see Appendix A).

11. QSW 129:182, 187–188.

12. QSW 129:183.

13. Kohn 2000:209; Pregadio 2007:733–734; MSZ 26.2a (DZ 5.665A); QSW 137:8, 129:183. On another occasion their discussion touched on the Two Xu (Xu Mi and Xu Hui), important in the Highest Clarity tradition because of their role in the revelation of the central scriptures in the fourth century (QSW 164:49).

14. QSW 163.262.

15. QSW 129:183; Mollier 2008:136–173. On Personal Destiny, see also Liu Changdong 2005:391–446.

16. Mollier 2008:142.

17. QSW 164:104. This letter is dated 1107/7/29.

18. BDBM; Mollier 2008:1551–1556; Pregadio 2007:1053–1055; Schipper and Verellen 2004:952–955. Although it presents itself as Laozi's sermon to the Han

Daoist master Zhang Daoling, modern scholars think that this scripture was probably written during the Song period.

19. QSW 137:8 (MSZ 26.1b–2a; DZ 5.664C–665A); QSW 129:183.

20. See Bokenkamp 1997:373–438; Schipper and Verellen 2004:214–225; T. Yamada 2000:240–241; Strickman 1978.

21. Bokenkamp 1997:417–418. Later in his reign, a vastly expanded version of this scripture was made the first scripture in the Daoist canon. See Strickmann 1978.

22. QSW 129:187; Kohn and Kirkland 2000:362–363; Kohn 1993:24–29.

23. Kohn 1993:25–27.

24. For some possibilities, see Pregadio 2007:695–697.

25. MSZ 3.3a–22b, 4.1–6a (DZ 5:562A–570). The letters have been punctuated in the *Quan Song wen*, arranged by date. On the letters, see Gyss-Vernande 1995. The *Maoshan zhi* was compiled in 1329, but drew on earlier versions, one of 1150, and is considered a generally reliable source. See Boltz 1987:103–105; Pregadio 2007:736–738.

26. This was the name subsequently given to the central hall of the temple complex (QSW 137:8).

27. QSW 163:318; MSZ 3.4a (DZ 5:562B).

28. QSW 164.51, 67; MSZ 3.12b–14a (DZ 5:566A–C).

29. QSW 129:183, 188; 137:8–9 (MSZ 26; DZ 5.665A–67C).

30. QSW 129:183, 164:104, 122; MSZ 4.1b, 4b (DZ 5:568C, 569C). In the Southern Song a painting by Huizong of the Mao Lords hung in a temple in Hangzhou, perhaps this one (CYZJ 2.80).

31. Most likely the three mountains referred to here are Penglai, Fangzhang, and Yingzhou, traditionally viewed as lands of immortality. See S. Jang 1992:83.

32. QSS 1495.17075; QSW 166:390 (both from MSZ 3.13b [DZ 5:566B]).

33. The letter is in QSW 164:61–62 (MSZ 3.12b [DZ 5:566A]).

34. Based on a line in the *Laozi*, D. C. Lau 1963:69: "he who makes a present of the way without stirring from his seat."

35. This line is from the *Book of Songs*, poem 165: Legge 1961 4:254, "spiritual beings will then harken to them"; Waley 1937:204, "For the spirits are listening."

36. QSS 1495.17074–17075.

37. There are also three undated letters.

38. QSW 164:48–49.

39. MSZ 11.11a (DZ 5.605B).

40. QSW 164:85, 48–49, 72–73.

41. QSW 164:51.

42. QSW 164:85.

43. Talisman-like writings are found in Later Han tombs and the *History of the Later Han* mentions experts who could use talismans to control demons and spirits. See Seidel 1982; HHS 72.2744, 2747; Csikszentmihalyi 2000:69–70. On talismans in Daoism, see Despeux 2000; Pregadio 2007:35–38; Campany 2002:61–70.

44. MSZ 26.11a (DZ 5:668C); QSW 129:187, 163:398, 164:44, 50, 62, 73, 84, 94, 111, 117, 122; MSZ 4.2a (DZ 5:569A).

45. Several scholars, including Boltz 1993 and E. Davis 2001:54–66, point to officials and members of the educated class learning how to perform as Daoist exorcists themselves rather than seek the help of Daoist priests. By contrast,

Huizong, like most lay devotees, turned to experts for help rather than master the rituals and other techniques himself.

46. The Water-and-Land ceremony was a popular Buddhist salvation ritual. See E. Davis 2001:236–241 and the sources he cites.

47. QSW 164:83–84; MSZ 3.15a–b (DZ 5:567B). The code mentioned here is probably what was eventually called *New Forms of the Five Categories of Rites of the Zhenghe Period*. Huizong's efforts to exclude Buddhist practices in its compilation are discussed in Chapter 9.

48. QSW 164:84.

49. QSW 129:186–187; MSZ 11.13a–b (DZ 5.605B).

50. Robinet 1993:97–117 (quote p. 105), Kohn 2000:201; Schipper and Verellen 2004:1043–1045.

51. On the illustrations in Daoist texts, see S. Huang 2012.

52. QSW 129:188, 164:66, 84, 85, 94, 97, 101, 104, 112.

53. QSW 129:189–190, 166:387–388.

54. While I do not doubt that Da Jingzhi sent a final will-like memorial to Huizong, I do think it is likely that a later Daoist historian "improved" it to make it seem that the Daoist establishment did not deserve any of the blame for Huizong's extravagance.

55. QSW 137:303–304; MSZ 26.13b–15b (DZ 5:669C–670B).

56. See Schafer 1977; Baldrian-Hussein 1996–1997.

57. Cai Tao noted this, contrasting Huizong to the First Emperor of Qin and Emperor Wu of the Han (TWSCT 1.6).

58. SHY Chongru 6.34b; Li Liliang 2006:109–110.

59. LSZX 51 (DZ 5:394C–395C), 52 (DZ 402B–C, 403C). Some are also recorded in standard historical sources, such as CBBM 127.2143–2144.

60. For the custom of celebrating emperors' birthdays, see Ebrey 2002; Naba 1974:28–34; Benn 1987:136–137; Weinstein 1987:54; Halperin 2006:130–138; Wang Shengduo 2010:510–534; CFYG 2.6b–8b.

61. CFYG 2.6b–26a; Zhu Ruixi et al. 1998:431–433. For the elaborate banquets in the palace, see DJMHLZ 9.225–229.

62. SHY Li 5.15a–b. On this system, see Chikusa 1982:83–109, esp. 95–97.

63. SHY Li 5.15b–16a; 23a–24a.

64. SHY Li 5.23b; Wang Shengduo 1991:227–228.

65. Guiji had both a Buddhist and a Daoist one. The Daoist one was three *li* east of the prefectural seat and had the Personal Destiny Hall (GJZ 7.3a). In Fuzhou, the Honoring Calm / Heavenly Calm temple was a major scenic site, on the top of a hill to the south of the city (SSZ 38.25a–b [p. 8069]). The Buddhist temple selected in Xin'an for this designation was also a major one with a thirteen-story pagoda over one hundred room-units at its base (XAZ 3.16b–17a.). Siming had four different Honoring Calm / Heavenly Calm temples. Three were Daoist, one in the prefectural seat and one each in two of the county seats (SMZYY 18.30a, 38a, 38b; 16.13a). For a Buddhist temple that petitioned to be converted into a Chongning temple, see Halperin 2006:134–137.

66. QSW 104:34–36. The temple was in Chuzhou, in modern Zhejiang.

67. SHY Li 57.24a–b.

68. Strickmann 1978:341–342.

69. JLZTJY 9.1 (DZ 9:133C); Van der Loon 1984:39.

70. JLZTJY (DZ 9:133A–B); Schipper and Verellen 2004:995–996. Tang Daijian 2003:47 sees one three-*juan* work and five one-*juan* texts, each beginning "Golden Registers," as edited by Zhang Shangying, all extant in the canon.

71. Schipper and Verellen 2004:1039; Chen Guofu 2004:284–285; DZ 5:765–772.

72. QSS 1494.17067.

73. QSS 1494.17064–17065. Three poems in the sequence "Pacing the Void" are translated in Ebrey 2013.

74. Schipper 1989:110, 119–120.

75. Sue 1994:119. The 764 recorded in the *Song Collected Documents* is not a complete list of every award given during his quarter-century rule. Of twelve temples with inscriptions that referred to government honors, only five were listed in the SHY. Hansen 1990:79–80 found the SHY listed even fewer of the Huzhou temples she learned of from other sources.

76. SHY Li 20.100b–101a.

77. QSW138:319–20. For some other examples of lengthy inscriptions that fill in the background of brief listings in SHY, see QSW 154:279–281 and SHY Li 20.121b–122a; QSW 167:73–74 and SHY Li 20.70b; QSW 167:75–76 and SHY Li 20.25b.

78. SHY Li 20.7b.

79. Zheng Zhenman and Ding Hesheng 1995:11. For a full translation of this inscription, see Clark 2005.

80. SHY Zhiguan 13.23a.

81. SHY Li 20.9b–10a. Hansen 1990:90–91n.13 lists inscriptions that mention later edicts calling for systematic reporting of gods deserving titles.

82. See McKnight 1992:75–79.

83. LJ 13.9a–b; compare Legge 1967 1:237–238.

84. SHY Xingfa 2.48b. On Manichaeism in China, see S. Lieu 1998.

85. SHY Xingfa 2.50a, Li 20.14b–15a.

86. SHY Xingfa 2.43b–44a.

87. SHY Xingfa 2. 61b–62a, 63b, 64a–b.

6. Embracing and Revitalizing Tradition

Epigraph: SHY Ruiyi 1.19a–b.

1. LJ 37.3b (Legge 1967 2:93); ZL 18.27a.

2. SS 128.2997. On the music reform, see also J. Lam 2006 and Ebrey 2008:159–166.

3. CBSB 23.787–788; CBBM 135.2280–2281. This memorial is translated in J. Lam 2006:429–430.

4. SDZLJ 149.551; CBSB 29.986; SCSS 14.223–224. See also Ebrey 2008:159–166, 2010; Li Youping 2004.

5. GCSB 3.6b–7a. On the failure of officials during Renzong's reign to cast chime bells that worked properly, see Ebrey 2010.

6. Chen Mengjia 1964; Chen Fangmei 2001:95–99; Li Youping 2004. See also Zhongguo yinyue wenwu daxi zongbian jibu 1996–2001, especially the volumes on Beijing, Henan, Shanghai, and Shaanxi.

7. Because these bells were seized by the Jurchen as booty in 1127, some of them had their name changed in 1174 because the word *sheng*, here translated as "brilliance," violated the taboo of the Jin emperor. See Chen Mengjia 1964 and Rudolph 1948.

8. SS 129:3017–3018, 356.11206–11207; J. Lam 2006:435–436.

9. SS 129:3001.

10. CBSB 25.851–853; SCSS 14.222.

11. CBSB 29.985–986. See also J. Lam 2006:417–418. Some examples of hand-drafted edicts on the new music are in SDZLJ 149.551–552.

12. SS 129.3018.

13. SS 104.254, 128.2997–2998. On the ancient Nine Cauldrons, see Barnard 1973:468–479; K. C. Chang 1983:95–101; H. Wu 1995:4–10.

14. The main sources for the Nine Cauldrons cast by Huizong are CBBM 128.2154–2157; CBSB 25.834–836; SHY Li 51.22a–24a, SHY Yufu 6.14a–16b; RZSB San 13.570–571; NGZML 12.352–353; TWSCT 1.11–12. See also Kojima 1992:468–471.

15. On Li Jie's role, see QSW 155:431–433.

16. HCBNBY 27.679; CBSB 23.790; TWSCT 1.11–12.

17. SHY Li 51.23a; SS 104.2544; TWSCT 1.11–12; SCSS 14.222; Fang Chengfeng 2011:236–237.

18. SHY Li 51.22b–23a; SS 104.2544–2545.

19. CBBM 128.2154 says that Cai Jing actually drafted the two inscriptions.

20. CBBM 128.2155; SHY Yufu 6.14a–16a.

21. SHY Li 51.23b–24a; SS 104.2545; ZHWLXY *juan* 68 and 69.

22. SHY Li 51.23b–24a; SS 104.2545.

23. SHY Yue 4.3b; YFL 6.17b; CBSB 25.836; SS 128.999. The sentence is 景鍾, 垂則為鍾, 仰則為鼎.

24. On auspicious signs and the political culture of Huizong's court, see Fang Chengfeng 2011.

25. For the development of Han thought on these subjects, see Loewe 1994:85–111, 121–141; Csikszentmihalyi 2000.

26. CQFL 4.101–103. Queen 1996:101–104 views the chapters on Five Phases as probably not by Dong Zhongshu.

27. See Beck 1990:111–174.

28. Political manipulation of the reporting of portents has been studied for the Han period by Eberhard 1957 and Bielenstein 1950, 1984. Sivin 1969:53–64 is less inclined to see political manipulation. On the celebration of signs, see Kern 2000.

29. H. Wu 1989:76–77.

30. HS 22.1065. For the poem, see H. Wu 1989:77; Lippiello 2001:76.

31. SShu 28.813, 851, 853; Lippiello 2001:102. See also H. Wu 1989:240 on the appearance of these predictions on a second-century stone shrine.

32. Dull 1966; Bielenstein 1984; Wechsler 1985:55–77; M. Poo 1998:152–156; Kern 2000.

33. HS 30.1773. For Tang examples of skeptics, see Wechsler 1985:60. On Wang Anshi, see Skonicki 2007:440–457.

34. TLD 4.114–115. On omens reported to the court in Tang times, see also Schafer 1963, which concentrates on bird omens.

35. SHY Ruiyi 1.88a–b and Ruiyi, *passim.*
36. SHY Ruiyi 1.11a; YH 200.29b–30a.
37. SHY Ruiyi 1.10b–13a; CB 67.1506. Compare S. Cahill 1980:25. For a different interpretation, see Kubota 2006, 2007a–b, 2008 (in 2008, pp. 100–101). For more on Zhenzong's auspicious signs, see Fang Chengfeng 2011:216–226.
38. CB 498.11840–11841, 11848; SDZLJ 2.9; SHY Yufu 3.1b; QSW 121:74–75.
39. SS 352.11124; SZFBNL 12.790, 796, 797.
40. QSW 102:139; SHY Ruiyi 1.19a–b. QSS 16:11004–11005. For the allusion to the *Book of Songs* (Mao 161), see Legge 1961 4:255–258.
41. QSS 26:17051 (poem 113).
42. See S. Nakayama 1966 and Sivin 1969:5–7. On early Chinese astronomy and astrology, see also Needham and Wang 1959.
43. Schafer 1977:44–53.
44. SHY Ruiyi 1.18a. For the allusion, see HS 26.1291.
45. SHY Ruiyi 2.4b–5a, Yufu 3.2a; QSW 136:193, 136:197, 146:249–250, 155:135–136. For other auspicious heavenly phenomena, see SHY Yizhi 7.3b, Ruiyi 1.22b; QSW 146:263–264.
46. SShu 28.813. See Lippiello 2001:102–104; Harper 1998:394.
47. For examples of references to sweet dew in early Daoist texts, see Bokenkamp 1997:221, 222.
48. NGZML 11.328. See also SHY Ruiyi 1.18b–19a, which dates the appearance of the dew to the thirteenth day of the eleventh month.
49. QSW 146:266.
50. SS 20.379, 20.381, 20.383, 21.397, 22.405; SHY Ruiyi 1.18b, 1.23a–b, Yizhi 7.4a.
51. QSW 136:197–198.
52. QSS 26:17053; trans. Egan 2006a:383, slightly modified.
53. This phrase, referring to the emperor's face as the face of Heaven, is borrowed from Du Fu.
54. TWSCT 2.28. The Weiyang palace was the palace of Emperor Wu in the Han period. For another poem Chao Duanli did on an auspicious omen, see NGZML 16.479. Others are found in QSC 1.418–443.
55. JSCB 146.16b–22b.
56. SJ 6.257, 12.477; BHTSZ 6.284; T. Som 1952 I:241–242, modified; SShu 29.860; Lippiello 2001:141.
57. TSLBZCP 38a (DZ 34:328B). See also Schipper and Verellen 2004:770–771. The *Benzao* that Huizong issued in 1116 quotes a book in the *Daozang* called *Classic of the Numinous Mushrooms of the Gods and Immortals* (Shenxian zhicao jing, CXBC 6.5b).
58. QSS 26:17044 (poem 11). For Emperor Wu's song, see Lippiello 2001:76. The Unicorn Pavilion was a Han palace hall decorated with portraits of eminent officials.
59. QSW 146:288.
60. Schafer 1963:199.
61. Translation from Hartman, n.d., slightly modified. The colophon is transcribed in Xu Bangda 1984:225. The current whereabouts of the painting is unknown, but a black and white illustration is found in Xie Zhiliu 1957, pl. 34, 1989:20–21, and Bickford 2006, fig. 11.9.

62. SHY Ruiyi 1.23b, SHY Yizhi 7.4a.

63. HZL Yuhua 1.273.

64. Most likely, this album was a copy of a well-known wall painting by Huang Quan, a painter Huizong admired. See Rowland 1954.

65. SHY Ruiyi 1.22b.

66. SS 129.3019.

7. *Welcoming Masters and Experts*

Epigraph: Plate 8.

1. See McMullen 1988.

2. On the long-term decline in the status of technical officials, see Zhang Bangwei 2005:100–141.

3. On the system of rank titles, see K. Umehara 1986 and Lo 1987. For the low rank of technical offices, see the list in Shimada 1981:118–121.

4. T. Lee 1985:91–93.

5. For the civil service examinations, the major classics were the *Book of Songs, Record of Ritual, Rites of Zhou,* and *Zuo Commentary.* The minor ones were the *Documents, Changes,* and the *Guliang* and *Gongyang* commentaries to the *Spring and Autumn Annals* and the *Etiquette and Ritual.* See SS 155.3620.

6. T. Lee 1985:94–97.

7. Yu Hui 2008:124.

8. Goldschmidt 2009:22–31. For a brief overview of government sponsorship of medicine in earlier periods, see, for example, Needham, Lu, and Sivin 2000:95–105.

9. Goldschmidt 2009:30.

10. Goldschmidt 2009:46–50.

11. See Goldschmidt 2006:288 for a list.

12. SHY Chongru 3.11b–26a; Needham et al. 2000:105–111; Goldschmidt 2006:278–294, 2009:51–61. In 1110, with Cai Jing's dismissal, the Medical School returned to the supervision of the Medical Service, but in 1113, with Cai Jing's return, it was once again placed under the Directorate of Education.

13. QSW 146:288.

14. Goldschmidt 2006:290–294, 2009:55–56.

15. Goldschmidt 2009:121–123, 158–163.

16. Needham, Lu, and Huang 1986:283–287.

17. Goldschmidt 2009:116–121; Needham et al. 1986:282–283; Okanishi 1969 3:799.

18. Goldschmidt 2006:319–321, 2009:181–182. For Huizong's preface to this book, see Okanishi 1969 3:797–798; Goldschmidt 2006:315.

19. Goldschmidt 2009:183.

20. Goldschmidt 2006:314–319, 2009:180–183. For Huizong's preface to this work, see Okanishi 1969 3:790. See also Schipper and Verellen 2004:765–769 for a similar book included in the Daoist canon.

21. See SSLF for medical writings by Su and Shen.

22. According to SS 85.2099, it was built in 1097.

23. ZGYL 9. 255. This conversation, with minor variations, is also in CBSB 15.575 and HCBNBY 25.621.

24. SHY Zhiguan 36.20b.

25. On this book, see Glahn 1975, 1981; Q. Guo 1998, 1999. For briefer but still interesting treatments, see Needham et al. 1971:84–85, 107–110; Steinhardt 1997:182–183; Ledderose 2000:132–137; Yetts 1927:476–478.

26. SS 165.3918

27. See the diagrams in Liang Sicheng 1983.

28. YZFSZS 16.190, 19.205.

29. BSJ 33.16b–18a (QSW 155:431–433).

30. BSJ 33.18b (QSW 155:432).

31. HJ 10.417. Compare R. Maeda 1970b:60.

32. SDJK 9.157.

33. SZJSZ 17.31a.

34. SHY Li 24.70b–72a.

35. See Acker 1954:260–263, 232–237, 248–250.

36. SHY Zhiguan 36.95a, 106b; W. Ho 1980:xxviii.

37. HJ 10.417; R. Maeda 1970b:60. HJ refers to the Temple of the Five Marchmounts, first built under Zhenzong. Some scholars believe Deng Chun was referring to the disappointment of Zhenzong, then skipped ahead to Huizong. Others propose that Deng Chun misremembered the name of the building under construction, as there were others that Huizong had built before 1104. Shimada 1981:133, 148n.88 points out that in 1101 one of the halls of the Temple of the Five Marchmounts burned down, which might well have been promptly rebuilt, though there is no explicit reference to rebuilding.

38. On training of painters by the Song court, see Suzuki 1965; Shimada 1981; Li Huishu 1984; She Cheng 1988; W. K. Ho 1980; Egan 2005:122–129.

39. SS 157.3688; CBBM 135.2286–2287; SHY Chongru 3.26a–27a.

40. SS 157.3688; YLMC 2.50. See also W. K. Ho 1980:xxviii–xxix; Shimada 1981:132–139.

41. HJ 10.421; compare R. Maeda 1970b:63.

42. HJ 1.269–270. Suzuki 1965:173 identifies the line on the hidden temple as from a poem by Kou Zhun (961–1023) and points out the advantage a person who recognized the poem would have.

43. HJ 6.378. Su Wu was a Han official who was kept as a captive by the Xiongnu for nineteen years and made to tend flocks of sheep.

44. A Ming source, HSWY 2.33a, reported that the well-known painter Li Tang was the one who scored the highest on that assignment.

45. YXCS 1.6–7.

46. CJSL Xu 40; trans. Egan 2005:123.

47. HSWY 2.32b–33a. One problem with this anecdote is that the painter listed as coming in first is Liu Songnian, who entered the academy in the Chunxi period (1174–1189), several decades after Huizong's time. Possibly an anecdote about the tests used during the Southern Song got mixed in with ones about ones from Huizong's reign. See She Cheng 1988:37–38; Suzuki 1965:175.

48. Egan 2005:124.

49. For some examples, see J. Cahill 1996b:20–71.

50. TWSCT 4.78; HJ 1.269; trans. Bush and Shih 1985:134. In some sources Mi Fu is said to be professor of both calligraphy and painting, in others only calligraphy. See Shimada 1981:131–132. See Sturman 1997:182–184 and 245n.22 on the likelihood that Cai Jing advanced Mi Fu's career.

51. Trans. Sturman 1997:218, modified.

52. CZJW 7.9a–b. The anecdote that follows this one is translated in Sturman 1997:219 and concerns another occasion when Huizong called on Mi Fu to write for him.

53. Shimada 1981.

54. HJ 10.421; R. Maeda 1970b:63.

55. For lists of painters and summaries of what is known of them, see She Cheng 1988:109–135 and Linghu Biao 1982:55–57. Their lists are not identical, as some painters are difficult to date with any certainty.

56. HJ 10. 421; R. Maeda 1970b:64.

57. HJ 1.270.

58. HJ 10.417. Compare R. Maeda 1970b:60. There is also another story of Huizong demanding exactitude on the same page.

59. THJWZ 6.236; Soper 1951:95–96; MXBT 17.541; J. Cahill 1996a:166.

60. Sullivan 1999:177; Li Huishu 1984; J. Cahill 1996b:22–72; Yu Hui 2008:98–99.

61. Another reason that there are few attributions to Huizong's court artists is that several of the most famous painters of Huizong's court, such as Li Tang and Su Hanchen, were able to relocate to Hangzhou after the fall of Kaifeng in 1127. Since their signed paintings are rarely dated, most art historians, to be cautious, attribute their undated paintings to the Southern Song. The case of Li Tang has been extensively discussed (see Edwards 1958; Barnhart 1972; Suzuki 1981, 1982). His case is particularly complicated because of contradictions in the sources. Although Li Tang had been active as an artist for more than twenty years when Kaifeng fell, and his one dated painting falls within Huizong's reign (1124), art historians assign almost all of his other extant paintings to the Southern Song. Since it is unlikely that someone fifty or older would abruptly change his painting style, such attributions seem based primarily on a vague notion that the paintings seem "Southern Song." Gaozong went to great efforts to recreate a palace establishment comparable to the one lost at Kaifeng—trying to reconstruct a painting and calligraphy collection, for instance, and he seems to have offered employment to all of Huizong's former court artists who presented themselves. It therefore seems unlikely that he would insist that they cease painting in their established styles.

62. For scholars who argue it was most likely done at Huizong's court, see Murray 1997 and Ihara 2001 and 2012. For ones who place it in mid- or late eleventh century, see H. Liu 1997:147–190; Whitfield 1998; and H. Tsao 2003. Hansen 1996 argues for a Southern Song date. I might add that the failure of the *Xuanhe Painting Catalogue* to mention the painter Zhang Zeduan lends support to the idea that the painting was done during Huizong's reign as he listed none of his court painters (nor himself or his sons). If a painter of this much talent and skill had worked at the court of his father, he should have been listed (even if this particular painting was no longer in the palace).

63. For a larger illustration, see Lin Boting 2006:156–163. On this painting, see Y. Chen 2007; Yi Ruofen 2006, 2008; Xie Zhiliu 1989; and Xu Bangda 1979:226–227. Xie and Xu see *Literary Gathering* as a painting of Huizong's period with genuine inscriptions but painted by a court artist. In their view, there was no intention to present it as a painting by Huizong (that is, it is not a *daibi*, "substitute brush" painting), rather it is an imperially inscribed painting. This view has also

been accepted by scholars at the National Palace Museum (Lin Boting 2006:161–163). Yi Ruofen 2008 reports that Fu Shen judged the calligraphy by Cai Jing to be genuine. Earlier, some scholars judged it a Ming copy; see Sirén 1956 II.81; Ecke 1972:149–151; and J. Cahill 1980:100.

64. The other paintings are *Eight Princes on a Spring Excursion, Zhu Yun Breaking the Balustrade,* and *Telling the Concubine Where to Sit,* all in the Palace Museum Taipei. They are all illustrated along with *Literary Gathering* in Y. Chen 2007.

65. On Song depictions of the eighteen scholars, see S. Jang 1999:43–53.

66. Trans. Y. Chen 2007:59.

67. On narrative painting, see Murray 2007.

68. XHHP 15.239; Bush and Shih 1985:127–128.

69. Bickford 2002–2003, 2006.

70. Trans. Hartman 2001:482.

71. Hartman 2001:482.

72. J. Cahill 1996a:164.

73. Trans. J. Cahill 1996a:165.

74. Y. Wang 1988. Another bird painting by Huizong's artists, *White Hawk,* is discussed in Chapter 6 and two done to document auspicious signs are discussed in Chapter 9.

75. Bush and Shih 1985:153.

76. Murck 2000:34, 36. In a similar vein, Heping Liu sees the Northern Song paintings of watermills as powerful imperial symbols that celebrated state involvement in commerce and engineering (H. Liu 2002:586–588).

77. The full painting, with the colophon, is published in Fu Xinian 1988:103–127. A larger reproduction of the full painting is in Gugong 1981:94–132. For a recent appreciation of it, see Ma Xianyu 2012.

78. Hay 1991:189 says that the painting "must have been reflecting the emperor's obsession with Taoist paradises, as embodied in the man-assembled splendors of the famous garden, the Ken-yüeh-yuan. But the brilliant greens and blues of Wang's painting overlie a painting of unforgiving rationality. There is much cartography and little poetry." See also W. Fong 1992:104, where he writes that mineral-blue and green colors were used in Daoist alchemy and that "the malachite-green color scheme is also associated with the representation of the theme of Taoist immortals."

79. See esp. Loehr 1961:242; Hall 1989:64; and Vinograd 1979:102.

80. Murck 2000:123.

81. National Palace Museum 1981 is a ninety-six-page book devoted to this painting with dozens of enlarged details.

82. Among the many who have written on this painting are Loehr 1939, 1961:246; Sirén 1956 2:93–94; Edwards 1958; Barnhart 1972, 1997:127–129; National Palace Museum 1961:90; Sullivan 1979:74–76; W. Fong 1984:52–53, 1996:134; Lin Boting 2006:103–104. On the skimpy evidence of Li Tang's period of activity, see note 61 above.

83. W. Fong 1996b:134.

84. Barnhart 1997:127. There is an exception to this positive treatment. Michael Sullivan (1979:74–76) presents Li Tang as a good example of the retreat from realism and the formation of a frozen "official court style." "The man most

directly responsible for this freezing process was the enormously influential Li Tang." In the 1124 painting "the intense yet sensitive brushwork of Fan Kuan has hardened into a formula." He sees the axe-cut stroke as one easy to imitate and "completely impersonal."

85. P. Foong 2006:125–126

86. Ebrey 2008:260–272.

8. Crafting an Image as an Artist

Epigraph: RZSB Si 2.636.

1. See National Palace Museum 1970:14a–20a; Shui Laiyou 1995:11–12.

2. Trans. by Charles Mason in J. Cahill 1996a:165, modified.

3. Sullivan 1974:7.

4. XHSP 12.89–90. On the tremulous brush style, see Soper 1951:165n.456.

5. XHHP 17.267.

6. HSSL 1.6b; SHY Zhiguan 18.22a–23b. For illustrations of Huizong's calligraphy, see Duan Shu'an 1986–2001 15:33; Song Huizong 1997.

7. The earliest use of the term "Slender Gold" that I can trace is by Zhou Mi (1232–1308) at the end of the Southern Song or early Yuan (GXZZ Bie 2.218). A late Yuan, early Ming writer Tao Zongyi (fl. 1360–1368) says that Huizong himself chose the term, a claim several scholars accept (S. Chuang 1967; J. Cahill 1996a:165). Examples of Slender Gold calligraphy datable to early in Huizong's reign include the 1104 standard script *Thousand Character Classic*, the 1104 Biyong stele, the 1108 stele for the Eight Conducts, and several inscriptions on paintings dated 1107. In addition, the transcription of poems beginning "Wish to borrow" is very close in style. See Ebrey 2006a.

8. National Palace Museum 1961:219.

9. TWSCT 1.5–6; Ebrey 2006a:263–264.

10. Ecke 1972:59; Sturman 1997:189–190; Y. Tseng 1993:182.

11. See McNair 1998:79–82.

12. The style of Huizong's calligraphy is pursued more fully in Ebrey 2006a:261–266.

13. SHY Li 5.23b; HQL 2.57; Ebrey 2006a. The coins are discussed in Chapter 11.

14. QSW 143:61–65, 146:244–245; HSSL 1.6b; Ebrey 2008:126–127; HZL Hou 7.164–165; XNYL 76.1259–1260.

15. Ebrey 2008:232–240, 26, 30. The Two Wang style referred to the calligraphy of the father and son, Wang Xizhi and Wang Xianzhi.

16. Yu Hui 2008:150–151.

17. On Gaozong as a calligrapher, see Murray 1993:10–31.

18. HJ 1.264.

19. Ebrey 2008:125–127.

20. CLJ 1.21b–22a (QSS 24:15979). This poem is translated in Chapter 10.

21. HLGY 1a–b.

22. HJ 1.263–264.

23. NSGGL Xu 3.179–180; Chen Gaohua 1984:618–620.

24. HJian 419–20, 422–423; trans. D. Chou 2005:140–141, 148, 149, modified.

25. In a few cases unsigned, unsealed paintings have been ascribed to Huizong, particularly by the Jin emperor Zhangzong (r. 1189–1208), who had inherited the collection of paintings removed by the Jurchen from Kaifeng in 1127. See Ebrey 2008:326–327.

26. Scholars who have contributed to the sorting out of Huizong's paintings include Rowland 1951; Sirén 1956; Xie Zhiliu 1957 and 1989; Deng Bai 1958; Ecke 1972; Xu Bangda 1979; J. Cahill 1980; Li Huishu 1984; Sturman 1990; Chen Baozhen 1993; Bo Songnian 1998; Bickford 2002–2003, 2006; Yu Hui 2008. J. Cahill 1980 lists most of the attributed paintings, generally with brief indications of his degree of confidence in the work. See also J. Cahill 1994:136–139. Ecke 1972 also goes through most of his attributed paintings, labeling most as questionable but declaring some degree of confidence in a few. Yu Hui 2008:129–163 divides paintings attributed to Huizong into ones he thinks Huizong did himself and ones he thinks Huizong had a court painter do for him *(daibi)*. He classes the National Palace Museum's *Two Birds* as *daibi*, but accepts the same museum's *Ducks and Lotus* and the Shanghai Museum's *Willow and Ducks*, which some other art historians doubt. Bickford 2002–2003, 2006 is by far the most cautious, arguing that no particular painting can be accepted as personally painted by Huizong ("holding the brush"), but accepting a half-dozen or more as by him in a looser sense.

27. There has not been much written about this painting, but J. Cahill 1980:102 calls it "an important early painting."

28. W. Fong 1996a:34.

29. Ebrey 2008:262.

30. XHHP 15.239.

31. XHHP 15.243; Ebrey 2008.292.

32. See Xie Zhiliu 1989:23–26, 46–53; Gugong bowuyuan et al., 2002:377–387; National Palace Museum 1995:15:365–368; Yu Hui 2008:134–136.

33. For the Taipei landscape, see National Palace Museum 2000:212.

34. *Returning Fishing Boats* is widely published (Gugong bowuyuan 1981:84–91; Bo Songnian 1998:26–27; Xie Zhiliu 1989:6–18; Fu Xinian 1988, pl. 45), but Xu Bangda 1979:64 suggests it was done by a court artist, and James Cahill 1980:100 thinks it a Ming work. Ecke 1972:131, 109–113 thought it reflected Huizong's style and was impressed by the number of early references to a work with this title. On this painting, see also H. Pang 2009. For an illustration of the Wang Shen painting, see Fu Xinian 1988:68–71.

35. The colophon is reproduced in Gugong 1981:13 and transcribed in Zhang Guangbin 1984 2:140–141.

36. QSS 26:17076.

37. CTSH 2485–2486.

38. QSS 24:15974–15981. For more on these poems, see Chapter 10.

39. HZL Yuhua 1.271–273; YH 28.16b–17a. XNYL 167.2729 says 155 *shi* poems.

40. Preface in QCCS, *Song Huizong ci* preface; trans. Ecke 1972:38.

41. BSXL 8.

42. J. Chen 2010:5; Kahn 1971:11.

43. Egan 2006a.

44. QSS 26:17045; trans. Egan 2006a:385, modified.

45. QSS 26:17059; trans. Egan 2006a:391.

46. QSC 897; trans. Landau 1994:154, slightly modified.

47. CTSH 2485–2486. Even though Cai Tao started his book with effusive praise, as mentioned in Chapter 4 it got him into trouble because it also expressed appreciation for the poetry of Su Shi and Huang Tingjian.

48. RZSB Si 2.636 (see the epigraph to this chapter).

49. J. Chen 2005:58. J. Chen 2010:161–190 provides an overview of emperor poets through the Sui dynasty.

50. On poetry and painting at the Southern Song court, see Edwards 1991; J. Cahill 1996b; H. Lee 2001 and 2010.

9. Pursuing the Monumental

Epigraph: TWSCT 2.26.

1. LJ 21.21b; compare Legge 1967 1:375.

2. SS 20.377, 98.2423; SHY Zhiguan 5.21b.

3. On the state cult in Tang times, see Wechsler 1985; McMullen 1987, 1988:113–158; and V. Xiong 2000:129–164.

4. CBBM 133.2247–2248; CBSB 28.947–948; ZHWLXY Shou 14a; SHY Zhiguan 5.21b–22a.

5. ZHWLXY Xu 2a–b.

6. SDZLJ 148.547–548; QSW 164:161–163; ZHWLXY Shou 10a–12a; SHY Li 14.61b–62a.

7. On Sima Guang and Zhu Xi on capping, see Ebrey 1991a:131, 1991b:36.

8. All the references in the SHY to capping of princes date from Huizong's reign or later. See SHY Dixi 2.18b–19a, Li 14.73b, Yizhi 7.3b, Zhiguan 5.22b.

9. Measurement: ZHWLXY Shou 23a–b, 29a–30a; SHY Shihuo 41.30b–31b, Shihuo 69.5a–6a. Clothing: SHY Yufu 4.22a–b; SS 105.2553. Silk: SHY Li 26.3b–4a. Statues of Confucius: CBBM 133.2254–2255; WXTK 44.415. Vessels: SHY Li 15.13b–14a; SS 108.2600; CBBM 133.2255–2256. Tablets: CBBM 133.2256. Orchestra: CBBM 133.2256. Sequence: ZHWLXY Shou 23b–24a. Abstention: ZHWLXY Shou 31a–b.

10. CBBM 133.2257; ZHWLXY Shou 31b–32b; QSW 164:259–260.

11. The history of this festival is analyzed in Teiser 1988.

12. CBBM 133.2257; ZHWLXY Shou 32b–33a, 34a; QSW 164:259–260.

13. ZHWLXY Shou 35a–39a; SS 20.385.

14. ZHWLXY Shou 40a–41a, 44b–54a, 54b–55a, 58b–59a, 61a–62b.

15. There are ten references in the prefatory chapter and seventeen elsewhere in the book.

16. McMullen 1987:222–225.

17. ZHWLXY 68, 69, 72, 73. See also Kojima 1992:471–476.

18. ZHWLXY 191.2a.

19. ZHWLXY 8.1a–3a.

20. ZHWLXY 4.1a.

21. ZHWLXY 4.5a, 5.7a–b. For other ways Daoism colored the state sacrificial program in the ZHWLXY, see Zhu Yi 2009a:314–318.

22. SS 98.2423; see also Ebrey 1989:295–296.

23. Hayashi 2003:11.

24. McDermott 1999:13.

25. Schipper and Verellen 2004:25–28.

26. All of these refer to groups of Daoist texts.

27. SDZLJ 223.862; QSW 165:71. Compare CBBM 127.2130 for the date in the twelfth month. See also Van der Loon 1984:40. For a prefect who was energetic in getting the magistrates under him to search for Daoist texts, see YJZ Jia 6.50.

28. The number of volumes is from Van der Loon 1984:30–32. SHY Li 5.23a gives 5,587. On this canon, see Strickmann 1978; Van der Loon 1984; Chen Guofu 1963 1:135–1138 and passim.

29. SHY Chongru 6.35a–36; XHHP 4.91, 92; LSZX 51.4b–5a (DZ 5:395C–396A, ZHDZ 47:558A).

30. QSW 138:54–55. On this text, see Skar 2000:433–434; Schipper and Verellen 2004:1057–1060; E. Davis 2001:23–24 and passim.

31. On this project, see Bickford 2002–2003.

32. See, e.g., QSS 26:1491.17044.

33. SS 371.11517; HJ 1.266. Compare Ecke 1972:99.

34. YH 200.32b–33a; HJian 419–420. See also the translation, D. Chou 2005:141.

35. On these paintings, see Bickford 2002–2003 and 2006.

36. QSS 26:17078–17079. Translation from Tomita 1933:78, modified.

37. Sturman 1990; Bickford 2006:477.

38. QSS 26:17069.

39. QSS 26:17069; trans., Sturman 1990:33, slightly modified. Sturman explains all the allusions in the poem.

40. Sturman 1990; Bickford 2002–2003. On *Cranes of Good Omen*, see also Itakura 2004.

41. These paintings could be compared to the many huge scrolls made by the early Qing emperors to record their birthdays, hunts, and travels, which took many man-years to make but after the emperor viewed them were rarely unrolled.

42. Huizong's collections are dealt with in detail in Ebrey 2008.

43. Ebrey 2008:210–217.

44. HLSZ 20a–b; Sturman 1997:183; Ebrey 2008:409n.31; Nakata 1977–1995: 6:234–236.

45. GCSB 2.14b–15a; SS 319.10388–10389, 472.13722; SSWJHL 27.214; Ebrey 2008:105–112.

46. CBBM 133.1b–2a; CBSB 28.950, 32.1057, 1062.

47. SS 356.11206–11207.

48. LXJ 168:3b–4b; SS 443.13105–13106.

49. ZHJ Fulu 2b–3a, 21b–23a.

50. Compare Bush 1971:74–82; Chen Xiang 1992; Yi Ruofen 1999.

51. XHSP 12.89–90.

52. On the cultural accomplishments of clansmen, see Chaffee 1999:267–271.

53. XHHP 20.307; Ebrey 2008:297–301.

54. Ebrey 2008:301–306.

55. BHTSZ 6.263; trans. Lewis 2006:269, slightly modified.

56. The passages in the classics and traditional scholarship on the Bright Hall can be found many places, such as WXTK *juan* 73; QSKS *juan* 28; MTDDL; GJTSJC Liyi dian *juan* 170–178. For modern scholars who have investigated the literature on the Bright Hall above all for what it can tell us about ancient China,

see Soothill 1952 and M. Hwang 1996. For the way the Bright Hall entered into political thought in the Warring States and Han periods, see H. Wu 1995:176–187; Lewis 2006:260–273.

57. SLTJZ 4.2b–3a, 4.24b; LiS 40.3a. For diagrams by modern scholars, see V. Xiong 2003.

58. On Wang Mang's Bright Hall, see H. Wu 1995:176–187. For examination of the Bright Hall built in Tang times by Empress Wu, see Forte 1988 and Wechsler 1985:195–211. Bright Halls were also constructed during the Northern and Southern Dynasties, but the sources are relatively scanty. See V. Xiong 2003.

59. H. Wu 1995:177–178; Forte 1988:153–160; KYL *juan* 10. Empress Wu's Bright Hall burned down, but she had it rebuilt on the same model.

60. SS 101.2465–2466.

61. J. Liu 1973.

62. CBBM 125.2099–2102.

63. CBSB 25.848–851; SHY Li 24.70b–73a; CBBM 125.2099–2101. On Cai Jing's role in Huizong's building projects, see also Kubota 2005:624–626.

64. SS 66.1417; SHY Li 24.70a, 71b–72a; QSW 165:134; CBBM, 125.2102–2104.

65. QSW 146.243–244, 273–274; CLJ 4.48a–b; YH 196.10b–11a; SHY Ruiyi 1.21a.

66. SHY Li 24.68b–70b; CBBM 125.2102–2104; SS 101.2472–2473. Several other sources, probably drawing on SS or a common source, also give the round number of ten thousand.

67. SDZLJ 124.427–428; SHY Li 24.68b–70a; QSW 165:133–134.

68. SDZLJ 124.427–428; QSW 165:120–121, 128.

69. For a picture of a roof with this sort of ornament, see Figure 9.2.

70. QSW 149:246–251; SHY Li 24.72b–76b.

71. ZHWLXY *juan* 30 and 31.

72. SS 117.2771–2772; SHY Li 24.78a–81b, Li 24.58a–64b.

73. QSW 146:246–247.

74. QSW 165:210–211; SDZLJ 124.428; SHY Li 24.77b–78a.

75. SHY Li 24.58a, 64b–65a.

76. SHY Li 24.66a, 81b–83a; QSW 165:229; SS 101.2477; CBBM 125.2104; SDZLJ *juan* 126–133.

77. SHY Li 24.66b–67a, Xingfa 1.31a; SDZLJ 124.428; QSW 165:271.

78. On Genyue, see Hargett 1988–1989; Kubota 2005:632–635.

79. C. Heng 1999:137 reports that Chang'an's Palace City was 4.2 square kilometers before Daming Palace was built, and 7.5 square kilometers afterwards. Kaifeng's palace amounted to only about 0.4 square kilometers.

80. To put this in proportion, V. Xiong 2006:82 reports that the largest palace hall built by the Sui emperor Yangdi in Luoyang was 120 meters long, so more than three times as long.

81. SS 85.2100; RZSB San 13.568–569.

82. SS 85.2101; CBSB 32.1061; HCBNBY 28.709. For more on the objects stored at this site, see Ebrey 2008:112–113.

83. Schafer 1968:325–331; Lewis 2006:177–178; Ledderose 1983:166.

84. V. Xiong 2006:98. Closer in size to Huizong's park was the northern extension of the Tang Palace City in Chang'an, known as the Daming Palace, which was

about seven kilometers in circumference. In subsequent dynasties as well, the imperial gardens/parks took up a good chunk of space in the capital (Naquin 2000:129, 132–136). To give a non-Chinese comparison, Phillip II of Spain in the sixteenth century had a sixteen-square-kilometer park created at Casa de Campo, complete with fountains and artificial lakes and another further from Madrid at Aranjuez, where he had 223,000 trees planted, many shipped from far and wide (Parker 1978:39–41).

85. For contradictory evidence on its height, see Hou Naihui 1994:260–261 and Hargett 1988–1989:19n.78.

86. HZL Hou 2.74.

87. An allusion to *Mencius* 1 B; see D. Lau 1970:16–17.

88. Numinous Tower and Numinous Pond are mentioned in the *Book of Songs*, Daya, "Lingta" (Mao 242). See Legge 1961 4:456–457; Schafer 1977:322.

89. The terms "Golden Tower" and the "Jade Capital" appear thousands of times in the Daoist canon, with quite a few references in the "Longest Daoist Scripture" that was placed first in the Daoist canon edited at Huizong's court.

90. HZL Hou 2.72–73. Zuxiu said the stele was three *zhang*, or thirty Chinese feet tall, and done in Huizong's calligraphy (Hargett 1988–1989:41). Hargett translates about half of Huizong's inscription, the part that was included in Zhang Hao's later record, which does not include the opening or closing parts of Huizong's text.

91. These translations are all from Hargett 1988–1989.

92. Hargett, 1988–1989:36, slightly modified.

93. Ledderose 1983:170; V. Xiong 2006:98.

94. Schafer 1961:7.

95. See Schafer 1961:8–9, 16–17.

96. Trans. Hargett 1988–89:41–42, slightly modified. On Huizong's use of stones in his garden, see also Keswick 1978:53–56.

97. ZHL Hou 2.80–84.

98. HZL Hou 2.87.

99. Schafer 1968:336.

100. For some of those who worked on the project, see SHY Zhiguan 5.22a.

101. SHY Xingfa 2.70a–b; SDZLJ 145.532.

102. On the "Flower and Rock Network" that Zhu Mian directed, see Y. Kao 1962–1963 and Hargett 1988–1989:10–15.

103. ZHWLXY shou 38b–39a.

104. Ebrey 2008:356–370.

105. Ebrey 2008:293–297.

106. QSW 165:162; SHY Li 51.11a–b; SDZLJ 136.481.

107. HZL Hou 2.75.

10. Finding Pleasure in Court and Palace Life

Epigraphs: SHY Dixi 8.39b; HZL Hou 1.280.

1. On Han Wudi, see Knechtges 1994; on the Liang court, see X. Tian 2007; on Tang Taizong, see J. Chen 2005 and 2010; on Li Yu, see Chen Baozhen 2009, P. Chen 1999. On court poets' panegyric poetry, see F. Wu 2008.

2. TWSCT 2.27–28; DXZZ 4.36.

3. Zhuge Yibing 2001. On Zhou Bangyan as a writer of *ci* verse, see J. J. Y. Liu 1974:161–194; Hightower 1977; Egan 2006b:330–347.

4. Hargett 1993:113–114; Egan 2005:118–122.

5. HZL Houlu 4.121–124; QBZZ 6.245–246; CLJ 1.6a–11a; QSS 24:15971–15974; SS 352.11126. HZL Hou 4.121 dates the banquet to Xuanhe 7 (1125), which must be an error; see QBZZ 6.247–248. SS 352.11126 mentions Wang Anzhong's poetic contribution, but does not give the date.

6. YJ 10.4a–5a.

7. On poetic games, including matching rhymes, see Hawes 2005, esp. 31–50.

8. SS 445.13130; FXWC Fulu 2b–3a. Unfortunately none of his poems were preserved.

9. XHSP 12.93–94.

10. Other occasions can be seen from the poems written by Murong Yanfeng CWTJ 2.4b–8a and by Cai Jing, mentioned in HZL Yuhua 1.271–273. See also SSJS 1.11a–12b. In a couple of cases, Murong Yanfeng has poems using the same rhyme words as Wang Anzhong (CWTJ 2.5b, 6a).

11. QSS 24:15974–15981 (CLJ 1.1a–24a).

12. CLJ 1.21b–22a (QSS 24:15979).

13. CLJ 1.17a–b (QSS 24:15977). For examples of songs on the Lantern Festival written by poets who served in the Music Bureau, see Zhuge Yibing 2001:49.

14. ZSKS 1b–2a. For another occasion when Wang Anzhong wrote a poem during the lantern festival with a long preface, see QBZZ 6.245–248 and HZL Hou 4.121–124.

15. MXSZYXLG 19.18b–19a. For other occasions of Huizong laughing at humorous poems, see QBZZ 6.277.

16. MXSZYXLG 19.18a–b.

17. SS 113.2698–2699.

18. An allusion to the *Li ji* (LJ 25.20b; trans. Legge 1967 I:425–426).

19. This ritual was performed at the winter solstice, so it marked the shift from shorter to longer days and thus more sunlight (*yang*).

20. The second half of this line could also mean "who writes about willow catkins?" [as did the female Eastern Jin poet Xie Daoyun, who compared snow to willow catkins].

21. HZL Yuhua 1:271–273. This group of poems, written near the end of 1119, suggests strongly that Huizong had no inkling that the tide of history would soon turn against him.

22. See Magdalino 1993:413–470 on panegyrics in Byzantium and their roots in Rome.

23. J. Chen 2010:380.

24. See F. Wu 2008:5–6.

25. SCBM 7 Zhengxuan shang 7.60.

26. QSS 31:19676; BLJ 1.1a–4b; HZL Hou 2.98.

27. See Zhuge Yibing 2001; Egan 2006b:237–347. Huizong's contemporary Ye Mengde records a rather far-fetched story that in the Zhenghe period (1111–1117), on one occasion an official with no talent for poetry proposed that poetry should be banned as "Yuanyou learning." Later that year, however, when Huizong was delighted at the first snowfall, his councilor Wu Juhou presented to Huizong

three poems on the snowfall and Huizong responded with one of his own, making it clear that writing poetry could not be an offense (BSLH 2.35a–b).

28. ZGYL 8.155–156.

29. SS 142.3348. On female musicians, see Bossler 2008 and 2013:13–19.

30. YJZ Zhiyi 4.822–823. See also Idema and West 1982:175–176.

31. SHY Li 45.16a.

32. Reference to the two princes is from JLB 2.62.

33. QSW 109:169; trans. Hennessey 1981:26.

34. HZL Yuhua 1.273–276; QSW 109:168–171.

35. QBZZ 8.364; HSSCGY 17.14a. On the halls that they passed through, see Fujimoto 2007.

36. On Zhao Zhonghu, see Ebrey 2008:83, 109, 419n.112.

37. HZL Yuhua 1.277; QSW 109:172–175, with some readings from CBSB 40.1251–1252.

38. For other occasions when parties were held there, see SHY Li 45.16a–b.

39. HZL Yuhua 1.279–281; QSW 109:173–175. Referring to the ruler and his subjects sharing their joys is an allusion to *Mencius* 1A.2.

40. HZL Yuhua 1.279–280. QSW 109:178–179 records this essay as a work of Cai Jing, but from the text it seems more likely that Li Bangyan wrote it. Wang Anzhong wrote an account of the banquet at a different, probably later, Lantern Festival; see QSS 24:15971–15973.

41. See TWSCT 6.106; Shen Dongmei 1999.

42. DGCL 13a–14b; trans. Blofeld 1985:34–37, slightly modified.

43. SCZCZY 11.101–103.

44. P. Chung 1981; Ebrey 2003a, 2003b:177–193.

45. This is the number given in SS 246.8725–8729, 248.8763–8787. It does not include children born to Huizong while in captivity, which one source says included six boys and eight girls, bringing the total to seventy-nine (SFJ 253). For the number of children each of his consorts bore and comparisons to other Northern Song emperors, see Ebrey 2003b:177–193.

46. Jia Huchen 1967, passim. From Jia's charts, thirty-nine emperors reigned twenty years or longer. Of them only four had more than thirty children.

47. Compare Ebrey 2003b:190.

48. SS 243.8639; SS 19.359.

49. SS 243.8638.

50. HSSCGY 15.1b–2b. I am using the translations for consorts' titles in P. Chung 1981:81.

51. SS 243.8639.

52. SHY Houfei 3.16b.

53. SS 243.8638.

54. SS 111.2661.

55. SS 243.8643.

56. Posthumous promotions were used mainly when an emperor came to the throne who was not a child of the empress, but of a lower-ranking consort. If neither the empress nor his mother was still alive, he could promote his mother to empress posthumously.

57. TWSCT 5.88. See also WYXP 8.80.

58. LSZX 53.6a–b (DZ 5:409A). BTL 1.4 has a shorter account of the séance.

59. SS 243.8645; HZL Hou 3.115–116; SDZLJ 24.118.

60. HSSCGY 15.2a–b.

61. These women are all listed as Huizong's. Those attached to Qinzong were listed separately. There were many fewer of them because he had been on the throne only a year and seems not to have been as inclined toward multiple partners as his father or his younger brother Kai, who had already had quite a few children born to several of his consorts.

62. KFFZ 104–111; SFJ 254–261. The ages given in these sources for the women and the evidence in other historical sources does not always match. Although He Zhongli 1994 has argued that in the case of Consort Wei (the mother of Gaozong), the Jurchen's records are probably more correct because Gaozong had reason to present his mother as older than she actually was, in the cases of princesses whose awards of titles are given in the SHY, showing them to be several years older than the Jurchen records, it seems likely that the Jurchen sometimes made estimates, or that some women misreported their ages.

63. QSS 1492.17053, 17055, 1493.17057; trans. Egan 2006:389–392.

64. SHY Dixi 2.18a–b; SHY Fangyu 3.22a.

65. SHY Zhiguan 7.25b–26a.

66. QSW 143.55–56.

67. JKYL 6.117.

68. CBBM 146.2454–2455; SS 21.393–394, 111.2666; SHY Dixi 2.18b–19a; SD-ZLJ 25.123, 129–130; CB 470.11227. Since Consort Zhu had not wanted Huizong to succeed to the throne, it is surprising that Huizong forged a new link to her family.

69. ZHWLXY Zhenghe yuzhi guanli, passim.

70. TWSCT 2.23, 5.89.

71. SHY Dixi 8.39b; TWSCT 1.2.

72. SS 246.8729; SHY Dixi 2.28a.

73. SS 246.8725; SHY Dixi 2.20b–21a; Chaffee 1999:164.

74. TWSCT 1.1; HZL Yuhua 1.281; trans. Djang and Djang 1989:78–79.

75. SHY Dixi 8.39a–b, 8.56b. Zeng Yin's age is inferred from the listing of him as twenty-eight in 1127 in KFFZ 119.

76. She received her first title in 1103/3, meaning that she was born late in 1102 or early in 1103. According to the record of the ages of the captives in 1127, Cai Tiao was then twenty-one *sui* (KFFZ 119), which would mean that he was born in 1107. Of course, there could have been errors in that list, but it is not impossible that Cai Tiao was still quite young. Perhaps his age was overlooked because Huizong wanted to make a match and only Cai Jing's youngest son was still unmarried.

77. SHY Dixi 8.57a–b.

78. KFFZ 3.114–116. His married daughters were included in the group to be transported, along with their husbands. Whether their children were left behind, or just considered too unimportant to list, is unclear.

79. CBSB 38.1197–1198.

80. HZL Yuhua 1.277–278.

81. GEJ 2.46; trans. Djang and Djang 1989:550–552.

82. See Hennessey 1984.

83. Hennessey 1981:35. In other sources, it is a different Daoist master, Wang Zixi, who gets into contact with her.

84. Hennessey 1981:42–44.

85. XHYS Hengji 15–16; trans. Hennessey 1981:69–70, modified.

86. ZGYL 9.294–295; SHY Dixi 1.17a; SCZCZY 32.319–320; SS 351.11099.

87. SHY Dixi 2.17b. Prince Si died in 1106 (SS 30.377).

88. On the Song imperial clan, see Chaffee 1999. The numbers of clansmen is found on p. 31.

89. Ebrey 2008:297–301.

90. SHY Dixi 5.25a–b; Chafee 1999:106.

11. Working with Councilors

Epigraph: SDZLJ 179:649.

1. Pines 2009; Twitchett 1996:63–75; OYXQJ Jushiji 17.126–128; J. Liu 1967a:118.

2. On Wei Zheng and Tang Taizong, see Wechsler 1974. On Sima Guang's views on ruler–minister relations, see X. Ji 2005:36–49.

3. DDSL 105.2a; SS 348.11024–11025, which records other conversations as well.

4. FXJ 24.275–276. Another example of an official whose conversations with Huizong were included in his funerary biography is Jiang You. See FXJ 27.344–348.

5. LQGZ 56–57; P. Foong 2006:125–126.

6. Here I am not counting Cai Jing's brief return in 1124 when he was well into his seventies, nearly blind, and not able to reestablish his power.

7. See Chaffee 2006.

8. SDZLJ 196:723–734. One reason for the renewed attacks was the appearance of a comet in 1110/5. See Chaffee 2006:49.

9. SHY Zhiguan 1.33a–b, Li 47.8a–b; SDZLJ 70:339–340.

10. See Hartman 2006. On the writing of history in the early decades of the Southern Song, see also Hartman 1998b, 2003.

11. XHSP 12:92–93; Nakata 1977–1995 5:321–323. On this catalogue, see Ebrey 2008:223–256. For more extensive translations from it, see Ebrey 2006b.

12. XHSP 12.92.

13. QSW 143:61–65.

14. SHY Zhiguan 5.13a–b; SHYBB 308; SS 180.4386–4387; Chaffee 2006:36–40; and Goldschmidt 2006:300.

15. For other evidence of Huizong matching his poems, see QDYY 16.292–293.

16. SS 343:10921–10922; QSW 143:61–65. SS 343.10921–10922 and SZFBNL 12.770 give his age as seventy-nine *sui*, but the funerary inscription (QSW 143:65) says seventy-seven.

17. HZL Hou 7.164–165; SHY Chongru 6.11a–12a.

18. SHY Li 12.3a–b, Li 44.17b; SS 351.11100; CLJ 3.18b–24a, 4.40b–46b, 49a–52b; HZL Qian 3.26–27; CBSB 35.1130–1131; Ebrey 2008:168–169. The recipients included Cai Jing, Zheng Juzhong, Deng Xunwu, Yu Shen, Hou Meng, Xue Ang, Bai Shizhong, and Tong Guan. How many vessels they received depended on their rank (1a, 1b, or 2a). One vessel, given to Tong Guan, is still extant. For an illustration, see Ebrey 2008:171.

19. BTL 1.12; TWSCT 2.26–27.

20. SHY Fangyu 4.23a–b; SS 351.11102; HLYL Yi 5.200; LXABJ 5.63, 8.106; NGZML 12.320. In Wang Fu's case, he received two houses, a smaller one in 1116, replaced with a larger one in 1122 (NGZML 12.368; SHY Chongru 6.12b–13a).

21. SS 351.11109; SZFBNL 12.747–767. See also Chaffee 2006:46–49.

22. SS 351.11101–11103; CBSB 29.988; HCBNBY 27.699–700; HZL Hou 3.119.

23. This was also true of other dominant grand councilors both earlier and later in Song history. See Twitchett and Smith 2009, passim.

24. SSWJL 5.44; SS 471.13716–13717; SHY Zhiguan 68.7a–b.

25. HZL Yuhua 1.278; SZJSZ 17:29a–31a; GXZZ Bie 2:218; Ebrey 2006a: 241–248; Ebrey 2006b. See also Zhan Kaiqi 2011.

26. XHSP 12.92–94.

27. HZL Yuhua 1.277.

28. QSW 109:177–178 or JLB 2.62–64.

29. SHY Zhiguan 10.2a–b, Fangyu 4.23a.

30. The standard biographical sources on Wang Fu are DDSL 106.1a–3a; SS 470.13681–13684; SZFBNL 12.786–789; and SCBM 31 Jingkang zhong 6.305–309.

31. Chaffee 2006:54–55.

32. SHY Zhiguan 4.28a–b; QWJW 10.225.

33. On the sons of councilors as courtiers, see SS 361.11316; SHY Zhiguan 69.21b–22a. On Cai You in Huizong's initial years as a companion to Huizong, see HZL Hou 3.109–111 and Fujimoto 2007.

34. See, for instance, SHY Yue 4.1b–2a; SHY Li 24.72b; 34.13a–b, 18b; SHY Chongru 4.10b.

35. SS 472.13730–13732.

36. E. A. Kracke, John Chaffee, and Thomas Lee have looked in detail at the shifts in the educational and recruitment policies (Kracke 1977; Chaffee 1985:77–84; T. Lee 1985:64–65, 77–80, 126–127, 256–257). Chaffee has also investigated the reforms of the imperial clan (Chaffee 1999:95–111). Hugh Scogin, Silvia von Eschenbach, and Asaf Goldschmidt have studied the charitable institutions (Scogin 1978; Von Eschenbach 1994; Goldschmidt 2006).

37. There is a large literature, mostly in Chinese and Japanese, on the Song monetary system. For brief introductions in English, see von Glahn 2004 and Oberst 1996:345–408. For a more detailed exposition, see X. Peng 1994:332–457; Wang Shengduo 2003:352–386. Nakajima Satoshi wrote articles on each of Huizong's currency measures, collected in his 1988 book. For the location of mints and their output, see X. Peng 1994:335–336. On regional differences in currencies, see Gao Congming 1990.

38. CBSB 31.734; SS 180.4387. On these currency issues, besides SS 180. 4386–4394, other good sources are QSKS Hou 60.20a–30a; WXTK 9.96B–97C; CBBM 136.2291–2305.

39. See Wang Shengduo 1995:385–386. According to X. Peng 1994:344–345, the point of making coins of a tin-iron alloy is that it would discourage melting coins down to make utensils from the metal. On the identification of these coins as tin-iron rather than tin-copper, see Nakajima 1988:44–45 and Hua Jueming and Zhao Kuanghua 1986.

40. SS 180.4387. SHY Shihuo 52.15b gives larger numbers, six hundred thousand strings of the ten-*qian* coins, worth six million one-*qian* coins.

41. SS 180.4387; SHY Shihuo 52.15b; CBSB 25.837; CBBM 136.2293; WXTK 9.96B–C.

42. SHY Shihuo 24.34b–35b. On paper money during Huizong's reign, see Wang Shengduo 2003:632–636. Scattered evidence suggests price inflation throughout Huizong's reign, but the evidence is not good enough to identify the periods when it was worst or how high it reached. Moreover, most price inflation was specific to particular places and varied in terms of the currency in question, with the one-*qian* copper coins the most stable and paper money the least. For evidence on Northern Song prices, see X. Peng 1994:380–403. For more analytic treatment, see Gao Congming 1991.

43. CBBM 136.2294–2295; CBSB 26.868, 869, 870, 874–878; QSKS 60.24b; SHY Shihuo 24.34b–35b. On paper money during Huizong's reign, see Wang Shengduo 2003:632–636; CBSB 26.887. On the paper money issued, see Nakajima 1988:61–63.

44. CBBM 136.2295–2296; QSW 135:265–266.

45. CBSB 26.885–886; CBBM 136.2296. DXZZ 9.86–87 offers a different reason for Huizong to abolish the ten-*qian* coins. During a banquet the entertainers did a skit making fun of the policy, which moved Huizong.

46. SS 180.4389–4390; see also Wang Shengduo 2003:367–371.

47. QSW 137.77–78; SHY Shihuo 13.23b–24a.

48. SS 180.4390–4391; CBSB 29.983–984; QSW 102:136–137. HCBNBY 27.699–700 says that Zhang Shangying directed funds from coining money to the general government funds rather than the Privy Purse, where they had previously gone.

49. SDZLJ 184.669; CBSB 30.1004–1006.

50. QSW 102:138; CBSB 29.987–988.

51. For an anecdote about how people responded to the ten-*qian* coins, see PZKT 2.27.

52. SS 180.4393; CBSB 31.10029; QSKS Hou 60.29a–b.

53. SDZLJ 184.668–669; CBSB 30.1005.

54. YYYML 5.46.

55. BZZFSZ 2.17–18; SS 85.2101–2102; 468.13552, 13661–13663; CBSB 43.1324–1325; Bickford 2006:505–510; Ebrey 2008:114, 133–134, 139; HCBNBY 28.713; HZL Houlu 2.73.

56. On eunuchs' military roles, see Labadie 1981:174–176, or, for more detail, Chai Degeng 1941. On Tong Guan as a military man, see Wyatt 2009:207–214.

57. CBSB 19.676; SS 468.13658; SS 468.13658. Cai Jing had served on a mission to Liao during Shenzong's reign (SS 472.13721).

58. SCBM 52 Jingkang zhong 27.518–519; SHY Zhiguan 1.12b; SZFBNL 12.772–774, 800–801.

59. Fully illustrated in Wang Pingchuan and Zhao Menglin 2002:6–35, among other places.

60. SCBM 52 Jingkang zhong 27.520; TWSCT 1.2. One source reports that when Tong Guan was attending court, he wore official dress, but after court sessions he would enter the palace and change into the dress of the eunuchs and perform their duties of attendance (TWSCT 1.2). No other source, however, confirms this and it may reflect anti-eunuch gossip rather than fact. For an example of strongly anti-eunuch sentiments, see the memorial of An Yaochen, dating to 1118 (SCBM 2 Zhengxuan shang 2.12–18, esp. pp. 16–18).

61. XHHP 12.205–206.

62. SS 372.11544; QSW 125:100–113; SCBM 159 Yanxing xia 59.336.

63. For memorials warning against eunuch abuse, see SCZCZY *juan* 61–63. Eunuchs during Huizong's reign are the subject of two memorials by Yang Shi written for Qinzong soon after he succeeded to the throne. See SCZCZY 63.704–705.

64. TWSCT 5.89, 6.109–111.

12. Accepting Divine Revelations, 1110–1119

Epigraph: QSW 138:54–55.

1. TWSCT 5.87–88; SS 462.13527; LSZX 52 (DZ 5:403A–B). See also H. Liao 2005:356–357.

2. Xu Xun was a fourth-century immortal whose cult was popular in Song times; see Boltz 1987:72–73.

3. CBBM 127.2144; TWSCT 5.89; QBZZ 3.110; SHY Yufu 6.16b.

4. CBBM 127.2129–2130; Ebrey 2013:16. On the dream, see also QBZZ 11.461–462. SHY Zhiguan 76.28b–29a refers to Huizong's illness in 1111/7/11, serious enough for officials to make measures to change his fortune, such as reducing penalties on officials. On traditions about dreams in Daoism, see Strickmann 1988 and Wagner 1988.

5. SHY Li 28.16a; SS 21.392.

6. SHY Li 28.16b; SDZLJ 136:482; trans. Ebrey 2013:22.

7. SHY Li 28.16b–18b.

8. SDZLJ 144.524.

9. From the *Rites of Zhou;* ZL 22.17b, slightly abbreviated.

10. SHY Li 28.59b–61b.

11. TWSCT 5.87–88.

12. See, e.g., Tang Daijian 2003:28–29.

13. SS 20.380; CBBM 127.2130.

14. SHY Li 51.14b–16b SHY Bubian 802A; Ebrey 2013.

15. SHY Li 5.2a–b; TWSCT 6.104–105; HCBNBY 28.714–715; Tang Daijian 2003:52–53; HJ 1.270. On the date the temple was built, see Kubota 2005:15.

16. For examples of Daoist masters invited to meet Huizong, see LSZX 51, 52, and 53 (ZHDZ 47:556, 557, 558, 563, 564, 565, 566, 567, 568, 576).

17. Huizong's relationship with Lin Lingsu has been treated by many scholars. Among pioneering works are Jin Zhongshu 1966 and 1967; Miyakawa 1975a and 1975b; and Strickmann 1978. Notable among recent treatments are Xiao Baifang 1990a, 1990b; Tang Daijian 1992, 1994, 1997, and 2003:26–57; S. Chao 2003, 2006; and Li Liliang 2006.

18. Buddhist views of Lin are included in two Buddhist general histories dated 1269 and 1341 respectively (FZTJ [T49, 2035] 46.421b; FZLDTZ [T49, 2036] 681A–19.684B). Lu You's account is in JSJW 2.218–219.

19. Much is included on Lin in CBBM 127, which sometimes cites its sources, the most relevant of which is Cai Tao's *Supplement to the History of the Dynasty* [*Guo shi houbu*]. Another detailed account, recorded in Zhao Lingshi's (1175–1231) BTL 1.4–6, is said to have originally been written by Geng Yanxi, who was active during the early Southern Song (see also Tang Daijian 1996:60).

20. LSZX; on this book, see Schipper and Verellen 2004:887–892; Boltz 1987:56–59; Katz 1999.

21. Sources differ on Lin's early career, including whether he started training as a Buddhist, where he traveled, and from whom he learned Thunder Rites and acquired the texts of the Divine Empyrean. Some sources are clearly wrong, such as the statement in the hagiography that he had been a servant of Su Shi, found in LSZX 53.1b (DZ 5:403B). (See Li Liliang 2006:90–91 on the impossibility of the dates.)

22. See LSZX 53.2a–b, 5a–b (DZ 5:407C, 408C); BTL 1.4; WXTK 225:1808C; Tang Daijian 2003:50; E. Davis 2001:26–27.

23. BTL 1.4. Xu Zhichang, then employed on the canon-editing project, was a talented poet, knowledgeable in both the Daoist and Confucian texts, and expert at curing illnesses without the use of drugs (XHHP 4.91); LSXZ puts Xu Zhichang's recommendation in 1116/10; FZLDTZ (T49.2036) 19.681A puts the introduction in 1117/1 and has Xu Zhichang work through Cai Jing, rather than approach Huizong himself. Tang Daijian 1992:24–25 argues for 1115 as the most likely date. Li Liliang 2006:106 argues that Cai Jing probably also recommended Lin Lingsu. According to BTL 1.4, Xu Zhichang's recommendation was in response to a query from Huizong, who had dreamt that the Eastern Florescence Sovereign summoned him to a Divine Empyrean Palace. When he awoke, he asked Xu Zhichang to find out what the terms referred to, and someone informed the latter of a Daoist from Wenzhou named Lin Lingsu then living in the Eastern Grand Unity Temple who talked of the Divine Empyrean and had written poems about it. Huizong then summoned Lin Lingsu. The version in Lin's hagiography gives a fuller description of Huizong's dream, but places it earlier, in 1106, and credits Liu Hunkang with recommending Lin Lingsu before he died in 1108, with Huizong not encountering Lin Lingsu until 1116 (LSZX 53.2b–4a [DZ 5:407C–408B]).

24. BTL 1.4; LSZX 53.4a–b (DZ 5:408B).

25. On confusion about the date of the revelation, see Tang Daijian 1992:25. The revelation is recorded in CBBM 127.2130–31 (drawing on Cai Tao's *Supplement*) and SS 462.13528–13529. JSJW 2.218 says the Jade Emperor rather than Shangdi, as do the Buddhist sources.

26. GSSXZS; SS 462.13528–13529; compare CBBM 127.2130–2131; JSJW 2.218–219; Strickmann 1978:334–340; Boltz 1987:26–27. As pointed out in Schipper and Verellen 2004:1085–1086, this text must have been put in final form after Huizong's reign as it refers to him as "Huizong," not used during his lifetime. It not only portrays Huizong as playing a key role in the revelation of the Divine Empyrean, but also refers to his commentaries, his other Daoist writings, such as his hymns, and his direction of the Daoist canon project.

27. There is a sizable literature on the divinization of kings in the ancient world; see Birsch 2008.

28. Tang Daijian 1996. Strickmann 1978:335, instead of pointing to Lin Lingsu, argues that "Huizong himself was in a sense the founder of the Divine Empyrean (Shenxiao) order of Taoism." Li Yuanguo 2003, by contrast, accepts the internal accounts and begins his history of Divine Empyrean Daoism in the Tang period.

29. For a summary of Divine Empyrean teachings, see Robinet 1997:180; Tang Daijian 1996:64–65. Boltz 1983 gives a translation and analysis of a short Divine

Empyrean text. Skar 1996–1997 provides a translation and analysis of a Southern Song Thunder Ritual text connected to Divine Empyrean teachings.

30. BTL 1.4; YJZ Bing 18.518; JSJW 2.218.

31. BTL 1.4; LSZX 53.4b (DZ 5:408B); FZLDTZ (T49.2036) 19.681C; JSJW 2.218; SS 462.13528. SSQW 14.817 has cranes appearing in 1117/2 when Lin Lingsu reported the descent of the celestial spirits. SHY Ruiyi 1.23b reports cranes appeared at the temple in 1118. Wang Anzhong congratulated Huizong on an undated occasion when a thousand cranes arrived at Precious Registers Temple (QSW 146:268–269).

32. CBBM 127.2131; CBSB 36.1138; Ebrey 2013.

33. Fu Xilie was one of those who had carried messages and gifts between Huizong and Liu Hunkang. See QSW 164:49; Li Liliang 2006:123.

34. See CBBM 127.2131–2132; CBSB 36.1140. On Zhang Xubai, see LSZX 51 (DZ 5:394C–395A; ZHDZ 47:556C).

35. CBBM 127.2132; CBSB 36.1142. See also the edict of 1118/2/20 (SDZLJ 179.649–650), in which Huizong states that he had been visited both by the Lord on High and by lofty Perfected Ones.

36. SS 21.399; Yao Sheng 1965:147; SXJSZ Buyi 1.37a–b; trans. Ebrey 2006:253. SXJSZ Buyi 1.37a gives the height of the part inscribed in Huizong's hand as four feet five inches, but from the rubbing in Yao Sheng 1965:147, that would account for about only four-sevenths of the whole. Its width is given as three feet five inches.

37. Zhang Jixian was the Thirtieth Celestial Master, that is, the leader of Celestial Masters sect.

38. LSZX 53.8a–b (DZ 5:409C).

39. LSZX 53.8b–9a (DZ 5.409C–410A). Huizong's painting catalogue lists ten paintings of Zhenwu under his various titles (XHHP 1.33, 1.38, 1.39, 2.65, 4.90, 6.112, 7.129, 19.295).

40. LSZX 53.6a–b (DZ 5:409A). She went on to warn Huizong of coming difficulties in the year 1126, another example of the hagiography taking pains to show that Lin Lingsu bore no responsibility for the fall of the Northern Song. BTL 1.4 has a shorter account of the séance.

41. LSZX 53.10a–b (DZ 5:410B).

42. SS 462.13529, 472.13731–13732; Li Liliang 2006:138–140.

43. E. Davis 2001:35–36; CBBM 127.2131.

44. CBBM 127.2133; CBSB 37.1185–86. The text of the stele in Putian is transcribed in Zheng and Ding 1995:9–10; trans. in Ebrey 2006a:254–255. CBBM 127.2141 (CBSB 40.1248–1249) gives a summary of the text.

45. QSW 146:193–194 or CLJ 3.21b–24a; CBBM 127.2141. See also Li Liliang 2006:180–181; Tang Daijian 1996:63–64, 2003:33, 34–35, 49–50. There is nothing in the current Daozang that matches this very closely.

46. CBBM 127.2140, 131.2227–2228; CBSB 38.1199. People who resisted receiving the registers were sometimes later viewed as particularly courageous or at least independent-minded. See Lu You's statement on Li Gang and two others who pleaded illness to avoid going to the ceremony to confer the registers (LFWQJ Weinan wenji 32.201; SS 381.11767).

47. CBBM 127.2132; CBSB 35.1123; BTL 1.4; SS 104.2546; RZSB San 13.570–571; Tang Daijian 1996:62.

48. SDZLJ 179.649–650; CBBM 127.2139.

49. SHY Li 5.4a. See also Tang Daijian 1994; Li Liliang 2006:44–65; and S. Chao 2006 on Divine Empyrean temples. For evidence that Buddhist temples were taken over, see LXABJ 9.115; YJZ 3 Ji 7.1352–1354, Zhiding 1.972; HQJSJ 32.17. See also the survey in Li Liliang 2006:149–165, which finds most of the Divine Empyrean temples recorded in local histories and other sources to have been converted from Buddhist temples.

50. FZTJ 46 (T49:2035) 46.421B; SDZLJ 223.863.

51. Li Liliang 2006:144; CBSB 38.1213; SHY Li 5.4a, Daoshi 2.3b; SDZLJ 219.843; trans. S. Chao 2006:350–51, modified. Huizong also wrote a record on the establishment of these clinics (SHY Li 5.2a–b).

52. SDZLJ 179.649–650. S. Chao 2006:346 translates this edict. For some examples of perfunctory prefects, see S. Chao 2006:344–348.

53. FXJ 20.225–227; LXABJ 9.115. On the paraphernalia, see also ZHJ 6.6a (or QSW 149:135).

54. GJZ 7.17a–19a.

55. This text is titled "Great Magic from the Purple Book of the True King of the Highest Divine Empyrean Jade Clarity." On it see Boltz 1987:27, Schipper and Verellen 2004:1094–1095. The text was likely compiled after the Song period, but the rituals for Huizong's birthday probably date to his period, when they would have been performed. See also Tang Daijian 1996:65.

56. GSSX 1.21a, 2.1a (DZ 28:565A–B); SS 112.2680–2681.

57. SS 157.3690; CBBM 127:2135; S. Chao 2003:9–15. Government involvement in Daoist education was not new. During the Tang, under Emperor Xuanzong, Daoist schools and examinations had been established (Barrett 1996:65–73). In 1080 Shenzong had set up an examination in Daoist subjects, which was used to select Daoists for temple appointments (S. Chao 2003).

58. CBBM 127.2132–2136; CBSB 37.1185–1187. As Shin-yi Chao 2003:20 argues, most likely it was Wang Anshi's promotion of the *Mencius* that led to it being promoted over the *Analects* as the essential Confucian text.

59. SDZLJ 224.864–868. For the titles and their equivalent in the civil hierarchy, see S. Chao 2003:28–31.

60. Strickmann 1978.

61. SS 21.400–401, 356.11220; HYSJ 9.49b (DZ 17:883A); Chen Guofu 1963:137–138; SHY Chongru 6.35b.

62. JZDSZ 5A:616; LBFT; LBWL; Boltz 1987:27; DZ 3:62–92. Tang Daijian 2003:45–47 provides a lengthy list of Huizong's Daoist writings.

63. Strickmann 1978:345–346. Schipper and Verellen 2004:1084–1085 raise doubts about Huizong's authorship of the preface on the grounds of the use of the pronoun *wo*, which Li Liliang 2006:179–180 argues reflects the language in the *Book of Salvation* and does not rule out Huizong as author. On the visual power of talismans, see Despeaux 2000:511–513, 525–526; S. Huang 2012:135–177.

64. DZ 11:489–512; ZHDZ 8:227–251; Boltz 1987:214–215; Schipper and Verellen 2004:648–649.

65. Kohn 1991:32–33. Kohn offers a translation and analysis of the book.

66. SDZLJ 224.864; CBBM 127.2133, 2138. Huizong's commentary to the *Liezi* was printed in 1123.

67. CXZDZJ 1.8b (DZ 15.3B).

68. On Liang Wudi, see X. Tian 2007:47. Liang Wudi and Tang Xuanzong, however, both also wrote commentaries on the *Classic of Filial Piety* and Buddhist sutras. More generally on commentaries on the *Laozi*, see Kohn 1998.

69. Xuanzong's commentary on the *Laozi* is still extant. See Schipper and Verellen 2004:284–286. On commentaries to the *Laozi* in Tang and Song times, see Robinet 1998.

70. SHZYJ (DZ 11:843–884); T. Liu 1974; see also his longer Liu Cunren 1991.

71. Robinet 1998:135; Schipper and Verellen 2004:647–649.

72. SHZYJ 1.39a (DZ 11:855C); trans. T. Liu 1974:15.

73. CBBM 127.2133, 2136–2137; CBSB 39.1218–1224; SDZLJ 223.863; FZLDTJ (T49:2036) 19.683–684. See also BTL 1.4; SS 462.13529. Tang Daijian 2003:42–43 gives cases where force was used or other excessive measures taken. Interestingly, the hagiography of Lin carefully disassociates him from these unpopular measures (LSZX 53 [DZ 5:407–412]).

74. JSJW 2.219; LDXZ 53.8a–9a, 13a.16b (DZ 5.409C–410A, 411B, 412B). Wang Wenqing wrote several extant Divine Empyrean texts preserved in later Daoist compendia. He lived into the Southern Song and appears in several of Hong Mai's anecdotes. He once brought on rain by performing the Pace of Yu. See Boltz 1987:47–48; Schipper and Verellen 2004:1107–1108; Skar 1996–97:171–172; E. Davis 2001:28–29, 54–56. On Wang Wenqing's association with Thunder Rites, see YJZ Bing 14.487, Zhiyi 5.832, Zhiding 10.1049; LSZX 53.16a–21b (DZ 5:412B–414A).

75. NGZML 12.356.

76. FZTJ (T49:2035) 46.421B.

77. FZTJ (T49:2035) 46.421A–B.

78. BTL 1.5; Schmidt-Glintzer 1989; SS 470.13685, 328.10584, 462.13528; Tang Daijian 1996:66, 2003:44–45; TWSCT 5.91.

79. FZTJ (T49:2035) 46.421B; BTL 1.4–5; LSZX 53.10b–11b (DZ 5. 410B–C). SS 462.13529 says that Lin Lingsu did not yield on the road to the princes, creating friction.

80. BTL 1.4–5; SS 462.13529; CBBM 127.2146–2147; BTL 1.5; FZTJ (T49:2035) 46.421C. On the severity of the flood, and the more conventional efforts to control it by diverting the water, see SS 61.1329; CBSB 39.1236–1241. The hagiography, by contrast, has Lin Lingsu solving the flood problem (LSZX 53.12a–13a [DZ 5:411A–B]). Another reason Huizong may have lost confidence in Lin Lingsu is recorded by Wang Mingqing: he failed to introduce Huizong to a young man with exceptional abilities who was studying with him (TXL 1.30a–31b.).

81. FZTJ (T49:2035) 46.421C; CBBM 127.2138; CBSB 41.1267; FZLDTZ (T49, 2036) 19.682A.

82. CBBM 127.2138; CBSB 43.1341; XHFSGLTJ 34.133; S. Chao 2006:354–355; Li Liliang 2006:188–189.

83. YH 158.18b–22b; SDJK 12.214; LSZX 51.1a–b (DZ 5:394C); QSW 109:158.

84. S. Chao 2003:25.

85. See Naquin 2000:146.

86. Strickmann 1979:3–4; Schipper and Verellen 2004:1082–1083; Boltz 1983:493; E. Davis 2001:29–30, 37 (quotation on p. 37). See also Strickmann 1978, which is less explicit but more widely available.

87. Ren Jiyu 1990:482–483; Tang Daijian 1993, 2003:4–5.

13. Allying with Jin

Epigraph: QBBZ 1.124–125.

1. For a basic description of the Song military institutions, see Labadie 1981 and Wang Zengyu 1983. For a brief interpretative history of the military during the Northern Song, see Lorge 2005:17–57. For fuller accounts of military campaigns, see the relevant chapters in Twitchett and Smith 2009.

2. On routine embassies, see Franke 1983; Ang 1983; and D. Wright 2005.

3. Some surviving reports from earlier in the Song are translated in D. Wright 1993:236–367.

4. See Tackett 2008:128–133.

5. Smith 1991:16–17 gives 760,000 horses as a high figure for the early Tang and 200,000 for the Song in 1008, after which numbers dropped to 153,000 in 1069. See also Zhang Tianyou 1980:186–188.

6. Twitchett and Tietze 1994:73–74; Standen 2005, 2009:103. The most convenient account of Liao is Mote 1999:31–91. See also Twitchett and Tietze 1994; J. Tao 1988; Barfield 1989:167–177; Standen 2007; and Wittfogel and Feng 1949.

7. Twitchett and Tietze 1994:85–87; N. Lau and K. Huang 2009:248–251; J. Tao 1988:10–14.

8. D. Wright 2005:145–152; N. Lau and K. Huang 2009:262–270; Twitchett and Tietze 1994:104–110; Lorge 2005:33–35.

9. J. Tao 1988:57–66.

10. JLB 3.89–90; Ren Chongyue 1990:81.

11. See Hartwell 1988, esp. pp. 66, 71. Total Song revenues in the eleventh century were generally at least one hundred million units (strings of cash or ounces of silver, etc.).

12. Shiba 1983:98; Smith 2009a:20; Lorge 2005:35.

13. Forage 1991; Smith 2009b:64–78.

14. Forage 1991:18.

15. On these wars, see Li Huarui 1998:91–96, 193–197; Levine 2009a:548–551; Smith 2006; Smith 1991:42–47.

16. CBBM 141.2370, 2375; Mostern 2011:210–215; Von Glahn 1987, esp. 118–124.

17. CBBM 140.2354; Li Huarui 1998:98–99. Compare Smith 2006:108–119.

18. Li Huarui 1998:100–102.

19. CBBM 140.2359–2361; SS 350.11082; Smith 2006:119–125.

20. SS 317:10351, 348.11038–11039.

21. CBSB 26.891–892. For Feng Xie's memorial and Huizong's response, see Smith 2006:117–118. On these campaigns, see also Ren Chongyue 1996b:53–55.

22. Li Huarui 1998:103; Levine 2009b:622.

23. SS 22.404, 486.14020–14021; SHY Bing 14.20b–21b, Zhiguan 1.3a; CLJ 6.1a–11b (QSW 146:364–370).

24. Several sources date Huizong's first encounter with this defector (Ma Zhi, later named Zhao Liangsi) to 1111 (e.g., SSJSBM 53.539), but others give 1115, a more plausible date in terms of the rise of Jurchen power. For the arguments for the later date, see XNYL 1.2–3 and Zhang Tianyou 1980:207–208. On the Jurchen, see J. Tao 1976 and Franke 1994.

25. J. Tao 1976:15; Franke 1994:220–221.

26. On Zhao, see SCBM 1 Zhengxuan shang 1.1–3; SS 472.13733–13734; SSJSBM 53.539–540.

27. SS 468.13659, 472.13734; SCBM 1 Zhengxuan shang 1.3; QBBZ 1.124–125.

28. SCBM 19 Zhengxuan shang 19 jia 181; Li Tianming 2000b:113.

29. SHY Fanyi 2.30b–31a.

30. SS 470.13682–13683; Xu Yuhu 1958:231. See also Li Tianming 2000b.

31. SSJSBM 52.519–526. See also Twitchett and Tietze 1994:139–144; Mote 1999:201–202.

32. SCBM 1 Zhengxuan shang 1.1–4.

33. CBBM 142.2381–2382; SCBM 1 Zhengxuan shang 1.1–4; SSJSBM 53.540.

34. HZL Hou 4.124.

35. SCBM 2 Zhengxuan shang 2.18–19; CBBM 142.2382–2383.

36. SS 351.11106; SCBM 2 Zhengxuan shang 2.12–18, 20. See also QBBZ 3.150–151.

37. SCBM 1 Zhengxuan shang 1.4–11, 2 Zhengxuan shang 2.12–20; SS 335.10750, 351.11100; CBSB 39.1225–1226; QBBZ 3.150; TWSCT 2.32–33. Some authors, including Ren Chongyue 1996b:174 and Levine 2009b:628, treat Cai Jing as a supporter of the alliance, but the evidence seems stronger that he was against it. See Appendix A.

38. SCBM 1 Zhengxuan shang 1.4–7; CBSB 39.1125–1128.

39. At this time, Cai Jing came to court only every fifth day.

40. If this occurred after the arrival of the Jin envoys in 1119, as stated, Zheng Juzhong should not have been in attendance, as he was in retirement from 1118/9 to 1121/5.

41. QBBZ 1.124–125. See also CBSB 44.1363–1364.

42. XNYL 1.4; Zhang Tianyou 1980:190; Yang Xiaomin and Zhang Zifu 2011:102.

43. SHY Zhiguan 1.41b–42a.

44. SCBM 2 Zhengxuan shang 2.19. On Ma Zheng see Franke 2003:107; Huang Kuanchong 1993:1–18; Jiang Qingqing 2008.

45. SCBM 2 Zhengxuan shang 2.19–20; CBSB 37.1166–1167. On the Song–Jin diplomatic negotiations, see Thiele 1971, which includes translations into German of all of the state letters.

46. JS 2.30; SCBM 2 Zhengxuan shang 2.20; CBSB 37.1166–1167.

47. SCBM 3 Zhengxuan shang 3.21; CBSB 39.1220–1221. See J. Tao 1988:87–97 or Zhang Tianyou 1980 for a narrative.

48. JS 2.31–32; SSJSBM 52.527; CBSB 39.1221–1222.

49. SCBM 4 Zhengxuan shang 4.30–31; CBSB 39.1220. It is also possible that Huizong was purposely delaying to see if Jin and Liao reached a peace settlement. According to the modern scholar Jing-shen Tao (1988:95), Huizong may have preferred to see Liao survive, hoping to balance Liao and Jin against each other, in the way Song had earlier been able to balance Liao and Xi Xia.

50. SCBM 4 Zhengxuan shang 4.30–31.

51. CBSB 41.1267–1269. The Jurchen later quoted a sentence from this imperial brush instruction. See SCBM 4 Zhengxuan shang 4.35, Chen Lesu 1933.18.

52. SCBM 4 Zhengxuan shang 4.31–34; CBBM 142.2387–2388; CBSB 41.1273–1274.

53. Added to this, there was considerable confusion concerning the identity of the sixteen prefectures, since prefecture boundaries had been altered since the tenth century. CBSB 41.1280–1283. See also Chen Lesu 1933:3–4.

54. SCBM 4 Zhengxuan shang 4.35–36.

55. SCBM 4 Zhengxuan shang 4.36–37.

56. On Ma Kuo, see Franke 2003 and Jiang Qingqing 2008.

57. SCBM 4 Zhengxuan shang 4.38–40; CBSB 42.1297–1300. Franke 2003 gives a full translation of this passage into German.

58. On Aguda as a negotiator, see Zhao Yongchun 2005:33–34.

14. Adjusting to Military Setbacks, 1121–1125

Epigraph: TWSCT 1.21.

1. SCBM 5 Zhengxuan shang 5.42–43.

2. SS 470.13682; HCBNBY 29.738.

3. SHY Bing 10.16b–17a; trans. Y. Kao 1966:234–235, slightly modified.

4. SS 447.13181.

5. QXKG 109; SS 468.13660, 470.13682; CBSB 43.1311.

6. Kao Yu-kung's 1962 and 1966 studies remain very useful, but do not reflect more recent scholarship. The secondary literature in Chinese is huge. For a review of it, and how politics since 1949 has shaped it, see Zhu Ruixi and Cheng Yu 2006:97–102. For some major historians who have worked on the issue, see Li Yumin 1980; Yang Weisheng 1980; Deng Guangming 1982; Chikusa 1982.

7. CBSB 42.1302; XZZTJ 93.2424; QXKG 112. The author of the last text reports that Fang La aimed to break the country in two, so that the south would no longer have to subsidize the north. This, he realized, would be devastating to the Song: "If we occupy the country south of the Yangzi, the people of the Central Plain will be cruelly deprived; unable to stand [the extra burden], they will revolt. Once they learn of this situation, the two enemies [Liao and Xia] will certainly take the opportunity to move in. When the government is attacked from both front and back, even such great ministers [of ancient times] as Yi Yin and Lü Shang could not help" (trans. Y. Kao 1966:221, slightly modified). In this account Fang La went on to predict that after the fall of the Song he would have the country reunified in about ten years.

8. QXKG 108; CBSB 42.1293–1297, 1302–1306.

9. CBBM 141.2377.

10. SS 470.13686; CBSB 43.1313.

11. CBSB 43.1312; CBBM141.2377.

12. CBBM 141.2377–2380; QXKG 108; CBSB 43.1329–1330; trans. Y. Kao 1966:232–233, slightly modified; SS 22.408.

13. SS 468.13660. On the discrepancies in the number of prefectures and counties reported involved, see Yang Weisheng 1980.

14. QXKG 109; CBBM141.2378; SHY Bing 10.18a–b; trans. Y. Kao 1966:237, slightly modified.

15. CBSB 42.1304–43.1332 passim cites many of these stories in its notes, mainly from LZMXL.

16. His letter to Wang Fu is found in QSW 171:22–25, to Bai Shizhong in QSW 171:26–28, to Zheng Juzhong in QSW 171:28–31, to Feng Xizai in QSW 171:32–33, to Wang Anzhong in QSW 171:34–36. Because Tong Guan had already left, he did not write to him.

17. SCBM 4 Zhengxuan shang 4.38.

18. SCBM 5 Zhengxuan shang 5.42; CBSB 43.1315–1316.

19. SCBM 5 Zhengxuan shang 5.45; SSJSBM 52.528–532.

20. SSJSBM 52.530–532; Li Tianming 2000b:122.

21. SCBM 214 Yanxing xia 114.205–208; Li Tianming 2000b:125–129, which also has other examples of memorials against starting military action.

22. LS 40.493–494; Wittfogel and Feng 1949:79–81.

23. SCBM 5 Zhengxuan shang 5.47–48.

24. SCBM 6 Zhengxuan shang 6.49.

25. SCBM 6 Zhengxuan shang 6.51, 7 Zhengxuan shang 7.60; DXZZ 5.45. See also Ren Chongyue 1996b:181 for his interpretation of these poems. Some have argued that Cai Jing wrote this poem as an insurance policy, so that if the plan failed, he could prove that he had been against it. The weight of the evidence, however, is that he was consistently against the campaign.

26. SCBM 8 Zhengxuan shang 8.74–76, 9 Zhengxuan shang 9.77–78.

27. SCBM 6 Zhengxuan shang 6.57–59.

28. SCBM 6 Zhengxuan shang 6.53–54, 7 Zhengxuan shang 7.63–64. This report may derive from DXZZ 10.91, or both from common gossip. For a blow-by-blow account of the fight and a helpful map, see Li Tianming 1996:288–299, 304.

29. HCBNBY 29.743.

30. SCBM 9 Zhengxuan shang 9.79–80.

31. SCBM 9 Zhengxuan 9.82–83; CBBM 143.2394–2396; CBSB 45.1377–1382. See also DJGZ 2.25–26.

32. SCBM 9 Zhengxuan shang 9.83–84.

33. SCBM 10 Zhengxuan shang 10.89–90; HCBNBY 29.744.

34. SCBM 10 Zhengxuan shang 109.93.

35. SCBM 10 Zhengxuan shang 10.88–95.

36. SCBM 10 Zhengxuan shang 10.96–SCBM 11 Zhengxuan shang 11.99.

37. SCBM 11 Zhengxuan shang 11.100–101. For an analysis of the reasons for Song's defeat from a military standpoint, see Li Tianming 1996:297–299.

38. SCBM 11 Zhengxuan shang 11.102–104 for Zhao Liangsi's report, 11.104–105 for Ma Kuo's.

39. SCBM 11 Zhengxuan shang 11.102–105.

40. SCBM 11 Zhengxuan shang 11.104–105.

41. CBBM 143.2401–2402; CBSB 45.1394–1395. The author saw these two letters, then in the collection of the professor of a prefectural school.

42. CBSB 45.1397; J. Tao 1988:92; SCBM 12 Zhengxuan shang 12.111–12; Franke 2003:112; SSJSBM 52.533–534.

43. CBBM 143.2402–2404. The epitaph for Zhou Liangsi records the discussions in detail, probably taken from his own writings (GSJ 36.7b–12a).

44. SCBM 13 Zhengxuan shang 13.117–118; CBSB 46.1406–1407.

45. SCBM 13 Zhengxuan shang 13.118–119.

46. SHY Zhiguan 41.20a; SS 352.11125.

47. SCBM 15 Zhengxuan shang 15.137–138; CBBM 143.2408–2409. Compare Chen Lesu 1933:30.

48. CBBM 143.2407; J. Tao 1988:92–93.

49. Franke 1970:60–64, which has a translation of the oath-letter.

50. CBSB 46.1420–1422; SCBM 15 Zhengxuan shang 15.135–136; Franke 2003:113.

51. SCBM 16 Zhengxuan shang 16.145, 150–152.

52. SCBM 17 Zhengxuan shang 17.158; SHY Zhiguan 1.3b, Chongru 6.12b–13a; NGZML 12.368.

53. SCBM 17 Zhengxuan shang 17.158.

54. SCBM 17 Zhengxuan shang 17.161–162.

55. SCBM 17 Zhengxuan shang 17.158–159; CBSB 47.1449.

56. CBSB 47.1455.

57. HZL Hou 1.49.

58. SCBM 31 Jiankang zhong 6.306, 308.

59. On the economic deterioration of Hebei during the eleventh century due to changes in the course of the Yellow River and deforestation that resulted from dike building, see L. Zhang 2009.

60. SCBM 19 Zhengxuan shang 19.175–176, 23 Zhengxuan shangjia 23.224–225, 99 Jingkang zhong 74.402; SSJSBM 53.553; CBSB 48.1474–1475, 1497.

61. See the report of a Korean envoy in SCBM 20 Zhengxuan shang 20.187. See also Li Tianming 2000a:188–189.

62. CBSB 48.1476.

63. CBSB 48.1477. Some sources, such as SSJSBM 53.553 give the fee as thirty strings per man.

64. TWSCT 1.21; CBSB 48.1477 offers several different readings, which have been used here.

65. CBSB 48.1475–1476, 1482–1484.

66. XZZTJ 95.2478; CBSB 48.1486–1489; SS 179.4362–4363. Lamouroux 2003:200–202 translates and annotates the full memorial.

67. XZZTJ 95.2480, 2485; CBSB 48.1493, 1513; SSJSBM 53.554.

68. CBSB 49.1511–1534.

69. SCBM 19 Zhengxuan shang 19.174; CBSB 48.1472; Zhao Yongchun 2005:41–44.

70. For a full list, see Ang 1983:105–106.

71. SCBM 20 Zhengxuan shang 2010.185–195. See also Franke 1983.

72. SCBM 22 Zhengxuan shang 22.208–213.

73. CBSB 50.1560; SCBM 24 Zhengxuan shang 24.236–237.

74. SCBM 23 Zhengxuan shang 23.225; CBBM 144.2431.

75. Zhao Yongchun 2005:16 makes this argument.

15. Abdicating the Throne, 1125–1126

Epigraph: TS 8.93.

1. SCBM 23 Zhengxuan shang 23.219–221; CBSB 50.1546, 1550.

2. SS 468.13661.

3. CBSB 50.1552–1558. For a detailed analysis, see Li Tianming 2000a:208–217.

4. SSJSBM 56.568–569; SCBM 25 Zhengxuan shang 25.246.

5. CBBM 146.2458–2459. Ma Kuo had advocated that if the Yellow River border could not be held, the emperor should retreat to Sichuan, citing Tang precedent. SCBM 23 Zhengxuan shang 23.224; CBSB 50.1552.

6. SCBM 25 Zhengxuan shang 25.246; CBSB 50.1562.

7. XZZTJ 95.2494; SCBM 23 Zhengxuan shang 23.225 dates this encounter earlier, connecting it to Li Ye's proposal on 1125/12/8.

8. XZZTJ 95.2496; SS 371.11526–11527. For one such memorial, see SCBM 9 Zhengxuan shang 98.80–81.

9. CBBM 146.2457; CBSB 51.1571.

10. SCBM 25 Zhengxuan shang 25.247–248; CBSB 51.1568–1571; SS 22.417.

11. SCBM 25 Zhengxuan shang 25.249; SS 371.11527.

12. SS 358.11241; SCBM 56 Jingkang zhong 31.557–558.

13. CBBM 146.2459–2460; CBSB 51.1577–1578.

14. Hebei literally means north of the [Yellow] river; Jiangnan literally means south of the [Yangzi] river.

15. Taishang was used as the term of reference for a retired emperor, meaning something like "extremely exalted."

16. Mengzi usually referred to the follower of Confucius of that name, usually Latinized as Mencius. *Meng*, however, was used for the eldest of a series of brothers, and *zi* was a common term for son.

17. CBBM 146.2460–2461; CBSB 51.1578.

18. CBBM 146.2461.

19. CBBM 146.2462; CBSB 51.1579–1580.

20. A Jin source records it (DJDFL 93–97).

21. SCBM 25 Zhengxuan shang 25.250.

22. CBBM 146.2462–2463; CBSB 51.1580–1581. Some less detailed sources, such as SS 471.13732, make Cai You more important than Wu Min in this drama. See also Chen Lesu 1936a:261–262 and SCBM 228 Yanxing xia 128.343–344.

23. CBBM 146.2463–2464; CBSB 51.1581–1582.

24. Compare JKYL 1.5. On JKYL, a key source for this period, see S. Chao 1979:145–146.

25. CBBM 146.2459; CBSB 51.1583–1584. Compare SDZLJ 7.29, which dates the edict to the twenty-fourth and has variant wording in a few places. A story circulated that a group of eunuchs, knowing Prince Huan disapproved of their behavior, tried to have Prince Kai, perhaps Huizong's favorite son, placed on the throne instead of Huan. The night of the abdication, several dozen of them took Prince Kai to the palace. When they got there, the general He Guan, then in command of the palace guard, refused entry. Another source associated Wang Fu with an earlier plan to have Prince Kai made heir apparent and the eunuch Liang Shicheng with defending the heir apparent's interests (HZL Yuhua 1.282; XZZTJ 96.2511).

26. This temple was Huizong's former princely mansion, which had been first converted to Dragon Virtue Palace in 1100, then in 1118 dedicated to the Daoist deity Northern Grand Unity (SDJK 1.14, 20.357).

27. TS 8.93, trans. in full in Ebrey 2013. Later Huizong gave a copy of this prayer to Li Gang when he visited him in 1126/3, and JKYL 4.74–75 records it after describing that visit, but does not mention when the prayer was first written.

28. SS 357.11228–11229. Ruizong abdicated to his son Xuanzong in 712.

29. SCBM 26 Jingkang zhong 1.256.

30. SCBM 26 Jingkang zhong 1.259–260.

31. JKYL 1.6, 1.8, 8.155; SCBM 27 Jingkang zhong 2.261–262; JLB 3.107; SSJSBM 56.571; CBSB 52.1609.

32. SCBM 27 Jingkang zhong 2.262–270; QSW 182:260–261; JKCXL 1.2–3; CBSB 52.1614; JKYL 1.10.

33. All of these men have been mentioned except for Li Yan, a eunuch who was hated for his role in collecting taxes from confiscated land made into public lands, most of it in regions near the capital. See Y. Suto 1965. On Chen Dong, see also Haeger 1978.

34. SSJSBM 55.559–560; CBSB 51.1594–1599, 52.1610; JKYL 1.7–8.

35. SCBM 28 Jingkang zhong 3.275.

36. SCBM 28 Jingkang zhong 3.275–276, 78–29, Jingkang zhong 4.288; CBSB 52.1619, 1622. WZRY 53 differs on some of the figures, giving ten thousand bolts of silk and satin and omitting the camels.

37. SCBM 28 Jingkang zhong 3.278–280, Jingkang zhong 5.294, 297–928; JKYL 1.19–20; WZRY 55. See also Franke 1970.

38. CBSB 52.1624–1625; SCBM 30 Jingkang zhong 5.299, 31 Jingkang zhong 6.304–305; WZRY 54; JKYL 1.18.

39. SCBM 32 Jingkang zhong 7.312–313; WZRY 55; JKYL 1.19 says two hundred thousand ounces of gold and does not say how much silver.

40. SSJSBM 56.579; JKQXL 2.13–14.

41. SSJSBM 56.580–581.

42. HZL Hou 1.64, San 2.240; JKYL 1.16.

43. SSJSBM 55.560–561; SCBM 31 Jingkang zhong 6.304.

44. SCBM 32 Jingkang zhong 7.315–320; CBSB 52.1633–1634. On the discourse about Qinzong's filial duties, see also Ebrey 2004.

45. Interestingly, Qinzong still had enough uncommitted money to give Li Gang a gift of five hundred ounces of silver and five hundred thousand strings of cash when he dismissed him (CBSB 53.1648).

46. SCBM 33 Jingkang zhong 8.325–334, SCBM Jingkang zhong 9.341; CBSB 53.1648–1656. See also Wang Jianqiu 1965:266–283.

47. SCBM 37 Jingkang zhong 12.367.

48. SCBM 39 Jingkang zhong 14.389–394, 43 Jingkang zhong 18.423–425; JKYL 3.46–50, 55, 57, 58–62, 4.76–77, 81–83, 87–88, 6.123; CBSB 54.1688–1689, 1697–1698, 1701–1705.

49. SCBM 43 Jingkang zhong 18.425–427.

50. CBSB 54.1691.

51. SCBM 43 Jingkang zhong 18.425–426.

52. SCBM 43 Jingkang zhong 18.427; JKYL 3.62–63.

53. JKYL 4.67, 69–70; SCBM 43 Jingkang zhong 18.430–432; CBSB 54.1694–1695.

54. JKYL 4.69–70.

55. JKCXL 2.16.

56. JKYL 3.63–66; JKCXL 2.16–17.

57. JKCXL 2.18–19.

58. JKCXL 2.18. Li Gang later showed this document to Qinzong, who added his own thanks to it and returned it to Li Gang. Gang not only treasured it, but also had copies of it printed (LXJ 161.1a–2b).

59. SCBM 44 Jingkang zhong 19.440–441, 45 Jingkang zhong 20.445, 99 Jingkang zhong 74.400.

60. JKYL 5.93; SCBM 45 Jingkang zhong 20.445, 47 Jingkang zhong 22.471.

61. JKYL 5.106–107, 6.116–117; SHY Zhiguan 69.23b–24b; SCBM 48 Jingkang zhong 23.481–483, 50 Jingkang zhong 25.506–551 Jingkang zhong 26.507.

62. SSJSBM 55.562–563; SCBM 49 Jingkang zhong 24.493–495, 52 Jingkang zhong 27.517, 56 Jingkang zhong 31.557–558; CBSB 55.1738–1745, 56.1771; HZL Hou 8.185. XNYL 1.16 has somewhat different dates, with Zhao Liangsi killed in the fourth month, Tong Guan in the seventh, Zhu Mian and Cai You in the tenth. On Tong Guan's execution, see Wyatt 2009:212–214. QBBZ 2.42 says Cai You and Cai Xiao committed suicide when they heard the death sentence.

63. SCBM 56 Jingkang zhong 31.558–560.

64. BSJWL 5.

65. SS 335.10754–10755; SCBM 47 Jingkang zhong 22.466–467, 48 Jingkang zhong 23.475, 485; SSJSBM 56.582–583.

66. SSJSBM 56.584–585; CBSB 56.1772–7179.

67. SCBM 57 Jingkang zhong 32.565.

68. SCBM 57 Jingkang zhong 32.564.

16. Losing Everything, 1126–1127

Epigraph: SCBM 79 Jingkang zhong 54.229.

1. SSJSBM 56.587. DJGZ 4.64 says only seventy thousand residents remained in the city, which cannot be literally true.

2. SCBM 58 Jingkang zhong 33.4, 60 Jingkang zhong 35.18; SS 335.10753; CBSB 56.1781–1782.

3. SCBM 62 Jingkang zhong 37.47–49, 63 Jingkang zhong 38.55–57; XNYL 1.16–17; JKJW 1; CBSB 57.1799, 1801.

4. SCBM 63 Jingkang zhong 38.60, 64 Jingkang zhong 39.67–69; JKJW 2; CBSB 57.1802, 1805–1806.

5. SCBM 65 Jingkang zhong 40.74, 79–80; JKJW 3–4; SS 353.11137.

6. SCBM 65 Jingkang zhong 40.84.

7. JKJW 4.

8. JKJW 3–4; JKYL 13.256–263; WZRY 63; SS 23.434; SCBM 66 Jingkang zhong 41.92.

9. SCBM 68 Jingkang zhong 43.109–112. See also JKJW 6; CBSB 58.1817–1820.

10. WZRY 64–65; SSJSBM 56.591.

11. For the events of this day, see also S. Chao 1979.

12. JKJW 8–9; JKYL 13.265–268; SCBM 69 Jingkang zhong 44.120. On the strange weather in this period, see Cheng Minsheng 2011 and H. Pang 2009.

13. SSJSBM 56.591; SCBM 69 Jingkang zhong 44.120–125, 70 Jingkang zhong 45.130; Zhou Baozhu 1992:612; WZRY 69; JKCYQY 1; JKJW 8–10; JKYL 13.267, 14.273, 274.

14. JKYL 14.273.

15. JKJW 9–10.

16. CBBM 149.2489–2490; CBSB 58.1829–1830; NZLH 126–127; DJDFL 334.

17. NZLH 126, 129; SCBM 70 Jingkang zhong 45.135, 137; DJDFL 335–336.

18. XNYL 1.14, 12.244; SSJSBM 59.609; Kaplan 1970:41–56; J. Tao 1989:532–534.

19. JKJW 11–12.

20. SCBM 71 Jingkang zhong 46.140–143; DJDFL 384–385, 500; NZLH 130; JKYL 14.275, 277–278; JKJW 12–14. On Sun Di drafting the surrender letter, see Hartman 2003:112–118.

21. JKYL 14.276–277.

22. JKYL 14.278. DJGZ 4.65 and CBSB 58.841–842 give different but equally astronomical figures: ten million bars of gold, twenty million bars of silver, and twenty million bolts of silk. Gold was worth about fourteen times as much as silver, since a few weeks later an exchange of cash for silver was announced at 35,000 cash for an ounce of gold, 2,500 for an ounce of silver (JKJW 23). SCBM 71 Jingkang zhong 46.144 reports that Qinzong visited Huizong and Empress Zheng at Dragon Virtue Palace on this day, after returning from the Jin camp, but other sources indicate that he remained within the Palace City at Extended Blessings Palace, which seems more plausible.

23. SCBM 71 Jingkang zhong 46.145–146.

24. That the horses had not been slaughtered for food is evidence that the capital could have survived a longer siege.

25. SCBM 72 Jingkang zhong 47.149, 153, 73 Jingkang zhong 48.160, 163, 77 Jingkang zhong 52.209; JKYL 14.279.

26. JKJW 22; SCBM 74 Jingkang zhong 49.176, 77 Jingkang zhong 52.209–211, 78 Jingkang zhong 53.211–214, 81 Jingkang zhong 56.241–242, 244; JKYL 15.297, 302–304, 307.

27. SCBM 99 Jingkang zhong 74.408; JKJW 16.

28. SCBM 72 Jingkang zhong 47.152–153, 48.161–163; JKJW 18.

29. SCBM 74 Jingkang zhong 49.171–172; JKJW 21.

30. SCBM 72 Jingkang zhong 47.156, 159, 73 Jingkang zhong 48.163, 165–166; JKJW 17, 18.

31. SCBM 74 Jingkang zhong 49.168.

32. JKYL 15.297; SCBM 74 Jingkang zhong 49.172. The heir was born in 1117/10, so in 1127/1 he was nine years and two or three months old.

33. NZLH 133–134; CBSB 59.1859; SHY Dixi 8.57a–b, 41a–b. According to KFFZ 98, in 1127 Fujin was twenty-two and Cai Tiao was twenty-one, which would have made them thirteen and twelve in 1118, but Fujin had to be at least sixteen in 1118, as she received her first title in 1103 (SHY Dixi 8.40a).

34. NZLH 134; SCBM 74 Jingkang zhong 49.173–175, 177; 99 Jingkang zhong 74.409; CBSB 59.1863; WZRY 77.

35. SCBM 74 Jingkang zhong 49.175–176, 74 Jingkang zhong 49.178; JKJW 22.

36. JKJW 25; WZRY 78; CBSB 59.1862–1863. JKYL 15.302 says two million ounces of silver.

37. SCBM 96 Jingkang zhong 71.378. One source said a third of the students at the Imperial Academy contracted beriberi, half of them eventually dying of it (SCBM 99 Jingkang zhong 74.401–402).

38. SCBM 77 Jingkang zhong 52.202–203; 77 Jingkang zhong 52.209, 87 Jingkang zhong 62.294; JKJW 26.

39. NZLH 136.

40. SCBM 77 Jingkang zhong 52.209–210; JKYL 15.303; NZLH 139.

41. SCBM 76 Jingkang zhong 51.198, 77 Jingkang zhong 52.201, 78 Jingkang zhong 53.216–217; NZLH 140.

42. NZLH 141.

43. SCBM 78 Jingkang zhong 53.219.

44. NZLH 141; JKJW 39.

45. On discrepancies among them, see XNYL 2.40–42.

46. SCBM 79 Jingkang zhong 54.224.

47. SCBM 79 Jingkang zhong 54.224–225.

48. BSJWL 1–2.

49. NZLH 141; JKJW 29. This contradicts the statement of Cai Tiao, quoted above, that the residents, weeping, tried to block their exit. In all likelihood, the truth is somewhere between the two. Those residents who realized what was going on gathered in protest, but significant numbers of people were oblivious to what was happening.

50. SCBM 99 Jingkang zhong 74.401.

51. NZLH 141.

52. SCBM 79 Jingkang zhong 54.225. Xiao Qing and Wang Rui had formerly worked for Liao but now were working for Jin.

53. Or perhaps, "We [no longer] approve a marriage alliance with you, as you are now all captives."

54. NZLH 141–142.

55. SCBM 79 Jingkang zhong 54.225; DJDFL 501.

56. JKJW 30. Similar sentiments appear in SCBM 79 Jingkang zhong 54.229.

57. SCBM 80 Jingkang zhong 55.2322–2333; JKJW 36.

58. JKJW 36–37; Chaffee 1999:31–32, 95–103. SFJ 243–244 says four thousand members of the imperial clan *(zongshi)* and five thousand nobles *(guiqi)* were taken prisoner, but some of these would have died at the camp and others may have been released as too ill to make the trip. It also reports that the convoy with the imperial clan and nobles included 5,600 people, of whom 2,200 were men.

59. SCBM 81 Jingkang zhong 56.239; 83 Jingkang zhong 58.258; JKJW 38.

60. NZLH 146, 154.

61. SFJ 243–244; NZLH 154; JKJW 40.

62. This is not the princess who had married Cai Tiao, but rather the one who had married Tian Pi (different characters romanized the same way). See KFFZ 99.

63. NZLH 155–156.

64. NZLH 156, 160, 164.

65. SCBM 79 Jingkang zhong 54.226; 81 Jingkang zhong 56.241–242.

66. SCBM 79 Jingkang zhong 54.229–231.

67. NZLH 156–157; SCBM 81 Jingkang zhong 56.245, 99 Jingkang zhong 74.410. JKJW 38–39 says the four that survived were beaten fifty strokes.

68. BSJWL 2.

69. NZLH 162, 167; JKYL 16.326, 331, 332; WZRY 87. Plunder continued even after the wagon train started.

70. DJGZ 5.72; NZLH 168–169; JKJW 43. JKYL 16.333 says Qinzong requested ten thousand strings.

71. SCBM 86 Jingkang zhong 61.286–288; KFFZ 121–122. The women are listed by name and age (KFFZ 97–118). The DJGZ 32.455 gives different totals (three million *ding* of gold and eight million of silver) as does CBSB 59.1880.

72. See West 1999:36.

73. SCBM 97 Jingkang zhong 72.385.

74. Franke 2003:108.

17. Enduring Captivity, 1127–1135

Epigraph: BSJWL 4.

1. SCBM 87 Jingkang zhong 62.293–294. This story is similar to the one reported to have occurred ten days earlier by NZLH 155–156, cited in the previous chapter. It could be that Huizong kept repeating the matter because he considered it important, but it is also possible that one source records the wrong date. Another difference is that this account has Empress Zheng securing the release of all of her relatives, but the other only a single one.

2. SCBM 87 Jingkang zhong 62.293; BSJWL 3.

3. R. Davis 2004:162–75; Standen 2005:155.

4. SFJ 244–245.

5. SFJ 244–250.

6. SCBM 99 Jingkang zhong 74.401, 89 Jingkang zhong 64.313; BSJWL 6.

7. SYY 192, 201; BSJWL 6.

8. BSJWL 6–7.

9. QGYY 177.

10. QGYY 177.

11. QGYY 178.

12. QGYY 179.

13. QGYY 180.

14. QGYY 183.

15. QGYY 185.

16. BSJWL.

17. BSXL.

18. SCBM 98 Jingkang zhong 73.393–399.

19. SYY.

20. NZLH 172. BSJWL 3–4 adds that the consort committed suicide.

21. SYY 193; BSJWL 6.

22. SYY 194.

23. SYY 195; BSJWL 4; SFJ 285; SS 246.8723.

24. BSJWL 6.

25. BSJWL 6; trans. J. Liu 1985:211–212.

26. BSJWL 4.

27. SYY 197. This version of these events makes more sense than the versions in SS 447.13182–13183 or SCBM 95 Jingkang zhong 70.370. See Cui Wenyin 1988:18–19.

28. BSJWL 4–5; SS 379.11700; SCBM 101 Yanxing xia 1.416.

29. SS 246.8728–8729 records Prince Zhen's escape and the subsequent capture of his camp. SFJ 268, 271, however, records that Prince Zhen was in Five Nations Fort and that the person who fought against Jin was an imposter. Still other sources—Tao Jinsheng 1970, Huang Kuanchong 1993:1–40, and Herbert Franke 2003:117–118—believe that Ma Kuo was not deceived and this was in fact the prince.

30. SYY 198–199. SCBM 98 Jingkang zhong 73.394 says Huizong arrived on 5/18.

31. BSXL 1. Cai Tiao in BSXL 1 says he distributed all of the ten thousand pieces of silk that he had received, Zhao Zizhi in SCBM 98 Jingkang zhong 73.395 that he distributed 150 pieces of it.

32. On Xiebao as a younger son of Nianhan, see SFJ 246. Xiebao had traveled with the third convoy, which included Qinzong's empress and consorts.

33. SCBM 98 Jingkang zhong 73.394; SYY 199–200. According to Cai Tiao, at this or another meeting with Wolibu, Huizong discussed his views on the north–south situation and his desire to see a peace treaty concluded. He talked passionately of the significance of the dynasty continuing, moving those who heard him, even bringing some to tears. Wolibu remained silent, merely nodding. BSXL 1.

34. XNYL 5.135; TWSCT 1.2–3.

35. SYY 200.

36. BSXL 8.

37. QSS 1495.17070.

38. QSC *juan* 898; trans. Ecke 1972:42.

39. SYY 200, 203; SFJ 262. SYY 203 says Wolibu's death occurred in the eighth month, but JS 3.57 says in the sixth month.

40. SCBM 98 Jingkang zhong 73.394–395; SYY 202, 203.

41. SYY 204; SCBM 98 Jingkang zhong 73.395.

42. SYY 204, 206; SCBM 98 Jingkang zhong 73.395; SFJ 253.

43. BSXL 3–5.

44. All of these events are well-known ones, discussed in Barfield 1989. On Yelü Deguang, see Standen 2005.

45. BSXL 1–3; XNYL 16.333–334.

46. W. Lo 1996:108–112.

47. SYY 209; compare JS 3.59.

48. SYY 209–210.

49. SYY 207, 211; SCBM 98 Jingkang zhong 73.395, 116 Yanxing xia 16.560.

50. BSXL 4–5.

51. SYY 214, 216–218; DJDFL 529–531.

52. DJDFL 533.

53. SFJ 271.

54. SYY 216; XNYL 35.676–677; 40.744; BSXL 5; JSJSBM 7.156.

55. SYY 219; BSXL 4.

56. GEJ 3.45; Djang and Djang 1989:68.

57. BSJWL 4.

58. SYY 223 and SFJ 272 have 1132. BSXL 6–7 gives the same date, but in 1133. JS 3.65 lists this under the eighth month of 1133, perhaps when it was settled.

59. BSXL 7, 8.

60. XNYL 40.751; SYY 221; BSXL 9.

61. SYY 224–226; JSJSBM 7.157–158; SYY 228 says Nianhan was strangled in jail. JS 4.71 merely says that he died.

62. SYY 240; RZSB San 8.503.

63. For some temples recorded in local histories, see JKZ 45.3a–b; GJZ 7.16a–17a; PLZ 25.11b–12a. See also SHY Daoshi 1.12b; Halperin 2006:127–128, 134–138.

64. SFJ 244–245. For a listing as of about 1142, see SCBM 99 Jingkang zhong 74.404–405. Chen Lesu 1936b:300–301 thinks this document may have been brought back by someone in the party of Consort Wei when she returned in 1142.

65. JS 10.234.

66. SYY 229–230.

67. SFJ 284–285.

68. SFJ 254–261; KFFZ 104–112.

69. SFJ 285–287.

70. On these books, see Hennessey 1984 and West 2006. For a scholar who emphasizes how well Huizong and the other imperial captives were treated, see Liao Huaizhi 2007.

71. BSXL 6, 8.

72. SYY 220–221.

73. RZSB San 3.443–444.

Afterword

1. SS 22.417–418.

2. DJTS Hou 88b–89a, 91a, 96a. On this book, see Murray 2001, 2005.

3. On Wang Fuzhi, see de Bary and Lufrano 2000:26–35.

4. On the stereotype of Yangdi as the dissolute last emperor, see A. Wright 1960. Li Linfu was the chief minister under the Tang emperor Xuanzong and held responsible for the rebellion of An Lushan, which nearly toppled the dynasty.

5. SL *juan* 8.

6. See A. Wright 1960.

7. Shaberg 2001:224–225.

8. Owen 1998:14.

9. Owen 1998:16. See also J. Chen 2010:73, 76.

10. On court expenses in Europe, see Burke 1992:135–149; Vale 2001:69–135, and Duinham 2003:45–89. For the variety among the courts of Europe, see Dickens 1977 and Adamson 1999.

11. SS 19.357.

12. SS 20.378.

13. SS 16.312, 102.2484–2485, 243.8632.

14. In bibliographies and book catalogues the only title that appears to be a biography of an emperor is the *Han Wudi neizhuan*, which is not the sort of biography under discussion, but a Daoist text.

15. Compare R. Huang 1981:95–100.

16. One could point to bans on books of prognostication on the grounds that those rising in rebellion used them. However, those bans were explicit, apparently not the case with emperors' biographies.

17. For examples of ruler-centered histories contemporaneous with the Song dynasties, see the Byzantine works Choniates 1984 and Psellus 1966.

18. See Hegel 1981:84–111 for analysis of a late Ming example.

19. The body of scholarship on Chinese emperors is now quite substantial. Books in English devoted to particular emperors include Spence 1974; S. Wu 1979;

De Heer 1986; S. Tsai 2001; V. Xiong 2006; M. Elliott 2009; J. Chen 2010; H. Chan 2011. There are also books that have given considerable attention to particular emperors within studies of related topics, such as Wechsler 1974; A. Wright 1978; R. Huang 1981; P. Kuhn 1990. For imperial sovereignty more generally and the political ideas behind it, see Mote 1961; Loewe 1965:70–92; 1986, 1994:85–111; Nylan 2008; Pines 2009. Recently, imperial courts have also been the focus of a few studies (Rawski 1998; Robinson 2008).

20. To give a few Ming examples, the Ming founder and his son, the Hongwu and Yongle emperors, both had many officials executed (see H. Tsai 2001:30, 51, 70–71), and later in the Ming ordering officials beaten was not rare (e.g., R. Huang 1981:17, 24, 59, 99).

21. For some Ming examples, see R. Huang 1981:121–124.

22. R. Huang 1981:86. See also p. 93 where he refers to the Wanli emperor realizing that "he was less the Ruler of All Men than a prisoner of the Forbidden City."

23. See Lewis 2006:79–80. Nylan 2008:59 suggests that keeping the Han ruler out of sight might have been in part because "the ruler invisible" "can be all things to all people" and also that "the hidden ruler" motif might have been "devised to screen from view the everyday realities of the Han court," such as power in the hands of maternal relatives.

24. See Allsen 2006:14. On hunting at medieval European courts, see also Vale 2001:179–184.

25. Wechsler 1974:130.

26. See N. Lau and K. Huang 2009:260–272.

27. CB 160.3866–3867; SCZCZY 11.95–96. See also Kubota 2007b.

28. C. Zhang 2011.

29. On this discourse, see also Knechtges 1999, esp. 55–59, M. Chang 2007:45–54.

30. See Allsen 2006:207–208 for some comparative cases of assassinations during hunts.

31. Allsen 2006:109. See also J. Chen 2010:35–36.

32. DX *juan* 4–6, DJTS.

33. See R. Davis 1996:135–151; N. Lau and K. Huang 2009.

Appendix A

1. Modern authors who cited this as fact include Yu Hui 2008:90 and Zhang Qifeng 2008:183.

2. QDYY 11.193; and GXZZ Hou 104–105; YSHB 2.52.

3. See HSSCGY 8.2a–b.

4. For modern scholars who accept this anecdote, see Hargett 1988–1989:8–9 and W. Fong 1996a:31.

5. HZL Hou 2.72.

6. HZL Hou 2.72; trans. Djang and Djang 1989:61–62, modified.

7. Examples include Ren Chongyue 1996b:77; Wang Ruilai 2004:38; H. Pang 2009:20n.

8. SS 468.13658.

9. SS 472.13722; trans. Hartman 2006:539.

10. SCBM 52 Jingkang zhong 27.518.

11. SZFBNL 12.773; Hartman 2006:539. This discrepancy was noted by traditional historians. See CBSB 18.665. Hayashi 2003:8–9 also notes the contradiction.

12. HZL Yuhua 1.276–279.

13. See, e.g., Wang Ruilai 2004; Levine 2009b:61–62; He Zhongli 2007:221–223. A scholar who gives a more nuanced picture is Zhang Bangwei 2002. For more on Empress Xiang, see Ebrey 2012.

14. SS 242.8630.

15. On this issue, see footnote 60 in Chapter 30.

16. CB 520.12378–12379; ZGYL 9.227–228.

17. ZGYL 9.269–270; CBSB 15.584–585.

18. CBSB 16.603; SS 471.13713.

19. CBSB 16.606–607.

20. SZFBNL 12.732–734.

21. See, e.g., Li Tianming 2000b:120.

22. SCBM 2 Zhengxuan shang 2.12–18.

23. JKYL 3.46–47.

24. SZFBNL 13.836.

25. DDSL 101.1a.

26. SHY Fanyi 2.30b–31a.

27. SCBM 1 Zhengxuan shang 1.4–11, 2 Zhengxuan shang 2.12–20; SS 335.10750; CBSB 39.1225–1226.

28. SCBM 2 Zhengxuan shang 2.18–19; CBBM 142.2382–2383.

29. QBBZ 1.124–125.

30. QBBZ 1.124–125. See also CBSB 44.1363–1364.

31. SZFBNL 13.841. Some scholars have recognized that the decision to continue pursuing an alliance with Jin went against Cai Jing's advice. Hayashi 2003:16–17 sees it as a sign that Cai Jing gradually lost in a power struggle with Wang Fu, Cai You, and possibly key eunuchs.

32. TWSCT 2.33.

33. DJMHLZ 5.137–140; MZML 8.222–223.

34. KCZ 1.1.

35. GEJ 3.46; Djang and Djang 1989:550–552.

36. HRZYT 3.13b.

37. Although the memorial does not survive, there is a record that Cai Jing wrote on Huizong's fourth visit. See QSW 109.177–178.

38. SS 352.11128–11129.

39. See LDMCZY 287, which includes Cao Fu's memorial and many others.

40. For some examples, see Ren Chongyue 1996a; Liu Kongfu; Pan Liangzhi 1994.

41. XHYS 1.27a–28a; trans. Hennessy 1981:64.

42. GEJ 2.46; trans. Djang and Djang 1989:550–552, modified.

43. XNYL 151.2433. Zhu Xi, in ZZYL 127.3050, said of the accounts of the abdication that Wu Min's was the most detailed.

References

Works frequently cited have been abbreviated in the notes as follows:

CBETA   Chinese Buddhist Electronic Texts (www.cbeta.org).
CSJC   *Congshu jicheng* 叢書集成. Shanghai: Commercial Press,
        1936–1939.
DZ   *Daozang* 道藏. 36-vol. edition of Beijing: Wenwu chubanshe,
        Shanghai: Shanghai shudian, and Tianjin: Guji chubanshe, 1988.
SKQS   *Siku quanshu* 四庫全書. Taipei: Commercial Press, 1983.
SKSLXB *Shike shiliao xinbian* 石刻史料新編. Taipei: Xinwenfeng, 1977.
SYDFZCS *SongYuan difang zhi congshu* 宋元地方誌叢書. Taipei: Guotai wenhua
        shiye, 1980.
TC   Used to number texts in the Daoist canon, from Schipper and
        Verrellen, *The Taoist Canon.*
XXSKQS *Xuxiu siku quanshu* 續修四庫全書. Shanghai: Guji chubanshe,
        1995–1999.

Primary Sources

BDBM   *Taishang xuanling beidou benming changsheng miaojing* 太上玄靈北斗本命
        長生妙經 (TC 623; DZ 11:34950).
BGT   *Chongxiu Xuanhe bogu tu* 重修宣和博古圖, 30 *juan*, attributed to Wang Fu
        王黼 (d. 1126). 1528 ed.
BHTSZ   *Baihutong shuzheng* 白虎通疏證, 12 *juan*, by Ban Gu 班固, edited by
        Chen Li 陳立 and Wu Zeyu 吳則虞. Beijing: Zhonghua shuju, 1994.
BLJ   *Binglü ji*, 枡欄集, 25 *juan*, by Deng Su 鄧肅 (1091–1132). SKQS ed.
BQS   *Baqiong shi jinshi buzheng* 八瓊室金石補正, 130 *juan*, by Lu Zengxiang 陸增祥
        (1816–1882). SKSLXB ed. Taipei: Xinwenfeng, 1977 reprint.
BSJ   *Beishan ji* 北山集, 40 *juan*, by Cheng Ju 程俱 (1078–1144). SKQS ed.

BSJWL   *Beishou jianwen lu* 北狩見聞錄, 1 *juan*, by Cao Xun 曹勳 (1098–1174). CSJC ed.

BSLH   *Bishu luhua* 避暑錄話, 2 *juan*, by Ye Mengde 葉夢得 (1077–1148). SKQS ed.

BSXL   *Beishou xinglu* 北狩行錄, 1 *juan*, by Cai Tiao 蔡絛 (fl. 1100–1130). CSJC ed.

BTL   *Bintui lu* 賓退錄, 10 *juan*, by Zhao Lingshi 趙令時 (1175–1231). Songyuan biji congshu ed. Shanghai: Shanghai guji chubanshe, 1983.

BZZFSZ   *Baozhen zhai fashu zan* 寶真齋法書贊, 28 *juan*, by Yue Ke 岳珂 (1183–1240). Yishu congshu ed. Taipei: Shijie shuju, 1962.

CB   *Xu zizhi tongjian changbian* 續資治通鑑長編, 520 *juan*, by Li Tao 李燾 (1115–1184). Beijing: Zhonghua shuju, 1985.

CBBM   *Huang Song Tongjian changbian jishi benmo* 皇宋通鑑長編紀事本末, 150 *juan*, by Yang Zhongliang 楊仲良 (fl. ca. 1170–1230). Harbin: Heilongjiang renmin chubanshe, 2006.

CBSB   *Xu zizhi tongjian changbian shibu* 續資治通鑑長編拾補, edited by Huang Yizhou 黄以周 (1828–1899). Beijing: Zhonghua shuju, 2004.

CFYG   *Cefu yuangui* 冊府元龜, 1,000 *juan*, edited by Wang Qinruo 王欽若 (962–1025) et al. Taipei: Zhonghua shuju reprint of Ming ed.

CJSL   *Chuijian silu* 吹劍四錄, 4 *juan*, by Yu Wenbao 俞文豹 (1200–1260). In *Song-ren zhaji bazhong* 宋人劄記八種. Taipei: Shijie shuju, 1963.

CLJ   *Chuliao ji* 初寮集, 8 *juan*, by Wang Anzhong 王安中 (1076–1134). SKQS ed.

CQFL   *Chunqiu fanlu yizheng* 春秋繁露義證, 82 *juan*, by Dong Zhongshu 董仲舒 (179–104 BCE), edited Su Yu 蘇輿 and Zhong Zhe 鍾哲. Beijing: Zhonghua shuju, 1992.

CTSH   *Cai Tao shihua* 蔡絛詩話 , 1 *juan*, by Cai Tao 蔡絛 (?–1147+). In *Song shihua quanbian* 宋詩話全編. Nanjing: Jiangsu guji chubanshe, 1998.

CWTJ   *Chiwentang ji* 摛文堂集, 15 *juan*, by Murong Yanfeng 慕容彥逢 (1067–1117). SKQS ed.

CXBC   *Chongxu Zhenghe jingshi zhenglei beiyong bencao* 重修政和經史證類備用本草, 30 *juan*, edited by Tang Shenwei 唐慎微 (fl. 1086–1093) and Cao Xiaozhong 曹孝忠 (fl. 1116). Beijing: Renmin weisheng chubanshe, 1957.

CXZDZJ   *Chongxu zhide zhenjing yijie* 沖虛至德真經義解, 8 *juan*, by Huizong 徽宗, part of *Chongxu zhide zhenjing sijie* 沖虛至德真經四解, edited by Gao Shouyuan 高守元 (1189) (TC 732; DZ 15:1–161).

CYLY   *Chaoye leiyao* 朝野類要, 5 *juan* (1234), by Zhao Sheng 趙升 (?–1236+). Beijing: Zhonghua shuju, 2007.

CYZJ   *Jianyan yilai chaoye zaji* 建炎以來朝野雜記, 40 *juan*, by Li Xinchuan 李心傳 (1166–1243). Beijing: Zhonghua shuju, 2000.

CZJW   *Chunzhu jiwen* 春渚紀聞, 10 *juan*, by He Wei 何薳 (1077–1145). SKQS ed.

DDSL   *Dongdu shilue* 東都事略, 130 *juan*, by Wang Cheng 王偁 (twelfth century). Songshi ziliao cuibian ed. Taipei: Wenhai, 1967.

DGCL   *Daguan chalun* 大觀茶論, 1 *juan*, by Song Huizong 宋徽宗. *Shuofu* ed.

DJDFL   *Da Jin diaofa lu* 大金弔伐錄, 4 *juan*, anon. Beijing: Zhonghua shuju, 2001.

DJGZ   *Da Jin guozhi* 大金國志, 40 *juan*, by Yuwen Maozhao 宇文懋昭. Beijing: Zhonghua shuju, 1986.

DJMHL   *Dongjing menghua lu* 東京夢華錄, 10 *juan* (1147), attributed to Meng Yuanlao 孟元老 (fl. 1126–1147). In *Dongjing menghua lu wai si zhong* 東京夢華錄外四種. Shanghai: Zhonghua shuju, 1962.

DJMHLJZ   *Dongjing menghua lu jianzhu* 東京夢華錄箋注, 10 *juan* (1147), attributed to Meng Yuanlao 孟元老 (fl. 1126–1147), ed. Yi Yongwen 伊永文 (b. 1950). Beijing: Zhonghua shuju, 2006.

DJMHLZ   *Dongjing menghua lu zhu* 東京夢華錄注, 10 *juan* (1147), attributed to Meng Yuanlao 孟元老 (fl. 1126–1147), ed. Deng Zhicheng 鄧之誠 (1887–1960). Beijing: Commercial Press, 1959.

DJTS   *Dijian tushuo* 帝鑒圖説, 2 *juan*, by Zhang Jucheng 張居正 (1525–1582). In *Siku quanshu cunmu congshu*. Jinan: Qi Lu shushe chubanshe, 1997.

DX   *Di xue* 帝學, 8 *juan*, by Fan Zuyu 范祖禹 (1041–1098). SKQS ed.

DXJ   *Daoxiang ji* 道鄉集, 40 *juan*, by Zou Hao 鄒浩 (1060–1111). SKQS ed.

DXZZ   *Duxing zazhi* 獨醒雜志, 10 *juan*, by Zeng Minxing 曾敏行 (1118–1175). SongYuan biji congshu ed. Shanghai: Shanghai guji chubanshe, 1986.

DYJ   *Danyang ji* 丹陽集, 24 *juan*, by Ge Shengzhong 葛勝仲 (1072–1144). SKQS ed.

DZ   *Daozang* 道藏 (36 vols.) Beijing: Wenwu chubanshe, 1988.

FXJ   *Fuxi ji* 浮溪集, 32 *juan*, by Wang Zao 汪藻 (1079–1154). CSJC ed.

FXWC   *Fuxi wencui* 浮溪文粹, 15 *juan*, by Wang Zao 汪藻 (1079–1154). SKQS ed.

FZLDTZ   *Fozu lidai tongzai* 佛祖歷代通載, 22 *juan*, by Nianchang 念常 (b. 1282). CBETA ed.

FZTJ   *Fozu tongji* 佛祖統紀, 54 *juan*, by Zhipan 志磐. CBETA ed.

GCSB   *Guangchuan shuba* 廣川書跋, 10 *juan*, by Dong You 董逌. SKQS ed.

GEJ   *Guier ji* 貴耳集, 3 *juan*, by Zhang Duanyi 張端義 (1179–1250). CSJC ed.

GJTSJC   *Gujin tushu jicheng* 古今圖書集成, edited by Chen Menglei 陳夢雷 (1726). Shanghai: Zhonghua shuju, 1934 reprint.

GJZ   *Guiji zhi (Jiatai)* 會稽志 嘉泰), 20 *juan* (1201), by Shi Su 施宿 (d. 1213). SYDFCS ed.

GSJ   *Guishan ji* 龜山集, 42 *juan*, by Yang Shi 楊時 (1053–1135). SKQS ed.

GSSX   *Gaoshang shenxiao yuqing zhenwang zishu dafa* 高上神霄玉清真王紫書大法, 12 *juan* (TC 1219; DZ 28:557–68).

GSSXZS   *Gaoshang Shenxiao zongshi shoujing shi* 高上神霄宗師受經式, 1 *juan* (TC 1282; DZ 32:637–39).

GXZZ   *Guixin zazhi* 癸辛雜識, by Zhou Mi 周密 (1232–1308). Beijing: Zhonghua shuju, 1988.

HS   *Han shu* 漢書, 100 *juan*, by Ban Gu 班固 (32–92 CE). Beijing: Zhonghua shuju, 1962.

HCBNBY   *Huangchao biannian gangmu beiyao* 皇朝編年綱目備要, 30 *juan*, by Chen Jun 陳均 (ca. 1165–1236+). Beijing: Zhonghua shuju, 2006.

HHS   *Hou Han shu* 後漢書, 120 *juan*, by Fan Ye 范曄 (398–445 CE). Beijing: Zhonghua shuju, 1971.

HJ   *Huaji* 畫繼, 10 *juan*, by Deng Chun 鄧椿 (fl. 1127–1167), edited by Pan Yungao 潘運告. In *Tuhua jianwen zhi, Huaji* 圖畫見聞志, 畫繼, Changsha: Hunan meishu chubanshe, 2000.

HJian   *Hua jian* 畫鑑, 1 *juan*, by Tang Hou 湯垕 (fl. 1322). In *Huapin congshu*, edited by Yu Anlan 于安瀾. Shanghai: Renmin meishu chubanshe, 1982.

HLGY   *Hualu guangyi* 畫錄廣遺, by Zhang Cheng 張澂 (1139). In *Meishu congshu*, 4th collection. Shanghai: Shenzhou Guoguangshe, 1928.

HLSZ   *Helinsi zhi* 鶴林寺志, 1 *juan*, by Mingxian 明賢. Late Ming ed., microfilm of Rare Books in the National Library Peiping, roll 501.

HLYL   *Helin yulu* 鶴林玉露, 16 *juan*, by Luo Dajing 羅大經 (?–1248+). Beijing: Zhonghua shuju, 1983.

HQJSJ   *Hongqing jushi ji* 鴻慶居士集, 42 *juan*, by Sun Di 孫覿 (1081–1169). SKQS ed.

HQL   *Hou qing lu* 侯鯖錄, 8 *juan*, by Zhao Lingzhi 趙令畤 (1064–1134). Beijing: Zhonghua shuju, 2002.

HRZYT   *Haoran zhai yetan* 浩然齋野談, 3 *juan*, by Zhou Mi 周密 (1232–1308). SKQS ed.

HSSCGY   *Huang Song shichao gangyao* 皇宋十朝綱要, 25 *juan*, by Li Zhi 李埴 (1161–1238). Songshi ziliao cuibian ed. Taipei: Wenhai chuban she, 1980.

HSSL   *HuangSong shulu* 皇宋書錄, by Dong Shi 董史 (thirteenth century) (1242). Zhibuzuzhai congshu ed.

HSWY   *Huishi weiyan* 繪事微言, 2 *juan*, by Tang Zhiqi 唐志契 (1579–1651). SKQS ed.

HYSJ   *Hunyuan shengji* 混元聖紀, 9 *juan*, by Xie Shouhao 謝守灝 (TC 770; DZ 17:779–883).

HZL   *Huizhu lu* 揮麈錄, 20 *juan*, by Wang Mingqing 王明清 (1127–1214+). Beijing: Zhonghua shuju, 1961.

JKCXL   *Jingkang chuanxin lu* 靖康傳信錄, 3 *juan*, by Li Gang 李綱 (1083–1140). CSJC ed.

JKCYQY   *Jingkang chaoye qianyan* 靖康朝野僉言, 1 *juan*, anon. CSJC ed.

JKJW   *Jingkang jiwen* 靖康紀聞, 1 *juan*, by Ding Teqi 丁特起 (d. 1135+). CSJC ed.

JKYL   *Jingkang yaolu* 靖康要錄, 16 *juan*, anon. CSJC ed.

JKZ   *Jiankang zhi (Jingding)* 建康志 (景定), 50 juan (1261). Ed. Zhou Yinghe 周應合 (1213–1280). SYDFZCS ed.

JLB   *Ji le bian* 雞肋編, 3 *juan*, by Zhuang Chuo 莊綽 (1078–1143+). Beijing: Zhonghua shuju, 1983.

JLZSDZYY   *Jinlu zhai sandong zanyong yi* 金籙齋三洞讚詠儀, edited by Zhang Shangying 張商英 (1043–1121) (TC 310; DZ 5:764–71).

JLZTJY   *Jinlu zhai toujian yi* 金籙齋投簡儀, edited by Zhang Shangying 張商英 (TC 498; DZ 9:131–33).

JS   *Jinshi* 金史, 135 *juan*, edited by Tuo Tuo 脫脫 (1313–1355) et al. Beijing: Zhonghua shuju, 1975.

JSCB   *Jinshi cuibian* 金石萃編, 160 *juan*, by Wang Chang 王昶 (1725–1806). SKSLXB ed. Taipei: Xinwenfeng, 1977 reprint.

JSJSBM   *Jinshi jishi benmo* 金史紀事本末, 52 *juan*, by Li Youtang 李有棠. Beijing: Zhonghua shuju, 1980.

JSJW   *Jiashi jiuwen* 家世舊聞, 2 *juan*, by Lu You 陸游 (1125–1210). Beijing: Zhonghua shuju, 1998.

JZDSZ   *Junzhai dushu zhi* 郡齋讀書志, 4 *juan*, by Chao Gongwu 晁公武 (d. 1171). Taipei: Commercial Press reprint, 1978.

KCZ   *Kuiche zhi* 暌車志, 5 *juan*, by Guo Tuan 郭彖 (ca. 1165). CSJC ed. .

KFFZ   *Kaifeng fuzhuang* 開封府狀, 1 *juan*, anon. In *Jingkang baishi jianzheng* 靖康稗史箋証, compiled by Cui An 確庵 and Nai An 耐庵, edited by Cui Wenyin 崔文印. Beijing: Zhonghua shuju, 1988.

KYL   *Da Tang Kaiyuan li* 大唐開元禮, 150 *juan*, edited by Xiao Song 蕭嵩 (eighth century) et al. SKQS ed.

LBFT *Lingbao wuliang duren shangpin miaojing futu* 靈寶無量度人上品妙經符圖, 3 *juan* (TC 147, DZ 3:62–87).

LBWL *Lingbao wuliang duren shangpin miaojing* 靈寶無量度人上品妙經, 61 *juan* (TC 1; DZ 1:1–416).

LDMCZY *Lidai mingchen zouyi* 歷代名臣奏議, 350 *juan*, by Yang Shiqi 楊士奇 (1365–1444). SKQS ed.

LFWQJ *Lu Fangweng quanji* 陸放翁全集, 186 *juan*, by Lu You 陸游 (1125–1210). Hong Kong: Guangzhi shuju punctuated ed., n.d.

LiS *Li shu* 禮書, 150 *juan*, by Chen Xiangdao 陳祥道 (1053–1093). SKQS ed.

LJ *Li ji* 禮記, 63 *juan*, Shisan jing zhushu ed. Taipei: Yiwen yinshu guan, 1981.

LQGZ *Linquan gaozhi* 林泉高致, by Guo Si 郭思 (ca. 1050–1130+). In *Songren hualun* 宋人畫論, ed. Pan Yungao 潘運告. Changsha: Hunan meishu chubanshe, 2000.

LS *Liao shi* 遼史, 116 *juan*, edited by Tuo Tuo 脫脫 (1313–1355) et al. Beijing: Zhonghua shuju, 1974.

LSZJ *Lüshi zaji* 呂氏雜記, 2 *juan*, by Lü Xizhe 呂希哲 (1036–1114). Quan Song biji ed. Zhengzhou: Daxiang chubanshe, 2003.

LSZX *Lishi zhenxian tidao tongjian* 歷世真仙體道通鑑, 53 *juan*, by Zhao Daoyi 趙道一 (preface 1294) (TC 296; DZ 5:99–413).

LXABJ *Laoxuean biji* 老學庵筆記, 10 *juan*, by Lu You 陸游 (1125–1210). Beijing: Zhonghua shuju, 1979.

LXJ *Liangxi ji* 梁溪集, 180 *juan*, by Li Gang 李綱 (1083–1140). SKQS ed.

LZMXL *Liang Zhe mingxian lu* 兩浙名賢錄, 54+8 *juan*, by Xu Xiangmei 徐象梅 (seventeenth century). XXSKQS ed.

MSZ *Maoshan zhi* 茅山志, 33 *juan*, edited by Liu Dabin 劉大彬 (fl. 1317–1328) (TC 304; DZ 5:548–702).

MTDDL *Mingtang dadao lu* 明堂大道錄, 8 *juan*, by Hui Dong 惠棟 (1697–1758). CSJC ed.

MXBT *Mengxi bitan jiaozheng* 夢溪筆談校證, 26 *juan*, by Shen Gua 沈括 (1031?–1095?), edited by Hu Daojing 胡道靜. Shanghai: Shanghai chuban gongsi, 1956.

MXSZYXLG *Mingxian shizu yanxing leigao* 名賢氏族言行類稿, 61 *juan*, by Zhang Ding 章定 (thirteenth century). SKQS ed.

MZLX *Minzhong lixue yuanyuan kao* 閩中理學淵源考, 92 *juan*, by Li Qingfu 李清馥 (eighteenth century). SKQS ed.

MZML *Mozhuang manlu* 墨莊漫錄, 10 *juan*, by Zhang Bangji 張邦基 (Song). Beijing: Zhonghua shuju, 2002.

NGZML *Nenggai zhai manlu* 能改齋漫錄, 18 *juan* (1157), by Wu Zeng 吳曾 (d. 1170+). Taipei: Muduo, 1982.

NSGGL *NanSong guange lu, xulu* 南宋館閣錄, 續錄, both 10 *juan*, by Chen Kui 陳騤 (1128–1205) and anon. Beijing: Zhonghua shuju, 1998.

NZLH *Nanzheng luhui* 南征錄彙, by Li Tianmin 李天民 (Jin). In *Jingkang baishi jianzheng* 靖康稗史箋証, compiled by Cui An 碻庵 and Nai An 耐庵, edited by Cui Wenyin 崔文印. Beijing: Zhonghua shuju, 1988.

OYXQJ *Ouyang Xiu quanji* 歐陽修全集, 157 *juan*, by Ouyang Xiu 歐陽修 (1007–1072). Taipei: Shjie shuju, 1961.

PLZ *Piling zhi (Xianchun)* 毘陵志 (咸淳), ed. Shi Nengzhi 史能之 (fl. 1241–1268). SYDFZCS ed.

PZKT *Pingzhou ketan* 萍州可談, 3 *juan*, by Zhu Yu 朱彧 (Song). CSJC ed.

QBBZ   *Qingbo biezhi* 清波別志, 3 *juan*, by Zhou Hui 周輝 (1127–1198+). CSJC ed.

QBZZ   *Qingbo zazhi* 清波雜志, 12 *juan*, by Zhou Hui 周輝 (1127–1198+). Beijing: Zhonghua shuju, 1994.

QCCS   Qiangcun congshu 彊村叢書, by Zhu Zumou 朱祖謀 (1857–1931). Guian Zhushi ed., 1922.

QDYY   *Qidong yeyu* 齊東野語, 20 *juan*, by Zhou Mi 周密 (1232–1308). Beijing: Zhonghua shuju, 1983.

QFJ   *Qufu ji* 曲阜集, 4 *juan*, by Zeng Zhao 曾肇 (1047–1107). SKQS ed.

QGYY   *Qinggong yiyu* 青宮譯語, by Wang Chengdi 王成棣 (Jin). In *Jingkang baishi jianzheng* 靖康稗史箋証, compiled by Cui An 確庵 and Nai An 耐庵, edited by Cui Wenyin 崔文印. Beijing: Zhonghua shuju, 1988.

QSC   *Quan Song ci* 全宋詞, edited by Tang Guizhang 唐圭璋. Beijing: Zhonghua shu ju, 1965.

QSKS   *Qunshu kaosuo* 群書考索, 4 parts, total 212 *juan*, by Zhang Ruyu 章如愚 (*jinshi* 1196). SKQS ed.

QSS   *Quan Song shi* 全宋詩, edited by Fu Xuancong 傅璇琮 (b. 1933) et al., Beijing: Beijing Daxue chubanshe, 1991–?

QSW   *Quan Song wen* 全宋文, edited by Zeng Zaozhuang 曾棗莊 (b. 1937) et al. Shanghai: Shanghai Cishu chubanshe, 2006.

QWJW   *Quwei jiuwen* 曲洧舊聞, 10 *juan*, by Zhu Bian 朱弁 (?–1138). Zhonghua shuju, 2002.

QXKG   *Qingxi kougui* 青溪寇軌, 1 *juan*, by Fang Shao 方勺 (1066–1141+), included in the same author's *Bozhai bian* 泊宅編. Beijing: Zhonghua shuju, 1983.

RZSB   *Rongzhai suibi* 容齋隨筆, 74 *juan*, by Hung Mai 洪邁 (1123–1202). Shanghai: Shanghai guji chubanshe, 1978.

SCBM   *Sanchao beimeng huibian* 三朝北盟會編, 250 *juan*, by Xu Mengxin 徐夢莘. Taipei: Dahua shuju reprint of the Shixue yanjiushe punctuated ed., 1939.

SCSS   *Songchao shishi* 宋朝事實, 20 *juan*, by Li You 李攸. CSJC ed.

SCZCZY   *Songchao zhuchen zouyi* 宋朝諸臣奏議, 150 *juan*, edited by Zhao Ruyu 趙汝愚 (1140–1196). Shanghai: Shanghai guji chubanshe, 1999.

SDCNB   *Song dachen nianbiao* 宋大臣年表, 2 *juian*, by Wan Sitong 萬斯同 (1638–1702). In *Ershiwu shi bu bian* 二十五史補編. Taipei: Kaiming shuju, 1974.

SDJK   *Song Dongjing kao* 宋東京考, by Zhou Cheng 周城. Beijing: Zhonghua shuju, 1988.

SDZLJ   *Song dazhaoling ji* 宋大詔令集, 196 *juan*. Beijing: Zhonghua shuju, 1962.

SFJ   *Song fuji* 宋俘記, by Kegong 可恭 (Jin). In *Jingkang baishi jianzheng* 靖康稗史箋, compiled by Cui An 確庵 and Nai An 耐庵, edited by Cui Wenyin 崔文印. Beijing: Zhonghua shuju, 1988.

SHY   *Song huiyao jigao* 宋會要輯稿, 460 *juan*, edited by Xu Song 徐松 (1781–1848) et al. Beijing: Zhonghua shuju, 1957.

SHYBB   *Song huiyao jigao bubian* 宋會要輯稿補編, edited by Xu Song 徐松 (1781–1848). Beijing: Xinhua, 1988.

SHZYJ   *Song Huizong yujie daode zhenjing* 宋徽宗御解道德真經, 4 *juan*, by Song Huizong 宋徽宗 (1082–1135) (TC 680; DZ 11:489–512).

SJ   *Shiji* 史記, 130 *juan*, by Sima Qian 司馬遷 (145?–86? bce). Beijing: Zhonghua shuju, 1962.

SL   *Song lun* 宋論, 15 *juan*, by Wang Fuzhi 王夫之 (1619–1692). Guoxue jiben congshu ed.

SLT   *Sanli tu* 三禮圖, 20 *juan*, by Nie Chongyi 聶崇義 (tenth century). Shanghai: Tongwen shuju, ca. 1910.

SLTJZ   *Sanli tu jizhu* 三禮圖集注, 20 *juan*, by Nie Chongyi 聶崇義 (tenth century). SKQS ed.

SLYY   *Shilin yanyu* 石林燕語, 10 *juan*, by Ye Mengde 葉夢得 (1077–1148). Beijing: Zhonghua shuju, 1984.

SMCYXL   *Song mingchen yanxing lu* 宋名臣言行錄, 24 *juan*, by Zhu Xi 朱熹 (1130–1200) and Li Youwu 李幼武 (fl. 1261). SKQS ed.

SMZYY   *Siming zhi (Yanyou)* 四明志 (延祐), edited by Yuan Jue 袁桷 (1266–1327) SYDFZCS ed. ed. Taipei: Guotai wenhua shiye, 1980.

SQDDZJ   *Shangqing dadong zhenjing* 上清大洞真經, 6 *juan* (TC 6; DZ 1:513–55).

SS   *Song shi* 宋史, 496 *juan*, edited by Tuo Tuo 脫脫 (1313–1355) et al. Beijing: Zhonghua shuju, 1977.

SShu   *Song shu* 宋書, 100 *juan*, by Shen Yue 沈約 (441–513). Beijing: Zhonghua shuju, 1974.

SSJS   *Songshi jishi* 宋詩紀事, 100 *juan*, by Li E 厲鶚 (1692–1752). SKQS ed.

SSJSBM   *Songshi jishi benmo* 宋史紀事本末, 40 *juan*, by Chen Bangzhan 陳邦瞻 (d. 1623). Beijing: Zhonghua shuju, 1977.

SSLF   *Su Shen liangfang* 蘇沈良方, 10 *juan*, by Su Shi 蘇軾 (1036–1101) and Shen Gua 沈括 (1031?–1095?). CSJC ed.

SSQW   *Songshi quanwen* 宋史全文, 36 *juan*, anon., edited by Li Zhiliang 李之亮. Harbin: Heilongjiang renmin chubanshe, 2005.

SSWJ   *Su Shi wenji* 蘇軾文集, 73 *juan*, by Su Shi 蘇軾 (1036–1101). Beijing: Zhonghua shuju, 1986.

SSWJHL   *Shaoshi wenjian hou lu* 邵氏聞見後錄, by Shao Bowen 邵伯溫 (1056–1134). Beijing: Zhonghua shuju, 1983.

SSWJL   *Shaoshi wenjian lu* 邵氏聞見錄, 20 *juan*, by Shao Bowen 邵伯溫 (1056–1134). Beijing: Zhonghua shuju, 1983.

SSZ   *Sanshan zhi* 三山志, 42 *juan*, by Liang Kejia 梁克家 (1128–1187). SYDFZCS ed.

STD   *San tendai godaisan ki* 参天台五臺山記, by Jōjin 成尋 (1011–1081). Tokyo: Tōyō bunko, 1937.

SXJSZ   *Shaanxi jinshi zhi* 陝西金石志, 32 *juan*, by Wu Shushan 武樹善. SKSLXB ed. Taipei: Xinwenfeng, 1977.

SYXA   *Song Yuan xuean* 宋元學案, 100 *juan* by Huang Zongxi 黃宗羲 (1610–1695) et al. Shanghai: Commercial Press, 1928.

SYY   *Shenyin yu* 呻吟語, anon. In *Jingkang baishi jianzheng* 靖康稗史箋証, compiled by Cui An 碻庵 and Nai An 耐庵, edited by Cui Wenyin 崔文印. Beijing: Zhonghua shuju, 1988.

SZFBNL   *Song zaifu biannian lu jiaobu* 宋宰輔編年錄校補, 20 *juan*, by Xu Ziming 徐自明 (d. 1220+), edited by Wang Ruilai 王瑞來. Beijing, Zhonghua shuju, 1986.

SZJSZ   *Shanzuo jinshizhi* 山左金石志, 24 *juan*, by Bi Yuan 畢沅. SKSLXB ed. Taipei: Xinwenfeng 1977 reprint.

THJWZ   *Tuhua jianwenzhi* 圖畫見聞誌, by Guo Ruoxu 郭若虛 (fl. 1070–1075). In *Tuhua jianwenzhi*, *Huaji* 圖畫見聞誌, 畫繼, edited by Pan Yungao 潘運告 and Mi Tianshui 米田水. Changsha: Hunan meishu chubanshe, 2000.

TLD   *Tang liu dian* 唐六典, 30 *juan* (739), by Li Linfu 李林甫 (683–752) et al., Beijing: Zhonghua shuju, 1992.

TPZJTL   *Taiping zhiji tonglei* 太平治績統類, 30 *juan*, by Peng Baichuan 彭百川 (Song). SKQS ed.

TS   *Tingshi* 庭史, 15 *juan*, by Yue Ke 岳珂 (1183–?). Beijing: Zhonghua shuju, 1983.

TSLBWFX   *Taishang lingbao wufu xu* 太上靈寶五符序, 3 *juan*, anon. (TC 388; DZ 6:315–42).

TSLBZCP   *Taishang lingbao zhicao pin* 太上靈寶芝草品 (TC 1406; DZ 34:316–36).

TWSCT   *Tiewei shan cong tan* 鐵圍山叢談, 6 *juan*, by Cai Tao 蔡絛 (?–1147+). Beijing: Zhonghua shuju, 1983.

TXL   *Touxia lu* 投轄錄, by Wang Mingqing 王明清. SKQS ed.

WCZL   *Wenchang zalu* 文昌雜錄, 6 *juan*, by Pang Yuanying 龐元英 (fl. 1078–1082). Quan Song biji ed. Zhengzhou: Daxia chubanshe, 2006.

WXTK   *Wenxian tongkao* 文獻通考, 348 *juan*, by Ma Duanlin 馬端臨 (ca. 1250–1325). Taipei: Xinxing shuju reprint of Shitong ed., 1963.

WYXP   *Wengyou xianping* 甕牖閒評, 8 *juan*, by Yuan Wen 袁文 (1119–1190). CSJC ed.

WZRY   *Wengzhong renyu* 甕中人語, 1 *juan*, anon. (Song). In *Jingkang baishi jianzheng* 靖康稗史箋証, compiled by Cui An 確庵 and Nai An 耐庵, edited by Cui Wenyin 崔文印. Beijing: Zhonghua shuju, 1988.

XAZ   *Xin'an zhi* 新安志, 10 *juan* (1175), by Luo Yuan 羅願 (1136–1184). SYDFCS ed.

XHFSGLTJ   *Xuanhe fengshi Gaoli tu jing* 宣和奉使高麗圖經, by Xu Jing 徐競 (1091–1153). Quan Song biji edition. Zhengzhou: Daxiang chubanshe, 2008.

XHHP   *Xuanhe huapu* 宣和畫譜, 20 *juan*, edited by Yu Jianhua 俞劍華. Beijing: Renmin meishu, 1964.

XHSP   *Xuanhe shupu* 宣和書譜, 20 *juan*. Shanghai: Shanghai shuju, 1984.

XHYS   *Da Song Xuanhe yishi* 大宋宣和遺事, anon. Shanghai: Commercial Press, 1937.

XNYL   *Jianyan yilai xinian yaolu* 建炎以來繫年要錄, 200 *juan*, by Li Xinchuan 李心傳 (1166–1243). Beijing: Zhonghua shuju, 1956.

XTJ   *Xitai ji* 西臺集, 20 *juan*, by Bi Zhongyou 畢仲游 (1045–1119). CSJC ed.

XZZTJ   *Xu zizhi tongjian* 續資治通鑑, 220 *juan*, by Bi Yuan 畢沅 (1730–1797) et al. Beijing: Zhonghua shuju, 1957.

YFL   *Yan fan lu* 演繁露, 16 *juan*, by Cheng Dachang 程大昌 (1123–1195). SKQS ed.

YH   *Yuhai* 玉海, 204 *juan*, by Wang Yinglin 王應麟 (1223–1296). Shanghai: Shanghai shudian, 1987.

YJ   *Yu jian* 寓簡, 10 *juan*, by Shen Zuozhe 沈作喆. SKQS ed.

YJZ   *Yijian zhi* 夷堅志, 207 *juan*, by Hong Mai 洪邁 (1123–1202). Beijing: Zhonghua shuju, 1981.

YLMC   *Yunlu manchao* 雲麓漫鈔, 15 *juan*, by Zhao Yanwei 趙彥衛 (?–1206+). Beijing: Zhonghua shuju, 1996.

YSHB   *Songren yishi huibian* 宋人軼事彙編, 20 *juan*, edited by Ding Chuanjing 丁傳靖. Taipei: Commercial Press, 1935.

YXCS   *Yingxue congshuo* 螢雪叢說, 2 *juan*, by Yu Cheng 俞成 (1195–1200). CSJC ed.

YYDRZ   *Yuanyou dangren zhuan* 元祐黨人傳, 10 *juan*, by Lu Xinyuan 陸心源 (1834–1894). 1889 ed.

YYYML   *Yanyi yimou lu* 燕翼詒謀錄, 5 *juan*, by Wang Yong 王栐 (?–1227+). Beijing: Zhonghua shuju, 1981.

YZFS *Li Mingzhong Yingzao fashi* 李明仲營造法式, 34 *juan*, by Li Jie 李誡. Shanghai: Commercial Press, 1929.

YZFSZS *"Yingzao fashi" zhushi*《營造法式》註釋, edited by Liang Sicheng 梁思成. Beijing: Zhongguo jianzhu gongye chubanshe, 1983. 北京: 中國建築工業出版社, 1983.

ZGYL *Zeng Gong yilu* 曾公遺錄, 3 *juan*, by Zeng Bu 曾布 (1035–1107). Quan Song biji edition. Zhengzhou: Daxiang chubanshe, 2003.

ZHDZ *Zhonghua da Daozang* 中華大道藏. Beijing: Huaxia chubanshe, 2004.

ZHJ *Zhonghui ji* 忠惠集, 10 *juan*, by Zhai Ruwen 翟汝文 (1076–1141). SKQS ed.

ZHWLXY *Zhenghe wuli xinyi* 政和五禮新儀, 220 *juan*, edited by Zheng Juzhong 鄭居中 (1059–1123) et al. SKQS ed.

ZL *Zhou li* 周禮, 42 *juan*, Shisanjing zhushu ed.

ZS *Zhou shi* 籀史, 1 *juan*, by Zhai Qinian 翟耆年 (twelfth century). Shoushan ge congshu ed.

ZSKS *Zhangshi keshu* 張氏可書, 1 *juan*, anon. SKQS ed.

ZZYL *Zhu Zi yulei* 朱子語類, 140 *juan* (1270), by Zhu Xi 朱熹 (1130–1200). Beijing: Zhonghua shuju, 1986.

Secondary Sources

Acker, William, trans. 1954. *Some T'ang and Pre-T'ang Texts on Painting.* 2 vols. Leiden: E. J. Brill.

Adamson, John, ed. 1999. *The Princely Courts of Europe, 1500–1750.* London: Seven Dials.

Allsen, Thomas T. 2006. *The Royal Hunt in Eurasian History.* Philadelphia: University of Pennsylvania Press.

Anderson, James A. 2008. "Treacherous Factions: Shifting Frontier Alliances in the Breakdown of Sino-Vietnamese Relations on the Eve of the 1075 Border War." In *Battlefronts Real and Imagined: War, Border, and Identity in the Chinese Middle Period,* edited by Donald J. Wyatt, pp. 191–226. New York: Palgrave Macmillan.

Ang, Melvin Thlick. 1983. "Sung-Liao Diplomacy in Eleventh-and-Twelfth-Century China: A Study of the Social and Political Determinants of Foreign Policy." PhD diss., University of Pennsylvania.

Baldrian-Hussein, Farzeen. 1996–1997. "Alchemy and Self-Cultivation in Literary Circles of the Northern Song Dynasty—Su Shi (1037–1101) and His Techniques of Survival." *Cahiers D'Extreme Asie* 9: 15–53.

Bao Weimin 包偉民. 1989. "Songdai de chaoting qianwu ji qi zhucun de zhu ku wu" 宋代的朝廷錢物及其貯存的諸庫務. *Hangzhou daxue xuebao* 19, no. 4: 135–43.

Barfield, Thomas J. 1989. *The Perilous Frontier: Nomadic Empires and China, 221 BC to AD 1757.* Cambridge, MA: Blackwell.

Barnard, Noel. 1973. "Records of Discoveries of Bronze Bessels in Literary Sources—and Some Pertinent Remarks on Aspects of Chinese Historiography." *Journal of the Institute of Chinese Studies of the Chinese University of Hong Kong* 6, no. 2: 455–544.

Barnhart, Richard. 1972. "Li T'ang (c. 1050–c. 1130) and the Kōtō-in Landscapes." *The Burlington Magazine.* EXIV, no. 830: 305–14.

———. 1983. "Wang Shen and Late Northern Sung Landscape Painting." In *International Symposium on Art Historical Studies 2: Ajia ni okeru sansui hyōmen ni tsuite.* Kyoto: Kyoto National Museum and Taniguchi Foundation.

———. 1997. "The Five Dynasties and the Song Period." In *Three Thousand Years of Chinese Painting*, edited by Yang Xin et al., pp. 87–137. New Haven: Yale University Press.

———. 1998. "Three Song Landscape Paintings." *Orientations* 29, no. 2: 54–58.

Barrett, Timothy Hugh. 1996. *Taoism under the T'ang: Religion and Empire during the Golden Age of Chinese History*. London: Wellsweep.

Beck, B. J. Mansvelt. 1990. *The Treatises of Later Han: Their Author, Sources, Contents and Place in Chinese Historiography*. Leiden: E. J. Brill.

Benn, Charles David. 1987. "Religious Aspects of Emperor Hsüan-tsung's Taoist Ideology." In *Buddhist and Taoist Practice in Medieval Chinese Society*, edited by David W. Chappell, pp. 127–45. Honolulu: University of Hawai'i Press.

Bickford, Maggie. 2002–2003. "Emperor Huizong and the Aesthetic of Agency." *Archives of Asian Art* 53: 71–104.

———. 2006. "Huizong's Paintings: Art and the Art of Emperorship." In *Emperor Huizong and Late Northern Song China: The Politics of Culture and the Culture of Politics*, edited by Patricia Buckley Ebrey and Maggie Bickford, pp. 453–513. Cambridge, MA: Harvard Asia Center.

Bielenstein, Hans. 1950. "An Interpretation of the Portents in the Ts'ien Han Shu." *Bulletin of the Museum of Far Eastern Antiquities* 22: 127–43.

———. 1984. "Han Portents and Prognosticatis." *Bulletin of the Museum of Far Eastern Antiquities* 56: 97–112.

Birsch, Nicole, ed. 2008. *Religion and Power: Divine Kingship in the Ancient World and Beyond*. Chicago: The Oriental Institute of the University of Chicago.

Blofeld, John. 1985. *The Chinese Art of Tea*. Boston: Shambhala.

Bo Songnian 薄松年. 1998. *Zhao Ji* 趙佶. Beijing: Wenwu.

Bokenkamp, Stephen R. 1997. *Early Daoist Scriptures*. Berkeley: University of California Press.

Bol, Peter K. 2001. "Whither the Emperor? Emperor Huizong, the New Policies, and the Tang-Song Transition." *Journal of Song-Yuan Studies* 31: 103–34.

———. 2006. "Emperors Can Claim Antiquity Too—Emperorship and Autocracy under the New Policies." In *Emperor Huizong and Late Northern Song China: The Politics of Culture and the Culture of Politics*, edited by Patricia Buckley Ebrey and Maggie Bickford, pp. 173–205. Cambridge, MA: Harvard Asia Center.

Boltz, Judith M. 1983. "Opening the Gates of Purgatory: A Twelfth-Century Taoist Mediation Technique for the Salvation of Lost Souls." In *Tantric and Taoist Studies in Honour of R. A. Stein*, vol. 2., edited by Michel Strickmann, pp. 487–511. Brussels: Institut Belge des Hautes Études Chinoises.

———. 1987. *A Survey of Taoist Literature, Tenth through Seventeenth Centuries*. Berkeley: Institute of East Asian Studies.

———. 1993. "Not by the Seal of Office Alone: New Weapons in Battles with the Supernatural." In *Religion and Society in T'ang and Sung China*, edited by Patricia Buckley Ebrey and Peter N. Gregory, pp. 241–305. Honolulu: University of Hawai'i Press.

Borgen, Robert. 1987. "*San Tendai Godai San ki* as a Source for the Study of Sung History." *Bulletin of Sung Yuan Studies* 19: 1–16.

———. 2007. "Jōjin's Travels from Center to Center (with Some Periphery in Between)." In *Heian Japan: Centers and Peripheries*, edited by Mikael S Adolphson, Edward Kamens, and Stacie Matsumoto, pp. 384–413. Honolulu: University of Hawai'i Press.

Bossler, Beverly. 2008. "Gender and Entertainment at the Song Court. In *Servants of the Dynasty: Palace Women in World History*, edited by Anne Walthall, pp. 261–279. Berkeley: University of California Press.

———. 2013. *Courtesans, Concubines, and the Cult of Female Fidelity*. Cambridge, MA: Harvard Asia Center.

Burke, Peter. 1992. *The Fabrication of Louis XIV*. New Haven: Yale University Press.

Bush, Susan. 1971. *The Chinese Literati on Painting: Su Shih (1037–1101) to Tung Ch'i-ch'ang (1555–1636)*. Cambridge, MA: Harvard University Press.

Bush, Susan, and Hsih-yen Shih. 1985. *Early Chinese Texts on Painting*. Cambridge, MA: Harvard University Press.

Cahill, James. 1980. *An Index to Early Chinese Paintings*. Berkeley: University of California Press.

———. 1994. *The Painter's Practice: How Artists Lived and Worked in Traditional China*. New York: Columbia University Press.

———. 1996a. "The Imperial Painting Academy." In *Possessing the Past: Treasures from the National Palace Museum, Taipei*, edited by Wen C. Fong and James C. Y. Watt, pp. 159–99. New York: Metropolitan Museum of Art.

———. 1996b. *The Lyric Journey: Poetic Painting in China and Japan*. Cambridge, MA: Harvard University Press.

Cahill, Suzanne. 1980. "Taoism at the Sung Court: The Heavenly Text Affair of 1008." *Bulletin of Sung and Yüan Studies* 16: 23–44.

Campany, Robert Ford. 2002. *To Live as Long as Heaven and Earth: A Translation and Study of Ge Hong's* Traditions of Divine Transcendents. Berkeley: University of California Press.

Capitanio, Joshua. 2008. "Dragon Kings and Thunder Gods: Rainmaking, Magic, and Ritual in Medieval Chinese Religion." PhD diss., University of Pennsylvania.

Chaffee, John W. 1985. *The Thorny Gates of Learning in Sung China: A Social History of Examinations*. Cambridge, UK: Cambridge University Press.

———. 1990–1992. "Chao Ju-yu, Spurious Learning, and Southern Sung Political Culture." *Journal of Sung-Yüan Studies* 22: 23–61.

———. 1991. "The Marriage of Clanswomen in the Sung Imperial Clan." In *Marriage and Inequality in Chinese Society*, edited by Rubie S. Watson and Patricia Buckley Ebrey, pp. 133–169 Berkeley: University of California Press.

———. 1999. *Branches of Heaven: A History of the Imperial Clan of Sung China*. Cambridge, MA: Harvard University Asia Center.

———. 2006. "Huizong, Cai Jing, and the Politics of Reform." In *Emperor Huizong and Late Northern Song China: The Politics of Culture and the Culture of Politics*, edited by Patricia Buckley Ebrey and Maggie Bickford, pp. 31–77. Cambridge, MA: Harvard Asia Center.

Chai Degeng 柴德賡. 1941. "Song huanguan canyu junshi kao" 宋宦官參預軍事考. *Furen xuezhi* 10, nos. 1–2: 187–225.

Chan, Hok-lam. 2011. *Ming Taizu (r. 1368–98) and the Foundation of the Ming Dynasty in China*. Burlington, VT: Ashgate.

Chang Bide 昌彼得 et al. 1977. *Songren zhuanji ziliao suoyin* 宋人傳記資料索引. Revised edition. Taipei: Dingwen shuju.

Chang, K. C. 1983. *Art, Myth, and Ritual: The Path to Political Authority in Ancient China*. Cambridge, MA: Harvard University Press.

Chao, Samuel H. 1979. "The Day Northern Sung Fell," *Zhongyuan xuebao* 8:144–57.

Chao, Shin-yi. 2003. "Daoist Examinations and Daoist Schools during the Northern Song Dynasty." *Journal of Chinese Religions* 31: 1–37.

———. 2006. "Huizong and the Divine Empyrean Palace Temple Network," in *Emperor Huizong and Late Northern Song China: The Politics of Culture and the Culture of Politics*, edited by Patricia Buckley Ebrey and Maggie Bickford, pp. 324–58. Cambridge, MA: Harvard Univeristy Asia Center.

Chen Baozhen 陳葆真 [see also Chen Pao-chen]. 1993. "Song Huizong huihua de meixue tezhi—jianlun qi yuanyuan he yingxiang" 宋徽宗繪畫的美學特質—兼論其淵源和影響. *Wenshizhe xuebao* 40, no. 6: 293–344.

———. 2009. *Li Houzhu he tade shidai* 李后主和他的時代. Beijing: Beijing Daxue chubanshe.

Chen Fangmei 陳芳妹. 2001. "Song guqi wuxue de xingqi yu Song fanggu tongqi" 宋古器物學的興起與宋仿古銅器. *Meishu shi yanjiu jikan* 10:37–160.

Chen Gaohua 陳高華. 1984. *Song Liao Jin huajia shiliao* 宋遼金畫家史料. Beijing: Wenwu.

Chen Guofu 陳國符. 1963. *Daozang yuanliu kao* 道藏源流考. Beijing: Zhongguo shuju.

———. 2004. *Daozang yanjiu lunwen ji* 道藏研究論文集. Shanghai: Shanghai guji chubanshe.

Chen, Jack. 2005. "The Writing of Imperial Poetry in Medieval China." *Harvard Journal of Asiatic Studies* 65, no. 1: 57–98.

———. 2010. *The Poetics of Sovereignty: On Emperor Taizong of the Tang Dynasty.* Cambridge, MA: Harvard University Asia Center.

Ch'en, Kenneth K. S. 1956. "The Sale of Monk Certificates during the Sung Dynasty: A Factor in the Decline of Buddhism in China." *Harvard Theological Review* 49, no. 4: 307–27.

Chen Lesu 陳樂素. 1933. "Song Huizong moufu Yanyun zhi shibai" 宋徽宗謀復燕雲之失敗. *Furen xuezhi* 4, no. 1: 1–47.

———. 1936a. "Sanchao beimeng huibian kao (shang)" 《三朝北盟會編》考（上）. *Shiyusuo jikan* 6, no. 2: 197–279.

———. 1936b. "Sanchao beimeng huibian kao (xia)" 《三朝北盟會編》考（下）. *Shiyusuo jikan* 6, no. 3: 281–341.

———. 1983. "Guilin shike 'Yuanyou dangji'" 桂林石刻《元祐黨籍》. *Xueshu yanjiu* 1983, no. 6: 63–71.

Chen Mengjia 陳夢家. 1964. "Song Dasheng bianzhong kaoshu" 宋大晟編鐘考述. *Wenwu* 1964, no.2: 51–53.

Chen Pao-chen [see also Chen Baozhen]. 1999. "Emperor Li Hou-chu as a Calligrapher, Painter, and Collector," in *Selected Essays on Court Culture in Cross-Cultural Perspective*, edited by Lin Yaofu, pp. 133–69. Taipei: National Taiwan University Press.

Chen Xiang 陳翔. 1992, "*Xuanhe huapu* de huihua meixue sixiang" 《宣和畫譜》的繪畫美學思想. In *Zhongguo huihua yanjiu lunwen ji* 中國繪畫研究論文集, edited by Duoyun 朵雲. Shanghai: Shanghai shudian. Reprinted from *Duoyun* 25, no. 2 (1990): 70–77, 23, where the author is listed as Jie Han 頡翰.

Chen, Yunru. 2007. "At the Emperor's Invitation: 'Literary Gathering' and the Emergence of Imperial Garden Space in Northern Song Painting. *Orientations* 38, no. 1: 56–61.

Cheng Minsheng 程民生. 1999. "Lun Songdai shidafu zhengzhi dui huangquan de xianzhi" 論宋代士大夫政治對皇權的限制. In *Songdai yanjiu lunwenji* 宋代研究論文集, ed. Qi Xia 漆俠 and Wang Tianshun 王天順, pp. 61–78. Yinchuan: Ningxia renmin chubanshe.

———. 2011. "Jingkang nianjian Kaifeng de yichang tianqi shulue" 靖康年間開封的異常天氣述略. *Henan shehui kexue* 19, no. 1: 147–50.

Chien, Cecelia Lee-fang. 2004. *Salt and State: An Annotated Translation of the Songshi Salt Monopoly Treatise*. Ann Arbor: University of Michigan Center for Chinese Studies.

Chikusa Masaaki 竺沙雅章. 1982. *Chūgoku bukkyō shakai shi kenkyū* 中國佛教社會史研究. *Tōyōshi kenkyū sōkan* 34. Kyoto: Dōhōsha.

Choniates, Niketas. 1984. *O City of Byzantium, Annals of Niketas Choniates*. Translated by Harry J. Magoulias. Detroit: Wayne State University Press.

Chou, Diana Yeongchau. 2005. *A Study and Translation from the Chinese of Tang Hou's* Huajian *(Examination of Painting): Cultivating Taste in Yuan China, 1279–1368*. Lewiston, ME: Edwin Mellen Press.

Chuang, Shang-yen. 1967. "The Slender Gold Calligraphy of Emperor Sung Hui Tsung." *National Palace Museum Bulletin* 2: 1–9.

Chung, Priscilla Ching. 1981. *Palace Women in the Northern Sung*. Monographies du T'oung Pao, 12. Leiden: E. J. Brill.

Clark, Hugh R. 2001. "An Inquiry into the Xianyou Cai: Cai Xiang, Cai Que, Cai Jing, and the Politics of Kinship." *Journal of Song-Yuan Studies* 31: 67–101.

———, trans. 2005. "Fang Lue, 'Inscription for the Temple of Auspicious Response.'" In *Hawai'i Reader in Traditional Chinese Culture*, edited by Victor H. Mair, Nancy S. Steinhardt, and Paul R. Goldin, pp. 392–98. Honolulu: University of Hawai'i Press.

Csikszentmihalyi, Mark. 2000. "Han Cosmology and Mantic Practices." In *Daoism Handbook*, edited by Livia Kohn, pp. 53–73. Leiden: E. J. Brill.

Cui Wenyin 崔文印. 1988. "Qianyan" 前言. In *Jingkang baishi jianzheng* 靖康稗史箋証, compiled by Cui An 確庵 and Nai An 耐庵, ed. by Cui Wenyin 崔文印, pp. 1–29. Beijing: Zhonghua shuju.

Davis, Edward L. 2001. *Society and the Supernatural in Song China*. Honolulu: University of Hawai'i Press.

Davis, Richard L., 1996. *Wind against the Mountain: The Crisis of Politics and Culture in Thirteenth-Century China*. Cambridge, MA: Council on East Asian Studies.

———, trans., 2004. *Historical Records of the Five Dynasties* by Ouyang Xiu. New York: Columbia University Press.

———. 2009. "The Reigns of Kuang-tsung (1189–1194) and Ning-tsung (1194–1224)." In *The Cambridge History of China*, vol. 5, part 1: *The Sung Dynasty and Its Precursors, 907–1279*, edited by Denis Twitchett and Paul Jakov Smith, 756–838. Cambridge, UK: Cambridge University Press.

de Bary, Wm. Theodore, and Richard Lufrano, eds. 2000. *Sources of Chinese Tradition*, vol. 2. 2nd edition. New York: Columbia University Press.

de Heer, Ph. 1986. *The Care-Taker Emperor: Aspects of the Imperial Institution in Fifteenth-Century China as Reflected in the Political History of the Reign of Chu Ch'i-yü*. Leiden: E. J. Brill.

de Pee, Christian. 2010. "Purchase on Power: Imperial Space and Commercial Space in Song-Dynasty Kaifeng, 960–1127." *Journal of the Economic and Social History of the Orient* 53: 149–84.

de Weerdt, Hilde. 2006. "Byways in the Imperial Chinese Information Order: The Dissemination and Commercial Publication of State Documents." *Harvard Journal of Asiatic Studies* 66, no. 1: 145–88.

———. 2009. "Court Gazettes and 'Short Reports': Official Views and Unofficial Readings of Court News." *Hanxue yanjiu* 漢學研究 *(Chinese Studies)* 27, no. 2: 167–200.

Deng Bai 鄧白. 1958 (1986 reprint). *Zhao Ji* 趙佶. Shanghai: Shanghai renmin chubanshe.

Deng Guangming 鄧廣銘. 1982. "Guanyu Song Jiang de touxiang yu zheng Fang La wenti" 關於宋江的投降與征方臘問題. *Zhonghua wenshi luncong*, 1982, no. 4: 1–9.

Despeux, Catherine. 2000. "Talismans and Sacred Diagrams." In *Daoism Handbook*, edited by Livia Kohn, pp. 498–540. Leiden: E. J. Brill.

Dickens, A. G., ed. 1977. *The Courts of Europe: Politics, Patonage, and Royalty, 1400–1800*. London: Thames and Hudson.

Djang, Chu, and Jane C. Djang, trans. 1989. *A Compilation of Anecdotes of Sung Personalities*. Compiled by Ting Ch'uan-ching. [New York]: St. John's University Press.

Duan Shu'an 段書安, ed. 1986–2001. *Zhongguo gudai shuhua tumu* 中國古代書畫图目. 24 vols. Beijing: Wenwu.

Duinham, Jeroen. 1994. *Myths of Power: Norbert Elias and the Early Modern European Court*. Amsterdam: Amsterdam University Press.

———. 2003. *Vienna and Versailles: The Courts of Europe's Dynastic Rivals, 1550–1780*. Cambridge, UK: Cambridge University Press.

Dull, Jack L. 1966. "A Historical Introduction to the Apocryphal (ch'an-wei) Texts of the Han Dynasty." PhD diss., University of Washington.

Eberhard, Wolfram. 1957. "The Political Function of Astronomy and Astronomers in Han China." In *Chinese Thought and Institutions*, edited by John K. Fairbank, pp. 33–70. Chicago: University of Chicago Press.

Ebrey, Patricia Buckley. 1989. "Education through Ritual: Efforts to Formulate Family Rituals during the Sung Period." In *Neo-Confucian Education: The Formative Stage*, edited by Wm. Theodore de Bary and John W. Chaffee. Berkeley: University of California Press.

———. 1990. "Cremation in Sung China." *American Historical Review* 95, no. 2: 406–28.

———, trans. 1991a. *Chu Hsi's Family Rituals: A Twelfth-Century Chinese Manual for the Performance of Cappings, Weddings, Funerals, and Ancestral Rites*. Princeton: Princeton University Press.

———. 1991b. *Confucianism and Family Rituals in Imperial China: A Social History of Writing About Rites*. Princeton University Press

———. 1997. "Portrait Sculptures in Imperial Ancestral Rites in Song China." *T'oung Pao* 83: 42–92.

———. 1999. "Taking Out the Grand Carriage: Imperial Spectacle and the Visual Culture of Northern Song Kaifeng." *Asia Major* 12, no. 1: 33–65.

———. 2000. "Taoism and Art at the Court of Song Huizong," in *Taoism and the Arts of China*, ed. Steven Little and Shawn Eichman, pp. 95–111. Chicago: Art Institute of Chicago.

———. 2002. "The Emperor and the Local Community in the Song Period." In *Chūgoku no rekishi sekai—tōgō no shisutemu to tagen teki hatten* 中國の歷史世界 :

統合のシステムと多元的發展, pp. 373–402. Tokyo: Tokyo toritsu daigaku shuppankai.

————. 2003a. "Record, Rumor, and Imagination: Sources for the Women of Huizong's Court before and after the Fall of Kaifeng." In *Tang-Song nüxing yu shehui*, edited by Deng Xiaonan, pp. 46–97. Shanghai: Shanghai cishu chubanshe.

————. 2003b. *Women and the Family in Chinese History*. London: Routledge.

————. 2004. "Imperial Filial Piety as a Political Problem." In *Filial Piety in Chinese Thought and History*, edited by Alan K. L. Chan and Sor-hoon Tan, pp. 122–40. London: Routledge.

————. 2006a. "Huizong's Stone Inscriptions." In *Emperor Huizong and Late Northern Song China: The Politics of Culture and the Culture of Politics*, edited by Patricia Buckley Ebrey and Maggie Bickford, pp. 229–274. Cambridge, MA: Harvard Asia Center.

————. 2006b. "Literati Culture and the Relationship between Huizong and Cai Jing." *Journal of Song-Yuan Studies* 36: 1–24.

————. 2006c. "Succession to High Office: The Chinese Case." In *Culture, Technology and History: Implications of the Anthropological Work of Jack Goody*, edited by David R. Olson and Michael Cole, pp. 49–71. Mahwah, NJ: Erlbaum.

————. 2008. *Accumulating Culture: The Collections of Emperor Huizong*. Seattle: University of Washington Press.

————. 2010. "Replicating Zhou Bells at the Northern Song Court." In *Reinventing the Past: Archaism and Antiquarianism in Chinese Art and Visual Culture*, edited by Wu Hung, pp. 179–99. Chicago: Art Media Resources.

————. 2011. "Empress Xiang (1046–1101) and Biographical Sources beyond Formal Biographies." In *Beyond Exemplar Tales: Cultural Politics and Women's Biography in China*, edited by Hu Ying and Joan Judge, pp. 193–211. Berkeley: University of California Press.

————. 2013. "Emperor Huizong as a Daoist." *Institute of Chinese Studies Visiting Professor Lecture Series* (III), pp. 47–90. Hong Kong: Institute of Chinese Studies, Chinese University of Hong Kong.

Ecke, Betty Tseng Yu-ho [see also Tseng Yuho]. 1972. "Emperor Hui Tsung, the Artist: 1082–1136." PhD diss., New York University.

Edwards, Richard. 1958. "The Landscape Art of Li T'ang." *Archives of the Chinese Art Society of America* 12: 48–60.

————. 1991. "Painting and Poetry in the Late Sung." In *Words and Images: Chinese Poetry, Calligraphy, and Painting*, edited by Wen C. Fong and Alfreda Murck, pp. 405–430. Princeton: Princeton University Press.

Egan, Ronald C. 1994. *Word, Image, and Deed in the Life of Su Shi*. Cambridge, MA: Council on East Asian Studies, Harvard University.

————. 2005. "The Emperor and the Ink Plum: Tracing a Lost Connection between Literati and Huizong's Court." In *Rhetoric and the Discourses of Power in Court Culture: China, Europe, and Japan*, edited by David R. Knechtges and Eugene Vance, pp. 117–48. Seattle: University of Washington Press.

————. 2006a. "Huizong's Palace Poems." In *Emperor Huizong and Late Northern Song China: The Politics of Culture and the Culture of Politics*, edited by Patricia Buckley Ebrey and Maggie Bickford, pp. 361–394. Cambridge, MA: Harvard Univeristy Asia Center.

———. 2006b. *The Problem of Beauty: Aesthetic Thought and Pursuits in Northern Song Dynasty China.* Cambridge, MA: Harvard Univeristy Asia Center.

Elliott, J. H. and L. W. B. Brockliss, eds. 1999. *The World of the Favourite.* New Haven: Yale University Press.

Elliott, Mark C. 2009. *Emperor Qianlong: Son of Heaven, Man of the World.* New York: Longman.

Fang, Chengfeng 方誠峰. 2011. "Xiangrui yu Bei Song Huizong chao de zhengzhi wenhua" 祥瑞与北宋徽宗朝的政治文化, *Zhonghua wenshi luncong* 2011, no. 4:215–253.

———. n.d. "Yubi yu yubi shouzhao" 御筆與御筆手詔. Unpublished paper.

Feros, Antonio. 2000. *Kingship and Favoritism in the Spain of Philip III, 1598–1621.* Cambridge, UK: Cambridge University Press.

Fong, Wen C. 1984. *Images of the Mind.* Princeton: The Art Museum, Princeton University.

———. 1992. *Beyond Representation: Chinese Paintings and Calligraphy, 8th–14th Centuries.* New York: Metropolitan Museum of Art.

———. 1996a. "The Emperor as Artist and Patron." In *Mandate of Heaven: Emperors and Artists in China*, edited by Richard Barnhart, Wen C. Fong, and Maxwell K. Hearn, pp. 31–35. Zurich: Museum Rietberg.

———. 1996b. "Monumental Landscape Painting." In *Possessing the Past: Treasures from the National Palace Museum, Taipei*, edited by Wen C. Fong and James C. Y. Watt, pp. 120–37. New York: Metropolitan Museum of Art.

Foong, Ping Leong. 2006. "Monumental and Intimate Landscape by Guo Xi." PhD diss., Princeton University.

Forage, Paul C. 1991. "The Sino-Tangut War of 1081–1085. *Journal of Asian History* 25: 1–27.

Forte, Antonino. 1988. *Mingtang and Buddhist Utopias in the History of the Astronomical Clock: The Tower, Statue and Armillary Sphere Constructed by Empress Wu.* Rome: Istituto Italiano per Il Medio ed Estremo Oriente.

Franke, Herbert. 1970. "Treaties between Sung and Chin." In *Études Song in Memoriam Étienne Balazs*, Ser. I:1, edited by Francoise Aubin, pp. 55–84. Paris: Mouton.

———, ed. 1976. *Song Biographies.* 3 vols. Munchener Ostasiatische Studien, 16. Wiesbaden: Franz Steiner Verlag.

———. 1983. "Sung Embassies: Some General Observations." In *China among Equals: The Middle Kingdom and Its Neighbors, 10th–14th Centuries*, edited by Morris Rossabi. Berkeley: University of California Press.

———. 1994. "The Chin Dynasty." In *The Cambridge History of China*, vol. 6: *Alien Regimes and Border States, 907–1368*, edited by Herbert Franke and Denis Twitchett, pp. 215–320. Cambridge, UK: Cambridge University Press.

———. 2003. *Krieg und Krieger in Chinesischen Mittlealter (12. bis 14. Jahrhundert): Drei Studien.* Wiesbaden: Franz Steiner Verlag.

Fu Xinian 傅熹年. 1988. *Zhongguo meishu quanji* 中國美術全集 *Huihua bian* 繪畫編 3. Beijing: Wenwu chubanshe.

Fujimoto Takeshi 藤本猛. 2007. "HokuSō matsu no Genwaden—Kotei Kisō to gakushi Sai 北宋末の宣和殿—皇帝徽宗と學士蔡攸—. *Tōhō gakuhō* 81: 1–68.

Gao Congming 高聰明. 1990. "BeiSong xibei diqu de tongtieqian zhidu" 北宋西北地區的銅鐵錢制度. *Hebei daxue xuebao* 1990, no. 3: 21–29.

———. 1991. "BeiSong wujia biandong yuanyin zhi yanjiu" 北宋物價變動原因之研究. *Hebei xuekan* 1991, no. 4: 95–100.

Glahn, Else. 1975. "On the Transmission of the *Ying-tsao fa-shih.*" *T'oung Pao* 61, nos. 4–5: 232–65.

———. 1981. "Chinese Building Standards of the 12th Century." *Scientific American* 144, no. 10: 162–73.

Golas, Peter J. 1988. "The Song Economy: How Big?" *Bulletin of Sung-Yuan Studies* 20: 90–94.

———. n.d. "The Song Fiscal Administration." In *Cambridge History of China*, edited by John Chaffee and Denis Twitchett, forthcoming.

Goldschmidt, Isaf Moshe. 2006. "Huizong's Impact on Medicine and Public Health." In *Emperor Huizong and Late Northern Song China: The Politics of Culture and the Culture of Politics*, edited by Patricia Buckley Ebrey and Maggie Bickford, pp. 275–323. Cambridge, MA: Harvard Univeristy Asia Center.

———. 2009. *The Evolution of Chinese Medicine: Song Dynasty, 960–1200*. London: Routledge.

Goody, Jack. 1966. *Succession to High Office.* Cambridge, UK: Cambridge University Press.

Gregory, Peter S. and Patricia Buckley Ebrey. 1993. "Historical and Religious Landscape." In *Religion and Society in T'ang and Sung China*, edited by Patricia Buckley Ebrey and Peter S. Gregory, pp. 1–44. Honolulu: University of Hawai'i Press.

Guarino, Marie. 1994. "Learning and Imperial Authority in Northern Sung China (960–1126): The Classics Mat Lectures." PhD diss., Columbia University.

Gugong bowuyuan canghuaji bianji weiyuanhui 故宮博物院藏畫集編輯委員會. 1981. *Zhongguo lidai huihua* 中國歷代繪畫, II. Beijing: Palace Museum.

Gugong bowuyuan 故宮博物院, Liaoningsheng bowuguan 遼寧省博物館, Shanghai bowuguan 上海博物館, eds. 2002. *JinTangSongYuan shuhua guobao teji* 晉唐宋元書畫國寶特集. Shanghai: Shanghai shuhua chubanshe.

Guo, Qinghua. 1998. "*Yingzao Fashi:* Twelfth-Century Chinese Building Manual." *Architectural History* 41: 1–13.

———. 1999. *The Structure of Chinese Timber Architecture*. London: Minerva Press.

Gyss-Vermande, Caroline. 1995. "Lettres de Song Huizong au maître du Maoshan Liu Hunkang, ou le patronage impérial comme pratique de dévotion." In *Hommage à Kwong Hing Foon: Études d'histoire culturelle de la Chine*, edited by Jean-Pierre Diény, pp. 239–53. Paris: College de France, Institute des hautes études chinoises.

Haeger, John Winthrop. 1978. "Li Kang and the Loss of K'ai-Feng: The Concept and Practice of Political Dissent in Mid-Sung." *Journal of Asian History* 12, no. 1: 30–57.

Hall, Dickson. 1989. *Chinese Paintings in the Palace Museum, Beijing 4th–14th Century.* Hong Kong: Joint Publishing Co.

Halperin, Mark. 2006. *Out of the Cloister: Literati Perspectives on Buddhism in Sung China, 960–1279.* Cambridge, MA: Harvard Asia Center.

Hansen, Valerie. 1990. *Changing Gods in Medieval China, 1127–1276.* Princeton: Princeton University Press.

———. 1996. "The Mystery of the Qingming Scroll and Its Subject: The Case Against Kaifeng." *Journal of Sung-Yuan Studies* 26: 183–200.

Hargett, James M. 1987. "A Chronology of Reigns and Reign-Periods of the Song Dynasty (960–1279). *Bulletin of Sung Yuan Studies* 19: 26–34.

———. 1988–1989. "Huizong's Magic Marchmount: The Genyue Pleasure Park of Kaifeng." *Monumenta Serica* 38: 1–48.

———. 1993. "*Song Biographies*, Supplementary N. 1: Chen Yuyi (1090–1139)." *Journal of Sung-Yuan Studies* 23: 110–22.

Harper, Donald J. 1998. *Early Chinese Medical Literature: The Mawangdui Medical Manuscripts*. London: Kegan Paul International.

Hartman, Charles. 1990. "Poetry and Politics in 1079: The Crow Terrace Poetry Case of Su Shih." *Chinese Literature: Essays, Articles, Reviews* 12: 15–44.

———. 1998a. "Bibliographic Notes on Sung Historical Works: *Topical Narratives from the Long Draft Continuation of the Comprehensive Mirror that Aids Administration (Hsü tzu-chih t'ung-chien ch'ang-pien chi-shih pen-mo* 續資治通鑑長編紀事本末*)* by Yang Chung-liang 楊仲良 and Related Texts." *Journal of Sung-Yuan Studies* 28: 177–200.

———. 1998b. "The Making of a Villain: Ch'in Kuei and Tao-hsueh." *Harvard Journal of Asiatic Studies* 58: 59–146.

———. 2001. "Poetry and Painting." In *Columbia History of Chinese Literature*, edited by Victor H. Mair, pp. 466–90. New York: Columbia University Press.

———. 2003. "The Reluctant Historian: Sun Ti, Chu Hsi, and the Fall of Northern Sung." *T'oung Pao* 89: 100–48.

———. 2006. "A Textual History of Cai Jing's Biography in the *Songshi*." In *Emperor Huizong and Late Northern Song China: The Politics of Culture and the Culture of Politics*, edited by Patricia Buckley Ebrey and Maggie Bickford, pp. 517–564. Cambridge, MA: Harvard Asia Center.

———. n.d. "Chinese Hawks: An Untitled Portrait." Unpublished paper.

Hartwell, Robert M. 1967. "A Cycle of Economic Change in Imperial China: Coal and Iron in Northeast China, 750–1350." *Journal of the Economic and Social History of the Orient* 10, no. 1: 102–59.

———. 1988. "The Imperial Treasuries: Finance and Power in Song China." *Bulletin of Sung-Yuan Studies* 20: 18–89.

Hawes, Colin S. C. 2005. *The Social Circulation of Poetry in the Mid-Northern Song: Emotional Energy and Literati Self-Cultivation*. Albany, NY: SUNY Press.

Hay, John. 1991. "Poetic Space: Ch'ien Hsüan and the Association of Painting and Poetry." In *Words and Images: Chinese Poetry, Calligraphy, and Painting*, edited by Alfreda Murck and Wen C. Fong. New York: Metropolitan Museum of Art.

Hayashi Daisuke 林大介. 2003. "Cai Jing to sono seiji shūdan: Sōdai no keitei-saishō kankai rikai no tame no ichi kōsatsu" 蔡京とその政治集團‐宋代の皇帝‐宰相關係理解のための一考察. *Shihō* 35: 1–28.

He Zhongli 何忠禮. 1994. "Huanrao Song Gaozong shengmu Weishi nianling de ruogan wenti" 環繞宋高宗生母韋氏年齡的若干問題. *Wenshi* 39: 135–47.

———. 2007. *Songdai zhengzhi shi* 宋代政治史. Hangzhou: Zhejiang daxue chubanshe.

Hegel, Robert E. 1981. *The Novel in Seventeenth-Century China*. New York: Columbia University Press.

Henansheng wenwu kaogu yanjiusuo 河南省文物考古研究所. 1997. *Bei Song huang-ling* 北宋皇陵. Zhongzhou: Zhongzhou guji chubanshe.

Heng Chye Kiang. 1999. *Cities of Aristocrats and Bureaucrats: The Development of Medieval Chinese Cityscapes*. Honolulu: University of Hawai'i Press.

Hennessey, William O. 1984. "Classical Sources and Vernacular Resources in *Xuanhe Yishi*: The Presence of Priority and the Priority of Presence." *Chinese Literature: Essays, Articles, and Reviews* 6: 33–52.

———, trans. 1981. *Proclaiming Harmony*. Ann Arbor: Center for Chinese Studies, University of Michigan.

Hightower, James R. 1977. "The Songs of Chou Pang-yen." *Harvard Journal of Asiatic Studies* 37, no. 2: 233–72.

Ho, Wai-kam. 1980. "Aspects of Chinese Painting from 1100 to 1350." In *Eight Dynasties of Chinese Painting: The Collections of the Nelson Gallery-Atkins Museum, Kansas City, and the Cleveland Museum of Art*, edited by Wai-kam Ho, et al., pp. xxv–xxxiv. Cleveland: Cleveland Museum of Art.

Hou Naihui 侯迺慧. 1994. "Shi lun Song Huizong Bianjing Genyue de zao yuan chengjiu" 試論宋徽宗汴京艮岳的造園成就. *Zhonghua xue yuan* 44, no. 4: 259–83.

Hua Jueming 華覺明 and Zhao Kuanghua 趙匡華. 1986. "Jiaxi qian shi tieqian, bushi tongqian" 夾錫錢是鐵錢不是銅錢. *Zhongguo qianbi* 3: 21–22.

Huang Kuanchong 黃寬重. 1993. *Songshi conglun* 宋史叢論. Taipei: Xinwenfeng chuban gongsi.

Huang, Ray. 1981. *1587: A Year of No Significance*. New Haven: Yale University Press.

Huang, Shih-shan Susan. 2012. *Picturing the True Form: Daoist Visual Culture in Medieval China*. Cambridge, MA: Harvard Asia Center.

Hwang, Ming-Chorng. 1996. "Ming-Tang: Cosmology, Political Order and Monuments in Early China." PhD diss, Harvard University.

Hymes, Robert P. 2002. *Way and Byway: Taoism, Local Religion, and Models of Divinity in Song and Modern China*. Berkeley: University of California Press.

Hymes, Robert P., and Conrad Schirokauer. 1993. "Introduction." In *Ordering the World: Approaches to State and Society in Sung Dynasty China*, edited by Robert P. Hymes and Conrad Schirokauer. Berkeley: University of California Press.

Idema, Wilt. L. and Stephen West. 1982. *Chinese Theater, 1100–1450: A Source Book*. Wiesbaden: Steiner.

Ihara Hiroshi 伊原弘. 1991. *Chūgoku Kaifū no seikazu to saiji—egakareta Sōdai no toshi seikazu* 中國開封の生活と歳時—描かれた宋代都市生活. Tokyo: Sansen shūkkbansha.

———. 2001. "The *Qing ming shang he tu* by Zhang Zeduan and its Relation to Northern Song Society: Light and Shadow in the Painting." *Journal of Song-Yuan Studies* 31: 135–56.

———, ed. 2012. *Seimei jōkazu" to Kisō no jidai—soshite kagayuki no zanshō* 「清明上河図」と徽宗の時代: そして輝きの残照. Tokyo: Bensei Shuppan. Itakura Masaaki 板倉聖哲. 2004. "Hotei no mesashi—Kisō no 'Zuitsuru tokan' o megutte" 皇帝の目差し一 徽宗《瑞鶴圖卷》をめぐって. *Ajia yūgaku* 64: 128–39.

Iwasaki, Tsutomi. 1986. "A Study of Ho-hsi Tibetans during the Northern Song Dynasty." *The Memoirs of the Toyo Bunko* 44: 57–132.

Jang, Scarlett. 1992. "Realm of the Immortals: Paintings Decorating the Jade Hall of the Northern Song." *Ars Orientalis* 22: 81–96.

———. 1999. "Representations of Exemplary Scholar-Officials, Past and Present." In *Arts of the Sung and Yüan: Ritual, Ethnicity, and Style in Painting*, edited by Cary Y. Liu and Dora C. Y. Ching. Princeton: The Art Museum, Princeton University.

———. 2008. "The Eunuch Agency Directorate of Ceremonial and the Ming Imperial Publishing Enterprise." In *Culture, Courtiers, and Competition: The Ming Court (1368–1644)*, edited by David M. Robinson, pp. 116–85. Cambridge, MA: Harvard University Asia Center.

Ji, Xiao-bin. 2005. *Politics and Conservatism in Northern Song China*. Hong Kong: The Chinese University Press.

Jia Huchen 賈虎臣. 1967. *Zhongguo Lidai diwang puxi huibian* 中國歷代王譜系彙編. Taipei: Zhengzhong shuju.

Jiang Qingqing 姜青青. 2008. *Ma Kuo yanjiu* 馬擴研究. Beijing: Renmin chubanshe.

Jin Zhongshu 金中樞. 1966, 1967. "Lun Bei Song monian zhi chongshang Daojiao" 論北宋末年之崇尚道教. *Xinya xuebao* 7, no. 2: 323–414; 8, no. 1: 187–257.

Kahn, Harold. 1985. "A Matter of Taste: The Monumental and Exotic in the Qianlong Reign." In *The Elegant Brush: Chinese Painting Under the Qianlong Emperor 1735–1795*, pp. 288–302. Phoenix: Phoenix Art Museum.

Kao, Yu-kung. 1962–1963. "A Study of the Fang La Rebellion." *Harvard Journal of Asiatic Studies* 24: 17–63.

———. 1966. "Source Materials on the Fang La Rebellion." *Harvard Journal of Asiatic Studies* 26: 211–40.

Kaplan, Harold. 1970. "Yueh Fei and the Founding of Southern Sung China." PhD diss., Iowa State University.

Katz, Paul R. 1999. *Images of the Immortal: The Cult of Lü Dongbin at the Palace of Eternal Joy*. Honolulu: University of Hawai'i Press.

Kawai, Senro 河井荃廬. 1937. *Shina nanga taisei* 支那南畫大成. Tokyo: Kobunsha.

Kern, Martin. 2000. "Religious Anxiety and Political Interest in Western Han Omen Interpretation: The Case of the Han Wudi Period (141–87 BC)." *Chūgoku shigaku* 10: 1–31.

Keswick, Maggie. 1978. *The Chinese Garden: History, Art, and Architecture*. New York: Rizzoli.

Knechtges, David R. 1994. "The Emperor and Literature." In *Imperial Rulership and Cultural Change in Traditional China*, edited by Frederick P. Brandauer and Chun-chieh Huang, pp. 51–76. Seattle: University of Washington Press.

———. 1999. "Criticism of the Court in Han Dynasty Literature." In *Selected Essays on Court Culture in a Cross-Cultural Perspective*, edited by Lin Yaofu, pp. 51–77. Taipei: National Taiwan University.

Kohn, Livia. 1991. *Taoist Mystical Philosophy: The Scripture of Western Ascension*. Albany, NY: SUNY Press.

———. 1993. *The Taoist Experience: An Anthology*. Albany, NY: SUNY Press.

———. 1998. *God of the Dao: Lord Lao in History and Myth*. Ann Arbor: University of Michigan, Center for Chinese Studies.

———, ed. 2000. *Daoism Handbook*. Leiden: E. J. Brill.

Kohn, Livia and Russell Kirkland. 2000. "Daoism in the Tang (618–907)." In *Daoism Handbook*, edited by Livia Kohn, pp. 339–83. Leiden: E. J. Brill.

Kojima Tsuyoshi. 小島毅. 1992. "Sōdai no kokka" 宋代の國家祭祀 「政和五禮新儀」 の特徵. In *Chūgoku reihō to Nihon ritsuryōsei* 中國禮法と日本律制, edited by Ikeda On 池田溫, pp. 463–484. Tokyo: Tōhō shuppan.

Kondō, Kazunari 近藤一成. 1994. "Sai Kei no kakyō—gakkō seisoku" 蔡京の科擧學校政策. *Tōyōshi kenkyū* 53, no. 1: 24–49.

———. 1999. "Sōdai shidaifu seiji no tokushoku" 宋代士大夫政治の特色. In *Iwanami koza Sekai rekishi 9: Chuka no bunretsu to saisei, san-jusan* seiki 岩波講座世界歷史9: 中華の分裂と再生, edited by Kabayama Kōichi 樺山紘一, pp. 305–26. Tokyo: Iwanami shoten.

Kracke, Edward A. Jr. 1975. "Sung K'ai-feng: Pragmatic Metropolis and Formalistic Capital." In *Crisis and Prosperity in Sung China*, edited by John Winthrop Haeger, pp. 49–77. Tucson: The University of Arizona Press.

———. 1977. "The Expansion of Educational Opportunity in the Reign of Hui-tsung and Its Implications." *Sung Studies Newsletter* 13: 6–30.

Kubota Kazuo 久保田和男. 2005. "HokuSō Kisō jidai to Kaifū" 北宋徽宗時代と首都開封. *Tōyōshi kenkyū* 63, no. 3: 1–35.

———. 2006. "Hoku Sō no keitei koko ni tsuite: Shoto kūkan ni okeru o chūshi to shite" 北宋の皇帝行幸について — 首都空間における行幸を中心として, 一. In *Sōdai shakai no kūkan to komyunikēshon* 宋代社会の空間と 首都空間における行幸を中心として—とコミュニケーション, edited by Hirata Shigeta 平田茂樹, et al., pp. 69–96. Tokyo: Kyūko Shoin.

———. 2007a. *Sōdai Kaifū no kenkyū* 宋代開封の研究. Tokyo: Kyūshoin.

———. 2007b. "Sōdai no 'tenryō' o megutte—bunji seiji kakuritsu no ichi sokumen" 宋代の「畋獵」を巡って—文治政治確立の一側面. In *Kodai higashiajia no shakai to bunka: Fukui Shigemasa sensei koki taishoku kinen ronshū* 古代東アジアの社会と文化: 福井重雅先生古稀・退職記念論集, edited by Fukui Shigemasa sensei koki taishoku kinen ronshū kankōkai, pp. 487–506. Tokyo: Kyūko Shoin.

———. 2008. "Guanyu BeiSong huangdi de xingxing—yi zai shoudu kongjian de xingxing wei zhongxin" 關於北宋皇帝的行幸—以在首都空間的行幸為中心. In *Songdai shehui de kongjian yi jiaoliu* 宋代社會的空間與交流, edited by Hirata Shigeki 平田茂樹. Kaifeng: Henan Daxue chubanshe. (Translation into Chinese of the same author's 2006 article above).

Kuhn, Dieter. 2009. *The Age of Confucian Rule: the Song Transformation of China*. Cambridge, MA: Harvard University Press.

Kuhn, Philip A. 1990. *Soulstealers: The Chinese Sorcery Scare of 1768*. Cambridge, MA: Harvard University Press.

Labadie, John Richard. 1981. "Rulers and Soldiers: Perception and Management of the Military in Northern Sung China (960–ca. 1060)." PhD diss., University of Washington.

Lam, Joseph S. C. 2005. "Huizong's Ritual and Musical Insignia." *Journal of Ritual Studies* 19, no. 1: 1–18.

———. 2006. "Huizong's Dashengyue, a Musical Performance of Emperorship and Officialdom." In *Emperor Huizong and Late Northern Song China: The Politics of Culture and the Culture of Politics*, edited by Patricia Buckley Ebrey and Maggie Bickford, pp. 395–452. Cambridge, MA: Harvard Asia Center.

Lamouroux, Christian. 2003. *Fiscalité, comptes publics et politiques financières dans la Chine des Song (960–1276): le chapitre 179 du Songshi*. Paris: Institut des Hautes Études Chinoises.

———. 2008. "'Old Models,' Court Culture and Antiquity between 1070 and 1125 in Northern Song China." In *Perceptions of Antiquity in Chinese Civilization*, edited by Dieter Kuhn and Helga Stahl, pp. 291–319. Heidelberg: Edition Forum.

Landau, Julie. 1994. *Beyond Spring Tz'u Poems of the Sung Dynasty*. New York: Columbia University Press.

Lau, D. C., trans. 1963. *Lao Tzu: Tao Te Ching*. New York: Penguin.

———, trans. 1970. *Mencius*. London: Penguin.

Lau, Nap-yin and Huang K'uan-chung. 2009. "Founding and Consolidation of the Sung Dynasty under T'ai-tus (960–976), T'ai-tsung (976–997), and Chen-tsung (997–1022)." In *The Cambridge History of China*, vol. 5, part 1: *The Sung Dynasty and Its Precursors, 907–1279*, edited by Denis Twitchett and Paul Jakov Smith, pp. 206–78. Cambridge, UK: Cambridge University Press.

Ledderose, Lothar. 1979. *Mi Fu and the Classical Tradition of Chinese Calligraphy*. Princeton: Princeton University Press.

———. 1983. "The Earthly Paradise: Religious Elements in Chinese Landscape Art." In *Theories of the Arts in China*, edited by Susan Bush and Christian Murck, pp. 165–83. Princeton: Princeton University Press.

———. 2000. *Ten Thousand Things: Module and Mass Production in Chinese Art*. Princeton: Princeton University Press.

Lee, Hermione. 2009. *Biography: A Very Short Introduction*. Oxford: Oxford University Press.

Lee, Hui-shu [see also Li Huishu]. 2001. *Exquisite Moments: West Lake and Southern Song Art*. New York: China Institute Gallery.

———. 2010. *Empresses, Art, and Agency in Song Dynasty China*. Seattle: University of Washington Press.

Lee, Thomas Hong-chi. 1985. *Government Education and Examinations in Sung China*. Hong Kong: The Chinese University of Hong Kong.

Legge, James, trans. 1865–1895 (1961 reprint). *The Chinese Classics*, 5 vols. Hong Kong: Hong Kong University Press.

———. 1885. (1967 reprint). *Li Chi, Book of Rites*, 2 vols. New York: University Books.

Levine, Ari. 2006. "Terms of Estrangement: Factional Discourse in the Early Huizong Reign, 1100–1104." In *Emperor Huizong and Late Northern Song China: The Politics of Culture and the Culture of Politics*, edited by Patricia Buckley Ebrey and Maggie Bickford, pp. 131–170. Cambridge, MA: Harvard Univeristy Asia Center.

———. 2008. *Divided by a Common Language: Factional Conflict in Late Northern Song China*. Honolulu: University of Hawai'i Press.

———. 2009a. "Che-tsung's Reign (1085–1100) and the Age of Faction." In *The Cambridge History of China*, vol. 5, part 1: *The Sung Dynasty and Its Precursors, 907–1279*, edited by Denis Twitchett and Paul Jakov Smith, pp. 484–555. Cambridge, UK: Cambridge University Press.

———. 2009b. "The Reigns of Hui-tsung (1100–1126) and Ch'in-tsung (1126–1127)." In *The Cambridge History of China*, vol. 5, part 1: *The Sung Dynasty and Its Precursors, 907–1279*, edited by Denis Twitchett and Paul Jakov Smith, pp. 556–643. Cambridge, UK: Cambridge University Press.

Lewis, Mark Edward. 2006. *The Construction of Space in Early China*. Albany, NY: SUNY Press.

Li, Cho-ying and Charles Hartman. 2011. "Primary Sources for Song History in the Collected Works of Wu Ne." *Journal of Song-Yuan Studies* 41: 295–341.

Li Huarui 李華瑞. 1998. *Song-Xia guanxi shi* 宋夏關係史. Shijiazhuang: Hebei renmin chubanshe.

Li Huishu 李慧淑 [see also Lee, Hui-shu]. 1984. "Songdai huafeng zhuanbian zhi qiji—Huizong meishu jiaoyu chenggong zhi shili" 宋代畫風轉變之契機—徽宗美術教育成功之實例 (上 , 下). *Gugong xueshu jikan* 14: 71–91; 2, no. 1: 9–36.

Li Liliang 李麗涼. 2006. "BeiSong Shenxiao daoshi Lin Lingsu yu shenxiao yun-dong" 北宋神霄道士林靈素與神霄運動. PhD diss., Chinese University of Hong Kong.

Li Tianming 李天鳴. 1996. "Song Jin lianhe gong Liao Yanjing zhi yi—Yanshan zhi yi" 宋金聯合攻遼燕京之役—燕山之役. In *Dierjie Songshi xueshu taolun wenji* 第二屆宋史學術討論文集, pp. 283–305. Taipei: Chinese Culture University, 1996.

———. 2000a. "Jin qin BeiSong chuqi zhanyi he Songting de juece" 金侵北宋初期戰役和宋廷的決策, In *Song Xuxuan jiaoshou bashi rongshou lunwenji* 宋旭軒教授八十榮壽論文集, pp. 183–236. Taipei: Committee to prepare the fest-scrift for the 80th birthday of Professor Song Xi.

———. 2000b. "Song Huizong beifa Yanshan shiqi de fandui yijian" 宋徽宗北伐燕山時期的反對意見. *Gogong xueshu jikan* 17, no. 4: 109–43.

Li Youping 李幼平. 2004. *Dasheng zhong yu Songdai huangzhong biaozhun yingao yanjiu* 大晟鍾與宋代黃鍾標準音高研究. Shanghai: Shanghai yinyue xueyuan chubanshe.

Li Yuanguo 李遠國. 2003. *Shenxiao leifa: Daojiao shenxiao pai yange yu sixiang* 神霄雷法: 道教神霄派沿革与思想. Chengdu: Sichuan renmin chubanshe.

———. 2007. "Lun Daojiao leifa de fazhan ji qi sixiang beijing" 論道教雷法的發展及其思想背景. In *Purposes, Means and Convictions in Daoism: A Berlin Symposium*, edited by Florian C. Reiter, pp. 201–20. Wiesbaden: Harrassovitz.

Li Yumin 李裕民. 1980. "Fang La qiyi xinkao" 方臘起義新考. *Shanxi daxue xuebao* 1980, no. 2: 44–52.

Liang Sicheng 梁思成. 1983. *Yingzao fashi zhushi* 營造法式註釋. Beijing: Zhong-guo jianzhu gongye chubanshe.

Liao Hsien-huei. 2002. "Visualizing the Afterlife: The Song Elite's Obsession with Death, the Underworld, and Salvation." *Hanxue yanjiu* 20, no. 1: 399–440.

———. 2005. "Exploring Weal and Woe: The Song Elite's Mantic Beliefs and Practices." *T'oung Pao* 91: 347–95.

———. 2007. "Encountering Evil: Ghosts and Demonic Forces in the Lives of the Song Elite." *Journal of Song-Yuan Studies* 37: 89–134.

Liao Huaizhi 廖懷志. 2007. "Cong Hui Qin er di de qiujin shenghuo kan Jinguo de fulu zhengce" 從徽欽二帝的囚禁生活看金國的俘虜政策. *Heilongjiang minzu congkan* 98, no. 3:94–98.

Lieu, Samuel N. C. 1998. *Manichaeism in Central Asia and China*. Leiden: E. J. Brill.

Lin Boting 林柏亭. 2006. *Daguan: BeiSong shuhua tezhan* 大觀: 北宋書畫特展. Taipei: National Palace Museum.

Linghu Biao 令狐彪. 1982. "Songdai huayuan huajia kaolue" 宋代畫院畫家考略. *Meishu yanjiu* 1982, no. 4: 39–40; 49–61.

Lippiello, Tiziana. 2001. *Auspicious Omens and Miracles in Ancient China: Han, Three Kingdoms, and Six Dynasties.* Nettetal, Germany: Steyler Verlag.

Liu Changdong 劉長東. 2005. *Songdai fojiao zhengce lungao* 宋代佛教政策論稿. Chengdu: Bashu shushe.

Liu Cunren 柳存仁 [see also Liu, Ts'un-yan]. 1991. "Daozang ben san sheng zhu Daode jing huijian" 道藏本三聖注道德經會箋. In Liu Cunren 柳存仁, *Hefeng tang wenji* 和風堂文集, pp. 223–495. Shanghai: Shanghai guji chubanshe.

Liu, Heping. 1997. "Painting and Commerce in Northern Song Dynasty China, 960–1126." PhD diss., Yale University.

———. 2002. "*The Water Mill* and Northern Song Imperial Patronage of Art, Commerce, and Science." *Art Bulletin* 84, no. 4: 566–95.

Liu, James J. Y. 1974. *Major Lyricists of the Northern Sung.* Princeton: Princeton University Press.

Liu, James T. C. [see also Liu Zijian]. 1959. *Reform in Sung China: Wang An-shih (1021–1086) and His New Policies.* Cambridge, MA: Harvard University Press.

———. 1962. "An Administrative Cycle in Chinese History: The Case of Northern Sung Emperors." *Journal of Asian Studies* 21, no. 2: 137–52.

———. 1967a. *Ou-yang Hsiu: An Eleventh-Century Neo-Confucianist.* Stanford: Stanford University Press.

———. 1967b. "The Sung Views on the Control of Government Clerks." *Journal of the Economic and Social History of the Orient* 10, nos. 2–3: 317–44.

———. 1973. "The Sung Emperors and the Ming-t'ang or Hall of Enlightenment." In *Études Song in Memoriam Étienne Balazs*, Ser. II, edited by Françoise Aubin. Paris: Mouton.

———. 1985. "Polo and Cultural Change: From T'ang to Sung China." *Harvard Journal of Asiatic Studies* 45, no. 1: 203–24.

———. 1988. *China Turning Inward: Intellectual-Political Changes in the Early Twelfth Century.* Cambridge, MA: Harvard University Press.

Liu Kongfu 劉孔伏 and Pan Liangzhi 潘良熾. 1994. "Li Shishi yishi bian" 李師師遺事辨. Qinghai shehui kexue, 1994, no. 2: 66–70.

Liu Meixin 劉美新. 2005. "Cai Jing yu Song Huizong chao zhi Zhengju" 蔡京與宋徽宗朝之政局. In *BeiSong zhonghouqi zhengzhi tansuo* 北宋中後期政治探索, edited by Zhang Qifan 張其凡, pp. 443–521. Hong Kong: Huaxia wenhua yishu chubanshe.

Liu, Ts'un-yan [see also Liu Cunren]. 1974. *On the Aart of Ruling a Big Country: Views of Three Chinese Emperors.* Canberra: Australian National University Press.

Liu Zijian 劉子建 [see also James T. C. Liu]. 1987. *Liang Song shi yanjiu huibian* 兩宋史研究彙編. Taipei: Lianjing.

Lo, Winston W. 1987. *An Introduction to the Civil Service of Sung China, with an Emphasis on Its Personnel Administration.* Honolulu: University of Hawai'i Press.

———. 1996. "Wan-yen Tsung-han: Jurchen General as Sinologist." *Journal of Sung-Yuan Studies* 26: 87–112.

Loehr, Max. 1939. "A Landscape by Li T'ang." *The Burlington Magazine for Connoisseurs* 74: 288–93.

————. 1961. "Chinese Paintings with Sung Dated Inscriptions." *Ars Orientalis* 4: 219–84.

Loewe, Michael. 1965. *Imperial China: The Historical Background to the Modern Age*. New York: Praeger.

————. 1986. "The Concept of Sovereignty." In *The Cambridge History of China*, vol. 1: *The Ch'in and Han Empires 221 BC–AD 220*, edited by Denis Twitchett and Michael Loewe, 726–46. Cambridge, UK: Cambridge University Press.

————. 1994. *Divination, Mythology and Monarchy in Han China*. Cambridge, UK: Cambridge University Press.

Lorge, Peter. 2005. *War, Politics and Society in Early Modern China, 900–1795*. London: Routledge.

Luo Jiaxiang 羅家祥. 1993. *Bei Song dangzheng yanjiu* 北宋黨爭研究. Taipei: Wenjin chubanshe.

————. 2003a. "Zeng Bu yu BeiSong Zhezong, Huizong tongzhi shiqi de zhengju yanbian" 曾布與北宋哲宗、徽宗統治時期的政局演變. *Huazhong keji daxue xuebao (shehui kexue ban)* 2003, no. 2: 51–57.

————. 2003b. "Lun BeiSong Huizong tongzhi chuqi de zhengju yanbian" 論北宋徽宗統治初期的政局演變. *Hebei xuekan* 23, no. 5: 151–56.

Ma Xianyu 馬嫻育. 2012. "Cong qianli jiangshan tu kan huajia chuanda de lixiang guo du" 從《千里江山圖》看畫家傳達的理想國度. *Lishi wenwu* 22, no. 2: 46–62.

Maeda, Robert J. 1970a. "The Chao Ta-nien Tradition." *Ars Orientalis* 8: 243–53.

————. 1970b. *Two Twelfth Century Texts on Chinese Painting*. Ann Arbor: Michigan Papers in Chinese Studies.

Magdalino, Paul. 1993. *The Empire of Manuel J. Komnenos, 1143–1180*. Cambridge, UK: Cambridge University Press.

Maguire, Henry, ed. 1997. *Byzantine Court Culture from 829 to 1204*. Washington, DC: Dunbarton Oaks Research Library and Collection.

Mateer, David. 2000. *Courts, Patrons and Poets*. New Haven: Yale University Press.

Matsumoto Kōichi 松本浩一. 1979. "Sōdai no raihō" 宋代の雷法. *Shakai bunka shigaku* 17: 45–65.

————. 2004. "Kisō to dōkyo seisaku" 徽宗と道教政策. *Ajia yūgaku* 64: 110–18.

————. 2006. *Sōdai no Dōkyō to minkan shinkō* 宋代の道教と民間信仰. Tokyo: Kyūko Shoin.

McDermott, Joseph P., ed. 1999. *State and Court Ritual in China*. Cambridge, UK: Cambridge University Press.

McKnight, Brian E. 1992. *Law and Order in Sung China*. Cambridge, UK: Cambridge University Press.

McMullen, David L. 1987. "Bureaucrats and Cosmology: The Ritual Code of T'ang China." In *Royalty: Power and Ceremonial in Traditional Societies*, edited by David Cannadine and Simon Price, pp. 181–236. Cambridge, UK: Cambridge University Press.

————. 1988. *State and Scholars in T'ang China*. Cambridge, UK: Cambridge University Press.

McNair, Amy. 1998. *The Upright Brush: Yan Zhenqing's Calligraphy and Song Literati Politics*. Honolulu: University of Hawai'i Press.

Miyakawa, Hisayuki 宮川尚志. 1975a. "Rin Reiso to Sō no Kisō" 林靈素と宋の徽宗. *Tokai daigaku kiyo (bunkaku bu)* 24: 1–8.

———. 1975b. "Sō no Kisō to dōkyō" 宋 の徽宗 と道教. *Tokai daigaku kiyo (bunkaku bu)* 23: 1–10.

Mollier, Christine. 2008. *Buddhism and Taoism Face to Face: Scripture, Ritual, and Iconogrpahic Exchange in Medieval China.* Honolulu: University of Hawai'i Press.

Mostern, Ruth. 2011. *"Dividing the Realm in Order to Govern": The Spatial Organization of the Song State (960–1276 CE).* Cambridge, MA: Harvard University Asia Center.

Mote, Frederick. 1961. "The Growth of Chinese Despotism: A Critique of Wittfogel's Theory of Oriental Despotism as Applied to China." *Oriens Extremus* 8.1:1–41.

———.1999. *Imperial China 900–1800.* Cambridge, MA: Harvard University Press.

Murck, Alfreda. 2000. *Poetry and Painting in Song China: The Subtle Art of Dissent.* Cambridge, MA: Harvard Asia Center.

Murray, Julia K. 1993. *Ma Hezhi and the Illustration of the Book of Odes.* Princeton: Princeton University Press.

———. 1997. "Water under a Bridge: Further Thoughts on the *Qingming* Scroll." *Journal of Sung-Yuan Studies* 27: 99–107.

———. 2001. "From Textbook to Testimonial: The Emperor's Mirror, an Illustrated Discussion (Di jian tu shuo/Teikan Zusetsu) in China and Japan." *Ars Orientalis* 31:65–101.

———. 2005. "Didactic Illustration in Printed Books." In *Printing and Book Culture in Late Imperial China,* edited by Cynthia J. Brokaw and Kai-wing Chow, pp. 417–50. Berkeley: University of California Press.

———. 2007. *Mirror of Morality: Chinese Narrative Illustration and Confucian Ideology.* Honolulu: University of Hawai'i Press.

Naba Toshisada 那波利貞. 1974. *Tōdai shakai bunkashi kenkyū* 唐代社會文化史研究. Oriental Studies Library, 8. Tokyo: Sōbunsha.

Nakajima Satoshi 中嶋敏. 1988. *Tōyō shigaku ronshū—Sōdaishi kenkyū to sono shūhen* 東洋史學論集—宋代史研究とその周邊. Tokyo: Kyūko Shūen.

Nakata Yujirō 中田勇次郎. 1977–1995. *Chūgoku shoron taikei* 中國書論大系 (18 vols.; vols. 5 and 6 include annotated translation into Japanese of XHSP). Tokyo: Nigensha.

Nakayama, Shigeru. 1966. "Characteristics of Chinese Astrology." *Isis* 57, no. 4: 442–54.

Naquin, Susan. 2000. *Peking: Temples and City Life, 1400–1900.* Berkeley: University of California Press.

National Palace Museum. 1961. *Chinese Art Treasures: A Selected Group of Objects from the Chinese National Palace Museum and the Chinese National Central Museum, Taichung, Taiwan.* Geneva: Skira.

———. 1970. *Song Huizong Gaozong moji* 宋徽宗高宗墨蹟. Taipei: National Palace Museum.

———. 1981. *Li Tang wanhe song feng tu* 李唐萬壑松風圖. Taipei: National Palace Museum.

———. 1995. *Gugong shuhua tulu* 故宮書畫圖錄, vol. 15. Taipei: Guoli Gugong bowuyuan.

————. 2000. *Qianxi nian Songdai wenwu dazhan* 千禧年宋代文物大展. Taipei: National Palace Museum.

Needham, Joseph, Lu Gwei-djen, and Huang Hsing-tsung. 1986. *Science and Civilisation in China*, vol. 6: *Biology and Biological Technology*, part 1: *Botany*. Cambridge, UK: Cambridge University Press.

Needham, Joseph, Lu Gwei-djen, and Nathan Sivin. 2000. *Science and Civilisation in China*, vol. 6: *Biology and Biological Technology*, part 6: *Medicine*. Cambridge, UK: Cambridge University Press.

Needham, Joseph, and Wang Ling. 1959. *Science and Civilisation in China*, vol. 3: *Mathematics and the Sciences of the Heavens and the Earth*. Cambridge, UK: Cambridge University Press.

Needham, Joseph, Wang Ling, and Lu Gwei-djen. 1971. *Science and Civilisation in China*, vol. 4: *Physics and Physical Technology*, part 3: *Civil Engineering and Nautics*. Cambridge, UK: Cambridge University Press.

Nylan, Michael. 2008. "The Rhetoric of 'Empire' in the Classical Era in China." In *Conceiving the Empire in China and Rome Compared*," edited by Fritz-Heiner Mutschler and Achim Mittag, pp. 39–64. Oxford: Oxford University Press.

Oberst, Zhihong Liang. 1996. "Chinese Economic Statecraft and Economic Ideas in the Song Period (960–1279). PhD diss., Columbia University.

Ogawa Hiromitsu 小川裕充. 1981. "Inchō no meiga—Dong Yu, Juran, Yan Su kara, Guo Xi made"「院中名畫」—董羽、巨然、燕肅から郭熙 まで—. In *Chūgoku kaigashi ronshū: Suzuki Kei Sensei kanreki kinen* 中国繪畫史論集: 鈴木敬先生還曆記念 C, pp. 23–85. Tōkyō: Yoshikawa Kōbunkan, 1981.

Okanishi Tameto 岡西爲人. 1969. *Song yiqian yiji kao* 宋以前醫籍考. 4 vols. Taipei: Guting.

Owen, Stephen. 1998. "The Difficulty of Pleasure." *Extrême-Orient, Extrême-Occident* 20: 9–30.

Pang, Huiping. 2009. "Strange Weather: Art, Politics, and Climate Change at the Court of Northern Song Emperor Huizong." *Journal of Song-Yuan Studies* 39: 1–41.

Parker, Geoffrey. 1978. *Phillip II*. London: Hutchinson.

Peng, Xinwei. 1994. *A Monetary History of China*. Translated by Edward H. Kaplan. Belllingham: Western Washington University, Center for East Asian Studies.

Pines, Yuri. 2009. *Envisioning Eternal Empire: Chinese Political Thoughts of the Warring States Era*. Honolulu: University of Hawai'i Press.

Poo, Mu-chou. 1998. *In Search of Personal Welfare: A View of Ancient Chinese Religion*. Albany, NY: SUNY Press.

Pregadio, Fabrizio, ed. 2007. *The Encyclopedia of Taoism*. London: Routledge.

Psellus, Michael (1018–1096). 1966. *Fourteen Byzantine Rulers*, trans. E. R. A. Sewter. New York: Penguin Books.

Queen, Sarah A. 1996. *From Chronicle to Canon: The Hermeneutics of the Spring and Autumn, according to Tung Chung-shu*. Cambridge, UK: Cambridge University Press.

Quigley, Declan. 2005. "Introduction: The Character of Kingship." In *The Character of Kingship*, edited by Declan Quigley, pp. 1–23. Oxford: Berg.

Rawski, Evelyn S. 1998. *The Last Emperors: A Social History of Qing Imperial Institutions*. Berkeley: University of California Press.

Reiter, Florian C. 2007. "The Management of Nature: Convictions and Means in Daoist Thunder Magic (Daojiao leifa)." In *Purposes, Means and Convictions in Daoism: A Berlin Symposium*, edited by Florian C. Reiter, pp. 183–200. Wiesbaden: Harrassovitz.

Ren Chongyue 任崇岳. 1990. "Luelun Song Jin guanxi de jige wenti" 略論宋金關係的幾個問題. *Shehui kexue jikan*, 1990 , no. 4: 41–49.

———. 1996a. "Li Shishi shengnian xiaokao" 李師師生年小考. *Henan daxue xuebao: shekeban* , 1996, no. 1: 57–60.

———. 1996b. *Song Huizong, Song Qinzong* 宋徽宗, 宋欽宗. Changchun: Jilin wenshi chubanshe.

Ren Jiyu 任繼愈. 1990. *Zhongguo daojiao shi* 中國道教史. Shanghai: Shanghai Renmin chubanshe.

Robinet, Isabelle. 1993. *Taoism Meditation: The Mao-shan Tradition of Great Purity*. Albany, NY: SUNY Press.

———. 1997. *Taoism: Growth of a Religion*. Translated by Phyllis Brooks. Stanford: Stanford University Press.

———. 1998. "Later Commentaries: Textual Polysemy and Syncretistic Interpretations." In *Lao-tzu and the Tao-te-ching*, edited by Livia Kohn and Michael LaFargue, pp. 119–142. Albany, NY: SUNY Press.

Robinson, David M. 2008. "The Ming Court." In *Culture, Courtiers, and Competition: The Ming Court (1368–1644)*, edited by David M. Robinson. Cambridge, MA: Harvard University Asia Center.

Rowland, Benjamin. 1951. "The Problem of Hui Tsung." *Archives of the Chinese Art Society of America* 5: 5–22.

———. 1954. "Hui-tsung and Huang Ch'uan." *Artibus Asiae* 17, no. 2: 130–34.

Rudolph, Richard C. 1948. "Dynastic Booty: An Altered Chinese Bronze." *Harvard Journal of Asiatic Studies* 11: 174–83.

Sanmenxiashi wenwu gongzuodui 三門峽市文物工作隊. 1999. *Bei Song Shanzhou louzeyuan* 北宋陝州漏澤園. Beijing: Wenwu.

Sariti, Anthony William. 1970. "The Political Thought of Ssu-ma Kuang: Bureaucratic Absolutism in the Northern Song." PhD diss., Georgetown University.

Schafer, Edward H. 1961. *Tu Wan's Stone Catalogue of Cloudy Forest*. Berkeley and Los Angeles: University of California Press.

———. 1963. "The Auspices of T'ang." *Journal of the American Oriental Society* 83, no. 2: 197–225.

———. 1968. "Hunting Parks and Animal Enclosures in Ancient China." *Journal of the Economic and Social History of the Orient* 11: 318–43.

———. 1977. *Pacing the Void: T'ang Approaches to the Stars*. Berkeley: University of California Press.

———. 1980. *Mao Shan in T'ang Times*. N.p.: Society for the Study of Chinese Religions.

Schipper, Kristofer. 1989. "A Study of Buxu (步虛): Taoist Liturgical Hymn and Dance." In *Studies of Taoist Rituals and Music of Today*, edited by Pen-Yeh Tsao and Daniel P. L. Law, pp. 110–120. Hong Kong: The Chinese Music Archive, Chinese University of Hong Kong.

Schipper, Kristofer, and Franciscus Verellen, eds. 2004. *The Taoist Canon: A Historical Companion to the Daozang*. Chicago: University of Chicago Press.

Schmidt-Glintzer, Helwig. 1989. "Zhang Shangying (1043–1122)—An Embarrassing Policy Adviser under the Northern Song." In *Liu Tzu-chien hakushi shoshū kinen Sōshi* kenkyū ronshū, edited by Kinugawa Tsuyoshi, pp. 521–530. Kyoto: Dohōsha.

Scogin, Hugh. 1978. "Poor Relief in Northern Sung China." *Oriens Extremus* 25, no. 1: 30–46.

Seidel, Anna K. 1982. "Tokens of Immortality in Han Graves." *Numen* 29: 79–122.

———. 1983. "Imperial Treasures and Taoist Sacraments: Taoist Roots in the Apocrypha." In *Tantric and Taoist Studies in Honour of R. A. Stein*, vol. 2, edited by Michel Strickmann, pp. 291–371. Brussels: Institut Belge des Hautes Études Chinoises.

Shaberg, David. 2001. *A Patterned Past: Form and Thought in Early Chinese Historiography*. Cambridge, MA: Harvard University Asia Center.

She Cheng 佘城. 1988. *Bei Song tuhua yuan zhi xintan* 北宋圖畫院之新探. Taipei: Wenshizhe chubanshe.

Shen Dongmei 沈冬梅. 1999. *Songdai cha wenhua* 宋代茶文化. Taipei: Xuehai chubanshe.

Shen Songqin 沈松勤. 1998. *BeiSong wenren yu dangzheng—Zhongguo shidafu qunti yanjiu zhi yi* 北宋文人與黨爭—中國士大夫群體研究之一. Beijing: Renmin chubanshe.

Shiba Yoshinobu. 1983. "Sung Foreign Trade: Its Scope and Organization." In *China among Equals: The Middle Kingdom and Its Neighbors, 10th–14th Centuries*, edited by Morris Rossabi, pp. 89–115. Berkeley: University of California Press.

Shimada Hidemasa. 島田英誠. 1981. "Kisō chō no gagaku ni tsuite" 徽宗朝の畫學について. In *Chūgoku kaigashi ronshū: Suzuki Kei sensei kanreki kinen*, pp. 109–50. Tokyo: Yoshikawa Kobunkan.

Shinno Reiko 秦玲子. 1993. "Sodai no ko to tei ken" 宋代の后と帝嗣決定權. In *Yanagida Setsuko sensei ko kinen: Zhugoku no dento shakai to kazoku* 柳田節子先生古 記念; 中國の伝統社会と家族, pp. 51–70. Tokyo: Kyūko Shoin.

Shui Laiyou 水賚佑. 1995. *Zhao Ji de shufa yishu* 趙佶的書法藝術. Beijing: Renmin meishu.

Sirén, Osvald. 1956. *Chinese Painting: Leading Masters and Principles*. 7 vols. London: Lund, Humphries and Co.

Sivin, Nathan. 1969. "Cosmos and Computation in Early Chinese Mathematical Astronomy." *T'oung Pao* 55: 1–73.

Skar, Lowell. 1996–1997. "Administering Thunder: A Thirteenth-Century Memorial Deliberating the Thunder Rites." *Cahiers d'Extrême-Asie* 9: 159–202.

———. 2000. "Ritual Movements, Deity Cults and the Transformation of Daoism in Song and Yuan Times." In *Daoism Handbook*, edited by Livia Kohn, pp. 413–463. Leiden: E. J. Brill.

Skonicki, Douglas Edward. 2007. "Cosmos, State and Society: Song Dynasty Arguments concerning the Creation of Political Order." PhD diss., Harvard University.

Smith, Paul. 1991. *Taxing Heaven's Storehouse: Bureaucratic Entrepreneurship and the Sichuan Tea and Horse Trade, 1074–1224*. Cambridge, MA: Council on East Asian Studies, Harvard University.

———. 2006. "Irredentism as Political Capital: The New Policies and the An-nexation of Tibetan Domains in Hehuang (the Qinghai-Gansu Highlands) under Shenzong and his Sons, 1068–1126)." In *Emperor Huizong and Late Northern Song China: The Politics of Culture and the Culture of Politics*, edited by Patricia Buckley Ebrey and Maggie Bickford, pp. 78–130. Cambridge, MA: Harvard Asia Center.

———. 2009a. "Introduction: The Sung Dynasty and Its Precursors, 907–1279." In *The Cambridge History of China*, vol. 5, part 1: *The Song Dynasty and Its Precursors, 907–1279*, edited by Denis Twitchett and Paul Jakov Smith, pp. 1–37. Cambridge, UK: Cambridge University Press.

———. 2009b. "Shen-tsung's Reign and the New Policies of Wang An-shih, 1067–1085." In *The Cambridge History of China*, vol. 5, part 1: *The Song Dynasty and Its Precursors, 907–1279*, edited by Denis Twitchett and Paul Jakov Smith, pp. 347–483. Cambridge, UK: Cambridge University Press.

Som, Tjan Tjoe, trans. 1952. *Po hu t'ung: The Comprehensive Discussions in the White Tiber Hall*. 2 vols. Leiden: E. J. Brill.

Song Huizong 宋徽宗. 1997. *Qianzi wen* 千字文. Shenyang: Liaoning Provincial Museum.

Soothill, William Edward. 1952. *The Hall of Light: A Study of Early Chinese King-ship*. New York: Philosophical Library.

Soper, Alexander C. 1948. "Hsiang-kuo-ssu, An Imperial Temple of Northern Sung." *Journal of the American Oriental Society*, 68, no. 1: 19–45.

———. 1951. *Kuo Jo-hsü's Experiences in Painting (T'u-hua chien-wen chih): An Eleventh Century History of Chinese Painting*. Washington, DC: American Council of Learned Societies.

Standen, Naomi. 2005. "What Nomads Want: Raids, Invasions and the Liao Con-quest of 947." In *Mongols, Turks, and Others: Eurasian Nomads and the Sedentary World*, edited by Reuven Amitai and Michal Biran, pp. 129–74. Leiden: E. J. Brill.

———. 2007. *Unbounded Loyalty: Frontier Crossings in Liao China*. Honolulu: Uni-versity of Hawai'i Press.

———. 2009. "The Five Dynasties." In *The Cambridge History of China*, vol. 5, part 1: *The Sung Dynasty and Its Precursors, 907–1279*, edited by Denis Twitchett and Paul Jakov Smith, pp. 38–132. Cambridge, UK: Cambridge University Press.

Steinhardt, Nancy. 1997. *Liao Architecture*. Honolulu: University of Hawai'i Press.

Strickmann, Michel. 1977. "The Mao Shan Revelations: Taoism and the Aristoc-racy." *T'oung Pao* 63, no. 1: 1–64.

———. 1978. "The Longest Taoist Scripture." *History of Religions* 17, nos. 3–4: 331–54.

———. 1979. "The Taoist Renaissance of the Twelfth Century." Paper presented at the Third International Conference of Taoist Studies, Unterägeri, (Swit-zerland, September 3–9, 1979.

———. 1988. "Dreamwork of Psycho-Sinologists: Doctors, Taoists, Monks." In *Psycholo-Sinology: The Universe of Dreams in Chinese Culture*, edited by Caro-lyn T. Brown, pp. 25–46. Washington, DC: Woodrow Wilson International Center for Scholars.

Sturman, Peter C. 1990. "Cranes above Kaifeng: The Auspicious Image at the Court of Huizong." *Ars Orientalis* 20: 33–68.

———. 1997. *Mi Fu: Style and the Art of Calligraphy in Northern Song China*. New Haven: Yale University Press.

Sue Takashi 須江隆. 1994. Tōsōki ni okeru shibyō no byōgaku, hōgō no kashi ni tsuite 唐宋期における祠廟の廟額　封號の下賜について. *Chūgoku—shakai to bunka* 9: 96–119.

Sullivan, Michael. 1974. *The Three Perfections: Chinese Painting, Poetry and Calligraphy*. London: Thames and Hudson.

———. 1979. *Symbols of Eternity: The Art of Landscape Painting in China*. Stanford: Stanford University Press.

———. 1999. *The Arts of China*. 4th edition. Berkeley: University of California Press.

Sun Kekuan 孫克寬. 1965. *Song Yuan daojiao zhi fazhan* 宋元道教之發展. Taipei: Sili Donghai daxue.

Suto, Yoshiyuki. 1965. "The Kung-T'ien-Fa of the Late Northern Sung." *Memoirs of the Research Department of the Toyo-Bunko* 24: 1–46.

Suzuki Kei 鈴木敬. 1965. "Gagaku o chūshin to shita Kisō Gaen no kaikaku to intai sansuiga yōshiki no seiritsu" 畫學 を中心とした徽宗畫院の改革と院體山水畫樣式の成立. *Tōyō bunka kenkyūjo kiyō* 38: 145–84.

———. 1981. "Li Tang no nanto, fukuin to sono yōshiki hensen ni tsuite no ichi shiron," 李唐の南渡 復院とその樣式變遷についての一試論, part 1, *Kokka* 88, no. 6: 5–20. A translation into Chinese is also available: "Shilun Li Tang nanduhou chong ru huayuan ji qi huafeng zhi yanbian, shang" 試論李唐南渡後重入畫院及其畫風之演變, 上. *Gugong jikan* 17, no. 3 (1983): 57–74.

———. 1982. "Li Tang no nanto, fukuin to sono yōshiki hensen ni tsuite no ichi shiron" 李唐の南渡 復院とその樣式變遷についての一試論, part 2. *Kokka* 88, no. 12: 13–23. A translation into Chinese is also available: "Shilun Li Tang nanduhou chong ru huayuan ji qi huafeng zhi yanbian, xia" 試論李唐南渡後重入畫院及其畫風之演變, 下. *Gugong jikan* 17, no. 4 (1983): 65–80.

Tackett, Nicolas. 2008. "The Great Wall and Conceptulizations of the Border under the Northern Song." *Journal of Song-Yuan Studies* 38: 99–138.

Tang Daijian 唐代劍. 1992. "*Songshi* 'Lin Lingsu zhuan' buzheng" 《宋史. 林靈素傳》補正. *Shijie zongjiao yanjiu* 49: 23–28.

———. 1993. "Lun Lin Lingsu yu 'Huizong shiguo'" 論林靈素與"徽宗失國." *Shijie zongjiao yanjiu* 49: 23–28.

———. 1994. "Bei Song Shenxiaogong jiqi weiyi gouji" 北宋神霄宮及其威儀鈎稽. *Zhongugo daojiao* 1994, no.3: 47–48.

———. 1996. "Lun Lin Lingsu chuangli shenxiaopai" 論林靈素創立神霄派. *Shijie zongjiao yanjiu* 1996, no.2: 59–67.

———. 1997. "Songdai daojiao fazhan yanjiu" 宋代道教發展研究. *Guangxi daxue xuebao (Zhexue shehui ke xuebao)* 73: 63–95.

———. 2003. *Songdai daojiao guanli zhidu yanjiu* 宋代道教管理制度研究. Beijing: Xianzhuang shuju.

Tao, Jing-shen [see also Tao Jinsheng]. 1976. *The Jurchen in Twelfth-Century China: A Study of Sinification*. Seattle: University of Washington Press.

———. 1988. *Two Sons of Heaven: Studies in Sung-Liao Relations*. Tucson: University of Arizona Press.

———. 1989. "The Personality of Sung Kao-tsung (r. 1127–1162)." In *Liu Tzu-chien hakushi shoshū kinen Sōshi kenkyū ronshū*, edited by Kinugawa Tsuyoshi, pp. 531–543. Kyoto: Dohōsha.

Tao, Jinsheng 陶晉生 [see also Tao Jing-shen]. 1970. "Nan-Song chu xinwang Zhen kang Jin shimo" 南宋初信王榛抗金始末. *Zhonghua wenhua fuxing yuekan* 3, no. 7: 18–20.

Teiser, Stephen F. 1988. *The Ghost Festival in Medieval China*. Princeton: Princeton University Press.

Thiele, Dagmar. 1971. *Der Abschluss eines Vertrages: Diplomatie zwischen Sung-und Chin-Dynastie 1117–1123*. Wiesbaden: Franz Steiner Verlag.

Tian, Xiaofei. 2007. *Beacon Fire and Shooting Star: The Literary Culture of the Liang (502–557)*. Cambridge, MA: Harvard University Asia Center.

Tokunaga Yosuke 德永洋介. 1998. "Sōdai no gyohitsu shushō" 宋代の御筆手詔. *Tōyōshi kenkyū* 57, no. 3: 393–426.

Tomita, Kojiro. 1933. "The Five Colored Parakeet of Hui Tsung (1082–1135)." *Bulletin of the Museum of Fine Arts* 31: 75–79.

Tomota Kōmei 富田孔明. 2002. "HokuSō shidaifu no kōtei-saishitsu ron" 北宋士大夫 の皇帝-宰執論. *Tōyō bunka kenkyū* 4: 33–60.

Tsai, Shih-shan Henry. 2001. *Perpetual Happiness: The Ming Emperor Yongle*. Seattle: University of Washington Press.

Tsao, Hsingyuan. 2003. "Unraveling the Mystery of the Handscroll *Qingming shanghe tu*." *Journal of Song-Yuan Studies* 33: 155–79.

Tseng Yuho [see also Ecke, Betty Tseng Yu-ho]. 1993. *A History of Chinese Calligraphy*. Hong Kong: The Chinese University Press.

Twitchett, Denis. 1961. "Chinese Biographical Writing." In *Historians of China and Japan*, edited by W. G. Beasley and E. G. Pulleyblank, pp. 95–114. Oxford: Oxford University Press.

———. 1962. "Problems in Chinese Biography." In *Confucian Personalities*, edited by Arthur F. Wright and Denis Twitchett, pp. 24–42. Stanford: Stanford University Press.

———. 1992. *The Writing of Official History under the T'ang*. Cambridge, UK: Cambridge University Press.

———. 1996. "How to be an Emperor: T'ang T'ai-tsung's Vision of His Role." *Asia Major*, 3rd series, 9: 1–102.

Twitchett, Denis, and Paul Jakov Smith, eds. 2009. *The Cambridge History of China*, vol. 5, part 1: *The Sung Dynasty and Its Precursors, 907–1279*. Cambridge, UK: Cambridge University Press.

Twitchett, Denis, and Klaus-Peter Tietze. 1994. "The Liao." In *The Cambridge History of China*, vol. 6: *Alien Regimes and Border States, 907–1368*, edited by Herbert Franke, and Denis Twitchett, pp. 43–153. Cambridge, UK: Cambridge University Press.

Umehara Kaoru 梅原郁. 1976. "Songdai de neizang yu zuozang—Junzhu ducaizhi de caiku" 宋代的内藏與左藏—君主獨裁的財庫, trans. Zheng Liangsheng 鄭樑生. *Shihuo yuekan* 6, nos. 1–2: 34–66.

———. 1985. *Sōdai kanryō seido kenkyū* 宋代官僚制度研究. Kyoto: Dōhōsha.

———. 1986. "Civil and Military Officials in the Sung: The Chi-lu-kuan System." *Acta Asiatica* 50: 1–30.

Vale, Malcolm. 2001. *The Princely Court: Medieval Courts and Culture in North-West Europe, 1270–1380*. Oxford: Oxford Univeristy Press.

Van der Loon, Piet. 1984. *Taoist Books in the Libraries of the Sung Period: A Critical Study and Index*. London: Ithaca Press.

Vinograd, Richard. 1979. "Some Landscapes related to the Blue-and-Green Manner from the Early Yuan Period." *Artibus Asiae* 41, nos. 2–3: 101–31.

Vittinghoff, Helmolt. 1975. *Proskription und Intrige gegen Yüan-yu-Parteigänger: ein Beitrag zu den zur Kontroversen nach den Reformen des Wang An-shih, dargestellt an den Biographien des Lu Tien (1042–1102) und des Ch'en Kuan (1057–1124)*. Frankfurt: Peter Lang.

Von Eschenbach, Silvia Freiin Ebner. 1994. "Public Graveyards of the Song Dynasty." In *Burial in Song China*, edited by Dieter Kuhn, pp. 215–52. Heidelberg: Edition Forum.

Von Glahn, Richard. 1987. *The Country of Streams and Grottoes: Expansion, Settlement, and the Civilizing of the Sichuan Frontier in Song times*. Harvard East Asian Monographs, 123. Cambridge, MA: Council on East Asian Studies, Harvard University.

———. 2004. *The Sinister Way: The Divine and the Demonic in Chinese Religious Culture*. Berkeley: University of California Press.

Wagner, Rudolph. 1988. "Imperial Dreams in China." In *Psycholo-Sinology: The Universe of Dreams in Chinese Culture*, edited by Carolyn T. Brown, pp. 11–24. Washington, DC: Woodrow Wilson International Center for Scholars.

Waley, Arthur, trans. 1937. *The Book of Songs*. London: Allen & Unwin.

Wang Jianqiu 王建秋. 1965. *Songdai taixue yu taixuesheng* 宋代太學與太學生. Taipei: Commercial Press.

Wang Mingsun 王明蓀. 1981. "Tan Songdai de huanguan" 談宋代的宦官. *Dongfang zazhi* 15, no. 5: 57–60.

Wang Pingchuan 王平川, and Zhao Menglin 趙夢林, eds. 2002. *Song Huizong shufa quanji* 宋徽宗書法全集. Beijing: Chaohua chubanshe.

Wang Ruilai 王瑞來. 1989. "Lun Songdai huangquan" 論宋代皇權. *Lishi yanjiu* 197, no. 1: 144–60.

———. 2001. *Sōdai no kōtei kenryoku to shitaifu seiji* 宋代の皇帝權力と士大夫政治. Tokyo: Kyūko Shōin.

———. 2004. "Kisō to Saikyō—kenriki no karamiai" 徽宗と蔡京—権力の絡み合い. *Ajia yūgaku* 64: 34–44.

Wang Shengduo 汪聖鐸. 1991. "Songchao li yu daojiao" 宋朝禮與道教, *Guoji Songdai wenhua yantao hui lunwen ji*. Chengdu: Sichuan daxue.

———. 1995. *Liang Song caizheng shi* 兩宋財政史. 2 vols. Beijing: Zhonghua shuju.

———. 2003. *Liang Song huobi shi* 兩宋貨幣史. 2 vols. Beijing: Shehui kexue wenxian chubanshe.

———. 2010. *Songdai zhengjiao guanxi yanjiu* 宋代政教關係研究. Beijing: Renmin chubanshe.

Wang Yaoting. 1988. "Images of the Heart: Chinese Painting on a Theme of Love." *National Palace Museum Bulletin* 12, no. 6: 1–21.

Wang, Yugen. 2011. "The Limits of Poetry as Means of Social Criticism: The 1079 Literary Inquisition against Su Shi Revisited." *Journal of Song-Yuan Studies* 41: 29–65.

Wang Yuji 王育濟. 1987. "Lun BeiSong monian de 'Yubi xingshi'" 論北宋末年的 '御筆行事'. *Shandong daxue xuebao*, no.1: 54–62.

Wang Zengyu 王曾瑜. 1983. *Songchao bingzhi chutan* 宋朝兵制初探. Beijing: Zhonghua shuju.

———. 1994. "Bei Song wanqi zhengzhi jianlun" 北宋晚期政治簡論. *Zhongguoshi yanjiu* 1994 no.4: 82–87.

Wechsler, Howard J. 1974. *Mirror to the Son of Heaven: Wei Cheng at the Court of T'ang T'ai-tsung*. New Haven: Yale University Press.

———. 1985. *Offerings of Jade and Silk: Ritual and Symbol in the Legitimation of the T'ang Dynasty*. New Haven: Yale University Press.

Weinstein, Stanley. 1987. *Buddhism under the T'ang*. Cambridge, UK: Cambridge University Press.

Weng Tongwen 翁同文. 1968. "Wang Shen shengping kaolue" 王詵生平考略. *Nanyang daxue xuebao* 2: 172–82. Reprinted in *Song shi yanjiu ji* 5 (1970): 135–68.

West, Stephen H. 1985. "The Interpretation of a Dream: The Sources, Evaluation, and Influence of the Dongjing Meng Hua Lu." *T'oung Pao* 71: 63–108.

———. 1987. "Cilia, Scale and Bristle: The Consumption of Fish and Shellfish in the Eastern Capital of Northern Sung." *Harvard Journal of Asiatic Studies* 47: 595–634.

———. 1997. "Playing with Food: Performance, Food, and the Aesthetics of Artificiality in the Sung and Yuan," *Harvard Journal of Asiatic Studies* 57, no. 1: 67–106.

———. 1999. "The Emperor Sets the Pace: Court and Consumption in the Eastern Capital of the Northern Song During the Reign of Huizong." In *Selected Essays on Court Culture in a Cross-Cultural Perspective*, edited by Lin Yao-fu, pp. 25–50. Taipei: National Taiwan University.

———. 2005a. "Spectacle, Ritual, and Social Relations: The Son of Heaven, Citizens, and Created Space in Imperial Gardens in the Northern Song." In *Baroque Garden Cultures: Emulation, Sublimation, Subversion*, edited by M. Conan, pp. 291–321. Washington, DC: Dumbarton Oaks.

———. 2005b. "Recollections of the Northern Song Capital." In *Hawai'i Reader in Traditional Chinese Culture*, edited by Victor H. Mair, Nancy S. Steinhardt, and Paul R. Goldin, pp. 405–22. Honolulu: University of Hawai'i Press.

———. 2006. "Crossing Over: Huizong in the Afterglow, or the Deaths of a Troubling Emperor." In *Emperor Huizong and Late Northern Song China: The Politics of Culture and the Culture of Politics*, edited by Patricia Buckley Ebrey and Maggie Bickford, pp. 565–608. Cambridge, MA: Harvard Asia Center.

Whitfield, Roderick. 1998. "Material Culture in the Northern Song Dynasty— the World of Zhang Zeduan." In *Bright as Silver, White as Snow: Chinese White Ceramics from Late Tang to Yuan Dynasty*, edited by Kai-yin Lo, pp. 49–70. Hong Kong: Yongming tang.

Wilhelm, Richard, trans. 1967. *The I Ching or Book of Changes*. Princeton: Princeton University Press.

Wittfogel, Karl A., and Feng Chia-sheng. 1949. *History of Chinese Society, Liao (907–1125)*. Philadelphia: American Philosophical Society.

Wong, Hon-chiu. 1975. "Government Expenditures in Northern Sung China, 960–1270." PhD diss., University of Pennsylvania.

Wood, Alan T. 1995. *Limits to Autocracy: From Sung Neo-Confucianism to a Doctrine of Political Rights*. Honolulu: University of Hawai'i Press.

Wright, Arthur F. 1960. "Sui Yang-ti, Personality and Stereotype." In *The Confucian Persuasion*, edited by Arthur F. Wright, pp. 47–76. Stanford: Stanford University Press.

———. 1978. *The Sui Dynasty*. New York: Knopf.

Wright, David C. 1993. "Sung-Liao Diplomatic Practices." PhD diss., Princeton University.

———. 2005. *From War to Diplomatic Parity in Eleventh-Century China: Sung's Foreign Relations with Kitan Liao*. Leiden: E. J. Brill.

Wu, Fusheng. 2008. *Written at Imperial Command: Panegyric Poetry in Early Medieval China*. Albany, NY: SUNY Press.

Wu Hung. 1989. *The Wu Liang Shrine: The Ideology of Early Chinese Pictorial Art*. Stanford: Stanford University Press.

———. 1995. *Monumentality in Early Chinese Art and Architecture*. Stanford: Stanford University Press.

Wu, Silas H. L. 1979. *Passage to Power: K'ang-hsi and His Heir Apparent, 1661–1722*. Cambridge, MA: Harvard University Press.

Wyatt, Don J. 2009. "Unsung Men of War: Acculturated Embodiments of the Martial Ethos in the Song Dynasty." In *Military Culture in Imperial China*, edited by Nicola di Cosmo. pp. 192–28. Cambridge, MA: Harvard University Press.

Xiao Baifang 蕭百芳. 1990a. "Cong daozang ziliao tansuo Song Huizong chong dao de mudi" 從道藏資料探索宋徽宗崇道的目的. *Daoziao xue tansuo* 3: 130–83.

———. 1990b. "Song Huizong chong dao shenhua de tantao" 宋徽宗崇道神話的探討. *Daojiao xue tansuo* 3: 95–129.

Xie Zhiliu 謝稚柳. 1957. "Zhao Ji Tingqin tu he ta de zhenbi wenti" 趙佶聽琴圖和他的真筆問題. *Wenwu cankao ziliao* 1957. no. 3: 20–21.

———. 1989. *Song Huizong Zhao Ji quanji*. 宋徽宗趙佶全集. Shanghai: Shanghai Renmin chubanshe.

Xiong Mingqin 熊鳴琴. 2005. "Zeng Bu yu BeiSong houqi zhengzhi" 曾布與北宋後期政治. In *BeiSong zhonghouqi zhengzhi tansuo* 北宋中後期政治探索, edited by Zhang Qifan 張其凡, pp. 177–316. Hong Kong: Huaxia wenhua yishu chubanshe.

Xiong, Victor. 1996. "Ritual Innovations and Taoism under Tang Xuanzong," *T'oung Pao* 82, nos. 4–5: 258–316.

———. 2000. *Sui-tang Chang'an: A Study in the Urban History of Medieval China*. Ann Arbor: Center for Chinese Studies, the University of Michigan.

———. 2003. "Ritual Architecture under the Northern Wei." In *Between Han and Tang: Visual and Material Culture in a Transformative Period*, edited by Wu Hung, pp. 31–95. Beijing: Cultural Relics Publishing House.

———. 2006. *Emperor Yang of the Sui Dynasty: His Life, Times, and Legacy*. Albany, NY: SUNY Press.

Xu Bangda 徐邦達. 1979. "Song Huizong Zhao Ji qinbihua yu daibihua de kaobian" 宋徽宗趙佶親筆畫與代筆畫的考辨. *Gugong bowuyuan yuankan* 1979, no. 1: 62–67, 50.

———. 1984. *Gu shuhua wei'e kaobian* 古書畫偽訛考辨. Jiangsu: Jiangsu guji chubanshe.

Xu Yuhu 徐玉虎. 1958. "Song Jin haishang lianmeng de gaiguan" 宋金海上聯盟的概觀. In *Songshi yanjiu ji* 宋史研究集, vol. 1, pp. 227–42. Taipei: Guoli bianyi guan.

Xu Zhentao, David W. Pankenier, and Yaotiao Jiang. 2000. *East Asian / Archaeoastronomy: Historical Records of Astronomical Observations of China, Japan and Korea*. Amsterdam: Gordon and Breach Science Publishers.

Yamada, Toshiaki. 2000. "The Lingbao School." In *Daoism Handbook*, edited by Livia Kohn, pp. 225–255. Leiden: E. J. Brill.

Yamauchi Kōichi. 山內弘一. 1986. "BeiSong shiqi de jiaosi zhidu" 北宋時期的郊祀制度. *Daqing shizhuan xuebao: zhesheban* 1986, no. 1: 83.

———. 2000. "State Sacrifices and Daoism during the Northern Song." *Memoirs of the Research Department of the Toyo Bunko* 58: 1–18.

Yan Yongcheng 燕永成. 2001. "Bei Song zaifu chaozheng biji yanjiu" 北宋宰輔朝政筆記研究. *Wenxian* 2001, no. 3: 105–19.

Yang Shili 楊世利. 2007. "Lun BeiSong zhaolingzhong de neijiang, shouzhao, yubishouzhao" 論北宋詔令中的內降、手詔、御筆手詔. *Zhongzhou xuekan* 2007, no. 6: 186–88.

Yang Weisheng 楊渭生. 1980. "Guanyu Fang La qiyi ruogan wenti de zai tantao" 關於方臘起義若干問題的再探索. *Wenshi* 8, no. 3: 59–72.

Yang Xiaomin 楊小敏 and Zhang Zifu 張自福. 2011. "Lun BeiSong wanqi Huizong junchen shoufu Yan Yun zhi guoce" 論北宋晚期徽宗君臣收復燕雲之國策. *Tianshui shifan xueyuan xuebao* 31, no. 1: 99–104.

Yao Sheng 耀生. 1965. "Yaoxian shike wenzi lue zhi" 耀縣石刻文字略志. *Kaogu* 1965, no. 3: 134–51.

Yetts, W. Percival. 1927. "A Chinese Treatise on Architecture." *Bulletin of the School of Oriental Studies* 4, no. 3: 473–92.

Yi Ruofen 衣若芬. 1999. "*Xuanhe huapu* yu Su Shi huihua sixiang" 宣和畫譜與蘇軾繪畫思想. In *Zhongguo di shijie Su Shi yanjiu huiyi wenji* 中國第十屆蘇軾研究會議文集, ed. Li Zengpo 李曾坡, pp. 209–38. Jinan: Qilu shushe chubanshe.

———. 2006. "Hunjun yu jianchen de duihua—tan Song Huizong wenhui tu tishi" 「昏君」與「奸臣」的對話—談宋徽宗「文會圖」題詩. *Wen yu zhe* 8: 253–78.

———. 2008. "Tianlu qianqiu—Song Huizong wenhui tu jiqi tishi" 天祿千秋—宋徽宗「文會圖」及其題詩. *Kaichuang dianfan: BeiSong de yishu yu wenhua yantaohui lunwenji* 開創典範: 北宋的藝術與文化研討會論文集, edited by Wang 王耀庭, pp. 347–68. Taipei: National Palace Museum.

Yi Yongwen 伊永文. 2005. *Xingzou zai Songdai de chengshi* 行走在宋代的城市. Beijing: Zhonghua shuju.

Ying Yan 英嚴. 1991. "Songdai gongting de gongji zhidu" 宋代宮廷的供給制度. *Hebei xuekan* 1991, no. 5: 82–87.

You Biao 游彪. 2004. "Songchao de dibao yu shizheng" 宋朝的邸報與時政. *Zhongzhou xuebao* 2004, no. 6: 108–11.

Yu Hui 余輝. 2008. *Huali jiangshan yousheng: Bainian yishu jiazu zhi ZhaoSong jiazu* 畫裡江山猶勝:百年藝術家族之趙宋家族. Taipei: Shitou chubanshe.

Zhan Kaiqi 詹凱琦. 2011. "Cai Jing yu Huizong chao xin shufeng yanjiu" 蔡京與徽宗朝新書風研究. *Zhonghua hongdao shuxue hui huikan* 9, no. 6: 17–29.

Zhang Bangwei 張邦煒. 1993. *Songdai huangqin yu zhengzhi* 宋代皇親與政治. Chengdu: Sichuan renmin chubanshe.

———. 2002. "Guanyu jianzhong zhi zheng" 關於建中之政. *Sichuan shifan daxue xuebao (Shehui kexue ban)* 29, no. 6: 99–108.

———. 2005. *Songdai zhengzhi wenhua shilun* 宋代政治文化史論. Beijing: Renmin chubanshe.

Zhang, Cong Ellen. 2011. *Transformative Journeys: Travel and Culture in Song China*. Honolulu: University of Hawai'i Press.

Zhang Guangbin 張光賓, ed. 1984. *Zhonghua wuqian nian wenwu jikan* 中華五千年文物集刊. *Fashu pian* 法書篇. Taipei: Zhonghua wuqian nian wenwu jikan bianji weiyuanhui.

Zhang, Ling. 2009. "Changing with the Yellow River: An Environmental History of Hebei, 1048–1128." *Harvard Journal of Asiatic Studies* 69, no. 1: 1–36.

Zhang Qifeng 張其鳳. 2008. *Song Huizong yu wenren hua* 宋徽宗與文人畫. Beijing: Rongbaozhai chubanshe.

Zhang Tianyou 張天祐. 1980. "Song Jin haishang lianmeng de yanjiu" 宋金海上聯盟的研究. In *Songshi yanjiu ji* 宋史研究集, vol. 12, pp. 185–245. Taipei: Guoli bianyi guan.

Zhao Yongchun 趙永春. 2005. *Song Jin guanxi shi* 宋金關係史. Beijing: Renmin chubanshe.

Zheng Zhenman 鄭振滿 and Ding Hesheng 丁荷生 [Kenneth Dean]. 1995. *Fujian zongjiao beiming huibian*. 福建宗教碑銘彙編. Fuzhou: Fujian renmin chuban she.

Zhongguo yinyue wenwu daxi zongbian jibu 中國音樂文物大系總編輯部. 1996–2001. *Zhongguo yinyue wenwu daxi* 中國音樂文物大系. 9 vols. Zhengzhou: Daxiang chubanshe.

Zhou Baozhu 周寶珠. 1992. *Songdai dongjing yanjiu* 宋代東京研究. Kaifeng: Henan Daxue chubanshe.

Zhu Hong 朱鴻. 1991. "Songdai neiku de caizheng guanli shulun" 宋代內庫的財政管理述論. *Xibei shida xuebao* 1991, no. 4: 69–74.

Zhu Ruixi 朱瑞熙. 1994. "Songdai de gongting zhidu" 宋代的宮廷制度. *Xueshu yuekan* 1994, no. 44: 60–66, 26.

Zhu Ruixi 朱瑞熙 and Cheng Yu 程郁. 2006. *Songshi yanjiu* 宋史研究. Fuzhou: Fujian renmin chubanshe.

Zhu Ruixi 朱瑞熙, Zhang Bangwei 張邦煒, Liu Fusheng 劉復生, Cai Chongbang 蔡崇榜, and Wang Zengyu 王曾瑜. 1998. *Liao Song Xixia Jin shehui shenghuo shi* 遼宋西夏金社會生活史. Beijing: Chinese Academy of Social Sciences.

Zhu Yi 朱溢. 2009a. "Cong jiaoqiu zhi zheng dao tiandi fenhe zhi zheng—Tang zhi Bei Song shiqi jiaosi zhushenwei de bianhua" 從郊丘之爭到天地分合之爭——唐至北宋時期郊祀主神位的變化. *Hanxue yanjiu* 27 no. 2:267–300.

———. 2009b. "Tang zhi Bei Song shiqi de da si zhong si he xiao si" 唐至北宋時期的大祀、中祀和小祀. *Qinghua xuebao* 39 no. 2:287–324.

Zhuge Yibing 諸葛憶兵. 2000. *Songdai zaifu zhidu yanjiu* 宋代宰輔制度研究. Beijing: Zhongguo shehui kexue chubanshe.

———. 2001. *Huizong citan yanjiu* 徽宗詞壇研究. Beijing: Beijing chubanshe.

Chinese Character Glossary

Advisory Office 講義司
Agency for Deliberating on Ritual
 議禮局
Agency for Instituting Rituals 禮制局
Aguda 阿骨打 (r. 1115–1123)
Ai Xuan 艾宣 (fl. 1068–1077)
*Album for the Imperial Gaze of the
 Xuanhe [Hall or Reign Period]* 宣和睿
 覽冊
Altar of the Soil 社稷
An Dun 安惇 (1042–1104)
An Lushan 安祿山 (703–757)
An Tao 安濤 (fl. 1085–1100)
An Yaochen 安堯臣 (fl. 1118)
Antiquities Illustrated 博古圖
Ascension to the West 西昇經
Assembled Heroes Hall 集英殿
Assisting the State Monastery 相國寺
Atiji 阿替紀 (ca. 1127)

Bai Shizhong 白時中 (d. 1127)
Beseeching the Spirits Temple
 祈神觀
Bi 佀, Huizong's older brother
 (1082–1106)
biji 筆記
Biyong Academy 辟雍
Blessed Tranquility Hall 福寧殿

Bohai 渤海
Book for Saving Lives as at Nanyang
 南陽活人書
Book of Changes 易經
Book of Documents 尚書 / 書經
Book of Music 樂記
Book of Salvation 度人經
Book of Songs 詩經
Bright Gold Agency 明金局
Bright Hall 明堂
Broad Supply Granary 廣濟倉
Bureau of the Music of Great
 Brilliance 大晟樂府

Cai Bian 蔡卞 (1058–1117)
Cai Jing 蔡京 (1047–1126)
Cai Que 蔡確 (1037–1093)
Cai Shu 蔡儵 (fl. 1110s–1120s)
Cai Tao 蔡絛 (?–1147+)
 *Supplement to the History of the
 Dynasty* 國史後補
Cai Tiao 蔡脩 (fl. 1100–1130)
 Annals of the Young and Old 幼老春秋
Cai Xiao 蔡儵 (fl. 1100–1126)
Cai You 蔡攸 (1077–1126)
Calligraphy Bureau 書藝局
Calm Great Master of Peaceful
 Graciousness 安惠文靜大士

637

Cao Fu 曹輔 (*jinshi* 1063)
Cao Xiaozhong 曹孝忠 (fl. 1116)
Cao Xun 曹勛 (1098–1174)
Cao Zu 曹組 (fl. early 12th century)
Celestial Venerable 天尊
Chao Buzhi 晁補之 (1053–1110)
Chao Chongzhi 晁沖之 (fl. early 12th century)
Chao Duanli 晁端禮 (*jinshi* 1073)
Chen 陳, consort of Shenzong, Huizong's birth mother (fl. 1070s–1080s)
Chen 諶, Huizong's grandson, Qinzong's son (b. 1117)
Chen Cisheng 陳次升 (1044–1119)
Chen Dong 陳東 (1087–1127)
Chen Gongfu 陳公輔 (1077–1142)
Chen Gou 陳遘 (fl. early 12th century)
Chen Guan 陳瓘 (1060–1124)
Chen Prefecture Gate 陳州門
Chen Shixi 陳師錫 (fl. early 12th century)
Chen Xiangdao 陳祥道 (1053–1093)
Chen You 陳祐 (fl. 1100–1104)
Chen Yuyi 陳與義 (1090–1138)
Cheng Yi 程頤 (1033–1107)
Cheng Yu 程瑀 (1087–1152)
Chong Shidao 種師道 (1051–1126)
Chong Shizhong 種師中 (1059–1126)
Chongning 崇寧 reign period (1102–1106)
Chu 楚
Chu Hui 楮慧
ci 詞
Classic of Sagely Benefaction 聖濟經
cloud-seal (script) 雲篆
Collected Effective Prescriptions for Universal Benefit Compiled During Leisure 普惠乘閒集效方
Compassionate Virtue Hall 慈德宮
Complete Truth (Daoism) 全真
Comprehensive Manual for Sagely Benefaction of the Zhenghe Period 政和聖濟總錄
Comprehensive Mirror for Aid in Governing 資治通鑑
Cui Bo 崔白 (1024–1068)

Cultured Virtue Hall 文德殿
cursive script 草

Da Jingzhi 笪淨之 (1068–1113)
Daguan 大觀 (reign period, 1107–1110)
daibi 代筆
daode 道德
daoshi 道士
Dashilinya 大石林牙 (fl. 1122)
Dawn Radiance Gate 晨暉門
Deng Su 鄧肅 (1091–1132)
Deng Xunren 鄧洵仁 (fl. 1100–1113)
Deng Xunwu 鄧洵武 (d. 1121)
deshi 德士
diaomin fazui 弔民伐罪
ding 錠
Ding Fu 丁孚 (fl. 1127)
Ding Teqi 丁特起 (?–1135+)
Divine Empyrean 神霄
Divine Empyrean Jade Clarity Longevity Temple 神霄玉清壽宮
Divine Empyrean Jade Clarity Monarch 神霄玉清王
Divine Talismans of the Sexigesimal Jia 六甲神符經
Documents Lodge 名書館
Dong You 董逌 (fl. 1100–1130)
Dong Yu 董羽 (10th century)
Dong Zhongshu 董仲舒 (179–104 BCE)
Dragon Virtue Palace / Temple 龍德宮
Dreaming of Traveling to the Heavenly Palace 夢遊化城圖
Du Fu 杜甫 (712–770)
Du Guangting 杜光庭 (850–933)
Duan, Prince of 端王
Duan Gate 端門
Duke Cheng of Song 宋成公 (r. 636–620 BCE)
Duke of Zhou 周公 (11th century BCE)

E 楀, Huizong's fifteenth son (1110–1132)
Eastern Splendor Gate 東華門
Eastern Grand Unity Temple 東太一宮
Eastern Water Gate 東水門
Eight Immortals' Lodge 八仙館

Eight Virtues, Eight Offenses 八行
八刑

Eluguan 額魯觀 (fl. early 12th century)

Emperor Lord of the Dao 道君皇帝

Erya 爾雅

Establishing the Mean and Stabilizing
the State 建中靖國

Etiquette and Ritual 儀禮

Ever-Victorious Army 常勝軍

Exalted Protection Hall 隆祐宮

Examining Artisans 考工記

Extended Blessings Palace 延福宮

Extended Felicity Hall 延慶殿

Extended Harmony Hall 延和殿

Extended Longevity Temple 延壽寺

Extending to Heaven hat 通天冠

Fan Bolu 范百祿 (1030–1094)

Fan Chuncui 范純粹 (1046–1117)

Fan Chunli 范純禮 (1031–1106)

Fan Chunren 范純仁 (1027–1101)

Fan Kuan 范寬 (ca. 960–ca. 1030)

Fan Qiong 范瓊 (d. 1129)

Fan Tang 范鏜 (*jinshi* 1073)

Fan Zhen 范鎮 (1008–1088)

Fan Zhixu 范致虛 (d. 1129)

Fan Zhongyan 范仲淹 (989–1052)

Fan Zongyin 范宗尹 (1095–1131)

Fan Zuyu 范祖禹 (1041–1098)

Fang La 方臘 (d. 1121)

fangshi 方士

Fangzhang 方丈

Feng Hao 馮浩 (d. 1121)

Feng Xie 馮澥 (d. 1140)

Feng Xizai 馮熙載 (*jinshi* 1107)

First Emperor of Qin 秦始皇
(r. 221–210 BCE)

Five Phases 五行

Five Sacred Mountains 五嶽

Flower and Rock Network 花石綱

form-likeness 形似

Fu Ji 傅楫 (1042–1102)

Fu Xilie 傅希烈 (fl. early 12th century)

Fujin 福金, Huizong's daughter,
married to Cai Tiao 福金 (b. 1103)

Fujin 富金, Huizong's daughter,
married to Tian Pi (b. 1109)

Fuxi 伏羲

Gaitian, Great Prince (of Jin) 蓋天
大王 (fl. early 12th century)

Gao 高, empress of Yingzong, later
regent for Zhezong (1023–1093)

Gao Qingyi 高慶裔 (fl. early 12th
century)

Gao Qiu 高俅 (d. 1126)

Gao Wenjin 高文進 (fl. 960s–990s)

Gao Yaoshi 高藥師 (fl. 1118)

Gao Yijian 高一箭 (fl. 1122)

Gaozong, emperor of Song 宋高宗
(1107–1187, r. 1127–1162)

Gaozu, emperor of Han 漢高祖
(r. 202–195 BCE)

Ge Cizhong 葛次仲 (1063–1121)

Ge Shengzhong 葛勝仲 (1072–1144)

Ge Shouchang 葛守昌 (fl. 1068–1077)

Geng Nanzhong 耿南仲 (*jinshi* 1082)

Geng Yanxi 耿延禧 (fl. early to
mid-12th century)

Geng Yu 耿愚 (fl. 1100)

Golden Brilliance Lake Park 金明
池苑

Golden Immortal of Great
Enlightenment 大覺金仙

Golden Tower 金闕

gong 工

Gong Guai 龔夬 (1057–1111)

Gong Yuan 龔原 (1043–1110)

gongguan 宮觀

Grand Celebration Hall 大慶殿

Grand Clarity Edifice 太清樓

Grand Master of Health and Peace 和
安大夫

Grand Unity 太一 or 太乙

Grand Unity Temple 太一宮 or
太乙宮

Great Brightness Hall 大明殿

Great Brilliance 大晟

Great Clarity 太清

Great Completion Hall 大成殿

Great Interior 大內

Great Lord of Long Life 長生大帝

Great Peace and Prosperous Realm
Monastery 太平興國寺

Great Profundity Scripture 大洞經

Green Enclosure 青城

green verses 青詞

Guangwu, emperor of Han 漢光武帝 (r. 25–57)
Guo Jing 郭京 (fl. 1126–1127)
Guo Ruoxu 郭若虛 (fl. 1070–1075)
Guo Si 郭思 (early twelfth century)
Guo Xi 郭熙 (ca. 1001–ca. 1090)
Guo Yaoshi 郭藥師 (fl. 1120s)
Guolu 國祿 (d. 1127)

Hall for the Daoist Era 道紀堂
Hall of Complete Truth 全真殿
Hall of Flowers with Green Perianths 葛綠華堂
Han Gan 韓幹 (fl. 713–756)
Han Qi 韓琦 (1008–1075)
Han Wudi neizhuan 漢武帝內傳
Han Zhongyan 韓忠彥 (1038–1109)
Han Zongwu 韓宗武 (fl. 1101)
Hanging Hem Hall 垂拱殿
Hao 顥, Huizong's uncle (1050–1096)
Hao Sui 郝隨
Harmony Preserved Hall 保和殿
Harmony Revealed Gate 宣和門
Harmony Revealed Hall 宣和殿
He Guan 何灌 (1065–1126)
He Xin 何訢 (fl. early 12th century)
He Zhitong 何志同 (fl. 1110s–1120s)
He Zhizhong 何執中 (1044–1117)
He Zhuo 何桌 (fl. 1126–1127)
Heavenly Calm 天寧
Heavenly Calm Longevity Temple 天寧萬壽觀
Heavenly Felicity Temple 天慶觀
Heaven's Auspicious Signs 天祥
Heaven's Protection Hall 天保殿
Helu 曷魯 (Jin)
Highest Clarity 上清
Highest Clarity Precious Registers Temple 上清寶籙宮
Highest Truth Purple Void Primal Lord 上真紫虛元君
History of the Dao 道史
Holy Ancestor 聖祖
Hongwu, emperor of Ming 明洪武 (r. 1368–1398)
Honoring Calm 崇寧
Hou Meng 侯蒙 (1054–1121)
Hu Shunzhi 胡舜陟 (1083–1143)

Huan 桓, Huizong's eldest son (1100–1161, Qinzong)
Huang Bosi 黃伯思 (1079–1118)
Huang Chao 黃巢 (d. 884)
Huang Jingchen 黃經臣 (fl. ca. 1100)
Huang Jucai 黃居寀 (933–993+)
Huang Lü 黃履 (*jinshi* 1057)
Huang Quan 黃筌 (903–968)
Huang Tingjian 黃庭堅 (1045–1105)
Huanhuan 嬛嬛, Huizong's daughter (b. 1113)
Huayang, Master 華陽先生
Huizong 徽宗 (1082–1135, r. 1100–1125)
  Auspicious Dragon Rock 祥龍石圖
  Autumn Evening by a Pond 池塘秋晚圖
  Birds and Butterflies in an Autumn Garden 金英秋禽圖
  Cranes of Good Omen 瑞鶴圖
  Finches and Bamboo 竹禽圖
  Five-Colored Parakeet 五色鸚鵡圖
  Listening to the Qin 聽琴圖
  Pheasant on a Hibiscus Branch 英容錦雞圖
  Returning Fishing Boats 雪江歸棹圖
  Streams and Mountains in Autumn Hues 溪山秋色圖
  Two Birds on a Blossoming Wax-Plum Tree 臘梅山禽
Humane Aid Pavilion 仁濟亭
Huyan Qing 呼延慶 (fl. 1120s)

Illuminated Perfected One Who Observes the Marvelous 觀妙明真
Illustrations of the Three Ritual Classics 三禮圖
Imperial Academy 太學
Imperial Heir Apparent 皇太子
Imperial Way 御街
Incipient Clarity 始清
Initiating Treasure Monastery 開寶寺
Inner Classic of the Yellow Emperor 黃帝內經
Inner Treasury 內藏庫
Institutes of the Dao 道典

Jade Book of the Heavenly Altar of the Divine Empyrean 神霄天壇玉書
Jade Capital 玉京
Jade Carriage 玉輅
Jade Clarity 玉清
Jade Clarity Divine Empyrean Temple 玉清神霄宮
Jade Clarity Harmonious Yang Temple 玉清和陽宮
Jade Emperor 玉帝／玉皇大帝
Jade Ford Park 玉津園
Jade Hall 玉堂
Jade Registers 玉牒簿
Jade Splendor Pavilion 玉華閣
Jade True One of the Nine Splendors 九華玉真
Jade Truth Gallery 玉真軒
Jade Void Hall 玉虛殿
Jasper Ford Pavilion 瑤津亭
Ji 佶
Jia Xiang 賈祥 (fl. 1100–1120)
Jian Xuchen 蹇序辰 (fl. late 11th–early 12th centuries)
Jiang E 姜諤 (fl. early 12th century)
Jiang Gongwang 江公望 (fl. early 12th century)
Jiang Han 江漢 (fl. early 12th century)
Jiang You 蔣猷 (1065–1130)
Jiang Zhiqi 蔣之奇 (1031–1104)
Jianzhang Palace 建章宮
jin 斤 (unit of weight)
Jin 金 (dynasty)
Jingfu Palace Treasury 景福殿庫
Jingkang 靖康 reign period (1126–1127)
jinshi 進士
Joined Calm Hall 會寧殿
Jōjin 成尋 (1011–1081)
Joyous Meeting of Ruler and Subjects 君臣慶會
Jun 頵, Huizong's uncle (1056–1088)
Juran 巨然 (10th century)
Jurchen 女真

Kai 楷, Huizong's third son (1101–ca. 1130)
Kaiyuan 開元 reign period (713–742)

Kang, Prince of 康王 (1107–1187, Gaozong)
Kangxi 康熙 reign period (1662–1723)
Kitan 契丹
Kou Zhun 寇準 (961–1023)
Kou Zongshi 寇宗奭 (fl. early 12th century)
Kunlun Clouds Kiosk 崑雲亭
Kunning Hall 坤寧殿

Lan Congxi 藍從熙 (fl. early 12th century)
Laozi 老子
Learning for an Emperor 帝學
Li Anzhong 李安忠 (fl. early to mid-12th century)
Li Bangyan 李邦彥 (d. 1130)
Li Cheng 李成 (919–967)
Li Chuwen 李處溫 (d. 1122)
Li Derou 李得柔 (fl. early 12th century)
Li Gang 李綱 (1083–1140)
Li Gonglin 李公麟 (ca. 1041–1106)
Li Jie 李誠 (d. 1110)
Li Jing 李靖 (fl. 1122–1123)
Li Liang 李良 (Tang)
Li Linfu 李林甫 (d. 752)
Li Qingchen 李清臣 (1032–1102)
Li Ruoshui 李若水 (1093–1127)
Li Shanqing 李善慶 (fl. early 12th century)
Li Shi 李爽 (fl. 1127)
Li Shishi 李師師 (fl. early 12th century)
Li Sixun 李思訓 (651–716)
Li Tang 李唐 (early 12th century)
  Wind in the Pines amid Ten Thousand Valleys 萬壑松風圖
Li Xijing 李熙靖 (1075–1127)
Li Yan 李彥 (fl. early 12th century)
Li Ye 李鄴 (fl. early 12th century)
Li Yu 李煜 (937–978)
Li Zhaodao 李昭道 (fl. 670–730)
Li Zhi 李質 (fl. early 12th century)
Li Zongyan 李宗言 (fl. early 12th century)
Liang Congzheng 梁從政 (fl. late 11th century)

Liang Fangping 梁方平 (fl. 1125)

Liang Shicheng 梁師成 (ca. 1063–1126)

Liang Shimin 梁師閔 (early 12th century)

Liang Tao 梁燾 (1034–1097)

Liao 遼 (dynasty)

Liezi 列子

Lin Jiang xian 臨江仙

Lin Lingsu 林靈素 (1076–1120)

Lin Shu 林攄 (fl. late 11th and early 12th centuries)

Lin Xi 林希 (fl. 1085–1100)

Liu 劉, Empress Dowager (Zhenzong's empress) (969–1033)

Liu 劉, Empress/Empress Dowager (Zhezong's empress) (1079–1113)

Liu Ban 劉攽 (1022–1088)

Liu Biangong 劉卞功 (fl. early 12th century)

Liu Bei 劉備 (161–223)

Liu Bing 劉昺 (*jinshi* 1100)

Liu Chang 劉敞 (1019–1068)

Liu Dong 劉棟 (fl. early 12th century)

Liu Fengshi 劉奉世 (1041–1113)

Liu Guangshi 劉光世 (1089–1142)

Liu Hunkang 劉混康 (1035–1108)

Liu Kui 劉逵 (fl. 1100–1110)

Liu Mingda 劉明達 (d. 1113)

Liu Mingjie 劉明節 (d. 1121)

Liu Si 劉思 (fl. 1127)

Liu Songnian 劉松年 (d. 1224)

Liu Wenyan 劉文彥 (d. 1132)

Liu Yanqing 劉延慶 (1068–1126)

Liu Yi 劉益 (artist) (fl. early 12th century)

Liu Yi 劉益 (Daoist) (fl. early 12th century)

Liu Youduan 劉友端 (fl. early 12th century)

Liu Yuandao 劉元道 (fl. early 12th century)

Liu Zhen 劉鎮 (fl. 1121)

Liu Zhengfu 劉正夫 (1062–1119)

Liu Zhongwu 劉仲武 (fl. early 12th century)

liubo 六博

Longevity Daoist Canon of the Zhenghe Period 政和萬壽藏經

Longevity Mountain 萬歲山

Lord of Confused Virtue 昏德公

Lord of Double Confusion 重昏侯

Lord of Highest Heaven 昊天上帝

Lord of the Nine Old Immortals 九老仙都君

Lu Dian 陸佃 (1042–1102)

Lu Xinger 陸行兒 (fl. 1121)

Lu Yi 盧益 (fl. 1123)

Lu You 陸游 (1125–1210)

Lü Dafang 呂大防 (1027–1097)

Lü Duan 呂端 (935–1000)

Lü Gongzhu 呂公著 (1018–1081)

Lü Huiqing 呂惠卿 (1031–1110)

Lü Jiawen 呂嘉問 (fl. late 11th, early 12th century)

Lü Shang 呂尚 (Zhou dynasty)

Lü Yijian 呂夷簡 (979–1044)

Luan prefecture 灤州

Ma Juan 馬涓 (*jinshi* 1086)

Ma Kuo 馬擴 (d. 1151)

Ma Zheng 馬政 (fl. early 12th century)

Mao Ying 茅盈 (Han dynasty)

Maodun Shanyu 冒頓單于 (d. 174 BCE)

Master of the Cavern Tenuity 洞微先生

Master of Religion and Lord of the Dao 教主道君

Materia Medica of the Daguan Period, Classified and Verified from the Classics and Histories 經史證類大觀本草

Mathematical Canons 算經十書

Medical School 醫學

Mei Zhili 梅執禮 (1079–1127)

Mencius 孟子

Meng, Zhezong's empress, 孟皇后, 孟太后 (1077–1135)

mengzi (first son) 孟子

Mi Fu 米芾 (1051–1107)

Middle Prime 中元

Mirror for Governing along the Lines of the "Great Plan" Chapter of the Book of Documents 洪範政鑑

Mo Chou 莫儔 (1089–1164)

Morning Sun Gate 朝陽門

Most High Lord of the Dao 太上道君
Mount Juqu 句曲山
Mount Mao 茅山
mu 畝
Murong Yanfeng 慕容彥逢
  (1067–1117)
Music of Great Brilliance 大晟樂
Mysterious Primal Holy Ancestor 玄元
  聖祖

na 捺 (stroke)
Nanjin jiwen 南燼紀聞
New Forms of the Five Categories of
  Rites of the Zhenghe Period 政和五禮
  新儀
New Policies 新法
Nianhan 粘罕
  (1079/1080–1136/1137)
Nie Chongyi 聶崇義 (d. 962)
Nie Shan 聶山 (fl. early 12th century)
Nine Cauldrons 九鼎
Nine Completions 九成
Northeast Marchmount 艮嶽
Northern Grand Unity Temple 北太
  一官
Numinous Treasure 靈寶
Nurturing Goodness Hall 資善堂

Offices of Zhou 周官
Outer Document Storehouse
  文字外庫
Ouyang Xiu 歐陽修 (1007–1072)
Ouyang Xun 歐陽詢 (557–641)

Pace of Yu 禹步
palace lady 御侍
Palace Library 秘書監
palace poems 宮詞
paupers' graveyards 漏澤園
Pavilion of the Joyous Meeting of
  Ruler and Subjects 君臣慶會
Peace Achieved Hall 成平殿
Peace Reigns over the River 清明上河圖
Peaceful Consort of Nine-Splendored
  Jade Truth 九華玉真安妃
Penetrating Truth Temple 通貞宮
Peng Rulin 彭汝霖 (*jinshi* 1076)
Penglai 蓬萊

Permanent Benefit 永澤
Perpetual Happiness 永樂
Personal Destiny 本命
pie 撇 (stroke)
Ping prefecture 平州
Pity and Loyalty Shrine 愍忠祠
Plank Bridge 板橋
poorhouse system 居養法
Power of Yang Temple 陽德觀
Precious Registers Temple 寶籙宮
Preserving Harmony Palace 保和殿
Primal Tally Myriad Calm Temple
  元符萬寧宮
Prince 王
Promoting Governance Hall 崇政殿
Proper Sincerity Hall 端誠殿
Protecting the Spirits Temple 佑神觀
public apothecaries 和劑局
Pujienu Xiangwen 蒲結奴相溫 (fl.
  1120s)
Purple Asterism Hall 紫宸殿
Puxian 普賢

qi 氣
Qi 杞, son of Huizong (b. 1104)
qian 錢 (currency)
Qian Ji 錢即 (1054–1124)
Qian Yu 錢通 (1050–1121)
Qianlong 乾隆, reign period
  (1736–1796)
qin 琴
Qin Guan 秦觀 (1049–1100)
Qin Gui 秦檜 (1090–1155)
qing 頃
Qinzong, emperor of Song 宋欽宗 (r.
  1125–1127)
Queen Mother of the West 西王母

Rear Garden 後苑
Receiving Mist Kiosk 承嵐亭
Record of Auspicious Responses of the
  Zhenghe Period 政和瑞應記
Record of Ritual 禮記
Reflecting and Responding to the
  Realm of Jade Clarity Temple 玉清
  昭應宮
regular script 楷書
Ren Boyu 任伯雨 (ca. 1047–ca. 1119)

Sun Guoting 孫過庭 (646–691)
  Treatise on Calligraphy 書譜
Supreme Opening Heaven, Grasping
  the Talisman, Directing the
  Calendar, Containing the True,
  Embodying the Dao, Highest
  Heaven, Jade Emperor, Lord on
  High 太上開天執符御曆含真體道昊
  天玉皇上帝
Supreme Shrine 太廟
*Sutra on the Final Kalpa as Preached by
  the Buddha* 佛說末劫經
Suzong, emperor of Tang 唐肅宗
  (r. 756–762)
Sweet Spring Temple 醴泉觀

Tai Mausoleum 泰靈
Taiwu, emperor of Northern Wei 魏太
  武 (r. 424–452)
Taizong, emperor of Jin 金太宗
  (Wuqimai, r. 1123–1135)
Taizong, emperor of Song 宋太宗
  (r. 976–997)
Taizong, emperor of Tang 唐太宗
  (r. 626–649)
Taizu, emperor of Ming 明太祖
  (r. 1368–1398)
Taizu, emperor of Song 宋太祖
  (r. 960–976)
talisman-water 符水
*Talismans and Diagrams of the Book of
  Salvation* 靈寶無量度人上品妙經符
  圖
Tan Zhen 譚稹 (fl. 1112–1126)
Tang Xiya 唐希雅 (Northern Song)
Tao Xuangan 陶宣干 (12th century)
Temple of Spectacular Numina
  景靈宮
Temple of the Nine Completions 九成
  宮
Ten Exalted Perfected 十極高真
Thousand Character Essay 千字文
Three Clarities 三清
Three Dynasties 三代
Three Halls 三舍
Three Mao Lords 三茅君
Thunder Rites 雷法
Tian Pi 田丕 (fl. 12th century)

Tian Wei 田為 (fl. early 12th century)
Tianzuo, emperor of Liao 遼天祚
  (r. 1101–1125)
Ting 楟, Huizong's twenty-second son,
  Prince of Xiangguo (b. 1114)
Tong Guan 童貫 (1054–1126)
Transformation Revealed Gate
  宣化門
Treasured Compassion Hall 寶慈宮
Treasured Completion Temple
  寶成宮

Venerable Celestial of the Primal
  Beginning 元始天尊
Veritable Records 實錄
Vermilion Bird Gate 朱雀門
Virtue Revealed Gate 宣德門

Wan Siyong 萬俟詠 (fl. early 12th
  century)
Wang Anshi 王安石 (1021–1086)
Wang Anzhong 王安中 (1076–1134)
Wang Bing 王稟 (d. 1126)
Wang Cai 王寀 (1078–1118)
Wang Dan 王但 (957–1017)
Wang Di 王覿 (fl. late 11th century)
Wang, empress of Huizong 王皇后
  (1084–1108)
Wang Fan 王蕃 (fl. late 11th and early
  12th centuries)
Wang Fu 王黼 (1079–1126)
Wang Fuzhi 王夫之 (1619–1692)
Wang Gui 王珪 (1019–1085)
Wang Hou 王厚 (d. 1106)
Wang Laozhi 王老志 (fl. early 12th
  century)
Wang Mang 王莽 (r. 9–23)
Wang Mingqing 王明清 (1127–1214+)
Wang Nengfu 王能甫 (fl. early 12th
  century)
Wang Reng 王仍 (fl. early 12th
  century)
Wang Rui 王汭 (fl. early 12th century)
Wang Ruochong 王若冲 (fl. early 12th
  century)
Wang Shen 王詵 (ca. 1048–ca. 1103)
  Rivers and Mountains in Mist 煙江疊
  嶂圖

Wang Shiyong 王時雍 (fl. early 12th
century)
Wang Wei 王維 (699–759)
Wang Wenqing 王文卿 (1093–1153)
Wang Xianzhi 王獻之 (344–386)
Wang Ximeng 王希孟 (b. 1096)
  Thousand Li of Rivers and Mountains
  千里江山圖
Wang Xizhi 王羲之 (309–ca. 365)
Wang Yansou 王嚴叟 (1043–1093)
Wang Yongchang 王永昌 (fl. early 12th
century)
Wang Yun 王雲 (fl. early 12th century)
Wang Yuzhi 王與之 (fl. early 12th
century)
Wang Zao 汪藻 (1079–1154)
Wang Zixi 王仔昔 (d. 1117)
Wanli 萬曆 reign period (1573–1620)
Wei Hanjin 魏漢津 (fl. 1030s–1100s)
Wei Zheng 魏徵 (580–643)
Wen, king of Zhou 周文王 (11th
century BCE)
Wen Yanbo 文彥博 (1006–1097)
Wen Yi 溫益 (1037–1102)
Wenhao 文浩 (fl. early 12th
century)
Wenshu 文殊
Western Garden of Gathered Views
  擷景西園
Wolibu 斡離不 (d. 1127)
*The Wondrous Scripture on the Grand
  Unity's Preservation of the Embryo
  and the Jade Infant's Divine
  Transformation, Spoken by the
  Perfected King of the Divine
  Empyrean of the Highest Jade
  Clarity* 高上玉清神霄真王說太一保
  胎玉嬰神變妙經
Wu, emperor of Han 漢武帝
  (r. 141–87 BCE)
Wu, emperor of Liang 梁武帝
  (r. 502–549)
Wu, emperor of Northern Zhou 周武
  帝 (r. 560–578)
Wu, emperor of Tang 唐武宗
  (r. 840–846)
Wu, empress of Tang 唐武后
  (r. 689–705)

Wu 俁, brother of Huizong
  (1083–1128)
Wu Daozi 吳道子 (d. 792)
Wu Jian 吳开 (fl. early 12th century)
Wu Juhou 吳居厚 (1037–1113)
Wu Min 吳敏 (1089–1132)
Wu Ti 吳褆 (fl. early 12th century)
Wu Yuanyu 吳元瑜 (fl. 1080–1104)
Wuqimai 吳乞買 (r. 1123–1135)
Wushi 兀室 (fl. early 12th century)

Xi 奚
Xi Yi 席益 (fl. early 12th century)
Xianmu 賢穆, Huizong's sister
  (1075–1111)
Xiao Gan 蕭幹 (fl. early 12th century)
Xiao Qing 蕭慶 (fl. early 12th
century)
Xicisalu 錫喇薩魯 (fl. early 12th
century)
Xie Daoyun 謝道韞 (fourth century)
Xie Kejia 謝克家 (d. 1134)
Xiebao 斜保 (fl. early 12th century)
Xing Junchen 邢俊臣 (fl. early 12th
century)
Xing Shu 邢恕 (fl. 1090s–1110s)
Xizong, emperor of Jin 金熙宗
  (r. 1135–1150)
Xu Bingzhe 徐秉哲 (d. 1133)
Xu Churen 徐處仁 (1062–1127)
Xu Hui 許翙 (341–370)
Xu Ji 徐勣 (fl. late 11th and early 12th
  centuries)
Xu Jiang 許將 (1037–1111)
Xu Kangzong 許亢宗 (*jinshi* ca. 1114,
  fl. 1124)
Xu Mi 許謐 (305–376)
Xu Shen 徐伸 (fl. early 12th century)
Xu Xi 徐熙 (fl. 960s)
Xu Xun 許遜 (4th century)
Xu Zhichang 徐知常 (fl. 1110s)
Xuan, king of Zhou 周宣王 (r. 827–782
  BCE)
Xuanhe 宣和 reign period
  (1119–1126)
Xuanhe Calligraphy Catalogue 宣和
  書譜
Xuanhe Painting Catalogue 宣和畫譜

Xuanzong, emperor of Tang 唐玄宗 (r. 712–756)

Xue Ang 薛昂 (*jinshi* 1085, fl. 1100s–1120s)

Xue Ji 薛稷 (649–713)

Xujing 虛靜

Xunzi 荀子 (3rd century BCE)

Yan Anzhong 閻安中 (fl. 1101)

Yan Hui 顏回 (5th century BCE)

Yan Shouqin 閻守懃 (fl. 1101)

Yan Su 燕肅 (d. 1040)

Yan Zhenqing 顏真卿 (709–785)

Yanfeng granary 延豐倉

Yang Guifei 楊貴妃 (719–756)

Yang Jian 楊戩 (d. 1121)

Yang Keshi 楊可世 (fl. early 12th century)

Yang Qiu 楊球 (fl. early 12th century)

Yang Shi 楊時 (1053–1135)

Yang Xiong 楊雄 (53 BC–18 AD)

Yangdi, emperor of Sui 隋煬帝 (r. 605–618)

Yanjing 燕京

Yao 堯

Yao Gu 姚古 (fl. early 12th century)

Yao Pingzhong 姚平仲 (b. 1099)

Yao Shunren 姚舜仁 (*jinshi* 1085)

Yao You 姚祐 (fl. early 12th century)

Yao Youzhong 姚友仲 (fl. early 12th century)

Ye Tao 葉濤 (fl. late 11th and early 12th centuries)

Ye Zuqia 葉祖洽 (fl. 1100–1117)

Yellow Emperor 黃帝

Yelü Chun 耶律淳 (d. 1122)

Yelü Deguang 耶律德光 (r. 927–947)

Yi prefecture 易州

Yi Yuanji 易元吉 (11th century)

Ying 楑, son of Huizong (1115–1127)

Ying prefecture 營州

Yingtian fu 應天府

Yingzhou (land of immortals) 瀛洲

Yingzong, emperor of Song 宋英宗 (1032–1067, r. 1063–1067)

Yongle, emperor of Ming 明永樂 (r. 1402–1424)

Yongle dadian 永樂大典

Yu 禹

Yu Ce 虞策 (1047–1107)

Yu Shen 余深 (d. 1132)

Yu Xiyin 俞希隱 (fl. early 12th century)

Yuan Miaozong 元妙宗 (fl. 1116)

Yuanfeng 元豐 reign period (1078–1086)

Yuanfeng treasury 元豐庫

Yuanfu 元符 reign period (1098–1101)

Yuanyou 元祐 reign period (1086–1093)

yulanpen 盂蘭盆

Yuwen Cuizhong 宇文粹中 (d. 1139)

Yuwen Xuzhong 宇文虛中 (1079–1146)

Zeng Bu 曾布 (1035–1107)

Zeng Yin 曾黌 (fl. early 12th century)

Zeng Yu 曾紆 (1073–1135)

Zeng Zhao 曾肇 (1047–1107)

Zhai Ruwen 翟汝文 (1076–1141)

Zhan Dechun 戰德淳 (early 12th century)

Zhan Piyuan 詹丕遠 (fl. early 12th century)

Zhang Bangchang 張邦昌 (1081–1127)

Zhang Bu 張補 (fl. early 12th century)

Zhang Daoling 張道陵 (d. 156 CE)

Zhang Dun 章惇 (1035–1105)

Zhang Fu 章甫 (1045–1106)

Zhang Gen 張根 (1062–1121)

Zhang Jixian 張繼先 (1092–1126)

Zhang Jue 張覺 (d. 1124)

Zhang Juzheng 張居正 (1525–1582)

Zhang Kangguo 張康國 (1056–1109)

Zhang Lei 張耒 (1054–1114)

Zhang Liang 張良 (d. 186 BCE)

Zhang Linghui 張令徽 (fl. early 12th century)

Zhang Pu 張樸 (fl. early 12th century)

Zhang Shangying 張商英 (1043–1121)

Zhang Shunmin 張舜民 (*jinshi* 1065)

Zhang Shuye 張叔夜 (1065–1127)

Zhang Xu 張旭 (fl. 700)

Zhang Xuan 張萱 (fl. 730s)

Zhang Xubai 張虛白 (fl. early 12th century)

Zhang Yan 章縡 (fl. early 12th century)

Zhang Yanyuan 張彥遠 (fl. 847)
  Celebrated Painters of All the Dynasties
  歷代名畫記
Zhang Zeduan 張擇端 (Song)
  Peace Reigns over the River 清明上河圖
Zhangzong, emperor of Jin 金章宗 (r.
  1189–1208)
Zhao 趙
Zhao Liangsi 趙良嗣 (d. 1126)
Zhao Lingbi 趙令庇 (11th century)
Zhao Lingrang 趙令穰 (Danian 大年)
  (ca. 1070–ca. 1100)
Zhao Ruyu 趙汝愚 (1140–1196)
Zhao Shenzhi 趙甡之 (fl. early 12th
  century)
  Surviving Accounts 遺史
Zhao Tingzhi 趙挺之 (1040–1107)
Zhao Ye 趙野 (1084–1127)
Zhao Zhonghu 趙仲忽 (fl. 1090–1120)
Zhao Zizhi 趙子砥 (fl. early 12th
  century)
Zhen 榛, Huizong's eighteenth son,
  prince of Xin (b. 1117)
Zheng 鄭, Huizong's consort, empress,
  empress dowager (1081–1132)
Zheng Juzhong 鄭居中 (1059–1123)
Zheng Qian 鄭虔 (d. ca. 761)
Zheng Shen 鄭紳 (d. 1127)
Zhenghe 政和, reign period
  (1111–1118)

Zhenwu 真武
Zhenzong, emperor of Song 宋真宗 (r.
  997–1022)
Zhezong, emperor of Song 宋哲宗
  (r. 1085–1100)
Zhou Bangyan 周邦彥 (1056–1121)
Zhou Chang 周常 (fl. late 11th – early
  12th century)
Zhou Wuzhong 周武仲 (1074–1128)
Zhou Xingji 周行己 (*jinshi* 1091)
Zhou Xun 周訓 (fl. early 12th century)
Zhu 朱, Consort Dowager, mother of
  Zhezong (d. 1102)
Zhu, Empress of Qinzong 朱皇后
  (d. 1128)
Zhu Fu 朱紱 (d. 1107, Huizong's
  tutor)
Zhu Fu 朱服 (*jinshi* 1073)
Zhu Gong 朱肱 (1068–1165)
Zhu Mengshuo 朱夢說 (fl. early 12th
  century)
Zhu Mian 朱勔 (1075–1126)
Zhu Xi 朱熹 (1130–1200)
Zhuangzi 莊子
Zhuge Liang 諸葛亮 (181–234)
Zhuo prefecture 涿州
Zong Ze 宗澤 (1059–1128)
Zou Hao 鄒浩 (1060–1111)
Zuo Commentary 左傳
Zuxiu 祖秀 (fl. early 12th century)

Index